T. Hewitt Key

A Latin Grammar

T. Hewitt Key

A Latin Grammar

ISBN/EAN: 9783742807861

Manufactured in Europe, USA, Canada, Australia, Japa

Cover: Foto ©Andreas Hilbeck / pixelio.de

Manufactured and distributed by brebook publishing software (www.brebook.com)

T. Hewitt Key

A Latin Grammar

A

LATIN GRAMMAR

BY

T. HEWITT KEY, M.A., F.R.S.

LATE PROFESSOR OF LATIN IN UNIVERSITY COLLEGE, LONDON,
NOW PROFESSOR OF COMPARATIVE GRAMMAR, AND
HEAD-MASTER OF THE JUNIOR SCHOOL.

Fifth Thousand, corrected and somewhat enlarged.

LONDON:
BELL AND DALDY, 186 FLEET STREET.
CAMBRIDGE: DEIGHTON, BELL, AND CO.
1862.
[*The right of Translation is reserved.*]

By the same Author,

A SHORT LATIN GRAMMAR

ON THE SYSTEM OF CRUDE FORMS.

Crown 8vo, cloth, price 3s. 6d.

London: BELL and DALDY, 186 Fleet Street.

Also,

THE ALPHABET; TERENTIAN METRES; GOOD,

BETTER, BEST, WELL, &c. Second Issue, with a Paper on the Pronouns of the Third Person. Crown 8vo, price 7s. 6d.

London: WALTON and MABERLY, 28 Upper Gower Street.

By J. G. GREENWOOD, Esq., Fellow of University College, London; Professor of Classics in Owen College, Manchester,

THE ELEMENTS OF GREEK GRAMMAR

ADAPTED TO THE SYSTEM OF CRUDE FORMS.

Small 8vo, price 5s. 6d.

London: WALTON and MABERLY, 28 Upper Gower Street.

PREFACE.

THE chief changes which have been made in the present edition are as follows:

1. The principle involved in the new section, marked 451.1, has led to the introduction of forms which without explanation might offend the eye of the scholar, viz. *dĭc-* 'say,' *dŭc-* 'draw,' *fĭd-* 'trust,' *nŭb-* 'veil,' *ŏd-* or *ŏdi-* 'take an aversion to.' Yet these forms are as legitimate for the Latin language, as λιπ- (ἔλιπον) 'leave,' φυγ- (ἔφυγον) 'fly,' in Greek grammars. Precisely as from these bases are deduced the imperfect tenses λειπ-ω, λειπ-ειν; φευγω, φευγ-ειν; so we may likewise deduce in the sister language from the short bases the imperfect tenses *dĭc-o, dŭc-o, fĭd-o, nŭb-o,* and a perfect *ŏdi,*—forms which are no longer inconsistent with *maledīcus, fatīdīcus; dux dŭlcis, redux redŭcis, edŭcare; fīdes perfīdus; connŭbium, pronŭba;* or *ŏdium.*

2. It has been thought desirable to attach references to the quotations employed in the Syntax.

3. Some difference of arrangement has been made in the 'principal parts' of the verbs, and in the syntax of the dative.

4. Attention has been drawn to some inseparable prepositions which represent the Greek ανα in form and power, as well as to an inseparable preposition *inter,* of like origin and no way related to the ordinary preposition *inter* 'between' (§§ 834 *b.* and *d.,* 1308.1, 1342.1). It may here be noticed, that in order to retain as far as may be the original numerical headings of the paragraphs, such new paragraphs as were required have been distinguished by added digits, which have the appearance of a decimal notation. Instances have just been given.

5. To the crude forms a hyphen has been affixed (as in the Smaller Grammar), so as to imply that an addition to the word must be made before it is entitled to take a place in a Latin sentence.

6. The defence of the crude-form system, which appeared in the Preface of the first edition, has been enlarged and transferred to an Appendix.

7. A second Appendix touches on some new views, which were thought to be not sufficiently mature for admission into the body of the Grammar.

It will still be found that much which is important to the Latin scholar is wanting in these pages. But in reply to some objections on this head, it may truly be urged that a grammar is not the proper receptacle for the notice of peculiarities, which should find a place in the dictionary alone. The special office of grammar is to deal with general laws; and it was with justice that Cæsar gave to his work on this subject the title of *Analogia Latina*. There has therefore been an error on the side of excess in the admission of much matter relating to the prepositions, the excuse for which is the very unsatisfactory condition of our dictionaries in this department.

Lastly, the writer has to express his acknowledgments to Mr. John Power Hicks, of Lincoln College, Oxford, and to his son Mr. Thomas Key, of Lincoln's Inn, for much valuable assistance in the preparation of this edition.

UNIVERSITY COLLEGE, LONDON,
Feb. 15, 1858.

LATIN GRAMMAR.

ALPHABET.

1   THE Latin language was spoken in Rome and Latium, and afterwards spread with the Roman conquests over Italy, Sicily, and the greater part of France and Spain.

2   The alphabet consisted, as Cicero tells us (Nat. Deor. II. 37, 93), of twenty-one letters. These must have been: *a b c d e f g h i k l m n o p q r s t u* and *x*,—without any *j v w y z*. That the alphabet ended with *x* is implied in Suetonius (Aug. c. 88). *Y* and *z* were introduced at a late period from Greece, and for a long time limited to Greek or foreign words.

3   The vowels were *i e a o u*, to follow the natural* order of their sounds.

4   The liquid consonants, following the natural order of their formation from the back of the mouth towards the lips, were *r l n m*.

5   *X* is a double consonant, sounding as *ks*.

6   *K* is only used before *a*, as its modern name implies; for example, in the proper names Kasso, Volkanus; and in kalendae, dedikare.

   Q is used only before *u*, as its modern name implies; for example, in sequor; and in old inscriptions, pequnia, &c.

   Ph, ch, th, rh were not used in old Latin (Cic. Or. 48).

---

* See Professor Willis's experiments as detailed in the Cambridge Philosophical Transactions, vol. I. for Nov. 24, 1828 and March 16, 1829.

PRONUNCIATION.

7   The true pronunciation of the Latin language is no longer known. The vowels were probably pronounced as they now are in Italian.

8   In England the words are commonly pronounced nearly as they would be in English.

9   When *i* before a vowel commenced a syllable, it was called by the Romans *i consonans*; but was in fact a vowel *i* very shortly pronounced, like our *y* in *we*. But the English in such cases change it into a *j*. Thus i u n i o r (yunior) *younger* is commonly written and pronounced 'junior.'

10   When *u* before a vowel commenced a syllable, it was called *u consonans*; but was in fact a vowel *u* very shortly pronounced, like our *w* in *we*. But the English change it into a *v*. Thus, u i n u m (winum) *wine* is commonly written and pronounced 'vinum.'

11   *C* and *g* were probably always pronounced as in *cat* and *goose*, even before *i* and *e*. But the English follow their own rule. Thus Cicero, the Roman orator, is commonly supposed to have called himself *Sisero*.

12   The diphthongs, *ae*, *oe*, are generally pronounced as *e*.

13   A short syllable is pronounced rapidly, and is sometimes marked by a crescent (˘) over the vowel, as the *i* in dominus *master*.

14   A syllable or vowel is said to be *long by nature*, when the voice dwells upon the vowel, as vērus *true*.

15   A syllable or vowel is said to be *long by position*, when the vowel is followed by two consonants which do not both belong to the next syllable, as māgnus *great*, sūnt *they are*, ět mater *and the mother*.

16   A straight line (¯) over the vowel is sometimes used to denote a long syllable, as vērus *true*, māgnus *great*.

17   A diphthong is nearly always long by nature, as aurum *gold*, aes *bronze*, proelium *battle*. The few exceptions consist of words in which the diphthong is immediately followed by a vowel, as praeustus *burnt at the end*.

18   A vowel followed by a vowel in the next syllable is nearly always short, as filius *son*, filia *daughter*, aureus *golden*. The exceptions consist of words in which the long vowel has taken the

place of a diphthong, or of two vowels, as fīo (for fīio) *I become*, nullīus (for nullōīus) *of no one*, alīus (for alīius) *another's*: so especially with foreign names, as Darīus (for Darēīus), Medēa (for Medēīa).

19. A short vowel followed by a consonant should generally be pronounced with that consonant, as păt-er *father*.

20. A long vowel followed by a consonant should generally be pronounced separately from the consonant, as mā-ter *mother*.

21. If a vowel, itself short, be followed by two consonants which can be pronounced at the beginning of a syllable,—as *pr, cr, tr; br, gr, dr;* and *pl,*—there are often two ways of dividing the word. Thus fūnebris *connected with a corpse* is pronounced in prose fū-nĕ-bris; but in verse it may be pronounced fū-nĕb-ris. In the comic writers, however, such a syllable is always short.

A syllable which is sometimes long and sometimes short is said to be common, and is marked (˘) or (¯) over the vowel, as funĕbris or funēbris.

22. If the last syllable but one be long, it has the accent, as uīnum *wine*, árcus *bow*, regīna *queen*, sagítta *arrow*.

23. If the last syllable but one be short and the last syllable but two be long, this long syllable has the accent, as fīlia *daughter*, aṹnculus *a mother's brother*.

24. If two or more short syllables, exclusive of the last syllable, come together, the second of them (counting from the beginning of the word) has its vowel nearly dropped* in pronunciation. Thus ŏpĕra *work* should be pronounced almost as ŏp'ra; mĭsĕrĭa *wretchedness*, as mĭs'ria; exĭĕrat *he had gone out*, as exĭ'rat; lăcrŭma *tear*, probably as lă'r'ma.†

25. If the syllable to be so dropped be an *i* (or *e*) or *u*, pronounce the *i* (or *e*) like *y*, the *u* like *w*. Thus mŭlĭer *woman* should be pronounced múlyer; ărĭĕtis *of a ram*, áryĕtis; pĕrĭĭmus *we are ruined*, péryimus; flŭuĭŏrum *of rivers*, fluuyŏrum; Pŭtĕŏli *name of a town*, Pútyŏli; restĭtŭĕre *to set up again*, restĭtwĕre.

26. A long word has sometimes more than one accent: as, immortālis *immortal;* recŭpĕrāre (rĕco'perāre), *to recover, to get back*.

---

* See Bentley's Terence ad Eun. li. 2. 36; Hermann de Re Metrica, speaking of *miserum*, p. 206.

† Compare the French *larme*.

27. *Enclitics* are little words pronounced and sometimes even written with the word preceding: as, quŏ *and*, matĕr-que *and the mother*; uĕ *or*, matĕr-ue *or the mother*; nĕ in asking questions, as matĕr-ne abiit? *is the mother gone away?* Prepositions placed *after* a noun are of this kind: as, altis-de montibus *down from the high mountains*.

28. *Proclitics* are words pronounced and sometimes even written with the word following. Prepositions are of this kind: as, intĕr-nos *between us*, intĕr-se *between them*, in-primis *among the first*, á-me *from me*.

29. *Elision.* When one word ends with a vowel or a vowel and an *m*, and the next begins with a vowel or an *h*, the final vowel and *m* of the first word are not pronounced in poetry: thus,

Monstrum horrendum informe ingens cūi lūmĕn ădemptum

should be read,

Monstr', hŏrrend', inform', ingéns oūī lúmen adémptum.
Unearthly, ghastly, shapeless; reft of an eye immense.

WORD-BUILDING.

30. The simplest words consist of one syllable: as the verbs dūc- *draw*, ăg- *drive* or *put in motion*; or the substantives pĕd- *foot*, sāl- *salt*.

These are called *roots*.

32. A *suffix* is a syllable which is added to the end of a word and adds to or alters its meaning: as, dūc-* *draw*, duc-to- *drawn*; ăg- *drive*, ag-mĕn- *a drove*.

33. A short vowel, generally ĭ, seems sometimes to be inserted before the suffix: as in ăg-ĭ-li- *easily put in motion, active*.

34. Several suffixes may be added one after another to the same root: as, ăg- *put in motion*, ăg-ĭ-li- *active*, ăgĭlĭ-tăt- *activity*, ăgĭlĭtăt-ĭs *of activity*.

Words formed by suffixes are said to be *derived*.

35. A *prefix* is a syllable which is placed before a root, and adds to or alters its meaning: as, dūc- *draw*, dē-dūc- *draw down*; ăg- *drive*, ex-ăg- *drive out*.

* For the quantity see § 451. 1.

Words formed by prefixes are said to be *compounded*.

36 In the derivation and composition of words the letters are sometimes slightly altered: as, ĭg- *drive*, ac-to- *driven*, ex-ĭg- *drive out*; ŏpĕs- *work*, ŏpĕr-ĭs *of work*.

NOUNS.

i. e. Substantives and Adjectives.

37 The Latin language has no article, so that a Latin substantive may be translated in three ways: 1. without an article, as mŭliĕr, *woman*; 2. with the indefinite article, as mŭliĕr, *a woman*; 3. with the definite article, as mŭliĕr, *the woman*.

38 With Latin substantives there are three questions to be asked: What is the gender? What is the case? What is the number?

39 The genders are two, *masculine* and *feminine*. If a noun be of neither gender, it is called *neuter*.

See tables of genders, §§ 191, &c.

40 Little suffixes with the meaning of prepositions are added to nouns. Thus Sulmōn- was the name of a town in Italy. Add the suffix *em* to it, and e-ŏ Sulmōn-em means *I am going to Sulmon*. Add the suffix *i*, and Sulmōn-ī hăbĭt-ŏ means *I reside at Sulmon*.

41 A noun, before these suffixes are added, is said to be in the *crude form*. A crude form is here printed with a final hyphen.

42 The word made up of a noun and one of these suffixes is called a *case*.

43 There are five suffixes, which being added to a crude form make five cases: the nominative, accusative, genitive, dative, and ablative. To these is generally added the vocative.*

44 The *nominative* is commonly formed by the suffix *s*: as, trăb-a *beam*, nom. trabs.

The nominative marks the quarter *from* which an action proceeds, *i. e.* the agent. Thus, in the sentence, 'the master strikes the slave,' the blow comes *from* the master: this word *master* in Latin would be in the nominative case.

* The case so called is in reality, so far as the Latin language is concerned, a nominative; except perhaps in the singular of the *o* declension, viz. *us*. But even with this compare the nominatives *is*, *ille*, *ipse*.

The nominative is called the *subject* in English grammar.

The *vocative* is used in addressing people.

45. The *accusative* is formed by the suffix *em*: as, trăb- *a beam*, acc. trăb-em.

46. The accusative answers to the question *whither?* or marks the quarter *to* which an action is directed: as, eō Sulmōnem, *I am going to Sulmon*. Or again in the sentence, 'the master strikes the slave,' the blow goes *to* the slave: this word *slave* in Latin would be in the accusative case.

The accusative is often used with prepositions: as, In urbem vēnit, *he came into the city*.

The accusative is called the *object* in English grammar.*

47. The *genitive* is formed by the suffix *iŭs* or *is*: as, quo- *who*, gen. quŏ-iŭs; trăb- *beam*, gen. trăb-is.

The genitive answers to the question *whence?* or signifies *from*: as, călor sōl-is, *the heat from the sun*. It is commonly translated by *of*: as, călor sōlis, *the heat of the sun*; or by the English suffix *'s*: as, călor sōlis, *the sun's heat*.†

48. The nominative and genitive both signify *from*: but they differ in this; the nominative belongs to a *verb*, the genitive to a *noun*.

49. The *dative* is formed by the suffix *ŏi* or *i*: as, i- *this*, I-bi *in this place*; trăb- *beam*, dat. trăb-i.

The dative answers to the question *where?* and is translated by *at* or *in*: as, Sulmōn-i, *at Sulmon*; ăli-bi, *in another place*. It is used also for *to*, if there is no motion: as, haeret tĭbi, *it clings to you*.

50. The ablative has two very different meanings, and perhaps two different origins. Sometimes it answers to the question *whence?* sometimes, like the dative, to the question *where?* In the former sense it had originally a final *d*, as, from Gnaivo-, the old form of the praenomen Cneio- (Cneius), abl. Gnaivod. This form became quite obsolete. In the classical writers the ablative in form, whatever be its sense, is very like to or identical with the dative; but the *i* is often changed into an *ē*: as, trăb- *beam*, abl. trăb-ē; or lost altogether, leaving the preceding vowel long: as, ăla- *wing*, abl. ălā.

---

* The English language has the accusatival suffix in *him*, the accusative of *he*; and in *whom*, the accusative of *who*.

† The English language has the genitival suffix in *his*, the genitive of *he*; and in *whose*, the genitive of *who*.

The ablative sometimes signifies *from*, as, Cŏrintho- *Corinth*, abl. Cŏrinthŏ *from Corinth*; sometimes it agrees in meaning with the dative, as, rūs- *country*, D. rūr-ī, or Ab. rūr-ē, *in the country*; D. Sulmōn-ī, or Ab. Sulmōn-ē, *at Sulmon*.

51. The ablative is often used with prepositions: as, ex urbĕ, *out of the city*; cum rēg-ĕ, *with the king*; in urb-ĕ, *in the city*.

52. *Number.*—The *plural* is generally marked in English by *s* or *en*, as, *dogs*, *oxen*; in Latin sometimes by *s*, sometimes by *em*. These suffixes are added to the case-suffixes; as in the genitives servō-r-um for servō-'s-um, *of slaves*; rē-r*-um for rē-'s-um, *of things*; or in the datives, vō-bī-s, rē-bū-s.

53. In adding these case-suffixes and plural-suffixes to the crude forms, some changes take place, particularly if the crude form end in a vowel.

54. These changes depend chiefly upon the last letter of the noun. Nouns are therefore divided, according to the last letter, into classes called *declensions*.

55. CONSONANT (*or* THIRD)† DECLENSION.

MASCULINE AND FEMININE NOUNS.

Latin c.f. Gender. English.	Trăb- fem. *tree, beam.*	Princĕp- masc. or fem. *first, chief.*	Aucĕp- masc. or fem. *bird-catcher.*	Rēg- masc. *king.*	Nŭc- fem. *nut.*
Singular.					
Nom.	trabs	princeps	auceps	rex	nux
Voc.	trabs	princeps	auceps	rex	nux
Acc.	trăbem	princĭpem	aucŭpem	rēgem	nŭcem
Gen.	trăbĭs	princĭpĭs	aucŭpĭs	rēgĭs	nŭcĭs
Dat.	trăbī	princĭpī	aucŭpī	rēgī	nŭcī
Abl.	trăbĕ	princĭpĕ	aucŭpĕ	rēgĕ	nŭcĕ
Plural.					
Nom.	trăbēs	princĭpēs	aucŭpēs	rēgēs	nŭcēs
Voc.	trăbēs	princĭpēs	aucŭpēs	rēgēs	nŭcēs
Acc.	trăbēs	princĭpēs	aucŭpēs	rēgēs	nŭcēs
Gen.	trăbum	princĭpum	aucŭpum	rēgum	nŭcum
Dat.	trăbĭbŭs	princĭpĭbŭs	aucŭpĭbŭs	rēgĭbŭs	nŭcĭbŭs
Abl.	trăbĭbŭs	princĭpĭbŭs	aucŭpĭbŭs	rēgĭbŭs	nŭcĭbŭs

* The *r* for *s* in the genitive is seen in the English genitives *her* and *their*.

† The numbers of the declensions are given, because they are so arranged in nearly all grammars and dictionaries.

CONSONANT DECLENSION.

MASCULINE AND FEMININE NOUNS—(continued).

Latin c.r. Gender. English.	Lăpĭd- masc. a stone.	Custōd- masc. or fem. guard.	Ariēt- masc. ram.	Cŏm-ĭt- masc. or fem. companion.	Aetāt- fem. age.
Singular.					
Nom.	lăpĭs	custōs	ărĭēs	cŏmĕs	aetās
Voc.	lăpĭs	custōs	ărĭēs	cŏmĕs	aetās
Acc.	lăpĭdem	custōdem	ărĭĕtem	cŏmĭtem	aetātem
Gen.	lăpĭdĭs	custōdĭs	ărĭĕtĭs	cŏmĭtĭs	aetātĭs
Dat.	lăpĭdī	custōdī	ărĭĕtī	cŏmĭtī	aetātī
Abl.	lăpĭdĕ	custōdĕ	ărĭĕtĕ	cŏmĭtĕ	aetātĕ
Plural.					
Nom.	lăpĭdēs	custōdēs	ărĭĕtēs	cŏmĭtēs	aetātēs
Voc.	lăpĭdēs	custōdēs	ărĭĕtēs	cŏmĭtēs	aetātēs
Acc.	lăpĭdēs	custōdēs	ărĭĕtēs	cŏmĭtēs	aetātēs
Gen.	lăpĭdum	custōdum	ărĭĕtum	cŏmĭtum	aetātum
Dat.	lăpĭdĭbŭs	custōdĭbŭs	ărĭĕtĭbŭs	cŏmĭtĭbŭs	aetātĭbŭs
Abl.	lăpĭdĭbŭs	custōdĭbŭs	ărĭĕtĭbŭs	cŏmĭtĭbŭs	aetātĭbŭs

Latin c.r. Gender. English.	Mōs- masc. custom.	Pulvĭs- masc. dust.	Pătĕr- masc. father.	Clāmŏr- masc. shout.	Hĭĕm- fem. winter.
Singular.					
Nom.	mōs	pulvĭs	pătĕr	clāmŏr	hiemps
Voc.	mōs	pulvĭs	pătĕr	clāmŏr	hiemps
Acc.	mōrem	pulvĕrem	pătrem	clāmōrem	biĕmem
Gen.	mōrĭs	pulvĕrĭs	pătrĭs	clāmōrĭs	hiĕmĭs
Dat.	mōrī	pulvĕrī	pătrī	clāmōrī	hiŏmī
Abl.	mōrĕ	pulvĕrĕ	pătrĕ	clāmōrĕ	hiĕmĕ
Plural.					
Nom.	mōrēs	*No Plural.*	pătrēs	clāmōrēs	biĕmēs
Voc.	mōrēs		pătrēs	clāmōrēs	hiĕmēs
Acc.	mōrēs		pătrēs	clāmōrēs	hiĕmēs
Gen.	mōrum		pătrum	clāmōrum	biĕmum
Dat.	mōrĭbŭs		pătrĭbŭs	clāmōrĭbŭs	hiĕmĭbŭs
Abl.	mōrĭbŭs		pătrĭbŭs	clāmōrĭbŭs	hiĕmĭbŭs

* An acc. pulvĕrĕs in Horace.

CONSONANT DECLENSION.

Masculine and Feminine Nouns—(continued).

Latin c.f. Gender. English.	Sōl- masc. sun.	Consŭl- masc. consul.	Rătiōn- fem. account.	Ordōn- masc. rank.	Sanguĭn- masc. blood.
Singular.					
Nom.	sōl	consŭl	rătiō	ordō	sanguĭs
Voc.	sōl	consŭl	rătiō	ordō	sanguĭs
Acc.	sōlem	consŭlem	rătiōnem	ordĭnem	sanguĭnem
Gen.	sōlĭs	consŭlĭs	rătiōnĭs	ordĭnĭs	sanguĭnĭs
Dat.	sōlī	consŭlī	rătiōnī	ordĭnī	sanguĭnī
Abl.	sōlĕ	consŭlĕ	rătiōnĕ	ordĭnĕ	sanguĭnĕ
Plural.					
Nom.	sōlēs	consŭlēs	rătiōnēs	ordĭnēs	No Plural.
Voc.	sōlēs	consŭlēs	rătiōnēs	ordĭnēs	
Acc.	sōlēs	consŭlēs	rătiōnēs	ordĭnēs	
Gen.	——*	consŭlum	rătiōnum	ordĭnum	
Dat.	sōlĭbŭs	consŭlĭbŭs	rătiōnĭbŭs	ordĭnĭbŭs	
Abl.	sōlĭbŭs	consŭlĭbŭs	rătiōnĭbŭs	ordĭnĭbŭs	

Neuter Nouns.

Neuter nouns differ from others only in the N. V. and Acc., which are always alike. In the singular these cases are nearly always short in the last syllable, and in the plural always end in ā.

Latin c.f. English.	Nōmĕn- name.	Opĕs- work.	Frĭgŭs- cold.	Rōbŏr- hardness.	Căpŭt- head.
Singular.					
Nom.	nōmĕn	ŏpŭs	frĭgŭs	rōbŭr	căpŭt
Voc.	nōmĕn	ŏpŭs	frĭgŭs	rōbŭr	căpŭt
Acc.	nōmĕn	ŏpŭs	frĭgŭs	rōbŭr	căpŭt
Gen.	nōmĭnĭs	ŏpĕrĭs	frĭgŏrĭs	rōbŏrĭs	căpĭtĭs
Dat.	nōmĭnī	ŏpĕrī	frĭgŏrī	rōbŏrī	căpĭtī
Abl.	nōmĭnĕ	ŏpĕrĕ	frĭgŏrĕ	rōbŏrĕ	căpĭtĕ
Plural.					
Nom.	nōmĭnă	ŏpĕră	frĭgŏră	rōbŏră	căpĭtă
Voc.	nōmĭnă	ŏpĕră	frĭgŏră	rōbŏră	căpĭtă
Acc.	nōmĭnă	ŏpĕră	frĭgŏră	rōbŏră	căpĭtă
Gen.	nōmĭnum	ŏpĕrum	frĭgŏrum	rōbŏrum	căpĭtum
Dat.	nōmĭnĭbŭs	ŏpĕrĭbŭs	frĭgŏrĭbŭs	rōbŏrĭbŭs	căpĭtĭbŭs
Abl.	nōmĭnĭbŭs	ŏpĕrĭbŭs	frĭgŏrĭbŭs	rōbŏrĭbŭs	căpĭtĭbŭs

* Not found.

CONSONANT DECLENSION.

Neuter Nouns—(continued).

Latin c.f. English.	Ŭbĕr- stream.	Os- mouth.	Os- bone.	Crūs- leg.	Cord- heart.
Singular.					
Nom.	ŭbĕr	ōs	ŏs	crūs	cŏr
Voc.	ŭbĕr	ōs	ŏs	crūs	cŏr
Acc.	ŭbĕr	ōs	ŏs	crūs	cŏr
Gen.	ŭbĕrĭs	ōrĭs	ossĭs	crūrĭs	cordĭs
Dat.	ŭbĕrī	ōrī	ossī	crūrī	cordī
Abl.	ŭbĕrĕ	ōrĕ	ossĕ	crūrĕ	cordĕ
Plural.					
Nom.	ŭbĕră	ōră	ossă	crūră	cordă
Voc.	ŭbĕră	ōră	ossă	crūră	cordă
Acc.	ŭbĕră	ōră	ossă	crūră	cordă
Gen.	ŭbĕrum	——*	ossĭum†	crūrum	——*
Dat.	ŭbĕrĭbŭs	ōrĭbŭs	ossĭbŭs	crūrĭbŭs	cordĭbŭs
Abl.	ŭbĕrĭbŭs	ōrĭbŭs	ossĭbŭs	crūrĭbŭs	cordĭbŭs

57 *Remarks on the Consonant Declension.*

The nominative, as has been already said, is most regularly formed by the addition of *s*: as, trăb- *beam*, N. trabs.

58 If the crude form end in *g* or *c*, *x* is written instead of *gs* or *cs*: as, rēg- *king*, N. rex ; nŭc- *nut*, N. nux.

59 If the crude form end in *d* or *t*, this letter is omitted: as, lăpĭd- *stone*, N. lăpis ; cŏmĭt- *companion*, N. cŏmĕs.

60 If in Greek words the crude form end in *ant, ent*, or *unt*, the Nom. will end in *as, es*, or *us* respectively.

61 Even in Latin words, this change is sometimes found: as, infant- *infant*, N. infans or infās.

62 If the crude form end in *r* or *l*, the *s* is omitted: as, pătĕr- *father*, N. pătĕr ; consŭl- *consul*, N. consŭl : if in *n*, either the *n* or the *s* is omitted, as sanguĭn- *blood*, N. sanguis, or in old writers sanguen.

63 If the crude form end in *ŏn* or *ōn*, both *n* and *s* are omitted: as, hŏmŏn- *human being*, N. hŏmŏ ; rătiōn- *an account*, N. rătiō. In Greek names in *on* or *ont*, the *n* is often retained, but not by the best writers: as, Lăcōn-, Xĕnŏphont-, N. Lăcōn, Xĕnŏphōn ; better Lăcō, Xĕnŏphō.

* Not found. † Observe the irregular *i*.

CONSONANT DECLENSION.   11

64   If the crude form end in *s* or *ss*, only one *s* is left at the end of the nominative: as, mūs- *mouse*, ōs- *mouth*, oss- *bone*; N. mūs, ōs, ōs.

65   If the crude form end in *ll*, *rr*, or *rd*, the second of these consonants is omitted in the nominative: as, mell- *honey*, farr- *spelt*, cord- *heart*; N. mĕl, făr, cŏr.

66   If the word be neuter, the *s* is not added: as, ālēc- *pickled herring*, N. ālēc. Many adjectives however take the *s* even for the neuter N. V. Ac.: as, fĕrōc- *haughty*, praesent- *present*; N. V. Ac. neut. fĕrox, praesens.

67   Neuters in *mat*, borrowed from the Greek language, imitate that language in dropping the *t* in the N. V. Ac.: as, poēmăt- *a poem*, N. V. Ac. poēmă.

68   If the crude form has a short *i* before the final consonant, this is often changed in the N. into *e*: as, mīlĭt- *soldier*, N. mīlĕs.

69   If the crude form end in *ĕs* or *ŏs*, the N. and V. generally prefer *ŭs*: as, vĕnĕs- *beauty*, corpŏs- *flesh, body*; N. and V. vĕnŭs, corpŭs. Neuter words retain the *ŏs* in the Ac. also. Greek words prefer *ŏs* in the N. V. Ac. of neuters.

70   The crude form of comparative adjectives ends in *ĭs*; whence the neuter N. V. Ac. end in *ĭs*, the masculine and feminine N. and V. in *ŏr*: as, mĕliōs- *better*, N. and V. m. and f. mĕliŏr, N. V. Ac. neut. mĕliŭs.

71   *When the nominative is left with a single consonant at the end, the quantity of the preceding vowel generally remains as in the crude form: as, sălūt- *safety*, custōd- *keeper*, N. sălūs, custōs; and again, ănăt- *duck*, lăpĭd- *stone*, pătĕr- *father*, have in the N. ănăs, lăpĭs, pătĕr.

72   But the crude forms in *ōr* have a short nominative: as, tĭmōr- *fear*, N. tĭmŏr. Yet such a form as tĭmōr also occurs.

73   Crude forms in *s* coexist for the most part with crude forms in *r*: as, arbōs- or arbōr- *a tree*, ŏdōs- or ŏdōr- *scent*. Of these, the form with *r* is preferred in those cases where a vowel follows: as, G. arbŏris *of a tree*, ŏdŏris *of the scent*.

---

* In old writers, such as Ennius, Plautus, Terence (and occasionally even Virgil), nominatives, which should be short according to this rule, are at times long: as, pătēr, like the Greek πατήρ. So the nominatives āēr, sŏnĭpēs, ăbiēs, ăriēs, părĭēs, Cĕrēs, sanguīs, pulvīs, from the crude forms āĕr-, sŏnĭpĕd-, ăbiĕt-, ăriĕt-, părĭĕt-, Cĕrĕs-, sanguĭn-, pulvĭs-, have some of them always, others at times, a long vowel.

74 If the crude form end in *ĭs, ĕr* takes its place in those cases where a vowel follows: as, *pulvĭs- dust*, G. *pulvĕris*.

75 If the crude form end in *ŏn, ĕn, ăl*, &c., the short vowel is often changed into *ĭ* in those cases where a vowel follows: as, *ordōn- rank*, *căpŭt- head*, G. *ordĭnĭs*, *căpĭtĭs*. *Cărōn- flesh* drops the vowel altogether in those cases: as, G. *carnĭs*.

76 V.—Greek words in *ant* form the V. in *ā*: as, Atlant- *Atlas*, N. Atlās, V. Atlā.

77 Ac.—Greek words often form the Ac. in *ă*: as, Pallăd- *the goddess Pallas*, N. Pallăs, Ac. Pallădă; āēr- *air*, Ac. āěrǎ; aethěr- *the region of fire* (above the air), Ac. aethěrǎ.

78 G.—Greek words often form the G. in *ŏs* or *ĕs*: as, Pallăd-, G. Pallădŏs.

79 D.—The dative sometimes takes an *ĭ* instead of an *ī*: as, aes- *bronze*, D. aerī, and rarely aerě.

80 D.—Greek words sometimes form the D. in *ĭ*: as, Pallăd-, D. Pallădĭ.

81 Ab.—The ablative sometimes takes an *ī* instead of an *ĕ*: as, căpŭt- *head*, Ab. căpĭtě, and rarely căpĭtī.

82 N. and V. pl.—Greek words often shorten the last syllable of the N. and V. pl.: as, rhētŏr- *orator*, N. and V. pl. rhētŏrěs.

83 N. V. Ac. pl.—Greek neuter nouns whose crude form ends in *ěs* form the N. V. and Ac. pl. in *ěă* or *ē*: as, ěpěs- *an heroic poem*, N. sing. ěpŏs, N. V. Ac. pl. ěpěǎ *or* ěpē.

84 Ac. pl.—Greek words often form the Ac. pl. in *ăs*: as, rhētŏr- *orator*, Ac. pl. rhētŏrǎs.

85 G. pl.—There is an old form of the G. pl. in *ěrum*: as, nūc- *nut*, G. pl. nūcěrum.

86 D. and Ab. pl.—Greek nouns in *măt* often form this case in *mătĭs*, rather than in *mătĭbŭs*: as, poěmăt- *a poem*, N. sing. poěmă, D. and Ab. pl. poěmătĭbŭs, or poěmătĭs.

87 D. and Ab. pl.—Greek nouns sometimes form the D. and Ab. pl. in *sĭn* or *sī*, with the final consonant of the crude form omitted, so as to leave the preceding vowel short: as, Trōǎd- *a Trojan woman*, N. sing. Trōǎs, D. and Ab. pl. Trōǎsĭn *or* Trōǎsī.

VOWEL DECLENSIONS.

1. Masculine and Feminine Nouns.

Last let. Declen.	a 1	o 2	i 3	u 4	e 5
Latin. Gender. English.	Ala- fem. *wing.*	Auo- masc. *grandfather.*	Aui- fem. *bird.*	Acu- fem. *needle.*	Rē- fem. *thing.*
Sing.					
Nom.	ălă§	ăuŏs, ăuŭs	ăuĭs‡	ăcŭs	rēs
Voc.	ălă†	ăuĕ	ăuĭs	ăcŭs	rēs
Acc.	ălam	ăuom, ăuum	ăuim, ăuem	ăcum	rem
Gen.	ălae	ăuī*	ăuĭs	ăcŭs	rĕī, rē
Dat.	ălae	ăuō	ăuī	ăcuī, ăcū	rĕī, rē
Abl.	ălā	ăuō	ăuī, ăuĕ	ăcū	rē
Plural.					
Nom.	ălae	ăuī	ăuēs	ăcūs	rēs
Voc.	ălae	ăuī	ăuēs	ăcūs	rēs
Acc.	ălās	ăuōs	ăuīs, ăuēs	ăcūs	rēs
Gen.	ălārum	ăuōrum	ăuium	ăcuom	rērum
Dat.	ălīs†	ăuīs	ăuībŭs	ăcŭbŭs	rēbŭs
Abl.	ălīs	ăuīs	ăuībŭs	ăcŭbŭs	rēbŭs

* The o of the crude form may be traced even in those cases which appear commonly without it. Compare the gen. sing. *guā-ius* with the Homeric λογοιο; the old nom. pl. *ăloe* for *illi* with the Greek λογοι; the dat. and abl. pl. *duobus*, and *ŏloes* for *illis*, with the Greek λογοις.

† The a of the crude form is visible through all this declension except in the dative and ablative plural. That it once existed here also is proved by the old forms *equābūs*, &c., and by the Greek dative μουσαις.

‡ Compare this declension with the Greek πολι-, N. πολις.

§ The a of these cases was perhaps at first long, like Greek χωρα, *orad*, Andâ. So *aquilā*, Enn. Ann. 140; *amicta*, *filiā*, Liv. Andr. ap. Prisc. vi. 42; *liberā*, Plaut. Ep. iii. 4. 67; especially in Greek words, as *Iluricā*, Trin. iv. 2. 10; *epistulā*, Asin. iv. 1. 17; *Casshari*, Ep. iv. 1. 40.

VOWEL DECLENSIONS.
2. Neuter Nouns.

Last letter. Declension.	a 1	o 2	i 3	u 4	e 5
Latin. English.		Bello- war.	Mări- sea.	Cornu- horn.	
Singular. Nom. Voc. Acc. Gen. Dat. Abl.	There are no neuters of this declension.	bellum bellum bellum bellī bellō bellō	mărĕ mărĕ mărĕ măris mărī mărī	cornū cornū cornū [cornūs]* cornuī, cornū cornū	There are no neuters of this declension.
Plural. Nom. Voc. Acc. Gen. Dat. Abl.		bellă bellă bellă bellōrum bellīs bellīs	mărĭă mărĭă mărĭă mărĭum măribŭs măribŭs	cornuă cornuă cornuă cornuum cornŭbŭs cornŭbŭs	

Remarks on the First, or A Declension.

90 A very large number of feminine adjectives are of this declension, while the masculine and neuter forms end in o : as, bŏnŭ-l. *good,* bŏno- masc. and neuter.

91 N.—Four words add an e to make the feminine nominative: quae ; haec ; istaec ; illaec. In the last three the e has nothing to do with the case-suffix.†

92 N.—The nominative in Greek proper names sometimes has an s : as, Aeneā- *Aeneas,* N. Aeneās ; but the best prose writers prefer the N. and V. in ā : as, Aristagorā.

93 V.—The vocative of Greek proper names sometimes has a long ā : as, Aeneā-, voc. Aeneā.

94 Ac.—The accusative of Greek proper names sometimes has an n : as, Aeneā-, ac. Aeneān ; Maiā-, ac. Maiān.

95 G.—The genitive has an old form in i : as, alaī.

96 G.—The genitive sometimes takes an s : as, fămĭlĭa- (făm'lia) *a gang of slaves, an establishment of slaves,* gen. fămĭlĭas.

* Not found.   † See § 239.

D.—The dative has an old form in *i*: as, ălāī.

G. pl.—The plural genitive sometimes has a short form: as, caelĭcŏla- *inhabitant of heaven*, G. caelĭcŏlum, instead of caelĭcŏlārum; amphŏra- *a measure of content*, G. amphŏrum. And in foreign proper names ŏn, as in Greek, is sometimes written instead of um.

D. and Ab. pl.—The dative and ablative have an old form in *būs*: as, ĕqua- *mare*, D. and Ab. ĕquābūs. This form is often retained to distinguish the sex; otherwise, ĕquŏ- *horse*, and ĕqua- *mare*, would have the same dative and ablative plural; so also dua- f. *two*, amba- f. *both*, have D. and Ab. duābūs, ambābūs.

Remarks on the Second, or O Declension.

The Greek words Trō- *a Trojan*, and hērō- *a demigod*, are declined like Greek words of the consonant declension.

If the crude form end in *ĕro*, the *e* is often dropped in those cases where a vowel follows the *r*: as, lĭbĕro- *the inner bark of a tree, a book*, N. and V. lĭbĕr, Ac. lĭbrum, &c. See § 124. 1.

N. and Ac.—The nominative and accusative prefer an *o*, if *u* precede, as ăuo- *grandfather*, N. ăuŏs, Ac. ăuom; otherwise *u* is preferred, as hāmo- *hook*, N. hāmŭs, Ac. hāmum. But if the crude form end in *quo*, then *cus* and *cum* are preferred to *quus* or *quos*, and to *quum* or *quom*: as, ĕquo- *horse*, N. ĕcus, Ac. ĕcum; antīquo- *old*, N. antīcŭs, Ac. antīcum.

N.—In Greek words *o* is preferred to *u*: as, Dēlo- *the island Delos*, N. Dēlŏs.

N. and V.—If the crude form of a masculine noun end in *ro*, the N. and V. often drop the letters that follow *r*: as, lĭbĕro- *book*, N. and V. lĭbĕr; ŭīro- *man*, N. and V. uĭr.

N.—Three nouns form the N. in *ŏ*: ipso- *self*, N. ĭpsĕ, more commonly ipsĕ; isto- *that near you*, N. istĕ; illo- *yonder*, N. illĕ. If nominatives so formed take after them the enclitic *ce*, *look* or *lo*, they have an *i* instead of an *e*: hence ho- *this*, N. hĭc; isto-, N. istĭc; illo-, N. illĭc.

V.—The vocative from proper names in *io* contracts *iĭ* into ī: as, Antōnio- *Antonius* or *Antony*, V. Antōnī. So gĕnio- *a guardian spirit*, V. gĕnī; fīlio- *son*, V. fīlī.

V.—Meo- *mine* contracts the V. into mī.

V.—The nominative is sometimes used as a vocative: as, Deo- *God*, N. or V. Deŭs.

Ac.—Greek proper names sometimes form the accusative with *n*: as, Dēlo- *the island Delos*, Ac. Dēlŏn.

110 G. and D.—The following adjectives form their genitives in *ius*, their datives in *i*, for the masculine, feminine, and neuter, though some of them have occasionally the more common forms.

C.F.	G.	D.	C.F.	G.	D.
eo-	ējŭs	eī	ipso-	ipsīŭs	ipsī
quo- *or*	quoīŭs *or*	quoi, cuī*	ălĭo-	ălīŭs	ălĭī
cu-	cūīŭs	*or* cūī	altĕro-	altĕrīŭs	altĕrī
ūtĕro-	utrīŭs	utrī	ūno-	ūnīŭs	ūnī
neutĕro-	neutrīŭs	neutrī	ullo-	ullīŭs	ullī
ho-	hūīŭs	hūi-c*	nullo-	nullīŭs	nullī
isto-	istīŭs	istī	sōlo-	sōlīŭs	sōlī
illo-	illīŭs	illī	tōto-	tōtīŭs	tōtī

111 Many of these genitives in *ius* are found in poetry with a short penult, as illĭŭs; but the genitive ălīŭs (contracted from aliius) is always long. Altĕrīŭs with a long *i* is found in old writers (*Ter.* And. IV. 1. 4 and *Enn.* ap. Donat. ad *Ter.* Ph. II. 2. 25): in prose it is usual to pronounce the *i* short: altĕrĭŭs.

112 G.—Substantives in *io* contract *ii* into **I**: as, ōtio- *leisure*, G. ōtī. This final *i* is sometimes written so as to overtop the other letters, as otI.

113 G.—Greek words sometimes form the genitive in *ǒ*: as, Měnandro- *the poet Menander*, G. Měnandrū.

114 D.—Names of places form a dative in *ĭ* with the meaning *at*: as, Mīlēto- *the town Miletus*, D. Mīlētī *at Miletus*; so hūmo- *ground*, D. hūmī *on the ground*; dŏmo- *house*, D. dŏmī *at home*; bello- *war*, D. bellī *in war*: and some adjectives in certain phrases, as quintī diē *on the fifth day*, &c.

115 N. pl.—The old nominative ended in *e*: as, oloe from olo- *yonder*, instead of illī from illo-. So also in Greek words: as, Adelpho- *brother*, N. pl. Adelphoe.

116 N. pl.—Deo- *God* has the plural N. Deī, Diī, or more commonly Dī; and eo- *this* or *that* has a plural N. iī, ī, or more commonly hī.

117 N. and Ac. pl.—Duo- *two* and ambo- *both* have for the masculine N. duŏ and ambŏ, Ac. duŏs or duŏ, ambŏs or ambŏ; for the neut. N. and Ac. duŏ and ambŏ.

* Pronounced as monosyllables: cui (ki), huic (hīk).

† These words may be recollected by the following rhymes:
    Ius and I *from* ălĭo- altĕro-, { eo- *and* quo-, ūno- *and* ullo-,
    sōlo- tōto-, ūtĕro- neutĕro-, { ho- isto- illo-, ipso- *and* nullo-.

118 G. pl.—The genitive sometimes has a short form, especially in numbers weights and measures: as, duo- *two*, G. pl. duōrum or duum; mŏdĭo- *a bushel*, G. pl. mŏdium.
119 G. pl.—Greek words form the G. pl. in ōn: as, Georgico- *belonging to agriculture*, G. pl. Georgĭcōn.
120 D. and Ab. pl.—The dative and ablative of duo- and ambo- are in the masculine and neuter duōbŭs, ambōbŭs.
121 D. and Ab. pl.—An old form of the D. and Ab. pl. is in eis: as, ōloes from ōlo- *yonder*, instead of illīs from illo-.
122 D. and Ab. pl.—Deo- has in the D. and Ab. pl. Deīs, Dīīs, or more commonly Dīs; and eo- has eīs, iīs, īs, or more commonly his.
123 Four neuters in o have a d in the N. and Ac. singular: quo-, quŏd; isto-, istŭd; illo-, illŭd; Klio-, ălĭŭd.
124 Ho-, isto-, illo-, when compounded with the enclitic cĕ, *look* or *lo*, take neither d nor m in the N. and Ac. neut.: as, hŏc, istŏc or istūc, illŏc or illūc.

124.1 IRREGULAR O DECLENSION.

Latin c.f. Gender. English.	Puĕro- masc. *boy*.	Vīro- masc. *man*.	Lībēro- masc. *inner bark*.	Fīlio- masc. *son*.	Equo- masc. *horse*.
Singular. *Nom.* *Voc.* *Ac.* *Gen.* *Dat.* *Abl.*	puĕr puĕr puĕrum puĕrī puĕrō puĕrō	vĭr vĭr vĭrum vĭrī vĭrō vĭrō	lībĕr lībĕr lībrum lībrī lībrō lībrō	fīlĭŭs fīlī fīlium fīlĭī or fīlī fīliō fīliō	ĕcŭs* ĕquĕ ĕcum* ĕquī ĕquō ĕquō
Plural. *Nom.* *Voc.* *Ac.* *Gen.* *Dat.* *Abl.*	puĕrī puĕrī puĕrōs puĕrōrum puĕrīs puĕrīs	vĭrī vĭrī vĭrōs vĭrōrum vĭrīs vĭrīs	lībrī lībrī lībrōs lībrōrum lībrīs lībrīs	fīliī fīliī fīliōs fīliōrum fīliīs fīliīs	ĕquī ĕquī ĕquōs ĕquōrum ĕquīs ĕquīs

* So our best Mss. for the best authors; but editors in their timidity generally print *equus, equum*.

Remarks on the Third, or I Declension.

125   Many words belong partly to the *i* declension, partly to the consonant declension: as, sorti- or sort- *a lot* or *ballot*. In such words the singular is generally formed according to the consonant declension, the plural according to the *i* declension. (See § 148.1)

126   Many words belong partly to the *i* declension, partly to the *e* declension: as, aede- or aedi- *temple*. (See § 148.1) The forms from *e* are seldom used except in the nom. and voc. But fame- or fami- *hunger* has an Ab. fămē with the *e* long, as in the *e* declension.

126.1   N.—Although neuter nominatives of this declension commonly end in *ĕ*, pŏti- *possible* has 'for the neuter in old writers pŏtis, as well as pŏtĕ.

127   N. and V.—If a crude form end in *ri*, the letters which should follow *r* are often dropped in the nom. and voc.: as, lintĕri- *a wherry*, N. and V. lintĕr; Arāri- *a river in Gallia*, N. and V. Arăr or Arăris.

128   N. and V.—Some adjectives ending in *ĕri* have both forms: as, ācĕri- *sharp*, N. and V. ācĕr for the masculine, ācris for the feminine; but ācris is sometimes used even for the masculine.

129   If the crude form end in *ĕri*, the *e* is often dropped in those cases which do not end in *er*: as, lintĕri- *wherry*, G. lintris.

130   N. and V.—If the crude form ends in *li*, the letters which should follow *l* in the N. and V. are sometimes dropped: as, vigĭli- *a night-sentinel*, N. and V. vigĭl. This word is in origin an adjective.

131   N. V. Ac.—If the crude form of a neuter substantive end in *āri* or *āli*, the N. V. Ac. generally drop the final *i* and shorten the *a*: as, calcāri- *spur*, N. V. Ac. calcăr. These words are in origin neuter adjectives.

132   N. and Ac.—Three pronouns form the neut. sing. N. and Ac. in *d*: qui- quid; i- id; illi- illid.

133   Ac.—Some few substantives are found only with the Ac. in *im*: as, vi-m *force*, siti-m *thirst*; but *em* is in more general use. With adjectives *em* alone is found, as from lēni- *smooth*, Ac. masc. and fem. lēnem.

134   Ac.—Greek words often form the accusative in *n*: as, Pări- *Paris*, N. Păris, Ac. Părin.

135   G.—Greek words sometimes form the gen. in *ŏs*: as, mäthēsi- *knowledge*, G. mäthēseōs.

136   Ab.—Neuter substantives (with the exception of names of towns) and also adjectives of all genders prefer the ablative in *i*:

as, mări- *sea*, Ab. mărī;* lēni- *smooth*, Ab. lēnī. But adjectives used as masc. or fem. substantives admit the Ab. in *e*: as affīnī- *a relative by marriage*, Ab. affīnē. Participles in *enti-* when used as substantives, and also in the construction called the ablative absolute (§ 1013), require the form in *e*.

136.1 Ac. pl.—A form in *eis* (= īs) also occurs in inscriptions.

137 G. pl.—Some nouns drop the *i* in the G. pl.: as, căni- *dog*, jŭvĕni- *young man*, cĕlĕri- quick; G. pl. cănum, jŭvĕnum, cĕlĕrum. This is often the case in poetry: as, ăgresti- *of the country*, G. pl. ăgrestium, or in poetry ăgrestum; and generally with those adjectives which have no neuter plural: as, ĭnŏp- *helpless*, G. pl. ĭnŏpum.

138 G. pl.—Greek words sometimes form the G. pl. in *ōn*: as, mĕtămorphōsi- *change of form*, N. sing. mĕtămorphōsis, G. pl. mĕtămorphōseōn.

139 G. pl.—Plural names of festivals often form the G. pl. as if from a c.F. in *io*: as, Baccănāli- *of Bacchus*, N. pl. Baccănālĭă, G. pl. Baccănālium or Baccănāliōrum.

130.1   IRREGULAR *I* DECLENSION.

Lat. c.F. Gender. English.	Lintĕri- fem. *wherry*.	Vĭgĭli- masc. *a night-sentinel*.	Affīni- mas. or fem. *relative by marriage*.	Ănĭmāli- neut. *living being*.	Calcări- neut. *spur*.
Sing.					
Nom.	lintĕr	vĭgĭl	affīnis	ănĭmăl	calcăr
Voc.	lintĕr	vĭgĭl	affīnis	ănĭmăl	calcăr
Acc.	lintrem	vĭgĭlem	affīnem	ănĭmăl	calcăr
Gen.	lintris	vĭgĭlis	affīnis	ănĭmālis	calcăris
Dat.	lintrī	vĭgĭlī	affīnī	ănĭmālī	calcārī
Abl.	lintrī or lintrĕ	vĭgĭlī or vĭgĭlĕ	affīnī or affīnē	ănĭmālī or ănĭmālĕ	calcārī or calcārĕ
Plural.					
Nom.	lintrĕs	vĭgĭlēs	affīnēs	ănĭmālĭă	calcărĭă
Voc.	lintrĕs	vĭgĭlēs	affīnēs	ănĭmālĭă	calcărĭă
Acc.	lintrīs or lintrĕs	vĭgĭlīs or vĭgĭlēs	affīnīs or affīnēs	ănĭmālĭă	calcărĭă
Gen.	lintrium	vĭgĭlum†	affīnium	ănĭmālium	calcărium
Dat.	lintrĭbŭs	vĭgĭlĭbŭs	affīnĭbŭs	ănĭmālĭbŭs	calcărĭbŭs
Abl.	lintrĭbŭs	vĭgĭlĭbŭs	affīnĭbŭs	ănĭmālĭbŭs	calcărĭbŭs

* But *mărĕ* as an abl. occurs in poetry after prepositions: as, *ē mărĕ* Lucr. 1. 162, *dē mărĕ* Ov. Trist. v. 2. 20.

† Observe the omission of the *i* before the *u*.

Remarks on the Fourth, or U Declension.

140. Two monosyllabic nouns, su- *a boar* or *sow*, gru- *a crane*, are not contracted like the longer nouns of this declension, and are therefore declined as in the consonant declension; but su- has both sŭbŭs and sŭbŭs in the D. and Ab. pl.

141. Many crude forms in *u* coexist with crude forms in *o*: as, lauro- or laura- *laurel*. Hence the genitives sĕnātī, tŭmultī, &c. as well as sĕnātūs, tŭmultūs, &c. are found. See § 148. 1.

142. G.—From ănu- *an old woman* the uncontracted Gen. ănuĭs is used.

143. G. pl.—One *u* is sometimes omitted in the G. pl.: as, curru- *chariot*, G. pl. curruum, or in poetry currum.

144. D. and Ab. pl.—Many words change the penult *ŭ* into *ĭ*: as, cornu- *horn*, D. and Ab. pl. cornĭbŭs.

Remarks on the Fifth, or E Declension.

145. Many crude forms in *e* coexist with crude forms in *a*: as, mătĕria- or mătĕriē- *timber*. See § 148. 1.

146. G.—Old forms of the genitive, such as diēs and diī from die- *day*, are found.

147. G. and D.—The penult *e* in the G. and D. was originally long in all the nouns of this declension; but if no *i* precede, it is considered to be short in prose: as, from fĭde- *faith*, G. and D. fĭdĕī; but from dĭē- *day*, G. and D. diēī.

148. Few nouns in *e* have a plural, and still fewer a G. D. and Ab. pl.

MIXED DECLENSIONS.

Latin. English.	Consonant and i.		i and e.	
	urb- or urbi-, *f.* city.	part- or parti-, *f.* part.	nūbi- or nūbe-, *f.* cloud.	torqul- or torque-, *m.* or *f.* twisted chain.
Sing.				
Nom.	urbs	pars	nūbēs or nūbis	torquēs or torquis
Voc.	urbs	pars	nūbēs	torquēs
Acc.	urbem	partem*	nūbem	torquem
Gen.	urbis	partis	nūbis	torquis
Dat.	urbī	partī	nūbī	torquī
Abl.	urbĕ	partĕ	nūbĕ	torquĕ
Plural.				
Nom.	urbēs	partēs	nūbēs	torquēs
Voc.	urbēs	partēs	nūbēs	torquēs
Acc.	urbīs or urbēs	partīs or partēs	nūbīs or nūbēs	torquīs or torquēs
Gen.	urbium	partium	nūbium	torquium
Dat.	urbībūs	partībūs	nūbībūs	torquībūs
Abl.	urbībūs	partībūs	nūbībūs	torquībūs

Latin. English.	e and a.	u and o.	o and u.
	mătĕria- or mătĕrie-, *f.* timber.	bŏno- or bŏna- good.	fīco- or fīcu-, *f.* fig-tree.
Sing.			
Nom.	mătĕriēs or mătĕriă		fīcūs
Voc.			
Acc.	mătĕriem or mătĕriam		fīcum
Gen.	—————— mătĕriae	See Adjectives, § 212	fīcī or fīcūs
Dat.	—————— mătĕriae		fīcō or fīcuī
Abl.	mătĕriē or mătĕriā		fīcō or fīcū
Plural.			
Nom.			fīcī or fīcūs
Voc.			
Acc.	No Plural		fīcōs or fīcūs
Gen.			fīcōrum or fīcuum
Dat.			fīcīs or fīcūbūs
Abl.			fīcīs or fīcūbūs

* Rarely *partim* unless used adverbially.

DEFECTIVE AND IRREGULAR NOUNS.

149. Some nouns are not declined: as, nihil *nothing*, fas *permitted by Heaven*, nequam *good for nothing*, quŏt *how many*, tŏt *so many*, and many numerals. See Numerals, § 252. Substantives undeclined are seldom used except as nominatives or accusatives.

150. Some want the plural: as, sĕnectūt- *old age*, vēr- n. *spring*, sŭperbia- *pride*, prōle- *offspring*, auro- n. *gold*, ōleo- n. *oil*.

151. Some want the singular: as, tĕnĕbra-, N. pl. tĕnĕ-brae *darkness*; castrŭ- n., N. pl. castrā *camp*; armo- n., N. pl. armā *arms*; Pŭteōlo-, N. pl. Pŭteōlī *Little wells*, the name of a town.

152. Some have both singular and plural, but with different meanings: as,

SING.		PLUR. NOM.	
aedi- or aede-	*a room or temple*,	aedēs	*a house*.
ăqua-	*water*,	ăquae	*medicinal springs*.
auxĭlio- n.	*help*,	auxĭliă	*allied troops*.
cōpia-	*abundance*,	cōpiae	*military forces*.
fini-	*end*,	fīnēs	*boundaries, territory*.
fortūna-	*fortune*,	fortūnae	*property*.
grātia-	*favour*,	grātiae	*thanks*.
littĕra-	*a letter of the alphabet*,	littĕrae	*a letter or epistle*.
ŏpĕra-	*work, assistance*,	ŏpĕrae	*labourers or hired men*.

153. Some nouns are deficient in one or more cases: thus, vīc- *turn* has no N. or D. sing.; ŏp- *help* has no nominative.

154. Some nouns form their cases partly from one crude form, partly from another. Thus, volgŏs- n. *mob* supplies a N. V. Ac. sing. volgŭs, and volgo- n. the G. volgī, D. and Ab. volgō; Itĕr- n. *route* supplies a N. V. Ac. sing. Itĕr, and Itĭnĕr- n. the other cases; praecĭp- *head-foremost* supplies praeceps for the N. and V. sing. of all genders and the Ac. neut. sing., the other cases being formed from praecĭpĭt-; vās- n. *a vessel* is declined in the singular along with vāso- n. in the plural.

155. Some nouns have one gender in the singular, another in the plural. Thus,

dĭe-	*day*	is m. or f. in the singular, but m. in the plural.					
caelo-	*air, sky*	is n.	,,	,,	,,	m.	,,
frāno-	*bridle*	is n.	,,	,,	,,	m. or n.	,,
rastro-	*rake*	is n.	,,	,,	,,	m. or n.	,,
jŏco-	*joke*	is m.	,,	,,	,,	m. or n.	,,
lŏco-	*place*	is m.	,,	,,	,,	m. or n.	,,

DEFECTIVE AND IRREGULAR NOUNS.

156 Some adjectives are deficient in gender. Thus, mĕmŏr- *mindful*, paupĕr- *earning-little*, have no neuter; victrīci- or victrīo- *victorious* is only fem. in the sing., only fem. or neut. in the plur.

Some Irregular Nouns declined.

157 Bŏu- *ax* or *cow*, N. V. bōs, Ac. bŏuem, G. bŏuĭs, D. bŏuī, Ab. bŏuē. Pl. N. V. Ac. bŏuēs, G. bŏuum or boum, D. and Ab. bōbŭs or būbŭs.

158 Deo- *God*, N. V. Deŭs, Ac. Deum, G. Dei, D. Ab. Deō. Pl. N. V. Dei, Dii, more commonly Dī, Ac. Deōs, G. Deōrum or Deum, D. Ab. Deis, Diis, more commonly Dīs.

159 Dōmo- or dŏmu- *f.*, *house*, N. V. dŏmŭs, Ac. dŏmum, G. dŏmūs, D. dŏmui, dŏmō, with dŏmī *at home*, Ab. dŏmū or dŏmō. Pl. N. V. dŏmŭs, Ac. dŏmūs or dŏmōs, G. dŏmuum or dŏmōrum, D. Ab. dŏmĭbŭs.

160 Iou-pĭtĕr- (= pater-) *Jupiter*, N. V. Iuppĭtĕr or Iūpĭtĕr, Ac. Iŏuem, G. Iŏuĭs, D. Iŏuī, Ab. Iŏuē.

161 Iūs-iūrando- *n.*, *oath* (really two words), N. V. Ac. iūsiūrandum, G. iūrisiūrandi, D. iūriiūrandō, Ab. iūreiūrandō.

162 Nĭg- or nĭu- *snow*, N. V. nĭx, Ac. nĭuem, G. nĭuĭs, D. nĭuī, Abl. nĭuē. Pl. N. Ac. nĭuēs, Ab. nĭuĭbŭs.

163 Rē-publica- *common-wealth* (really two words), N. V. res-publĭcă, Ac. rem-publĭcam, G. D. rei-publĭcae, Ab. rē-publĭcā. Pl. Ac. res-publĭcās, G. rērum-publĭcārum, Ab. rēbus-publĭcīs.

164 Sĕnĕo- or sĕn- *an old man*, N. V. sĕnex, Ac. sĕnem, G. sĕnĭs, D. sĕnī, Ab. sĕnē. Pl. N. V. Ac. sĕnēs, G. sĕnum, D. Ab. sĕnĭbŭs.

165 Vīsi- uĭs- or uī- *force*, N. V. uĭs, Ac. uim, G. uĭs, D. Ab. uī. Pl. N. V. Ac. uīrēs, G. uīrium, D. Ab. uīrĭbŭs.

Some Foreign Proper Names declined.

166 Αἰνεια- Aeneā- *Aeneas*, N. Aenēās, V. Aenēā, Ac. Aenēān or -am, G. D. Aenēae, Ab. Aenēā.

167 Αγχισα- or -η- Anchisā- or Anchisē- *Anchises*, N. Anchisēs, V. Anchisē or -ā, Ac. Anchisēn or -am, G. D. Anchisae, Ab. Anchisē or -ā.

168 Ὀρεστη- Oresto- or -tā- *Orestes*, N. Orestēs, V. Orestē, Ac. Orestēn or -em, G. D. Orestae, Ab. Orestē.

169 Μεναδρο- Mĕnandēro- *Menander*, N. Mĕnandrŏs or -drŭs or -dĕr,

V. Měnandrē or -děr, Ac. Měnandrŏn or -drum, G. Měnandrū
or -drī, D. Ab. Měnandrō.
170 Πανθοο- Panthoo- *Panthus*, N. Panthūs, V. Panthū, Ac. Panthūn
or Panthum, G. Panthī, D. Ab. Panthō.
171 Αθω- Athō- or Athōn- (and perhaps Athŏ-) *Mount Athos*, N. Athōs,
Ac. Athōn Athō Athōnem (and perhaps Athōn), G. D. Athō,
Ab. Athō or Athōnā.
172 Δειδοι- Dīdoi- *Dido*, N. V. Ac. Dīdō, G. Dīdūs, D. Ab. Dīdō. Also
from Dīdōn- N. V. Dīdō, Ac. Dīdōnem, &c.
173 Κοω- or Κω- Coo- *the island Cos*, N. Cōs, Ac. Coon or Cōn, G. Coī
or Cō, D. Ab. Coō or Cō.
174 Παρι- or Παριδ- Pări- or Părīd- *Paris*, N. Păris, V. Păris or Pări,
Ac. Părim or -ĭn, Păridem or -dă, G. Păridŏs or -dis, D. Păridī
or -dī, Ab. Păridĕ.
175 Αχιλλεύς- Achilleŭ- or -lē- *Achilles*, N. Achillēs, V. Achillē, Ac.
Achillēn or -lan or -lem, G. Achilleŏs -leī -lis and in the best
prose Achillī, D. Achilleī or -leī or -lī, Ab. Achillē.
176 Ορφεύς- Orpheŭ- or Orpheo- *Orpheus*, N. Orpheus, V. Orpheu, Ac.
Orphēă or -eum, G. Orpheŏs or -eī or -ei or -ī, D. Orpheī or -eī
or -eo, Ab. Orpheo.
177 Ιλιονεύς- Iliōneŭ- *Ilioneus*, N. Iliōneus, V. Iliōneu, Ac. Iliōneă, G.
Iliōneŏs or Iliōnei, D. Iliōneī or -ei or -eo, Ab. Iliōneo.
178 Περσεύς- Perseŭ- or Persē- *Perseus*, like Orpheŭ-: but also N.
Persēs, V. Persē, Ac. Persēn, G. D. Persae, Ab. Persē or -sā.
179 Σωκρατεσ- Socrătes- or Socrătē- *Socrates*, N. Socrătēs, V. Socrătēs or
-tēs or -tē, Ac. Socrătēn or -tem, G. Socrătis or rather Socrătī,
D. Socrătī, Ab. Socrătā.
180 Περικλεισ- Pěriclē- *Pericles*, N. Pěriclēs, V. Pěriclēs or -clē, Ac.
Pěriclēă or -clem, G. Pěriclis or rather Pěriclī, D. Pěriclī, Ab.
Pěricle.
181 Θαλησ- Thălēt- or Thălē- *Thales*, N. Thălēs, V. Thălēs or -lē, Ac.
Thălētă or -tem, Thălēn or -em, G. Thălētis Thălis or -lī, D.
Thălētī or Thălī, Ab. Thălētĕ or Thălē.
182 Ατυ- Aty- *Atys*, N. Atys, V. Aty, Ac. Atyn or Atym, G. Atyŏs or
Atyis or Atys, D. Atyi or Aty, Ab. Atyē or Aty.

GENDER.

183 It has been already stated that there are two genders, masculine and feminine, and that those nouns which are of no gender are called neuter.

184 The gender may be determined partly by the meaning, partly by the suffix or termination.

Gender determined by Meaning.

185 Males, months,* winds, and rivers, are generally masculine.

186 Females, countries,* islands,* and trees, are generally feminine.

187 Nouns undeclined, as fās *right*, nĕfas *wrong*, gummi *gum;* words belonging to the other parts of speech used for the time as substantives, as hoc ipsum 'diu' *this very word 'diu';* sentences used as substantives; and the produce of trees, are generally neuter.

188 Many substantives denote both the male and female, and are therefore called *common:* as, săcerdōt- *priest* or *priestess*. These are for the most part really adjectives.

189 Sometimes there are two different words or two different terminations, one for the male, the other for the female: as, tauro- *bull,* vacca- *cow;* ĕquo- *horse,* ĕqua- *mare*.

190 At other times the natural gender of animals is forgotten for a fanciful gender. Thus, the words uolpe- *fox,* căni- or căne- *dog,* ănăt- *duck,* are generally considered to be feminine. On the contrary, ansĕr- *goose,* lĕpŏs- *hare,* are masculine. Those words which under one grammatical gender are applied to both male and female are called *epicenes.* If the real gender must be noticed, the words mās- *male,* and fōmina- *female,* are added.

---

* The names for the months are really adjectives agreeing with the masculine noun, mens- 'month,' understood. The names of countries and islands are also often adjectives agreeing with the feminine nouns, terra- 'land,' and insula- 'island.' So the names of ships (*navi-* understood) and plays (*fabula-* understood) are treated as feminines.

Gender determined by Suffixes.

MASCULINE SUFFIXES.

191. The following suffixes produce masculine nouns. They are arranged alphabetically according to their last letters.

Suffix	Added to	Gives a subst. meaning	Thus from	English	Is derived	English
a*	verbs	a person	incŏl-	*inhabit*	incŏl-a-	*inhabitant.*
ta	—	a person	naut-	*ship*	naul-ta-	*sailor.*
ic	—	—	uort-	*turn*	uort-ic-	*eddy.*
ōn	subst.	—	nāso-	*nose*	Nās-ōn-	*big-nose.*
ōn	verbs	man	bīb-	*drink*	bīb-ōn-	*tippler.*
ōn	verbs	—	turbā-	*whirl*	turb-ōn-	*whirlwind.*
ot	verbs	act	lūd-	*play*	lūd-o-	*play.*
iot	verbs	—	flu-	*flow*	flŭu-io-	*river.*
ŭlot	verbs	little	tŭm-e-	*swell*	tŭm-ŭlo-	*mound.*
ŭlot	nouns	little	fŏco-	*fire*	fŏc-ŭlo-	*a little fire.*
cŭlot	nouns	little	frātēr-	*brother*	frāter-cŭlo-	*little brother.*
lnot	—	little	—	—	ŭs-lno-	*ass.*
ero	—	little	—	—	nŭm-ĕro-	*number.*
tĕrot	verbs	means	cŏl-	*cul. dig*	cul-tĕro-	*ploughshare.*
to‡	verbs	one —ed	lĕgā-	*depute*	lĕgā-to-	*deputy.*
ŏr	verbs	state	time-	*fear*	tĭm-ŏr-	*fear.*
tŏr	verbs	man	ārā-	*plough*	ārā-tŏr-	*ploughman.*
tŏr	subst.	man	iānua-	*gate*	iāni-tŏr-	*gatekeeper.*
tu§	verbs	—ing	audī-	*hear*	audī-tu-	*hearing.*

192. It would be a useful exercise to collect examples of each suffix. Thus, for the suffix *a*, from verbs, denoting a person:

conuīu-a- *a messmate* or *guest*, from cŏn *together* and utu- *live.*
aduĕn-a- *a stranger*, „ ăd *to* and uĕn- *come.*
scrīb-a- *a secretary*, „ scrīb- *write.*
parrīcīd-a- *a parricide*, „ pătĕr- *father* and caed- *slay.*
trānsfŭg-a- *a deserter*, „ trans *across* and fŭg- *fly.*
caelīcŏl-a- *heaven-inhabiting*, „ caelo- *sky* and cŏl- *inhabit.*
ignīgĕn-a- *fire-born*, „ igni- *fire* and gĕn- *produce.*

* Words of this class may perhaps be considered as common, but the masculine is generally meant.
† See the neuter suffixes.
‡ These are really masculine participles.
§ These are often called supines.

FEMININE SUFFIXES.

Suffix	Added to	Gives a subst. meaning	Thus from	English	Is derived	English
a	verbs	act	fŭg-	fly	fŭg-a-	flight.
a	male	female	hospĭt-	stranger	hospĭt-a-	female stranger.
ia	subst.	collective	fămŭlo-	slave	famĭl-ia-	family.*
ia	people	a country	Gallo-	a Gaul	Gall-ia-	Gallia.
ia	adj.	quality	mĭsĕro-	wretched	mĭsĕr-ia-	wretchedness.
Ïtia∥	adj.	quality	ămīco-	friendly	ămīc-ĭtia-	friendship.
ēla	verbs	act	quĕr-(r.)	complain	quĕr-ēla-	complaint.
ēla	subst.	state	clienti-	vassal	client-ēla-	vassalage.
tēla	verbs	act	tuĕ-(r.)	protect	tū-tēla-	protection.
āla	nouns	little	ănĭma-	breath	ănĭm-ăla-	little breath.
cŭla	nouns	little	sŏrŏr-	sister	sŏror-cŭla-	little sister.
ma	verbs	act	fa-	speak	fā-ma-	report.
ĭna	—	—	pāto-	be spread	pāt-ĭna-	dish.
ĭna	male	female	rēg-	king	rēg-ĭna-	queen.
īna	verbs	act	ru-	rush	ru-īna-	downfall.
bra	verbs	—	lāte-	be hid	lătĕ-bra-	hiding-place.
ēra	—	—	pāte-	be spread	pāt-ēra-	bowl.
ūra	verbs	act	fĭg-	model	fĭg-ūra-	shape.
tūra†	verbs	act	pĭg-	paint	pic-tūra-	painting.
ta	verbs	act	ulu-	live	uī-ta-	life.
ta	adj.	quality	louăni-	young	iŭuen-ta-	youth.
īci	-tŏr‡	female	uic-tŏr-	conqueror	uictr-īci-	conqueress.
e	verbs	act	fīd-	trust	fīd-e-	faith.
ĭtie	adj.	quality	trīsti-	sad	trīst-ĭtie-	sadness.
ti	verbs	act	mŏr-(r.)	die	mor-ti-	death.
dōn∥	verbs	quality	dulcē-	be sweet	dulcē-dōn-	sweetness.
gōn§	verbs	act	ŏrī-(r.)	rise	ŏrī-gōn-	origin.
tūdōn	adj.	quality	longo-	long	longĭ-tūdōn-	length.
lōn§	verbs	act	ŏpīna-(r.)	fancy	ŏpīn-iōn-	opinion.
tiōn	verbs	act	dīc-	speak	dic-tiōn-	speaking.
tāt∥	nouns	quality	cīuĭ-	citizen	cīuĭ-tāt-	citizenship.
tūt	nouns	quality	seruo-	slave	scruī-tūt-	slavery.

* Literally, 'a slave-gang.'

† Perhaps more immediately from nouns in *tŏr*, as from *pictŏr-*'painter,' *pictūra-* 'painting.'

‡ i. e. a substantive in *tor*. § See Appendix II.

∥ But -iōn as a suffix of material objects is masculine, as:

| iōn | verbs | little | pŭg- | pierce | pŭg-iōn- | dagger |
| — | subst. | little | căballo- | horse | căball-iōn- | hippocampus |

194   NEUTER SUFFIXES.

Suffix	Added to	Gives a subst. meaning	Thus from	English	Is derived	English
li*	subst.	—	ănĭmă-	life	ănĭmă-li-	animal.
ri*	subst.	—	puluīno-	cushion	puluīnā-ri-	shrine.
ĕn	verbs	—	ungu-	anoint	ungu-ĕn-	ointment.
mĕn	verbs	instrument	tĕg-	cover	tĕg-mĕn-	covering.
o	verbs	—	jŭg-	yoke	jŭg-o-	yoke.
io	verbs	act, &c	gaude-	rejoice	gaud-io-	joy.
Iŭo	nouns	—	seruo-	slave	seru-Iŭo-	slavery.
ŭlo	verbs	instrument	iăc-	throw	iăc-ŭlo-	dart.
ŭlo	nouns	little	paulo-	a little	paul-ŭlo-	a very little.
bŭlo†	verbs	instrument	uĕnā-	hunt	uĕnā-bŭlo-	hunting-spear.
bŭlo†	subst.	instrument	tūs-	incense	tūrĭ-bŭlo-	censer.
cŭlo‡	verbs	instrument	uĕh-	carry	uĕhĭ-cŭlo-	carriage.
cŭlo	nouns	little	ŏpĕs-	work	ŏpus-cŭlo-	a little work.
īno	—	—	rēg-	king	rēg-no-	royal power.
ĕro	verbs	instrument	scalp-	scratch	scalp-ro-	graving-tool.
b'ro†	verbs	instrument	cĕr-	sift	crī-bro-	sieve.
c'ro‡	verbs	instrument	sĕpĕl-	bury	sĕpul-cro-	burial-place.
t'ro	verbs	instrument	rād-	scrape	rās-tro-	rake.
to	verbs	thing done	lēg-	leave	lēgā-to-	legacy.
to	trees	collective	arbŏs-	tree	arbus-to-	vineyard.
ĕto§	trees	collective	quercu-	oak	querc-ēto-	oak-grove.
ento	verbs	—	ungu-	anoint	ungu-ento-	ointment.
mento	verbs	instrument	ornā-	equip	ornā-mento-	equipment.
ĕr¶	verbs	—	it- or i-	go	ĭt-ĕr-	route.
Inĕr	verbs	—	it- or i-	go	ĭt-Inĕr-	route.
ŭr	verbs	—	fulg-	shine	fulg-ŭr-	lightning.
ĕs	verbs	—	gĕn-	produce	gĕn-ĕs-	race, birth.
ŏs	verbs	—	frīg-e-	be cold	frīg-ŏs-	cold.
Inŏs	verbs	—	făc-	do	făc-Inŏs-	deed.

195   The tables of suffixes here given are far from sufficient to determine the gender of all words. Indeed, some of the suffixes

* These are really neuter adjectives, and the two suffixes are closely related; puluīnāri- being preferred to puluīnāli- because the word has already got an l.

† bŭlo and b'ro are probably the same suffix, the latter being preferred after a preceding l. See Appendix II.

‡ The same may be said of cŭlo and c'ro, and perhaps t'ro.

§ But ĕs, ŏs, ōs, ŭs, together with ĕr, ăr, ŏr, ŭr and ŭl, are mere varieties of the same suffix. So also Inĕr, Inŏs, Inŭr, &c. are of one origin. Compare the last three with the Greek τέμενος- 'sacred ground.'

|| More strictly ecto, the first syllable of which is the diminutival ec, see § 207. 1. Indeed the form ecto is preserved in uirueto- n., olīveto- n.

¶ See Appendix II.

will be found common to the masculine and neuter tables: as, o, io, alo, ino, ero, iro, to.

195.1 Suffixes which denote an abstract quality or act are at times used in the sense of collective nouns, as from

 ĕquĭta- *ride*, ĕquĭta-tu- m., *a body of riders, cavalry.*
 Ităllo- *an Italian*, Ităl-ĭa- *the body of Italians, Italy.*
 sĕqu- (r.) *follow*, sec-ta- *a body of followers, a school.*
 gĕn- *produce*, gen-ti- *or* gent- *a race.*
 multo- *many*, multĭ-tūdŏn- *a multitude, a mob.*
 lĕg- *choose*, lĕg-iōn- *picked men, a legion.*
 cĭuĭ- *citizen*, cĭuĭ-tāt- *a body of citizens, a state.*
 nōbĭli- *noble*, nōbĭlĭ-tāt- *a body of nobles, a nobility.*
 iŭuĕnĭ- *young*, iŭuen-tūt- *a body of young men, youth.*
 consŭl- *consult*, consĭl-io- n., *a body of persons consulting.*

196 It will be observed that a large number of substantives in *a* are feminine. But the rule is far from universal; as may be seen in the masculines: Belga- *a Belgian*, Sulla- *the Roman dictator*, Matrōna- m. *the river Marne*, Hadria- *the Hadriatic*, nauta- *sailor*, incŏla- *inhabitant*.

197 The nouns in *i* occasion much trouble. The majority are feminine, but the exceptions are numerous. These may perhaps be remembered by the following acrostic:

  M ascŭlĭnĭ gĕnĕrĭs crīnĭ-
  A mnĭ-* axĭ- fūnĭ-* finĭ-*
  S entĭ-* dentĭ- callĭ-* collĭ-
  O aulĭ- fascĭ- fustĭ- follĭ-
  V t'rĭ- uent'rĭ- uermĭ- assĭ-
  L nĭ- postĭ- torrĭ- cassĭ-
  I gnĭ- imb'rĭ- piscĭ- pontĭ-
  N atalĭ- uectĭ- fontĭ- montĭ-
  E nsĭ- mensĭ- pānĭ-* orbĭ-
  S angul- anguĭ-* unguĭ- curbĭ-.

197.1 Lat. c.r.	Nom.	English.	Lat. c.r.	Nom.	English.
amni-	amnis	*river*	axi- *or*	axis *or*	*axle or*
angui-	anguis	*snake*	assi-	assis	*pole*
assi-	as	*unit*	calli-	callis	*path*

 * Many e'en of these, as fīnĭ-,
 Are also gĕnĕrĭs fēmĭnīnĭ.

30 DIMINUTIVES.

Lat. c.f.	Nom.	English.	Lat. c.f.	Nom.	English.
ansi- (pl.)	assēs	net	mensi-	mensis	month
cauli-	caulis	stalk	monti-	mons	mountain
colli-	collis	hill	nātāli-	nātālis	birthday
corbi-	corbis	basket	orbi-	orbis	round
crīni-	crīnis	band of hair	pāni-	pānis	loaf
ensi-	ensis	sword	pisci-	piscis	fish
fasci-	fascis	bundle	ponti-	pons	bridge
fīni-	fīnis	end	posti-	postis	door-post
folli- (pl.)	follēs	bellows	sangui-†	sanguis	blood
denti-	dens	tooth	senti-	sentis	thorn
fonti-	fons	spring	torri-	torris	brand
fūni-	fūnis	rope	uecti-	uectis	pole
fusti-	fustis	club	uentri-	uenter	belly
igni-	ignis	fire	uermi-	uermis	worm
imbēri-	imber	shower	ungui-	unguis	nail
lēni-*	lēnis	wine-press	ūtĕri-	ūter	skin.

FORMATION AND GENDER OF DIMINUTIVES.

198 Diminutives denote strictly small size, but are also used to denote sometimes contempt, sometimes affection.

198.1 The gender of a diminutive is the same as that of the noun from which it is formed: as, frātĕr- m. *brother*, frātercŭlo- m. *little brother;* cŏrōna- f. *a circular wreath or chaplet*, cŏrolla- f. *a small chaplet;* corpŏs- n. *body*, corpusculo- n. *a small body.*

199 Hence the gender of a diminutive will often assist the memory to the gender of the primitive or word from which it is derived. Thus tūber-cŭlo- n. *a little bump* proves that tūbĕr- *bump* is neuter.

200 If the noun be of the first or second declension, that is, if it end in *a* or *o*, the diminutive ends in *ŭla* or *ŭlo* (older form *ĕla*, *ĕlo*). Thus from ănĭma- *breath* or *life,* dim. ănĭmŭla-.

201 If the letter before *o* and *a* be *u, e* or *i*, *ŏlo* and *ŏla* are preferred. Thus from seruo- *slave*, linea- *line*, seruŏlo-, lineŏla- are derived.

202 If the letter before *a* and *o* be an *r, l,* or *s,* a contraction gene-

* Lēni- = λήνο-, whence *Lēnaeus* 'the God of the wine-press, Bacchus.'
† Hence nom. sanguis, acc. sanguem, Inscr. Or. 2270, 3054, the diminutive sangui-culo- m., and the adj. ex-sangui- 'bloodless.' Otherwise sangula-, nom. sanguis, &c. is in use.

rally takes place producing a termination *lla* or *llo*. Thus from puĕra- *girl*, ŏcŭlo- *eye*, uĭno- *wine*, are derived (puĕrŭla-) puella- f., (ŏcŭlŭlo-) ŏcello- m., (uĭnŭlo-) nillo- n.

203. If the letter before *a* or *o* was an *l*, and that *l* was itself preceded by a long vowel or diphthong, the diminutive ends in *xilla* or *xillo*. Thus āla- *wing*, axilla- *armpit*; māla- *jaw*, maxilla- ; paulo- n. *little*, pauxillo- n. ; pālo- m. *stake*, paxillo- m. ; talo- m. *ancle*, taxillo- m. ; uōlo- n. *sail*, uexillo- n. *flag*.*

204. If the noun be not of the first or second declension, the diminutive generally ends in *cŭla* or *cŭlo* (older form *cŭla*, *cŭlo*). Thus from cănĭ- f. *dog*, frā-tŏr- m. *brother*, gĕnu- n. *knee*, spē- f. *hope*, are derived cănĭcŭla- f., frātercŭlo- m., gĕnĭcŭlo- n., spēcŭla- f.

205. But if the noun end in *c* or *g*, *t* or *d*, the form *ŭla* or *ŭlo* is generally preferred. Thus from cornĭc- f. *crow*, rēg- m. *king*, căpŭt- n. *head*, lăpĭd- m. *stone*, are derived cornĭcŭla- f., rēgŭlo- m., căpĭtŭlo- n., (lăpĭdŭlo- contracted into) lăpillo- m.

206. If the noun end in *ōn* or *ōn*, the *o* is changed into *u*. Thus from hŏmōn- *man*, rătiōn- f. *account*, are derived hŏmuncŭlo- m., rătiuncŭla- f.

206.1 If the noun end in any of the five terminations *ŭs, ŏr, ŭs, ŏr, ĕs*, this syllable becomes *us*. Thus from rŭmŭs- or rŭmŏr- m. *report*, arbŏs- or arbŏr- f. *tree*, ŏpĕs- n. *work*, are derived rŭmuscŭlo- m., arbuscŭla- f., ŏpuscŭlo- n.

207. These rules for forming diminutives are applicable to adjectives also: as, paupĕr- *poor*, paupercŭlo- ; mĭsĕro- *wretched*, misello- ; ūno- *one*, ullo- ; molli- *soft*, mollĭcŭlo- ; paruo- *little*, paruŏlo- ; aureo- *golden*, aureŏlo-.

207.1 Diminutives are also formed by the addition of suffixes *ăc* or *ĭc*, *e* or *i*, and *u*.† Thus from sĕn- *an old man* (which forms ac. sĕnem, gen. sĕnĭs, &c.) comes sĕn-ĕc- *a little old man* (with nom. sĕnex). Many of these diminutives have wholly superseded the primitives whence they were derived, so that the latter have disappeared: as, cŭl-ĕc- m. *gnat*, cĭm-ĕc- m. *bug*, pŭl-ĕc- m. *flea*, săl-ĭc- f. *willow*, răd-ĭc- f. *root*, torqu-i- or torqu-e- f. *twisted chain*, ăp-i- f. *bee*, ăn-u- f. *old woman*, ăc-u- f. *needle*, măn-u- f. *hand*, gĕn-u- n. *knee*.

* In these nouns a guttural has probably been lost before the *l*. Comp. pauco- '*few*,' and *tēla*- '*web*' from *tex*- '*weave*.'

† These suffixes correspond to our English suffixes *ock* ; *ie* or *ee* ; *ow, ue*, and *ow*: as seen in *hillock*, *bullock*; *lassie*, *knee, tree*; *shrew, crew*; *clue*; *sparrow*, *willow*, *crow*. See Phil. Soc. vol. iii.

207.2 A diminutival suffix *leo* also occurs. Thus from ĕquo- or ŏco- *horse*, ĕcŭleo-. So also there are ăcŭleo- m. *a sting*, mal-leo m. *a mallet*. Probably *deo* in hordeo- or fordeo- *barley* is virtually the same suffix, added to the root far- *spelt*.

207.3 Diminutives may be formed from diminutives: as cista- *a box*, cistŭla- *a little box* or *casket*, cistella- *a little casket*, cistellŭla- *a very little casket*. So from ŏcŭlo- *an eye* (itself formed from an obsolete ŏco-)* come ŏcello- *a little eye*, and ŏcellŭlo- *a dear little eye*.

208 The feminine diminutives in *io* declined like neuters, as Glȳ- cĕrio- N. Glȳcĕrium, from Glȳcĕra- *Sweet one*, belong to the Greek language.

209 To the same language belong the masculine diminutives in *isco* and *astĕro*: as, Sȳrisco- N. Sȳriscŭs *little Syrus*, părăsĭtastĕro- *a little parasite*.

210 Many adjectives are used as substantives, the real substantive being understood. Thus:

Mĕdĭcina-, arti- *art* understood, *the art of healing*.
Arithmētĭca-, arti- *art* understood, *the art of numbers*.
Mĕdĭcina-, tăberna- *shop* understood, *the doctor's shop*.
Agnīna-, cărōn- *flesh* understood, *lamb's flesh, lamb*.
Bellōna-, dea- *goddess* understood, *the goddess of war*.
Africa-, terra- *land* understood, *the land of the Afri*.
Annōna-, cōpia- *supply* understood, *the year's supply*.
Corōna-, vitta- *fillet* understood, *circular fillet, chaplet*.
Compĕd-, cătēna- *chain* understood, *foot-chain, fetter*.
Mănĭca-, cătēna- *chain* understood, *hand-chain, hand-cuff*.
Annāli-, lĭbro- *book* understood, *year-book*.
Natāli-, die- *day* understood, *birth-day*.
Dĕcembāri-, mensi- *month* understood, *the tenth month (from March), December*.
Stătuārio- m. (*a man*) *of statues, a sculptor*.
Praetōrio- n. (*the place*) *of the praetor, the general's tent*.
Grānārio- n. (*the place*) *for grain, granary*.
Ovīli- n. (*the place*) *for sheep, sheep-fold*.

210.1 Such compounds in *io* as triennĭo- n. (from tri- *three*, anno- *year*) *a space of three years*, interlŭnĭo- n. (from intĕr *between*,

---
* Compare osso- or occo- and the German *auge*.

lūna-*moon*) *the time when no moon is visible*, are probably in origin neuter adjectives.

ADJECTIVES.

211 Adjectives are declined like substantives.

212 Adjectives with crude forms in *o* for the masculine and neuter, in *a* for the feminine, are often called adjectives of three terminations.

213 Bŏno- m. and n., bŏna- f. *good.*

	Singular.				*Plural.*	
	Masc.	*Fem.*	*Neut.*	*Masc.*	*Fem.*	*Neut.*
N.	bŏnŭs	bŏnă	bŏnum	N. bŏnī	bŏnae	bŏnă
V.	bŏnĕ	bŏnă	bŏnum	V. bŏnī	bŏnae	bŏnă
Ac.	bŏnum	bŏnam	bŏnum	Ac. bŏnōs	bŏnās	bŏnă
G.	bŏnī	bŏnae	bŏnī	G. bŏnōrum	bŏnārum	bŏnōrum
D.	bŏnō	bŏnae	bŏnō	D. bŏnīs	bŏnīs	bŏnīs
Ab.	bŏnō	bŏnā	bŏnō	Ab. bŏnīs	bŏnīs	bŏnīs

214 Atĕro- m. and n., ātĕra- f. *black.*

	Singular.				*Plural.*	
	Masc.	*Fem.*	*Neut.*	*Masc.*	*Fem.*	*Neut.*
N.	ātĕr	ātră	ātrum	N. ātrī	ātrae	ātră
V.	ātĕr	ātră	ātrum	V. ātrī	ātrae	ātră
Ac.	ātrum	ātram	ātrum	Ac. ātrōs	ātrās	ātră
G.	ātrī	ātrae	ātrī	G. ātrōrum	ātrārum	ātrōrum
D.	ātrō	ātrae	ātrō	D. ātrīs	ātrīs	ātrīs
Ab.	ātrō	ātrā	ātrō	Ab. ātrīs	ātrīs	ātrīs

215 Aspĕro- m. and n., aspĕra- f. *rough.*

	Singular.				*Plural.*	
	Masc.	*Fem.*	*Neut.*	*Masc.*	*Fem.*	*Neut.*
N.	aspĕr	aspĕră	aspĕrum	aspĕrī	aspĕrae	aspĕră
V.	aspĕr	aspĕră	aspĕrum	aspĕrī	aspĕrae	aspĕră
Ac.	aspĕrum	aspĕram	aspĕrum	aspĕrōs	aspĕrās	aspĕră
G.	aspĕrī	aspĕrae	aspĕrī	aspĕrōrum	aspĕrārum	aspĕrōrum
D.	aspĕrō	aspĕrae	aspĕrō	aspĕrīs	aspĕrīs	aspĕrīs
Ab.	aspĕrō	aspĕrā	aspĕrō	aspĕrīs	aspĕrīs	aspĕrīs

216 Adjectives with crude form in *i* are often called adjectives of two terminations.

217 Tristi- *bitter.*

	Singular.				Plural.	
	Masc.	Fem.	Neut.		Masc. Fem.	Neut.
N.	tristis	tristis	tristĕ	N. tristēs	tristēs	tristiă
V.	tristis	tristis	tristĕ	V. tristēs	tristēs	tristiă
Ac.	tristem	tristem	tristĕ	Ac. tristīs or -ēs tristīs or -ēs tristiă
G.	tristis	tristis	tristis	G. tristium	tristium	tristium
D.	tristī	tristī	tristī	D. tristĭbŭs	tristĭbŭs	tristĭbŭs
Ab.	tristī	tristī	tristī	Ab. tristĭbŭs	tristĭbŭs	tristĭbŭs

218 Acri- *sharp.*

	Singular.				Plural.	
	Masc.	Fem.	Neut.	Masc.	Fem.	Neut.
N.	acĕr or acris	acris	acrĕ	acrēs	acrēs	acriă
V.	acĕr or acris	acris	acrĕ	acrēs	acrēs	acriă
Ac.	acrem		acrem acrĕ	acrīs or acrēs acrīs or -acrēs acriă
G.	acris	acris	acris	acrium	acrium	acrium
D.	acrī	acrī	acrī	acrĭbŭs	acrĭbŭs	acrĭbŭs
Ab.	acrī	acrī	acrī	acrĭbŭs	acrĭbŭs	acrĭbŭs

218.1 Celĕri- *quick.*

	Singular.				Plural.	
	Masc.	Fem.	Neut.	Masc.	Fem.	Neut.
N.	celĕr or celĕris	celĕrĕ	N. celĕrēs	celĕrēs	celĕriă
	celĕris					
V.	celĕr or celĕris	celĕrĕ	V. celĕrēs	celĕrēs	celĕriă
	celĕris					
Ac.	celĕrem celĕrem celĕrĕ	Ac. celĕrīs or celĕrīs or celĕriă
				celĕrēs	celĕrēs	
G.	celĕris	celĕris	celĕris	G. celĕrum	celĕrum	celĕrum
D.	celĕrī	celĕrī	celĕrī	D. celĕrĭbŭs	celĕrĭbŭs	celĕrĭbŭs
Ab.	celĕrī	celĕrī	celĕrī	Ab. celĕrĭbŭs	celĕrĭbŭs	celĕrĭbŭs

219 Adjectives with one crude form in a consonant, and another in i, form the singular chiefly from the former, the plural from the second: as,

Praesenti- *or* praesent- *present.*

	Singular.	
	Masc.	Fem.	Neut.
N.	praesens	praesens	praesens
V.	praesens	praesens	praesens
Ac.	praesentem	praesentem	praesens
G.	praesentis	praesentis	praesentis
D.	praesentī	praesentī	praesentī
Ab.	praesentī *or* -tĕ	praesentī *or* -tĕ	praesentī *or* -tĕ

ADJECTIVES.

	Masc.	Plural. Fem.	Neut.
N.	praesentēs	praesentēs	praesentiā
V.	praesentēs	praesentēs	praesentiā
Ac.	praesentīs or -tēs	praesentīs or -tēs	praesentiā
G.	praesentium	praesentium	praesentium
D.	praesentĭbŭs	praesentĭbŭs	praesentĭbŭs
Ab.	praesentĭbŭs	praesentĭbŭs	praesentĭbŭs

219.1 Nouns in *tŏr* are often used as masculine adjectives; nouns in *trīci* or *tric* as feminine adjectives, and also in the plural as neuter adjectives.

Victŏr- *and* uictrici- *or* uictrīc- *conquering.*

Singular.			Plural.		
Masc.	Fem.		Masc.	Fem.	Neut.
N. uictŏr	uictrix		N. uictōrēs	uictrīcēs	uictrīciā
V. uictŏr	uictrix		V. uictōrēs	uictrīcēs	uictrīciā
Ac. uictōrem	uictrīcem		Ac. uictōrēs	uictrīcēs	uictrīciā
G. uictōris	uictrīcis		G. uictōrum	uictrīcium	uictrīcium
D. uictōrī	uictrīcī		D. uictōrĭbŭs	uictrīcĭbŭs	uictrīcĭbŭs
Ab. uictōrĕ	uictrīcē		Ab. uictōrĭbŭs	uictrīcĭbŭs	uictrīcĭbŭs

220 Adjectives with the crude form in a consonant are sometimes called adjectives of one termination.

221   Vĕtŭs- *old.*

Singular.			Plural.		
Masc.	Fem.	Neut.	Masc.	Fem.	Neut.
N. uĕtŭs	uĕtŭs	uĕtŭs	uĕtĕrēs	uĕtĕrēs	uĕtĕrā
V. uĕtŭs	uĕtŭs	uĕtŭs	uĕtĕrēs	uĕtĕrēs	uĕtĕrā
Ac. uĕtĕrem	uĕtĕrem	uĕtŭs	uĕtĕrēs	uĕtĕrēs	uĕtĕrā
G. uĕtĕris	uĕtĕris	uĕtĕris	uĕtĕrum	uĕtĕrum	uĕtĕrum
D. uĕtĕrī	uĕtĕrī	uĕtĕrī	uĕtĕrĭbŭs	uĕtĕrĭbŭs	uĕtĕrĭbŭs
Ab. uĕtĕrĕ or uĕtĕrī	uĕtĕrĕ or uĕtĕrī	uĕtĕrĕ or uĕtĕrī	uĕtĕrĭbŭs	uĕtĕrĭbŭs	uĕtĕrĭbŭs

221.1   *Dīuĭt- rich.*

	Singular.	
Masc.	Fem.	Neut.
N. dīuĕs	dīuĕs	dīuĕs
V. dīuĕs	dīuĕs	dīuĕs
Ac. dīuĭtem	dīuĭtem	dīuĕs
G. dīuĭtis	dīuĭtis	dīuĭtis
D. dīuĭtī	dīuĭtī	dīuĭtī
Ab. dīuĭtĕ or dīuĭtī	dīuĭtĕ or dīuĭtī	dīuĭtĕ or dīuĭtī

30 ADJECTIVES.

	Masc.	Plural Fem.	Neut.
N.	diultēs	diultēs	not found
V.	diultēs	diultēs	———
Ac.	diultēs	diultēs	———
G.	diultum	diultum	diultum
D.	diultĭbŭs	diultĭbŭs	diultĭbŭs
Ab.	diultĭbŭs	diultĭbŭs	diultĭbŭs

There is also in the poets a contracted form, dit- or diti-; whence N. m. f. dis, Ac. m. f. ditem, &c.; but for the neuter of the N. V. Ac. sing. ditĕ, plur. ditiă.

222 Tristiŭs- or tristiŏr- *more bitter.*

Singular.

	Masc.	Fem.	Neut.
N.	tristiŏr	tristiŏr	tristiŭs
V.	tristiŏr	tristiŏr	tristiŭs
Ac.	tristiōrem	tristiōrem	tristiŭs
G.	tristiōris	tristiōris	tristiōris
D.	tristiōrī	tristiōrī	tristiōrī
Ab.	tristiōrĕ*	tristiōrĕ*	tristiōrĕ*

Plural.

	Masc.	Fem.	Neut.
N.	tristiōrēs	tristiōrēs	tristiōrā
V.	tristiōrēs	tristiōrēs	tristiōrā
Ac.	tristiōrēs	tristiōrēs	tristiōrā
G.	tristiōrum	tristiōrum	tristiōrum
D.	tristiōrĭbŭs	tristiōrĭbŭs	tristiōrĭbŭs
Ab.	tristiōrĭbŭs	tristiōrĭbŭs	tristiōrĭbŭs

223 Adjectives whose crude form ends in a consonant rarely have a neuter plural.

224 Some adjectives have a crude form in *i* as well as that in *o* or *a*: as,

bĭjŭgo-	*yoked-two-together*	or	bĭjŭgi-
hĭlăro-	*cheerful*	,,	hĭlări-
imbēcillo-	*weak*	,,	imbēcilli-
inermo-	*unarmed*	,,	inermi-
infrēno-	*unbridled*	,,	infrēni-
ūnănimo-	*of-one-mind*	,,	ūnănimi-

* Seldom *tristiōrī*.

231. SUFFIXES OF ADJECTIVES.

Suffix	Added to	Gives an adjective meaning	Thus from	English	In derived	English
āci or āx	verbs	full	fĕr-	bear	fēr-āci-	fruitful.
ōci or ōx	verbs	full	fĕr-	raise	fĕr-ōci-	haughty.
ici or īx	nouns in trīx	female	uictr-	victorious	uictr-īci-	victorious.
ĭdi (—idus)	verbs	full	ūir-	be green	ūir-idi-	green.
ĭli or īli	verbs	fit to	ūt-	use	ūt-ĭli-	useful.
. . .	nouns	like	quoz or quā-	what	quā-li-	like what, of what kind.
. . .	nouns	of the same	fĕr-	tribe	tribo-li-	of the same tribe.
. . .	nouns	full	fīdĕ-	faith	fīdē-li-	faithful.
. . .	nouns	belonging to	ūirgŏn-	river	fluuiā-li-	belonging to a river.
(āli) *	nouns &c.	like, &c.	ūirgŏn-	maiden	uirgin-āli-	maiden-like.
bili;	verbs	belonging to	ām-	love	āmā-bili-	lovely.
ēli;	nouns &c.	of, like, &c.	āqua-	water	āquā-tili-	belonging to water.
ĭli (—ilis)	nouns	of, like, &c.	puellā-	girl	puellā-ri-	girl-like.
(ari),* (—āli)	nouns	state	Apollŏn-	Apollo	Apollōn-āri-	of Apollo.
ĕri	. . .	full	[ac- oís.	sharpen]	ācri-	sharp.
bĕri (—bilis)†	verbs &c.	fit to	lūgē-	mourn	lūgū-bĕri-	mournful.
ulĕri;	verbs	belonging to	uolā-	fly	uolā-cĕri-	able to fly.
ensi‡	nouns	belonging to	castro- pl.	camp	castr-ensi-	belonging to this neuter.
ēni	. . .	belonging to	Arpīno-	Arpinum	Arpīnā-ti-	belonging to a camp.
'ti or 'tī	(uerna ino(n.)	—ing	flu-	flow	flu-enti- }	belonging to Arpinum.
unti or ent	verbs	full	ul-		ul-ŏlemli-	flowing.
ŏlenti	nouns	belonging to	caelo-	sky	cael-esti-	violent. belonging to the sky.

*See § 232. ‡See Appendix II. †These are participles

SUFFIXES OF ADJECTIVES—(continued).

Suffix	Added to	Gives an adjective meaning	Thus from	English	Is derived	English
o	verbs	state	uhu-	live	uhu-o	alive.
ico	nouns	belonging to	Nilo-	Nile	Nil-ico-	of the Nile.
ico	nouns	belonging to	civi-	citizen	civ-ico-	of citizen.
tico	nouns	belonging to	Ligus-	a Ligurian	Ligus-tico-	of the Ligurians.
tico	verbs	ready to	cad-	fall	cad-uco-	ready to fall.
ido	verbs	full	tim-	fear	tim-ido-	fearful.
endo*	verbs	being ——ed	doma-	tame	doma-ndo-	taming, being tamed.
bundo‖	verbs	full of play	ludi-	play	ludi-bundo-	full of play.
cundo‖	verbs	full	ira-	be angry	ira-cundo-	passionate.
eo	nouns	made of	oss-	bone	oss-eo-	of bone.
eo	nouns	made of	membran-	skin	membran-eo-	of skin or parchment.
ceo	nouns, &c.	...	ilic-	ilex, a tree	ilic-eo-	of ilex-wood.
io	verbs	belonging to	ex-im-	take out	ex-im-io-	select, excellent.
io	verbs	belonging to	reg-	king	reg-io-	royal.
ia	nouns	belonging to	Romulo-	Romulus	Ramuli-io-	name of a Roman gens.
icio	nouns	belonging to	tribuno-	tribune	tribun-icio-	of the tribunes.
icio	participles	that has been ——ed	facto-	made	fact-icio-	artificial.
ilio	nouns	—— sort	Servio-	Servius	Servi-lio-	name of a Roman gens.
rio	praenomen	dealing in	statua-	statue	statua-rio-	of statues, a sculptor.
(ário)¶	nouns	belonging to	carbōn-	coal	carbōn-ário-	coal-(merchant).
ulo	adj.	diminutive	longo-	long	long-ulo-	rather long.
ilo	verbs	diminutive	cred-	believe	cred-ilo-	rather credulous.
clo	adj.	diminutive	longiōs-	longer	longius-clo-	rather long.

* These are participles. † So that what was originally a patronymic became a praenomen; like our Johnson, &c.
‡ For quantity compare translatio, Phaedr. v. 8. 24. § See Appendix II. ¶ See § 254.

SUFFIXES OF ADJECTIVES.

imo, timo	prep.	most	pri-	forward	primo-*	first.
issimo	adj.	most	[longo- [piè- obs.	long	long-issimo-	longest or very long.
no, ino	...	state	klomā-	full or fill	plē no-	full.
no, ino	nouns	belonging to	moat-	Rome	klāmā-no-	belonging to Rome.
(āno)†	nouns	belonging to	Ocn-	mountain	mont-āno-	of the mountain.
āno	towns	belonging to	(āgo-	town in Spain	Ocē-āno-	belonging to Ocn.
āno	nouns	made of	cra-	beech	fāg-ino-	made of beech.
ino	nouns	belonging to	nudi-	tomorrow	crā-tīno-	belonging to tomorrow.
(ino)‡	nouns	belonging to	nous-	goat	nudi-ino-	belonging to a goat.
terno	nouns	belonging to	diu-	age	aeul-terno-¶	eternal.
turno	nouns	state	ab	day, time	dih-turno-	lasting.
āro	verbs	state	lib-	touch	in-tāg-āro-	untouched, entire.
āro	prep.	of two			tāct- āro-	
dro	verbs ?	belonging to	quo-	up	āltēro-	higher.
cǒro (—dǐri)?	adj. or prep.	of two	āquo-	which	dūp-lǐco-	belonging to grmat.
tǎro			bello-	water	quo-tēro-	which of the two.
ǎco	nouns	full	krni-	war	āqu-āco-	watery.
ǎco	nouns	full		land	bellī-cōso-	warlike.
oso	verbs	— of	cornu-¶ obs.	horn	krnī-to-	loud.
to	nouns	provided with	[cru-¶ ob.		cornī-to-	horned.
		full	ul-	gore]	cru-ento-	gory.
ento	nouns	full	ā-, ēd-	force	e-ellēnto-	violent.
ōlento	verbs	fit to	ulo-	eat	ule-uc-	eatable.
uo	verbs	state	ulo-	be empty	ule-uno-	empty.
fuo	verbs	state	flāg-	be empty	ule-uno-	empty.
tuo	verbs	state	stō-	fly	flag. fluo-	runaway (slave).
tur	verbs	male agent		compare	uic-lōr-	victorious.
ior	adj.	more	longo-	long	long-ior-	longer.

* Instead of pro-imo. † See § 520.
‡ See § 531. ¶ Contracted into octervus.
§ These are called participles. See the Verbs. ¶ Of crā-do, crū-do.
∥ See Appendix II.

226. Of these suffixes many are closely connected: as, *āc* and *ŏc*; *li, ri,* and *rio*; *bŭli* and *bĕri*; *estri* and *esti*; *tīco, luo, uo,* and *io,* from verbs; *āvo* and *cīvo*, &c.

227. In adding the suffixes, the last vowel of the preceding word must not be neglected. Thus, with the suffix *īno* or *no*, the following derivatives are formed:

 Rōma- *Rome,*   Rōmā-no- *of Rome.*
 pōmo- *apple,* &c., Pōmō-na- *(goddess) of fruit.*
 māri- *sea,*   māri-no- *of the sea.*
 trĭbu- *tribe,*   trĭbū-no- *(commander) of a tribe, tribune.*
 ĕgo- (verb) *want,* ĕgē-no- *in want.*

228. Or, with a slight change:

 dīuo- *a god,* (diuoino-) dīuīno- *belonging to a god.*
 uīpĕra- *a viper,* (uiperaino-) uīpĕrīno- *belonging to a viper.*

229. And, lastly, since *o* is readily interchanged with *a*:

 Pompeio- *Pompey,* Pompeia-no- *belonging to Pompey.*

230. Now, as by far the greater number of Latin nouns end in *a* or *o*, and the latter itself is often changed to *a*, the result was, that of the adjectives formed with the suffix *īno* or *no*, a large majority were found to end in *āno*. Hence *āno* was itself mistaken for a suffix, and from mont- *mountain* was formed montāno- *belonging to the mountains,* &c.

231. Again, as the nouns ending in *o* or *a*, when the suffix *īno* is added, often suffer a contraction so as to form adjectives in *īno*, and as the same termination resulted from adding the same suffix to nouns in *i*, the consequence was that *īno* was mistaken for a suffix. Hence from anser- *goose* was formed anserīno- *belonging to a goose,* &c.

232. Similarly, with the suffix *li*, or after a preceding *l, ri* are formed:

 ancŏra- *anchor,* ancŏrā-li- *of the anchor.*
 puella- *girl,*   puellā-ri- *girl-like.*
 flŭuio- *river,*   flŭuiā-li- *of the river.*
 pōpŭlo- *state,*   pōpŭlā-ri- *of the same state.*
 cĭui- *citizen,*   cĭuī-li- *like a citizen.*
 trĭbu- *tribe,*   trĭbū-li- *of the same tribe.*
 fĭde- *faith,*   fĭde-li- *faithful.*

233. Again, of adjectives so formed, the greater number will be

found to end in *ali* or *ari*. Hence these were mistaken for suffixes; and, accordingly, from căpŭt- *head*, virgōn- *maid*, rēg- *king*, &c. were formed căpŭt-āli-, virgĭn-āli-, rēg-āli-.

In the same way *ario* was supposed to be a suffix in place of *rio*, and from carbōn- *coal* was formed carbōn-ārio- *coal-dealer*.

Adjectives are also formed as follows:—*a*. By prefixing a particle to a substantive: as,

from In *not*, genti- or gent- *nature*, in-genti- *unnatural, immense*.
,, sē *apart*, cord- *heart*, sē-cord- *senseless*.
,, ss *apart*, cūra- *care*, sē-cūro- *unconcerned*.
,, cŏn *together*, mūni- *share*, com-mūni- *common*.

b. By prefixing a substantive or adjective to a substantive: as,

from căpŏro- *goat*, pĕd- *foot*, căpri-pĕd- *goat-footed*.
,, [quădr-] *four*, pĕd- *foot*, quădrŭ-pĕd- *four-footed*.
,, centum *hundred*, mănu- *hand*, centi-māno- *hundred-handed*.
,, magno- *great*, ănĭmo- *mind*, magn-ănĭmo- *great-minded*.
,, misĕro- *wretched*, cord- *heart*, misĕri-cord- *tender-hearted*.

c. By prefixing a particle to an adjective: as,

from In *not*, ūtĭli- *useful*, ĭn-ūtĭli- *useless*.
,, pĕr *thorough*, magno- *great*, per-magno- *very great*.
,, prae *praeeminently*, clāro- *bright*, prae-clāro- *very illustrious*.

d. By prefixing a substantive, adjective, or particle to a verb: as,

from tūba- *trumpet*, căn- *sing*, tūbĭ-căn- *trumpeter*.
,, parti- *part*, căp- *take*, partĭ-cĕp- *partaking*.
,, cărōn- *flesh*, vōra- *devour*, carnĭ-uŏro- *flesh-eating*.
,, [bĕno-] *good*, gĕn- *produce*, bĕni-g'no-* *generous*.
,, mălo- *bad*, dĭc-† *speak*, mălĭ-dĭco- *abusive*.
,, dē *down*, sĕd- *sit*, dē-sĭd- *slothful*.
,, cŏm *with*, [It- *obs.*, *go*] cŏm-ĭt- *accompanying*.

Adjectives are also formed from prepositions. See the table of words derived from prepositions, § 838.

COMPARATIVES AND SUPERLATIVES.

The suffixes which form the Comparatives and Superlatives are so much used, that they must be spoken of more at length.

The simple adjective is said to be in the positive degree: as, longo- or -a- *long*.

* Literally *well-born*.   † See § 451. 1.

ADJECTIVES.

241. The comparative degree takes the suffix iōs or iōr: as, long iōs-* or long-iōr- *longer* or *more long*.

242. The superlative degree takes the suffix ǐssǐmo or ǐmo, issǔmot or ǔssǐmo: as, long-issǐmo-* *longest* or *most long*.

243. If the adjective ends in ĕro, ĕri, or ĕr, the superlative suffix is slightly changed: as, nĭgĕro- *black*, nĭgĕr-rŭmo- *blackest*; lĭbĕro- *free*, lĭberrŭmo-; ăcŭri- *sharp*, ăcerrŭmo-; cĕlĕri- *quick*, cĕlerrŭmo-; paupĕr- *poor*, pauperrŭmo-; uĕtĕs- *old*, uĕterrŭmo-.

244. If the adjective ends in ǐli, the superlative suffix is slightly changed: as, făcĭli- *easy*, făcil-lŭmo- *easiest*; diffĭcĭli- *difficult*, diffĭcillŭmo-; grăcĭli- *slender*, grăcillŭmo-; sĭmĭli- *like*, sĭmillŭmo-; dissĭmĭli- *unlike*, dissĭmillŭmo-.

245. The following comparatives and superlatives are irregular:

Pos.	Comp.	Sup.
bŏno- *good*,	mĕliōs- *better*,	optŭmo- *best*.
mălo- *bad*,	pēiōs- (=ped-iōs-) *worse*,	pessŭmo- *worst*.
mag-no- *great*,	maiōs- (=mag-iōs-) *greater*,	maxŭmo- *greatest*.
paruo- *little*,	minōs- *less*,	minŭmo- *least*.
multo- *much*,	plūs-‡ n. *more*,	plūrŭmo- n. *most*.
multo-§ pl. *many*,	plūr- pl. *more*,	plūrŭmo-§ pl. *most*.

See also the table of words derived from prepositions, § 838.

246. Sometimes one or more of the positive, comparative, and superlative are deficient: as,

Pos.	Comp.	Sup.
———	ōc-iōs- *quicker*,	ōc-issŭmo- *quickest*.
———	nēqu-iōs- *worse*,	nēqu-issŭmo- *worst*.
nŏuo- *new*,	———	nŏu-issŭmo- *newest*.
falso- *false*,	———	fals-issŭmo- *most false*.
ingenti- *immense*,	ingent-iōs- *more immense*.	———
dēsĭd- *slothful*,	dēsĭd-iōs- *more slothful*.	———
iŭuĕni- *young*,	iūniōs- *younger*.	———

Sĕniōs- *older* has no corresponding positive: see § 207. 1.

* In adding the suffixes of the comparative and superlative the vowels *a*, *o*, *i*, at the end of the crude form of the positive are discarded.

† The forms with *s* are the oldest. They were used by Terence, &c., down to Cicero, inclusive.

‡ From ple- 'full,' the root of plē-no-, is formed ple-ios- contracted into plous- and plūs-. Compare the Greek πλε-ιων and πλε-ον.

§ These are used in the singular in poetry.

NUMERALS.

247 Cardinal numbers answer to the question, quŏt ? (undeclined) *how many?* as, *one, two, three,* &c.; or tŏt (undecl.) *so many.*

248 Ordinal numerals state the place occupied in a rank or series. They answer to the question quŏto- or -ta- N. quŏtŭs, -tă, -tum ? *occupying what place in the series?** answer, *first, second, third,* &c.; or tŏto- or -ta- *occupying such a place.*

249 Distributives answer to the question, quŏtēno- or N. pl. quŏtēnī, -ae, -ă ? *how many at a time?* *one at a time, two at a time,* &c.; or the preposition *by* may be used, *by twos, by threes,* &c.; or the word *each,* as, *two each, three each,* &c.

250 The numeral adverbs answer to the question, quŏtiens or quŏtiēs ? *how often?* *once, twice, thrice, four-times,* &c.; tŏtiens or tŏtiēs *so often.*

251 *Roman Symbols.*—The symbols for 1, 10, 100, 1000, seem to have consisted of one, two, three, and four lines respectively: viz. I, X, ⊏, M; for the last two of which the more easily written symbols, C, and ⋔ or ⋀, were afterwards substituted. The mark for 1000 seems to have suggested those for 10 000, 100 000, &c. viz. ⋀⋀, or ⋀ ⋀, &c. The next step was to find symbols for the halves of these numbers, and the most easy course was to take the half of the symbols themselves. Thus, V, L, ⋂ or ⋀, ⋂ or ⋀, ⋂ or ⋀, severally denoted 5, 50, 500, 5000, 50 000. Lastly, modern printers found it convenient to use the existing types for letters, to avoid the expense of new types for the numerical symbols. Hence, in modern Latin books, we find the letters I, V, X, L, C, D, M, and the inverted Ɔ, all used in the representation of Latin numerals. It was probably an accident, that of these seven letters, two were the initials of the words for which they stood: viz. C and M, of centum and millĕ.†

---

* No single English word corresponds to *quoto-*. Such a form as *what-th*, like *fif-th, six-th,* would best suit it.

† When a symbol of a smaller number precedes one of a greater, the smaller is to be subtracted, as IIX = 8, IX = 9, XXIX = 29, CD = 400. Further, a bar over a symbol denotes multiplication by 1000: thus $\overline{V}$ = 5000.

253. Numerals.

Arabic Symbols	Roman Symbols	Cardinal	Ordinal	Distributive Masc. N. pl. from —ą-ā	Adverbs
1	I.	ūno	prīmo-	singŭli	sĕmel
2	II.	dŭo	sĕcundo- or altĕro-	bĭn.1	bis
3	III.	tri-	tertio-	terni or trīni	tĕr
4	IIII. or IV.	quattuŏr	quarto-	quaterni	quătĕr
5	V.	quinque	quinto-	quīni	quinquiens
6	VI.	sex	sexto-	sēni	sexiens
7	VII.	septem	septĭmo-	septēni	septiens
8	VIII. or IIX.	octō	octāvo-	octōni	octiens
9	VIIII. or IX.	nŏvem	nōno-	nŏvēni	nŏviens
10	X.	dĕcem	dĕcĭmo-	dēni	dĕciens
11	XI.	undĕcim	undĕcĭmo-	undēni	undĕciens
12	XII.	duŏdĕcim	duŏdĕcĭmo-	duŏdēni	duŏdĕciens
13	XIII.	trĕdĕcim	tertio- dĕcĭmo-	terni dēni	terdĕciens
14	XIIII. or XIV.	quattuordĕcim	quarto- dĕcĭmo-	quaterni dēni	quatordĕciens
15	XV.	quindĕcim	quinto- dĕcĭmo-	quīni dēni	quindĕciens
16	XVI.	sēdĕcim	sexto- dĕcĭmo-	sēni dēni	sēdĕciens
17	XVII.	septendĕcim	septĭmo- dĕcĭmo-	septēni dēni	septiens dĕciens
18	XVIII. or XIIX.	duŏdēvigintī	duŏdēvicēsĭmo-	duŏdēvicēni	duŏdēviciens
19	XVIIII. or XIX.	undēvigintī	undēvicēsĭmo-	undēvicēni	undēviciens
20	XX.	vīgintī	vicēsĭmo- er vīcēsĭmo-	vīcēni	vīciens
21	XXI.	vīgintī ūnis	ş prīmo-et-vīcēsĭmo-	vīcēni singŭli	sĕmĕl-et-vīciens
22	XXII.	vīgintī dŭo	{ altĕro-et-vīcēsĭmo-	vīcēni bīni	bis-et-vīciens

NUMERALS.

23	XXIII. &c.	uīgintī trēs &c.	‡uīcēnsimō- tertiō- &c.	uīcēnī ternī &c.	tēr-et-uīciēns &c.
30	XXX.	trīgintā	trīcēnsimō-	trīcēnī	trīciēns
40	XXXX. or XL.	quādrāgintā	quādrāgēnsimō-	quādrāgēnī	quādrāgiēns
50	L.	quīnquāgintā	quīnquāgēnsimō-	quīnquāgēnī	quīnquāgiēns
60	LX.	sexāgintā	sexāgēnsimō-	sexāgēnī	sexāgiēns
70	LXX.	septuāgintā	septuāgēnsimō-	septuāgēnī	septuāgiēns
80	LXXX. or XXC.	octōgintā	octōgēnsimō-	octōgēnī	octōgiēns
90	XC.	nōnāgintā	nōnāgēnsimō-	nōnāgēnī	nōnāgiēns
100	C.	centum	centēnsimō-	centēnī	centiēns
200	CC.	dūcentō-	dūcentēnsimō-	dūcēnī	dūcentiēns
300	CCC.	trēcentō-	trēcentēnsimō-	trēcēnī	trēcentiēns
400	CCCC. or CD.	quādringentō-	quādringentēnsimō-	quādringēnī	quādringentiēns
500	D. or IↃ.	quīngentō-	quīngentēnsimō-	quīngēnī	quīngentiēns
600	DC.	sescentō-	sescentēnsimō-	sescēnī	sescentiēns
700	DCC.	septingentō-	septingentēnsimō-	septingēnī	septingentiēns
800	DCCC.	octingentō-	octingentēnsimō-	octingēnī	octingentiēns
900	DCCCC.	nōngentō-	nōngentēnsimō-	nōngēnī	nōngentiēns
1,000	M. or CIↃ.	mīlī- (n.)	mīllēnsimō-	singūlā mīlīā (n.)	mīliēns
2,000	MM.	**duō or bīnā mīlīā	bis mīllēnsimō-	bīnā mīlīā	bis mīliēns
5,000	IↃↃ.	quīnquēorquīnā mīlīā	quīnquiēs mīllēnsimō-	quīnā mīlīā	quīnquiēs mīliēns
10,000	CCIↃↃ.	dēcem or děnā mīlīā	dēciēns mīllēnsimō-	dēnā mīlīā	dēciēns mīliēna

* The last four are neut. N. pl.
† Often written and perhaps commonly pronounced *quīnquiēs, sextīs*, &c.
‡ Often written in later writers *septimō-, decimō-* &c. § Both parts must be declined.
∥ So also *trīcēsimō-* &c. ¶ In later writers *orīgintā, quadrāgintā*, &c.
** The last three are neut. N. pl.

253. *Cardinal Numbers.*—Those from quattuŏr to centum, both inclusive, are not declined. Mīli- is both substantive and adjective. If no smaller number accompany it, it is more commonly used as a substantive. Hence the phrases mille hŏmĭnum or mille hŏmĭnēs; triă mīlia hŏmĭnum, triă mīliă trŏcenti hŏmĭnēs.

254. The three first numerals are declined. Ūno- *one* makes G. ūnīūs, D. ūnī. The other cases are regular. The plural is used with those substantives which with a plural form have a singular meaning: as, N. pl. ūnă castră *one camp.*

255. Duo- dua- *two* is declined thus: Plur. N. duŏ duae duŏ, Ac. duŏ or duŏs, duās, duŏ, G. duōrum duārum duōrum or m. f. n. duum, D. and Ab. duōbūs duābūs duōbūs. In the same way is declined ambo- amba- *both*, except as to the quantity of ambō.*

256. Tri- *three* is declined regularly.

257. Milli- or mīli- *thousand* is declined: Sing. for all cases millĕ, Plur. N. V. Ac. mīliă, G. mīlium, D. and Ab. mīlībūs.†

258. From 13 to 19 there occur also dŏcem et trĭa, &c. Between 20 and 100 there are two forms, viz. uīgintī unūs or unūs et uīgintī, &c. Above 100, the greater number precedes: as, trĕcentī sexăgintă sex or trĕcenti et sexăgintă sex.

259. The practice of prefixing the smaller number to the greater in order to denote subtraction, as IV (one from five), IIX (two from ten), extended also to the names. Hence duŏdēuīgintī, 18; undēuīgintī, 19; duŏdētrīgintă, 28; undētrīgintă, 29; duŏdēquādrāgintă, 38; undēquādrāgintă, 39; and so on to duŏdēcentum, 98; undēcentum, 99. Series of the same kind belong to the ordinals, distributives and adverbs.

260. The high numbers were chiefly required for representing money. Here abbreviations were found convenient. Thus millions of *sesterces* were commonly denoted by adverbs alone, the words centēnă mīliă being omitted: as, dĕciens *ten times (a hundred thousand) sesterces*, that is, *a million sesterces*; uīciens *twenty times &c.*, or *two million sesterces.*

261. *Ordinal Numbers.*—From 13 to 19 there are also sometimes found dĕcĭmus tertĭŭs and dĕcĭmŭs et tertĭŭs, &c. Between 20

---

* See Prof. Ramsay's Latin Prosody. Yet duă, Plaut. Mil. iv. 9. 7.
† A single *l* was preferred before the vowel *i*; so that from *uilla-* 'a farm' comes *uilico-* m. 'a farm-bailiff.'

and 100 there are two forms; ulcensŭmus quartŭs or quartŭs et ulcensŭmŭs, &c. For 21, 31, 41, &c., ūnŭs et ulcensŭmŭs, ūna et ulcensŭmă or ūnctulcensŭmă, &c. frequently occur.

262 *Distributive Numerals.*—These are also used as cardinal numbers with those nouns which with a plural form have a singular meaning: as, N. binae aedēs *two houses*, binae littěrae *two letters* or *epistles.* Duae aedēs, duae littěrae, would signify *two temples, two letters of the alphabet.* With ūno- there could not be the same confusion: hence ūnă littěră, ūnae littěrae, signify respectively *one letter of the alphabet, one letter* or *epistle.* The distributives* are often used by the poets for the cardinals.

263 *Adverbs.*—Between 20 and 100 there are three expressions: bis et ulciens, ulciens et bis, ulciens bis. Bis ulciens would mean *twice twenty* or *forty times.*

264 There is a series formed from plĭca- *a flat surface* or *fold*, answering to quŏtŭ-plĭci- or -plěc-, N. quŏtŭplex *how many fold?* viz. sim-plĭci-†, dŭ-plĭci-, trĭ-plĭci-, quădrŭ-plĭci-, quincŭ-plĭci-, ——, septem-plĭci-, ——, ——, děcem-plĭci-, and centum-plĭci-.

265 There is a series of similar meaning, with crude form ending in plo- (=to our *full*) and answering to quŏtŭplo- ? viz. simplo-, dŭplo-, trĭplo-, quădrŭplo-, quincŭplo-, ——, septŭplo-, octŭplo-.

266 There is a series with suffix rio formed from the distributives, *containing two, three*, &c.: viz. ——, bĭnārio-, ternārio-, quăternārio-, quīnārio-, sēnārio-, septēnārio-, octōnārio-, &c.

267 There is a series with suffix no, formed from ordinal series, *belonging to the first, second*, &c.: viz. primāno-, sěcundāno-, tertiāno-, &c. These terms are chiefly used to denote the legion to which a soldier belongs. Hence, in the higher numbers are found such forms in the nom. as tertia-děcŭmā-nŭs, tertia-et-ulcensŭmānŭs; where the feminine form of the first part seems to be determined by the gender of the Latin word lēgiōn-.

268 Fractions are expressed by the ordinal series with parti- or

* The distributives are also used in phrases of multiplication, as *quater quini* 'four times five men.'

† Not from *sinŭ piled*, but from an old root *sĭm* or *sĕm* 'one;' which is also found in *singulo-, simplo-, simili-, sincerro-, sěmel, sĭmul*; Gr. ἅμα, ὁμόσε, ὁμοῦ; Eng. *same*; Germ. *sammlung*, &c.

part- *part* expressed or understood: as, nom. $\frac{1}{3}$, tertiā pars; $\frac{3}{7}$, tres septūmae.

269. But many shorter forms were employed. Thus, when the numerator is one less than the denominator: as, nom. $\frac{2}{3}$, duae partēs, *two parts out of three;* $\frac{3}{4}$, tres partēs, *three parts out of four,* &c.

270. Again, when the denominator is 12, the unit or whole being represented by assi-, N. as (our *ace*), the parts are

$\frac{1}{12}$ uncia- (our *ounce* and *inch*)	$\frac{7}{12}$ septunci-, n. septunx
$\frac{2}{12}$ or $\frac{1}{6}$ sextanti-, nom. sextans	$\frac{8}{12}$ or $\frac{2}{3}$ bessi-, n. bes
$\frac{3}{12}$ or $\frac{1}{4}$ quādranti-, n. quādrans	$\frac{9}{12}$ or $\frac{3}{4}$ dōdranti- (from dē-quādranti-)
$\frac{4}{12}$ or $\frac{1}{3}$ trienti-, n. triens	$\frac{10}{12}$ or $\frac{5}{6}$ dextanti- (from dē-sextanti-)
$\frac{5}{12}$ quincunci-, n. quincunx	$\frac{11}{12}$ de-unci-, n. deunx
$\frac{6}{12}$ or $\frac{1}{2}$ sēmissi-, n. sēmis	

271. Fractions were also expressed by the addition or multiplication of other fractions: as, nom. tertiā septūmā, $\frac{1}{3}$ of $\frac{1}{7}$, or $\frac{1}{21}$; tertia et septūmā, $\frac{1}{3} + \frac{1}{7}$, or $\frac{10}{21}$.

272. Mixed numbers were denoted by the Latin for the fractional part accompanied by that number of the ordinal series which exceeds by unity the given whole number. Thus, nom. 3¼ is quadrans quartūs; 5½, sēmis sextūs; 2½, sēmis tertiūs, or rather, by contraction, sestertiūs. The last quantity, viz. 2½, was represented in symbols by adding *s*, the initial letter of *sēmis*, to the symbol for *two*, with a line running through the whole symbol, as in our own ℔, £, for pounds; thus, IIS̶. But printers have found it convenient to substitute the letters HS.

PRONOUNS.

273. Pronouns are, strictly speaking, substantives, adjectives, adverbs, &c., and therefore belong to those heads of grammar; but it is convenient to discuss them separately, partly because they sometimes exhibit the suffixes in a more complete, sometimes in a less complete form than other words belonging to the same parts of speech, and partly because they are so much used.

PERSONAL PRONOUNS.

FIRST PERSON.
c.f. not known,* *I, &c.*

	Sing.	Plur.
N.	ĕgo	nōs
V.	—	—
Ac.	mē	nōs
G.	meī	nostrum *or* -rī
D.	mihi *or* mī	nōbīs
Ab.	mē	nōbīs

275. SECOND PERSON.
c.f. tŭb- *thou, &c.*

	Sing.	Plur.
N.	tū	uōs
V.	tū	uōs
Ac.	tē	uōs
G.	tuī	nostrum *or* -rī
D.	tĭbi	uōbīs
Ab.	tē	uōbīs

For the pronoun of the third person, viz. *he, she, it,* the several parts of the adjective eo- or i- are used.

The nominatives of these pronouns are not expressed unless emphatic, because the personal suffixes of the verbs already denote the persons.

REFLECTIVE PRONOUNS.

Reflective pronouns refer to the person or thing expressed in the nominative case. In English the word *self* is used for this purpose.

Reflective pronouns, from their very nature, can have no nominative or vocative.

In the first and second persons, the common personal pronouns are used, viz. mē, meī &c., tē, tuī &c. For the third person the several cases formed from the crude form sĕb- *self* are used without any distinction for number or gender, to signify *himself, herself, itself, themselves.*

c.f. sĕb-† *self.*
Ac. sē, G. suī, D. sĭbi, Ab. sē.

Remarks on the Pronouns EGO, TU, SE.

Ac.—Med and ted are used by old writers, as Plautus, for mē and tē. Mē, tē, sē, are also doubled, as mēmē, tētē, sēsē. The two first are rare, and only used to give emphasis. Sēsē is not uncommon. Mehe is an antiquated form for mē.

* Probably *ĕgŏmĕt* (corresponding to the Sanscrit *asmdi*), or rather *mĕgŏmĕt*. Compare too the Greek ἡμερ- (for ἀσμερ-) of ἡμέτερος, implied also in (ἄμμες) ἄμμις.

† The same as the old English adjective *sib* 'related,' still preserved in Scotch. In Greek the form is σφ-, whence σφι, σφέτερος, &c.

282 G.—Mis and tis are antiquated forms, found in Plautus.
283 D.—Mi is rarely used in prose writers. Mē, tē or tĭbe, sĭbe, are severally antiquated forms for mihi, tĭbi, sĭbi.
284 Ab.—Mēd and tēd are found in old writers.
285 G. pl.—These are merely genitives of the possessive adjectives nostĕro-, uostĕro-. Indeed nostrōrum, uostrōrum for the m., and nostrārum, uostrārum for the f., are found in old writers. Vestrum, uestri, with an e, are used by later writers. The genitives nostrī, uostrī are used only in the objective sense. (See § 927.) Nostrum, uostrum are required in partitive phrases. (See § 932.)
285.1 D. and Ab. pl.—Nīs for nōbīs is given in Festus.

Demonstrative Pronouns.

286 The three demonstrative pronouns are adjectives, which point as it were with the finger to the place occupied: as, ho- *this near me*, isto- *that near you*, illo- *that yonder*.

287 Illo- (older form ŏlo-* *or* ollo-) *that yonder*.

	Singular.			Plural.		
	Masc.	Fem.	Neut.	Masc.	Fem.	Neut.
N.	illĕ	illă	illŭd	illī	illae	illă
Ac.	illum	illam	illŭd	illōs	illās	illă
G.	illīŭs	illīŭs	illīŭs	illōrum	illārum	illōrum
D.	illī	illī	illī	illīs	illīs	illīs
Ab.	illō	illā	illō	illīs	illīs	illīs

288 In the same manner is declined isto- *that near you*.†

289 To the three demonstratives, and to the adverbs derived from them, the demonstrative enclitic cĕ or c (*look, lo*) is often added for the sake of greater emphasis.

290 Illo- with enclitic cĕ.

	Singular.			Plural.		
	Masc.	Fem.	Neut.	Masc.	Fem.	Neut.
N.	illĭc	illaec	illŏc *or* illŭc	illīcĕ	illaec	illaec
Ac.	illunc	illanc	illŏc *or* illŭc	illōscĕ	illascĕ	illaec
G.	illīuscĕ	illīuscĕ	illīuscĕ	illōruncĕ	illāruncĕ	illōruncĕ
D.‡	illīc	illīc	illīc	illīscĕ	illīscĕ	illīscĕ
Ab.	illōc	illāc	illōc	illīscĕ	illīscĕ	illīscĕ

* See § 1173.1.
† The Nn. often drop the *i*, as Hor. Ep. 11. 2.163, *sempŭ mědŏ sto*. (See Lachmann's Lucretius.) *Istus* as a nom. m. is in *Pl*. Mil. iv. 6.18.
‡ The dative *illic* is only used as an adverb.

PRONOUNS.

291 In nearly all those cases which end in c, the e may be added: as, Ac. m. illuncĕ, &c.

292 In the same manner is declined isto- with cĕ.

293 If, besides the enclitic cĕ, the enclitic nĕ *whether* is also added, the first enclitic takes the form cĕ throughout: as, illicĭnĕ illaecĭnĕ illōcĭnĕ &c.; istĭcĭnĕ istaecĭnĕ istōcĭnĕ &c.; hĭcĭnĕ haecĭnĕ hōcĭnĕ &c.

294 Many of the cases from ho- alone, have disappeared from the language, their places being supplied by those formed from ho- with cĕ. Hence in part the irregularities of the following declension.

295 Ho- *this*, partly with, partly without the suffix cĕ.

	Singular.				*Plural.*		
	Masc.	*Fem.*	*Neut.*		*Masc.*	*Fem.*	*Neut.*
N.	hĭc	haec	hŏc	N.	hī	hae	haec
Ac.	hunc	hanc	hŏc	Ac.	hōs	hās	haec
G.	hŭiŭs	hŭiŭs	hŭiŭs	G.	hōrum	hārum	hōrum
D.*	huīc	huīc	huīc	D.	hīs	hīs	hīs
Ab.	hōc	hāc	hōc	Ab.	hīs	hīs	hīs

296 Those cases which do not end in c, as here declined, may have that enclitic added: as, G. hūiuscĕ; N. pl. m. hīcĕ, f. haecĕ or haec; Ac. hōscĕ, &c. An old N. pl. is hisce, *Pl.* Mil. III. 6. 9.

297 An old form of the D. or Ab. pl. is hĭbŭs.

298 The adverbs from illo- (or ōlo-) are illō or illōc or illūc *to yonder place, thither*; illim or illinc *from yonder place*; illī or illīc *in yonder place, yonder, there*; illā or illāc *by yonder road, along that line*; and ōlim† *formerly* or *hereafter, in those days.* See also Table of words derived from prepositions.

299 The adverbs from isto- are, istō or istōc or istūc *to the place where you are, to your part of the country*; istim or istinc *from the place where you are*; istī or istīc *where you are*; istā or istāc *along the place or country where you are.*

300 The adverbs from ho- are, hōc or hūc *hither, towards me*; hinc *hence, from me, from this time*; hīc *here, near me*; hāc *along this road, by me*; and sī (very rare), more commonly sīc, *so, thus, in this way.*

---

* Illic is the form of the dative when used as an adverb.

† Unless olim be the equivalent in form of our *whilom*, an old dative of *while*, and signifying 'at times.'

LOGICAL PRONOUNS.

301 Logical pronouns refer only to the *words* of a sentence. To these belong i- or eo- *this or that*, and qui- or quo- *which, &c.*

302 I- *or* eo-* *this or that.*

	Singular.			Plural.		
	Masc.	Fem.	Neut.	Masc.	Fem.	Neut.
N.	is	eă	id	N. iī *or* ī *or rather* hī	eae	eă
Ac.	eum	eam	id	Ac. eōs	eās	eă
G.	ēiŭs	ēiŭs	ēiŭs	G. eōrum	eārum	eōrum
D.	eī	eī	eī	D. {eīs iīs *or* is *or rather* hīs *for all genders.*		
Ab.	eō	eā	eō	Ab.		

303 Old forms are N. hīs,† Ac. im *or* em, D. *or* Ab. pl. Ibŭs and eābŭs.

304 The adverbs from i- or eo- are, eō *to this or to that place or degree, thither;* indĕ (in compounds im or in, as exim or exin) *from this*‡ ——, *from that* ——, *thence;* Ibi *in or at this* ——, *in that* ——, *there, then;* eā *along this or that line or road;* Itā *thus, so;* iam *now, already, at last.*

305 Qui- *or* quo-§ *which, what, who, any.*

Singular.

	Masc.	Fem.	Neut.
N.	quĭs *or* quī	quae *or* quī	quĭd *or* quŏd
Ac.	quem	quam	quĭd *or* quŏd
G.	quōiŭs *or* cūiŭs *for all genders*		
D.	quoi *or* cuī *or* cūī *for all genders*		
Ab.	quō *or* quī	quā *or* quī	quō *or* quī

Plural.

	Masc.	Fem.	Neut.
N.	quī	quae	quae *or* quĭă
Ac.	quōs	quās	quae *or* quĭă
G.	quōrum	quārum	quōrum

D. Ab. quībŭs *or* quīs *for all genders.*

---

* An older c.p. was is, whence in-dĕ adv. 'from this place.' Compare the Greek ἐν-θεν, as illustrated by ἐκεῖ-θεν, ἐμέ-θεν.

† Fest. sub voce 'Muger.'

‡ For the blanks insert *time, place, &c.*, as it may be.

§ An older c.p. was quin *or* cun, whence un-dĕ (for cundĕ, compare ăli-cundĕ) 'from what place.'

306. Of the double forms, qui N. and quŏd are adjectives; quis commonly a substantive, rarely an adjective; quid a substantive only.

307. Qui- or quo- is called a *relative* when it refers to a preceding word, as, *the person who* ——, *the thing which* ——, *the knife with which* ——, &c. To the relative belong all the forms except quis quă and quid.

308. It is called *a direct interrogative* when it asks a question, as, *who did it?* and *an indirect interrogative* when it only speaks of a question, as, *we do not know who did it.* To the interrogative belong all the forms, except quă.

309. It is said to be used *indefinitely* when it signifies *any*. In this case it is placed after some word to which it belongs; very commonly after sī, nē, num, eo, ălī. All the forms are used in this sense, but quă is more common than quae.

310. N. Ac.—Quis and quem in old writers are sometimes feminine.

311. G. D.—Quŏiŭs and quoi are older than the other forms. They appear to have been used by Cicero. An old genitive cui occurs in the word cui-cui-mŏdī *of whatever kind.*

312. Ab.—Qui is the older form, and is only used by the later writers in particular phrases: as, 1. quīcum = quōcum m. or n.; 2. without a substantive in the sense *wherewith*; 3. as an interrogative, *by what means, how?*

313. N. pl.—Quēs is a very old form.

314. D. and Ab. pl.—Quis, sometimes written queis, is the older form of the two.

315. The adverbs from quo- or qui- are, quō *whither, to what* ——; undĕ (formerly cundĕ) *from what* ——, *whence;* ŭbi (formerly cŭbi) *in what* ——, *where, when;* quā *along what road or line,* &c.

316. The conjunctions from quo- or qui- are, quom quum or cum *when;* quando *when;* quam *how;* quārē (quā rē) quŏr or cŭr *why;* ŭt (formerly oŭt) or ŭtī *how, that, as;* quŏd *that, because,* &c.

OTHER PRONOMINAL ADJECTIVES, &c.

317. The following adjectives are derived from quo- or qui-: quanto- *how great;* quāli- *like what, of what kind;* quŏt (undeclined) *how many* (whence quŏtiens *how often*); quŏto- *occupying what place in a series.*

318. From an old root, to- *this,* are derived the adjectives, tanto- *so great;* tāli- *like this, of this kind;* tŏt (undecl.) *so many* (whence

tŏtiens *so often*); tŏto- *occupying this place*; also the adverbs tam *so*; tum or (with the enclitic că) tunc *then*.

319   Of pronominal origin are, nam *thus* or *for*, and num *now* (Greek νυν), an old word still used in ĕtiam-num *even now, still*, and in nūdius tertiŭs *now the third day, two days ago*. In common use the enclitic că is always added, as, nunc *now*.

320   Ali is prefixed to many of the relative forms: as, ălĭqui- *any, some* (emphatic), declined like qui- *any*; N. n. ălĭquantum *some, a considerable quantity*; ălĭquŏt (undeclined) *some, a considerable number*, &c.

321   Eo is prefixed: as, ecqui- &c. *whether any?* ecquando *whether at any time?*

322   Num *whether*, sī *if*, nē *not*, are also prefixed: as, numqui- *whether any*, sīqui- *if any*, nēqui- *lest any*. N. numquis, sīquis, nēquis, &c.

323   Of the adverbs formed from ălĭqui-, nēqui-, numqui-, sīqui-, many take the old initial c, as ălĭ-cūbi, ălĭ-cundĕ, &c.

324   Vtĕro- (originally oŭ-tĕro-)—generally an interrogative, *which of the two?* and sometimes a relative, *he of the two, who*; and after sī, *either*, as, sī ūtĕro- *if either*—has G. ūtrīūs, D. ūtri. Hence neutĕro- N. neutĕr, &c. (formerly ne-cūtĕr) *neither*.*

325   Ipso- ipsa- *self, very*, is declined, N. ipsŭs or ipsē ipsă ipsum, Ac. ipsum ipsam ipsum, and the rest like illo-.

326   The N. ipsŭs is found only in old writers, as Terence. Apsē or 'psē undeclined is sometimes found in old writers instead of the proper case of ipso-: as, re-apsē for re-ipsā, eampsē for eam ipsam, &c.

327   Alio- *one, another*, has G. ălīŭs, D. ălĭī, and N. and Ac. neut. sing. ălĭŭd, and the rest like illo-. From a crude form ăli- are derived the old N. m. f. ălis, n. ălid, and the adverbs ălĭbi *elsewhere*, ălĭtĕr *otherwise*.

* The plural of those words which have the suffix tĕro must be carefully distinguished from the singular. Thus,
    N. sing. *ŭtĕr* which of the two individuals.
    N. pl. *ŭtri* which of the two classes, parties, nations, armies, &c.
    N. sing. *altĕr* one of the two individuals.
    N. pl. *altĕri* one of the two classes, parties, nations, armies, &c.
    N. sing. *ŭterquĕ* both of the two individuals.
    N. pl. *ŭtriquĕ* both of the two classes, parties, nations, armies, &c.
    N. sing. *neutĕr* neither of the two individuals.
    N. pl. *neutri* neither of the two classes, parties, nations, armies, &c.

328 When ălĭo- is used in two following sentences, it is translated by *one* ——, *another* ——; or *some* ——, *others* ——: as, ălĭus rīdet, ălĭus lăcrŭmat *one laughs, another cries;* ălĭōs caedit, ălĭos dīmittit *he kills some, and lets others go.*

329 When ălĭo- is used twice in the same sentence, that sentence is commonly translated twice over: as, ălĭūd ălĭō tempŏrē *one thing at one time, another at another;* or by *each other:* as, ălĭi ălĭis prōsunt *they do good to each other.*

330 Altĕro- (from ăli-) *one of two, another of two, the second,* has G. altĕrīŭs, D. altĕrī; but altĕrĭūs occurs in poetry.*

331 When altĕro- is used in two following sentences, it is translated by *the one* ——, *the other* ——: as, alter rīdet, alter lăcrŭmat *the one laughs, the other cries.*

332 When altĕro- is used twice in the same sentence, it is commonly translated by *each—other:* as, altĕr altĕrum volnĕrat *each wounds the other.*

333 As ăli- and qui- form ăliqui-, so from altĕro- and ūtĕro- is formed altĕr-ūtĕro- *one of the two,* which is declined in both parts; but elision generally takes place if the first part end in a vowel or *m:* as, N. altĕrūtĕr altĕr'ūtră altĕr'ūtrum &c., but G. altĕrĭŭs-ūtrĭŭs.

334 Ullo- *any* (a diminutive from ūno- *one*) has G. ullĭūs, D. ullī &c. It is accompanied by a substantive, and is used only in negative sentences. Hence nullo- *none,* declined like ullo-.

335 Many enclitics are added to the pronouns to give emphasis to them: viz.

336 Quidem: as, ĕquĭdem, for ĕgŏ quĭdem *I at least.*

337 Mĕt: as, ĕgŏmĕt *I myself;* uosmĕt *you yourselves.* It is commonly followed by ipsĕ: as, suismĕt ipsī praesīdīis *they themselves with their own troops.*

338 Tĕ, only with the nominative tū: as, tūtĕ *thou thyself.*

339 Cĕ, only with the demonstrative pronouns. See §§ 266–300.

340 Pŏtĕ: as, ut-pŏtĕ *inasmuch as, as.*

341 Ptĕ, in certain old forms: as, mihĭptĕ, meptĕ; and above all with the ablatives, meoptĕ, meaptĕ, suoptĕ, suaptĕ, &c.

342 Dem, with the pronoun i- or eo-: as, ī-dem *the same.* The N. m. drops the *s,* but leaves the vowel long; the N. and Ac. neut. take no *d,* and have the vowel short. In the Ac. sing. and

* See note p. 54.

G. pl. the final *m* becomes *n* before *d.* Thus, N. idem eā-dem idem, Ac. eun-dem ean-dem idem &c. So also with tŏt, tŏtidem (undecl.) *precisely as many;* and with tanto-, N. m. tantusdem, &c. *of the same magnitude.*

343. Dam, with quo- or qui-. N. qui-dam quae-dam quid-dam or quod-dam, Ac. quen-dam quan-dam quid-dam or quod-dam &c. *a certain person or thing.* It is used when a person cannot or will not state whom or what he means, and often serves to soften adjectives which would express too much: as, divīnă quaedam ēlŏquentiă *a certain godlike eloquence, a sort of godlike eloquence, I had almost said a godlike eloquence.* From quidam is derived quondam *at some former or future time, formerly, hereafter.*

344. Quam, with quo- or qui-: as, N. quisquam quaequam quidquam or quicquam &c. *any,* in negative sentences. It is commonly used without a substantive. See ullo- above. From quisquam are formed the adverbs umquam or unquam (originally cumquam) *ever;* from whence nunquam *never,* nē-quiquam *in vain,* haudquāquam *in no way, by no means,* neutiquam or rather nūtiquam *in no way, by no means,* usquam *any where,* nusquam *no where.*

345. Piam (probably another form of preceding suffix), with quo- or qui-: as, N. quispiam quaepiam quidpiam or quodpiam &c. *any* (emphatic). From qui-piam comes the adverb uspiam *any where.*

346. Nam: as, N. quisnam or quinam quaenam quidnam or quodnam &c. *who, which?* in interrogations (emphatic); and N. ūternam *which of the two?* in interrogations (emphatic).

347. Quĕ (this enclitic is probably a corruption of the relative itself): as, N. quisquĕ quaequĕ quidquĕ or quodquĕ &c. *every, each;* whence the adverbs ūbiquĕ *every where,* undiquĕ *from every side,* ūtīquĕ *any how, at any rate,* usquĕ *every step, every moment;* also N. ūterquĕ ūtrăquĕ ūtrumquĕ *each of two, both.*

348. Quisquĕ in old writers is used in the same sense as quicunquĕ.

349. Quisquĕ is generally placed—1. after relatives and relative conjunctions: as, ut quisquĕ uēnit *as each arrived;* 2. after reflective pronouns: as, prō sē quisquĕ *each for himself;* 3. after superlatives and ordinal numerals: as, optĭmus quisquĕ *all the best men,* dĕcĭmus quisquĕ *every tenth man,* quŏtus quisquĕ ? (*every how manyeth*) *how few?*

350. Cumquĕ or cunquĕ (an old variety of quisquĕ): as, N. quicunquĕ quaecunquĕ quodcunquĕ &c. *whoever, whosoever, whichever, whatever:* so also N. ūtercunquĕ ūtrăcunquĕ ūtrumcunquĕ &c.

whichever of the two; N. m. quantuscunquĕ &c. *how great soever,* quandōcunquĕ *whensoever* &c. Cunquĕ may be separated from the other word: as, qui mē cunquĕ uīdit *whoever saw me.* Quicunquĕ is rarely used as an indefinite, *any whatever.*

351. Vīs (*thou wishest,* from uŏl- *wish*): as, N. quīuīs quaeuīs quiduīs or quoduīs &c. *any one you please* (the best or the worst), a universal affirmative; whence quamuīs *as much as you please, no matter how ——, though ever so ——;* and ūteruīs ūtrāuīs ūtrumuīs *whichever of the two you please.*

352. Lŭbet or lĭbet (*it pleaseth*): as, N. m. quilŭbet &c. *any one you please;* and N. m. ūterlŭbet &c. *whichever of the two you please.*

353. Relative forms are often doubled. Thus, qui- doubled: as, N. m. quisquis,* n. quidquid or quicquid *whoever, no matter who;* whence cuicuimŏdi, a genitive, *of whatever kind,* and quōquō mŏdo *in any way whatever.*

355. Quanto- doubled: as, N. m. quantusquantŭs &c. *how great soever, no matter how great.*

356. Quāli- doubled: as, N. m. quālisquālīs &c. *whatever-like, no matter what-like.*

357. Quŏt doubled: as, quotquŏt (undeclined) *how many soever, no matter how many.*

358. So also there are the doubled adverbs or conjunctions: quamquam *however, no matter how, although, and yet;* ŭtŭt *however, no matter how;* quōquō *whithersoever;* undĕundĕ *whencesoever;* ŭbiŭbi *wheresoever;* quāquā *along whatsoever road.*

Possessive Pronouns.

359. Meo- mea- *mine, my.*
Tuo- tua- *thine, thy, your, yours* (referring to one person).
Suo- sua- *his, hers, her; its; theirs, their.*
Nostĕro- nostĕra- *ours, our;* N. nostĕr nostrā nostrum &c.
Vostĕro- uostĕra- or uestĕro- uestĕra- *yours, your* (referring to more than one); N. uostĕr uostrā uostrum &c.
Cūio- cūia- *whose.*

360. These are all declined regularly, except that the m. V. of meois mī.

361. Suo- is a reflective pronoun, and can only be used when it refers to the nominative (see § 280). In other cases *his, her* or *its* must be translated by the genitive ūiŭs from i-, and *their* by the genitive eōrum or eārum.

* No special form for the feminine in use.

362   The adjective cūio- is rarely met with, the genitives cūiūs, quōrum, quārum, being used in its place.

363   The possessive pronouns, if not emphatic, are placed after the noun they belong to. If they are emphatic, they are placed before it.

364   From the possessive pronouns are derived:

    Nostrāti- or nostrāt-,   N. nostrās *of our country.*
    Vostrāti- or uostrāt-,   N. uostrās *of your country.*
    Cūiāti- or cūiāt-,   N. cūiās *of whose country.*

365   Formed in the same way are iufūmāti- *belonging to the lowest*, summāti- *belonging to the highest.* All those are declined like Arpīnāti- or Arpīnāt- *belonging to Arpīnum.*

366   TABLE OF PRONOMINAL ADVERBS.

Ending in	bī or ī. dat.	ō (=om) acc.	dē (=θεν)° old gen.	ā, abl. fem.
Meaning	*where*	*whither*	*whence*	*along what road*
ho-	hīc	hō,† hōc,‡ hūc	hinc	hāc
isto-	istī, istīc	istō, istōc,‡ istūc	istim, istinc	istā, istāc
illo-	illī, illīc	illō, illōc,‡ illūc	illim, illinc	illā, illāc
i- *or* eo-	ibī	eō	inde	eā
i- *or* eo- + dem	ībīdem	eōdem	indīdem	eādem
qui- *or* quo-	ūbī	quō	unde	quā
ūtŏro-	ūtrōbī	ūtrō	ūtrinde	ūtrā
ālio-	aliūbī	aliō	aliunde	aliā
ali-	alibī			
altĕro-		altrōş	altrinde(f)‖	
neutĕro-	neutrūbī	neutrō		
ali- + qui- *or* quo-	alicūbī	aliquō	alicunde	aliquā
sī + qui- &c.	sicūbī	siquō	sicunde	siquā
nē + qui- &c.	nēcūbī	nēquō	nēcunde	nēquā
num + qui- &c.	numcūbī	numquō		
qui- doubled	ūbiūbī	quōquō	undeunde	quāquā
qui- *or* quo- + uis	ūbīuīs	quōuīs	undēuīs	quāuīs
qui- &c. + lūbet	ūbīlūbet	quōlūbet	undēlūbet	quālūbet
qui- &c. + quē	ūbīquē	quōquē¶	undīquē	
ūtĕro- + quē	ūtrōbīquē	ūtrōquē	ūtrinquē	ūtrāquē
qui- &c. + quam		quōquam		quāquam**
qui- &c. + nam	ūbīnam	quōnam		quānam

* See § 790.
† Occurring in *horsum* for *hō-uorsum* 'hitherwards.'
‡ Less used than the other forms.
§ Occurring in *alīrō-uorsīs* 'towards the other side.'
‖ Virtually occurring in *altrinsēcūs* 'from the other side.'
¶ In *quōquōuorsūs* 'in every direction.'
** In *nēquāquam* and *haudquāquam* 'in no way, by no means.'

VERBS.

367   An *active* verb denotes action, that is, movement: as, caed-
   fdl, *cut or strike*, cŭr- *run*.
368   The person (or thing) from whom the action proceeds is called
   the *nominative to the verb*.
369   The object to which the action is directed is called the *accusative after the verb*.
370   A verb which admits a nominative is called *personal*: as, caed-
   strike; whence uir caedit *the man strikes*.
371   A verb which does not admit a nominative is called *impersonal*:
   as, tŏna- *thunder*; whence tŏnăt *it thunders*.
372   A *transitive* verb is one which admits an object or accusative
   after it: as, caedit puĕrum *he strikes the boy*.
373   An *intransitive* verb is one which does not admit an accusative:
   as, cŭr- *run*; whence currit *he runs*.
374   The object of a transitive verb may be the agent himself: as,
   caedo mē *I strike myself*, caedis tē *you strike yourself*, caedit sē *he
   strikes himself*, &c.   A verb is then said to be used as a *reflective*.
375   In Latin a reflective suffix is added to a transitive verb, so as
   to give it the reflective sense: as, uertō *I turn*, uertŏr *I turn myself*; uertis *you turn*, uertĕris *you turn yourself*; uertit *he turns*,
   uertĭtŭr *he turns himself*.
376   A reflective verb then denotes an action upon oneself, and in
   Latin is conjugated in the imperfect tenses with a suffix *s* or *r*.[*]
   It will be denoted by an *r* between brackets: as, uert-(r.) *turn
   oneself*.
377   The perfect tenses of a reflective verb are supplied by the verbs
   ĕs- and fu- *be*, united with the participle in *to-*.
378   An intransitive verb is generally in meaning reflective: as,
   cŭr- *run* i. e. *put oneself in a certain rapid motion*, ambŭla- *walk*

---

[*] This suffix is no doubt the pronoun *sē* 'self,' which, as it is not limited
in number and gender, was probably at first not limited in person. In
some of the Slavonic languages the same pronoun is actually applied to
all the persons ; and in the Lithuanian the reflective verb is formed from
the simple verb through all the persons by the addition of *s*. The interchange of *s* and *r* has been seen already in the nouns; another example
presents itself in *uertĭr-is*, which is formed from *uertĭs*, precisely as the
gen. *pulvĕr-is* from the o.f. *pulvis*, and the old pl. gen. *nucĕr-um* (see
§ 85) from the sing. gen. *nucis*. So also *lapidĕrum*, *regĕrum* (Charisius,
p. 40 Putsch.), *bouĕrum* (Cato R. R. 62).

i. e. *put oneself* in a *certain moderate motion;* but as the object in these cases cannot easily be mistaken, no reflective pronoun or suffix is added.

379   When the source of an action (*i. e.* the nominative) is not known, or it is thought not desirable to mention it, it is common to say that the action proceeds from the object itself. A reflective so used is called a *passive;* thus uertĭtŭr, literally, *he turns himself,* is often used for *he is turned.**

380   This passive use of a verb with a reflective suffix is more common than the proper reflective use.

381   The nominative to the passive verb is the same as the accusative after the transitive verb, caedunt puĕrum *they strike the boy,* or caedĭtur puĕr *the boy is struck.*

382   Hence passive verbs can be formed only from transitives.

383   An impersonal passive verb however is formed from intransitives† : as, from nŏce- *do damage,* nŏcĕtŭr *damage is done;* from rĕsist- *stand in opposition, offer resistance,* rĕsistĭtŭr *resistance is offered.* When the intransitive verb can be thus expressed by an English verb and substantive, the passive impersonal may be translated by what is also strictly impersonal, the person who does the damage, or offers the resistance, &c. not being mentioned. At times this is impracticable, and it is necessary to use the word *they* or *people* with the active, as from i- *go,* ĭtŭr *they go.*

384   Transitive verbs also may form a passive impersonal : as, from dic- *say,* dicĭtŭr‡ *they say;* but in this case the words of the sentence that follow dicĭtŭr may perhaps be considered as a nominative to it. See Syntax, § 1240.

* Many European languages will afford examples of this strange use of the reflective; as the German: *Das versteht sich von selbst,* 'that is understood of itself;' the French: *Le corps se trouva,* 'the body was found;' the Italian: *Si loda l'uomo modesto,* 'the modest man is praised;' the Spanish: *Las aguas se secaron,* 'the waters were dried up.' There is something like this in our own language: *the chair got broken in the scuffle.* Nay, children may often be heard to use such a phrase as *the chair broke itself.*

† Where the action of an intransitive verb is to be expressed without mentioning the nominative, the artifice of supposing the action to proceed from the object is of course impracticable, because an intransitive verb has no object. Here a second artifice is adopted, and the action is supposed to proceed from itself; thus, *nocetur,* literally translated, is 'damage does itself.'

‡ In Italian, *si dice;* in Spanish, *se dice.* In German it is expressed by *man sagt,* 'man says;' from which the French have literally translated their *on dit,* originally *hom dit.*

A *static* verb denotes a state: as, ĕs- *be*, dormi- *sleep*, iăce- *lie*, ŭĭgĭla- *be awake*, mĕtŭ- *fear*.

Static verbs generally end in *e*, by which they are sometimes distinguished from active verbs of nearly the same form and meaning: as,

iăo- or iăci-	*throw*,	iăce-	*lie*.
pend-	*hang or suspend*,	pende-	*hang or be suspended*.
sĭd- (sīdĕre)	*alight or sink*,	sĕde-	*sit or be seated*.
căp- or căpi-	*take*,	hăbe-	*hold or have*.
possĭd-	*enter upon possession*,	posside-	*possess*.
ferv-	*boil*,	ferve-	*be boiling hot*.
[cand-	*set on fire*],	cande-	*blaze*, & căle- *be hot*.
tend-	*stretch, strain*,	tĕne-	*hold tight*.
alba-	*whiten*,	albe-	*be white*.

A static imperfect is nearly equivalent to the perfect of an active: as, possēdit *he has taken possession*, and possĭdet *he possesses* or *is in possession*; possēdĕrat *he had taken possession*, and possĭdēbat *he possessed* or *was in possession*; possēdĕrit *he will have taken possession*, and possĭdēbit *he will possess* or *be in possession*.

Hence many static verbs in *e* have no perfect; and even in those which appear to have one, the perfect by its meaning seems to belong to an active verb. Thus frige- *be cold* is said to have a perfect frix-. The compound rēfrixit does exist, but not with a static meaning: thus ŭīnum rēfrixit *the wine got or has got cold again*. The form of the perfect itself implies a present rē-frig-, not rēfrige-.

Hence two perfects from active verbs are translated as static imperfects: as, gno- or gno-sc- *examine*, whence perf. gnōuit *he has examined* or *he knows*, gnōuĕrat *he had examined* or *he knew*; consue- or consuesc- *acquire a habit* or *accustom oneself*, whence perf. consuēuit *he has acquired the habit* or *is accustomed*, consuē-uĕrat *he had acquired the habit* or *was accustomed*.

Two verbs have only the perfect in use, and these translated by English imperfects of static meaning, viz. ōd-*, mĕmĭn-, whence ōdit *he hates*, ōdĕrat *he hated*, ōdĕrĭt *he will hate*; mĕmĭnit *he*

---

* These imply an imperfect crude form ŏd- or ŏdĭ- 'take an aversion to,' whence ŏdio- sb. n. 'hatred;' and mĕn- 'mind' or 'notice,' whence the sb. f. men-ti- or ment- 'mind.'

remembers, mĕmĭnĕrat *he remembered,* mĕmĭnĕrĭt *he will remember.*

391   Static verbs are for the most part intransitive; but some are transitive, as those which denote possession, hăbe- *hold,* tĕne- *hold tight, keep,* possĭde- *possess,* sci- *know;* and verbs of feeling, as, ăma- *love,* tĭme- *fear.*

Irregularities of Form and Meaning.

392   A static intransitive has sometimes a reflective or passive perfect. Such a verb is commonly called a *Neuter-Passive:* as,

Lat.	English.	Pres. 3 pers.	Perf. 3 pers. masc.
aude-	*dare,*	audet	ausŭs est.
gaude-	*rejoice,*	gaudet	gāvīsŭs est.
fīd-	*trust,*	fīdit	fīsŭs est.
sŏle-	*be wont,*	sŏlet	sŏlĭtŭs est.

393   To the same class belong several impersonal verbs of feeling, &c.: viz.

mĭsĕre-	denoting	*pity,*	mĭsĕret	mĭsĕrĭtum *or* mĭsertum est.
pŭde-	„	*shame,*	pŭdet	pŭduit *or* pŭdĭtum est.
pĭge-	„	*reluctance,*	pĭget	pĭguit *or* pĭgĭtum est.
taede-	„	*weariness,*	taedet	taeduit *or* per-taesum est.
lŭbe-	„	*pleasure,*	lŭbet	lŭbuit *or* lŭbĭtum est.
plăce-	„	*approbation,*	plăcet	plăcuit *or* plăcĭtum est.
lĭce-	„	*permission,*	lĭcet	lĭcuit *or* lĭcĭtum est.

394   Some transitive verbs are used without a reflective pronoun or suffix, yet with a reflective or intransitive meaning: as, fortūnă uertĕrat *fortune had turned* i. e. *had turned herself.* In these cases the pronouns mē, tē, sē &c. are said to be understood.

395   This use of a transitive form with a reflective or intransitive meaning is more common in the perfect tenses: as, rĕuortĭtŭr *he returns,* rĕuortēbātŭr *he was returning,* rĕuortētŭr *he will return;* but rĕuertit *he has returned,* rĕuertĕrat *he had returned,* rĕuertĕrit *he will have returned.* So dēuortĭtŭr *he turns out of the road into an inn,* but dēuertit (perf.) *he has done so;* plangĭtŭr *he beats himself,* but planxit *he has beaten himself.*

396   Some of the principal verbs which are thus used with both a transitive, and reflective or intransitive meaning, are the following:

Lat.	Trans.	Intrans.	Lat.	Trans.	Intrans.
mōve-	move,	move.	plang-	beat,	beat oneself.
auge-	increase,	increase.	incipi-	begin,	begin.
laxa-	loosen,	get loose.	inclīna-	slant,	slant.
lāva-	wash,	wash.	abstine-	keep away,	abstain.
mūta-	change,	change.	rěmit-	let go again,	relax.
sta-	set up,	stand.	suppědita-	keep filling up,	abound.
ru-	put in violent motion,	rush.	præcipita-	throw headlong,	rush headlong.*

In some verbs the transitive meaning, though originally belonging to the word, has become nearly or quite obsolete, as in prŏpěra- *hasten*, trans. or intrans., prŏpinqua- *make near* or *approach*.

The reflective form seems to have been originally given to some verbs to denote reciprocal action: as,

amplect-ĭmŭr	*we embrace each other.*	parti-mŭr	*we share together.*
convicĭā-mŭr	*we abuse each other.*	proeliā-mŭr	*we fight each other.*
fābŭla-mŭr	*we talk together.*	rixā-mŭr	*we snarl at each other.*
lŏqu-ĭmŭr	*we talk together.*	sōlā-mŭr	*we comfort each other.*
luctā-mŭr	*we wrestle together.*	sorti-mŭr	*we cast lots together.*
oscŭlā-mŭr	*we kiss each other.*	suāviā-mŭr	*we kiss each other.*

Many reflective verbs are translated by an English intransitive: as, prŏflīc-isc- (r.) *set out*, laeta- (r.) *rejoice*, which have still a reflective sense. These are called *Intransitive Deponents*.

Many reflective verbs have so far thrown off the reflective meaning, that they are translated by an English transitive and take a new accusative: as, mira- (r.) *admire*, věre- (r.) *fear*, amplect- (r.) *embrace*, indu- (r.) *clothe oneself*, *put on*, sěqu- (r.) *follow*, ĭmĭta- (r.) *make oneself like*, *imitate*. These are called *Transitive Deponents*.

Some intransitive verbs, by a slight change of meaning, are used transitively: as, from horre- *bristle* or *shudder*, horret těněbrās *he dreads the dark*; māne- *wait*, mānet aduentum ēius *he awaits his arrival*; ōle- *smell*, ōlet unguentis *he smells of perfumes*. This

---

* It is in this way that *fi-*, only a shortened form of *făci-*, first signified 'make myself,' and then 'become' or 'am made.' It is indeed probable that the *c* in *făcio* was not always pronounced. This would account for its disappearance in the Italian infinitive *fare* and French *faire*; and would also account for the fact that *fi* is commonly long before a vowel, as *fī-o* 'I am made,' for *faï-o*.

is particularly the case with some neuter pronouns: as, from lăbōra- *labour*, id lăbōrat *he is labouring at this*. (See § 900.)

402. Intransitive verbs may have an accusative of a noun which has the same meaning: as, uītam iūcundam uīuit *he is living a delightful life*. This is called the *Cognate Accusative* (§ 894).

403. Intransitive verbs when compounded sometimes become transitive: as, uād-* *go*, ēuād- *go out, escape;* whence ēuādĕrĕ pĕrīcŭlō or ex pĕrīcŭlō *to make one's way out of danger*, or ēuādĕrĕ pĕrīcŭlum *to escape danger;*— uĕni- *come*, conuĕni- *come together, meet;* whence conuĕnīre ăliquem *to meet one, to go and see a person;*— grăd- or grădi- (r.) *march*, ēgrŏd- or ēgrĕdi- (r.) *march out, leave;* whence ēgrĕdi urbĕ or ex urbĕ *to march out of the city*, or ēgrĕdi urbem *to leave the city*.

404. Some transitive verbs when compounded take a new transitive sense, nearly allied to the original meaning, and thus have a double construction: as, da- *put*, circumda- *put round* or *surround;* whence circumdărĕ mūrum urbi *to throw a wall round the city*, or circumdăre urbem mūrō *to surround the city with a wall;*— sĕr- *sow* or *plant*, insĕr- *plant in, graft;* whence insĕrĕrĕ pĭrum ornō (dat.) *to graft a pear on a wild ash*, or insĕrĕre ornum pĭrō (abl.) *to engraft a wild ash with a pear;*— du- *put*, indu- *put on, clothe;* indŭĕrĕ uestem ălicui *to put a dress on one*, or indŭĕre ăliquem ueste *to clothe one with a dress*.

405. The verb then has two forms or *voices:* the *simple voice* (commonly called the *active*), which does not take the reflective suffix; the *reflective voice* (commonly called the *passive*), which does take it.

Personal Suffixes to Verbs.

406. In English the pronouns *I, you* or *thou, he, she, it*, &c. are prefixed to a verb. In Latin, as in Greek, little syllables with the same meaning are attached to the end of a verb so as to form one word with it.

407. The Greek verb in its oldest shape formed from the pronouns me- *me*, su- or tu- *thou*, and to- *this*, the three suffixes mi, si, ti, or, with a short vowel prefixed, ŏmĭ, ĕsĭ, ĕtĭ.† Now the Latin language has its personal suffixes not unlike these: viz. ŏm, ĭs, ĭt.

* See § 451.1.

† Compare the old verb εμμι (εσ-μι), εσ-σι, εσ-τι, with the old reflective verb τυπτ-ομ-αι, τυπτ-εσ-αι, τυπτ-ετ-αι.

408 The suffix ŏm, belonging to the first person, is but little altered in sum (=ĕs-um) *I am*, or in inqu-am* *I say*.

409 More commonly the suffix *om* undergoes one of two changes. Either the *m* is lost, as, scrib-o *I write*, for scrib'om†; or, if a vowel precede, the *o* sometimes disappears, leaving the *m*, as, scribēba'm *I was writing*.

410 The final *o* of the first person is always long in Virgil‡, but common in later poets.

411 The suffixes of the second person, tĭs, and of the third person, tĭ, also lose their vowel, if the verb itself end in one. Thus, scrib-ĭs *you write*, and scrib-ĭt *he writes*; but scribēba's *you were writing*, ărā's *you plough*, scribēba't *he was writing*, ără't *he ploughs*. So also the ĭ is lost in fers *you bring*, fert *he brings*; ĕs (for ĕs-ĭs) *you are*, est *he is*; and nolt *he wishes*.

412 When the suffix tĭ thus loses its vowel by contraction, as, ără-ĭt, ărăt *he ploughs*, it might be expected that the syllable would be long; but it is in fact nearly always short. Still in the reflective the right quantity is preserved, scribēbāt-ūr, ărāt-ūr; and the old poets, including even Virgil, have examples of a long quantity in such words as verāt, nugeāt, accĭdēt.

413 The form of the second person suffix in the perfect is tī for ĭs: as, scripsĭs-tī *you have written*.

414 The suffixes of plurality for the nouns were *s* and *um*. (See § 52.) Those employed for the verbs are nearly the same.

415 From ŏmŭ and *s* is formed the double suffix ŏmĕs 'we' for the old Greek verb. The old Latin prefers ŭmŭs, as in vŏl-ŭmŭs *we wish*, sŭmŭs (=ĕs-ŭmŭs) *we are*, quaes-ŭmŭs *we ask*. Commonly ĭmŭs is written, as scrib-ĭmŭs *we write*.‖

---

* The English language still retains a trace of the first person suffix in the verb *am*. See also § 1158. 1, note †, about *solem*.

† See the adverbs of motion towards, where *om* final is similarly reduced to *o*.

‡ *Spondeo* and *nescio* appear to have a short *o* in Virgil, but in reality are to be considered as words of two syllables, *spondo* or *spondyo* and *nescyo*. *Scio* in Italian has become *so*.

§ The English language still retains its suffix of the second person *est*, and of the third person *eth* or *s*, as in *sendest* and *sendeth* or *sends*.

‖ See the same interchange of *ĭs* as and *ĭmus* in the superlatives (§ 242), and in the ordinal numerals (§ 252). Nay the Emperor Augustus wrote *simus* (i.e. *sīmŭs*) for *sumus* in the indicative.

416 The *s* is lost after a vowel: as, scrībēbā-mŭs *we were writing*, ărā-mŭs *we plough*.

417 From *tu* or *ti* and *s* is formed the double suffix *tĭs* 'you' (pl.); or, with a short vowel prefixed, *ĭtĭs*: as, scrīb-ĭtĭs *you* (pl.) *write*.

418 The prefixed *i* is lost after a vowel: as, scrībēbā-tĭs *you* (pl.) *were writing*, ărā-tĭs *you* (pl.) *plough*. So also in es-tĭs *you are*, fer-tĭs *you bring*, and uol-tĭs *you wish*.

419 The syllable attached to the verb to form the third person plural is *unt*: as, scrīb-unt *they write*.

420 The *u* is always lost if the verb end in *a* or *e*, and sometimes if it end in *i*. Thus, scrībēba-nt *they were writing*, scrībe-nt *they will write*, scripsĕri-nt *they will have written*; but audi-unt *they hear*.

421 In the imperative mood the suffixes of the second person singular and plural change the *ĭs* into *ĕ*, and *ĭtĭs* into *ĭtŏ*: as, scrīb-ĕ and scrīb-ĭtŏ *write*, scrībĭtŏ-tŏ *ye shall write*.*

422 The final *ĕ* is lost after a vowel: as, ără *plough*; also in fĕr *bring*, făc *make*, dīc *say*, dūc *lead*, ĕs *be*.

Moods, &c.

423 The *indicative* mood is used for the main verb of a sentence, whether it be affirmative, negative, or interrogative. It is also used in some secondary sentences.

The indicative mood has no special suffix.

424 The *imperative* mood *commands*. Its suffix in the future tense is the syllable *tŏ* or *ĭtŏ*: as, scrīb-ĭtŏ *thou shalt write*.

426 The two tenses of the imperative are commonly united as one.

427 The *subjunctive* mood, as its name implies, is used in secondary sentences subjoined to the main verb.

428 In some sentences it is not uncommon to omit the main verb, and then the subjunctive mood *seems* to signify *power, permission, duty, wish, purpose, result, allegation, hypothesis*; whereas in fact these notions rather belong to the verb which is not expressed. Thus the phrase, Quid făciam? is translated by *What should I do?* or *What am I to do?* But the full phrase is Quid uis făciam? *What do you wish me to do?*

---

* So in the Greek, even the indicative has τυπτετε for τυπτετις. Compare also the double form *s* tristis and tristī, magis and magī, and above all the second persons of reflective verbs: uidĕrĭs, uidĕrē; uidēbarĭs, uidēbarē, &c.

429 The suffix of the subjunctive mood cannot be easily separated from those of the subjunctive tenses.

430 The *infinitive* mood is also used in secondary sentences subjoined to the main verb. It differs from the subjunctive in that it does not admit the personal suffixes to be added to it.

431 The suffix of the infinitive mood is *ĕsĕ* or *ĕrĕ*: as, es-sĕ *to be*, scrib-ĕrĕ *to write*.

432 The infinitive mood may also be considered as a neuter substantive undeclined, but differing from other substantives in that it has the construction of a verb with a noun following.

433 The *supines* are the accusative and ablative cases of a masculine substantive formed from a verb with the suffix *tu* or *tu*. The accusative supine has occasionally the construction of a verb with the noun following.

434 The accusative supine is in many grammars called the supine active; and the ablative supine, the supine passive.

435 The *gerund* is a neuter substantive formed from a verb with the suffix *endo* or *undo*; of which the first vowel is lost after *a* and *e*. In the old writers it has the construction of a verb with the noun following.

436 A *participle* is an adjective in form, but differs from adjectives, first, because an adjective speaks of a quality generally, while a participle speaks of an act or state at a particular time; secondly, because a participle has the construction of a verb with the noun following.

On Tenses in General.

437 *Tense* is another word for time. There are three tenses: *past*, *present*, and *future*.

438 The past and future are boundless; the present is but a point of time.

439 As an act may be either past, present, or future, with respect to the present moment, so *yesterday* had its past, present, and future; and *to-morrow* again will have its past, present, and future.

Thus, first in reference to the present moment, we have: Past, *he has written to A;* Pres. *he is writing to B;* Fut. *he is going to write to C.*

Secondly, in reference to yesterday or any other moment now

gone by: Past, *he had written to D*; Pres. *he was writing to E;* Fut. *he was going to write to F*.

Thirdly, in reference to tomorrow or any moment not yet arrived: Past, *he will have written to G*; Pres. *he will be writing to H*; Fut, *he will be going to write to I*.

440. Or the same ideas may be arranged as follows:

Action finished, or *perfect*: at a past time, *he had written to D*; at the present moment, *he has written to A*; at a future time, *he will have written to G*.

Action going on, or *imperfect*: at a past time, *he was writing to E*; at the present moment, *he is writing to B*; at a future time, *he will be writing to H*.

Action intended: at a past time, *he was going to write to F*; at the present moment, *he is going to write to C*; at a future time, *he will be going to write to I*.

441. Or lastly, the same ideas may be represented by the lines in the following diagram:

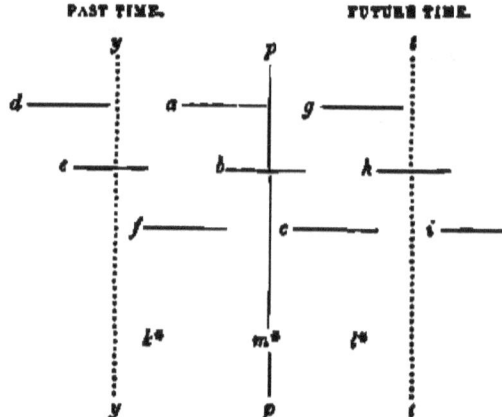

A point in the vertical line *pp* denotes present time; a point in *yy* denotes yesterday or some past time; a point in *tt*, tomorrow or some future time.

The several horizontal lines *a, b, c*, &c. denote the time occupied in writing to *A, B, C*, &c. respectively. Thus,

a is wholly to the left of *pp*, and signifies *he has written*—present perfect.

b partly on the left, partly on the right: *he is writing*—present imperfect.

c wholly to the right: *he is going to write*—present intention

d wholly to the left of *yy*: *he had written at time y*—past perfect.

e partly on the left, partly on the right: *he was writing at time y*—past imperfect.

f wholly to the right: *at time y he was going to write*—past intention.

g wholly to the left of *tt*: *he will have written at time t*—future perfect.

h partly on the left, partly on the right: *he will be writing at time t*—future imperfect.

i wholly to the right: *at time t he will be going to write*—future intention.

442   The word 'perfect' in all these phrases means *relatively* past: thus the present perfect *is* past, the past perfect *was* past, the future perfect *will be* past.

443   Again, the perfect tenses are used for events *recently* past, the consequences still remaining. *I have passed a good night, and feel refreshed; he had had his breakfast, and was putting on his boots; you will then have finished your letter, and will be ready to walk with me.* But we cannot say, *William the Conqueror has died in Normandy.*

444   So also the tenses of intention apply to a time *soon* to arrive.

445   The aorist, *he wrote*, is not thus limited; it may be applied to any past time; as, *Cicero wrote a history of his consulship*. It does not, like the past tenses which we have been considering, stand in any relation to any other point of time. The consequences of the act are not alluded to, as in the perfects; nor the duration of the act spoken of, as in the imperfects. On the contrary, the aorist treats the act as a mere *point* of past time.

446   In the diagram the aorist may be represented by the point *k*.

447   The simple future, *he will write*, corresponds in general character to the aorist of past time. It is equally independent of other points of future time, and speaks of the act as momentary.

448   In the diagram the future may be represented by the point *l*.

449   If the simple present were strictly limited to the mere point of time which belongs to it, it would seldom be used; but this, like some of the other tenses, is employed to denote a *state* of things,

customs, general truths, &c., the duration of which in fact is not limited to a mere moment.*

450 The true present may be represented in the diagram by the point *m* in *pp*.

TENSES OF THE LATIN VERB.

451 The Latin indicative has six leading tenses:—three perfect tenses, and three which, for convenience, but somewhat inaccurately†, are called imperfects; viz. the present, the past-imperfect, the future; the present-perfect, the past-perfect, the future-perfect.

451.1 The c.f. of a verb is often strengthened for the imperfect tenses: (*a.*) by lengthening the vowel: thus, dĭc- *say*, dŭc- *lead*, fĭd- *trust*, become in the imperfect tenses dīc-, dūc-, fīd-. (*b.*) by doubling the final consonant: thus, mĭt- *let go*, cŭr- *run*, uĕr- *sweep*, become mitt-, curr-, uerr-. (*c.*) by substituting two consonants for the final consonant: thus, rŭp- *burst*, scĭd- *tear*, tĕn- *stretch*, become rump-, scind-, tend-.

452 The present has no tense suffix: as, scrib- *write*, scribit *he writes*.

453 When an affirmation is made with emphasis, also in negative and interrogative phrases, the verb *do* is commonly used in the translation: as, *he does write; he does not write; does he write?*

454 The present-imperfect has the same form in Latin: as, scribit *he is writing.*

---

* An example of the true present, as applied to acts, occurs in Ivanhoe (c. XXIX.), where the agitated Rebecca, standing at the lattice, reports to the sick knight the proceedings of the siege. "He blenches not, he blenches not!" said Rebecca. "I see him now; he leads a body of men close under the outer barrier of the barbican. They pull down the piles and palisades; they hew down the barriers with axes. His high black plume floats abroad over the throng, like a raven over the field of the slain. They have made a breach in the barriers! they rush in! they are thrust back! Front-de-Bœuf heads the defenders; I see his gigantic form above the press. They throng again to the breach, and the pass is disputed hand to hand and man to man. God of Jacob! it is the meeting of two fierce tides—the conflict of two oceans moved by adverse winds." Such a use of the true present can only be looked for in dramatic writing. The *historic present*, as it is called, is an imitation of this dramatic excitement.

† Inaccurately, see § 459.

455 The present is sometimes employed in past narrative, both in English and Latin, as if the scene described were passing before one's eyes. This is called the *historic present*: as, *he then plunges into the river, swims across, and seeks the tent of the king*.

456 The present is also used in Latin when a state has continued for some time and still exists: as, iam tris mensis ăbest *he has been absent now three months*.

457 The present in Latin sometimes denotes not even the beginning of an act, but only the purpose, when the mind alone is employed upon it, or the matter at best is only in preparation: as, uxōrem dūcīt *he is going to be married*.

458 On the other hand, the present is at times used in Latin after certain conjunctions when past time is in fact meant: as,

A. Quid pater, uiuĭtne ? *B*. Vīuom, *quom* inde abĭmus,* liquĭmus (*Plaut.* Capt. II. 2. 32).

A. Well and your father, is he living ? *B*. We left him alive, *when* we *came* away.

Dŭm *studeo* obsequī tibi, paene inlūsi uitam filiae (*Ter.* And. v. 1. 3).

While I have endeavoured† to oblige you, I have almost trifled away my daughter's life.

So also with postquam, ŭbi, and ŭt, when they signify *the moment that*.

459 The past-imperfect has the suffix *ĕbā*: as, scrībēbā- *was writing*, scrībēbat *he was writing*.

460 But the *e* of *ĕbā* is lost after the vowels *a* and *e*: as, ărā'bat *he was ploughing*, dŏcē'bat *he was teaching*. While after the vowels *i* and *u* the *e* is commonly left: as, uĕni-ēbat *he was coming*, ăcuēbat *he was sharpening*.

461 The verb i- *go* loses the *e*: as, ī'bat *he was going*. The old writers and the poets often use this contracted form with other verbs in *i*: as, molli'bat *he was softening*.

462 Sometimes this tense is expressed in English by the simple past tense, *he wrote*. Thus, in answer to the question, *What used to be his duties in the counting-house?* the reply might be, *He wrote the foreign letters*. This would be expressed in the Latin by the tense in *ēbā*, because a continued state of things is meant,

---

* In editions generally abiīmus, which is against the metre (ăbyĭmus, see § 25). Some Mss. at any rate have abĭmus; and see § 1455 *e*.

† Or, 'In my endeavours.'

scrīb-ēbat *he used to write, he always wrote*. The Latin aorist would speak only of one act: *He wrote the foreign letters on a particular occasion*, scripsit.

463   The use of the English simple past tense for a continued state of things is very common with verbs of *static* meaning (see § 385): as, *he sat (all the time) on a rock; he loved frank and open conduct*.

464   The past-imperfect is also used in Latin when a state had continued for some time, and still existed at the moment spoken of: as, iam tris mensis āberat *he had been absent then three months*.

465   The past-imperfect sometimes denotes only a past purpose, or that a matter was in preparation: as, uxōrem dūcēbat *he was going to be married*.

466   The simple *future* appears to have had for its suffix the syllable db, which however loses its vowel after verbs in *a* or *e*, and its consonant* after verbs ending in a consonant, *i*, or *u*. Thus from verbs in *a* and *e* we have, arā'b- *will plough*, arā'b-it *he will plough*; docē'b- *will teach*, docē'b-it *he will teach*.†

467   Those verbs which retain only the vowel prefer *a* for the first person singular, and *e* for the rest: as, scrīb-a'm *I shall write*, scrīb-e's *you will write*, scrīb-e't *he will write*, &c.

468   The verbs in *i*, according to the preceding rules, form the future with *a* or *e* as, audi-a'm *I shall hear*, audi-e's *you will hear*, &c. But the verb i- *go* prefers the future in *b*: as, ī'b-it *he will go*. In the old writers many other verbs in *i* have a future of the same shape: as, scī'b-it *he will know*.

469   The Latin future from an active verb is not an imperfect future; thus scribet signifies *he will write*, not *he will be writing*.

---

* The loss of a *b* has been seen already in the datives of nouns.

† To the doctrines of § 439-61, 466-8, I now prefer the following: Scībam, scībo, are older than sciebam, sciam; dicebo (Naev.) than dicam. The *a* of am-ab-a-m, ten-eb-a-m, sc-ib-a-m (for sc-ib-am—where sco = sch- of German seh-en, our *see*) marks past time, as in er-a-m. The *ab eb ib* here, as in amabo tenebo dicebo scibo, denote imperfect action. But an imperfect pres. is akin to a fut. So er-o is in form a pres. The Keltic (Manx) has a general suffix of this power in *agh*, which plays a great part in Latin too, as tr-ah- (= German trag-en) 'bear' for tol-agh, from tol- (tollo); also in Greek, as γελ-α(χ)-, fut. γελαξω, our *laugh*. Here gh = f. So τρυφ- for ταρ-αφ-. But Greek φ = Latin b. Hence del-eb-ra-, vac-ab-ulo-, am-ab-ili-, plor-ab-undo-. The suffix-vowel, assimilated to root, gives ter-eb-ra i(e)r-ib-ulo- (τριβ-), gem-eb-undo-, rid-ib-undo-, jug-ab-ri-, vet-ub-ili-; and with final consonant lost we have am-a', ten-e', fin-i', aud-u'. See Appendix II. p. 439, &c.

470   The perfect tenses are formed by the addition of certain suffixes to a crude form of the perfect.

471   A crude form of the *perfect* is formed from the simple verb in three different ways:

   a. By *reduplication*, that is, by prefixing to the verb a syllable more or less like the verb itself: as, morde- *bite*, mŏmord- or mĕmord- *bit*; tend- *stretch*, tĕtend- *stretched*.*

   b. By a *long vowel*: as, făc- or făci- *make*, fēc- *made*; uĕni- or uĕni- *come*, uēni- *came*.†

   c. By a suffixed *s*: as, scrīb- *write*, scrips- *wrote*; dīc- *say*, dix- *said*.

   d. But many verbs, including nearly all those which end in a vowel, abstain from all these three changes.

472   All the perfect tenses of the three moods, indicative, subjunctive and infinitive, were formed by adding the tenses of the verb *es- be*. This is clearly seen in all but the present-perfect‡ of the indicative, and partly even here; as,

---

* The English language appears to have an example of this formation in what we may perhaps call one of its oldest verbs, *do*, perf. *did*, the original meaning of which verb was 'put,' whence *d'on* 'put on,' *d'off* 'put off,' *d'out* 'put out.' The German compounds of *thu'n* would confirm this view of the meaning. Thus our English verb corresponds to a Latin verb of kindred form and meaning, viz. *da-* 'put' (for such is its meaning), perf. *did-*. The Gothic abounds in perfects of reduplication: as, *hait* 'call,' perf. *haihait* 'called;' *skaid* 'separate,' perf. *skaiskaid* 'separated.'

† This formation also has its parallel in the English *come*, perf. *came*. It is not improbable that the long-vowel perfects originated in reduplication; as, *uĕni-* 'come,' perf. *uĕuĕn-* contracted into *uēn-* 'came;' *ăg-* 'drive,' *aag-* contracted into *ēg-* 'drove.' The last contraction is precisely the same as occurs in the subj. pres. of the verb *ama-* 'love,' c.f. *amaa-am?-*, 3d pers. *amaat*, *amet*. Compare also the so-called temporal augment of Greek verbs.

‡ In some parts of the present-perfect irregularities conceal the connection of the terminations with the present tense of *es-* 'be.' Yet the singular *scripe-isti* 'thou hast written' corresponds with great precision to the plural *scripe-istis* 'you have written.' Again, in the third person singular there is something peculiar in the occasional length of the suffix *it*, as *vendidīt Plaut.* Capt. prol. 9, *perrupīt Hor.* Od. 1. 3. 36, *despexīt Catull.* 64. 20; and especially in the compounds of *i-* 'go,' which have this syllable always long, as *praeterīit Ov.* A. A. III. 63 & 64; *rediīt Ov.* Her. vi. 31 and xiii. 29; *subīit Hor.* Sat. 1. 9. 21, *Ov.* Met. 1. 114. This peculiarity is accounted for, if *scripsit* had an older form *scripa-ist* corresponding to *est* 'he is.' The loss of the *s* in this position would resemble that which occurs in the French tense *fusse, fusses, fût* (old French *fust*). Indeed the *s* is silent in the French *est*. Lastly, *scripsi* must be regarded

74 VERBA.

INDIC.—*Present.*	*Present-Perfect.*
estis *you are,*	scrips-istis *you have written,*
(ĕsunt* or) sunt *they are,*	scrips-ĕrunt† *they have written,* &c.
Past.	*Past-Perfect.*
ĕram *I was,*	scrips-ĕram *I had written,*
ĕrās *thou wast,*	scrips-ĕrās *thou hadst written,* &c.
Future.	*Future-Perfect.*
ĕro *I shall be,*	scrips-ĕro *I shall have written,*
ĕris *thou wilt be,*	scrips-ĕris *thou wilt have written,* &c.
SUBJUNC.—*Present.*	
(ĕsim or) sim *I am,*	scrips-ĕrim *I have written,*
(ĕsis or) sis *thou art,*	scrips-ĕris *thou hast written,* &c.
Past.	
essem *I was,*	scrips-issem *I had written,*
essēs *thou wert,*	scrips-issēs *thou hadst written,* &c.
INFINITIVE.	
esse *to be,*	scrips-isse *to have written.*

472. 1 Many Latin verbs, particularly those which end in *a, e, i,* or a liquid, have a s‡ in the perfect immediately before the suffix borrowed from es- *be :* as,

    as a corruption of *scripsim,* and that of *scrips-ism,* where *ism* would represent the old Latin *ĕsum* 'I am.' The loss of the *s* in this position is what has occurred in the Greek ειμι 'I am' for εσμι, and in our own *em*. Nay, the Gothic form is *im*. If *scripsim* then be admitted as a theoretical form, the plural *scripsimus* is also explained.

    * See § 722. 4, note.

    † Though *scripsērunt* is the ordinary pronunciation, the short penult is not rare in the poets.

    ‡ This *u* (pronounced as our *w*) was no doubt an original part of the verb *ĕs-* 'be,' in the form *ŭs-*. Thus, the Gothic had *vis-an* 'to be,' the Icelandic *ver-a* 'to be.' So the German *wes-en* 'existence' is but an infinitive mood; and from a form *wes* is deduced our own past tense *was,* precisely as the Germans form *er las* 'he read' from *les-en* 'to read.' We have said that the original meaning of *esse* was 'to eat.' So the form *ues* also means to eat in the Latin *vescor* 'I feed myself,' whence the sub. n. *visc-er-* 'flesh.' In the old Latin writers *viscera* did not mean 'entrails.' We have said nothing of the origin of the suffix *s* as seen in *scrip-s-* &c. If this be a genitival suffix signifying 'from,' the formation of all the perfect tenses is simple enough; as, *scripsi* 'I am from writing,

ăru- *plough*,	ărā-uistis *you have ploughed.*
dŏc-e- *teach*,	dŏc-uistis *you have taught.*
audi- *hear*,	audi-uistis *you have heard.*
sĕr- *put*,	sĕr-uistis *you have put.*
cŏl- *till*,	cŏl-uistis *you have tilled.*
gĕn- *produce*,	gĕn-uistis *you have produced.*
gĕm- *groan*,	gĕm-uistis *you have groaned.*

473 The present-perfect tense of the Latin is also used for an aorist: as, scripsit *he has written* or *he wrote*.

474 Thus the English language confounds the aorist and past-imperfect; while the Latin confounds the aorist and the present-perfect. See § 462.

475 For the formation of the past-perfect* and future-perfect, see § 472.

476 The future-perfect of the indicative bears a very close resemblance to the present-perfect of the subjunctive. Hence much confusion arose, so that even the first person of the indicative tense in *ero* is occasionally found where a subjunctive in *erim* was to have been expected. But the greatest confusion is in the quantity of the syllables. As the future-perfect is formed from *ĕro*, *ĕris*, &c., we ought to have had in the indicative scripsĕris, scripsĕrimŭs, scripsĕritis; and on the other hand, as the present-perfect subjunctive is formed from sim, sis, &c. we ought to have had in the subjunctive scripsēris, scripsērimŭs, scripsēritis; but the two tenses are commonly confounded in respect of quantity.

477 The perfect tenses of some intransitive verbs are expressed in

I have written'; scripseram 'I was from writing, I had written'; scripsero 'I shall be from writing, I shall have written.' The use of a preposition in forming tenses is seen in our periphrastic futures 'I am *to* write,' 'I am going *to* write'; and also in our periphrastic present 'I am *a*-writing,' where *a* represents the old preposition *an*, now written *in*. 'I am a-writing' is the old form of the language, now corrupted to 'I am writing.' Compare also the French *je viens d'écrire*, literally 'I come from writing,' *i. e.* 'I have just written.'

* The formation of the past-perfect scripsĕram agrees with that of the Greek ετετυφεα, which had once a σ, ετετυφεσα-, as may be seen from the third pers. pl. ετετυφεσα-ν. Thus, the Greek suffix of this tense is εσα corrupted into εα, and the Latin is ĕra, itself a corruption from ĕsa. Consequently the two tenses have the same suffix, viz. the past tense of the verb *ἐσ*- 'be.' Nay, in the first person of the present-perfect τε-τυφ-α the α represents αμ, that is our first person of the verb 'to be;' and probably the preceding aspirate represents the suffixed *s* of scrips-, or in other words is a genitival suffix = 'from.'

English not only by the auxiliary verb *have*, but also by the tenses of *be*. Thus, rĕdiĭt *he has returned* or *he is returned*, rĕdiĕrat *he had returned* or *he was returned*, rĕdiĕrit *he will have returned* or *he will be returned*. These perfect tenses expressed by the auxiliaries *is*, *was*, *will be*, are often mistaken by beginners for passives. But a little reflection would of course satisfy them that the verbs in question do not admit of a passive.

478   The perfect tenses are often expressed in English without the perfect form. Thus, in the three phrases:

If a Roman soldier *left* his post, he *was* put to death,
If an English soldier *sleep* on his post, he *is* shot,
If you *receive* a letter, you *will* send it on to me,

the verbs *left*, *sleep*, *receive*, would be expressed in Latin by perfect tenses: viz. *left* by a past-perfect; *sleep* by a present-perfect; *receive* by a future-perfect; for an offence precedes in order of time the punishment, and of course a letter must be received before it is forwarded. (See § 1159.)

479   The *imperative* has two tenses, a present and a future; but the so-called present might be more fitly named an immediate future.

480   The imperative, mŏmentŏ, mŏmentŏtŏ, *you will remember*, is derived from a perfect crude form, like all the other tenses of the same verb. (See § 390.)

481   The *subjunctive* mood has four tenses: the present, the past, the present-perfect, and the past-perfect. Of these, the two former are often called the imperfect tenses.

482   The *subjunctive present* has the suffix ă, as scrīb-ă-, whence the third person, scrībat. When the suffix ă follows another ă, the two are contracted into ē, as ără- *plough*, subj. pres. ărāa- contracted into ărē-, whence the third person ăret. An old suffix of this tense was iă or ī, as siē- or sī- from ĕs- *be*, third person siet or sit. So also uĕli-m, nōli-m, māli-m, ĕdi-m, dui-m, and parhaps ausim, from the several verbs uŏl- *wish*, nōl- *be unwilling*, māl- *prefer*, ĕd- *eat*, da- or du- *put*, aude- *dare*.

483   The *subjunctive past* has the suffix ĕsĕ or ĕrĕ, as from ĕs- *be*, subj. past es'sē-, from scrib- *write*, subj. past scrībĕrĕ-, whence the third person esset, scrībĕret. The suffix ĕrĕ loses its short vowel after ă, ē, ī, as third person ără-'ret, dŏcē-'ret, audī-'ret; and sometimes after a consonant, as fer-'ret.

For the formation of the perfect tenses of the subjunctive see § 472.

The translation of the subjunctive tenses has various forms, which depend chiefly upon the meaning of the verb to which the subjunctive is attached.

If the preceding words denote a *command*, the subj. pres. and past are translated respectively by *shall* and *should*, or by *to*. Impĕro ut mittat *I command that he shall send* or *I command him to send;* impĕrāui ut mittĕret *I commanded that he should send* or *I commanded him to send*.

If the preceding words denote *permission*, the subj. pres. and past are translated respectively by *may* and *might*, or more commonly by *to*. Concēdo ut mittat *I grant that he may send* or *I permit him to send;* concessi ut mittĕret *I granted that he might send* or *I permitted him to send*.

If the preceding words denote a *purpose*, the subj. pres. and past are translated respectively by *may* and *might*, or *is to* and *was to*. Ob eam causam scribo ut sciās *I write for this reason, that you may know;* ob eam causam scripsi ut scirēs *I wrote for this reason, that you might know*. Mittit qui dicant *he sends persons (who are) to say;* misit qui dicĕrent *he sent persons (who were) to say*.

When the preceding words speak of the cause which leads to the *result* expressed in the following subjunctive, the latter mood is translated as an indicative. Tantus est terrŏr ut fŭgiant *so great is the alarm that they fly*.

The subjunctive in all its tenses may be translated as an indicative in passages where the *assertions* or *thoughts* of another are expressed. Qui scribat *who is writing (they say)*, qui scribĕret *who was writing (they said)*, qui scripsĕrit *who has written (they say)* or *who wrote (they said)*, qui scripsisset *who had written (they said)*.

The subjunctive in all its tenses, after certain conjunctions, may be translated as an indicative. Quum scribat *as he is writing*, quum scribĕret *while he was writing*, quum scripsĕrit *as he has written*, quum scripsisset *when he had written*.

The subjunctive in all its tenses may be translated as an indicative in indirect interrogatives: as, nescio quid făciat *I know not what he is doing*, nesciebam quid facĕret *I knew not what he was doing*, nescio quid fēcĕrit *I know not what he has done* or *what he did,* nesciēbam quid fēcisset *I knew not what he had done.*

495   When the two verbs in these phrases have the same nominative, the meaning is ambiguous: as, nescio quid făciam *I know not what I am doing* or *I know not what to do,* nescis quid făcias *you know not what you are doing or what to do* &c.

496   In *hypothetical* sentences, the subjunctive, which marks the *condition,* is expressed by English *past* tenses: as,

   si scribat,   *if he were writing* or *were to write.*
   si scriberet, *if he had been writing.*
   si scripserit, *if he were to write.*
   si scripsisset, *if he had written.*

497   With verbs of static meaning, the past indicative of the English is still used, but somewhat differently: as,

   si sciat,   *if he knew.*
   si sciret,   *if he had known.*
   si adsit,   *if he were present.*
   si adesset, *if he had been present.*

498   In *hypothetical* sentences, the subjunctive, which marks the *consequence,* is translated in the pres. by *should* or *would,* in the past and past-perfect by *should have* or *would have*: as,

   scribat,   *he would write.*
   scriberet,   *he would have been writing.*
   scripserit, *he would write.*
   scripsisset, *he would have written.*

499   In elliptical sentences, with quăsi *as if,* tanquam *as if* &c., the subjunctive is translated nearly in the same way: as, tanquam dormiat *as if he were asleep* (when in fact he *is* not), tanquam dormiret *as if he had been asleep* (when in fact he *was* not); quăsi nunquam antehac proelio adfuĕris *as if you had never before this been present at a battle* (when in fact you *have been*); quăsi nunquam antea proelio adfuisset *as if he had never before that been present at a battle* (when in fact *he had been*).*

500   The subjunctive mood has no special future tenses; still all its four tenses are at times used as future tenses.

501   The so-called subjunctive present is used for a future after a pres. or fut.: as, mitto qui rŏgent *I am sending persons to ask,*

---

* The clauses in the brackets are useful guides to the Latin tenses.

mittam qui rŏgent *I shall send persons to ask*, misi qui rŏgent *I have sent persons to ask*.

502. The so-called subjunctive past is used for a future after past tenses: as, mittēbam qui rŏgārent *I was sending persons to ask*, misi qui rŏgārent *I sent persons to ask*, misĕram qui rŏgārent *I had sent persons to ask*.

503. The so-called subjunctive present-perfect is used for a fut.-perf. after a pres. or fut., and the so-called subj. past-perf. is used for a fut.-perf. after a past. Thus, in the phrase, is cŏrōnam accipiet qui primŭs escendĕrit *the man shall receive a chaplet who first climbs up*, the word escendĕrit is the indicative future-perfect. But, by making the sentence depend upon such a word as dicit *he says*, or dixit *he said*, the indicative escendĕrit will be changed for a subj.: as, dicit eum cŏrōnam acceptūrum qui primŭs escendĕrit *he says that the man shall receive a chaplet who first climbs up*, dixit eum cŏrōnam acceptūrum qui primŭs escendisset *he said that the man should receive a chaplet who first climbed up*.

504. Thus, when the subjunctive perfect tenses are used as future-perfects, the present-perf. of the Latin is translated by the English ind. pres., the past-perf. of the Latin by the English ind. past.

505. If then we unite the different uses of the tenses in the subjunctive as so far explained, we shall have—

Tense in d	Pres.	or Fut. after Pres. or Fut.
"	3rd	Past	" Fut. after Past.
"	2rd	Pres.-Perf.	" Fut.-Perf. after Pres. or Fut.
"	4ad	Past-Perf.	" Fut.-Perf. after Past.

505.1 The subjunctive past is often used in phrases denoting a result with the power of an aorist, as, accidit ut primus nuntiāret *it happened that he was the first to bring word*. Hence, although the present-perfect indicative is habitually employed as an aorist, the present-perfect subjunctive is rarely so used. Still examples occur (see § 1182, ex. 5; § 1189, last two examples), especially in negative clauses.

506. The Infinitive has strictly but two forms, the imperfect and perfect.

507. The *infinitive imperfect* has for its suffix *tǎl* or *ĕrĕ*: as, from *ba* *be*, inf. es'sĕ; from scrīb- *write*, inf. scrībĕrĕ.

508 Slightly irregular are the infinitives, fer'rĕ, from fĕr- *bear;* nol'lĕ, nol'lŏ, mal'lŏ, from uŏl- or uĕl- *wish*, nŏl- *be unwilling*, mal- *prefer*. Plautus, Mil. i. 1. 27, iv. 8. 0, has dicerĕ; iii. 2. 34, promerĕ.†

509 The infinitive imperfect may be translated in three ways:—by *to:* as, incipit ridērĕ *he begins to laugh:* in some phrases the English language omits this *to*, as, pŏtest ridērĕ *he can laugh* i.e. *is able to laugh*, uidi eum ridērĕ *I saw him laugh*;—by *ing:* as, incipit ridērĕ *he begins laughing*, or uidi eum ridērĕ *I saw him laughing*;—as an indicative, with *that* before the English nominative: as, scio eum ridērĕ *I know that he is laughing*, sciēbam eum ridērĕ *I knew that he was laughing*.

510 For the formation of the *infinitive perfect*, see § 472.

511 The infinitive perfect may be translated in three ways:—by *to have:* as, scripsissĕ dicitŭr *he is said to have written*;—by *having:* as, risisse exitiō fuit *the having laughed was fatal*;—as an indicative, with *that* before the English nominative: as, scio eum scripsissĕ *I know that he wrote* or *that he has written*, sciēbam eum scripsissĕ *I knew that he had written*.

512 Thus the infinitive imperfect scribĕrĕ corresponds to two indicative tenses, scribit and scribēbat; and the infinitive perfect scripsissĕ also to two, scripsit and scripsĕrat.

513 The infinitive imperfect is sometimes used as a future, where the preceding verb itself implies a reference to futurity: as, pollicētur dărĕ *he promises to give*.

514 The participle in *enti* or *ent* is an imperfect, and belongs alike to past, present and future time.

515 The participle or gerund in *endo* is also an imperfect, and belongs alike to past, present and future time.

516 The participle in *to* is a perfect, and belongs alike to past, present and future time.

517 The participle in *tūro* denotes intention or destiny, and belongs alike to past, present and future time.

CONJUGATIONS.

518 As the changes which take place in adding the suffixes to a verb depend in a great measure upon the last letter, verbs may be divided into the following classes or conjugations*, viz.:

* See a similar division of nouns into declensions, §§ 84, 85, 86, 88, 89.   † Compare as of the Greek inf., as δώσειν.

The consonant (or third*) conjugation, as scrīb- *write*, whence scrībĕrĕ *to write*, and scrībĭs *thou writest*.

The *a* (or first) conjugation, as ărā- *plough*, whence ărārĕ *to plough*, and ărās *thou ploughest*.

The *e* (or second) conjugation, as dŏco- *teach*, whence dŏcērĕ *to teach*, and dŏcēs *thou teachest*.

The *u* (or third†) conjugation, as ăcu- *sharpen*, whence ăcuĕrĕ *to sharpen*, and ăcuĭs *thou sharpenest*.

The *i* (or fourth) conjugation, as audi- *hear*, whence audīrĕ *to hear*, and audīs *thou hearest*.

519 The *o* conjugation has nearly disappeared from the Latin language. There remain however fragments of two or three verbs of this conjugation, viz.:

gno- *examine*, whence gno-sco, gnŏ-ui, gnŏ-tum, or, as they are more commonly written, no-sco, nŏ-ui, nōtum; also the substantives nŏ-mĕn- *n.*, nŏ-tiōn- *f.* &c.; po-‡ *drink*, whence the participle pŏ-to- *drunk*, the substantives pŏ-cŭlo- *n. drinking-cup*, pŏ-tiōn- *f. drinking*, and the adjective pŏ-cŭlento- *drinkable*, &c.; aegro- *make sick*, implied in the participle or adj. aegrŏ-to- *sick*.

520 The other verbs, which might have been expected to end in *o*, have changed that vowel for *a* (see § 229): as from auro- *gold* is formed the verb in-aurā-rĕ‡ *to gild*.

521 The monosyllabic verbs ending in a consonant generally denote an act, and may be considered as belonging to the old verbs of the language: as dŭc- *draw*. (See § 30.)

522 The verbs in *a* are generally formed from substantives or adjectives of the *a* or *o* declension, and have a *factitive* meaning, that is, signify *to make* ——: as from albo- or alba- *white*, alba- *make white*; from mĕdico- *physician*, mĕdīca- (r.) *make oneself a physician, act the physician, cure*.

523 The two monosyllabic verbs, da- *put*, and sta- *stand*, must be classed with the old verbs of the language. So also many other

---

* The numbers of the conjugations are given, because they are so arranged in nearly all grammars and dictionaries.

† Observe that the *u* and consonant conjugations are united to form the third conjugation, just as the *i* and consonant nouns are united to form the third declension.

‡ Compare the Greek verb πυ-ω ' I drink,' or rather the tenses πυ-σω, πυυ-κα.

§ The Greek language retained many verbs of the *o* conjugation: as δουλο-ω ' to enslave,' χρυσο-ω ' to gild.'

G

verbs ending in *a* had older forms without that final *a*, which therefore belonged to the consonant conjugation and the old verbs. See those verbs of the first or *a* conjugation, which are said to form their perfects and supines irregularly, as cŭba- *lie*, &c.

524   The verbs in *e* generally denote a state, as iăce- *lie;* and often correspond to a consonant verb, as iăc- *throw.* (See § 388.)

525   The monosyllabic verbs, fle- *weep,* ne- *spin,* &c. should perhaps be classed with the old verbs of the language. So also many other verbs in *e* had older forms without that final *e*, which therefore belonged to the consonant conjugation and the old verbs, as ride- or rid- *laugh.*

526   The verbs in *u* are often derived from substantives in *u*, as from mĕtu- *fear* is formed mĕtu-ĕrĕ *to fear;* from tribu- *a division,* tribu-ĕrĕ *to allot.*

527   The monosyllabic verbs, nu- *nod,* su- *sew,* &c. must be classed with the old verbs of the language.

528   The verbs in *i* are often derived from substantives or adjectives in *i,* as from tussi- *a cough* is formed tussi-rĕ *to cough;* from molli- *soft,* molli-rĕ *to soften.*

529   The monosyllabic verbs, sci- *know,* i- *go,* ci- *rouse,* must be classed with the old verbs of the language. So also those verbs which had an old form without the *i,* as uĕni- or uĕn- *come.*

530   An attention to the final vowel of a verb is required in the formation of the derivatives, particularly as regards the quantity.

tĕg-	*cover,*	tĕg-ŭ-mento-	*covering.*
arma-	*equip,*	armă-mento-	*equipment.*
[cre-]	*grow,*	in-crĕ-mento-*	*increase.*
argu-	*prove,*	argŭ-mento-	*proof.*
ĕ-mŏli-	*heave up,*	ĕmŏli-mento-†	*great effort.*
[gno-]	*examine, know,*	co-gnŏ-mento-	*surname.*

Principal Parts of a Verb.

531   When the infinitive, the indicative present, the perfect, and the supine or verbal in *tu* of a Latin verb are known, there is

* *Monŭmento-, docŭmento-,* said to be derived from the verbs *mone-, doce-,* imply rather verbs of the consonant conjugation, viz. *mon-, doc-,* as do also the perfects and supines of the same.

† Not to be confounded with *ĕ-mŏl-ĭ-mento-* ' outgrinding or profit (of the miller, who pays himself by the excess of bulk in grinding his customer's corn).

seldom any difficulty in conjugating it. They are therefore called the *principal parts* of the verb.

532. In the following lists the crude form of the verb with its translation, the infinitive, the first person of the present and perfect are given, and the accusative of the supine, or for reflective verbs the nominative masculine of the perfect participle. In most of the compounds the infinitive has been omitted for the sake of brevity.

533   THIRD or CONSONANT CONJUGATION.

LIP-LETTERS, B, P.

scăb- *scratch*	scăbĕre	scăbo	scăbi
lăb- *lick*	lambĕre	lambo	lambi
bĭb- *drink*	bĭbĕre	bĭbo	bĭbi
scrīb- *write*	scrībĕre	scrībo	scripsi	scriptum
cŭb- *lie down*	[cumbĕre	cumbo]	cŭbui	cŭbĭtum
nūb- *veil oneself**	nūbĕre	nūbo	nupsi	nuptum
căp- or căpi- *take*	căpĕre	căpio	cēpi	captum
răp- or răpi- *seize*	răpĕre	răpio	răpui	raptum
rēp- *creep*	rēpĕre	rēpo	repsi	reptum
strĕp- *resound*	strĕpĕre	strĕpo	strĕpui	strĕpĭtum
scalp- *scratch*	scalpĕre	scalpo	scalpsi	scalptum
carp- *nibble, pluck*	carpĕre	carpo	carpsi	carptum
serp- *creep*	serpĕre	serpo	serpsi	serptum
cŭp- or cŭpi- *desire*	cŭpĕre	cŭpio	cŭpīui	cŭpītum
rŭp- *burst*	rumpĕre	rumpo	rŭpi	ruptum

534   THROAT-LETTERS, C, G, H, Q, X.

făc- or făci- *make, do*	făcĕre	făcio	fēci	factum
iăc- or iăci- *throw*	iăcĕre	iăcio	iēci	iactum
pĕc- *comb*	pectĕre	pecto	pexi	pexum
flĕc- *bend*	flectĕre	flecto	flexi	flexum
plĕc- *plait*	plectĕre	plecto	plexi	plexum
nĕc- *link, join*	nectĕre	necto	nexi†	nexum
ĭc-‡ *strike*	ĭcĕre	ĭco	ĭci	ictum
dīc- *show, say*	dīcĕre	dīco	dixi	dictum
uĭc- *conquer*	uincĕre	uinco	uīci	uictum

* As a female in the marriage ceremony.

† But *in-nexuit* Virg.   ‡ Another form of *iac-* ' throw.'

VERBS.

parc- *spare*	parcĕre	parco	pĕperci	parsum
posc- *pray, demand*	poscĕre	posco	pŏposci	
dŭc- *draw, lead*	dūcĕre	dūco	duxi	ductum
535 ăg- *drive*	ăgĕre	ăgo	ēgi	actum
plăg-* *strike*	plangĕre	plango	planxi	planctum
păg- *fix*	pangĕre	pango	pĕpĭgit	pactum
frăg- *break*	frangĕre	frango	frēgi	fractum
tăg- *touch*	tangĕre	tango	tĕtĭgi	tactum
lĕg- *sweep, read*	lĕgĕre	lĕgo	lēgi	lectum
rĕg- *make straight*	rĕgĕre	rĕgo	rexi	rectum
tĕg- *thatch, cover*	tĕgĕre	tĕgo	texi	tectum
fīg-‡ *fix*	fīgĕre	fīgo	fixi	fixum
fĭg- *mould, invent*	fingĕre	fingo	finxi	fictum
pĭg- *paint*	pingĕre	pingo	pinxi	pictum
strĭg- *grasp, graze*	stringĕre	stringo	strinxi	strictum
tĭg- *dye*	tingĕre†	tingo	tinxi	tinctum
fulg- *flash*	fulgĕre	fulgo	fulsi	
ang- *strangle*	angĕre	ango	anxi	
cing- *gird*	cingĕre	cingo	cinxi	cinctum
ung- *grease*	ungĕre§	ungo	unxi	unctum
sparg- or spăr-‖ *scatter*	spargĕre	spargo	sparsi	sparsum
merg- or măr-¶ *sink*	mergĕre	mergo	mersi	mersum
terg-** or tĕr- *wipe*	tergĕre	tergo	tersi	tersum
fŭg- or fŭgĭ- *flee, fly*	fŭgĕre	fŭgio	fūgi	fŭgĭtum
iŭg- *yoke, join*	iungĕre	iungo	iunxi	iunctum
pŭg- *puncture*	pungĕre	pungo	pŭpŭgi	punctum
sŭg- *suck*	sūgĕre	sūgo	suxi	suctum
536 trăh- *drag*	trăhĕre	trăho	traxi	tractum
uĕh- *carry*	uĕhĕre	uĕho	uexi	uectum
537 līq- *leave*	linquĕre	linquo	līqui	
cŏq- *cook*	cŏquĕre	cŏquo	coxi	coctum
538 tex- *weave*	texĕre	texo	texui	textum

* For the quantity compare πλάγιος.
† But *panxit* Enn., *pegi* Pacuv.
‡ Fīg- 'fix' and fĭg- 'mould' may perhaps be originally one, with the sense 'squeeze,' like σφίγγω. See Paley's Propertius. Observe too that *fictus* for *fixus* was preferred by Varr. R. R. III. 7. 4, *affictus* III. 3. 2, &c.
§ Also *tinguĕre*, *tinguo*; *unguĕre*, *unguo*.
‖ Comp. *spar-* of *σπείρω*.   ¶ Comp. *mari-* 'sea.'
** Also *tergĕre*-. Comp. *τερ-* of *τείρω*, and *ter-ra* 'dry-land.'

VERBS.

539 ulu- or ulg- *lie*   uluĕre   uluo   uixi   uictum
    flu- or fluc- *flow*   fluĕre   fluo   fluxi   fluxum
    stru- or struc- *pile, build* struĕre   struo   struxi   structum

TEETH-LETTERS, D, T.

540 cād-* *fall*   cădĕre   cădo   cĕcĭdi   cāsum†
    rād- *scrape*   rādĕre   rādo   rāsi   rāsum†
    ĕd- or ĕs- *eat*   ĕdĕre or esse ĕdo   ēdi   ēsum†
    caed- *fell, strike, cut*   caedĕre   caedo   cĕcĭdi   caesum
    laed- *strike, hurt*   laedĕre   laedo   laesi   laesum
    cēd- *go quietly, yield*   cēdĕre   cēdo   cessi   cessum
    sĕd- *sit down*   sĭdĕre   sĭdo   sēdi   sessum
    scĭd- *tear, cut*   scĭdĕre   scindo   scĭdi‡   scissum
    fĭd- *cleave*   fĭndĕre   findo   fīdi   fissum
    strĭd-§ *hiss, screech*   strĭdĕre   strido   strīdi
    scand- *climb*   scandĕre   scando   scandi   scansum
    mand- *chew*   mandĕre   mando   mandi   mansum
    pand- or păd- *spread*   pandĕre   pando   ——   passum‖
    pend- *hang, weigh*   pendĕre   pendo   pĕpendi   pensum
    tend- or tĕn- *stretch*   tendĕre   tendo   tĕtendi   tentum¶
    fŏd- or fŏdi- *dig*   fŏdĕre   fŏdio   fōdi   fossum
    rūd- *gnaw*   rōdĕre   rōdo   rōsi   rōsum
    clūd- *shut*   claudĕre   claudo   clausi   clausum
    plaud- *clap*   plaudĕre   plaudo   plausi   plausum
    cūd- *hammer, coin*   cūdĕre   cūdo   cūdi   cūsum
    fūd- *pour*   fundĕre   fundo   fūdi   fūsum
    lūd- *play*   lūdĕre   lūdo   lūsi   lūsum
    trūd- *thrust*   trūdĕre   trūdo   trūsi   trūsum
    tūd- *hammer, thump*   tundĕre   tundo   tŭtŭdi   tunsum
    quăt- or quăti- *strike*   quătĕre   quătio   ——   quassum
    mĕt- *mow*   mĕtĕre   mĕto   messui   messum
    pĕt- or pĕti- *go, seek*   pĕtĕre   pĕto   pĕtīui   pĕtītum
    mĭt- *let go, send*   mittĕre   mitto   mīsi   missum

* Akin to *caed-*, just as our *fall* to *fell*.
† The forms with *s* seem to have been originally in use with old writers, and even with Cicero, Virgil, &c. as *casum*, *esum*.
‡ *Scicidi* and *fifidi* were probably the older forms of these perfects. Ennius has the former. Comp. *tetuli*, afterwards *tuli*.
§ Also *stride-*. ‖ But *pansis* in Germanicus and Vitruvius.
¶ *Tensus* in Quintilian and late writers.

stert- *snore*	stertĕre	sterto	stertui	
uort- or uert- *turn*	uortĕre	uorto	uorti	uorsum
sist- *make to stand*	sistĕre	sisto	stĕti or stiti	stătum

542. The compounds of da-* *put* or *give*, with prepositions of one
syllable, are all of the third conjugation; as, with

ăb, *put away, hide*	abdĕre	abdo	abdĭdi	abdĭtum
ăd, *put to, add*	addĕre	addo	addĭdi	addĭtum
cŏn, *put together*	condĕre	condo	condĭdi	condĭtum
dē, *put down, surrender*	dēdĕre	dēdo	dēdĭdi	dēdĭtum
dis, *distribute*	dīdĕre	dīdo	dīdĭdi	dīdĭtum
ēo, *put out, utter*	ēdĕre	ēdo	ēdĭdi	ēdĭtum
ĭn, *put on*	indĕre	indo	indĭdi	indĭtum
pĕr, *fordo, destroy*	perdĕre	perdo	perdĭdi	perdĭtum
ŏb, *put to (as a bar)*	obdĕre	obdo	obdĭdi	obdĭtum
prō, *abandon, betray*	prōdĕre	prōdo	prōdĭdi	prōdĭtum
rĕd, *put back, restore*	reddĕre	reddo	reddĭdi	reddĭtum
sŭb, *put up*	subdĕre	subdo	subdĭdi	subdĭtum
trans, *hand over*	tradĕre	trado	tradĭdi	tradĭtum †

To these add two other compounds of da- *put*:

| uend-‡ *exhibit for sale* | uendĕre | uendo | uendĭdi | uendĭtum |
| crēd- *trust, believe* | crēdĕre | crēdo | crēdĭdi | crēdĭtum |

L, M, N.

543. ăl- *raise, rear, feed* | ălĕre | ălo | ălui | ălĭtum or altum |
făl- *cheat*	fallĕre	fallo	fĕfelli	falsum
săl- *salt*	sallĕre	sallo	—	salsum
pĕl- *push, drive*	pellĕre	pello	pĕpŭli	pulsum
uŏl- *pull, pluck*	uellĕre	uello	uelli	uolsum
cŏl- *dig, till*	cŏlĕre	cŏlo	cŏlui	cultum
mŏl- *grind*	mŏlĕre	mŏlo	mŏlui	mŏlĭtum

* Some Sanscrit scholars would lay it down that *da-* in these compounds represents the root θε- of τίθημι, not δο- of δίδωμι. They forget that the archaic forms *perduim, creduim* claim immediate connection with the archaic *duim* of *da-*. Besides θε- or rather θες- (θες-μος) is represented in Latin by *ser-* 'put,' whence *exser-, inser-* &c.

† *Praedĭto-*, 'armed' or 'endowed (with),' implies a vb. *prae-dere*.

‡ Literally 'put in the window.' The first syllable is an abbreviation of *uēnum*, which occurs in *uēnum i-re, uēni-re, uēnun-dă-re*.

VERBS.

tŏl- *raise, bear*	tollĕre*	tollo	tŭlit	lātum†
uŏl- *wish*	uelle	uŏlo	uŏlui	
544 ĕm- *take, buy*	ĕmĕre	ĕmo	ēmi	emptum
gĕm- *groan*	gĕmĕre	gĕmo	gĕmui	gĕmĭtum
frĕm- *roar*	frĕmĕre	frĕmo	frĕmui	frĕmĭtum
prĕm- *press*	prĕmĕre	prĕmo	pressi	pressum
trĕm- *tremble*	trĕmĕre	trĕmo	trĕmui	
545 căn- *sing*	cănĕre	căno	cĕcĭni	cantum
gĕn- *produce*	gignĕre	gigno	gĕnui	gĕnĭtum
lĭn- *smear*	lĭnĕre	lĭno	lēui	lĭtum‡
sĭn- *put, permit*	sĭnĕre	sĭno	sīui *or* sii	sĭtum‡

R, S.

546 păr- *or* pări- *produce*	părĕre	părio	pĕpĕri	partum
quaer-, quaes-§ *seek, ask*	quaerĕre	quaero	quaesīui	quaesītum₁
cĕr- *sift, separate*	cernĕre	cerno	crēui	crētum
fĕr- *raise, bear*	ferre	fĕro	tŭli	lātum
gĕr- *or* gĕs- *wear, carry*	gĕrĕre	gĕro	gessi	gestum
spĕr- *reject, despise*	spernĕre	sperno	sprēui	sprētum
sĕr-‖ *put*	sĕrĕre	sĕro	sĕrui	sertum
sĕr-‖ *plant, sow*	sĕrĕre	sĕro	sēui	sătum‡
tĕr- *rub*	tĕrĕre	tĕro	trīui¶	trītum
stĕr- *strew*	sternĕre	sterno	strāui**	strātum**
uĕr- *sweep*	uerrĕre	uerro	uerri	uersum
ūr- *or* ūs- *burn*	ūrĕre	ūro	ussi	ustum
cŭr- *run*	currĕre	curro	cŭcurri	cursum
547 păs- *or* pa- *feed*	pascĕre	pasco	pāui	pastum
ĕs- *be*	esse	sum	fui	

* In meaning the following go together: *tollere, tollo, sustuli, subla-tum*. See *fer-*.

† An old form of the perfect is *tĕtŭli*. *Latum* is for *tlatum*. Comp. τλῆμι, ταλας, τολμη.

‡ Observe the quantity of *lĭtum, sĭtum, sătum*.

§ *Quaeso* is used in the sense, ' I pray' or ' prithee.' A form *quaesii*- is implied in *quaesitum*; as also in *quaesitor* ' a commissioner' or ' judge.'

‖ *Sĕr-* ' put' and *sĕr-* ' sow' are one in origin.

¶ *Triui, tritum* imply a secondary verb *trīb-*, whence *tribulo-* sb. n. ' a threshing harrow.' Comp. τρίβ- of τρίβω.

** From a secondary verb *strag-* (= *ster-ag-*), whence *strag-*- sb. f., *strag-ulo-* adj.; also *strāmen-* ' straw.' Comp. our verb *strew*, old form *strow*.

68 VERBS.

uis- *go to see*	uisĕre	uiso	uisi	
lăcess-* *provoke*	lăcessĕre	lăcesso	lăcessĭui	lăcessītum
făcess-* *perform, cause*	făcessĕre	făcesso	făcessi	
arcess-* *send for*	arcessĕre	arcesso	arcessĭui	arcessītum
căpess-* *take*	căpessĕre	căpesso	căpessĭui	căpessītum
pōs- *put*	pōnĕre	pōno	pŏsui	pŏsĭtum

V.

548 lău-† *wash*	lăuĕre	lăuo	lăui	lautum *or* lōtum
trĭbu- *distribute*	trĭbuĕre	trĭbuo	trĭbui	trĭbūtum
ăcu- *sharpen*	ăcuĕre	ăcuo	ăcui	ăcūtum
argu- *prove*	arguĕre	arguo	argui	argūtum
solu- *loosen*	soluĕre	soluo	solui	sŏlūtum
uolu- *roll*	uoluĕre	uoluo	uolui	uŏlūtum
mĭnu- *lessen*	mĭnuĕre	mĭnuo	mĭnui	mĭnūtum
sternu- *sneeze*	sternuĕre	sternuo	sternui	
spu- *spit*	spuĕre	spuo	spui	spūtum
ru- *make to rush, rush*	ruĕre	ruo	rui	rŭtum ‡
su- *sew*	suĕre	suo	sui	sūtum
stătu- *set up*	stătuĕre	stătuo	stătui	stătūtum
mĕtu- *fear*	mĕtuĕre	mĕtuo	mĕtui	mĕtūtum

FIRST OR A CONJUGATION.

549 da-§ *put, give*	dăre	do	dĕdi	dătum
sta-‖ *make to stand, stand*	stăre	sto	stĕti	stătum
cŭba-¶ *lie*	cŭbāre	cŭbo	cŭbŭi	
nĕca- *stifle, kill*	nĕcāre	nĕco	nĕcăui**	nĕcātum
sĕca- *cut*	sĕcāre	sĕco	sĕcui	sectum
plĭca- *fold*	plĭcāre	plĭco	plĭcăui	plĭcātum

* These four verbs are formed from *lăc-* or *lăci-*, *făc-* or *făci-*, *arci-* (compound of *ci-* 'call'), *căp-* or *căpi-*. So also *plĕcess-* 'seek,' from *pĕt-* or *pĕti-*.

† See also *lăua-* § 549, and *dilu-* § 533. 2.

‡ Observe the short vowel of *rŭtum*. *Rultŭro-* is the participle in *turo*.

§ *Da-* stands apart from the other verbs in *a* by the irregularity of its quantity. See § 732.

‖ The derivatives from *sta-* have often a short vowel, as *stătu-* sb., *stăbĭli-* adj., *stătĭm* adv.

¶ See also *cŭb-* § 533.   ** *Necuit* Enn. and Phaedr.

VERBS.

mĭca- *vibrate*	mĭcāre	mĭco	mĭcui	
frĭca- *rub*	frĭcāre	frĭco	frĭcui	frictum
dŏma- *tame*	dŏmāre	dŏmo	dŏmui	dŏmĭtum
sŏna- *sound*	sŏnāre	sŏno	sŏnŭi	sŏnātum
	or sŏno	sŏnŭi	sŏnĭtum	
tŏna- *thunder*	tŏnāre	tŏnat	tŏnuit	tŏnĭtum
crĕpa- *creak, chatter*	crĕpāre	crĕpo	crĕpui	crĕpĭtum
vĕta-* *forbid*	vĕtāre	vĕto	vĕtui	vĕtĭtum
lăua- *wash*	lăuāre	lăuo	lăuăui	lăuātum
iŭua- *assist*	iŭuāre	iŭuo	iŭui	iŭtum†

551 The thirteen disyllabic verbs given in the preceding section were probably at one time all monosyllabic, and consequently of the consonant or third conjugation. The verbs lăuĕre, abluĕre, prŏcumbĕre, plectĕre, &c. are met with in the best authors; and in the older writers there occur such forms as sŏnĕre, sŏnĭt, sŏnunt, tŏnĭmŭs, &c. Observe too that the same thirteen verbs have all the first vowel short.

552 The other verbs in *a* form their principal parts like

ăra- *plough*	ărāre	ăro	ărāui	ărātum

SECOND or E CONJUGATION.

553 hăb-e- *hold, have*	hăbēre	hăbeo	hăbui	hăbĭtum
sorb-e- *suck up*	sorbēre	sorbeo	sorbui	
iŭb-e- *bid, order*	iŭbēre	iŭbeo	iussi	iussum
iăc-e- *lie*	iăcēre	iăceo	iăcui	‡
tăc-e- *be silent*	tăcēre	tăceo	tăcui	tăcĭtum
dŏc-e- *teach*	dŏcēre	dŏceo	dŏcui	doctum
nŏc-e- *do damage*	nŏcēre	nŏceo	nŏcui	nŏcĭtum
arc-e- *confine, keep off*	arcēre	arceo	arcui	§
misc-e- *mix*	miscēre	misceo	miscui	mixtum
suād-e- *recommend*	suādēre	suādeo	suāsi	suāsum
rīd-e- *laugh*	rīdēre	rīdeo	rīsi	rīsum
uīd-o- *see*	uīdēre	uīdeo	uīdi	uīsum
prand-e- *breakfast*	prandēre	prandeo	prandi	pransum
pend-e- *hang* (intrans.)	pendēre	pendeo	pĕpendi	

* Old form uĕto-. Persius has uetauit.

† *Iuuaturo-* in Sal. and Plin. ep.

‡ *Iacituro-* Stat. § *Aruto-* or *arto-* as an adj. ' confined.'

spond-e- *promise*	spondēre	spondeo	spŏpondi	sponsum
tond-e- *shear*	tondēre	tondeo	tŏtondi	tonsum
mord-e- *bite*	mordēre	mordeo	mŏmordi	morsum
urg-e- *press*	urgēre	urgeo	ursi	
aug-e- *increase* (trans.)	augēre	augeo	auxi	auctum
lūg-e- *mourn*	lūgēre	lūgeo	luxi	
ci-e- *rouse*	ciēre	cieo	cīvi	cītum
fle- *weep*	flēre	fleo	flēvi	flētum
ōl-e- *smell*	ōlēre	ōleo	ōlui	
dŏl-e- *ache*	dŏlēre	dŏleo	dŏlui	dŏlĭtūs
tim-e- *fear*	timēre	timeo	timui	
ne- *spin*	nēre	neo	nēvi	nētum
măn-e- *remain*	mănēre	măneo	mansi	mansum
tĕn-e-* *hold*	tĕnēre	tĕneo	tĕnui	
mŏn-e- *warn*	mŏnēre	mŏneo	mŏnui	mŏnĭtum
torque- *or* tor- *twist*, *hurl*	torquēre	torqueo	torsi †	tortum†
cār-e- *be without*	cārēre	cāreo	cārui	
pār-e- *wait on, obey*	pārēre	pāreo	pārui	pārĭtum
haer-e- *stick*	haerēre	haereo	haesi	haesum
mĕr-e-‡ *earn, deserve*	mĕrēre	mĕreo	mĕrui	mĕrĭtum
torre- *or* tŏr- *roast*	torrēre	torreo	torrui	tostum
con-se- *or* cēn-§ *count*	censēre	censeo	censui	censum
lăt-e- *lie hid*	lătēre	lăteo	lătui	
nit-e- *shine*	nitēre	niteo	nitui	
cău-e- *be on one's guard*	căuēre	căueo	cāui	cautum||
fău-e- *wish well*	făuēre	făueo	fāui	fautum||
pău-e- *fear*	păuēre	păueo	păui	
fŏu-e- *keep warm*	fŏuēre	fŏueo	fōui	fōtum
mŏu-e- *move*	mŏuēre	mŏueo	mōui	mōtum
uŏu-e- *vow*	uŏuēre	uŏueo	uōui	uōtum
feru-e- *boil* ¶	feruēre	ferueo	ferbui	

* Comp. *tend-* 'stretch.'

† From a root *ter-* or *tor-*, whence *tor-tor-, tor-men-*.

‡ Also *mere-ri* (r.).

§ The literal sense of *cen-* was 'puncture,' and so 'count.' Hence *cen-tro-* sb. n. 'centre.'

|| *Cauitum* and *fauitum* were preferred by Cicero.

¶ Also *feru-ĕre*.

FOURTH or I CONJUGATION.*

554	i- *go*	īro	eo	iui *or* ii	ĭtum
	fulci- *prop*	fulcīre	fulcio	fulsi	fultum
	sanci- *hallow*	sancīre	sancio	sanciui	sancītum
			or sancio	sanxi	sanctum
	uinci- *bind*	uincīre	uincio	uinxi	uinctum
	farci- *cram*	farcīre	farcio	farsi	farctum
	sarci- *mend*	sarcīre	sarcio	sarsi	sartum
	sali- *leap*	sălīre	sălio	săluí *or* sălii	saltum
	sĕpĕli- *bury*	sĕpĕlīre	sĕpălio	sĕpĕlīui	sĕpultum
	uĕni- *come*	uĕnīre	uĕnio	uĕni	uentum
	saepi- *hedge in*	saepīre	saepio	sepsi	septum
	ăpĕri- *open*	ăpĕrīre	ăpĕrio	ăpĕrui	ăpertum
	ŏpĕri- *cover*	ŏpĕrīre	ŏpĕrio	ŏpĕrui	ŏpertum
	hauri- *draw (water)*	haurīre	haurio	hausi	haustum

555 The other verbs in *i* form their principal parts like

	audi- *hear*	audīre	audio	audīui	audītum

555.1 Some inceptive verbs with a suffix *esc* or *isc*:

	lang- *droop, flag*	languesco	langui	
	dic-† *learn*	disco	didici	
	luc- *get light*	lūciscit	luxit	
	ard-‡ *blaze up*	ardesco	arsi	
	put- *become putrid*	pūtesco	pūtui	
	căl- *get hot*	călesco	călui‖	
	ual- *get strong*	ualesco	ualui‖	
	sil- *become silent*	silesco	silui	
	quie- *become quiet*	quiesco	quiĕui	quiĕtum
	cre- *grow*	cresco	crĕui	crĕtum

* The irregular supines of the verbs in § 554 imply verbs of the consonant conjugation; and indeed such forms as *suenet*, &c. for the imperfect tenses occur in Ennius and Plautus. Perhaps in Hor. Od. iv. 4, 65 we should read *pulchrior euenet*.

† *Dic-* 'learn,' originally identical with *dic-* 'say,' or more properly 'show.' Comp. δεικ- of δείκνυμι 'show.' *Doce-* 'teach' is also of the same family. *Disco* is for *dic-sco*.

‡ *Ard-* is probably akin to *al-* 'raise,' so often used with *flammam*. Compare as to form *arduus-* 'lofty,' which is immediately formed from *al-* 'raise.' Comp. too *ap-* of *sups*.

‖ *Calituro-, ualituro-*.

sue- *become accustomed*	suesco	suēvi	suētum
rĕ+sĭp-* *come to one's senses again*	rĕsĭpisco	rĕsĭpŭi	
rĕ+frig- *get cold again*	rĕfrigesco	rĕfrixi	
rĕ+vīvu- *come to life again*	rĕvīvisco	rĕvixi	
re+sci- *find out (a secret)*	rescisco	rescīvi	rescītum
cŏn+ăl- or ŏl- *grow together*	cŏălesco	cŏălŭi	cŏălĭtum
ăd+ŏl- or ōle- *grow up*	ădōlesco	ădōlŭi	ădultum
ăb+ŏle- *grow out of use*	ăbōlesco	ăbōlŭi	
ob+sŏlc-† *get covered with dirt*	obsŏlesco	obsŏlŭi	obsŏlētum

555.2   Compound verbs:

prō+cŭb- *lie down*	prōcumbo	prōcŭbŭi	prōcŭbĭtum
rĕ+cĭp- or căpi- *take back*	rĕcĭpio	rĕcēpi	rĕceptum
ab+rĭp- or răpi- *carry off*	abrĭpio	abrĭpŭi	abreptum
dis+carp- *pull to pieces*	discerpo	discerpsi	discerptum
per+făc- or făci- *finish*	perfĭcio	perfēci	perfectum
cŏn+iăc- or iăci- *hurl*	cōnĭcio	coniēci	coniectum
rĕ+iăc- or iăci- *throw back*	rēĭcio	rēĭēci	rēiectum
ad+lăc- or lăci- *draw to*	allĭcio	allexi	allectum
ec+lăc- or lăci- *draw out*	ēlĭcio	ēlĭcŭi	ēlĭcĭtum
in+spĕc- or spĕci- *look in*	inspĭcio	inspexi	inspectum
rĕd+ăg- *drive back*	rĕdĭgo	rĕdēgi	rĕdactum
cŏn+ăg- *drive together*	cōgo	coēgi	coactum
con+păg- *fix together*	compingo	compēgi	compactum
per+frăg- *break through*	perfringo	perfrēgi	perfractum
con+tăg- *touch closely*	contingo	contĭgi	contactum
con+lĕg- *sweep together*	colligo	collēgi	collectum
rĕ+lĕg- *read again*	rĕlĕgo	rĕlēgi	rĕlectum
inter+lĕg- *pick up, perceive*	intellĕgo	intellexi	intellectum
di+lĕg- *esteem*	diligo	dilexi	dilectum
neg+lĕg- *leave behind*	neglĕgo	neglexi	neglectum
por+lĕg- *lay out (a corpse)*	pollingo	pollinxi	pollinctum
por+rĕg- *stretch forth*	porrĭgo	porrexi	porrectum
por+rĕg- *keep straight on*	pergo	perrexi	perrectum
sub+rĕg- *rise*	surgo	surrexi	surrectum
ab+flīg- *dash down*	affligo	afflixi	afflictum

* Read the symbol (+) as *plus* or 'with.'

† The root of this verb is connected with *sŏlo-* sh. n. 'soil,' also with *sordes* and *sordido-*. It appears again in the French *sale* 'dirty,' *souiller*; and in the Eng. *soil* vb. or sb., as well as *sully* and *slush*.

con+flīg- *dash together*	conflīgo	conflīxi	conflictum
ec+stīg- *stamp out*	extinguo	extinxi	extinctum
dis+stīg- *spot*	distinguo	distinxi	distinctum
ec+mūg- *wipe (nose)*	ēmungo	ēmunxi	ēmunctum
con+sparg- *bespatter*	conspergo	conspersi	conspersum
con+pūg- *puncture forcibly*	compungo	compunxi	compunctum
rĕ+līq- *leave*	rĕlinquo	rĕliqui	rĕlictum
ob+cĭd- *set (as sun), die*	occĭdo	occĭdi	occāsum*
rĕ+cĭd- *fall back*	rĕcĭdo	reccĭdi†	rĕcāsum
ec+nīd- *come out*	ēnīdo	ēnīsi	ēnīsum
ob+caed- *cut down, kill*	occīdo	occīdi	occīsum
con+laed- *dash together*	collīdo	collīsi	collīsum
re+scid- *cut away again*	rescindo	rescĭdi	rescissum
dis+fīd- *cleave in two*	diffindo	diffīdi	diffissum
rĕ+sīd- *subside*	rĕsīdo	rĕsēdi	rĕsessum
di+uīd- *divide*	diuīdo	diuīsi	diuīsum*
sub+cand- *set fire to from below*	succendo	succendi	succensum
ec+scand- *climb up*	escendo	escendi	escensum
dē+fend- *ward off*	dēfendo	dēfendi	dēfensum
ex+pend- *weigh out*	expendo	expendi	expensum
prae+hand- *take hold of*	prehendo	prehendi	prehensum
or	prendo	prendi	prensum
obs+tend- *hold towards*	ostendo	ostendi	ostensum‡
ex+clūd- *shut out*	exclūdo	exclūsi	exclūsum
con+tūd- *hammer to pieces*	contundo	contūdi	contūsum
per+quāt- *strike violently*	percūtio	percussi	percussum
rĕ+sist- *stand against*	rĕsisto	restĭti	restĭtum
per+cēl- *overturn*	percello	percŭli	perculsum
con+pĕl- *drive together*	compello	compŭli	compulsum
rĕ+pĕl- *drive back*	rĕpello	reppŭli†	rĕpulsum
con+sŏl-|| *sit together, consult*	consŭlo	consŭlui	consultum
ex+ĕm- *take out*	eximo	exēmi	exemptum
de+ĕm- *take down*	dēmo	dempsi	demptum
con+ĕm- *arrange (the hair)*	cōmo	compsi	comptum
pro+ĕm- *bring out*	prōmo	prompsi	promptum

* Also in the older writers *occassum, diuissum, &c.*

† For *re-occidi, re-pepuli.* Hence the double consonant.

‡ *Ostenso-* in Lucan; but in Ter. Ph. v. 4, 7. and in Varr. *sstento-.*

|| *Sōl-*, an obsolete verb, is the parent of *sŏllo-* sb. n. 'a seat.' It is also akin to *sĕdo-* sb. f., *sĕde-* vb., *sŏdali-, sella-, subsellio-.*

VERBS.

sŭb+ĕm- *take up*	sūmo	sumpsi	sumptum
rĕ+prĕm- *press back*	rĕprimo	rĕpressi	rĕpressum
con+tĕm- *(cut up) despise*	contemno	contempsi	contemptum
con+căn- *sing together*	concĭno	concĭnui	concentum
dē+sĭn- *(put down) leave off*	dēsĭno	dēsii	dēsĭtum
con+quaer- *get together*	conquīro	conquisīui	conquisītum
ab+fĕr- *carry off*	aufĕro	abstŭli	ablātum
ec+fĕr- *carry out*	effĕro	extŭli	ēlātum
ob+fĕr- *present*	offĕro	obtŭli	oblātum
rĕ+fĕr- *bring back*	rĕfĕro	rettŭli*	rĕlātum†
con+sĕr- *plant all over*	consĕro	consēui	consĭtum
con+būr- *burn up*	combūro	combussi	combustum
ob+cŭr- *run towards*	occurro	occurri‡	occursum
in+du- *put on*	induo	indui	indūtum
ec+du- *put off*	exuo	exui	exūtum
dis+lu- *or* lŭu- *dissolve*	dīluo	dīlui	dīlūtum
ob+ru- *overwhelm*	obruo	obrui	obrŭtum
in+su-; *sew in*	insuo	insui	insūtum
re+stătu- *set up again*	restĭtuo	restĭtui	restĭtūtum
ec+năc- *kill off*	ĕnĕco	ĕnĕcāui	ĕnĕcātum
	or ĕnĕco	ĕnĕcui	ĕnectum
ex+plĭca- *unfold*	explĭco	explĭcāui	explĭcātum
	or explĭco	explĭcui	explĭcĭtum
in+crĕpa- *chide*	incrĕpo	incrĕpāui	incrĕpātum
	or incrĕpo	incrĕpui	incrĕpĭtum
pro+hăbe- *keep off*	prohĭbeo	prohĭbui	prohĭbĭtum
de+hăbe- *owe, ought*	dēbeo	dēbui	dēbĭtum
prae+hăbe- *present*	praebeo	praebui	praebĭtum
co+arce- *confine*	coerceo	coercui	coercĭtum
ex+arce-§ *work out, drill*	exerceo	exercui	exercĭtum
re+spondo- *answer*	respondeo	respondi	responsum
in+dulge-‖ *be kind*	indulgeo	indulsi	indultum
dē+le- *or* līn- *blot out*	dēleo	dēlēui	dēlētum
ăb+ŏle- *abolish*	ăbŏleo	ăbŏlēui	ăbŏlĭtum

* For *re-tetuli*, *re-peperi.* Hence the double consonant.

† *Rellatum* also in old writers. Comp. *reddis-*, *redd-*.

‡ Also *occucurri*.

§ *Erce-* or *arce-* is an obsolete vb. akin to the Greek ϝεργ-, whence ϝε(ρ- and the neut. sb. ἐργο-.

‖ *Dulge-* must be an obsolete vb. akin to the adj. *dulci-*.

VERBS.

ex+ple- *fill up*	expleo	explēvi	explētum
rĕ+tĭne- *hold back*	rĕtĭneo	rĕtĭnui	rĕtentum
rĕ+cense- *review*	rĕconsco	rĕcensui	rĕcensĭtum
ex+i- *go out*	exeo	exii	exĭtum
ăm+ĭci- *throw round one*	ămĭcio	ămĭcui	ămictum
in+farci- *cram in*	infercio	infersi	infertum
rĕ+pări- *find*	rĕpărio	reppĕri*	rĕpertum
con+pări- *find out*	compĕrio	compĕri	compertum

555.3 Reflective verbs:

lăb- *slip*	lăbi	lăbor	lapsus
am-plect- *embrace*	amplecti	amplector	amplexus
lice- *bid at an auction*	licĕri	liceor	licĭtus
plāg- *beat oneself*	plangi	plangor	
fung- *discharge oneself*	fungi	fungor	functus
sĕq- *follow*	sĕqui	sĕquor	sĕcūtus
lŏq- *talk†*	lŏqui	lŏquor	lŏcūtus
fru- or frug- *enjoy*‡	frui	fruor	fruĭtus
grăd- or grădi- *march*	[grădi]	grădior	gressus
co+grăd- *march out*	ĕgrădi§	ĕgrădior	ĕgressus
ordi- *begin weaving*	ordīri	ordior	orsus
făt-e- *confess*	fătĕri	făteor	fassus
pro+făt-e- *profess*	profĭtĕri	profĭteor	professus
păt- or păti- *suffer*	păti	pătior	passus
per+păt- *suffer to the last*	perpĕti	perpĕtior	perpessus
nio-‖ *kneel, lean*	nīti	nītor	nisus or nixus
mēn- or menti- *measure*	mētiri	mētior	mensus
ad+sĕn- or senti- *agree with*	assentīri	assentior	assensus
ūt- *use*	ūti	ūtor	ūsus
ex+pĕri- *try*	expĕrīri	expĕrior	expertus
ob+pĕri- *wait for*	oppĕrīri	oppĕrior	oppertus¶
quĕr- *complain*¶	quĕri	quĕror	questus

* See note * p. 94.
† See § 398.
‡ More literally 'feed oneself.'
§ Old form gnītor &c. from gĕnu- (or gĕnic-) ' a knee.' See Festus.
‖ But Plautus has opperītus.
¶ Literally 'beat oneself;' for quăs- is but a variety of quăt- ' strike.'
Comp. plāg- (r.) and verr- (r.) 'beat oneself.'

ŏr- or ŏri- *rise*	ŏrīri	ŏrior	ortus
mŏr- or mŏri- *die*	mŏri	mŏrior	mortuus
re- *reckon*	rēri	ror	rătus
mĕr-e- *earn*	mĕrēri	mĕreor	mĕritus
uĕr-e- *fear*	uĕrēri	uĕreor	uĕrĭtus
tu- or tue- *guard*	tuēri	tueor	tuĭtus or tūtus
ăp- *obtain*	ăpisci	ăpiscor	aptus
ăd+ăp- *obtain*	ădipisci	ădipiscor	ădeptus
pro+fĭco- *set out*	prŏfīcisci	prŏfīciscor	prŏfectus
năc- *win, obtain*	nancisci	nanciscor	nanctus*
păc- *fix, bargain*	păcisci	păciscor	pactus
ulc- *avenge*	ulcisci	ulciscor	ultus
ex+por+rĕg- *wake up*	exporgisci	exporgiscort	exporrectus
dē+făt- *give in*	dēfĕtisci	dēfĕtiscor	dēfessus
con+mĕn- *invent*	comminisci	comminiscor	commentus
ob+līu- *forget*	obliuisci	obliuiscor	oblĭtus

* So rather than *nactus* in mss.

† Literally 'I begin to stretch myself out.'

CONJUGATION OF IMPERFECT TENSES.

Last letter Conjugation	ā 1	ē 2	consonant 3	ŭ 3	ĭ 4
Lat. a.v. English	ărā- plough	dŏcē- teach	scrīb- write	ăcŭ- sharpen	audī- hear
Indicative Mood *Present Tense*	S. ăro ărās ărăt* P. ărāmŭs ărātĭs ărant	dŏceo dŏcēs dŏcēt* dŏcēmŭs dŏcētĭs dŏcent	scrībo scrībĭs scrībĭt scrībĭmŭs scrībĭtĭs scrībunt	ăcuo ăcŭĭs ăcŭĭt ăcŭĭmŭs ăcŭĭtĭs ăcŭuŭt†	audio audīs audīt* audīmŭs audītĭs audiunt
Past Imperfect	S. ărābam ărābās ărābăt* P. ărābāmŭs ărābātĭs ărābant	dŏcēbam dŏcēbās dŏcēbăt* dŏcēbāmŭs dŏcēbātĭs dŏcēbant	scrībēbam scrībēbās scrībēbăt* scrībēbāmŭs scrībēbātĭs scrībēbant	ăcuēbăm ăcuēbās ăcuēbăt* ăcuēbāmŭs ăcuēbātĭs ăcuēbant	audiēbam audiēbās audiēbăt* audiēbāmŭs audiēbātĭs audiēbant
Future Tense	S. ărābo ărābĭs ărābĭt P. ărābĭmŭs ărābĭtĭs ărābunt	dŏcēbo dŏcēbĭs dŏcēbĭt dŏcēbĭmŭs dŏcēbĭtĭs dŏcēbunt	scrībam scrībēs scrībĕt* scrībēmŭs scrībētĭs scrībent	ăcuam ăcuēs ăcuĕt* ăcuēmŭs ăcuētĭs ăcuent	audiam audiēs audiĕt* audiēmŭs audiētĭs audient
Imperative Mood *Present*	S. 2. ărā P. 2. ărātĕ	dŏcē dŏcētĕ	scrībĕ scrībĭtĕ	ăcuĕ ăcuĭtĕ	audī audītĕ
Future	S. 2. ărāto 3. ărāto P. 2. ărātōtĕ 3. ăranto	dŏcēto dŏcēto dŏcētōtĕ dŏcento	scrībĭto scrībĭto scrībĭtōtĕ scrībunto	ăcuĭto ăcuĭto ăcuĭtōtĕ ăcuunto	audīto audīto audītōtĕ audiunto
Subjunctive Mood *Present Tense*	S. ărem ărēs ărĕt* P. ărēmŭs ărētĭs ărent	dŏceam dŏceās dŏceăt* dŏceāmŭs dŏceātĭs dŏceant	scrībam scrībās scrībăt* scrībāmŭs scrībātĭs scrībant	ăcuam ăcuās ăcuăt* ăcuāmŭs ăcuātĭs ăcuant	audiam audiās audiăt* audiāmŭs audiātĭs audiant
Past Tense	S. ărārem ărārēs ărārĕt* P. ărārēmŭs ărārētĭs ărārent	dŏcērem dŏcērēs dŏcērĕt* dŏcērēmŭs dŏcērētĭs dŏcērent	scrībĕrem scrībĕrēs scrībĕrĕt* scrībĕrēmŭs scrībĕrētĭs scrībĕrent	ăcuĕrem ăcuĕrēs ăcuĕrĕt* ăcuĕrēmŭs ăcuĕrētĭs ăcuĕrent	audīrem audīrēs audīrĕt* audīrēmŭs audīrētĭs audīrent

* But see for quantity § 412 and note. † Or *acuunt*.

Last letter Conjugation	a 1	e 2	consonant 3	u 3	i 4
Lat. c.F. English	ără- *plough*	dŏce- *teach*	scrib- *write*	ăcu- *sharpen*	audi- *hear*
INFINITIVE MOOD.	ărărĕ	dŏcērĕ	scrībĕrĕ	ăcuĕrĕ	audīrĕ
PARTICIPLE.*	ărantĭ- or ărant-	dŏcentĭ- or dŏcent-	scrībentĭ- or scrībent-	ăcuentĭ- or ăcuent-	audientĭ- or audient-
PART. FUTURE.	ărātūro- or —a-	doctūro- or —a-	scrīptūro- or —a-	[ăcuĭtūro- or —a-]	audītūro- or —a-
GERUND.†	ărando-	dŏcendo-	scrībendo-	ăcuendo-	audiendo-

557 There are certain verbs which mix together the consonant and *i* conjugations in the imperfect tenses, viz.:

făc- or făci- *make* fŏd- or fŏdi- *dig* săp- or săpi- *taste*
iăc- „ iăci- *throw* fŭg- „ fŭgi- *flee* cŭp- „ cŭpi- *desire*
[lĭc-‡ „ lĭci- *draw*] căp- „ căpi- *take* păr- „ pări- *produce*
[apĕc-‡ „ spĕci- *look*] răp- „ răpi- *seize* quăt- „ quăti- *shake.*

Together with the reflective verbs:

grăd- or grădi- *march* mŏr- or mŏri- *die* pŏt- or pŏti- *make*
ŏr- „ ŏri- *rise* păt- „ păti- *suffer* *oneself master.*

Observe too that all these seventeen verbs have the vowel short.

558 MIXED CONSONANT AND *I* CONJUGATION.

INDICATIVE MOOD.

Present Tense.
S. fugio fugis fugit;   P. fugimus fugitis fugiunt.
Past-Imperfect.   *Future.*
S. fugiebam, fugiebas &c.   S. fugiam fugies &c.

* Declined like *praesenti-* or *praesenti-*. See § 219.
† Declined like a neuter noun in a. ‡ Only used in compounds.

IMPERATIVE MOOD.
Present. S. fugĕ ;   P. fugĭte.
Future.
S. 2. fugĭto, 3. fugĭto ;   P. 2. fugĭtote, 3. fugiunto.
SUBJUNCTIVE MOOD.
Present Tense.   *Past Tense.*
S. fugiam fugias &c.   S. fugĕrem fugĕres &c.

INFINITIVE, fugĕre.   PARTICIPLE, fugienti- *or* fugient-.

PARTICIPLE FUTURE, fugĭturo-.   GERUND, fugiendo-.

559   Observe that those forms, which have the vowel after *g* marked short, follow the consonant conjugation ; the others are derived as from a verb in *i*.

560   In old writers such forms as capīre, fodīre, parīre &c. occur.

561   CONJUGATION OF PERFECT TENSES.
Crude form of perfect, krăuĭs-.
INDICATIVE MOOD.
Present-Perfect or Aorist.
S. krăuī krăuistī krăuit ;   P. krăuĭmŭs krăuistĭs krăuērunt
              or krăuērĕ.
Past-Perfect.
S. krăuĕram krăuĕras krăuĕrat ;   P. krăuĕrămŭs krăuĕrātĭs kră-
                uĕrant.
Future-Perfect.
S. krăuĕro krăuĕrĭs krăuĕrĭt ; P. krăuĕrĭmŭs krăuĕrĭtĭs krăuĕrint.*
SUBJUNCTIVE MOOD.
Present-Perfect or Aorist.
S. krăuĕrim krăuĕrĭs krăuĕrit ; P. krăuĕrĭmŭs krăuĕrĭtĭs krăuĕrint.*
Past-Perfect.
S. krăuissem krăuissēs krăuisset ; P. krăuissēmŭs krăuissētĭs kră-
                uissent.
INFINITIVE MOOD.
krăuissē.

562   The conjugation of a perfect which takes the suffix *ĭs*, instead of *ŭĭs*, differs solely in the absence of the *u*. See §§ 584, 588, 590, 613, 620, 628.

* These two tenses are often confounded by Latin writers as regards the quantity of the *i*. See § 476.

563	The perfect tenses often undergo a contraction: as,

ărăuī	ărăuĭmŭs
ărăuĭstī or ărāstī	ărăuĭstĭs or ărāstĭs
ărăuĭt	ărăuērunt or ărārunt or ărăuērĕ.

  ărăuĕram or ărāram &c.
  ărăuĕro ,, ărāro &c.
  ărăuĕrim ,, ărārim &c.
  ărăuissem ,, ărāssem &c.
  ărăuissē ,, ărāssē.

564	In the perfects of the *i* conjugation similar contractions occur: as,

audīuī or audiī	audīuĭmŭs or audīmŭs
audīuĭstī, audīstī, or audīstī	audīuĭstĭs, audīstĭs, or audīstĭs
audīuĭt or audiĭt	audīuērunt or audiērunt, or audīuērĕ or audiērĕ.

  audīuĕram or audiĕram &c.
  audīuĕro ,, audiĕro &c.
  audīuĕrim ,, audiĕrim &c.
  audīuissem ,, audiissem or audissem &c.
  audīuissē ,, audiissē or audissē.

565	If the crude form of the perfect have *x* or *s* before *is*, as dix-is-, the following contractions are found:

dixī	diximŭs
dixistī or dixtī	dixistĭs or dixtĭs
dixit	dixērunt or dixērĕ.

  dixissem or dixem &c.
  dixissē ,, dixē &c.

566	As the future-perfect of the indicative originally ended in *so*, rather than *ero*, and the subjunctive perfect in *sim*, rather than *erim*, the following contractions, which occur in old writers, are explained:

  Ind. fut.-perf. faxo, faxis &c. *for* fēcĕro &c.
  Subj. pres.-perf. faxim, faxis &c. ,, fēcĕrim &c.
  Subj. past-perf. faxem*, faxēs &c. ,, fēcissem &c.

567	So again, ărasso, ărassis &c. for ărāuĕro &c.

---

* See § 1209 f. note.

568 From this future-perfect is formed an old infinitive future árampéró.

569 The gerund of the consonant and *i* conjugations often ends in *undo*, rather than *endo*; as scribundo-.

570   **REFLECTIVE OR PASSIVE VERBS.**
           CONJUGATION OF IMPERFECT TENSES.

Last letter Conjugation	a 1	e 2	consonant 3	u 3	i 4
Lat. o.F. English	orna- dress	doce- teach	uort- turn	metu- fear	audi- hear
INDICATIVE MOOD. Present Tense	S. ornŏr ornăris* ornātŭr P. ornāmŭr ornāminī ornantŭr	docĕor docĕris* docĕtŭr docēmŭr docēminī docentŭr	uortŏr uortĕris uortĭtŭr uortĭmŭr uortĭminī uortuntŭr	mētuŏr mĕtuĕris mĕtuĭtŭr mĕtuĭmŭr mĕtuĭminī mĕtuuntŭr†	audĭŏr audīris audītŭr audīmŭr audīminī audiuntŭr
Past-Imperfect	S. ornābăr ornābāris or ornābārĕ ornābātŭr P. ornābāmŭr ornābāminī ornābantŭr	docēbăr docēbāris or docēbārĕ docēbātŭr docēbāmŭr docēbāminī docēbantŭr	uortĕbăr uortĕbāris or uortĕbārĕ uortĕbātŭr uortĕbāmŭr uortĕbāminī uortĕbantŭr	mĕtuēbăr mĕtuēbāris or mĕtuēbārĕ mĕtuēbātŭr mĕtuēbāmŭr mĕtuēbāminī mĕtuēbantŭr	audiēbăr audiēbāris or audiēbārĕ audiēbātŭr audiēbāmŭr audiēbāminī audiēbantŭr
Future Tense	S. ornābŏr ornābĕris or ornābĕrĕ ornābĭtŭr P. ornābĭmŭr ornābĭminī ornābuntŭr	docēbŏr docēbĕris or docēbĕrĕ docēbĭtŭr docēbĭmŭr docēbĭminī docēbuntŭr	uortăr uortĕris or uortĕrĕ uortētŭr uortēmŭr uortēminī uortentŭr	mĕtuăr mĕtuēris or mĕtuērĕ mĕtuētŭr mĕtuēmŭr mĕtuēminī mĕtuentŭr	audiăr audiēris or audiērĕ audiētŭr audiēmŭr audiēminī audientŭr
IMPERATIVE MOOD. Present	S.2. ornārĕ P.2. ornāminī	docērĕ docēminī	uortĕrĕ uortĭminī	mĕtuĕrĕ mĕtuĭminī	audīrĕ audīminī
Future	S.2. } ornātŏr 3. P.3. ornantŏr	docētŏr docentŏr	uortĭtŏr uortuntŏr	mĕtuĭtŏr mĕtuuntŏr‡	audītŏr‡ audiuntŏr

* *Arbitrārī, nitīrī,* for *arbitrāris, nitēris,* occur. † Or *metuontur.*
‡ There was also for the 2d and 3d person of the singular an old form in *mino;* as *fā-mino, progredī-mino.* § Or *metuontor.*

Last letter Conjugation	a 1	e 2	consonant 3	u 3	i 4
Lat. o.F. English	orna- dress	doce- teach	vort- turn	metu- fear	audi- hear
Subjunctive Mood — *Present Tense*	S. orner ornëris or ornërë ornëtur P. ornëmur ornëmini orpentur	doceär docëaris or docëarë docëatur docëamur docëamini docëantur	uortar uortaris or uortarë uortatur uortamur uortamini uortantur	metuär metuaris or metuarë metuatur metuamur metuamini metuantur	audiär audiaris or audiarë audiatur audiamur audiamini audiantur
Past Tense	S. ornärër ornärëris or ornärërë ornärëtur P. ornärëmur ornärëmini ornärentur	docërër docërëris or docërërë docërëtur docërëmur docërëmini docërentur	uortërër uortërëris or uortërërë uortërëtur uortërëmur uortërëmini uortërentur	metuërër metuërëris or metuërërë metuërëtur metuërëmur metuërëmini metuërentur	audirër audirëris or audirërë audirëtur audirëmur audirëmini audirentur
Infinitive Mood*	ornärier or ornäri	docërier or docëri	uortier or uorti	motuier or metui	audirier or audiri
Participle†	ornando-	docendo-	uortendo-	metuendo-	audiendo-

571   MIXED CONSONANT AND *I* CONJUGATION.‡

Indicative Mood. *Present Tense.*
S. morior moreris moritur ;   P. morimur morimini moriuntur.

Past-Imperfect.   *Future.*
S. moriebar moriebaris &c.   S. moriar moriaris &c.

Imperative Mood.
Present Tense. S. morere ;   P. morimini.
Future. S. 2. moritor, 3. moritor ;   P. 3. moriuntor.

Subjunctive Mood.
Present Tense.   *Past Tense.*
S. moriar moriaris &c.   S. morerer morereris &c.
Infinitive, mori.   Participle, morienti- or morient-.
Participle Future, morituro-.   Gerund, moriundo-.

* The infinitives in *er* belong to the old language.
† The reflective verbs have also participles in *enti*- or *ent*- and in *tero*-.
‡ See § 537.

571.1 In old writers such forms as mŏrīmŭr and mŏrīrī occur.
572 Ori- (r.) *rise*, and pŏti- (r.) *make oneself master*, partake more of the *i* conjugation: as, ŏrīrĕr, ŏrīrī; pŏtīris, pŏtītŭr, pŏtīmŭr, pŏtīrĕr, pŏtīrī.
573 The perfect tenses of a reflective or passive verb are formed by the perfect participle in *to* and the verbs ĕs- or fu-.

574 CONJUGATION OF THE PERFECT TENSES OF A REFLECTIVE OR PASSIVE VERB.

Indicative Mood.

Present-Perfect or Aorist.

S. ornātus* sum   *or* fui   P. ornātī sŭmŭs *or* fuĭmŭs
   ornātŭs ĕs   „ fuistī   ornātī estis   „ fuistis
   ornātŭs est   „ fuit   ornātī sunt   fuērunt *or* fuērĕ.

Past-Perfect.

S. ornātŭs ĕram *or* fuĕram P. ornātī ĕrămŭs *or* fuĕrămŭs
   ornātŭs ĕrās   „ fuĕrās   ornātī ĕrătĭs   „ fuĕrātis
   ornātŭs ĕrat   „ fuĕrat   ornātī ĕrant   „ fuĕrant.

Future-Perfect.

S. ornātŭs ĕro   *or* fuĕro   P. ornātī ĕrĭmŭs *or* fuĕrĭmŭs
   ornātŭs ĕris   „ fuĕris   ornātī ĕrĭtis   „ fuĕritis
   ornātŭs ĕrit   „ fuĕrit   ornātī ĕrunt   „ fuĕrint.

Subjunctive Mood.

Present-Perfect or Aorist.

S. ornātus sim   *or* fuĕrim P. ornātī sīmŭs *or* fuĕrĭmŭs
   ornātus sīs   „ fuĕris   ornātī sītis   „ fuĕritis
   ornātus sit   „ fuĕrit   ornātī sint   „ fuĕrint.

Past-Perfect.

S. ornātŭs essem *or* fuĭssem P. ornātī essēmŭs *or* fuĭssēmŭs
   ornātŭs esses „ fuĭsses   ornātī essētis „ fuĭssētis
   ornātŭs esset „ fuĭsset   ornātī essent   „ fuĭssent.

Infinitive Mood.
ornātŭs esse *or* fuĭsse.

* *Ornātŭs, ornātā or ornātum*, to agree with the nominative.
† *Ornātī, ornātae or ornāta*, to agree with the nominative.

CONJUGATION OF A SIMPLE* VERB, WITH THE ENGLISH TRANSLATION.

575   c.f. scrib- *write.*
Principal parts: scrībĕrĕ scrībo scripsī scriptum.

INDICATIVE MOOD.

Present Tense, scrib-.

As a present-imperfect, *am ——ing*:

Ad frātrem meum scrībo,	*I am writing to my brother.*
Ad frātrem tuum scrībis,	*You are writing to your brother.*
Ad frātrem suum scrībit,	*He is writing to his brother.*
Ad frātrem nostrum scrībimus,	*We are writing to our brother.*
Ad frātrem vostrum scrībitis,	*You are writing to your brother.*
Ad frātrem suum scrībunt,	*They are writing to their brother.*

576 —— as an historic present:

Posterō die ad senem scrībo,   *The next day I write to the old man.*

577 —— as a present of custom:

Egŏ cālămō scrībo,	*I write with a reed.*
Tū pinnā scrībis,	*You write with a pen.*

578 —— as a present, translated by *do*:

Egŏ uērŏ scrībo,	*Yes I do write.*
Tū uērŏ scrībis,	*Yes you do write.*

579 —— as a present, including past time, *have been ——ing*:

Iam duās hōrās scrībo,   *I have been writing now two hours.*

580   *Past-Imperfect*, scrībēbă-†.

As a past-imperfect, *was ——ing*:

Scrībēbam cum puĕr intrāuit,   *I was writing when the boy came in.*

581 —— as a past tense of custom, *used to ——*:

Egŏ cālămō scrībēbam,	*I used to write with a reed.*
Tū pinnā scrībēbās,	*You used to write with a pen.*

---

* That is, not reflective or passive.
† Or 'I wrote,' &c.

582 ——— as a past tense, including time preceding, *had been ——ing:*

    Iam tris hōras scrībēbam,   *I had been then writing three hours.*

583   *Future Tense,* scrībă- *or* scrībĕ-.

    Translated by *shall, will:*

    Cras mānē scrībam,   *I shall write tomorrow morning.*
    Cras mānē scrībēs,   *You will write tomorrow morning.*

    Present-Perfect Tense, scrīpsĭs-.

584 As a present-perfect, *have ——en:*[*]

    Quattuŏr ĕpistŏlas scrīpsī,   *I have written four letters.*

585 ——— as an aorist, translated by the English past:

    Hĕri ad nĕgōtiātōrem scrīpsī,   *I wrote yesterday to the merchant.*

586 ——— as an aorist, translated by *did:*

    Egŏ uērŏ scrīpsī,   *Yes I did write.*
    Tū uērŏ scrīpsistī,   *Yes you did write.*

587 ——— as a present-perfect, translated by an English present:

    Egŏ sī scrīpsī, rescrībit,   *If I write, he writes again.*
    Tū sī scrīpsistī, rescrībit,   *If you write, he writes again.*

588   *Past-Perfect,* scrīpsĕrā-.

    Translated by *had ——en:*

    Ante id tempus scrīpsĕram,   *I had written before that time.*

589 ——— translated by an English past:

    Egŏ sī scrīpsĕram, rescrībēbat,   *If I wrote, he wrote again.*
    Tū sī scrīpsĕras, rescrībēbat,   *If you wrote, he wrote again.*

---

[*] That is, the perfect participle of the English verb.

106 VERB.

590   *Future-Perfect*, scripsĕr-.

Translated by *shall have ——en, will have ——en:*
Antĕ noctem scripsĕro,   *I shall have written before night.*
Antĕ noctem scripsĕris,*   *You will have written before night.*

591   —— translated by an English present :

Egŏ sī scripsĕro, rescribet,   *If I write, he will write again.*
Tū sī scripsĕris, rescribet,   *If you write, he will write again.*

592   IMPERATIVE MOOD.
              Present Tense.

Translated by the simple verb :
Scribe ad patrem tuum,   *Write to your father.*
Scribite ad patrem uestrum,   *Write to your father.*

593   *Future Tense.*

Translated by *shall, must, let;* or by the simple verb :
Scribito, *Thou shalt write.*   Scribitōtĕ, *Ye shall write.*
Scribito, *He shall write.*   Scribunto, *They shall write.*

594   SUBJUNCTIVE MOOD.
            Present Tense, scribā-.

As a present-imperfect, *am ——ing* (indirect interrogative) :
Nescio quid scribam,   *I know not what I am writing.*
Nescio quid scribās,   *I know not what you are writing.*

595   —— translated by an indicative present (result) :

Indĕ fit ut nihil de hac rē scri-   *Hence it happens that I write*
bam,   *nothing on this subject.*
Indĕ fit ut nihil de hac rē scribās,   *Hence it happens that you write*
                                  nothing on this subject.

596   —— translated by *do* (concession) :

Vt scribam, nōn est sătis,   *Even granting that I do write, it is not*
                                  enough.
Vt scribas, nōn est sătis,   *Even granting that you do write, it is*
                                  not enough.

* But see, as regards the quantity of the i after r, § 476.

597 ——— translated by *should, would* (hypothesis):

 Si pinna mihi sit, scribam, *If I had a pen, I would write.*
 Si pinna tibi sit, scribas, *If you had a pen, you would write.*

598 ——— translated by *were* ———*ing:*

 Sĕdeo hic, tanquam scribam, *I sit here, as if I were writing.*
 Sĕdes istic, tanquam scribas, *You sit there, as if you were writing.*
 Sĕdet illic, tanquam scribat, *He sits yonder, as if he were writing.*

599 ——— translated by *may* (purpose):

 Pinna dātur, quā* scribam, *The pen is given me, that I may write† with it.*

 Pinna dātur, quā scribas, *The pen is given you, that you may write with it.*

599.1 ——— translated by *must* or *shall* (command):

 Lex est ut scribam, *There is a law that I must write.*
 Lex est ut scribas, *There is a law that you must write.*

600 ——— translated by *to* (indirect interrogative):

 Nescio quid scribam, *I know not what to write.*
 Nescis quid scribas, *You know not what to write.*

601 ——— translated by *shall, will:*

 Puer timet ne scribam, *The boy is afraid I shall write.*
 Puer timet ne scribas, *The boy is afraid you will write.*

602 ——— translated by *from* ———*ing:*

 Hoc impĕdit ne scribam, *This prevents me from writing.*
 Hoc impĕdit ne scribas, *This prevents you from writing.*

602.1 ——— translated by English infinitive:

 Sine scribam, *Let me write.*   Sine scribamus, *Let us write.*
 Sine scribat, *Let him write.*   Sine scribant, *Let them write.*

---

* Literally, 'with which.'
† Or rather, 'to write with.'

108 VERBS.

602. 2 ——— translated by an English imperative:

Nē scrībam, *Let me not write.*   Nē scrībāmŭs, *Let us not write.*
Nē scrībās, *Do not write.*   Nē scrībātĭs, *Do not write.*
Nē scrībat, *Let him not write.*   Nē scrībant, *Let them not write.*

603   *Past Tense*, scrībĕre.

As a past-imperfect, *was ———ing* (indirect interrogative):

Nescĭēbam quid scrībĕrem,   *I knew not what I was writing.*
Nescĭēbam quid scrībĕrēs,   *I knew not what you were writing.*

604 ——— translated by an English past (result).

Indē factum est ut nihil de hāc   *Hence it happened that I wrote*
rē scrībĕrem,   *nothing on this subject.*
Indē factum est ut nihil de hāc   *Hence it happened that you wrote*
rē scrībĕrēs,   *nothing on this subject.*

605 ——— translated by *should* or *would have been ———ing* (hypothesis):

Sī pinnă mihi esset, scrībĕrem,   *If there had been a pen for me, I should have been writing.*
Sī pinnă tĭbi esset, scrībĕrēs,   *If there had been a pen for you, you would have been writing.*

606 ——— translated by *had been ———ing:*

Sĕdēbam hīc, tanquam scrībĕrem,   *I was sitting here, as if I had been writing.*
Sĕdēbās istīc, tanquam scrībĕrēs,   *You were sitting there, as if you had been writing.*
Sĕdēbat illīc, tanquam scrībĕret,   *He was sitting yonder, as if he had been writing.*

607 ——— translated by *might* (purpose):

Pinnă dăta est quā* scrībĕrem,   *The pen was given me, that I might write with it.*
Pinnă dăta est quā scrībĕrēs,   *The pen was given you, that you might write with it.*

* Literally, 'with which.'   † Or rather, 'to write with.'

VERBS. 109

608 ——— translated by *must* or *should* (command):

    Lex ĕrat ut scrībĕrem,   *There was a law that I must write.*
    Lex ĕrat ut scrībĕrēs,   *There was a law that you must write.*

609 ——— translated by *to* (indirect interrogative):

    Nescĭēbam quid scrībĕrem,   *I knew not what to write.*
    Nescĭēbas quid scrībĕrēs,   *You knew not what to write.*

610 ——— translated by *should* or *would*:

    Puer tĭmēbat nē scrībĕrem,   *The boy was afraid I should write.*
    Puer tĭmēbat nē scrībĕrēs,   *The boy was afraid you would write.*

611 ——— translated by *from* ———*ing*:

    Hoc impĕdĭēbat nē scrībĕrem,   *This prevented me from writing.*
    Hoc impĕdĭēbat nē scrībĕrēs,   *This prevented you from writing.*

612 ——— translated as a past order*:

    Nē scrībĕrem,   (*He bade*) *me not write.*
    Nē scrībĕrēs,   (*He bade*) *you not write.*

613   *Present-Perfect*, scrīpsĕrĭ-.

    As a present-perfect, *have* ———*en* (indirect interrogative):

    Nescĭo quid scrīpsĕrim,   *I know not what I have written.*
    Nescĭs quid scrīpsĕris†,   *You know not what you have written.*

614 ——— as an aorist (indirect interrogative):

    Nescĭo quid hĕrī scrīpsĕrim,   *I know not what I wrote yesterday.*
    Nescĭs quid hĕrī scrīpsĕris,   *You know not what you wrote yesterday.*

615 ——— translated by *may have* ———*en*:

    Forsĭtan nĭmium scrīpsĕrim,   *Perhaps I may have written too much.*
    Forsĭtan nĭmium scrīpsĕris,   *Perhaps you may have written too much.*

    * In reported speech.
    † But see, as regards the quantity of the i after r, § 476.

110 VERBS.

616 —— as a future-perfect after a present, translated by an English present (reported speech):

Caesar pollicētur sē, si scripsĕrim, rescriptūrum,   Caesar promises that if I write, he will write again.
Caesar pollicētur sē, si scripsĕris, rescriptūrum,   Caesar promises that if you write, he will write again.

617 —— translated by *were to* ——, or English past tense (hypothesis):

Si* scripsĕrim ād eum, rĕdeat,   *If I were to write† to him, he would return.*
Si scripsĕris ād eum, rĕdeat,   *If you were to write to him, he would return.*

618 —— translated by *should, would* (consequence of hypothesis):

Frustrā scripsĕrim,   *I should write in vain.*
Frustrā scripsĕris,   *You would write in vain.*

619 —— translated by *had* —— *en*:

Sĕdeo hic, tanquam ĕpistŏlam perscripsĕrim‡,   *I sit here, as if I had written the whole letter.*
Sĕdēs istic, tanquam ĕpistŏlam perscripsĕris,   *You sit there, as if you had written the whole letter.*
Sĕdet illic, tanquam ĕpistŏlam perscripsĕrit,   *He sits yonder, as if he had written the whole letter.*

620 —— translated as an imperative:

Id nunquam scripsĕrim,   *Let me never write that.*
Id nunquam scripsĕris,   *Never write that.*
Id nunquam scripsĕrit,   *Let him never write that.*

* This *si* might be omitted. Thus in the English too we might drop the *if*, and say, 'were I to write to him,' &c.

† Or, 'if I wrote,' &c.

‡ *Per-scrib-* literally signifies 'write through, write to the end.'

VERBS.

Past-Perfect, scripsisse-.

As a past-perfect, translated by *had ——en* (indirect interrogative):

Quaesitum est, ŭtrum scripsissem,	*The question was asked, whether I had written.*
Quaesitum est, ŭtrum scripsissēs,	*The question was asked, whether you had written.*

—— as a future-perfect after a past, translated by an English past (reported speech):

Caesar pollicēbătur sē, si scripsissem, rescriptūrum,	*Caesar promised that if I wrote, he would write again.*
Caesar pollicēbătur sē, si scripsissēs, rescriptūrum,	*Caesar promised that if you wrote, he would write again.*

—— translated by *had ——en* (hypothesis):

Etiamsi scripsissem, frustra esset,	*Even if I had written, it would have been in vain.*
Etiamsi scripsisses, frustra esset,	*Even if you had written, it would have been in vain.*

—— translated by *should have, would have* (consequence of hypothesis):

Tum* quŏquĕ scripsissem, *Even in that case* I should have written.*
Tum quŏquĕ scripsissēs, *Even in that case you would have written.*

INFINITIVE IMPERFECT, scrībĕrĕ.

Translated by an English infinitive:

Dēbeo scrībĕrĕ,	*I ought to write.*
Nĕqueo scrībĕrĕ,	*I cannot write.*

—— translated as an English indicative:

Scio cum scrībĕrĕ,	*I know that he is writing.*
Scisbam cum scrībĕrĕ,	*I knew that he was writing.*

—— translated by an English perfect infinitive:

Debebam scrībĕrĕ,	*I ought to have written.*

* Literally 'then.'

628   INFINITIVE PERFECT, scripsisse.
    Translated by an English perfect Infinitive:
      Scripsisse dicitur,   *He is said to have written.*

629   ——— translated by an English indicative:
      Scio eum scripsisse,   *I know that he has written.*
      Scio eum heri scripsisse,   *I know that he wrote yesterday.*
      Sciebam eum scripsisse,   *I knew that he had written.*

630   ——— translated by *the having* ——— *en:*
      Scripsisse exitio ei fuit,   *The having written was fatal to him.*

631   PARTICIPLE IMPERFECT, scribenti- or scribent-.
    Translated by ———*ing:*
      Senex epistolam scribens decidit, *The old man, while writing a letter, fell down.*

632   PARTICIPLE FUTURE, scripturo-.
    Translated by *about to* ———, *intending to* ———:
      Ad ipsum cras scripturus, haec   *Intending to write to himself to-*
        nunc omitto,   *morrow, I pass over these things now.*
632.1   Dico me scripturum esse,   *I say that I will write.*
       Dixi me scripturum esse,   *I said that I would write.*
632.2   Dixi me scripturum fuisse,   *I said that I would have written.*

633   ——— translated as an intention not fulfilled:
      Habebam ei gratias, scripturus* *I felt grateful to him, and should*
        quoque, nisi aegrotarem,   *have written too, if I had not been ill.*

634   GERUND, scribendo-.
    Translated by ———*ing:*
    N. Mihi est scribendum epistô- *To me belongs the writing the*
        las†,   *letters.*
    Ac. Deligitur ad scribendum   *He is selected for writing the*
        epistolas†,   *letters.*

      * See also the conjugation of the verb *fu-* with the participle in *turo.*
      † Most of these constructions are confined to the old writers. See the use of the Gerundive, § 1267.

G. Vēni ĕpistŏlas scribendi causā, *I came for the sake of writing the letters.*
D. Aptŭs est scribendo ĕpistŏlās*, *He is fit for writing letters.*
Ab. Scribendo† ĕpistŏlās ocŭpā- *He is engaged in writing letters.*
tŭs est,

SUPINE, scriptu-.

Translated as an English infinitive:

Ac. Eo illūc scriptum, *I am going yonder to write.*
Ab. Hae littĕrae difficĭles sunt *These letters are difficult to write.*
scriptū,

CONJUGATION OF A REFLECTIVE VERB, WITH THE ENGLISH TRANSLATION.

Arma- (r.), *arm oneself.*

Principal parts: armāri, armor, armātŭs.

INDICATIVE MOOD.

Present Tense, am arming myself, arm myself, &c.

Armor,	*I am arming myself.*
Armāris *or* armārĕ‡,	*You are arming yourself.*
Armātŭr,	*He is arming himself.*
Armāmŭr,	*We are arming ourselves.*
Armāmĭni,	*You are arming yourselves.*
Armantŭr,	*They are arming themselves.*

Past-Imperfect, was arming myself, &c.

Armābar,	*I was arming myself.*
Armābāris *or* armābārĕ,	*You were arming yourself.*
Armābātŭr,	*He was arming himself.*
Armābāmŭr,	*We were arming ourselves.*
Armābāmĭni,	*You were arming yourselves.*
Armābantŭr,	*They were arming themselves.*

---

* See note † p. 112.

† This form of the Gerund, although an ablative, is often shortened in late writers, as *vigilandŏ* (Juv. 3. 232).

‡ The form in *re* is not common for the present indicative; it may be from fear of confusion with the infinitive.

Future, shall or will arm myself, &c.

Armābor,	*I shall arm myself.*
Armābĕris or armābĕrĕ,	*You will arm yourself.*
Armābĭtŭr,	*He will arm himself.*
Armābĭmŭr,	*We shall arm ourselves.*
Armābĭmĭnī,	*You will arm yourselves.*
Armābuntŭr,	*They will arm themselves.*

Present-Perfect, have armed myself, &c. (or *Aorist*, armed myself.)

Armātus* sum,	*I have armed myself.*
Armātŭs* ĕs,	*You have armed yourself.*
Armātŭs* est,	*He has armed himself.*
Armātī† sŭmŭs,	*We have armed ourselves.*
Armātī† estis,	*You have armed yourselves.*
Armātī† sunt,	*They have armed themselves.*

Past-Perfect, had armed myself, &c.

Armātŭs ĕram‡,	*I had armed myself.*
Armātŭs ĕrās,	*You had armed yourself.*
Armātŭs ĕrat,	*He had armed himself.*
Armāti ĕrămŭs,	*We had armed ourselves.*
Armāti ĕrătis,	*You had armed yourselves.*
Armāti ĕrant,	*They had armed themselves.*

Future-Perfect, shall have armed myself, &c.

Armātŭs ĕro,§	*I shall have armed myself.*
Armātŭs ĕris,	*You will have armed yourself.*
Armātŭs ĕrit,	*He will have armed himself.*
Armāti ĕrĭmŭs,	*We shall have armed ourselves.*
Armāti ĕrĭtis,	*You will have armed yourselves.*
Armāti ĕrunt,	*They will have armed themselves.*

IMPERATIVE MOOD.
Present.

Armārĕ, *Arm yourself.*	Armămĭnī, *Arm yourselves.*

* *Armāta* if the nominative be feminine, *armātum* if it be neuter.
† *Armātae* if the nominative be feminine, *armāta* if it be neuter.
‡ Or *fuĕram*, &c.   § Or *fuĕro*, &c.

644

Future.

Armātor or armāmĭno,	*You must arm yourself.*
Armātor or armāmĭno,	*He must arm himself.*
Armantor,	*They must arm themselves.*

645   SUBJUNCTIVE MOOD.

Present. (See the several translations of *scriba-m.*)

Consŭl impĕrat ŭt armer,	*The consul commands me to arm myself.*
Consŭl impĕrat ŭt armēris or armērĕ,	*The consul commands you to arm yourself.*

646   *Past.* (See the several translations of *scribere-m.*)

Consŭl impĕrăuit ŭt armārer,	*The consul commanded me to arm myself.*
Consŭl impĕrăuit ŭt armārēris or armārērĕ,	*The consul commanded you to arm yourself.*

647   *Present-Perfect.* (See the several translations of *scripseri-m.*)

Nescio quāre armātus sim,	*I know not why I have armed myself.*
Nescio quāre armātus sis,	*I know not why you have armed yourself.*

648   *Past-Perfect.* (See the several translations of *scripsisse-m.*)

Nesciēbam quāre armātŭs essem,	*I knew not why I had armed myself.*
Nesciēbam quāre armātŭs esses,	*I knew not why you had armed yourself.*

649   INFINITIVE IMPERFECT.

Dĕbeo armāri,	*I ought to arm myself.*
Scio eum armāri,	*I know that he is arming himself.*
Sciēbam eum armāri,	*I knew that he was arming himself.*
Armāri signum belli est,	*To arm oneself is a sign of war.*
Dĕbēbam armāri,	*I ought to have armed myself.*

650   INFINITIVE PERFECT.

Scio eum armātum esse,	*I know that he has armed himself.*
Sciēbam eum armātum esse,	*I knew that he had armed himself.*
Scio eum armātum fŏrĕ,	*I know that he will have armed himself.*

651   PARTICIPLE IMPERFECT.
       Armanti- or armant-,   (While) arming oneself.

652   PARTICIPLE PERFECT.
       Armato-,   Having armed oneself.

653   PARTICIPLE FUTURE.
       Armaturo-,   About to arm oneself.

654   GERUND.
       Armando-,   Arming oneself.

CONJUGATION OF A PASSIVE VERB, WITH THE ENGLISH TRANSLATION.

Prĕm- *press.*

Principal parts: prĕmi, prĕmor, prĕssus.

INDICATIVE MOOD.

655   *Pres.* Prĕmor* *I am pressed,* prĕmĕris *you are pressed,* prĕmĭtŭr *he is pressed.* Prĕmĭmŭr *we are pressed,* prĕmĭmĭni *you are pressed,* prĕmuntŭr *they are pressed.*

656   *Past.* Prĕmēbart *I was pressed,* prĕmēbāris or prĕmēbārē *you were pressed,* prĕmēbātŭr *he was pressed.* Prĕmēbāmŭr *we were pressed,* prĕmēbāmĭni *you were pressed,* prĕmēbantŭr *they were pressed.*

657   *Future.* Prĕmar *I shall be pressed,* prĕmēris or prĕmērē *you will be pressed,* prĕmētŭr *he will be pressed.* Prĕmēmŭr *we shall be pressed,* prĕmēmĭni *you will be pressed,* prĕmentŭr *they will be pressed.*

---

* With many verbs this translation would not give the meaning, and indeed the English passive is defective in the imperfect tenses. Thus *domus aedificatur* means, not 'the house is built,' for that would imply that the building is completed, but 'the house is being built' or 'is a-building;' but of these two phrases, the first is scarcely English, and the second is obsolete. Again, such a verb as *occidor* must not be translated 'I am killed,' but rather 'I am on the point of being killed.'

† Similarly, *domus aedificabatur* would signify 'the house was being built' or 'was a-building.' So *occidebar* must not be translated 'I was killed,' but rather 'I was on the point of being killed.'

658   *Pres.-perf.* Pressus* sum† *I have been pressed*‡, pressus ĕs *you have been pressed*, pressus est *he has been pressed*. Pressi sŭmŭs *we have been pressed*, pressi estis *you have been pressed*, pressi sunt *they have been pressed*.

659   *Past-perf.* Pressus* eram§ *I had been pressed*‖, pressus ĕrās *you had been pressed*, pressus ĕrat *he had been pressed*. Pressi ĕrāmŭs *we had been pressed*, pressi ĕrātis *you had been pressed*, pressi ĕrant *they had been pressed*.

660   *Fut.-perf.* Pressus* ĕro¶ *I shall have been pressed*, pressus ĕris *you will have been pressed*, pressus ĕrit *he will have been pressed*. Pressi ĕrĭmŭs *we shall have been pressed*, pressi ĕrĭtis *you will have been pressed*, pressi ĕrunt *they will have been pressed*.

IMPERATIVE MOOD.

661   *Present.* Prĕmĕrĕ *be thou pressed*, prĕmĭmĭnī *be ye pressed*.

662   *Future.* Prĕmĭtor *thou shalt be pressed*, prĕmĭtor *he shall be pressed*. Prĕmuntor *they shall be pressed*.

663   ### SUBJUNCTIVE MOOD.

Present Tense. Rēs eō rĕdiit, ut mălis prĕmar, *Matters are come to this, that I am pressed with troubles.*

664   Rgŏ si tot mălis prĕmar, pĕream, *If I were pressed by so many troubles, I should die.*

665   Tum nimium prĕmar, *In that case I should be too much pressed.*

666   Timŏr est nē prĕmar, *The fear is that I shall be pressed.*

667   Stat per Caium, quōmĭnus prĕmar, *Caius prevents me from being pressed.*

668   Nītor nē prĕmar, *I am striving not to be pressed.*

669   *Past Tense.* Timŏr ĕrat nē prĕmĕrer, *There was a fear that I should be pressed.*

670   Rēs eō rĕdiĕrat, ut mălis prĕmĕrer, *Matters had come to this, that I was pressed with troubles.*

---

* i. e. Pressus, -d, or -um.

† Or as an aorist, 'I was pressed,' &c.

‡ With some verbs the translation 'is ——ed' is admissible. Thus *domus aedificata est* means 'the house is built' or 'the building is now completed.' *Occisus sum,* 'I am killed.'   § Or *fueram*, &c.

‖ With some verbs this tense may be translated 'was ——ed.' Thus, *domus tum aedificata erat,* 'the house was now built,' i. e. the building was completed.

¶ Or *fuero*, &c.

671. Egŏ sī tot mălīs prĕmĕrer, pĕrīrem, *If I had been pressed with so many troubles, I should have died.*

672. Tum nimium prĕmĕrer, *In that case I should have been too much pressed.*

673. Stĕtit per Caium, nē prĕmĕrer, *Caius prevented me from being pressed.*

674. Nītēbar nē prĕmĕrer, *I was striving not to be pressed.*

675. *Pres.-perf.* Nescit, quam grăvĭter pressus sim, *He knows not how heavily I have been pressed.*

676. *As an Aorist.* Nēmo scit, quantīs tum mălīs pressus sim, *No one knows with what great troubles I was then pressed.*

677. Sī pressus sim, cēdam, *If I were pressed, I should give way.*

678. Palleo, tanquam āb ursō pressus sim, *I look pale, as if I had been pressed by a bear.*

679. Nēquīquam pressus sim, *I should be pressed to no purpose.*

680. Scit mē, sī mălō pressus sim, tămen incŏlŭmem suāsūrum, *He knows that if I am pressed by trouble, still I shall come out unhurt.*

681. *Past-perf.* Nescīebat, quam grăvĭter pressŭs essem, *He knew not how heavily I had been pressed.*

682. Nēquīquam pressŭs essem, *I should have been pressed to no purpose.*

683. Scīēbat mē, sī mălō pressŭs essem, tămen nunquam cessūrum, *He knew that if I were pressed by trouble, still I should never yield.*

684. INFINITIVE IMPERFECT. Prĕmī *to be pressed.*
    INFINITIVE PERFECT. Pressūs* esse *to have been pressed.*
    PARTICIPLE IMPERFECT. Prĕmendo- *being pressed or to be pressed.*
    PARTICIPLE PERFECT. Presso- *pressed.*

685.   CONJUGATION OF A DEPONENT VERB.

c. F. Sĕqu- *follow.*

Principal parts: sĕquī, sĕquor, sĕcūtūs.

INDICATIVE MOOD.

686. *Present.* Sĕquor *I follow,* sĕquĕris *you follow,* sĕquĭtŭr *he follows.* Sĕquĭmŭr *we follow,* sĕquĭmĭnī *you follow,* sĕquuntŭr† *they follow.*

* The case and gender will vary with the sentence.
† The forms sequontur and secuntur also occur.

VERBS.   119

687 *Past.* Sĕquēbar *I was following,* sĕquĕbāris or sĕquĕbārĕ *you were following,* sĕquĕbātŭr *he was following.* Sĕquĕbāmŭr *we were following,* sĕquĕbāmĭnī *you were following,* sĕquĕbantŭr *they were following.*

688 *Future.* Sĕquar *I shall follow,* sĕquēris or sĕquērĕ *you will follow,* sĕquētŭr *he will follow.* Sĕquēmŭr *we shall follow,* sĕquēmĭnī *you will follow,* sĕquentŭr *they will follow.*

689 *Pres.-perf.* Sĕcūtus* sum *I have followed*†, sĕcūtŭs ĕs *you have followed,* sĕcūtŭs est *he has followed.* Sĕcūtī sŭmŭs *we have followed,* sĕcūti estis *you have followed,* sĕcūti sunt *they have followed.*

690 *Past-perf.* Sĕcūtus* ĕram§ *I had followed,* sĕcūtŭs ĕrās *you had followed,* sĕcūtŭs ĕrat *he had followed.* Sĕcūtī ĕrāmŭs *we had followed,* sĕcūti ĕrātis *you had followed,* sĕcūti ĕrant *they had followed.*

691 *Fut.-perf.* Sĕcūtus* ĕro‖ *I shall have followed,* sĕcūtŭs ĕris *you will have followed,* sĕcūtŭs ĕrit *he will have followed.* Sĕcūtī ĕrĭmŭs *we shall have followed,* sĕcūti ĕrĭtis *you will have followed,* sĕcūti ĕrunt *they will have followed.*

IMPERATIVE MOOD.

692 *Present.* Sĕquĕrĕ *follow thou,* sĕquĭmĭnī *follow ye.*
693 *Future.* Sĕquĭtor or sĕquĭmĭno *thou shalt follow,* sĕquĭtor or sĕquĭmĭno *he shall follow.* Sĕcuntor *they shall follow.*

694 SUBJUNCTIVE MOOD.¶

Present. Sĕquar, sĕquāris or sĕquārĕ, sĕquātŭr; sĕquāmŭr, sĕquāmĭnī, sĕquantŭr.

695 *Past.* Sĕquĕrer, sĕquĕrēris or sĕquĕrērĕ, sĕquĕrētŭr; sĕquĕrēmŭr, sĕquĕrēmĭnī, sĕquĕrentŭr.

696 *Pres.-perf.* Sĕcūtus sim**, sĕcūtus sīs, sĕcūtus sit; sĕcūtī sīmŭs, sĕcūtī sītis, sĕcūtī sint.

697 *Past-perf.* Sĕcūtŭs essem††, sĕcūtŭs essēs, sĕcūtŭs esset; sĕcūti essēmŭs, sĕcūti essētis, sĕcūti essent.

* *Secutus, -a, -um,* according to the gender of the nominative.
† Or as an aorist, 'I followed,' &c.
‡ *Secuti, -ae, -a,* according to the gender of the nominative.
§ Or *fueram,* &c.   ‖ Or *fuero,* &c.
¶ For the English translation, see the mode of translating *scribo-m,* &c. §§ 594-624; and observe that Deponent verbs are translated by English active verbs.
** Or *fuerim,* &c.   †† Or *fuissem,* &c.

608. INFINITIVE. Sĕquī *to follow.*
INFINITIVE PERFECT. Sĕcūtŭs essĕ *to have followed.*
PARTICIPLE IMPERFECT. Sĕquenti- *or* sĕquent- *following.*
PARTICIPLE and GERUND. Sĕquendo- *following.*
PARTICIPLE PERFECT. Sĕcūto- *having followed.*

699. CONJUGATION OF AN IMPERSONAL VERB.

G.V. Plu- *rain.*

INDICATIVE MOOD.

Present. Pluĭt *it rains.*
Past. Plŭēbat *it was raining.*
Future. Pluet *it will rain.*
Pres.-perf. Plūuit *it has rained,* or
As an Aorist. Plūuit *it rained.*
Past-perf. Plūuĕrat *it had rained.*
Fut.-perf. Plūuĕrit *it will have rained,* &c.

700. CONJUGATION, IN PART, OF AN IMPERSONAL VERB
OF THE FEELINGS. (See § 393.)

G.V. Pŭde- *shame.*

INDICATIVE MOOD.

Present.

Pŭdet me ignāuiae, *I am ashamed of my cowardice.*
Pŭdet te ignāuiae, *You are ashamed of your cowardice.*
Pŭdet eum ignāuiae, *He is ashamed of his cowardice.*

Pŭdet nōs ignāuiae, *We are ashamed of our cowardice.*
Pŭdet uōs ignāuiae, *You are ashamed of your cowardice.*
Pŭdet eōs ignāuiae, *They are ashamed of their cowardice.*

Past.

Pŭdēbat me ignāuiae, *I was ashamed of my cowardice.*
Pŭdēbat te ignāuiae, *You were ashamed of your cowardice,* &c.

Future.

Pŭdēbit me ignāuiae, *I shall be ashamed of my cowardice.*
Pŭdēbit te ignāuiae, *You will be ashamed of your cowardice,* &c.

701 Conjugation, in part, of a Passive Impersonal Verb:

c.v. Rĕsist- *stand against, make opposition, oppose.*

INDICATIVE MOOD.

Present.

Rĕsistĭtur mihi, *Opposition is made to me, or I am opposed.*
Rĕsistĭtur tĭbi, *Opposition is made to you, or you are opposed.*
Rĕsistĭtur ei, *Opposition is made to him, or he is opposed.*

Rĕsistĭtur nōbis, *Opposition is made to us, or we are opposed.*
Rĕsistĭtur uōbis, *Opposition is made to you, or you are opposed.*
Rĕsistĭtur eis, *Opposition is made to them, or they are opposed.*

Past. Rĕsistēbātur mihi, *Opposition was made to me, or I was opposed.**

Rĕsistēbātur tĭbi, *Opposition was made to you, or you were opposed,* &c.

Future. Rĕsistētur mihi, *Opposition will be made to me, or I shall be opposed.*

Rĕsistētur tĭbi, *Opposition will be made to you, or you will be opposed,* &c.

Pres.-perf. Restĭtum mihi est, *Opposition has been made to me, or I have been opposed.*†

Restĭtum tĭbi est, *Opposition has been made to you, or you have been opposed,* &c.

Past-perf. Restĭtum mihi ĕrat, *Opposition had been made to me, or I had been opposed.*

Restĭtum tĭbi ĕrat, *Opposition had been made to you, or you had been opposed,* &c.

702 Conjugation, in part, of the participle in *turo* with the verbs ĕs- and fu- *be* in the sense of intention or destiny.

INDICATIVE MOOD.

With the present of ĕs-, *intend to ——.*

Nihil actūrus sum, *I intend to do nothing.*

---

* I. e. 'All this time' or 'for a time.' This tense must not be confounded with the aorist.

† Or as an aorist, 'Opposition was made to me,' &c.

―― am destined to ――.

Quid tīmeam, sī beātus fūtūrus sum ? *What am I to fear, if I am destined to be happy ?*

703   With the Past of ĕs-, *intended to* ――.
Nihil actūrus ĕram, *I intended to do nothing.*

―― was destined to ――.

Quid tīmērem, sī beātus fūtūrus ĕram ? *What was I to fear, if I was destined to be happy ?*

705   With the Perf. of fu-, *intended to* ――, *and should have done so, if* ――.
Dēdītōs, occīsūrus fuī, *If they had been given up, I should have killed them.*

―― was destined to ――, and should have done so, if ――.
Nisi rĕuertissem, intĕritūrus fuī, *If I had not turned back, I should have perished.*

706   With the Past-perf. of fu-, *had intended to* ――, *and would have done so, if* ――.
Quam uim lātrō mihi fuĕrat illātūrus, in ipsum conuertī, *The violence which the robber had intended to direct against me, I turned against himself.*

707   SUBJUNCTIVE MOOD.
With the Pres. of ĕs-, *intend to* ――.
Scrībam quid actūrus sim, *I will write word what I intend to do.*

―― am destined to ――.
Nescio quandō sim moritūrus, *I know not when I am to die.*

708   With the Past of ĕs-, *intended to* ――.
Scrīpsī quid actūrus essem, *I wrote word what I intended to do.*

―― was destined to ――.
Nesciēbam quando essem moritūrus, *I knew not when I was to die.*

709   With the Perf. of fu-, *intended to, and should have done so,*
if ——.

Quis dŭbĭtat quin dēdĭtōs occĭsūrus fŭĕrim? *Who doubts but that, if they had been given up, I should have killed them?*

—— *was destined to, and should have done so, if* ——.

Sĕquĭtŭr ut nĭsĭ rĕuertissem, intĕrĭtūrus fŭĕrim, *It follows that if I had not turned back, I should have perished.*

710   With the Infinitive of ĕs-, *intend to* ——.

Scio* eum nĭhĭl actūrum essĕ, *I know* that he intends* to do nothing.*

         —— *is destined to* ——.

Scio omnēs hŏmĭnes mŏrĭtūrōs essĕ, *I know that all men are destined to die.*

711   With the Perf.-inf. of fu-, *intended to* ——, *and should have done so, if* ——.

Fama est mē dēdĭtōs occĭsūrum fuissĕ, *There is a report that if they had been given up, I should have killed them.*

         —— *was destined to* ——, *and should have done so, if* ——.

Certum est mē nĭsĭ rĕuertissem, intĕrĭtūrum fuissĕ, *It is certain that if I had not turned back, I should have perished.*

712   Conjugation of the participle in *endo* when used with the verb ĕs- and fu- *be* in the sense of duty or necessity.

INDICATIVE MOOD.
With the Pres. of ĕs-.

Mĭhi omnia ūnō tempŏrē sunt ăgenda, *I have every thing to do at once.*

713   With the Past of ĕs-.

Mĭhi omnia ūnō tempŏre ĕrant ăgenda, *I had every thing to do at once.*

714   With the Fut. of ĕs-.

Mĭhi omnia ūnō tempŏre ĕrunt ăgenda, *I shall have every thing to do at once.*

* After a past tense, as *sciebam* 'I knew,' the infinitive would be translated by 'intended' or 'were destined.'

124 VERBS.

715 With the Pres.-perf. of fu-.

Nisi firmāta extrēma agminis fuissent, ingens clādēs accipiendā fuit, *If the rear of the line of march had not been strengthened, a tremendous blow must have been received.*

Ab Alexamēnō fuit habenda ōrātiō, *The speech was to have been made by Alexamenus, (but as he is now dead) &c.*

716 With the Past-perf. of fu-.

Ab Alexamēnō fuĕrat habenda ōrātiō, *The speech was to have been made by Alexamenus, (but as he was then dead) &c.*

717 SUBJUNCTIVE MOOD.
With the Pres. of ĕs-.

Nescio quid sit nōbīs agendum, *I know not what we ought to do.*

718 With the Past of ĕs-.

Nesciēbam quid esset nōbīs agendum, *I knew not what we ought to do.*

719 With the Pres.-perf. of fu-.

Hoc haud dŭbium fĕcit quin nisi firmāta extrēma agminis fuissent, ingens clādēs accipiendā fuĕrit, *This made it certain that if the rear of the line of march had not been strengthened, a tremendous blow must have been received.*

720 INFINITIVE MOOD.
With Imperf. of ĕs-.

Sentit differendum esse in aestātem bellum, *He feels that the war must be put off to the summer.*

721 With the Perf. of fu-.

Hoc scio, nisi rĕvertisset, in illo ei conclāvī cŭbandum fuissĕ, *This I know, that if he had not turned back, he would have had to sleep in that chamber.*

722 SOME IRREGULAR AND DEFECTIVE VERBS CONJUGATED.

The verb ĕs- means, first, *eat*; secondly, *hiss*; thirdly, *exist* for the senses, *be*; fourthly, *exist* for the mind, *be*. In the first sense the forms in use are as follows:

ĕs- *eat.*

INDICATIVE MOOD. *Present.* S. ĕs *you eat,* est *he eats*; P. estis *you eat.*

IMPERATIVE. *Present.* S. ĕs* *eat thou*; P. estō *eat ye.*
Future. S. estō *thou shalt eat,* estō *he shall eat*; P. estōtō *ye shall eat.*

SUBJUNCTIVE. *Past.* S. essem esses esset; P. essēmus essētis essent.

INFINITIVE. essĕ *to eat.*†

PASSIVE. *Indic. Pres.* S. 3. estūr. *Subj. Past.* S. 3. essētūr.

1 The same forms exist for several of the compounds, as cŏmĕs- *eat up,* whence cŏmĕs, cŏmest, cŏmestis, cŏmessĕ.

2 The verb ĕd- *eat* is but a variety of ĕs- *eat.* It is declined regularly, except that for the subj. pres., besides the regular ĕdam &c. it has also an old form ĕdim, ĕdis &c.

ĕs- or fu- *be.*

(a) *Imperfect Tenses.*

INDICATIVE MOOD.

Present.		*Past.*		*Future.*	
S. sum	*I am*	S. ĕram	*I was*	S. ĕrō	*I shall be*
es‡	*you are*	ĕrās	*you were*	ĕris	*you will be*
est‡	*he is*	ĕrat	*he was*	ĕrit	*he will be*
P. sŭmŭs	*we are*	P. ĕrāmŭs	*we were*	P. ĕrĭmŭs	*we shall be*
estis	*you are*	ĕrātis	*you were*	ĕritis	*you will be*
sunt	*they are*	ĕrant	*they were*	ĕrunt	*they will be.*

IMPERATIVE.

Present. S. ĕs *be*; P. estō *be.*
Future. S. estō *thou shalt be,* estō *he shall be*; P. estōtō *ye shall be,* suntō *they shall be.*

---

* The quantity is not proved by the authority of any poet, but inferred from the statements of the grammarians Priscian (ix. 1, 11) and Servius (ad Aen. v. 785).

† Thus it appears that forms which begin with *es,* and these alone, are used with the double sense of 'eat' and 'br.'

‡ *Es* and *est* often lose the *e,* as *sonă's, inssī's,* for *sonăs īs, iussīs īs; bonūs'd, bonăst, bonumst,* for *bonūs est, bona est, bonum est; quantist* for *quanti est; umbrā's āmantem, l'laut.* Mil. III. 1. 31.

SUBJUNCTIVE.*

Present.		Past.		Or	
S. sim	*I am*	S. essem	*I was*	S. fŏrem	
sis	*you are*	esses	*you were*	fŏres	
sit	*he is*	esset	*he was*	fŏret	
P. simŭs	*we are*	P. essēmŭs	*we were*	P. ——	
sitis	*you are*	essētis	*you were*	——	
sint	*they are*	essent	*they were*	fŏrent.	

INFINITIVE.
essĕ *to be;* fŏrĕ *will be.*

PARTICIPLE FUTURE.
fŭtūro- *about to be.*

723. 1 **(b) Perfect Tenses.**

INDICATIVE.
Present-perfect.

S. fuī	*I have been*	P. fuĭmŭs	*we have been*
fuistī	*you have been*	fuistis	*you have been*
fuit	*he has been*	fuērunt *or* fuērĕ	*they have been.*

Or as Aorist.

S. fuī	*I was*	P. fuĭmŭs	*we were*
fuistī	*you were*	fuistis	*you were*
fuit	*he was*	fuērunt *or* fuērĕ	*they were.*

Past-perfect.

S. fuĕram	*I had been*	P. fuĕrāmŭs	*we had been*
fuĕrās	*you had been*	fuĕrātis	*you had been*
fuĕrat	*he had been*	fuĕrant	*they had been.*

Future-perfect.

S. fuĕrŏ	*I shall have been*	P. fuĕrĭmŭs	*we shall have been*
fuĕris	*you will have been*	fuĕritis	*you will have been*
fuĕrit	*he will have been*	fuĕrint	*they will have been.*

* For the other meanings of the subjunctive tenses see the conjugation of *scribam,* &c.

VERBS.   127

SUBJUNCTIVE.
Present-perfect.

S. fuĕrim   *I have been*   P. fuĕrimŭs *we have been*
   fuĕris   *you have been*   fuĕritis   *you have been*
   fuĕrit   *he has been*   fuĕrint   *they have been.*

Or as Aorist.

S. fuĕrim   *I was*   P. fuĕrimŭs *we were*
   fuĕris   *you were*   fuĕritis   *you were*
   fuĕrit   *he was*   fuĕrint   *they were.*

Past-perfect.

S. fuissem *I had been*   P. fuissemŭs *we had been*
   fuisses *you had been*   fuissetis *you had been*
   fuisset *he had been*   fuissent   *they had been.*

INFINITIVE.
fuisse *to have been, was* or *had been.*

724   As regards quantity, *a*. Es is often long in old writers (as Plautus, Mil. Gl. III. 1. 30), which agrees with the formation from esis (eis), with es *eat*, and with the Greek εἰς. *b*. For the quantity of the *i* after *r* in fuĕris, fuĕrimŭs, fuĕritis, of the indicative and subjunctive, see § 476.

725   Old forms are, *a*. esum *I am*, esumus, esunt, esim &c. (see *Varr.* L. L. IX. 57), which are in nearer agreement with the root es-. *b*. simus for sumus (comp. scribimus) was used by Augustus (*Suet.* Aug. 87). *c*. escit, an inceptive present (§ 732), occurs in old writings (as XII. Tab. ap. *Gell.* XX. 1. 25, *Lucr.* I. 612) as a future. So indeed the whole future tense ero, ĕris &c. is in form a mere present. Compare also fŏrĕ (=fuĕrĕ), a present in form, a future in meaning. *d*. A fuller form of the subjunctive present, siem, siēs &c., is common in the older writers. *e*. Another form of the present subjunctive, used in old writers, is S. fuam, fuas, fuat; P. fuant. *f*. The past subjunctive—S. fŏrem, fŏrēs, fŏret; P. fŏrent—sometimes takes the place of essem in classical writers, especially in hypothetical sentences (§ 1209), and those which denote a purpose (§ 1179). It also occurs in compound tenses for essem, but not in Cicero.* *g*. In the perfect tenses a fuller form,

* This from Madvig.

fū-uĭs- existed for the older writers, as fŭuĭmŭs (*Enn.* ap. *Cic. de Or.* III. 42), fŭuĭsset (*Enn.* ap. *Gell.* XII. 4. 4). A. An imperfect participle enti- (N. ens) is attributed to Caesar by Priscian. The compounds praesenti- *praesens*, absenti- *absens*, for prae-ĕs-enti-, ăb-ĕs-enti, are in form participles, in meaning adjectives. So also consentĕs for cŏn-ĕs-entĕs, in the phrase, DI consentĕs, literally *the united gods*. In late philosophical writings ens is used as a substantive for *a thing*.

727   Es- or fu- compounded with prŏ or prŏd, *be profitable*.

INDICATIVE. *Pres.* S. Prŏsum prŏdĕs prŏdest, P. prŏsŭmŭs prŏdestĭs prŏsunt. *Past.* S. Prŏdĕram prŏdĕrās &c. *Fut.* S. Prŏdĕrŏ prŏdĕrĭs &c. *Pres.-perf.* Prŏfuī &c. *Past-perf.* Prŏfuĕram &c. *Fut.-perf.* Prŏfuĕrŏ &c.

IMPERATIVE probably not in use.

SUBJUNCTIVE. *Pres.* Prŏsim &c. *Past.* Prŏdessem &c. *Pres.-perf.* Prŏfuĕrim &c. *Past-perf.* Prŏfulssem &c.

INFINITIVE. *Imperf.* Prŏdesse. *Perf.* Prŏfuisse.

PARTICIPLE. *Fut.* Prŏfŭtŭro-.

728   Es- or fu-, compounded with the adjective pŏti- or pŏt-, *be able, can*.

INDICATIVE. *Pres.* S. Possum pŏtĕs pŏtest, P. possŭmŭs pŏtestĭs possunt. *Past.* S. Pŏtĕram pŏtĕrās pŏtĕrat, P. pŏtĕrāmŭs pŏtĕrātĭs pŏtĕrant. *Fut.* S. Pŏtĕrŏ pŏtĕrĭs pŏtĕrit, P. pŏtĕrĭmŭs pŏtĕrĭtĭs pŏtĕrunt. *Pres.-perf.* Pŏtuī pŏtuistī &c. *Past-perf.* Pŏtuĕram &c. *Fut.-perf.* S. Pŏtuĕrŏ pŏtuĕrĭs pŏtuĕrit, P. pŏtuĕrĭmŭs pŏtuĕrĭtĭs pŏtuĕrint.

IMPERATIVE not in use.

SUBJUNCTIVE. *Pres.* Possim possīs &c. *Past.* Possem possēs &c. *Pres.-perf.* S. Pŏtuĕrim pŏtuĕrīs pŏtuĕrit, P. pŏtuĕrīmŭs pŏtuĕrītĭs pŏtuĕrint. *Past-perf.* Pŏtuissem pŏtuissēs &c.

INFINITIVE. *Imperf.* Posse (used sometimes as a future, *will be able*). *Perf.* Pŏtuisse.

PARTICIPLE. Pŏtenti-* or pŏtent-.

729   Fĕr- *bring*. (For the perfect tenses see § 548.)

INDICATIVE. *Pres.* S. Fĕrŏ fers fert, P. fĕrĭmŭs fertĭs fĕrunt. *Past-imp.* Fĕrebam &c. *Fut.* Fĕram &c.

  * This is used rather as an adjective than as a participle.

IMPERATIVE. *Pres. S.* Fĕr, *P.* fertĕ.   *Fut. S.* Fertŏ fertŏ, *P.* fertōtĕ fĕruntŏ.
SUBJUNCTIVE. *Pres.* Fĕram &c. *Past.* Ferrem &c.
INFINITIVE. Ferrĕ. *Part.* Fĕrenti- *or* fĕrent-. *Gerund.* Fĕrendo-.

The passive is regular except in the *indic. pres.* ferris, fertūr; *imperative* fertor; *subj. past* ferrēr &c.; *infin.* ferri; and *part. perf.* lāto-.

730   Inqu- *or* inqui- *say* has only IND. *Pres. S.* inquam iuquis inquit, *P.* inquimūs inquitis inquiunt. *Past-imperf.* —— —— inquiēbat. *Fut.* —— inquiēs inquiet. *Perf.* —— inquisti inquit.

IMPERAT. *Pres. S.* inquĕ. *Fut.* inquitŏ. The present inquam is only used in repeating a phrase, *I say, I tell you once more;* and inquit *says he or said he* introduces a direct speech, and always follows one or two words of this speech.

731   Cĕd- *give, tell,* only used in the imperative present.
     S. Cĕdŏ *give (me), tell (me); P.* cetīs *give (me), tell (me).*

732   Da- *put or give.*

INDICATIVE. *Pres. S.* Dŏ dās dat, *P.* dămūs dātis dant. *Past-imp.* Dăbam &c. *Fut.* Dăbŏ &c. *Pres.-perf.* Dĕdi &c. *Past-perf.* Dĕdĕram &c. *Fut.-perf.* dĕdĕrŏ &c.

IMPERATIVE. *Pres. S.* Dă, *P.* dătă. *Fut. S.* Dătŏ dătŏ, *P.* dătōtă dantŏ.

SUBJUNCTIVE. *Pres. S.* Dem dēs det, *P.* dēmūs dētis dent. *Past-imperf.* Dărem &c. *Pres.-perf.* Dĕdĕrim &c. *Past-perf.* Dĕdissem &c.

INFINITIVE. *Imperf.* Dărĕ. *Perf.* Dĕdissĕ.

PARTICIPLE. *Imperf.* Danti- *or* dant-. *Fut.* Dătūro-. GERUND. Dando-.

The Subj. *Pres.* has also an old form, duim, duis &c., from a crude form du-.

733   Vŏl- *or* uĕl- *wish.*

INDICATIVE. *Pres. S.* Vŏlŏ uīs uolt *or* uult, *P.* uŏlŭmūs uoltis *or* uultis uŏlunt. *Past-imp.* Vŏlēbam &c. *Fut.* Vŏlam uŏlēs &c. *Pres.-perf.* Vŏlui &c. *Past-perf.* Vŏluĕram &c. *Fut.-perf.* Vŏluĕrŏ &c.

K

IMPERATIVE not in use.
SUBJUNCTIVE. *Pres. S.* Vělim vŏlis vŏlit, *P.* vělīmŭs vělītis věllint. *Past.* Vellem vellēs &c. *Pres.-perf.* Vŏluĕrim &c. *Past-perf.* Vŏluissem &c.
INFINITIVE. *Imperf.* Vellĕ. *Perf.* Vŏluissĕ.
PARTICIPLE. *Imperf.* Vŏlenti- or vŏlent-. GERUND. Vŏlendo-.

734. Nĕuŏl- or nōl- *be unwilling*, a compound of ne or nōn and vŏl-.

INDICATIVE. *Pres. S.* Nŏlŏ nĕuīs* or nonuīs nĕuolt* or nonuolīt, *P.* nŏlŭmŭs nĕuoltīs* or nonuolūst nŏlunt. *Past-imp.* Nŏlēbam &c. *Fut.* —— nŏlēs nŏlet &c. *Pres.-perf.* Nŏluī &c. *Past-perf.* Nŏluĕram &c. *Fut.-perf.* Nŏluĕrŏ &c.
IMPERATIVE. *Pres. S.* Nŏlī, *P.* nŏlītĕ. *Fut. S.* Nŏlītŏ, *P.* nŏlītŏtĕ.
SUBJUNCTIVE. *Pres.* Nŏlim nŏlis &c. *Past.* Nollem &c. *Pres.-perf.* Nŏluĕrim &c. *Past-perf.* Nŏluissem &c.
INFINITIVE. *Imperf.* Nollĕ. *Perf.* Nŏluissĕ.
PARTICIPLE. *Imperf.* Nŏlenti- or nŏlent-. GERUND. Nŏlendo-.

735. Māuŏl- or māl- *prefer*, a compound of māgĕ *and* vŏl-.

INDICATIVE. *Pres. S.* Māuŏlŏ; or mālŏ māuīs māuoltǐ, *P.* mālŭmŭs māuoltīs; māuŏlunt; or mālunt. *Past-imp.* Mālōbam &c. *Fut.* ——mālēs mālet &c. *Pres.-perf.* Māluī &c. *Past-perf.* Māluĕram &c. *Fut.-perf.* Māluĕrŏ &c.
IMPERATIVE not in use.
SUBJUNCTIVE. *Pres.* Māuŏlim; or mālim mālis &c. *Past.* Māuellem; or mallem &c. *Pres.-perf.* Māluĕrim &c. *Past-perf.* Māluissem &c.
INFINITIVE. *Imperf.* Māuellĕ; or mallĕ. *Perf.* Māluissĕ.

736. Fī- *become*, used in the imperfect tenses as a passive of făci- or făc- *make* (see § 534).

INDICATIVE. *Pres. S.* Fīŏ fīs fit, *P.* —— —— fīunt. *Past-imp.* Fīēbam &c. *Fut.* Fīam fīēs &c.
IMPERATIVE. *Pres. S.* Fī, *P.* fītĕ.

* The forms with *ne* are found in the older writers.
† Or *nonuult* and *nonuultis*.
‡ The longer forms *mauolo* &c. are found in the older writers.
§ Or *mauult* and *mauultis*.

VERBS. 131

SUBJUNCTIVE. *Pres.* Fīam &c.   *Past.* Fĭĕrem* &c.
INFINITIVE. *Imperf.* Fĭĕrī.*

737   I- *go.*

INDICATIVE. *Pres.* S. Eŏ īs it, P. īmŭs ītis eunt.   *Past-imp.*
Ībam &c.   *Fut.* Ībō ībis &c.   *Pres.-perf.* Iŭī or iī īistī iit &c.
Past-perf. Iŭĕram or īĕram &c.   *Fut.-perf.* Iŭĕrō or īĕrō &c.
IMPERATIVE. *Pres.* S. I, P. ītĕ.   *Fut.* S. Itō ītō, P. itōtĕ euntĭ.
SUBJUNCTIVE. *Pres.* Eam eās &c.   *Past.* Irem &c.   *Pres.-perf.*
Iŭĕrim or īĕrim &c.   *Past-perf.* Iuissem or iissem or īssem &c.
INFINITIVE. *Imperf.* Irĕ.   *Perf.* Iuissĕ iissĕ or īssĕ.
PARTICIPLE. *Imperf.* Ienti- or ient-, N. Iens, Ac. euntem, G.
euntis &c.   *Fut.* Itūro-.   GERUND. Eundo-.

737. 1 The passive is used impersonally.   INDIC. Ītŭr, ĭbātŭr, ĭbītŭr,
Ītum est &c.   SUBJ. Eātŭr, īrētŭr, ītum sit &c.   INFIN. Irī, Ītum
essĕ.

737. 2 Some of the compounds being transitive form a passive, as ădi-
approach. Hence IND. *Pres.* S. ădeŏr ădīris ădītŭr, P. ădīmŭr
ădīmĭnī ădeuntŭr &c.

737. 3 Vēni- *for* uēnum i- *be offered for sale,* is a compound of i- *go,*
and consequently conjugated like it.

738   Qui- *be able,* and nĕqui- *be unable,* are conjugated as i- *go;* but
have no imperative, no participle imperfect or future, and no gerund.

739   Ai- *affirm, say,* is seldom used except in the following forms :
INDICATIVE. *Pres.* S. Aio ais or āis ait or āit, P. —— ——
aiunt.   *Past.* Aiĕbam *or* aibam aiĕbās &c.

740   DERIVATION &c. OF VERBS.

It has been stated that many substantives and adjectives in *a*
and *o* are used as verbs in *a* (§ 522) ; that some substantives in *u*
are used as verbs in *u* (§ 526) ; that some substantives and adjectives in *i* are used as verbs in *i* (§ 528).

* The *i* is sometimes long in old writers, as Terence (Ad. L. 2, 25)
and Plautus (Trin. II. 4. 131, and Men. v. 5, 24).

741. It has been stated (§ 224) that some adjectives have a crude form in *i* as well as that in *o* or *a*. Similarly some adjectives in *o* or *a* coexist with verbs in *i*; and some adjectives in *i* coexist with verbs in *a*. Thus there is

An adj. insano- *mad*, and a verb insani- *be mad*.
,, largo- *bountiful*, ,, largi- (r.) *lavish*.
,, celeri- *quick*, ,, celera- *quicken*.
,, levi- *light*, ,, leva- *lift*.
,, levi- *smooth*, ,, leva- *polish*.

742. As so large a number of substantives and adjectives ended in *o* or *a*, and these led to verbs in *a*, the consequence was, that there was a tendency to introduce an *a* in all such secondary verbs, even when the substantive or adjective ended in a consonant. Thus there is

A subst. nomen- *name*, and a verb nomina- *name*.
,, laud- *praise*, ,, lauda- *praise*.
,, onus-* *load*, ,, onera- *load*.
,, robor- *hardness*, ,, robora- *harden*.
,, exul- *an exile*, ,, exula- *be an exile*.
An adj. memor- *mindful*, ,, memora- *mention*.
,, exos- *boneless*, ,, exossa- *bone*.
,, praecip- or praecipit- *head foremost*, and a verb praecipita- *send head foremost*.

742.1 A few compound verbs take a final *a* although the simple verb ends in a consonant: as,

From spec- or speci- (obsolete) *look*, conspica- (r.) *behold*.
,, duc-† *lead*, educa- *bring up*, *nurse*.
,, spern- *despise*, asperna- (r.) *spurn*.‡

---

* Verbs formed in this way from nouns in *is*, *us* &c. are very numerous: as, pignera-, ucsera- (r.), frigora-, tempera-, volnera-, genera-, glomera-, modera- &c. The neuter noun modus- is obsolete, it is true, but its existence is proved by the adj. modesto-. Ramshorn erroneously considers *fer* as a verbal suffix, and even quotes as an example *oosifera-* (r.).

† See § 431.1.

‡ This class is probably formed directly from compounded nouns, as is certainly the case with remiga- 'row,' from remig- 'rower;' and that from rema- (m.) 'oar,' and ag- 'put in motion.' Velifica- (r.) 'make sail,' from velifico- 'making sail;' and that from velo- (n.) 'sail' and

DERIVATION OF VERBS.

742. 2 Some verbs in *a* from substantives signify to supply with the thing which the substantive denotes:* thus there is

A subst. tăbŭla- *plank,* and a verb contăbŭla- *cover with planks.*
" tigno- (n.) *beam,* and a verb contigna- *furnish with beams.*
" calceo- *shoe,* and a verb calcea- *shoe.*

743 Such verbs are often found only as perfect participles in *to:* thus,

From barba- *beard,* barbāto- *bearded.*
" ŏcŭlo- *eye,* ŏcŭlāto- *provided with eyes.*
" auri- *ear,* aurīto- *provided with ears.*
" cornu- *horn,* cornūto- *horned.*
" aes- *bronze,* aerāto- *armed with bronze.*
" denti- or dent- *tooth,* dentāto- *armed with teeth.*
" cord- *heart,* bŭnŏ cordāto- *good-hearted, i. e.,* in the Roman sense of the phrase, *clever.*

744 Certain reflective verbs from substantives also signify to provide oneself with what the substantive denotes. The verbs in question belong chiefly to military phraseology:

From ăqua- *water,* ăqua- (r.) *fetch water.*
" frūmento- (n.) *corn,* frūmenta- (r.) *fetch corn, forage.*
" pābŭlo- (n.) *fodder,* pābŭla- (r.) *fetch fodder, forage.*
" mătĕria- *timber,* mătĕria- (r.) *fetch timber.*
" ligno- *firewood,* ligna- (r.) *fetch firewood.*
" praeda- *booty,* praeda- (r.) *go plundering.*
" pisci- *fish,* pisca- (r.) *fish.*

744. 1 Again, certain reflective verbs from adjectives signify to regard as what the adjective denotes: as,

From grăui- *heavy,* grăua- (r.) *regard as heavy, be unwilling to bear.*
" digno- *worthy,* digna- (r.) *deem worthy of one, deign.*

---

fac- 'make.' *Vocifera-* (r.) 'raise one's voice,' from an obsolete adj. *uocifero-* 'raising the voice;' and that from *uoc-* 'voice' and *fer-* 'raise.' *Opitula-* (r.) 'bring help,' from an obsolete adj. *opitulo-* 'bringing help;' and that from *op-* 'help' and *tol-* 'bring.'

* The English language agrees in this use of substantives as verbs. Thus we use the phrases, to *shoe* a horse, to *water* a horse, to *horse* a coach.

From indigno- *unworthy*, indigna- (r.) *deem unworthy of one.*
" misĕro- *wretched*, miseĕra- (r.) *regard as wretched, pity.*

745 Verbs called frequentative, and they are very numerous, are formed by adding the suffix *tă* to the simple verb : as,

Ag- *put in motion*, ăgĭta- *put in constant motion.*
Quaer- *seek*, quaerīta- *seek perseveringly.*
Clāma- *cry out*, clāmĭta- *keep crying out.*
Mīna- (r.) *threaten*, mĭnĭta- (r.) *keep threatening.*
Flu- *flow*, fluĭta- *keep flowing.*
Sequ- (r.) *follow*, secta- (r.) *be in the habit of following.**

746 As this suffix *ĭta* is very similar to *tto*, the suffix of perfect participles, similar contractions and alterations commonly take place : thus,

Merg- *sink*, participle merso-, frequentative mersa-.†
Trăh- *draw*, participle tracto-, frequentative tracta-.
Pĕl- *drive*, participle pulso-, frequentative pulsa-.†

747 Some frequentatives are formed by the suffix *ĭtā* : as, from scrib- *write*, scriptĭta- ; from lĕg- *read*, lectĭta- ; from uīu- *live*, uictĭta-.

748 Many frequentatives have superseded the simple verb : thus, gus-ta- *taste* was formed from an obsolete verb gŭs- *taste*, which is also the root of the substantive gus-tu- *taste* ; ĭmĭta- (r.) *copy* was formed from an obsolete verb Ĭma- (r.), which is also the root of the substantive Ĭmā-gŏn- *likeness* ; pōta- *drink to excess*, was formed from an obsolete verb po- *drink*, which is also the root of the participle pōto- *drunk*, and of the substantive pō-cŭlo- (n.) *drinking-cup.*

749 A few verbs form, what are at once diminutives and frequentatives, with the suffix *ka* : as, fŏd- *dig*, fŏdĭca- *keep digging or nudging* ; uĕl- *pull*, uellĭca- *keep plucking.*

750 A few diminutive verbs are formed with a suffix *illa* or *tilla* : as, fŏue- *warm*, fōcilla- *cherish* ; scrib- *write*, conscribilla- *scribble over* ; sorbo- *suck*, sorbilla- *suck a drop or two* ; căn- *sing*, can-

---

* The so-called frequentatives in cĭna- (r.), as sermo-cĭna- (r.) 'converse,' patro-cĭna- (r.) 'act the patron,' uati-cĭna- (r.) 'act the prophet,' are probably formed upon the same principle from the verb can- 'sing,' just as medita- (r.) is at one time applied to music, at another to any repeated act.

† But the frequentatives mersa-, pulsa- are used by the old writers.

tilla- *wartle.* Ventīla- *fan,* from the subst. uento- *wind,* and ustūla- *singe,* from the verb ūs- or ūr- *burn,* are also diminutives.*

751 A few imitative verbs are formed from nouns, with a suffix in *issa:* as, from pătĕr- *father,* pātrissa- *take after one's father;* from Graeco- *a Greek,* Graecissa- *be in the Greek fashion.*†

752 Inceptive verbs are formed from verbs, substantives and adjectives, with the suffix *esc*‡ or *isc:* as,

  From ferv- *boil,* ferv-esc- or ferv-isc- *begin to boil.*
   „ [sĕn- *an old man*], sĕn-esc- *grow old.*
   „ lūc- *light,* lūcisc- or lūcesc- *get light.*

752.1 If the substantive or adjective end in *o* or *a,* the *e* of *esc* is sometimes omitted, and the vowel *a* prevails: as, from

  Puĕro- *a boy,* rĕ-puĕra-sc- *become a boy again.*
  Intĕgĕro- or -a- *whole,* rĕd-intĕgra-sc- *become whole again.*

753 But there are exceptions both ways, those verbs taking an *a* which are not entitled to it, and those which should have it dropping it: as,

  From mātūro- or -a- *ripe,* mātūresc- *ripen.*
   „ uĕtŭs- *old,* uĕtĕrasc- *become old.*

754 The suffix *ess* is added to a few verbs in *i* without any marked change of meaning: thus,

  From căpi- *take* is formed căpess- *take.*
   „ [lăci- obs. *draw*] „ lăcess- *provoke.*
   „ [arci- obs. *call to one*] „ arcess- *send for.*§

755 A few verbs, called desiderative, are formed from verbs with a suffix *tŭri,* which is liable to the same changes as the participial suffix *to:* thus,

---

* Ramshorn erroneously treats as diminutival verbs *exula-, iacula-* (r.), *opitula-* (r.), *uigila-, strangula-,* the last of which is probably formed from an obsolete subst. *strangula-* 'a halter,' corresponding to the Greek στραγγαλη-.

† These verbs are formed after the Greek verbs in ιζ: as, Μηδιζω. Indeed the later Latin writers use the *s* instead of ss, and write *patris-are.*

‡ In Greek σκ or ισκ.

§ *Petess-* 'seek' is formed in this way from the obsolete form *peti-* 'seek,' which is also the root of *petiui, petitus, petitor.*

From ĕm- *buy*, emptūri- *desire to buy*.
,, ĕd- *eat*, ĕsūri- *be hungry*.
,, păr- or pări- *bring forth*, partūri- *be in labour*.

So Sullătūri- *desire to play Sulla*, implies such a verb as Sulla-(r.) *play Sulla*. (See § 522.)

756. Compounds of făo- or făci- and fī- are made with prefixes commonly supposed to be verbs : as,

From tĕpe- *be warm*, tĕpĕfăc-* or tĕpĕfăci- *make warm*, tĕpĕfī- *become warm*.
,, lĭque- *melt*, lĭquĕfăo- or lĭquĕfăci- *melt, cause to melt*, lĭquĕfī- *melt, become melted*.

757. The compound verbs formed by prefixed prepositions are very numerous. (See prepositions in the Syntax.)

758. The verbs so compounded often undergo certain changes of the vowel : thus, ă frequently becomes ĭ before one consonant, ĕ before two consonants : thus,

From sĭstŭ- *set up*, is formed constĭtŭ- *establish*.
,, căd- *fall*, ,, occĭd- *set or die*.
,, săli- *leap*, ,, insĭli- *leap upon*.
,, căp- or căpi- *take*, ,, accĭp- or accĭpi- *receive*, and accepto- *received*.
,, iăo- or iăci- *throw*, ,, cŏnĭc- or cŏnĭci-† *hurl*, and conlecto- *hurled*.

But the compounds of căue- *beware*, măne- *wait*, trăh- *draw*, ămă- love, remain unaltered.

759. Again, ĕ generally becomes ĭ before a single consonant : as,

From sĕde- *sit*, assĭde- *sit near*.
,, rĕg- *make straight*, dirĭg- *guide*.
,, tĕne- *keep*, abstĭne- *keep away*.

But the compounds of pĕt- *go or seek*, tĕg- *cover*, tĕr- *rub*, gĕr- *wear or carry*, remain unaltered.

760. The diphthong *ae* becomes ī, and *au* becomes o or u : thus,

From caed- *cut*, occīd- *kill*.
,, laed- *strike*, illīd- *dash against*.

* In these words the vowel *e* before *f* is seldom long except in the older poets.
† Commonly written *confic-* or *confici-*.

From quaer- *seek*, exquir- *seek out*.
",, claud- or clūd-* *shut*, reclūd- *open*.
",, plaud- *clap* (the hands), explōd- *drive off* (the stage by clapping the hands).†

But the compounds of haere- *stick* retain the diphthong. Generally for the changes in compound verbs see § 555. 2, &c.

A few compound verbs are formed with a prefixed particle: thus,

From nē *not* and sci- *know*, nesci- *know not*.
",, nē *not* and qui- *be able*, nēqui- *be unable*.
",, nē *not* and uŏl- *wish*, nēuŏl- or nōl- *be unwilling*.
",, mălē *ill* and dīc- *speak*, mălēdīc- *abuse*.
",, bĕnē *well* and făc- *do*, bĕnēfăc- *do a kindness*.
",, măgē *more* and uŏl- *wish*, māuŏl- or māl- *prefer*.
",, săt *enough* and ăg- *do*, sătăg- *have enough to do*.

The negative *in* appears never to be prefixed to verbs‡, except to the participles, especially those in *to*, and even then the compound participle commonly becomes an adjective; except also the verbals in *tu*, which occur only as ablatives, as iniussu- *without orders*, incultu- *without cultivation*.

Docto- *taught*, indocto- *unlearned*.
Lōto- *washed*, illōto- *unwashed*.
Scienti- *knowing*, inscienti- *not knowing*.
Dīcenti- *speaking*, indīcenti- *not speaking*.

Many of these participles in *to* with *in* prefixed are to be translated by *not to be ——ed*: as,

uicto- *conquered*, inuicto- *invincible*.
menso- *measured*, immenso- *immeasurable*.
penso- *weighed*, impenso- *too enormous to be weighed*.

* Probably contracted from such a form as clăuid-. Compare the Greek substantive κλειϜιδ-, Latin clāui-, and *pseudo gauisus*.

† Corresponding in effect to the English 'hooting off, hissing off.'

‡ Hence it is probably an error to derive ignosc- 'pardon' from in 'not' and gnasc- 'take cognizance.' See § 1308. 2.

PARTICLES.

704. This term includes those secondary parts of speech which have little or no variety of form, and are called adverbs, prepositions, conjunctions and interjections.

705. It is not always possible to draw the line between these, as the same word may be at one time an adverb, at another a preposition; or again at one time an adverb, at another a conjunction. Thus, ante *before* or *formerly* may be either adverb or preposition; and simul *at the same time* or *as soon as* may be either an adverb or a conjunction.

766. A large number of the particles must be treated individually to show their origin. In a grammar, however, it is out of place to do more than exhibit those suffixes which apply to whole classes.

ADVERBS.

767. Adverbs are formed in Latin from adjectives and substantives, including pronouns, and also from verbs.

768. From adjectives in *o* or *a* are commonly formed adverbs in *ē*: as, from the adjective lāto- or -a- *wide*, the adverb lātē *widely*; from the adjective pĕrĭcŭlōso- or -a- *dangerous*, the adverb pĕrĭcŭlōsē *dangerously*.

769. From participles in *o* or *a*, used as adjectives, are formed in like manner adverbs in *ē*: as, from docto- *learned*, the adverb doctē *learnedly*; from ornāto- *dressed*, the adverb ornātē *with ornament*; from doctissimo- *most learned*, the adverb doctissimē *most learnedly*.

770. But mălo- *bad*, and bŏno- (old form bĕno-) *good*, form their adverbs, mălĕ *ill*, and bĕnĕ *well*, with a short *ĕ*. Infernĕ *below*, and supernĕ *above* also occur with a short *ĕ*. So also rĭtĕ *duly* has a short *ĕ*, though only a shortened form of ritē.

771. Some adjectives and participles in *o* or *a* form adverbs in *ō*:[*]

---

[*] In some cases this termination is the ablative of the noun; in others it probably corresponds to the Greek adverbs in ως, from adjectives of the same form. Thus, even in Greek, οὕτως and οὕτω 'thus,' ἀφνως and ἀφνω 'suddenly,' coexist.

as, from rāro- or -a- *scattered*, an adverb rārō *seldom*; from tūto- or -a- *safe*, an adverb tūtō *safely*, and tūtissŭmō *most safely*.

772. But cĭto- or -a- *quick* forms its adverb cĭtō *quickly* with ŏ.*

773. From adjectives and participles in *i* or a consonant are formed adverbs in tĕr or ĭtĕr: as,

    From molli- *soft*, the adverb mollĭtĕr *softly*.
      „ cĕlĕri- *swift*, cĕlĕrĭtĕr *swiftly*.
      „ fĕlĭci- or fĕlĭco- *fortunate*, fĕlĭcĭtĕr *fortunately*.
      „ mĕmŏr- *mindful*, mĕmŏrĭtĕr *from memory*.

774. If the adjective or participle end in *ti* or *t*, one *t* is omitted: thus, from ămanti- or ămant- *loving* is formed the adverb ămantĕr *lovingly*.

775. As adjectives in *o* or *a* sometimes coexist with adjectives in *i*, so adverbs in ĭtĕr or ĕtĕr are sometimes found in connexion with adjectives in *o* or *a*: as,

    From dūro- or -a- *hard*, the adverbs dūrē and dūrĭtĕr *severely*.
      „ largo- or -a- *bountiful*, the adverb largĭtĕr *bountifully*.†

776. Many adjectives, particularly comparatives, use their neuter singular as an adverb: thus,

    From făcĭli- *easy*, the adverb făcĭlē *easily*.
      „ multo- or -a- *much*, the adverb multum *much*.
      „ doctiŏr- *more learned*, the adverb doctiŭs *more learnedly*.‡

776.1 The neuter comparative should end in iŭs (= ios), as just seen; but in a few words a shorter form is produced by the omission of one of the vowels; thus without the *i* we have mĭnŭs (for mĭnĭŭs) *less*, plŭs (for ple-iŭs§) *more*; and without the *u*, măgĭs (for

---

* I'ero 'in truth,' sero 'late,' postremo 'at last,' have always a long *o* in the best writers. It is only in the late writers, such as Martial and Statius, that these words are used with a short *o*. Even *cito* has a long *o* in the old writers, as *Ter. And.* III. 1. 16, and elsewhere.

† Observe the same irregularity in the formation of the verb *largi-* (r.) 'lavish.' *Aliter* 'otherwise,' like *alibi* 'elsewhere,' is formed from the obsolete pronoun *ali-*, whence the nominatives *alis* and *alid*.

‡ The poets use adverbs of this form more freely than the prose writers, and even in the plural; as Virgil, *acerba tuens*, *crebra ferit*.

§ Comp. πλειω and πλεον (for πλε-ιον).

māgiūs) *more*, nimis *too much*, satis *enough*.* So priset for prius *before* enters into the formation of the adjective pris-tīno- *former*.

777   From adjectives and substantives are formed adverbs in *tŭs* or *tūs*†: thus we deduce from

   antiquo- *old*, antiquitūs *from of old*.
   caelo- *heaven*, caelitūs *from heaven*.
   diuino- *divine*, diuinitūs *from a divine source*.
   fundo- *bottom*, funditūs *from the foundation*.
   radio- *root*, radicitūs *from the roots*.
   publico- sb. n. *public money*, publicitūs *at the public cost*.

778   A few adjectives form adverbs with a suffix pĕr, denoting *time*: as, from nŏuo- or -a- *new*, nūpĕr *lately*. So also pĕrumpĕr and paulispĕr *for a little while*, tantispĕr *so long*, quantispĕr *as long as*, sempĕr§ *always*.

778.1   The adverbs of numerals have already been given in § 252, last column.

779   Adjectives and substantives form adverbs in *tim* with the sense of *one at a time* or *one by one*: thus, from the adj. singŭlo- or -a- *one at a time*, the adverb singŭlātim *or* singillātim *or* singultim *one at a time*; from paulo- (n.) *little*, paulātim *little by little*; from ulro- *man*, ulritim *man by man*; from tribu- *tribe*, tribūtim *tribe by tribe*; from grĕg- *flock*, grĕgātim *flock by flock*; from grădu- *step*, grădātim *step by step*.‖

780   From verbs also are formed adverbs in *tim*: as,
   From sta- *stand*, statim *constantly*, statim *immediately*.

* For the meaning of *nimis* compare the use of the comparative, § 1155.4, &c. *Satis* literally signifies ' rather full' (see § 1155.7).

† To this corresponds the Greek τρὶν (for πριον) 'before.' So also πλεω for πλειον. Πριν has more than once a long vowel in Homer.

‡ This termination corresponds in meaning to the suffix of the old Greek genitive θεν: as, ουρανοθεν 'from heaven.' Indeed the forms also are identical; for the θ must necessarily lose its aspirate in Latin, and the final syllable εν of the Greek would be as in Latin: compare τυπτομεν, scribimus. The corresponding Sanscrit suffix is *tās*.

§ The first syllable of *semper* is probably the same root which is spoken of in the note to § 263; so that it would signify 'one unbroken time.'

‖ Compare the irregularities of *paulatim*, *ulritim*, *gregatim* &c. with the irregularities in the formation of adjectives, §§ 227-229. This suffix *tim* is identical with the Greek δον: as, from αγελα- 'herd,' αγελαδον 'by herds.'

From prae *before* and sěr- *put*, praesertim *especially*.
,, caed- *cut*, caesim[*] *by cutting*.
,, pung- *pierce*, punctim *by piercing*.[†]

From substantives and verbs are formed a few adverbs in *ŭs:* thus from

Cŏn *together* and mănu- *hand*, cŏ-mĭn-ŭs *hand to hand*.
Ec *from* and mănu- *hand*, ē-mĭn-ŭs *from a distance*.

So from the verb ten- *stretch*, the adverb tĕnŭs[‡] *stretching;* whence prŏtĭnŭs *forthwith*.[§] And from the verb uort- *turn* the adverb uorsŭs[‖], which has also the form uorsum, corresponding in meaning to the English termination *-wards*.

From substantives and verbs are formed a few adverbs by adding the suffix *am*.[§]

Thus cŏn *together* and ōs- or ŏr- (n.) *mouth* or *face* form an adverb, cōram *face to face*.

The verb pand-[‖] *open* forms an adverb, pălam *openly*.

The verb cēla- *hide* forms an adverb, clam *secretly*.

In analogy with bis *twice* (for duis), we might have expected tris[¶] and quătris, but instead of these we have tĕr and quătĕr, an *s* being commonly rejected after an *r*.

The cases of adjectives and substantives, particularly pronouns, are often used as adverbs: thus the following, sometimes called adverbs, are in origin datives denoting *the time when* or *the place where* &c., hĕri *yesterday*, mănī *in the morning*, lūcī *in the daylight*, dŏmī *at home*, rūrī *in the country*, fŏrīs *out of doors*, multimŏdīs *in many a way*, quŏtannīs *every year*.

The pronominal adverbs in *bi* or *ĭ*, which answer to the ques-

---

[*] The *s* in this word represents the *t*, as it does so often in the perfect participle with verbs in *d*.

[†] This corresponds to the Greek suffix δην added to verbs: as, from γραφ- 'write,' γραβδην 'in writing.'

[‡] These are also prepositions.

[§] There is also a form *tenus* of the same meaning as *tenus*, whence *protenus* 'forthwith.'

[‖] Compare *scand-* 'climb' and *scala-* 'ladder;' *mand-* 'chew' and *mala-* 'jaw;' *sede-* 'sit' and *sella-* 'chair.'

[¶] Compare the Greek τρις, and perhaps τετρακις. For the loss of the *s* compare *linter* 'a boat' for *lintris*, *puer* for *puerus*, *uidebare* for *uidebaris*.

142   ADVERBS.

tion *where* or *when*, and may be seen in the second column of the table in § 300, are probably old datives.

786 Again, the following, sometimes called adverbs, are in origin accusatives:

Dŏmum *home* i. e. *to one's home*, rūs *into the country*, fŏrās *out of doors* i. e. *going out of doors*.

787 The pronominal adverbs in ō, which answer to the question *whither*, and may be seen in the third column of the table § 300, are probably old accusatives which have lost the final *m*.

788 Closely related to the pronominal adverbs in ō are the adverbs in *trō* from prepositions &c.: as,

> Rŏ-trō *backward*.
> Por-rō* *forward*.
> Cĭ-trŏt *towards the speaker*.
> Vl-trŏt *to a distance, forward, voluntarily*.
> In-trō *inwards*.
> Con-trō *towards*.‡

789 Adverbs in ŏ†, chiefly from pronouns, are used with comparative adjectives or comparative adverbs: as,

> Eō māgĭs *so much the more* or *the more*.
> Quō mĭnŭs *by how much the less* or *the less*.
> Hōc ūtĭlĭŭs *to this extent the more usefully*.
> Nihĭlō mĭnŭs *never the less*.

790 The terminations *indĕ*, *in*, and *im*, seen in the fourth column of the table § 300, must be considered as varieties of one suffix, since the compounds deindĕ, exindĕ &c. have also the shortened

---

* *Pŏr* is the old preposition, corresponding to our 'for,' whence comes *por-tro*, *por-ro*, and by contraction *pro*.

† Whence *ultro citroque* 'backwards and forwards,' in which the word 'backwards' is a translation of *citro*. The common derivation of *ultro* 'willingly,' from *vol-* 'wish,' is altogether indefensible.

‡ This word is seen in the compound verb *contro-vort-* 'turn against.' These adverbs in *tro*, though ultimately derived from prepositions, are immediately formed from adjectives, more or less obsolete, in *tero*.

¶ These are commonly held to be ablatives, and supposed to be translated literally when we say *multo maior* 'greater by much.' The Greek too uses πολλῷ μείζων. Still it is possible that they are in reality only the old accusatives in *o*, which have lost their final *m*: as *maior* 'the greater to this degree.'

forms dein, exin, exim* &c. The suffix is strictly dĭt, the n belonging to the pronominal base.

791. The adverbs in *am*, from pronouns, denote *how much*: as, tam *so*, quam *how*, quanquam *however, no matter how, although*, quamvis or quamlĭbet *as much as you please, although*.

792. The adverbs in *um*, chiefly from pronouns, denote the time *when*: as, tum or tuncǂ *then*, (num) or nuncǂ *now*, quom or quum or cum *when*, umquam or unquam (formerly cumquam) *ever*, numquam or nunquam (for ne-umquam) *never*, quondam (for quomdam) *at a certain time* (*past* or *future*), plūrumquĕ *generally*.

793. The adverbs in *dĭ* generally denote the *road along which* any thing is done. A large majority of these are from pronouns, as may be seen in § 300. Other examples are, rectā *in a straight line*, dextrā *along the road on the right*, sĭnistrā *along the road on the left*.

794. Some ablatives of nouns are used as adverbs: thus, ergō∥ *indeed, really, in the matter of*, is the ablative of an old Latin noun, ergo- (n.) *work*; and similarly mŏdō¶ *only* is literally *by measure*, being the ablative of mŏdo- (m.) *measure*. Likewise mānĕ *in the morning*, diū *in the daytime*, noctū or noctĕ *by night*, lūcĕ *in the daylight*, may be considered as ablatives.

795. The adverb quandō, from the relative, and those connected with it, denote *time*: as, quandō** *when*, ăliquandō** *sometime*, quandōcunquĕ *whenever*, quandōquĕ *whenever, some time or other*.

* This is the orthography used in Virgil.

† This suffix corresponds to θεν of εν-θεν, πο-θεν: and indeed the final ν of the suffix θεν disappears at times in Greek, as in ουτω-θε or ουτω-θα for ουτω-θεν.

‡ This *c* is the demonstrative enclitic: see § 289. And if the interrogative enclitic *ne* be added, *ci* is preferred to *c*, as in *nuncine*: see § 293.

§ It is generally held that these are feminine ablatives agreeing with *viā* 'road' understood.

∥ Corresponding to the Greek dative εργῳ 'in reality.'

¶ Whether we are speaking of a very great or a very small quantity, it adds weight to our assertion if we can speak of the quantity as known by measurement. Hence, with small quantities, modo 'by measure' may be translated by 'only.' On the other hand, with great quantities, admodum 'up to the measure' is equivalent to 'full, quite.' Observe that modo in old writers has a long final *o*, as in Ter. And. iv. 1. 6, Plaut. Asin. prol. 5, Aul. ii. 2. 62, Pseud. ii. 3. 23, Poen. i. 2. 7, Lucr. ii. 941 and 1135, Cic. Arat. N. D. ii. 42. 107.

** The later writers shorten the *o* in these two words.

706   The adverb ŭtī or ŭt *how, that, when* (itself connected with the relative), has many adverbs compounded with or derived from it: as, ŭtĭquĕ *anyhow, at least,* ŭtŭt *no matter how,* utcunquĕ *howsoever, whensoever,* neutīquam *or* nŭtīquam (for ne-ŭtĭquam) *in no way.* ŭtĭnam *O that!*

706.1   The adverbs in *us,* from pronouns of relative origin, commonly denote the place *where* or *whither:* as, usquam *any where or to any place,* uspiam *any where or in any place,* nusquam *no where or to no place.*

707   Many adverbs are nouns and prepositions written as one word: thus,

Prŏfectō* *indeed*† is from prō factō *for a thing done.*
Imprīmīs *specially,* from in prīmīs *among the first.*
Illicō *immediately,* from in lŏcō *on the spot.*
Indīēs *every day* (more and more), from in diēs.
Dēnuō *a-fresh,* from dē nŏuō.
Obĭtĕr *in passing* (or in French, *en passant*), from ŏb ĭtĕr *on the road.*
Intĕrim *meanwhile,* from intĕr im‡ *during this.*
Admŏdum *quite,* from ad mŏdum *up to the measure.*

708   Thus the preposition or adverb uorsūs *or* uorsŭs *-wards* is added to a number of adverbs in o, prepositions &c.: as,

Horsum *hitherward,* istorsum *towards your neighbourhood,* illorsum *towards yonder place,* quorsum *in what direction,* aliorsum *in another direction,* aliquŏuorsum *in some direction,* quōquōuorsum *in every direction,* ŭtrōquĕuorsum *in both directions,* aduorsum *towards,* prorsum§ *or* prōsum§ *forwards, downright,* rursum *or* rūsum§ (for reuorsum) *backward, again,* deorsum *downwards,* sursum *or* sūsum *upwards,* intrōuorsum *or* introrsum *inwards,* rĕtrorsum *backwards,* dextrōuorsum *or* dextrorsum *towards the right,* sinistrorsum *towards the left.*∥

* Plautus uses this word with the first syllable long.

† *Indeed* = in-deed is itself a parallel example from our own language; so also *forsooth.*

‡ An old accusative, or perhaps rather dative, of the pronoun i- 'this,' for an older form is *interibi.*

§ *Prosum* is preferred by Plautus, and *rursum* by Virgil. *Prorsus* and *rursus* occur even in Cicero, if we follow the Medicean Ms. ad Fam. xiii. 13. and ix. 9. 3.

∥ Most of these adverbs have also another form ending in *sorsus* instead of *sorsum,* and also in *uersum, uersus.*

799 Thus too prepositions that govern an accusative are attached to the pronominal adverbs in ŏ: as,

Adeŏ *to this* or *that degree, so; in addition to this, moreover.*
Quoăd *to what degree, how far; to what time, how long.*
Adhŭc *to this time, so far, as yet.*

800 The prepositions that govern an ablative are prefixed to the pronominal adverbs in dĕ, or their shortened forms in in (see § 366): as,

Proindĕ* or proin *henceforward, therefore, accordingly, at once then.*
Deindĕ or dein *after this, afterwards.*
Sŭbindĕ *soon after, ever and anon.*
Exindĕ, exin or exim *after this.*
Abhinc *from this time* (reckoning towards the past).
Dehinc *from this time forward, after this.*

801 Thus too the suffix sĕcŭs is added to pronominal and other adverbs in dĕ, or rather to the shortened forms in in: as,

Altrinsĕcŭs *from the other side.*   Extrinsĕcŭs *from without.*
Utrinquăsĕcŭs *from both sides.*   Intrinsĕcŭs *from within.*

802 Thus too the prepositions that govern an accusative are prefixed to pronouns in am or ā, which last also appear to have been corrupted from accusative pronouns in am: as,

Anteā *before this* or *that.*   Praeterquam *besides that....*
Posteā *after this* or *that.*   Sŭperquam *over and above that...*
Intĕreā *in the meanwhile.*   Antehāc *before this.*
Proptĕreā *for this* or *that reason.*   Posthāc *after this.*
Praetĕreā *besides this* or *that.*   Praetĕrhāc *besides this.*
Antĕquam *before that....*   Postillā *since that time, from that time.*
Postquam *after that....*

803 Thus too the preposition tĕnŭs *stretching*, is suffixed to pronominal forms in ā: as,

Eātĕnŭs *to this* or *that extent,*   Istactĕnŭs *so far as to reach your*
  so far.   *neighbourhood.*
Hactĕnŭs *to this extent.*   Quātĕnŭs *to what extent, so far as.*

---

* *Perinde* is only a corruption of *proinde* or rather *por-inde*, and in no way related to the preposition *per*. Indeed the Mss. generally have *proinde* where editions give *perinde*.

L

Aliquātĕnŭs *to some extent.* Quādamtĕnŭs *to a certain extent.*

804 Some so-called adverbs consist of an adjective and substantive written as one word : thus,

Quōmŏdō *how* is from quō mŏdō *in what manner.*
Magnŏpĕrĕ *greatly* is from magno ŏpĕrĕ *with great labour.*
Hŏdĭē, *or rather* hōdiē, *today,* is from hō* dĭē.
Quŏtĭdĭē *every day,* from quŏtĭt dĭē.

805 Nūdiustertiūs, *or rather* nūdiustertiūs, *the day before yesterday,* is for num‡ dius tertiŭs *now the third day.*

806 Some adverbs are formed by the addition of two or more particles : as, ĕtiam *even now, still, also,* from ĕt *even,* and iam *now;* and ĕtiamnum *even now-a-days,* from ĕt, iam, and num.

807 Scilicet, videlicet, ilicet, though called adverbs, are in origin verbs. When literally translated, they signify respectively :

Scilicet§ *one may know, of course.*
Videlicet *one may see, no doubt.*
Ilicet *one may go, it is all over.*

PREPOSITIONS.

808 Prepositions are particles that are prefixed‖ to substantives and verbs, and sometimes to other parts of speech. In their

* The old ablative before the enclitic *e* was added. We should probably pronounce *hodie* as a disyllable, *hŏjee;* or like the Italian *oggi.*

† An old dative case.

‡ The old form which with the enclitic *ce* produced *nunc* 'now.' *Dius* is that nominative of the *u* declension which has an ablative *diu* 'in the daytime.' Further, *dius* is but a monosyllable, just as *dies* often is (see *hodie* above). Hence *nudiustertius* should be pronounced something like *nūjustertius* (*Plaut.* Most. IV. 2, 40).

§ These words are actually employed as verbs. Thus *scilicet,* Plaut. Curc. II. 2, 10, Lucr. II. 468, Sal. Jug. 4; *videlicet,* Plaut. St. IV. 1, 49 and 81, Lucr. I. 210; *ilicet,* Ter. Ph. I. 4, 31. Similarly *licet* 'it is permitted,' became used as a conjunction in the sense of 'though.'

‖ The name preposition itself implies this. But in fact they occasionally follow (more particularly in the older authors); as in *me-cum* 'with me,' *quo-ad* 'to what degree,' *de quo* or *quo de* 'concerning which.' So in English we have *here-in, here-upon, &c.*

original sense they denote the relations of place: as, sŭb *up*, dē *down*, ŏb *towards*.

809. The letter *s* is often added as a prepositional suffix. Thus ăb *by* sometimes becomes abs, aps *or* as; sŭb *up* becomes sus; ŏb *towards*, obs *or* os; ēc *out*, ex; dĭ *different ways*, dĭs; [cĭ, obs., *this*], cĭs; [ŏl, obs., *yon*], uls.

810. The first three of these prepositions, viz. ăb *by or from*, sŭb *up*, ŏb *towards*, take this *s* more particularly in composition with verbs which begin with one of the letters *p*, *c* or *q*, *t*: as,

As-porta- *carry away*	Sus-pend- *hang up*	Os-tend- *stretch towards*.
Abs-cond- *put away*	Sus-cĭp- *take up*	
Abs-tĭne-* *keep away*	Sus-tĭne- *hold up*	

811. Ec *out* takes an *s* before the same consonants, and also before vowels: as,

    Ex-pōs-† *put out*   Ex-cŭr-† *run out*
    Ex-tend- *stretch out*   Ex-ĭm- *take out*.

812. Dĭ *different ways* takes an *s* before the same consonants, and takes *s*, or its substitute *r*, before vowels: as,

    Dis-pōs-† *put in different places*   Dis-ĭo-† *throw different ways*
    Dis-cēd-† *depart*   Dir-ĭm- *disperse*
    Dis-tĭne- *keep apart*.

813. Ec before a verb beginning with an *s* has two forms, as from sălĭ- *leap*, exsĭlĭ- *or* exĭlĭ- *leap up*, which do not differ in sound.‖

814. Dĭs is preferred to dĭ before a verb beginning with *s*, if that *s* be followed by a vowel: as, dis-sŏna- *sound a different note;* but

---

* Abs is found even before nouns in old authors, if a *tenuis* follow: as, abs te 'by you,' abs quivis homine 'by any man you please.'

† This form became obsolete, but was still preserved in the composition of verbs which begin with *f*: as, ec-fer- ' carry out,' ec-fod- ' dig out,' &c. Such at least was the orthography of Plautus, Terence, Cicero and Virgil. The Greek too has ἐκ.

‡ See § 451.1.

§ Commonly written disjĭc- or disjĭcĭ-. For the quantity of the preposition in the compounds of *jacĭ*-, as cōnicĭ-, sŭbicĭ-, see A. Gellius, iv. 17.

‖ XS, i.e. ΧΣ to use the Greek characters, was the symbol originally of the sound *chs;* but as the Romans never used the aspirate X in any other combination of letters, they eventually came to look upon X as representing the sound *cs*, and therefore discarded the superfluous *s*. Hence exsilĭ- may be looked upon as the older form, but representing *ech-sili*-.

not so if that *s* be followed by a consonant, as di-scrīb- *distribute in writing*.

815. The letter *d* is often added as a prepositional suffix. Thus prō *for*, ĭn *in*, rĕ *back*, become severally prōd, ind, rĕd*, as in prōd-ĭ-go *forward*, ind-ĭge- *be in want*, rĕd-ĭ- *go back*, red-d- *put back*, red-dūc- *bring back*, and by assimilation of *d* to the following *l* rellĭgiōn- *religion*, rellĭquiae N. pl. *remains*.

816. The prepositions often lose one of their final letters. Thus ăb becomes ā in the composition of verbs which begin with the letter m : as, ā-mŏve- *move away*. Before the verb fu- *be*, ăb and ā are both found : as, ab-fuit or ā-fuit *he was absent* ; while before the verbs fĕr- *carry*, and fŭg- *fly*, the form au is used : as, au-fĕr- *carry away*, au-fŭg- *fly away*. Similarly ā instead of ăb is used before many nouns beginning with a consonant.

817. In like manner ēc *out* becomes ē before other consonants than *p*, *c* or *q*. *t* : as, ē-bĭb- *drink up*, ē-dūc- *lead out*, &c.

818. Pōr *for* (see § 834), sŭpĕr *upon*, and Intĕr *up* (see § 834), before words beginning with *l*, assimilate the *r* to this *l*, as pollĭce- (r.) *bid beforehand, promise* ; polling-† *lay out* (a corpse) ; sŭpellĕg-† (nom. sŭpellex) and sŭpellectĭli-, strictly adjectives, *laid upon*, and hence as sb. f. *tapestry, furniture* ; intellĕg- *pick up* or *gather* (information), *perceive*.

819. Trans *across* before verbs sometimes takes the form trā : as, trā-dūc- *lead across*, trā-d- *hand over*.

820. Cum *with* before verbs becomes com or cŏn or co : as, cŏm-ĕd- *eat up*, con-cīd- *cut to pieces*, co-ĭ- *go together, meet*.

821. The other changes which prepositions sometimes undergo before verbs may be seen in the tables of perfects and supines, §§ 833-854.

822. From prepositions and two of the pronouns demonstrative are

---

* The preposition *si* 'aside' might have been added to these, as the conjunction *sĕd* 'but' is another form of that word. Sĕdĭtiōn- 'a division of the people,' or 'emeute,' implies the previous existence of a verb *si-d-* 'put apart, separate,' from *da-* 'put' (§ 542), rather than *sed-i-*, a compound of *i-* 'go,' as Madvig would have it (Lat. Gr. § 203), for then the *e* would be short. In old authors other prepositions take this *d* : thus *post, ante, supra, extra*, &c. become *postid, antid, suprad, extrad*, &c. Perhaps *apud* 'near' may be only another form of *ab*, or, as the Greeks wrote it, apo 'by.' This is consistent with the original meaning of *ab*, as may be seen in the Syntax.

† These compounds imply a simple verb *līg-* or *ling-*, corresponding to the Greek root λεγ-, German *lesen*, and our *lay*.

formed adjectives in *tĕro** and *ĕro*; and from these again, prepositions in *tĕr* or *ĕr*, and in *trā* or *rā*. Thus from sŭb *up* is formed the adjective sŭpĕro- *upper*; whence the prepositions sŭpĕr and suprā *above*. So from the obsolete root inf-, or rather ĕnŭf-, *below*, is formed first the adjective infĕro- *lower*, and secondly the preposition infrā *below*. Again, from ĭn *in* is formed first the obsolete adjective intĕro- *inner*, and thence the prepositions intĕr *between*, and intrā *within*, &c. From the obsolete preposition ĭd *again* is deduced a comparatival form ĭtĕrum *again*.†

823 From prepositions and two of the pronouns demonstrative are formed comparatives and superlatives. Thus from præ or prō *before*, a comparative priŏr- *former*, a superlative primo- *first*; from ĭn *in*, a superlative ĭmo- *inmost* or *lowest*; from sŭb *up*, a superlative summo-‡ *uppermost*; from post *after*, postŭmo-§ *last*; from ĕc or ex *out*, extŭmo- *outmost* or *uttermost*; from the obsolete pronominal root ci *this* or *near*, citŭmo-|| *hithermost, nearest*; from an obsolete ol *yon*, ultŭmo-|| *farthest*.

824 Comparatives and superlatives are also formed from the intermediate adjective in *tĕro* or *ĕro*. Thus from post *after* is formed first the adjective postĕro- *after*, and thence a comp. postĕriŏr- and a superl. postrēmo- ; from ex *out*, an adj. extĕro- *outer*, and thence a comp. extĕriŏr-, and superl. extrēmo- ; from dē *down*, an obsolete adj. dētĕro-, and thence a comp. dētĕriŏr-¶ *worse*, and superl. dēterrŭmo-¶ *worst*; from sŭb *up*, an adj. sŭpĕro- *upper*, and thence a comp. sŭpĕriŏr- *higher*, and a superl. sŭprēmo- *highest*, &c.

825 From the simple prepositions and from the adjectives in *tĕro* and *ĕro* are formed other adjectives in *no*; as,

Sŭpīno- *looking upward*, prōno- *looking downward*.

---

* These are in fact comparatives, as may be seen in the Greek πρό-τερο- &c.

† Compare the Welsh *ad*, old German *it* or *ita*, Danish *atter*, Swedish *åter*, all signifying 'again.' See § 1308. 3. a.

‡ For *subimo-* or *supimo-*. In the same way from *sub* 'up,' and *em-* 'take,' is formed the compound *sum-* 'take up.' Indeed the best Mss. more commonly have *summ-*.

§ The vulgar orthography is *posthumo-*, which is grounded upon a ludicrously erroneous derivation from *post humum*.

|| Related respectively to *ho-* 'this,' and *illo-* 'yonder.'

¶ Literally 'lower, lowest;' but they occur only in the sense of value

Sŭperno- *above*, inferno- *below*.
Externo- *without*, interno- *within*.

626 From some of the prepositions are formed adjectives in *ĭcus*. Thus,

Postico- *behind*, as postīcā jānuā *the back gate*.
Antico- *or* antiquo- *preceding* (either in time or value).

627 From some of the prepositional superlatives are formed adjectives in *tǐ* : as,

From summo- *highest*, summāti- *or* summāt- *of the highest rank*.
„ infimo- *lowest*, infūmāti- *or* infūmāt- *of the lowest rank*.

628 Adverbs in *tŭs* (§ 777) are formed from prepositions : as,
Intŭs *from within or within*, subtŭs *under*.

629 For the adverbs in *tro* and *trin* from prepositions, see § 838.

630 The prepositions* in use before substantives are the following. First, before accusatives alone :

ăd *to*	contrā *facing*	praetĕr *beside*
aduorsum *or* aduorsŭs	ergā *towards*	prŏpĕ *near*
towards	infrā *below*	prŏpiŭs *nearer*
antĕ *before*	intĕr *between*	proptĕr *near*
ăpŭd *near*	intrā *within*	proxŭmē *nearest*
circā *round*	iuxtā *near*	sĕcundum *following*
circĭtĕr *about*	ŏb *towards*	sūprā *above*
circum *round*	pĕnĕs *in the hands of*	trans *across*
cĭs *on this side of*	pĕr *through*	[ŭls, obs., *beyond*]
cĭtrā *on this side of*	post *after*	ultrā *beyond*.

631 Secondly, before ablatives alone :

ăb, abs, *or* ā *by or from*	[ăc], ex, *or* ē *out of*
absquē *without*	prae *before*
cum *with*	prō *before*
dē *down from*	sĭnĕ *without*.

632 Thirdly, before an accusative or ablative :

In *in*	subtĕr *under*
sŭb *up or under*	sŭpĕr *upon*.

* Many of these prepositions are common to the Greek language, viz.:
ab = απο.   ec = εκ.   con *or* cum = συν *or* ξυν.
ob = επι.   ante = αντι.   pro = προ.
sub and super = ύπο and ύπερ.   In = εν *or* εις.   post = μετα *or* πεδα?

833. Clam *secretly*, cōram *face to face*, pălam *openly*, sĭmŭl *at the same time*, tĕnŭs *extending*, uorsŭs or uersŭs *towards*, usquĕ *all the way or all the time*, are rather adverbs than prepositions. But see the syntax of prepositions.

833. 1 Some substantives in the ablative followed by genitives partake of the nature of prepositions, as causā *for the sake (of)*, grātiā *for the sake (of)*, and in old Latin ergō *on account (of)*. So instăr *instead (of)*, like its English equivalent, appears to be compounded of In and some substantive signifying 'station.'* This also is followed by a genitive: as, Plăto mihi ūnūs est instăr omnium (*Cic.* Brut. 51. 191) *Plato alone in my eyes is worth the whole lot*.

834 Other prepositions are found in the composition of verbs and adjectives, and therefore called *inseparable* prepositions, viz.:

a. Am† *round*, as, am-būr- *burn round*, *singe*; am-bĕd- *eat round*; and the adj. an-cĭp- or an-cĭpĭt- *two-headed*.

b. An‡ *up*, as ău-bŭla- *send up* (a blast of air). (See § 1308. 1.)

c. Dĭ† or dĭs *different ways*, as, dis-cĕd- *depart*, and from corda-*string*, the adj. dis-cordi- or dis-cord- *of a different note*.

d. Intĕr‖, inseparable prefix, *up*,—a corruption of an obsolete antĕr, and related to In or ău *up* (see two paragraphs above and § 1308. 1), as praetĕr to prae, and proptĕr to prŏpĕ (see § 822). —as intel-lĕg- *pick up* or *gather* (information), *perceive*. (See § 1312. 1.)

e. Pŏr *for* or *forth*, as por-rĭg- *stretch forth*, pol-lĭce- (r.) *bid beforehand*, *promise*; pol-ling- *lay out* (a corpse).

f. Rĕ or rĕd *back*, as, rĕ-pĕll- *drive back*, rĕd-i- *go back*, and the adj. rĕ-dŭc- *returning*.

g. Sē¶ or sēd *aside*, as, sē-pōs- *put aside*, and the adjectives sē-cūro- *unconcerned*, sē-cord- or sō-cord- *spiritless*.

* As if for *in-stāri* or *in-stārĕ*, where *star-* might be an obsolete neuter substantive derived from the verb *sta-*. Compare the German *an-stalt*.

† Related to the Greek αμφι, and German *um*.

‡ Related to the Greek ανα, German *auf*, and English *un*. See 'Transactions of the Philological Society,' for Jan. 27, 1854.

§ Related to the Greek δια, and the German *zer*.

‖ This *inter*, which must be carefully distinguished from *inter* 'between,' corresponds to the German inseparable *unter* in *unternehmen* &c., to our *under* in *undertake*, *understand*, and to *entre* in the French *entretenir* and *entreprise*.

¶ Related to the English *sund-er* and German *sond-ern*.

152 PREPOSITIONS.

     ă. Veh* or uĕ- *away*, as the adj. uĕ-cord- (*heartless*, i.e.) *senseless*, nehēmenti- or nehēment- (*devoid of mind*), *furious*.†

835   The prepositions in modern editions are usually written in immediate connection with verbs, but separately from nouns. The Romans themselves however generally wrote them in connection with nouns also: as, infŏrō *in the forum*.‡

836   Hence if an enclitic be inserted, it commonly follows the noun, not the preposition: as, infŏrōquĕ *and in the forum*, or, to copy the modern mode of printing, inforoque (*Cic.* ad Att. IV. 1. 5).

837   If the preposition be repeated, it has a stronger emphasis, and may be separated from the noun: in cūria inquō fŏrō§ *in the senate-house and in the forum*.

838   It will be convenient to exhibit a table‖ of words derived from prepositions:

   * Related to the German *weg*, and English *away*.

   † To these might be added the military example of *neg* 'after;' viz. *neg-leg-* ('leave behind,') 'neglect.' This prefix is identical with the German *nach*, and consequently with the English *nigh*.

   ‡ This consideration is of importance in the laws of metre.

   § Precisely on the same principle and under the same circumstances Lucretius separates the preposition even from a verb, and writes *disiectis disque supatis* (1. 652).

   ‖ The contents of this table may be usefully compared with similar formations in our own tongue. To the superlatives in *umo* correspond Anglo-Saxon superlatives in *ema*; as, *inn-ema*, *ut-ema*, *for-ma*, *aft-ema*, *mid-ema*, *nid-ema*, *lāt-ema*, *hind-ema*. The Latin language forms several comparatives and superlatives from words already in the comparative form. Nay, in *prim-ores* 'front-(men or teeth)' we see a comparative from a superlative. So the Anglo-Saxon formed superlatives upon superlatives, as *utem-est*, *midem-est*, *lātem-est*, or *form-ost*, *hindm-ost*, *utm-ost* (see Grimm, D. G. III. p. 630). Our own *form-er* agrees accurately with the Latin *prim-or-*; and in *near-er* we have a comparative formed upon a comparative; since *near* itself is but a compression of *nigh-er*, as *next* is of *nigh-est*. Under the head of pronominal prepositions we may compare *beyond*, *before*, *behind*, *beneath*, *beout* (obs.), *afore*, *amid*, *abaft*, *above*.

TABLE OF DERIVATIONS FROM PREPOSITIONS.

Prepositional root.	With s or d	em, tim.	er, ter.	rà, trà.	rò, nò.*	Comparative.	Superlative.	Comparative from ero, ero.	Superlative from ero, ero.
in	ind	[intēro-]	intĕr	intrā	intrō	—	īmo-† intimō-	intĕriŏr-	extrēmo-
(ŝc)	ex	extĕro-	—	extrā	—	—	extimō-	extĕriŏr-	sūprēmo-
sŭb	sŭm	sŭpĕro-	sŭpĕr } sŭbtĕr }	sŭprā	—	—	summo-	sūpĕriŏr-	dētĕrrĭmo-
dĕ	—	[dextĕro-] īnfĕro-	—	īnfrā	—	priŏr-	īnfĭmo- prīmo-	dētĕriŏr- īnfĕriŏr-	—
[inft]	prŏd	—§	—	—	porrō	—	—	—	—
[pōr]	rĕd	[retĕro-]	—	—	rĕtrō	—	—	—	—
cĭ	cis	[citĕro-]	—	citrā	citrō	—	citĭmo-	citĕriŏr-	—
ul	uls	[ultĕro-]	—	ultrā	ultrō	—	ultĭmo-	ultĕriŏr-	—
past	postid	postĕro-	—	—	—	—	postĭmo-	postĕriŏr-**	postrēmo-
antĕ	antĭd¶	—	—	—	—	—	—	—	—
cŏn	—	[contĕro-]	—	contrā††	contrō††	—	—	—	—

* Adverbs in *de* are implied in *indria-secus*, *extrin-secus*.
† 'Inmost or lowest.' Compare with the corresponding words in this column the Greek *ενγατω* (for *εχγατω*), *ὑπατω*, *πρωτω*.
‡ Or perhaps *half-*. Compare the English *south*, the Greek *ἀνα-ψω*, *ἐ-ναψω*, *νάψε*, *νπ-ερ*.
§ This place might be filled by the Greek *πρωτερο-*.
¶ From *he-* 'this,' *ille-* 'yonder.'

¶ For the rest of this column, as formed from other prepositions, see note *, p. 148.
** The word which naturally suggests itself for this place is of doubtful lucidity.
†† As *contra* is to *con* or *cum*, so is the German *wider* to the English *with*.
‡‡ This word is seen in the participial form *contraversus*-*opposed.*

CONJUNCTIONS.

839   The name 'conjunction' is commonly given to several classes of particles which require to be distinguished.

840   *Copulative* conjunctions are those which unite words, phrases or sentences, without making one dependent upon another. Such are ĕt *and*, the enclitic quĕ* *and*, atquĕ *and*; uĕl† *or*, auŧ‡ *or*; together with the interrogative particles ăn *or*, nĕ *or*.

841   There are several words compounded of the above particles which also serve as copulative conjunctions: for instance, nŏquĕ *nor*, nĕuĕ *nor*, siuĕ *or if*.

842   Many of these may be used in pairs: as, ĕt hoc ĕt illŭd *both this and that*, Dīque hŏmĭnesquĕ *both gods and men*, uĕl hoc uĕl illŭd *either this or that*, aut hoc aut illŭd *either this or that*, nĕque hoc nĕque illŭd *neither this nor that*, siue hoc siue illŭd *whether this or that*.

843   Several of the particles above mentioned admit of abbreviation. Thus, atquĕ, uĕl, nĕquĕ, nĕuĕ, siuĕ, may severally become ăc, uĕ, nĕc, neu, seu.

844   Many adverbs, when used in pairs, perform the part of copulative conjunctions: as, nunc hoc nunc illŭd *now this now that*, mŏdo hoc mŏdo illŭd *at one time this at another that*, tum săpiens tum fortis *on the one hand wise on the other brave*.

845   Certain phrases which run in pairs may also perform the office of copulative conjunctions: as, nŏn mŏdo hoc, sĕd ĕtiam illŭd *not only this, but also that*.

846   *Accessary* conjunctions are those which unite an accessary sentence to the main sentence: as antĕquam in the compound sentence, antĕquam lux nōs obprimat, ĕrumpămūs *let us sally out before daylight comes upon us*.

847   Accessary conjunctions are often formed by prefixing a preposition to some derivative from the pronoun quo- : as, quam, quŏd,

---

* The same as the Greek τε. Compare the interrogatives τις and quis.

† Probably an obsolete imperative of the verb uel- '*wish*.'

‡ Probably a corruption of *alterum*, as our *or* is of *other*. Compare the German *oder*.

CONJUNCTIONS.   155

ūt.* Thus there are: post-quam *after that* or *after*, antĕ-quam
   before that or *before*, super-quam *beyond what*, pro-ūt *according as*.

848   Conjunctions of this character perform for a secondary sentence
   the same office which simple prepositions perform for nouns. Thus
   the same idea might be expressed by antĕ lūcem ērumpāmŭs *let us
   sally out before daylight.* Or, again, we may say either post rĕdĭ-
   tum ŭĭus *after his return*, or postquam rĕdĭĭt *after he returned*.

849   Sometimes instead of a preposition, a comparative adjective or
   adverb, or other word of comparison, precedes the relative adverb:
   as, māior quam spērāuĕram *greater than I had hoped*, priusquam
   spērāuĕram *before I had hoped*, ălĭter quam spērāuĕram *differently
   from what I had hoped*, sĭmŭl ut uĭdi eum *the moment I saw him*.

850   Or some phrase may precede: as, eō consĭlio ut tē terrērem
   with the design that I might frighten you or *of frightening you*, hac
   lēge ut nē rĕdeās *with the condition that you shall not return*.

851   Sometimes the relative adverb is doubled: as, ultrā quam ut
   uĭdeam *beyond seeing*, super quam quod dissensĕrant *besides the
   fact that they had disagreed*.

852   Sometimes a derivative from eo- *this* is inserted between the
   preposition and the relative adverb: as, post-eā-quam *after*, pro

---

* This use of *quam, quod, ut* is probably to be explained on the principle on which Horne Tooke has explained the origin of the English conjunction *that*. ' I know that he is returned' may be resolved into two
sentences: ' He is returned, I know that fact.' So, in Greek, λεγω ὁτι
τεθνηκε ' I say this: he is dead.' The *quam, quod, ut* then have, in
the phrases we are speaking of, the signification *this* or *that*; a meaning
which accords with the use of the Greek relative in Homer. The particles in question enable the reader to pause before the words to which
they refer. So long as we have only a preposition and noun, no such
pause is requisite. In the same way the mathematician reads a x b,
a into b; but if we substitute for b a quantity containing more than one
term, a pause is required in reading, and a vinculum in writing: as,
a x b + c, which is read, a into . . . . b + c. Precisely in the same way, if
a long infinitive or subjunctive clause be employed after a Latin verb, it
adds to perspicuity if we insert near the main verb *hoc, ita* or *sic*. Thus
Cicero says, *Velim ita statutum habeas, me tui memoriam cum summa
beniuolentia tenere* (ad F. vi. 2. 1); and again, *Sic habeto, neminem esse
qui me amet quin idem te amet* (ad F. xvi. 4. 4): and Terence (Andr. i.
5. 46) says, *Hoc scio, esse meritam ut memor esses sui*. Lastly, the French
form in the same way their conjunctions *puis-que, sans-que, pour-quoi,
par-ce-que;* the Germans, *in-dem, nach-dem, dar-aus dass;* and the
English, *before that, beyond what, according as*. See ' Penny Cyclo-
pedia,' under the words Article and Conjunction.

† Sometimes the preposition is separated: thus we might say, *Ante
erumpamus quam hae nos obprimat.*

eō ūt *accordingly as*, pro-inde ūt *just as*, proptĕr-eā quŏd *for the reason that*, ex eō quŏd *from the fact that*, in eo ūt *in the act of*.

853. Sometimes the particle atquŏ* *or* āc occupies the place of the relative. Thus we may say simŭl ūt *at the same time that, as soon as*, or simŭl atquŏ *as soon as*; and in familiar Latin, māiŏr atquŏ *greater than*.

854. Sometimes the relative particle is omitted. Thus we may say simŭl ut rĕdiit *or* simul rĕdiit *as soon as he returned*.

855. Very frequently the prepositional word is omitted, and a solitary relative adverb performs the office of a conjunction: as, ūt *how, when, in order that*, quum *when*, quando *when*, quŏd *because*.

856. Or the relative may be accompanied by its noun: as quā-rē, or abbreviated cūr, *why*.

857. Or the relative adverb may have an enclitic particle attached to it: as, quandō-quidem† *since*, quŏn-iam (= quom iam) *since*.

858. These relative adverbs, with the exception of quum and quŏd, are used in direct questions, in which case they no longer perform the office of conjunctions, and may be more conveniently called interrogative adverbs: as, quando *when?* cūr *why?* ūt *how?* quoŭd *how long?* &c.

859. Many conjunctions have correlative adverbs in the main sentence which point to them; and these, in one sense, may also be called conjunctions.‡

Thus, itā *so*, and sīc *so*, answer to ūt *as*; tam *so much*, to quam *as*; tum *then*, to quum *when*; tămĕn *yet*, to quanquam *although*; itā *on the condition*, to sī *if*; sīc *on the condition*, to sī *if*; ĕt *yet*, to sī *if*, &c.

---

* This use of *atque* grows out of the abbreviation of a longer phrase. Thus, *Aliud ego dico atque aliud tu dicis* 'I say one thing and you say another,' easily degenerates into *Aliud ego dico atque tu*. See § 1148. 8.

† Perhaps this word was pronounced as a trisyllable, *quandŏquem*, for there is good reason to believe that *quidem* and *γε* represent the same word, as in *equidem* and *egōγε*. See 'Penny Cyclopædia,' under Terentian metres.

‡ In fact, they are to their conjunctions what the antecedent is to the relative; and the relative itself is the great conjunction of all languages.

INTERJECTIONS.

Interjections are abbreviated sentences which denote a sudden and hasty emotion of the mind. They are commonly inserted in another sentence as a parenthesis.

In respect of form, they are for the most part violently corrupted from what they were; yet a few admit of being analysed. Thus, the formula, *so may such a deity preserve me*, is the source of several.

Ità me Hercūlēs adiŭuet is corrupted into mehercūles, mehercūle, mohercle, meroūle, hercle.

Ità mē Deus Fidiŭs* adiŭuet, into mēdius-fĭdiŭs.

Ità mē Deus Pollux adiŭuet, into ēdēpol, ēpol, *or* pol.

And similarly, from the names of Castor, Iuno, Ceres, there arise the interjections mēcastor *or* ēcastor, ciŭno, ēcēre.

Some of the more common interjections are:

Ah, å, *ah, alas*.

Atāt (for ātātāt) denoting a sudden discovery, *ah ah*.

Aut † *don't, have done*.

Ecce ‡ *behold*.

Ehem, hem, denoting surprise, *ah*, often best translated by repeating the word which caused the surprise.

Eheu, heu *alas*.

Ehŏ§, calling a person's attention to a question, *here, answer me this*, or expressing surprise, *what!*

Eiā *do you hear!*

En, em, hem *behold, see*.

Eu and eugē *good, bravo* (ευ and ευγε, theatrical phrases).

Ha ha *or* ha ha ha *ha ha ha* (laughing).

Hei *or* ei *alas*.

---

* That is, 'the god of Faith,' like the Greek Ζευς ὅρκιος *or* Ζευς πιστιος. Some incorrectly derive this phrase from Διος φίλιος, i. e. *Hercules*.

† Perhaps for *aufer te* 'take yourself away.'

‡ Probably the imperative of an old verb.

§ Probably connected with ho *or* huc 'hither.'

Heus* *harkee, hollos.*
Hui *bless me!* or more strictly a whistle.
Ně *verily,* almost always at the beginning of a sentence, and followed by a pronoun.
Oh, o, denotes emotion, *oh.*
Ohě (ŏ) *avast.*
Păpae *ye gods.*
Pröh†, prō *avert it heaven, oh.*
St *hist, hush.*
Vae *woe,* as vae tǐbi *woe to you.*
Vah has various senses, depending upon the tone in which it is uttered, and must be translated according to the context.

863 There are also several neuter adjectives which are used as exclamations: as, mǎlum *ill betide you, the deuce;* infandum *unutterable thought,* &c.

864 A few unaltered verbs are used almost as interjections: as, ăgĕ *quick,* quaeso *prithee,* ămābo *please,* obsěcro *by all that's sacred,* ǎbi *that'll do.*

865 The preposition pěr with its accusative, in the sense of imploring, belongs to the class of interjections: as, per dextram hanc *by this right hand.* (See § 1350, *j* and *k*.)

---

* Probably the imperative of an old verb. Comp. the root-syllable of *aus-culta-* 'listen.'

† Perhaps for *prohibe* 'keep off.'

SYNTAX.

866 SYNTAX means the connection of words in a sentence. In treating this part of grammar the same order will be followed as in the former part.

NOUNS.

NOMINATIVE CASE.

867 The nominative* case marks the quarter from which an action† proceeds. Hence the nominative is commonly a living being: as,

Vĭpĕrā līmam mŏmordit (*Phaedr.* VIII. 5), *a viper bit a file.*
Aper sĕgĕtes prōculcat (*Ov.* Met. VIII. 290), *the wild boar tramples down the crops.*

868 Instead of living beings, inanimate‡ and abstract nouns are often used as the nominative: as,

Cursum mūtāuit amnis (*Hor.* ad Pis. 67), *the river has changed its course.*
Dies lēnit īrās (*Liv.* II. 45), *time assuages wrath.*
Verbĕrat imbĕr hŭmum (*Virg.* A. IX. 669), *lashes the ground the rain.*

869 The agent may act upon the agent. Hence the nominative is used with reflective verbs: as,

Rhēnus septentriōnāli ōceănō miscētūr (*Tac.* Ger. I.), *the Rhine mixes (itself) with the Northern Ocean.*

870 As the use of the passive§ has grown out of that of the reflective, the nominative is also found with passive verbs: as,

Insŭla adpellātur Monā (*Caes.* B. G. v. 13), *the island is called Mona*—more literally: *calls itself Mona.*

---

* See §§ 44, 48, 368, 381.
† The active verb is probably the oldest form of the verb.
‡ This savours of poetry, but language in its early state is always and of necessity what we call poetical. § See §§ 379–382.

871 As verbs of a static character have generally something of action* mixed up with them, the nominative is used before static verbs: as,

   Tūre cālent āræ (*Virg. A.* I. 421), *with incense glow the altars.*

872 The old construction of verbs of feeling is seen in §§ 700, 889, &c. But a large number of verbs which denote feeling have a nominative like other static verbs: as,

   Cicĕro eum ĕt ămābat et uĕrēbātŭr (*Cic.* ad Q. F. I. 3. 3), *Cicero both loved and respected him.*†

872.1 Impersonal verbs admit a nominative of a neuter pronoun, just as in English we use *it, there.*

   Lūciscĭt hoc (*Ter.* Haut. III. 1. 1), *it is getting light, look.*
   Non te hæc pŭdent ? (*Ter.* Ad. IV. 7. 36), *are you not ashamed of these things ?*

873 Thus the nominative is used before verbs of almost every kind. A very common use of it is before the verb signifying 'be:' as,

   Tu es trīstis (*Ter.* Ad. V. 1. 6), *you are out of spirits.*
   Sŏnectūs ipsast morbūs (*Ter.* Phor. IV. 1. 9), *old age itself is a disease.*

874 Some grammarians are in the habit of treating those sentences which have the verb *be* as the form to which all others are to be reduced. Hence they divide a sentence into three parts:

   The Subject, that of which you speak;
   The Predicate, that which you say of the subject; and
   The Copula, or verb *be*, which unites the subject and predicate.

   Thus, for instance, in the sentence or proposition, *man is an animal, man* is the subject, *animal* the predicate, *is* the copula.

   The subject, according to this system, is the nominative case. When, instead of the verb *be*, another verb is used, they resolve it into some part of the verb *be* and a participle. Thus, *Cicero writes a letter* is resolved into *Cicero is writing a letter,* where *Cicero* is the subject, *writing a letter* the predicate, *is* the copula.

---

   * Thus, he who sleeps often snores or drops his head, or dreams. At any rate, the going to sleep is commonly preceded by certain acts of preparation.
   † The old writers said *Cicero eius uerebatur,* or even *Ciceronem eius uerebatur.* Nay, Cicero himself has *quos non est ueritum* (de Fin. II. 13. 39).

875 The substantive, adjective, or participle that accompanies the verb *be* as a predicate, is in Latin made to agree in case with the subject nominative, and is called the nominative of the predicate.*
Thus,

> Săpientia est rērum dīuīnārum ĕt hūmānārum scientiă (*Cic. de Off.* I. 43. 153), *philosophy is the knowledge of things divine and human.*
> Insignis annūs hiĕmē nĭuŏsă fuit (*Liv.* v. 13), *the year was remarkable for a snowy winter.*
> Viae clausae, Tĭbĕris innāuĭgābĭlis fuit (*Liv.* v. 13), *the roads were blocked up, the Tiber not navigable.*

876 In the same manner other verbs have at times a nominative in the predicate referring to and agreeing in case with the subject nominative (see § 1050) : as,

> Mūnītiōnēs intĕgrae mănēbant (*Caes. B. G.* vi. 32), *the fortifications remained untouched.*
> Haud inrītae cĕcĭdĕrĕ mĭnae (*Liv.* vi. 35), *the threats did not fall without effect.*

876.1 Although a noun substantive or adjective with *ĕs- bĕ* usually constitutes the predicate, the place may be supplied by a descriptive word or phrase of a different form: as, *a*. a genitive or ablative of quality (§§ 928, 1010); *b*. dative of the light in which a thing is regarded (§ 983); *c*. a prepositional phrase; or *d*. an adverb : as,

> *a.* Nēmo ē dĕcem sānā mente est (*Cic. de Leg.* III. 10. 24), *not a man of the ten is of sound mind.*
> Nātūra hūmāna aeui brĕuis est (*Sal. Jug.* 1), *human nature is shortlived.*
> *b.* Cui bŏnō fuit ? (*Cic. p. Rosc. Am.* 30. 84), *to whom was it beneficial ?*
> *c.* Sunt in hŏnōrĕ (*Cic. p. Rosc. Am.* 28. 77), *they are held in honour.*
> *d.* Tūtō nōn ĕris (*Cic. ad Att.* xv. 11), *you will not be safe.*

See also § 1401.

---

* This nominative in the predicate must be referred to what grammarians call 'attraction.' The German language in such cases very properly divests the adjective of all case: *Der Mann ist gut,* not *guter.* See also § 1060.

877 The accusative with the active verb becomes a nominative with the passive: as,

    Rēgem cum appellant, *they salute him as king*—hence

    Rex ab suīs appellātūr (*Caes.* B. G. VII. 4), *he is saluted king by his friends.*

    Cāium Tĕrentium consŭlem creant, *they elect C. Terentius consul*—hence

    Cāius Tĕrentius consul creātŭr (*Liv.* XXII. 35), *C. Terentius is elected consul.*

    Doctiōrem făcĕrĕ ciuītātem, *to make the citizens more learned*—hence

    Disciplīnā doctior factast ciuītās (*Cic.* R. P. II. 19. 34), *by instruction the citizens were made (or became) more learned.*

878 Even when verbs are in the infinitive mood dependent upon another verb, the noun in the predicate referring to the subject nominative will still agree in case with the subject nominative, if no reflective pronoun in the accusative be interposed: as,

    Hŏmĭnes mĭnus crēdŭlī esse coepērunt (*Cic.* de Div. II. 57. 117), *men began to be less credulous.*

    Cum omnĭbus pŏtius quam sōlī pĕrīrĕ nōluĕrunt (*Cic.* in Cat. IV. 7. 14), *they resolved to perish with all rather than to perish alone.*

    Vis formōsă* uĭdērī (*Hor.* Od. IV. 13. 3), *you wish to appear beautiful.*

879 It is only in poetry that we find such phrases as

    Sensit† dēlapsŭs īn hostīs (*Virg.* A. II. 377), *he perceived that he had unwittingly fallen among the enemy.*

880 In the old authors, and in the poets, the nominative is found for the vocative: as,

    Agĕdum Pontĭfex Publĭcus praeī uerbă quĭbus mē prō lēgiōnĭbus dēuŏuĕam (*Liv.* VIII. 9), *come, Priest of the State, repeat (for me to follow) the words in which I am to devote myself for the legions.*

    Almae fīlius Maiae (*Hor.* Od. I. 2. 42), *thou son of fostering Maia.*

---

* The insertion of the pronoun *te* would require a change: thus, *Vis te formosam uideri*, 'you wish yourself to appear beautiful.'

† In prose it must have been *Sensit se delapsum in hostis.*

881 In interjectional phrases the verb is often understood : as,
Eccŏ littĕrae (i.e. mihi trăduntŭr) (*Cic.* ad Att. XIII. 16. 1),
behold, a letter is all at once put into my hand.*

VOCATIVE.

882 The vocative is used in addressing a person : as,
Dīc Marcĕ Tullī (*Cic.* ad Att. VII. 7. 7), *speak, Marcus Tullius.*

882. 1 The interjection *o* is only used in strong exclamations : as,
O Dī bŏnī, quid est in hŏmĭnis uitā diū ? (*Cic.* de Sen. 19. 60),
good heavens, what is there lasting in the life of man ?

882. 2 The vocative, if emphatic, commences the sentence; if not, it is usually preceded by a few words. It is also frequently placed immediately after the pronoun of the second person.

883 In the old writers, and in the poets, the vocative is sometimes used with verbs of the second person, instead of the nominative : as,
Mactĕ† uirtūte estō (*Liv.* IV. 14), *be increased in virtue,* i.e. *go on in thy virtuous course, and heaven bless thee.*
Quō mŏrĭtūrĕ ruis ? (*Virg.* A. x. 811), *whither dost rush to die ?*‡

ACCUSATIVE.

884 The accusative case answers to the question *whither*. Hence motion *to* towns§ or small islands is expressed by the accusative : as,
Căpuam concessit (*Liv.* XXIII. 18), *he withdrew to Capua.*
Nāuĭgābat Sȳrăcūsās (*Cic.* N. D. III. 34. 83), *he was sailing to Syracuse.*

885 With the names of countries the preposition *in* is usually employed.‖ But the poets use the simple accusative with names of countries, and even other words, after verbs of motion : as,

---

* For the nominative in apposition see below.

† The Romans, losing sight of this being a vocative, retain it in the construction of the infinitive, as, Iubērem macte uirtute esse (*Liv.* II. 12).

‡ For the vocative in apposition, &c., see below.

§ If any phrase be added by apposition to the name of the town, the preposition *in* is required : as, Se contulit Tarquinios in urbem Etruriae florentissimam (*Cic.* R. P. II. 19. 34). Peruenit in oppidum Cirtam (*Sal.* Jug. 102). See also Sal. Jug. 75.

‖ Thus, *Tarentum in Italiam uenit*, 'he came to Tarentum in Italy.'

Italiam fātō profŭgus Lāuīnăquĕ uēnit Littŏrĕ (*Virg. A.* 1. 2),
to Italia, by fate an outcast, and to the Lavine beach he came.

886 The accusatives dŏmum, rūs, fŏrās, uēnum, and in the old writers infĭtiās, mălam rem, are used after verbs of motion : as,

Dŏmum rĕuortĕrĕ (*Cic.* Tusc. v. 37. 107), *they returned home.*
Rūs ībō (*Ter.* E. 11. 1. 10), *I shall go into the country.*
Ecfūgī fŏrās (*Ter.* E. v. 4. 23), *I escaped into the street.*
Dărĕ uēnum (*Liv.* xxiv. 47. 6), literally *to put in the window (for sale)*—hence *to sell.*
Infĭtiās ībit (*Ter.* Ad. iii. 2. 41), *he will have recourse to subterfuges.**
Mălam rem hinc ībis ? (*Ter.* E. iii. 3. 30), *will you go and be hanged ?*

887 The verbal substantives in *tu* (called supines) are used in the accusative after verbs of motion (see also § 1299) : as,

Eō pābŭlātum uĕnient (*Caes.* B. G. vii. 18), *they will come here to get fodder.*
In eam spem ērectă cīuĭtās ĕrat, dēbellātum īrī (*Liv.* xxix. 14), *the citizens had been encouraged to hope that they were going to finish the war.*

888 After active verbs the object to which the action is directed is put in the accusative case : as,

Dŏmĭnus seruom uerbĕrāuit, *the master flogged the slave.*

889 The impersonal verbs of feeling have the accusative of the person who suffers that feeling : viz.

Mē mĭsĕret ĕiūs, et pĭget ;
Pŭdet taedetque ac paenĭtet : as,

Eōs infāmiae suae non pŭdet (*Cic.* i. Verr. 12. 35), *they are not ashamed of their infamy.*

890 So also certain other impersonals take an accusative of the person who suffers : viz.

Mē uel tē iŭuat dēcetquĕ,
Tum praetĕrit fŭgit lătetquĕ,
Fallīt ŏportet dēdĕcetquĕ : as,

---
* The usual translation is 'deny ;' but this is inconsistent with such a passage as *Liv.* vi. 40. 4 : *Neque nego neque infitias eo.*

Nēmĭnem uostrum praetĕrit (*Cic.* II. Verr. III. 5, 11), *it escapes no one among you.*

891   Many reflective verbs, called transitive deponents, take an accusative :* as,

Natūram sĕquĭt (*Cic.* de Off. I. 28. 100), *to follow nature.*

892   The so-called perfect participles are used, particularly by the poets, like those of reflective or deponent verbs, and so take an accusative case : as,

Membrā sŭb arbŭto Strătŭs (*Hor.* Od. I. 1. 21), *having spread his limbs under an arbute tree.*

Aduersum fĕmur trăgŭlă ictŭs‡ (*Liv.* XXI. 7), *wounded in the front of the thigh with a tragle.*

893   Similarly, some verbs, which are commonly intransitive, are occasionally used (by the poets more particularly) with an accusative: as,

Ingrāti ănĭmī crīmĕn horreo (*Cic.* ad Att. IX. 2 A. 2), *I shudder at the charge of ingratitude.*

Meum cāsum dōluĕrunt (*Cic.* p. Sest. 69. 145), *they lamented my misfortune.*

894   Some verbs, commonly intransitive, take an accusative of a noun related to the verb in form or meaning (called the *cognate accusative*), often in order to attach thereto an adjective : as,

Mirum sŏmniaui sŏmnium (*Plaut.* Rud. III, 1. 5), *I have dreamed a wonderful dream.*

Amānti hero qui sĕruitutem sĕruit (*Plaut.* Aul. IV. 1. 6), *he who is in the service of a master that is in love.*

Alium cursum petĭuit (*Cic.* ad Att. III. 8. 2), *he went another route.*

895   Similarly, the verbs of *smelling* and *taste*, and a few others, take an accusative which defines the nature : as,

Piscĭs ĭpsum mărĕ săpĭt (*Sen.* Q. N. III. 18), *the fish tastes of the very sea.*

---

* This and some of the following sections have been anticipated. See §§ 400 to 404. But the repetition was necessary for completeness.

† The compound *obsequ-* (v.) 'follow the wishes of any one, oblige,' requires a dative of the person obliged, agreeing thus with the Greek construction of the allied word ἕπ-ομαι (Aorist ἑ-σπ-ομην).

‡ *Ictus*, 'having it wounded.'

Olet peregrinum (*Cic. de Or.* III. 12. 44), *it has a foreign smell.*
Redolet antiquitatem (*Cic. Brut.* 21. 82), *it savours of antiquity.*

896   Verbs of *making, creating, electing,* have an accusative of the new condition or office (called the *factitive accusative*), besides the accusative of the object; as,

Me hebetem molestiae reddiderunt (*Cic. ad Att.* IX. 17), *for myself, troubles have made me dull of feeling.*

Recta prava faciunt (*Ter. Ph.* v. 2. 6), *they make straight things crooked.*

Ancum Marcium regem populus creauit* (*Liv.* I. 32), *the citizens elected Ancus Marcius king.*

897   So also verbs of *calling, thinking†, showing, seeing,* take two accusatives; as,

Octauium sui Caesarem salutabant (*Cic. ad Att.* XIV. 12. 2), *Octavius his own friends saluted as Cæsar.*

Socrates totius mundi se incolam et ciuem arbitrabatur (*Cic. Tusc.* v. 37. 108), *Socrates thought himself an inhabitant and citizen of the universe.*

Gratum me praebeo (*Cic. p. Planc.* 38. 91), *I show myself grateful.*

898   The verbs doce- *teach,* cela- *hide, keep in the dark,* may have two accusatives, one of the thing, one of the person: as,

Quid te litteras doceam? (*Cic. in Pis.* 30. 73), *what, am I to teach you your letters?*

Non te celaui sermonem Ampi (*Cic. ad Fam.* II. 16. 3), *I did not conceal from you the conversation with Ampius.*‡

899   With the passives of these verbs, the accusative of the person becomes the nominative, and the thing taught or concealed may be in the accusative: as,

---

* There is a sort of *motion to* in this construction: 'They put him into the office.' A German indeed would insert the preposition signifying 'to:' as, *Sie wählen ihn zum Führer,* 'they choose him leader.'

† With verbs of thinking the ablatives *numero* and *loco,* and the preposition *pro,* are also used: as, *in numero hostium eum habeo, in loco hostis habeo, pro hoste habeo.*

‡ These two verbs are also used with *de* of the matter referred to, or with an ablative alone of the means employed: as, *celare* or *docere de aliqua re, docere fidibus.*

Călăbăr (*Cic.* in Rull. II. 5. 12), *I was kept in the dark.*
Nosne hōc celatos tămdiu ? (*Ter.* Hea. IV. 4. 23), *to think that we, of all people, should have been kept in the dark about this so long.*
Dulcis doctă mŏdōs (*Hor.* Od. III. 9. 10), *taught sweet measures.*

900 Some transitive verbs of motion, compounded with trans, circum, praetĕr, ăd, may have two accusatives, one of the thing crossed &c., one of what is conveyed across &c.: as,

Ibĕrum cōpĭas trāiscit (*Liv.* XXI. 23), *he threw his forces over the Ebro.*
Equĭtătum pontem transdūcit (*Caes.* B. G. II. 10), *he leads the cavalry over the bridge.*
Idem iusiŭrandum ădĭgit Afrănium (*Caes.* B. C. 1. 76), *he compels Afranius to take the same oath.*
Arbĭtrum (alĭquem) ădĭgĕrĕ (*Cic.* Top. 10. 43), *to force (a person) to go before a judge.*

901 The thing crossed, &c. may, with the passive verb, be an accusative :* as,

Belgae Rhēnum transdūcuntŭr (*Caes.* B. G. II. 4), *the Belgae cross the Rhine.*
Scŏpŭlos praeteruectă uĭdētŭr ōrātĭō meă (*Cic.* p. Cael. 21. 51), *my speech seems now to have passed by the rocks.*
Tunc deindĕ cētĕră mandantur iusiŭrandum ădactis (*Sen.* ep. 95, p. 602 C.), *then and not till then the other duties are intrusted to them when they have been sworn.*

902 Many verbs of *asking, begging, demanding,* may have two accusatives, one of the person, the other of the thing : viz.

Rŏga- percontā- (r.) flagita-quĕ,
Posc- rĕposc- interrŏga-quĕ,
Quaes- ĕt ōra- postŭla-quĕ : as,

Pācĕm tē poscĭmŭs omnēs (*Virg.* A. XI. 362), *peace of thee ask we all.*†

---

* Or, so far as *traic-, traunit-* are concerned, in the nominative: as, *Rhodanus traiectus est,* 'the Rhone was crossed.' With the thing conveyed the nominative is required in the passive: as, *exercitus traiectus est.*

† *Pet-* 'beg,' and *quaer-* 'ask,' never take an accusative of the person, but employ a preposition ; the first *ab*, the second *ab, ex* or *de*.

Frūmentum Aeduos flāgitābat (*Caes.* B. G. 1. 16), *he kept demanding corn of the Aedui.*

903 The thing asked with the passive verb may be an accusative: as,

Scītō mē nōn ēmē rŏgātum sententiam (*Cic.* ad Att. 1. 13. 2), *you must know I was not asked my opinion.*

904 Many verbs which are originally intransitive[*] become transitive when compounded: as, from i- *go* is formed co-i- *go together* or *meet*, and hence

Coīre sŏciĕtātem (*Cic.* Phil. II. 10. 24), *to form a partnership.*[†]

So, from uersā-rī *to turn* is formed ā-uersā-rī *to turn away (in horror)*: and hence,

Fīlium āuersātūs (*Liv.* VIII. 7), *turning away in horror from his son.*

Āuersātur scĕlūs (*Curt.* VI. 7), *he turns away in horror from the (proposed) crime.*

905 Some transitive verbs, when compounded, slightly change their meaning, and thus have a changed construction: as, from sparg-[‡] *scatter, sprinkle,* spargĕre āquam *to sprinkle water;* but conspergĕre[§] ălĭquem āquā *to besprinkle any one with water.*

906 Hence some compound verbs have a double construction[||], one derived from the simple verb, one from the changed meaning of the compound, viz.

Adsperg- ĕt Insperg- indu-ō-quĕ,
Exu- circúmda- inpertī-ō-quĕ,
Addĕ circumfūd- insĕr-ō-quĕ.

907 Abstract nouns from verbs occasionally follow the construction of the verb, and take an accusative: as,

Dŏmum rĕdĭtiōnis spē sublātā (*Caes.* B. G. 1. 5), *the hope of returning home being taken away.*

Quid tibi hanc curātiost rem ? (*Plaut.* Am. I. 3. 21), *what business have you to trouble yourself about this matter ?*

---

* See § 403.

† Hence in the passive *societas coītur*, 'a partnership is formed.'

‡ Only the poets, and their prose imitators, use *sparg-* in the sense of 'besprinkle.'

§ The same difference exists between *spu-* and *conspu-*, between *ser-* and *conser-* or *obser-*.

|| See § 404.

Quid tibi istunc tactio est? (*Plaut.* Cas. II. 6. 54) *what business have you to touch that person?*

908 The adjectives propior- and proxumo-, and the adverbs propius and proxume, from the preposition propē, sometimes, like that preposition, take an accusative (as well as a dative): as,

Exercitum hăbērē quam proxŭme hostem (*Cic.* ad Att. VI. 5. 3), *to keep the army as near as possible to the enemy.*

Lăcōnĭcŭs ăger proxĭmus fĭnem eōrum est (*Liv.* XXXV. 27), *the territory of the Lacones is nearest to their frontier.*

909 The neuters of pronouns and of adjectives or substantives which denote quantity are often used in the accusative where other nouns in the accusative would be rare, or even inadmissible. In these cases the English language often requires the insertion of a preposition:

Id tĭbi suscensui (*Plaut.* Pers. III. 3. 26), *it was at this I took offence.*

Vnum omnes stŭdētis (*Cic.* Phil. VI. 7. 18), *you are all eager for one object.*

Cētĕra assentior Crassō (*Cic.* de Or. I. 9. 35), *as to the other points I agree with Crassus.*

Iam hoc ăliud est quod gaudeamus (*Ter.* E. V. 8. 11), *then again we have this other matter to rejoice at.*

Id ŏpĕram do (*Ter.* And. I. 1. 130), *I am labouring at this.*

Vtrumquē laetŏr (*Cic.* ad Fam. VII. 1. 1), *I am delighted at both things.*

Quid lăcrŭmās? (*Ter.* Ad. IV. 5. 45) *what are you crying for?*

Idne estis auctorēs mihi? (*Ter.* Ad. V. 8. 16) *is this what you recommend to me?*

Bĕnĭfĭcio isto nihĭl ūtĭtŭr (*Cic.* in Rull. II. 23. 61), *that advantage you offer he makes no use of.*

Ea quae ab nātūrā mŏnēmŭr (*Cic.* de Am. 24. 88), *those warnings which we receive from nature.*

And even unconnected with a verb: as,

Id tempŏris (*Cic.* de Fin. V. 1. 1), *at that time.*

Hŏmĭnēs id aetătis* (*Cic.* de Or. I. 47. 207), *men at that age.*

Ego istūc aetătis (*Ter.* Haut. I. 1. 58), *I at your time of life.*

* The phrase *hoc aetatis* was at last corrupted to *hoc aetati*. See Nonius, p. 192; and compare *magi, ueneri, for magis, ueneris.* In *Plaut.* Trin. IV. 2. 63, we should read *hoc aetate,* not *hoc aetate.* Compare also *illuc aetatis qui sit,* Pl. Mil. III. 1. 56; *quid tibi ego aetatis uideor?* Pl. Merc. II. 2. 19.

910. The possessive pronouns in *â* which accompany the impersonal verbs rēfert and intĕrest are in origin accusatives feminine singular. Thus,

> Meâ rĕfert, *it concerns me*, is a corruption of meam rem fert, *it carries with it something belonging to me.* So,
>
> Nostrâ* intĕrest is a corruption of nostram inter rem est, *it is in the midst of and consequently mixed up with something belonging to us.*

911. After many active verbs, instead of a single word, a whole sentence may take the place of the object, in which case the secondary verb is put in the infinitive mood, and the agent or subject of that verb is put in the accusative, called the *subject* accusative. Thus,

> Caesar rĕdiit, *Caesar is returned.*
>
> Nuntiant Caesărem rĕdiisse, *they bring word that Caesar is returned.*†

For other remarks on the construction of the accusative and infinitive see below.

912. Similarly, when a subordinate sentence is attached to a verb as its accusative, the nominative of that sentence is sometimes picked out and made the accusative of that verb‡ : as,

> Nosti Marcellum quam tardus sit (Caes. ap. Cic. ad Fam. VIII. 10. 3), *you know how slow Marcellus is.*
>
> Istam timeo ne illum talem praeripiat tibi (Ter. E. I. 2. 80),

---

* The use of *re-* in this sense of 'interest' is common; thus we find mea res agitur, 'my interest is at stake;' in rem meam est, 'it is to my advantage;' e re mea est, 'it is suggested by my interest.' The explanation above given applies equally to the use of the genitive of the person, as *Ciceronis rēfert*, *Ciceronis interest*; as well as the genitive of the value, as *magni rēfert*. The long quantity of the *a* is proved by Ter. Ph. v. 7. 47. and Haut. IV. 5. 45. Similarly, *postea*, from *posteam*, lengthens the *a* when the *m* is discarded. See also §§ 409, 767, 802.

† A mathematician might have expressed this by—*Ferunt* (Caesar rediit)em, attaching the symbol of the accusative case to the clause. As the Romans were afraid to do this, adopting what under the circumstances was perhaps the best make-shift, they selected for the addition of the suffix the chief substantive. Again, the passive construction should have been (Caesar rediit)s fertur ; but here again, by a similar make-shift, they wrote *Caesar rediisse fertur*; and even in the first person, *ego rediisse feror*.

‡ Hence even in the passive voice, *an dea sim dubitor* (Ov. Met. VI. 208), 'it is doubted whether I am a goddess.' So Cic. N. D. II. 44. 115, *intellegi qualis sint non possunt*; and 59. 147, *ex quo scientia intellegitur qualis sit*.

you are afraid that that girl you speak of will cut you out with that fine gentleman.

Impurúm uide Quantúm ualet (*Ter.* Ph. v. 7. 93), *see how strong the scoundrel is.*

Non sátis me pernosti ótiam qualis sim (*Ter.* And. III. 2. 23), *you do not quite thoroughly understand even yet what sort of person I am.*

Virtus tuă mē făcĭt ut te audacter mŏneam (*Ter.* Haut. I. 1. 4), *your own worth makes me boldly warn you.*

Fac me ut sciam (*Ter.* Haut. I. 1. 32), *mind you let me know.*

912. 1 Although the employment of the accusative as the agent or subject of a verb in the infinitive should, according to the explanation above given (§ 911), be limited to the case where such a clause follows a transitive verb as its object, this use of an accusative before an infinitive mood became general (see §§ 1239, 1240, 1246), and even when not expressed affected the case of words referring to it* : as,

Visumst útilius sōlum quam cum altĕrō regnārĕ (*Cic.* de Off. III. 10. 41), *it was thought better for one to hold royal power alone than to share it with another*—where in the indicative we should have had sōlus regnat.

913 The prepositions In and sŭb sometimes require the accusative, and always after a verb of motion : as,

In urbe est, *he is in the city;* but, In urbem uĕnit, *he came into the city.*

Sub mūrō stat, *he stands under the wall;* but, Sub mūrum uĕnit, *he came up to the wall.*

914 The majority of the other prepositions, which do not imply 'motion from,' also govern the accusative. See Prepositions†.

915 *Extent* of place or time or degree is commonly expressed in the accusative‡ : as,

* But see § 878.

† Those prepositions which require the ablative are included in the first two of the following lines; those which are found with both, in the third line. All others have the accusative alone.

Ābsque cum sine, ab coramque,
Prae pro de tenus, ec palamque ;
Both, super in sub, subter clamque.

But the use of *clam* with an ablative seems doubtful.

‡ Where a point of space is fixed by a distance from another point,

172 SYNTAX.

> A rectā conscientiā nōn transuorsum unguem discēdit (*Cic.* ad Att. XIII. 20. 4), *he departs not a nail's breadth from a right conscience.*
>
> Fossā quindĕcim pĕdes lātā (*Caes.* B. G. VII. 72), *a ditch fifteen feet broad.*
>
> Dĕcem annōs urbs oppugnāta est (*Liv.* V. 4), *for ten years was the city besieged.*
>
> Vndēuīgintī annōs nātūs (*Cic.* Brut. 64. 229), *nineteen years old.*
>
> Maxĭmam partem lactĕ uīuunt (*Caes.* B. G. IV. 1), *for the most part they live on milk.*

916   The accusative is occasionally used by the poets in connection with an adjective, to define the particular part, and is often called the Greek accusative. Cētĕrā *in other respects* is so used even in prose writers (Sallust, Livy, Velleius).

> Equus trĕmĭt artūs (*Virg.* G. III. 84), *the horse trembles in his limbs.*
>
> Vir cētĕrā ēgrĕgĭūs (*Liv.* L 35), *a man in other respects of distinguished merit.*
>
> Os hŭmĕrōsquĕ dĕō sĭmĭlis (*Virg.* A. L 593), *in face and shoulders like a god.*

917   The accusatives ulcem* *turn, lot,* gĕnus *kind,* and sĕcūs *sex,* are often used in an independent manner : as,

> Stŭpentīs et suam iam ulcem māgis anxīōs quam illīus (*Liv.* VIII. 35), *amazed and now more anxious about their own than the other's position.*
>
> In id gĕnus uerbīs (*Var.* L. L. X. 5. 180), *in words of that class.*
>
> Scis me ălĭquĭd id' gĕnus sŏlĭtum scrībĕrĕ (*Cic.* ad Att. XIII. 12. 3), *you know that I am in the habit of writing something of that kind.*
>
> Lībĕrōrum cāpĭtum uĭrīlĕ sĕcūs ad dĕcem mīlĭă captā (*Liv.* XXVI. 47), *of free persons of the male sex full 10,000 were taken.*

917. 1   The accusative partim is used even as a nominative to a verb: as,

> Partim ā nōbīs tĭmĭdī sunt, partim ā rēpublĭcae āuersī (*Cic.*

---

the ablative is used by good writers, and sometimes with the preposition ab. See also § 1018. 1.

* The equivalent perhaps in form and meaning of the German *wegen.*

Phil. viii. 11. 32), *some of us are timid, some ill-disposed to our country.*

In sentences of exclamation the accusative often appears, the word with which it should have been connected being suppressed: as,

Mē caecum* qui haec antĕ non uīdĕrim (*Cic.* ad Att. x. 10. 1), *my blindness, not to have seen all this before.*

Quo mi, inquit, mutam spéciem†, si uincŏr sono ? (*Phaedr.* iii. 18. 9), *what good, says she, is dumb beauty to me, if in song I am worsted ?*

Hem Dauom tĭbi‡ (*Ter.* And. v. 2. 1), *look, here is Davus at your service.*

Bĕnĕ tē pĭtĕr§ (*Ov.* Fast. ii. 637), *a blessing on thee, sire.*

Genitive.

The genitive, like the nominative, denotes 'from.' The difference between their uses is this, that the nominative denotes the source of the action expressed by a *verb*, while the genitive is used chiefly in connection with *substantives*. It will often be found that the preposition de with the ablative may be substituted for the genitive, and sometimes ăb or ex‖.

Genitive with Substantives.

The genitive is attached to another substantive to denote the origin of an action, and may be translated by *from*, *of*, or the English genitive in *s*: as,

Consŭlis iussū (*Cic.* in Cat. i. 1. 2), *by an order from the consul, by order of the consul, by the consul's order.*

This phrase corresponds to consul iussit, where consul would be called the subject of the verb iussit. Hence this genitive is often called the *subjective* genitive.

---

* Perhaps *dico* understood.

† Perhaps *das* understood. Literally thus: 'To what end do ye give me beauty ?'

‡ Perhaps *hem* itself (§ 662) is an old verb.

§ Perhaps *Di adiuuent* understood.

‖ Hence the substitution of *de*, or a word like it, in all the European languages derived from the Latin. In our own language too *of* appears to be only a variety of the preposition *off*.

922. When of or from a whole a certain part only is taken, that whole is expressed by the genitive.* This is often called the *partitive* genitive: as,

Pars mīlĭtum (*Caes.* B. G. VI. 40), *a part of the soldiers.*

Orātōrum praestantissĭmī (*Cic.* Opt. Gen. Or. 4. 13), *the most distinguished of orators.*

Vīs aurī (*Cic.* Tusc. v. 32. 91), *a quantity of gold.*

Nēmo nostrum (*Cic.* de Fin. II. 8. 23), *not one of us.*

Quī eōrum cūrūlīs gessĕrant măgistrātūs (*Liv.* v. 41), *such of them as had held curule magistracies.*

Rĕlĭquom aītas (*Liv.* XXXIX. 13), *the rest of his life.*

Dēlectī pĕdĭtum (*Liv.* XXVI. 5), *men chosen from among the infantry,* or *a picked body of infantry.*

Exĭguom campī (*Liv.* XXVII. 27), *a small portion of the plain.*

Vltŭmă Celtĭbērīae (*Liv.* XL. 47), *the farthest parts of Celtiberia.*

Dĕcemuĭrī ăgro Appŭlō, quŏd ĕius publĭcum pŏpŭlī Rōmānī ĕrat, dīuĭdendō (*Liv.* XXXI. 4), *ten commissioners for dividing the Apulian territory, i. e. so much of it as was the public property of the people of Rome.*

Id nĕgōtī (*Ter.* And. Prol. 2), *that piece of business,* or *that business.*

Alĭquid nŏuī (*Cic.* ad Att. v. 6. 2), *something of new matter,* or *some news.*

Quŏd† ĕius fĭcĕrĕ possum (*Cic.* ad Att. XI. 12. 4; ad Fam. III. 2. 2, and v. 8. 5; and de Inv. II. 6. 20), *so much of it as I can,* or *so far as is in my power.*

Obs. When the whole are included, the genitive in Latin cannot be used, although in English we still use the word 'of.' Thus, 'Three hundred of us have sworn'—if three hundred form the whole—must be expressed by Trĕcentī coniūrāuimūs (*Liv.* II. 12).

923. 1 Still, as the pronouns quisquĕ and ŭterquĕ deal with each unit of the whole number separately, though ultimately including the whole, they are entitled to a genitive of the whole: as,

Tuōrum quisquĕ nĕcessărĭōrum (*Cic.* ad Fam. I. 9. 25), *every one of your connections.*

---

* Instead of this partitive genitive, the prepositions of kindred meaning, such as *ex* and *de*, are often used, and even the preposition *inter*.

† In this construction our editions have *quoad*, but the best Mss. *quod*.

GENITIVE.

Vtrīquĕ nostrum grātum fĕcĕrĭs (*Cic.* de Am. 4. 16), *you will oblige both of us.*

Vterque eōrum exercĭtum ēdūcunt (*Caes.* B. C. III. 30), *both lead their armies out.*

The same partitive use of the genitive is found with adverbs: as,

Vbĭnam gentium ? (*Plaut.* Merc. II. 3. 97), *where among the nations ? in what part of the whole world ?*

Eō consuētūdĭnis rēs adductast (*Liv.* XXV. 8), *the thing was brought to that degree of habit.*

Nescīrĕ uĭdēmĭnĭ quo āmentiae prōgressi sītĭs (*Liv.* XXVIII. 27), *you seem not to know to what a degree of madness you have advanced.*

Intĕrĕā lŏcī (*Ter.* Haut. II. 3. 16), *in the meanwhile.*

Sulpīcĭŭs omnium nōbĭlium maxŭmē Graecis littĕris stŭduit (*Cic.* Brut. 20. 78), *Sulpicius of all our nobles applied himself most zealously to Greek literature.*

When a thing is said to belong to a person, it has generally come from him. Hence the owner to whom any thing belongs is in the genitive, which is then called the *possessive* genitive: as,

Thēbae pŏpŭlī Rōmānī iūrĕ bellī factae sunt (*Liv.* XXXIII. 13), *Thebes became the property of the Roman people by right of war.*

Prŏpĕ Caesăris hortos (*Hor.* Sat. I. 9. 18), *near Caesar's park.*

Omnia hostium ĕrant (*Liv.* XXI. 11. ad fin.), *the whole country belonged to the enemy.*

Plebs Hannĭbălis tōta ĕrat (*Liv.* XXIII. 14), *the commonalty were entirely at the disposal of Hannibal.*

The possessive or partitive† genitive is very common in speaking of a characteristic, office, part, duty‡: as,

---

* Instead of the genitive of the personal pronouns, the possessive adjectives are required: as, *est tuum uidere, quid agatur* (*Cic.* p. Mur. 38. 83), 'it does belong to you to see what is going on;' *nos nostri sumus* (*Plaut.* Mil. Gl. II. 5. 21), ' we belong to ourselves, we are our own masters.' So also *humanum, alienum, imperatorium, muliebre, regium,* &c. may be used instead of the genitives of the nouns whence they are derived.

† The term 'partitive' has been used, because in all these cases the notion of a part is perceptible. 'To make mistakes is one element in the character of man.' So again, 'it is one element towards constituting a perfect judge to' &c.

‡ A term for part, duty, &c. is often expressed: as, munus, negotium,

Cûiusuis hŏmĭnis est errārĕ*, nullīus nĭsi insĭpĭentĭs in errōrĕ persĕuĕrārĕ (*Cic.* Phil. xii. 2. 5), *it is in the character of every man to make a mistake, of none but a fool to persist in a mistake.*

Săpientis iūdĭcis* est, quid lex cōgat, cōgĭtārĕ (*Cic.* p. Clu. 58. 159), *it is the duty of a wise judge to consider what the law requires.†*

926   The genitive of *connection* is not unfrequent : as,

Sŏrōris suae utrum (*Cic.* in Cat. iv. 6. 13), *his sister's husband.*
Hūius āuŭs Lentūlī (ibid.), *the grandfather of this Lentulus.*
Diuom păter atque hŏmĭnum rex (*Virg.* A. i. 65), *sire of gods and king of men.*

926.1   A genitive is occasionally found where a case in apposition might have been expected (genitive of *definition*) : as,

Haec uox Vŏluptātis (*Cic.* de Fin. ii. 2. 6), *this word 'pleasure.'*
Aliis uirtūtĭbus—contĭnentiae, iustĭtiae, fĭdei—tē consŭlātū dignissĭmum iūdĭcāui (*Cic.* p. Mur. 10. 23), *in respect of other good qualities, as those of integrity, justice, honour, I thought you thoroughly fitted for the consular office.*
Vnum gĕnŭs est infestum nōbīs, eōrum quos Clōdī fūror răpīnis pāuit (*Cic.* p. Mil. 2. 3), *one class and but one regards us with deadly hostility, I mean those whom the demon of Clodius has fattened on rapine.*

927   The genitive of the *quality* or *quantity* requires an adjective or participle with it : as,

Vĭr et consĭlī magni et uirtūtĭs (*Caes.* B. G. iii. 5), *a man of great talent and great courage.*
Quattuor iūgĕrum ăgĕr (*Liv.* iii. 26), *a farm of four jugera.*
Fossā quindĕcim pĕdum (*Caes.* B. G. v. 42), *a ditch of fifteen feet (in width).*
Frūmentum diērum trīgintā (*Caes.* B. G. vii. 71), *30 days' corn.*
Hannĭbăl, annōrum fermē nŏuem (*Liv.* xxi. 1), *Hannibal, a boy of about nine years.‡*

---

officium, proprium, &c. ; but it is idle to talk of an ellipsis when no such noun is expressed.
* See note † p. 175.   † See note * p. 175.
‡ See also the ablative of the quality, § 1010. The use of the genitive in this sense is less common than that of the ablative, and limited to

928 The *objective* genitive is that where the genitive takes the place of what would be the object after a verb.* In this case the English often requires the substitution of another preposition† for 'of:' as,

Lectĭō lībrōrum (*Cic.* Acad. Pr. II. 2. 4), *the reading of books.*
Cŭpĭdĭtātēs immensae dīuĭtĭārum, glōrĭae, dŏmĭnātĭōnĭs (*Cic.* de Fin. I. 18. 59), *boundless desires, as for wealth, for glory, for power.*
Iniūriă mŭlĭěrum Săbīnārum‡ (*Liv.* L. 13), *the wrong done to the Sabine women.*

Which phrases severally correspond to lĭbrōs lĕgĕrĕ; dīuĭtĭās, glōrĭam, dŏmĭnātĭōnem cŭpĕrĕ; mŭlĭĕrēs iniūriā affĭcĕrĕ.

928.1 In the construction of the objective genitive, mei, tui, sui, nostri, uestri are required.

Grātă mihi uehĕmentēr est mĕmōrĭā nostrī tuĭ (*Cic.* ad Fam. XII. 17), *I am exceedingly pleased with your remembering us.*
Hăbētĭs dūcem mĕmŏrem uestri, oblītum suĭ (*Cic.* in Cat. IV. 9. 19), *you have a general who thinks of you, and forgets himself.*
Magnă mei Imāgo (*Virg.* A. IV. 654), *a great image of me.*

GENITIVE WITH ADJECTIVES.

929 Adjectives and participles are sometimes followed by a genitive of the cause§ in the poets and later writers: as,

Lassus mărĭs (*Hor.* Od. II. 6. 7), *weary of the sea.*
Interrĭtus lētī (*Ov.* Met. X. 616), *not frightened at death.*
Inuictus lăbōrĭs (*Tac.* Ann. I. 20), *unconquered by toil.*

permanent qualities; the ablative denotes both permanent and temporary conditions.

* Yet such phrases as *amor uirtutis, taedium laboris,* can scarcely be considered as objective phrases, seeing that the virtue and the labour are the causes or origin of the *amor* and the *taedium.*

† This objective genitive is far removed from the true meaning of the case; hence it is not surprising that our own language does not follow it.

‡ Sometimes the subjective and objective genitives are at once attached to the same noun: as, *Heluetiorum iniurias populi Romani* (*Caes.* B. G. I. 30), 'the wrongs done by the Helvetii to the Roman state,' where *Heluetiorum* is the subjective, *populi* the objective conex. as usual, last.

§ More commonly an ablative of the cause is preferred.

178   SYNTAX.

930 Adjectives or participles which denote *removal* or *separation* may be followed by a genitive in the poets:* as,

   Opĕrum sŏlūtŭs (*Hor.* Od. III. 17. 16), *set loose from work.*
   Liber lăbōrum (*Hor.* ad Pis. 212), *free from toils.*
   Scĕlĕris pūrŭs (*Hor.* Od. I. 22. 1), *clear of crime.*
   Văcuas caedis mănūs (*Ov.* A. A. I. 6. 42), *hands free from bloodshed.*

931 Adjectives of *fulness* may be followed by a genitive: as,

   Dŏmus plēna ĕbriōrum (*Cic.* Phil. II. 27. 67), *a house full of drunken men.*
   Lactis ăbundans† (*Virg.* Buc. II. 20), *abounding in milk.*

932 Some adjectives, formed from substantives, retain the substantive's power of being attended by a genitive: as,

   Stŭdiōsŭs ĕquōrum (*Ov.* Met. XIV. 321), *fond of horses.*
   Expers ĕrŭdĭtiōnĭs (*Cic.* de Or. II. 1. 1), *without any share of education.*
   Consors lăbōris (*Cic.* Brut. 1. 2), *having a common lot of labour.*
   Sĕcūrus fāmae (*Ov.* Trist. I. 1. 49), *without regard for what the world may say.*

933 Adjectives denoting *accusation, guilt*, or *innocence*, are followed by a genitive: as,

   Rĕus ăvărĭtĭae (*Cic.* p. Flac. 3. 7), *charged with avarice.*
   Sanguĭnĭs insons (*Ov.* Met. XIII. 149), *guiltless of blood.*

934 Many adjectives from verbs, and participles imperfect, are used as substantives‡, and followed by an objective genitive: as,

   Cŭpĭdus uĕrĭtātĭs (*Cic.* de Or. I. 11. 47), *eager for truth.*
   Avĭdus glōriae (*Cic.* p. Marc. 8. 25), *greedy of glory.*
   Tĕnax prŏpŏsĭtĭ (*Hor.* Od. III. 3. 1), *ever clinging to his purpose.*
   Edax rērum (*Ov.* Met. XV. 234), *devouring all things.*
   Efficiens uŏluptātĭs (*Cic.* de Off. III. 33. 116), *productive of pleasure.*

---

* More commonly an ablative with or without *ab* is preferred.

† This and many such adjectives prefer an ablative of the cause.

‡ Observe the difference between *laborem contemnens*, 'despising the labour,' and *laboris contemnens*, 'a despiser of labour;' the former speaking of the single occasion, the latter of an habitual feeling; which is the usual distinction between a participle and an adjective.

Gĕrens nĕgōtī (*Cic.* p. Quinct. 19. 62), *engaged in business as a merchant.*

Adjectives, more particularly in the later writers, take a genitive which may be translated by *in, in respect to, in point of** : as,

Vălĭdŭs ŏpum (*Tac.* Hist. II. 10), *strong in resources.*
Strēnuus mīlītīae (*Tac.* Hist. III. 42), *energetic in war.*
Intĕger ultae (*Hor.* Od. I. 22. 1), *pure (in point) of life.*

Some adjectives, which commonly govern the dative, being used as masculine or feminine substantives, take a genitive : viz.

  Sŏcio-, sŭperstĭt- affīni-quă.
  Fĭnĭt'mo-, cōgnāt(o-) aequāli-quă.
  Prŏpinquo-, sim'lī- consorti-quĕ.
  Pār-, fam'liāri- uĭcīno-quă.
  Nĕcessārio- contrārio-quă.
  Amīc(o-) et inuīd(o-) aemūlo-quă.†

In the same way some neuter adjectives have become substantives, and as such take a genitive : viz.

  Pār, prŏprium, sĭmĭlĕ and commūnĕ.

Genitive with Verbs.

The impersonal verbs of *feeling* (see § 889), together with the

---

* An ablative with or without *in* is preferred by the older and better writers. Ruddiman (Stallbaum's ed. II. 79) has given from Johnson a list of adjectives found with the genitive in addition to those which fall under his seven defined classes. In this list 133 are of that kind which are to be translated by 'in' or ' in point of.' But not one of these is from Terence, Lucretius, or Cicero, and only five from Plautus ; whereas, among the later writers, there are twenty-six from Tacitus, and forty-four from Silius. Again, of the whole 133, not less than fifty-five have the one word *animi*. For instance, of the five examples from Plautus, four have this word, one passage having also *mentis* (Trin. II. 4. 53, and this evidently corrupt); and of sixteen quoted from Apuleius, thirteen have the same. From these facts we are inclined to infer, that *animi* is in truth, what the sense requires, a dative (see § 114), as it certainly is when used with the verb *excrucior*, &c. (see § 982), and that the use of the genitive with this sense in later writers grew out of a false analogy from *animi*, and words of like form, aided by the ambiguity between the two cases in the first declension (see § 951). *Virg.* A. IX. 255. has *integer aevi* ; Albinovanus, III. 5, *integer aevo.*

† That many of these are substantives is confirmed by the fact, that they admit the possessive pronouns : as, *inuidos meos.* Even their superlatives are so used as substantives : as, *inimicissumorum suum*, *Cic.* p. Mil. 9. 25 ; *meus familiarissumus*, *Cic.* ad Fam. XIII. 35. 1.

personal verbs misĕre- (r.) and misĕresc-, take a genitive of the moving cause : as,

> Si duārum paenĭtēbĭt, addontur duae (*Plaut. St.* iv. 1. 45), *if you think two not enough, two more shall be added.*
> Hunc nostrum cōpiārum suppaenĭtet (*Cic.* ad Att. vii. 14), *our friend here half thinks that he has not force enough.*
> Frātris mē pŭdet (*Ter.* Ad. iii. 3. 37), *I'm ashamed of my brother.*
> Pŭdet deōrum hŏmĭnumquĕ (*Liv.* iii. 19), *I feel ashamed before heaven and before man.**

939   Occasionally in the older poets a genitive is found with other personal verbs of feeling : as,

> Fastīdit mei (*Plaut.* Aul. ii. 2. 67), *he has taken a dislike to me.*
> Stŭdet tui (quoted by *Cic.* N. D. iii. 29. 72), *he is fond of you.*
> Quae non nērētur†uiri (*Afran.* ap. Non. ix. 3), *who has no respect for her husband.*
> Instĭtiaenĕ prius mirer† bellīnĕ lăbōrum ? (*Virg.* A. xi. 126) *thy justice first should I admire or toils of war ?*
> Nec uĕtĕrum mĕmĭni laetorue† mălōrum (*Virg.* A. xi. 280), *nor their old griefs remember I or glory in.*
> Nĕque ille
> Sēpŏsĭti cicĕris nec longae inuĭdĭt ăuēnae (*Hor.* Sat. ii. 6. 84), *nor hoarded vetch nor taper oat he grudged.*

940   Occasionally verbs of *removal* or *separation* have a genitive of the *whence* in old writers and in poetry‡ : as,

> Abstĭnēto īrārum călĭdaequĕ rixae (*Hor.* Od. iii. 27. 69), *abstain shalt thou from wrath and heated fray.*
> Dēsĭnĕ mollium tandem quĕrĕlārum (*Hor.* Od. ii. 9. 17), *cease at last from plaints unmanly.*
> Tempus dēsistĕrĕ pugnae (*Virg.* A. x. 441), *'tis time to desist from battle.*

---

* The genitive of the person with *pudet* may be either one who has acted shamefully or one who has been dealt with shamefully, so that the sight of him in either case raises the feeling of shame.

† The reflective form of these verbs proves that the construction with an accusative could not originally have belonged to them. The idea of a Grecism is unnecessary. The genitive is the very case that might have been expected from the nature of the idea.

‡ The legal language here, as in so many cases, retained traces of the old construction : as, *liberare tutelae* (Dig. xxxii. 50. 2).

Manū significārĕ coepit, ut quiescĕrent pugnae (*Quadrig.* ap. Gell. IX. 13), *he began to make a signal with his hand that they should rest from battle.*

Me omnium iam laborum levas (*Plaut.* Rud. L 4. 27), *you at last relieve me of all my troubles.*

Nec sermōnis fallebăr tamen (*Plaut.* Ep. II. 2. 55), *nor yet was I cheated out of what they said.*

Miror morbi purgātum te illīūs (*Hor.* Sat. II. 3. 27), *I wonder thou art cleansed of that disease.*

941 Some verbs of *fulness*, *want*, and *need*, may have a partitive genitive (as well as an ablative): as,

Ollam dēnāriōrum implērĕ non pŏtĕs (*Cic.* ad Fam. IX. 18. 4), *you cannot fill the pitcher with denaries.*

Complētus iam mercātōrum carcĕr ĕrat (*Cic.* II. Verr. v. 57. 147), *the prison was at last filled with captains of trading ships.*

Non tam artis indigent quam lābōris (*Cic.* de Or. L 34. 156), *it is not so much skill they are in need of as industry.*

942 The verb pŏti-* (r.) *make oneself master* has a genitive (as well as an ablative): as,

Si explōrātum tĭbi est, possĕ te illīus regni pŏtīri (*Cic.* ad Fam. L 7. 5), *if you have ascertained that you really can make yourself master of that kingdom.*

Hi qui pŏtiuntur rērum (*Cic.* ad Fam. L 8. 4), *those who are now masters of every thing.*

943 Verbs of *memory*, although they take an accusative of the thing actually remembered, have a genitive† of that *about* which the memory is concerned‡: as,

Mĕmĭni Cinnam (*Cic.* Phil. v. 8. 17), *I remember Cinna* (i. e. *his person*).

Mĕmĭni ulvōrum (*Cic.* de Fin. v. 1. 3), *I remember* or *think of the living.*

---

* If the adjective poti- was ever used as a substantive, signifying 'the powerful one, the master,' as potenti- in fact was, the verb would naturally take the genitive. Tacitus uses a genitive with the reflective verbs apisc- (Ann. VI. 45) and adipisc- (Ann. III. 55).

† De with the ablative is also very common.

‡ Hence verbs of 'reminding,' 'making mention,' must have a genitive of the thing brought to mind, unless indeed it be a neuter pronoun. (See § 909.)

Nĕque unquam oblīvīscar noctis illīūs (*Cic. p. Planc.* 42. 101), *nor shall I ever forget (the occurrences) of that night.*

Vēnit mihi Plătōnis in mentem (*Cic. de Fin.* v. 1. 2), *the thought of Plato comes across me.*

Flāgĭtiōrum suōrum rĕcordābĭtŭr (*Cic. in Pis.* G. 12), *he will remember his scandalous proceedings.*

Dulcis rĕmĭnīscĭtŭr Argŏs (*Virg. A.* x. 782), *he remembers sweet Argi.*

Verbs* of *accusing, convicting, acquitting,* take a genitive† of the offence charged: as,

Altĕrum ambĭtūs accusant (*Cic. p. Cael.* 7. 16), *he accuses another of bribery.*

Pŏtestne hēres furti ăgĕrĕ ? (*Cic. ad Fam.* vii. 22) *can an heir bring an action for theft ?*

Prōdĭtiōnis eum insimŭlābant (*Caes. B. G.* vii. 20), *they were inclined to accuse him of treachery.*

The *penalty* is expressed in the genitive in a few phrases; as,

Arcessĕrĕ căpĭtis‡ (*Cic. p. Deiot.* 11. 30), *to bring a charge affecting a person's status as a citizen.*

Octŭplī§ damnātus (*Cic.* ii. *Verr.* iii. 12. 29), *he was condemned to a payment of eightfold.*

Damnātus lăbōris (*Hor. Od.* ii. 14. 19), *condemned to toil.*

With verbs of *buying, selling, costing,* the price is expressed by the genitives tantī§, quantī, mĭnōris, plūris; in all other cases by an ablative. (See Ablative.)

---

* For adjectives of this class see § 233.

† Or *de* with the ablative, which in some phrases is necessary, or at least more common: as, *de vi, de moribus, de testamento.* Cicero (p. Clu. 41. 114) says *de pecuniis repetundis*; Tacitus (Ann. iii. 33) *repetundarum* without the substantive.

‡ Also *capite damnare* (*Cic. Tusc.* i. 32. 50).

§ We have called these genitives, in deference to common opinion, but they are perhaps old datives; a supposition which will account for the use of the forms in *o* (see following note), and remove the strange contradiction of idioms which appears in *Hor. Sat.* ii. 3. 156:

Quanti emptae? Parvo. Quanti ergo? Octussibus.

The phrase too in Catullus (xvii. 17), *nec pili facit uni*, will no longer have a license in the last word. If our theory be right, *minoris, pluris, huius* and *suis* will afford another instance of an anomaly growing out of a false analogy (see § 235).

947 The *worth* or *value* is expressed by the same genitives, and also by parui, magnī, minīmī, maxīmī, and plūrīmī,* as well as the following, which generally are strengthened by the addition of a negative: viz.

      Huius et assis, flocci piliquē,
      Nauci nihili, torunciīquē.†

948 With the verbs refert and interest are employed tantī, quantī, parui, magnī, besides the ordinary adverbs of quantity.

949 *Of* being so commonly the translation of the genitive, it may be a useful caution to observe that the English phrases signifying *to talk of, to think of*, are to be translated with the preposition dē. Still certior fīerī, *to be informed*, often takes a genitive.

Dative.‡

950 The dative case answers to the question *where? in or near what place?* and to the time *when?* Hence its place is often supplied by such words as in or cum with the ablative, or by the ablative alone, seeing that the ablative is often only another form of the dative.

951 *At* a town or *in* a small island is expressed by the dative; but in the *o* (or second) declension the old dative in *i* is very generally preferred: as,

    Rōmae (*Liv.* XXI. 6), *at Roma* (or *Rome*);
    Athēnīs (*Cic.* de Sen. 13. 43), *at Athenae* (or *Athens*);
    Tārentī§ (*Cic.* de Sen. 12. 39), *at Tarentum*;

---

* Ablatives however are occasionally found, even in Cicero: as, in II. Verr. IV. 7.13, *tāle permagno aestumat*; de Fin. IV. 23. 62, *non nihilo aestumandum*. Festus has *bos centussibus, ovis decussibus aestimaretur*; and *asse carum est* is an old phrase.

† We have not added *pensi*, because the phrase *neque quidquam pensi habebat* is equivalent to *neque quidquam pendebat*, the word *pensi* being, according to the common idiom, attached to the neuter pronoun (§ 922). *Aequi boni consulere*, 'to take in good part,' has never, so far as the writer knows, been satisfactorily explained.

‡ As the order of the paragraphs under this head has been much altered, the numbers of the sections will not correspond with those of the previous edition.

§ In the phrase *habitat Mileti* (*Ter.* Ad. IV. 5. 20) Donatus saw no genitive case; he calls it *adverbium locale*. The dative of nouns in *o* ended at one time, like the Greek οικοι, λογῳ &c. in the diphthong *oi*, of which the old dative *quoi* is an example; and from this diphthong arose the two forms of the case, seen in *nullo* and *nulli*.

Tȳrō (*Virg.* A. IV. 36), *at Tyre;*
Lāuīniō (*Liv.* v. 52), *at Lavinium;*
Pūteōlīs (*Cic.* ad Att. XVI. 14. 1), *at Puteoli;*
Tībūrī* (*Cic.* ad Att. XVI. 3. 1), *at Tibur* (or *Tivoli*);
Cūrībūs (*Liv.* I. 18), *at Cures;*
Ithācae (*Cic.* de Off. III. 28. 97), *in Ithaca;*
Lemnī† (*Ter.* Ph. IV. 3. 75), *in Lemnos;*
Karthāgīnī* Nŏuae (Epil. of *Liv.* XXVIII.—for so the MSS.), *at New Carthage.*‡

952 The dative signifying *where?* maintained itself in certain words in spite of the increasing tendency to express this idea by in and an ablative. Such datives are: hŭmī *on the ground,* terrae (*Virg.* A. XI. 87) *on the ground,* dŏmī *at home,* rūrī *in the country* (in poetry also rūrē), fŏrīs *out of doors,* Achĕruntī (*Plaut.* Capt. III. 5. 31) *in Acheron* or *Tartarus,* cŏmitiīs *at the election,* lūdīs *at the games,* Lātīnīs (sc. fēriīs) *at the Latin festival,* glădiātōribŭs *at the gladiatorial exhibition,* ănimī *in the mind* (pl. ănĭmīs).

953 The so-called adverbs in *bi* and *i,* which denote *where,* as, ūbi *where,* ĭbi *there,* &c. (§ 366, col. 2), are all datives in origin.

954 The time *when* is put in the dative in certain words: as, hĕrī (also hĕrē) *yesterday,* mānī (or mānē) *in the morning,* uespĕrī (or uespĕrē) *in the evening,* lūcī *in the daylight,* diē quintī (or quintē) *on the fifth day* (see *Gell.* X. 24), diē pristīnī *the day before,* diē crastīnī *tomorrow,* īdĭbus martiīs *on the ides* (or 15th) *of March,* bellī *in war,* militiae *on military service,* ūbi *when,* ĭbi *then,* &c.

955 Adjectives which denote *nearness* take a dative: as,

* The poets take the liberty of shortening such forms as *Tīburī* to *Tiburī* (see § 990).

† See note §, p. 183.

‡ If the word *urb-* or *oppido-* be expressed, the preposition *in* must be used, as, *Milites Albae consisterent in urbe munita* (*Cic.* Phil. IV. 2. 6), *Ciuis Romanos Neapoli in celeberrimo oppido cum mitella uidimus* (*Cic.* p. Rab. Post. 10. 26). 'In a country' or 'In a large island' is commonly expressed by *in* with the ablative; yet there are passages where the dative is found, especially in the poets, as *Cretae* (*Virg.* A. III. 162), *Libyae* (*Virg.* A. IV. 36), and late prose writers, as the Pseudo-Nepos, *Chersonesi* (Milt. 2), *Cypri* (Chabr. 3). The passage in *Cic.* R. P. III. 9. 14 is not an example, for there *Graeciae,* as Madvig has pointed out, is a genitive in connection with *delubra.*

Belgae proximī sunt Germānīs (*Caes.* B. G. 1. 1), *the Belgae are nearest to the Germans.*

Heu quam vīcīna est ultimā terrā mihi (*Ov.* Trist. III. 4. 52), *alas, how near is the end of the world to me.*

Tibi gĕnĕrĕ prŏpinquī (*Sal.* Jug. 10), *those near akin to you.*

956 Verbs which denote *nearness* take a dative: as,

Pārēre* uŏluntātī architectī (*Cic.* N. D. I. 8. 19), *to wait upon the will of the architect.*

Cīuitātēs amīcitiā Caesarī conciliāre (*Caes.* B. C. III. 55), *to unite states in friendship with Caesar.*

Sī pŏpŭlus Rōmānus foedĕrĕ iungĕrētur rēgī (*Liv.* XXVI. 24. 13), *if the people of Rome should be united to the king by treaty.*

Currū iungit Hălaesūs ĕquōs (*Virg.* A. VII. 724), *to his car Halaesus yokes the steeds.*

Nescit ĕquo haerērĕt (*Hor.* Od. III. 24. 54), *he knows not how to cling to steed.*

Fortī ˈmiscēbat mellā Fălernō (*Hor.* Sat. II. 4. 24), *with strong Falernian he would honey mix.*

Luctantem Īcăriīs flucūbūs (*Hor.* Od. I. 1. 15), *wrestling with Icarian waves.*

Sōlus tibī certĕt Amyntas (*Virg.* Buc. 0. 8), *let Amyntas alone contend with thee.*

957 Adjectives compounded with prepositions of *rest* take a dative dependent upon that preposition: as,

Quī mihī consciīs essĕ sŏlēs (*Cic.* ad Att. I. 18. 1), *you who are wont to share my secrets with me.*

Mihī conscius sum (*Cic.* Tusc. II. 4. 10), *I share the knowledge with myself (alone)—or I am conscious.*

Eius mors consentānĕa uītae fuit (*Cic.* Phil. IX. 7. 15), *his death was in agreement with his life.*

Coenīsquĕ trĭbus iam pernā sŭperstes (*Mart.* X. 48. 17), *and a ham that had survived three dinners.*

* That 'to be present,' 'to wait upon,' rather than 'to obey,' is the true meaning of this verb, to say nothing of other evidence, is shown by the use of the verb *appare-* with such a dative as *magistratibus*, and by the noun *apparitor-* 'an officer in waiting.'

† This use of the dative with many of these verbs is limited to the poets: Cicero would rather have said *haerere in equo, miscere cum Falerno, luctari cum fluctibus, certare tecum.*

958 Verbs compounded with prepositions of *rest* take a dative*
dependent upon that preposition.

> Quem quóndam Ioui Iúno custodem áddidit (*Plaut.* Aul. III.
> 6. 20), *whom Juno of yore set as a watch o'er Io.*
>
> IIi scribendo affuērunt (*Cic.* ad Fam. VIII. 8. 0), *the following
> were present at the registration.*
>
> Iūdĭces sĭbi constāre dēbuērunt (*Cic.* p. Clu. 22. 60), *the jury
> ought to have been consistent with themselves.*
>
> Tū meo infēlici errōri sōlŭs illăcrŭmasti (*Liv.* XL. 50), *you
> alone have wept over my unfortunate mistake.*
>
> Campŭs interiăcens Tibĕri ac moenĭbus Rōmānĭs (*Liv.* XXI.
> 30), *the plain that lies between the Tiber and the walls of
> Rome.*
>
> Pŭdor nōn ŏbest ōrātiōnī (*Cic.* de Or. I. 26. 122), *modesty does
> not stand in the way of a speech, or is not prejudicial to it.*
>
> Omnĭbŭs ēius consĭlĭis obstĭtī (*Cic.* in Cat. III. 7), *all his plans
> I have thwarted.*
>
> Qui classĭbus praeĕrant (*Caes.* B. C. III. 25), *those who were in
> command of the fleets.*
>
> Hŏmĭnes bestiis praestant (*Cic.* de Inv. I. 4. 5), *men stand before
> (or* excel) *beasts.*
>
> Magnĭtūdĭne ănĭmī pŏtest rĕpugnārī fortūnae (*Cic.* de Fin. IV.
> 7. 17), *with magnanimity a battle may be maintained against
> fortune.*
>
> Sŭperfuit pătri (*Liv.* I. 34), *he survived his father.*

959 In the examples just quoted the verbs are of a static character; but even after verbs of *motion*, when the resulting position rather than the movement to attain it is before the mind, the dative is still used (see § 1336 *k*): as,

> Antětŭlissem uŏluntātem tuam commŏdō meō (*Cic.* ad Fam. V.
> 20. 1), *I should have preferred your wishes to my own advantage.*

---

* Thus the Latin here agrees with other languages in attaching a dative to prepositions of rest. So we have in the old language *postibi* and *interibi*, the latter of which was eventually corrupted to *inter-im*. So too in *postquam*, *antequam* &c., the *quam* is probably a dative in origin rather than an accusative, as is admittedly the case in the parallel forms of the German *nach-dem* &c. It is thus too that we find a dative in *suro contra*, § 1320 *f*.

Contiōnantī circumfundēbātur multitūdō (*Liv.* XXII. 14), *as he went on haranguing, a mob kept pouring round him.*

Vēnientī occurrītō morbō (*Pers.* III. 64), *hasten to meet the coming disease.*

Ōra ipsīs ōcūlīs prōpōnitō (*Cic.* p. Sest. 7. 17), *place their very faces before your eyes.*

Dum circumuentō fīliō subuēnit, interficitūr (*Caes.* B. G. v. 35), *as he advances to support his son who was surrounded, he is killed.*

Anātum ouā gallīnīs saepē suppōnimūs (*Cic.* N. D. II. 48. 124), *we often put ducks' eggs under hens.*

Even simple verbs at times take a dative to express the *where*; as,

Dumnōrigī custōdēs pōnit ut quae āgat scīrē possit (*Caes.* B. G. I. 20), *he places men about the person of Dumnorix to watch him, that he may know what he is doing.*

Custos frūmentō publicō est pōsitūs (*Cic.* p. Flac. 19. 45), *he was set as sentinel over the public corn.*

Fīnem ōrātiōnī facērē (*Cic.* II. Verr. II. 48. 118), *to set a limit to a speech.*

Adjectives, being in their very nature static, express the relation to an object by a dative: as,

Collīs aduersūs huic et contrāriūs (*Caes.* B. G. II. 18), *a hill facing and opposite to this.*

Sīta Antīcȳra est laeuā partē sinuum Cōrinthiācum intrantībūs (*Liv.* XXVI. 20), *Anticyra lies on the left as you enter the bay of Corinth.*

Aptum est tempōrī et persōnae (*Cic.* Or. 22. 74), *it is adapted to the time and to the person.*

Verbum Lātīnum par Graecō (*Cic.* de Fin. II. 4. 13), *a Latin word equal in force to the Greek one.*

Fīlius pātrī similis (*Cic.* de Fin. v. 5. 12), *a son like his father.*

Nihil tam dissimilē quam Cottā Sulpiciō (*Cic.* Brut. 56. 204), *there is nothing so unlike as Cotta to Sulpicius.*

Līuiūs Enniō aequālis fuit (*Cic.* Brut. 18. 73), *Livius was of the same age with Ennius.*

* But some verbs so compounded, especially with *ad*, are occasionally regarded as transitive verbs, taking an accusative; as, *allabitur aures* (*Virg.* A. IX. 474), *cum Tiberi genus miscuerretur* (*Tac.* Ann. I. 13).

Quŏd illī caussae maxŭmē est aliēnum (*Cic.* p. Caec. 9. 24), *what is most unfavorable for that side.*

Is dŏlor commūnis uōbis mēcum est (*Cic.* de Prov. Cons. 1. 2), *indignation at this is common to you with me.*

Rius căput Iŏuī sācrum estō (*Liv.* III. 55), *that man's head shall be devoted to Jupiter.*

Id uērō militĭbus fuit pergrātum (*Caes.* B. C. I. 86), *this indeed was most acceptable to the soldiers.*

Hŏmĭnēs omnĭbūs inīquī (*Cic.* p. Planc. 16. 40), *men unfriendly to every one.*

Virtus fructuōsa ălīīs, ipsī lābŏriōsa aut pērĭcŭlōsa, aut certē grătuītă (*Cic.* de Or. II. 85. 346), *energy full of fruit for others, for himself full of suffering or danger, or at best without reward.*

Nĕque ĭdeō tĭbi uīlis uīta esset mea (*Liv.* XL. 9), *nor would my life have been so cheap in your eyes.*

Nēquāquam spĕcĭe aestŭmantĭbus pārēs (*Liv.* VII. 10), *by no means equal in the eyes of those who judged of them from outward appearance.*

Hŏmērus Sceptrā pŏtītūs eădem āliīs* sōpītū quiētest (*Lucr.* III. 1036), *e'en Homer, who won our sceptre, was drugged by the same sleep (of death) with others.*

962 Similarly adverbs may have a dative of relation : as,

Conuĕnienter nātūrae uīuĕrĕ (*Cic.* de Off. III. 3. 13), *to live agreeably to nature.*

Quam sĭbi constanter dīcat, non lăbōrat (*Cic.* Tusc. v. 9. 26), *how far he talks consistently with himself, he heeds not.*

Imprŏbo et stulto et inertī nēmĭnī bĕne esse pŏtest (*Cic.* Parad. 2. 19), *with a villain or a fool or a sluggard things cannot be well.*

963 Static verbs express their relation to an object by a dative: as,

Hoc ūnum Caesărī dēfuit (*Caes.* B. G. IV. 26), *this one thing was wanting to Caesar.*

Qui dilĭgēbant hunc, illī fāuēbant (*Cic.* p. Rosc. Com. 10. 29), *those who esteemed this man wished well to the other.*

Aeduōrum cīuĭtātī praecĭpue indulsĕrat (*Caes.* B. G. I. 10), *he had been particularly indulgent to the state of the Aedui.*

* This construction occurs only in poets.

Irasci amicis non temere soleo (*Cic.* Phil. VIII. 5. 16), *I am not wont with light cause to be angry with friends.*

Nulla fuit civitas quin Caesari pareret (*Caes.* B. C. III. 81), *there was not a single state but was obedient to Caesar,* or *ready to obey his orders.*

Hoc omnibus patet (*Cic.* p. Mur. 13. 28), *this is open to all.*

Non placet Antonio consulatus meus, at placuit P. Servilio (*Cic.* Phil. II. 5. 12), *my consulship does not find favour with Antony, true, yet it found favour with Publius Servilius.*

Qui nec sibi nec alteri prosunt (*Cic.* de Off. II. 10. 36), *men who are useful neither to themselves nor to their neighbour.*

Sic noster hic rector studuerit legibus cognoscendis (*Cic.* R. P. V. 3), *so let this ruler of ours first devote himself to the study of the laws.*

Adulescenti nihil est quod suscenseam (*Ter.* Ph. II. 3. 14), *with the young man I have no reason to be offended.*

Quod tibi lubet, id mihi lubet (*Plaut.* Most. L 3. 138), *what pleases you, that pleases me.*

Catoni licuit Tusculi se delectare (*Cic.* R. P. I. 1), *it was permitted to Cato to amuse himself at Tusculum.*

964 In the older writers decet admitted a dative of the person, unless an infinitive followed the verb; but in other writers an accusative of the person is alone admissible.

Istuc facinus, quod tu insimulas, nostro generi non decet (*Plaut.* Am. II. 2. 188), *an act, such as that you complain of, would not be becoming in our family.*

965 Some verbs compounded with dis, which often require an English translation by *from*, and in Latin are usually accompanied by the prepositions ab or inter or cum, occasionally in the poets take a dative*: as,

Longe mea discrepat istis Et nox et ratio (*Hor.* Sat. L. 6. 92), *my words, my views are wholly out of harmony with them.*

Pede certo Differt sermoni (*Hor.* Sat. I. 4. 48), *by the fixed rhythm alone from prose it differs.*

Quantum Hypanis dissidet Eridano (*Prop.* I. 12. 4), *far as the Hypanis from the Eridanus is distant.*

---

* This construction is like that of the dative in connection with such adjectives as *dissimili-*, *dispar-*.

Scurrae distāt amīcus (*Hor.* Ep. I. 18. 4), *from the buffoon far different the friend.*

966 The verb ĕs- *be* stands out from among other static verbs by its frequent use of a dative of the person to denote relationship, connection of office and ownership.

Natūrā tu illī pāter es (*Ter.* Ad. I. 2. 46), *by nature you are his father.*

Mihī quaestŏr impĕrātōrī fuĕrat (*Cic.* post red. in S. 4. 35), *he had been my quaestor when I was commander-in-chief.*

Quĭbūs ōpes nullae sunt (*Sal.* Cat. 37), *those who have no property.*

967 From this idea of 'having' comes the use of ĕs- with a dative of the person in connection with a perfect participle and a gerundive; a use which was extended to phrases of apposition where the verb ĕs- is no longer expressed.

Quicquid mihi susceptumst (*Cic.* p. leg. Man. 24. 71), *whatever I have undertaken,*—less accurately, *whatever has been undertaken by me.*

Lĕgendus mihi saepĭūs est Cătō māiŏr (*Cic.* ad Att. XIV. 21), *I have to read again and again the 'de Senectute,'*—less accurately, *it must be read by me,* or *I must read it.*

967. 1 Participles often become virtually adjectives, and as such are entitled to a dative of relation : as,

Pinnās in littŏrĕ pandunt Dilectae Thĕtĭdi alcyŏnēs (*Virg.* G. I. 399), *their feathers on the beach spread out the kingfishers to Thetis dear.*

Notūs mihi nōmĭnĕ tantum (*Hor.* Sat. I. 9. 3), *known to me by name alone.*

968 It is rare, even in the poets, for a dative to be used of the agent with imperfect tenses of a passive. Some passages in prose writers, which seem to fall under this head, admit of a different explanation.

Carmĭnă quae scrĭbuntŭr ăquae pōtōrĭbūs (*Hor.* Ep. I. 19. 3), *verses that are written in the realm of water-drinkers.*

Scrībēris Vărĭō fortĭs (*Hor.* Od. I. 6. 1), *thy bravery shall be told in Varius' page.*

Hoc in lăbōrĭbus uīuentī nōn intellĕgĭtŭr (*Cic.* de Sen. 11.38), *this to one living immersed in labour is not perceptible.*

DATIVE. 191

Barbărŭs hic ĕgŏ sum, quiă nōn intellĕgŏr ulli (*Ov.* Trist. v. 10. 35), *a barbarian here am I, for to no one am I intelligible.*

969 Even substantives take a dative to denote the object referred to: as,

E bestiārum corpŏrĭbus multă rĕmĕdiă morbis et uolnĕrĭbŭs ĕlĭgĭmŭs (*Cic.* N. D. II. 64. 161), *from the bodies of beasts we select many remedies for diseases and wounds.*

Nĕque mihi ex cūiusquam altĭtūdĭne aut praesĭdiă pĕrīcŭlīs aut adiūmenta hŏnŏrĭbus quaerō (*Cic.* p. leg. Man. 24. 70), *nor do I seek in the exalted condition of any one whatever either protection against danger, or aid to political advancement.*

Tĕgĭmentă gălĕis mĭlĭtĕs ex uimĭnĭbus făcĕrĕ iŭbet (*Caes.* B. C. III. 62), *he bids the soldiers make coverings for their helmets of the osiers.*

Equĭtātum auxĭliō Caesări mīsĕrant (*Caes.* B. G. I. 18), *they had sent a body of cavalry as an aid to Caesar.*

970 Where an habitual state of things is expressed, a dative of the person is sometimes used to define those with whom the habit prevails: as,

Barbărĭs ex fortūnă pendet fĭdĕs (*Liv.* XXVIII. 17), *with barbarians fidelity depends upon fortune.*

Hŏnestă bŏnis uĭrĭs, nōn occultă quaeruntŭr (*Cic.* de Off. III. 9. 38), *with good men the honourable, not the mysterious, is the object sought.*

Etiam săpientĭbus cŭpĭdo glōriae nŏuissĭma exultŭr (*Tac.* Hist. IV. 6), *even among the wise the love of glory is the last thing discarded.*

971 Verbs of habitual action may in one sense be regarded as static, and so have a dative of the person to whom the habitual action refers. Such verbs are often reflectives.

Appius mihi blandītŭr (*Cic.* ad Q. Fr. II. 12. 2), *Appius performs the part of the 'blandus homo' to me,—is all smoothness to me.*

Nē quid pars altĕră grātĭfĭcārī pŏpŭlō Rōmānō* posset (*Liv.* XXI. 9), *for fear that the other party should do the obliging to*

---

* Instead of *populo Romano* the Mss. have *pro Romanis*, which, though nonsense, is retained in all the editions. *Populo Romano* was shortened as usual to *p-ro-*, and then mistaken for *pro*, which of course needed a noun, and to supply this need *Romanis* was added.

the Roman people, i. e. *should sacrifice any matter to oblige Rome.*

Caesārī supplĭcābo (*Cic.* ad Fam. VI. 14. 3), *I will play the part of suppliant to Caesar.*

Aliī glōriae seruiunt, aliī pĕcūniae (*Cic.* Tusc. V. 3. 9), *some are slaves to glory, some to money.*

972 Where an action is done to part of the body, the party suffering is expressed by the dative (though the English language prefers a possessive pronoun or possessive case): as,

Cui ego iam linguăm praecīdam atque ŏcŭlōs ecfodĭăm domi (*Plaut.* Aul. II. 2. 12), *I will at once cut off her tongue, and dig her eyes out here in the house.*

Tuō ultro ŏcŭlī dōlent (*Ter.* Ph. v. 8. 64), *your husband's eyes ache.*

Quid uīs tibi dari in manum ? (*Ter.* Ph. IV. 3. 29) *how much do you wish paid down into your hand ?*

Tĭbi sīcă dē mănĭbŭs extortast (*Cic.* Cat. I. 6. 16), *the dagger was wrested out of your hands.*

973 Thus verbs alike of giving and taking away have a dative of the person; but it must not be inferred from this that either motion to or motion from is really expressed by the dative.

Dĕdi ad tē lībertō tuō littĕrās (*Cic.* ad Att. VI. 3. 1), *I gave a letter to your freedman (to be delivered) to you.*

Reddĭdit mihi littĕrās (*Cic.* ad Att. V. 21), *he delivered the letter to me.*

Ingēns* cūi lūmĕn ădemptum (*Virg.* A. III. 658), *from whom a monstrous eye had been taken away.*

Id tōtum ēripĕrĕ uōbis cōnātust (*Cic.* in Rull. II. 7. 19), *all this he has endeavoured to tear from you.*

974 Verbs of *trusting*, for to trust is to put a thing into a person's hands†, have a dative of the person in whom the trust is placed: as,

---

* That *ingens* is the epithet of *lumen* is shown partly by the same epithet having been given to *lumen* in v. 636, *telo lumen terebramus acuto Ingens*; partly by Virgil's habit of making the relative in this part of his verse an enclitic attached to the preceding word. See § 1463 note. I had to thank a friend and then colleague for the suggestion.

† Indeed *cre-do*, *cre-didi*, *cre-ditum*, and the old subjunctive *cre-duim*, evidently belong to a compound of *do*.

DATIVE. 193

Sē suăque omnia aliēnissŭmis crēdidērunt (*Caes.* B. G. vɪ. 31), *they trusted themselves and all their property to perfect strangers.*

Credōn tibi hoc ? (*Ter.* And. ɪɪɪ. 2. 17) *am I to believe this that you tell me ?*

Mihī crēdō (*Cic.* in Cat. ɪ. 3. 0), *take my word for it.*

Quī sĭbī fīdīt* (*Hor.* Ep. ɪ. 19. 22), *who in himself confides.*

Multĭtūdo hostium nullī rei praetorquam nŭmĕrō frētā* (*Liv.* vɪ. 13), *the mob constituting the enemy's force, trusting to nothing but their numbers.*

975 Some verbs of *giving* are used with a dative of the person in the sense of doing something out of regard to that person, particularly in cases of forgiveness or concession: as,

Praetĕrĭta frātrī condōnat (*Caes.* B. G. ɪ. 20), *the past doings (of Dumnorix) he forgives out of regard to his brother (Diviciacus).*

Peccāta līberum pārentum misēricordiae concessērunt (*Cic.* p. Clu. 69. 195), *they have passed over the offences of sons out of pity to their parents.*

Tu inĭmĭcĭtias reipublicae dōnastī (*Cic.* ad Fam. v. 4), *you have dropped your enmities out of regard to the public welfare.*

Mĕmŏriam simultātum pătriae rĕmittĭt† (*Liv.* ɪx. 38), *he forgets his private quarrels out of regard to his country.*

Quantum consuētūdinī famaequē dandum sit (*Cic.* Tusc. ɪ. 45. 109), *how far we ought to make allowance for custom and what the world may say.*

976 Many verbs which denote an act done in the presence of or in reference to another concerned therein, take a dative of the person, in addition to the accusative of the thing, especially verbs of showing and telling.

Altĕri monstrant uiam (*Enn.* ap. Cic. de Div. ɪ. 58. 132), *they show a fellow-creature the way.*

---

* See also § 1092.

† Literally 'lets go back,' 'sends back.' The idea of punishment in the Latin language generally takes the form of a fine. The offender *dat, pendit, soluit poenam,* 'pays the fine ;' the injured party *sumit, exigit poenam,* 'takes, exacts the fine ;' or should any common friend succeed in assuaging his anger, then the offended party *remittit poenam intercessori,* 'returns the fine to the interceding party,' that the offender receiving it from him may know to whose kind offices he is indebted.

104   SYNTAX.

> Haec hĕrŏ dicam (*Plaut.* Am. I. 1. 304), *all this I will tell (to) my master.*
>
> Virgo nupsit Mĕtellō (*Cic.* de Div. I. 46. 104), *the maiden took the veil* to Metellus,* i. e. *married him.*

977   This dative of the person often denotes for his advantage or on his account, and is translated by *for*: as,

> Sic uos non nōbis mellĭfĭcātis ăpes (*Virg.* in ulta), *so ye too, bees, not for yourselves are honey-makers.*
>
> Non sōlum nōbis diuĭtēs esse nōlŭmus, sed lībĕris, prŏpinquis, ămīcis, maxŭmēquē reīpublĭcae (*Cic.* de Off. III. 15. 63), *it is not merely for ourselves we wish to be rich, but for our children, our relations, our friends, and above all our country.*
>
> Tū fors quid me fīat parui pendis, dum illi cōnsulas (*Ter.* Haut. IV. 3. 37), *you perhaps care little what becomes of me, so you provide for him.*
>
> Tĭbi tĭmui (*Ter.* Haut. III. 2. 20), *I was alarmed for you,* or *on your account.*
>
> Mĕliūs ei căuerē uŏlo quam ipse illis sŏlet (*Cic.* ad Fam. III. 1. 3), *I am determined to take better security for him than he himself is wont for others.*
>
> Nec tĭt tuă fūnĕră māter Prōduxi pressue ŏcŭlōs aut uolnĕră laui (*Virg.* A. IX. 486), *nor for thee led thine own mother forth the funeral pomp, or closed thine eyes, or bathed thy wounds.*

978   The dative of the personal pronouns more particularly, is used to denote an interest of the party (*datiuus ethicus*), and often ironically. In this case much latitude of translation is requisite to give the shade of meaning: as,

> Tongĭlium mihi ēduxit (*Cic.* in Cat. II. 2. 4), *Tongilius he has done me the favour to take out (of Rome) with him.*
>
> At tĭbi rĕpentē uēnit ad me Cănīnĭŭs† (*Cic.* ad Fam. IX. 2. 1), *but (what think you) all at once there comes to my house your friend Caninius.*

---

* The flame-coloured veil, *flammeolum*, used in the ceremony of marriage.

† *Te* a dative, and *tus* a nominative, the two pronouns being thrown together for the sake of emphasis. Another instance of *te* as a dative is seen in *Ter.* Haut. V. 2. 34, *te indulgebant.* See also p. 197, note †.

Haec nōbīs istōrum mīlitiā fuit (*Liv.* xx. 60), *this was the military service you have to thank your petitioners for.*

970 A dative and accusative seem to be rivals with each other in the construction of some verbs. The cases of this nature fall for the most part into two classes: *a.* those of older writers, who, adhering to the original meaning of a verb, employ a dative, which in later writers gives place to an accusative; or the two constructions may even coexist with a slight difference of meaning in the verb: *b.* those where, the verb being entitled originally to a dative of the person and accusative of the thing, the thing is in a manner personified, and so put in the dative.

Adūlā-rī, 'to wag the tail at,' hence 'to wheedle*, fawn on.'

Pōtentī ādūlātūs est (*Nep.* in Attico, 25), *he fawned on the powerful man.*

Praesentibūs ādūlandō (*Liv.* xxxvi. 7. 4), *by fawning on those present.*†

Aemūlā-rī, 'to play the rival,' hence 'to rival, envy.'

Hīs aemūlāmur, quī ea hăbent, quae nōs hăbērĕ cŭpĭmŭs (*Cic.* Tusc. i. 19. 44), *we envy those who possess what we are eager to possess.*‡

Ignōsc-ĕrĕ, literally 'to forget'§, and hence 'to forgive,' strictly with acc. of offence forgiven, dat. of person.

Vt eīs delicta ignōscas (*Plaut.* Bacch. v. 2. 68), *that you may forgive them their shortcomings.*

Hoc ignōscant dī immortālēs ŭtĭnam pŏpŭlō Rōmānō (*Cic.* Phil. i. 6. 13), *for this I would pray the immortal gods to forgive the Roman people.*

Inuidē-rē, 'to regard with an evil eye,' hence 'to envy, grudge;' originally it would appear with an acc. of the thing envied and a dat. of the owner.

---

* Observe that the German verb *wedel-n* means 'to wag the tail.'

† So again *plebi a.*, *Liv.* iii. 69. In *Cic.* in Pis. 41. 99, *omnibus a.* is justly preferred by Lambinus. But in later writers the acc. is used: as, *eosdem furem a.*, Col. vii. 12; *principem*, Tac. Hist. i. 32, *sui quem alium*, Ann. xvi. 19; *dominum*, Sen. de Ira, ii. 31. Hence in *Quint.* ix. 3, *huic non hunc adulari iam dicitur*, the words *huic* and *hunc* should be transposed.

‡ But *Pindarum ae.*, *Hor.* Od. iv. 2. 1; *virtutes*, Tac. Agr. 15; *uinum*, *Plin.* xiv. 2. 4.

§ 'To un-know,' if we had the word, would best suit.

Iampridem nōbīs caelī tē rēgiā, Caesar, īnuīdēt (*Virg.* G. 1. 503), *long, long has the palace of the sky envied us thy presence, Caesar.*

Africae sōlo ōleum et uīnum Nātūra inuīdit (*Plin.* xv. 2. 3), *nature grudged the soil of Africa oil and wine.**

Mĕdĭcā-rī and mĕdē-rī, literally 'to act the physician,' hence 'to cure, heal, remedy,' with a dat. of the patient or acc. of the disease.

Ego possum in hāc re medicari mihi (*Ter.* And. v. 4. 41), *in this matter I can play the part of physician to myself;*—but

Ego istum lĕpĭdē medĭcābōr metum (*Plaut.* Most. II. 1. 40), *I will cure that fear nicely.*

Dies stultis quŏque mĕdēri sōlet (*Cic.* ad Fam. vii. 28. 3), *time is wont to cure even fools;*—but

Eiusmodī ... cŭpĭdĭtātes, Quas quūm res aduorsaē sient, paulō mŏdĕrī pōssis (*Ter.* Ph. v. 4. 2), *desires of such a kind that when things go wrong, you can cure them at little cost.*

Mŏdĕrā-rī, 'to act as a limit or check (to)', hence 'to check, moderate,' and so generally 'to govern, control.'

Nōn uinum hominibūs moderari, sĕd uino homines ăssolent (*Plaut.* Truc. iv. 3. 57), *it is not the bottle for the most part that has control over the man, but the man that has control over the bottle;*—so at least the unfairly abused bottle would say if it could speak.

Mŏdĕrāri ĕt ănĭmo ĕt ōrātiōnī quum sīs īrātūs, est non mēdiŏcris ingĕnī (*Cic.* ad Q. Fr. I. 1. 13. 38), *to check both one's feelings and one's words when one is angry, is indeed the act of no ordinary character.*‡

Parc-ĕrĕ, 'to save, to spare,' originally with acc. of the thing and dat. of the person for whom.

Argenti atque auri memŏras quae multā tălenta Gnātiis parcē

---

* Thus i. *florem liberum* (= *liberorum*) in *Att.* ap. Cic. Tusc. iii. 9. 20; i. *nobis naturam* (as an instructress), *Cic.* Tusc. iii. 2 3, if the text be sound. As the evil eye might also be directed upon the owner himself, an acc. would not have been out of place; and so we have an explanation of the forms *inuideor* 'I am envied,' *Hor.* Ep. ii. 3, 56, and the participles *inuiso-* 'envied,' *inuidendo-* 'enviable.'

† Some good Mss. with Ritschl *medicabo.*

‡ In the general sense of 'governing' an acc. is common in Cicero; but even in the sense of 'checking' an acc. is found in later writers, as Tac. and Suet.

tuis (*Virg.* A. x. 532), *the silver, aye and gold of which thou speakest, all for thy children save.*

Suādē-rĕ, literally 'to sweeten'*, hence 'to recommend, give advice,' with acc. of thing recommended, dat. of person to whom the advice is given.†

Quód tĭbi suádeam, suádeam meó patri (*Plaut.* Capt. π. 1. 40), *any thing I would recommend to you, I would recommend to my own father.*

Tempĕrā-rĕ,‡ 'to act as a limit, to set bounds (to)', hence 'to check, spare,' and so 'to regulate, govern, mix in due proportion;' originally, it would seem, only with a dat.

Linguae témpera (*Plaut.* Rud. iv. 7. 28), *set limits to your tongue.*

Nĕque sibi hŏmĭnes fĕros tempĕrātūrōs existimābat quin &c. (*Caes.* B. G. i. 33), *nor did he think that, savages as they were, they would keep a check upon themselves so as not &c.*

Eum sibi crēdis ā mendācĭō tempĕrātūrum (Auct. ad Her. iv. 8. 25), *this man you suppose will refrain from a lie.*

Si cuiquam ulla in re unquam tempĕrāuĕrit, ut uos quōque ei tempĕrārētis (*Cic.* ii. Verr. π. 6. 17), *that if he ever spared any one in any thing, you also should spare him.*§

Of the extension of the dative from the person to the thing the following are examples:

Ignoscas uĕlim huic festīnātiōnī (*Cic.* ad Fam. v. 12. 1), *pray forgive my present haste.*

---

* From suaui- 'sweet,' Greek ἡδύ-. Advice is often represented under the idea of medicine, wholesome, yet bitter and so needing some sweet to disguise it, as in *Lucr.* i. 936, *sed ueluti pueris* &c.

† In *quis te persuasit* (*Enn.* ap. Serv. ad Aen. x. 10) *te* is a dative. But an acc. of the person was eventually used, as *uxorem eius suasi*, *Apul.* Met. ix. p. 286. Hence in the passive, *animus persuasus uidetur esse*, Auct. ad Her. i. 6; *persuasus erit*, Ov. A. A. iii. 679; *persuasa est*, *Phaedr.* i. 8.

‡ Perhaps originally, like *modera-ri*, a reflective verb. In the sense of 'regulate, mix in due proportion,' an acc. was soon used: as, *rempublicam*, (Cic. de Div. i. 43. 96; *acuta cum grauibus*, Cic. R. P. vi. 18; *iras*, *Virg.* A. i. 61).

§ That *imita-ri* 'to make oneself like (to)', and *sequ-i* 'to attach oneself (to)', must in some olden times have had a dative, seems to follow from their reflective form, as well as from the meaning. Thus the Greek ἕπεσθαι and Germ. *folg-en* always take a dat.

Hŏnōri inuīdērunt meō (*Cic.* in Rull. II. 3ᵛ. 103), *they looked with envy on the office I held.*
Cum căpĭtī mŏdērī dēbeō, rēdŭuiam cūrō (*Cic.* p. Rosc. Am. 44. 128), *when I ought to be doctoring the head, I am dressing an agnail.*
Rŏgō sumptŭ nē parcās (*Cic.* ad Fam. XVI. 4), *I beg you not to spare expense.*
Tēque his ērĭpē flammis (*Virg.* A. II. 289), *and thyself too rescue from these flames.*

981   When the active or simple verb requires a dative, care must be taken to use the passive as an impersonal.

Eius testĭmōniō crēdi ŏportet (*Cic.* II. Verr. III. 71. 166), *his evidence ought to be believed.**
Omnēs dēprĕcātōrēs quĭbus nōn ērat ignōtum, ētiam quĭbūs ērat, In Africam dīcuntur nāuĭgātūrī (*Cic.* ad Att. XI. 14. 1), *all the intercessors who have not been forgiven, even those who have been, are about to sail it is said for Africa.*
Inuĭdētŭr ēnim commŏdīs hŏmĭnum ipsōrum (*Cic.* de Or. II. 51. 207), *for even the advantages they themselves enjoy are regarded with an evil eye.*
Mihi nihil ăb istis nŏcēri pŏtest (*Cic.* in Cat. III. 12. 27), *I cannot be injured by your friends in any way.*
Cui ēnim parci pŏtuit ? (*Liv.* XXI. 14) *for who could have been spared ?*
Dictō pārētŭr (*Liv.* IX. 32), *the order is obeyed.*
His persuādēri ut diūtius mŏrārentur non pŏtĕrat (*Caes.* B. G. II. 10), *they could not be persuaded to stay any longer.*†

982   In Roman book-keeping, the account where an item was to be entered was expressed by a dative. Hence in phrases of this class two datives often present themselves, one pointing to the account, the other to the side of the account, whether Cr. or Dr.

---

* It is useful for beginners to translate verbs of this class by phrases which include a substantive and verb: as, *cred-* 'give credit,' *ignosc-* 'grant pardon,' *noce-* 'do damage.' By this contrivance an impersonal translation is obtained for the passive: *creditur* 'credit is given,' *ignoscitur* 'pardon is granted,' *nocetur* 'damage is done;' and thus a hint is given for putting the person 'to whom' in the dative.

† Still, exceptions occur: as, *credamur*, Ov. Fast. III. 351; *creditus*, Ov. Met. VII. 98. See also p. 196, note *, and p. 197, note †.

Mĭnus Dōlăbellă Verri acceptum rettŭlit,* quam Verrēs illi expensum tŭlĕrit (*Cic.* II. Verr. L 39. 100), *Dolabella placed to the credit of Verres a smaller sum than Verres placed to his (Dolabella's) debit.*

Quem fors diērum cumquĕ dăbit, lūcro Appŏnĕ (*Hor.* Od. I. 9. 14), *every day that fate shall give, set down to profit.*

Pŏstulare id grătiae appŏni sibi (*Ter.* And. II. 1. 32), *to expect that it should be set down to his credit as a favour received.*

Hoc ultiŏ mihi dant (*Cic.* ad Fam. XI. 28. 2), *this they set down against me as a fault.*

Nostram culpam illi (sc. terrae) impŭtămŭs† (*Plin.* XVIII. 1. 1. 2), *we debit her for our own misconduct.*

983 Hence a dative‡ is used to denote in what light a thing is regarded, what it serves as.

Nec eam rem hăbuit religiōni (*Cic.* de Div. I. 35. 77), *nor did he regard this as a warning from heaven.*

Vt sint rēliquis dŏcŭmentŏ (*Caes.* B. G. VII. 4), *that they may serve as a lesson to the rest.*

Vos eritis iūdices Laudin an uitio dūci id factum opŏrtuit (*Ter.* Ad. prol. 5), *you shall be judges whether this act a fault or credit should be deemed.*

Cui§ bŏnō fuit ? (*Cic.* p. Rosc. Am. 30. 84), *to whom was it an advantage ? or who was the gainer by it ?*

Mātronis persuāsit nē sĭbi ultio uertĕrent quŏd ăbessent ă pătriā (*Cic.* ad Fam. VII. 6), *she persuaded the matrons not to interpret her absence from her fatherland as a fault in her.*

984 Hence again the dative is sometimes used to denote the purpose: as,

---

* The first entries being made into the day-book (*aduersaria*), are thence carried to the proper heads in the ledger (*tabulae*). Hence the compound *re-fer-* used of the second entry. *Acceptum* and *expensum* mean 'received' and 'spent' by the book-keeper.

† Literally 'score against.'

‡ For this dative may be substituted *pro* or *in loco*. Often a mere nominative or accusative may be used; but the dative softens the phrase. *Sunt reliquis documentum* (Q. Curt. VIII. 14. 26) is, 'they are a lesson to the rest.' Still, in the English translation of this dative the 'as' is often omitted for brevity.

§ The favourite test of the old lawyer Cassius for discovering the author of a secret crime. A ridiculous blunder commonly marks the modern use of this quotation.

Quinquĕ cohortīs castrīs praesĭdĭō rĕlĭquit (*Caes.* B. G. vii. 60), *he left five battalions as a garrison for the camp,* or *to guard the camp.*
Hunc sĭbi dŏmĭcĭlĭō lŏcum dēlēgērunt (*Caes.* B. G. π. 29), *this place they selected as* (or *for*) *a residence.*
Hic nūptĭis dictŭst dĭes (*Ter.* And. i. 1. 75), *this is the day fixed for the marriage.*
Trĭumuir reī publĭcae constĭtuendae* (*Nep.* In Attico, 12), *one of three commissioners for regulating the state.*

985 The dative of a name is often used by attraction† to the dative of the object named : as,

Nōmen Arcturōst; mihi (*Plaut.* Rud. prol. 5), *my name is Arcturo.*
Cui nunc cognōmen Iūlo; Addĭtūr (*Virg.* A. 271), *to whom the surname Iulo now is added.* ‡
Lēges quĭbus ŭbŭlīs duŏdĕcim est nōmen (*Liv.* iii. 57), *the laws which have the name of the ! twelve tables.*§

986 The phrase soluendō nōn ĕrat, 'he was not able to pay, he was insolvent,' as in *Cic.* ad Fam. iii. 8. 2, seems difficult of explanation.

987 The poets use the dative (especially in nouns of the *o* declension) after verbs of motion : as,

It clāmor caelō‖ (*Virg.* A. v. 451), *rises the shout to heaven.*

ABLATIVE.

989 The ablative appears to unite in itself two cases of different origin, one similar in form and power to the dative, the other originally ending in a final *d*, signifying *from.* We commence with the former.

---

* Written briefly IIIVIR· R· P· C·
† Other instances of similar attraction are to be seen in § 1060.
‡ Can this construction have grown out of the use of the crude form, which in reason should have been used in such phrases?
§ Sometimes the name is in the same case as *nomen*. But in Cicero II. Verr. iv. 53. 118, *fons cui nomen Arethusast*, the letters *st* alone perhaps constitute the verb, leaving a dative *Arethusae*.
‖ Can this be a corruption of an accusative *caelom*, as the so-called adverbs *quo*, *eo*, &c. have also probably lost a final *m*. See also *tenus*, § 1384 *b.* note.

ABLATIVE. 201

990. At a town or in a small island the poets express by an ablative when the metre requires it, which can be only in the third or consonant declension: as,

Dardănĭumquē dūcem Tȳrĭā Karthāgĭnĕ* qui nunc Expectat (*Virg.* A. IV. 224), *and the Dardan chief at Tyrian Carthage who Now loitereth.*

991. The place *where* in some other phrases may also be expressed in the ablative, as rūrĕ *in the country*. Not unfrequently it is better to insert the preposition in. But this may be omitted at times, particularly if an adjective accompany the substantive. When that adjective is tōtō- *whole*, it would be wrong to use the preposition.

992. Time *when* is commonly expressed in the ablative: as,

Bellum eōdem tempŏrĕ mihi quŏque indixit (*Cic.* Phil. II. 1. 1), *he declared war at the same time against me too.*

993. The time *within* which any thing occurs is expressed by the ablative, whether the whole or any part be meant: as,

Saturnī stellā trigintā fĕrē annis cursum suum conficit (*Cic.* N. D. II. 20. 52), *the star of Saturn completes its course in about thirty years.*

Vrbēs Africae annis† prŏpē quinquāgintā nullum Rōmānum exercĭtum uīdērant (*Liv.* XXIX. 28), *the cities of the Afri during a space of nearly fifty years had seen no Roman army.*

994. Hence the interval *within* which one event follows another may be expressed by ablatives: as,

Mors Roscī quătriduō quoȚ is occisust Chrȳsŏgŏnō nuntiātūr (*Cic.* p. Rosc. Am. 36. 105), *the news of the death of Roscius is brought to Chrysogonus within four days after he is killed.*

---

* See Dative, § 951. That the ablative is only a license is stated by Servius on this passage: "*Carthagine pro Carthagini . . . Sic Horatius: Romae Tybur suam, ventosus Tybure Romam, pro Tyburi.*" In Livy the best Mss., where reported, have *Karthagini* &c.

† Hence the ablative is occasionally used when the accusative might have been expected. See § 1018. I.

‡ Literally 'the death of R. is reported to C. in the same four days in which he was killed,' the death occurring near the commencement of that period, the communication near the end of it.

905 Hence

Testāmentum fēcit, atque his diēbus paucīs est mortuā (*Cic.* p. Clu. 7. 22), *she made a will, and a few days after this died.*

906 From the notion of *where*, the ablative is used with the prepositions in and sūb if there be no motion implied, and also with prae, prō, &c. (See § 914, note.)

907 *In, in point of, in respect to,* is often the meaning of the ablative where it is used to define or limit the sense of any word or phrase : as,

Ennius fuit māior nātū* quam Plautūs (*Cic.* Tusc. L. 1. 3), *Ennius was older than Plautus.*

Scelērē pār est illi, industriā inferiōr (*Cic.* Phil. IV. 6. 15), *in wickedness he is equal to the other, in industry below him.*

Sunt ēnim quīdam hōmines non rē sed nōmine (*Cic.* de Off. L. 30. 105), *for there are, it must be confessed, some who are human beings not in reality, but in name.*

Lepōre omnibus praestĭtit (*Cic.* de Or. II. 67. 270), *in wit he excelled all.*

Victōriā suā glōriantŭr (*Caes.* B. G. I. 14), *they pride themselves on their victory.*

908 The ablatives of verbals in *tu*, called supines passive, are often so used with adjectives, though the more familiar translation is by an English infinitive : as,

Plērāquē dictū quam rē sunt facilĭōrā (*Liv.* XXXI. 38), *most things are easier in the saying than in the reality,* i. e. *easier to say than to do.*

Quid est tam iūcundum cognĭtū atque audītū? (*Cic.* de Or. I. 8. 31) *what is so delightful to see and to hear?*

909 The substantive ŏpĕs- (n.) *work,* and occasionally ŭsŭ- (m.) *advantage,* have an ablative† to express the object which it is necessary to obtain : as,

Opus: fuit Hirtiō conuentō (*Cic.* ad Att. X. 4. 11), *it was necessary to have an interview with Hirtius.*

---

* Literally 'greater in point of birth.'

† The nominative is also found in this construction, more particularly if it be a neuter pronoun. (See § 909.)

‡ 'The work to be done consisted in seeing Hirtius,' which accomplished, other things might follow. This might have been expressed by

Primum ĕrat nihil, cur prŏpĕrāto ŏpŭs esset (*Cic.* p. Mil. 19. 49), *in the first place there was nothing which made it necessary to hurry.*

Vbi mecum oriast tempestas, tum gūbernātōre* ŏpust (*Liv.* XXIV. 8), *when rough weather springs up, then there is need of a pilot.*

By, with, or *from,* &c. is frequently the translation of the ablative when it denotes the instrument, means, or cause: as,

Cornĭbus tauri, ăpri dentĭbus sē tūtantūr (*Cic.* N. D. II. 50. 127), *with his horns the bull, the boar with his tusks defends himself.*

Pătriae ignī ferrōquĕ mĭnĭtātūr (*Cic.* Phil. XIII. 21. 47), *he threatens his country with fire and sword.*†

Etĕsĭārum flātū nimii tempĕrantur călōrĕs (*Cic.* N. D. II. 53. 131), *by the blowing of the Etesian winds the excessive heat is moderated.*

The ablative of the means accompanies the five reflective verbs, ŭt-‡, nīt-, uesc-, fru-, pasc-: as,

Pellĭbŭs ūtuntūr (*Caes.* B. G. VI. 21), *they use skins.*

Pūrā quī nītītŭr hastā (*Virg.* A. VI. 760), *who rests him on a simple shaft.*

Lactĕ uescebantŭr (*Sal.* Jug. 89), *they lived upon milk.*

Lūcĕ fruīmŭr (*Cic.* p. Rosc. Am. 45. 131), *we enjoy the light of day.*

Frondĭbus pascuntūr (*Virg.* G. III. 528), *they feed themselves with branches.*

The ablative of the means in the same way accompanies the verbs, utu- *live,* fid- *trust,* and the participle frēto- *relying:* as,

---

a somewhat similar phrase in Greek: as, ἔργον ἦν συγγενέσθαι εἰς λόγους ἱέναι.

* Perhaps such a phrase as this had originally its participle also, as, for instance, *inuento.*

† 'Fire and iron' would be a more precise translation, the latter referring to the destructive axe quite as much as to the sword.

‡ The literal translation of these verbs would perhaps be, *utor* 'I assist myself with any thing,' *i. e.* 'I use it;' *nitor* 'I strain myself by acting upon something,' *i. e.* 'I lean upon it;' *uescor* 'I feed myself with,' or 'I eat' (used in speaking of human beings exclusive of slaves); *fruor* 'I feed myself with,' or 'I enjoy;' *pascor* 'I feed myself with,' or 'eat' (used in speaking of animals and slaves).

Lactĕ uīuunt (*Caes.* B. G. IV. 1), *they live upon milk.*

Prūdentiā consĭliōquĕ fīdens (*Cic.* de Off. I. 23. 81), *trusting in foresight and mental power.*

Ingĕniō frētī* (*Cic.* de Or. II. 24. 103), *relying upon their talent.*

1003 ' The ablatīve† of the means is used with the verbs făc- or făcĭmaīte *or do*, fī- *become*, and fu- *be*, especially in the participle fŭtŭro-.

Nĕscit quid făciat aurō (*Plaut.* Bac. II. 3. 100), *he knows not what to do with the gold.*

Quid hōc hŏmĭnĕ făciātis ? (*Cic.* II. Verr. I. 16. 42) *what are you to do with this fellow ?*

'Tuō quid factumst pallio ? (*Plaut.* Cas. v. 4. 9) *what is become of your cloak ?*

Quid Tulliōlā meā fīet ? (*Cic.* ad Fam. XIV. 4. 3) *what will become of my little Tullia ?*

Sī quid eō fuĕrit (*Plaut.* Trin. I. 2. 120), *if any thing happen to him.*

1004 The ablative of the means often accompanies verbs or adjectives of filling, increasing, mixing, joining, &c.: as,

Nāuīs cŏlōnīs pastōrĭbusquĕ complet (*Caes.* B. G. I. 50), *he fills the ships with farm-labourers and shepherds.*

Mactĕ uirtūte estō (*Liv.* IV. 14), *heaven bless thy noble deeds.*‡

Villa ăbundat; lactĕ, cāseō, mellĕ (*Cic.* de Sen. 16. 56), *the farmhouse abounds in milk and cheese and honey.*

Lăpĭdĭbus∥ plŭuit (*Liv.* I. 31), *it rained stones.*

1005 The price is the means by which any thing is obtained¶ in purchase, and hence the ablative accompanies verbs and adjectives of buying, selling, bidding and valuing:** as,

---

* Literally 'supported by,' *freto-* being in origin a participle of *fer-* ' bear.'

† In these phrases the preposition *de* is often used, as *quid de me fiet?*

‡ Literally 'be increased by thy manliness.'

§ This should perhaps have been referred to § 997.

∥ The accusative also is found.

¶ *Em-,* commonly translated 'buy,' means properly 'take,' as is seen in the compounds *dem-, exim-, sum-,* &c. See § 544.

** Or it would perhaps be more correct to be guided by the English preposition *at,* defining the point at which the price stands at a given

Eměre aquae sextārium cōguntur minā (*Cic.* de Off. II. 16. 56),
they are compelled to buy a pint of water for a mina.

Multō sanguĭnē Poenis uictōriā stětit (*Liv.* XXIII. 30), *the victory cost the Carthaginians much blood.**

Quod nōn ŏpūs est, assē cārum est (*Cato* ap. Sen. Ep. 94), *what you don't want is dear at a farthing.*

1005. 1 To affix a *penalty* implies an estimation of a crime. Hence the amount of penalties, like prices, is in the ablative :† as,

Děcem mīlĭbūs aeris dampnātūs (*Liv.* VII. 16), *sentenced to pay a penalty of 10,000 pieces of money.*

Multārō uitia hŏmĭnum dampnis, ignōmĭniā, uincŭlis, uerbĕrĭbŭs, exĭliis, mortĕ (*Cic.* de Or. I. 43. 194), *to punish the vices of men with fine, degradation, imprisonment, flogging, exile, death.*

1006 Verbs of *sacrificing* often take an ablative of the victim, that is, the means employed: as,

Cum fāciam uĭtŭlā prō frūgĭbŭs, ipsĕ uĕnīto (*Virg.* Buc. III. 77), *when I offer a calf for my crops, thyself shall come.*

Quīnquāgintā cāpris sācrĭfĭcārunt‡ (*Liv.* XLV. 16), *they sacrificed fifty goats.*

1007 Verbs signifying *to accustom*, take an ablative of the means, though in English the preposition *to* is prefixed: as,

Hŏmĭnes lăbōre adsĭduo et quŏtīdiāno adsuēti§ (*Cic.* de Or. III. 15. 58), *accustomed as they are to constant and daily labour.*

Crēdĕrē rēgii gĕnus pugnae quo assuērant fŏrĕ (*Liv.* XXXI. 35), *the king's troops thought the battle would be of the kind they were accustomed to.*

1008 *The road by which* any thing is moved is also a means, and therefore expressed by the ablative: as,

Frūmentum flūmĭne Arārī nāuĭbus subuexĕrat (*Caes.* D. G. L 16), *he had conveyed corn in ships up the river Arar.*

---

moment. We often talk of prices rising, falling, and being stationary. 'I bought consols at 63, and sold out at 94.'

* Literally 'stood them in much blood.'

† See also § 945.   ‡ The accusative is also used.

§ The dative also occurs after this word, as well as *ad* with the accusative.

1009   The attending *circumstances, manner, feelings,* are expressed by the ablative: as,

> Summā contentiōne dixit (*Cic.* Brut. 20. 80), *he spoke with the exertion of all his power.*
> Infestis armis concurrunt (*Liv.* I. 25), *they run together with their arms aimed at each other.*
> Expĕdītō* exercĭtu iter fēci (*Cic.* ad Fam. xv. 4. 8), *I proceeded with my army in light marching order.*
> Id aequō ănĭmō† non fĕret ciultās (*Cic.* de Or. II. 33. 144), *this the citizens will not bear calmly.*
> Duārum cohortium dampno exercĭtum rĕdūcĕre (*Caes.* B. G. vi. 44), *to lead the army back with the loss of two battalions.*

1009.1 In this construction, if no adjective accompany the noun, the preposition cum is commonly added, as summā cūrā *with the greatest care*, or cum cūrā *with care.* Yet certain ablatives have become virtually adverbs, and so are used without either adjective or preposition: as, ordĭne *in order,* rătiōne *rationally,* iūre *justly,* iniūria *without reason,* mōre *according to custom,* fraudĕ *fraudulently,* ui *forcibly,* ultrō *unduly,* silentiō *silently* (but also cum silentiō), sĕrēnō *with a cloudless sky,* austrō *with a south wind.*

1010   The ablative‡ of *quality* is the name usually given to that use of the case which denotes a condition of mind or body, &c. But it is essential that an adjective accompany this ablative:

> Tanta est ēlŏquentiā (*Cic.* de Or. II. 13. 55), *he is so eloquent.*
> Quā făcie fuit ? Crassis sūris, magnō căpĭte, admŏdum magnis pĕdĭbus (*Plaut.* Ps. IV. 7. 119), *how was he made ? He had thick calves, a great head, and very great feet.*
> Spēlunca infinĭta altĭtūdĭne (*Cic.* II. Verr. IV. 48. 107), *a cavern of boundless depth.*
> Hŏmĭnēs ēmĕrĭtis stipendiis (*Sal.* Jug. 84), *veterans who have served out their time.*

1011   This ablative is occasionally used when the state is not a permanent one: as,

> Nullō frigŏre addūcĭtŭr, ut căpĭte ŏpertō sit (*Cic.* de Sen. 10. 34), *no cold weather ever induces him to go with his head covered.*

---

* Literally 'unencumbered.'   † 'With a level or calm mind.'
‡ See also genitive of quality, § 927.

Magnō timōrĕ sum (*Cic.* ad Att. v. 14. 2), *I am in great alarm.*

Similar to this is the addition of the ablative of the name of the tribe or city to which a person belongs: as,

Ser. Sulpīcius Q.F.* Lemoniā† Rūfūs (*Cic.* Phil. IX. 7. 15), *Servius Sulpicius Rufus, son of Quintus, of the Lemonian tribe.*

Cn. Magius Crĕmōnā‡ (*Caes.* B. C. I. 24), *Cneius Magius of Cremona.*

Ablative absolute is the name commonly employed when an ablative of a noun is accompanied by a substantive, adjective, or participle, to denote the time when, the means by which, or any attending circumstances. It therefore belongs properly to the heads already given. There is however this peculiarity of translation, that the English often requires no preposition: as,

Abl. abs. of time when: Is, M.§ Messālā, M.§ Pīsōnĕ cōss.§ coniūrātiōnem fēcit (*Caes.* B. G. I. 2), *this man in the consulship‖ of Marcus Messala and Marcus Piso formed a conspiracy.*

Abl. abs. of means: Catāpultis dispŏsĭtis mūrōs dēfensōrĭbus nūdāuĕrat (*Liv.* XXL. 11), *by his catapults placed at different points he had cleared the wall of its defenders,* or *he had placed his catapults at different points and so had cleared &c.*

Abl. abs. of circumstances: Nātūrā dūce errāri nullō pactō pŏtest (*Cic.* de Leg. I. 6. 20), *with nature for our guide, the path can no way be mistaken.*

Quid dīcam hac iūuentūtĕ? (*Cic.* ad Att. X. 11. 3) *what am I to say with such young men as we have now-a-days?*

Vŏluntas tăcĭtis nōbīs¶ intellĕgi non pŏtĕrat (*Cic.* p. Caec. 18. 53), *our wish could not have been understood, had we been silent.*

That by which any thing is measured is a means of measurement, and therefore in the ablative: as,

---

* *Quinti filius.* † *Tribu* understood.

‡ Or the same might have been expressed by an adjective, *Cremonensis.*

§ To be read, *Marco, Marco, consulibus.*

‖ Literally 'M. Messala, M. Piso (being) consuls.'

¶ Literally 'we (being) silent.'

Vŏluptāte omniā dīrĭgĕrĕ* (*Cic.* de Fin. II. 22. 71), *to test every thing by pleasure.*

Non nŭmĕro haec iūdĭcantur, sed pondĕrĕ (*Cic.* de Off. II. 22. 79), *it is not by number that these things are estimated, but by weight.*

Discrīplus pŏpŭlus censū, ordĭnĭbŭs, aetātĭbŭs (*Cic.* de Leg. III. 19. 44), *the people distributed into different classes according to income and rank and age.*

1015 The *comparative* takes an ablative of the object with which the comparison† is made : as,

Viliūs argentumst aurō, ulrtūtĭbŭs aurum (*Hor.* Ep. I. 1. 52), *silver than gold is cheaper, gold than virtue.*

1016 Similarly the adjectives *digno- indigno-* and the verbs formed therefrom, take an ablative of the object with which the comparison is made : as,

Eum omnes cognĭtiōne ēt hospĭtiō dignum existŭmārunt (*Cic.* p. Arch. 3. 5), *this (foreigner) all deemed worthy of their acquaintance and friendship.*

Haud ēquĭdem tālī mē dignŏr hŏnōre (*Virg.* A. I. 339), *not in truth of such an honour do I deem me worthy.*

1017 The amount of distance or difference in time, space, or quantity is commonly expressed in the ablative.

Id uiginti annis ante ăpud nos fēcĕrat Cŏrĭŏlānŭs (*Cic.* de Am. 12. 42), *this Coriolanus had done among us twenty years before.*

Haec est aetas dĕcem annis minor quam consūlāris (*Cic.* Phil. v. 17. 48), *this age is ten years less than that required for a consul.*

Tribus tantis illi‡ minus redit quam obsēucris (*Plaut.* Trin. II.

---

* Literally ' to keep in a straight line as a carpenter does by applying his rule.'

† A comparison implies proximity of the things compared. Hence this use of the ablative flows easily from the original meaning of the dative. Observe too that all the verbs denoting comparison signify strictly the bringing together, as *com-para-*, *com-fer-*, *con-tend-*, *com-pos-*. So also the prepositions of proximity, ad (§ 1304 *h.*), prae (§ 1356 *d.*), prŏ (§ 1361 *g.*), are used in comparisons.

‡ The adverb.

4. 128), *for every bushel you sow on that land, you lose three bushels in the return.*

Milibus passuum sex ā Caesăris castris consēdit (*Caes.* B. G. I. 48), *he took a position six miles from Caesar's camp.*

1018   The ablatives† of pronouns and adjectives of quantity are much used in this way with comparatives : as,

Viā quantō tūtior, tantō fĕrē longiŏr (*Liv.* IX. 2), *a road longer in about the same proportion as it was safer.*

Quō māiŏr est In ănĭmīs praestantia, eō māiōre indĭgent dīlĭgentiā (*Cic.* Tusc. IV. 27. 58), *the greater the excellence in the soul, the more attention it needs.*

1018. 1   An ablative is occasionally used instead of an accusative (§ 915) to denote duration of time.

Quinque hōris proelium sustĭnŭērant (*Caes.* B. C. I. 47), *they had kept up the battle for five hours.*

Octōginta annis nixit (*Sen.* Ep. 93), *he lived to the age of eighty.*

1019   The form of an ablative is sometimes found in inscriptions, old writers, and certain phrases, where a dative would be expected : as,

IOVE OPTVMO MAXSVMO (Inscr. Grut. XVI. 8), *to Jupiter, the best, the greatest.*

Postquam mortĕ dātust Plautus, cōmoediā lūget (*Plaut.*‡), *now that Plautus is given to Death, Comedy is in mourning.*

Triumuĭri auro argento aerĕ flandō fĕriundō (Inscr. Orell. 560), *the three commissioners for smelting and stamping gold, silver and bronze.*

1020   Hence the poets, to accommodate their metres, occasionally substitute the form of the ablative where a dative might have been expected : as,

At si uirgineum suffūdĕrit ōrĕ rŭbōrem,
Ventŭs ĕrit (*Virg.* G. I. 430),

But if a maiden's blush she§ pour from beneath upon her cheek, Wind will there be.

---

* Literally ' less by three times as much.' Thus the extravagance of the phrase runs beyond possibility.

† But see § 789, note.

‡ First verse of the epitaph written by Plautus for himself. *Gell.* I. 24.

§ *i. e.* ' the moon.'

F

Mollī Cālēnum
Porrēctūrā ultrō miscet sitientī—rūbētam (Juv. I. 69),
*Mild Calene about to hand
To her thirsting lord, she mixes therein—a toad.*

A true ablative ending in the letter *d** belonged to the old language, and the loss of this *d* led to a form very similar to the weakened dative commonly called the ablative. Hence, *from a town* is sometimes expressed by a mere ablative: as,

Cŏrinthō† fūgit (*Cic*. Tusc. v. 37.109), *he fled from Corinth.*

Similarly the ablatives rūrĕ and dŏmō are used: as,

Cĭbārĭă sĭbi quemquĕ dŏmō effĕrrĕ iŭbent (*Caes*. B. G. I. 5), *they bid them bring food from home, every man for himself.*

Pāter rūrĕ rĕdiīt (*Ter*. E. III. 5. 63), *my father is returned from the country.*

Verbs and adjectives of *removal* and separation are followed by an ablative: as,

Signum non pŏtĕrat mŏuĕrĕ lŏcō (*Cic*. de Div. I. 35. 77), *he could not move the standard from where it was.*

Tuos culpā lībĕro (*Cic*. ad Att. XIII. 22. 3), *I free your people from blame.*

Praetūrā se abdīcat‡ (*Cic*. in Cat. IV. 3. 5), *he lays down the office of Praetor.*

Dēfunctī§ rēgis impĕriō (*Liv*. I. 4), *having discharged the king's order.*

His ăqua atque igni interdixĕrat (*Caes*. B. G. VI. 44), *these he had forbidden fire and water.*

Inuīdet ignĕ rŏgi misĕris (*Lucr*. VII. 798), *he grudges the poor wretches the fire of a funeral pile.*

* As, for example, on one of the epitaphs of the Scipios (Orelli 550), *Gnaiuod patre prognatus* for *Gnaeo* &c.

† More commonly *a Corintho*, as *a Gergouia discessit* (*Caes*. B. G. VII. 59). When a word denoting town is added, a preposition is necessary, as *Expellitur ex oppido Gergouia* (*Caes*. B. G. VII. 4); *Generis antiquitatem Tusculo ex clarissumo municipio profectam* (*Cic*. p. Font. 14. 41). See also §§ 884 note, and 951 note ‡.

‡ Literally 'he unbinds himself from,' the office being a sort of charge or burden which for security he had fastened to his person.

§ The reflective verbs *fung-*, *defung-*, probably meant originally to relieve oneself; and the burden, as with *abdico me*, will for the same reason be in the ablative. Hence the word 'discharge,' i.e. 'unload,' will be literally correct.

Rōmā cărēmŭs (*Cic. ad Att.* IX. 19.1), *we are deprived of Rome.*

1024 The verbs or participles which denote *birth* or origin take an ablative: as,

Mercŭrĭus, Iŏvĕ nātŭs et Maĭā (*Cic.* N. D. III. 22. 58), *Mercury born of Jupiter and Maia.*

1025 The prepositions which signify removal or separation have an ablative: as, ăb, dē, ēb, sĭnĕ, absquĕ, clam. See § 914, note.

NUMBER OF SUBSTANTIVES.

1026 Some substantives are used in the plural where the English translation has a singular*: as,

Cassī ădĭpĕm (*Cic. in Cat.* III. 7.16), *the fat of Cassius.*
Inĭmīcĭtĭae cum Rōscĭīs (*Cic. p. Rosc. Am.* 6. 17), *a quarrel with the Roscii.*
Cervīces‡ sĕcūrī subiēcit (*Cic.* Phil. II. 21. 51), *he presented his neck to the hatchet.*

1027 The terms of *weather* are sometimes used in the plural where the English language would almost require the singular: as, călōrēs, frīgŏră, grandĭnēs, imbrēs, nĭvēs, plŭvĭae, pruīnae. Thus,

Terrēre ănĭmos fulmĭnĭbus, nĭvĭbus, grandĭnĭbŭs (*Cic.* N. D. II. 5. 14), *to frighten the minds of men with thunder, and snow, and hail.*
Transcendĕre Apennīnum intŏlĕrandĭs frĭgŏrĭbŭs (*Liv.* XXII. 1), *to cross the Apennines when the frost was unbearable.*

1028 The plural is preferred in *general truths,* where the English has commonly a singular: as,

Vĭri ĭn uxōrēs ultae nĕcisquĕ hăbent pŏtestātem (*Caes.* B. G. VI. 19), *the husband (in that country) has the power of life and death over the wife.*

1029 The singular of some words is found where the English translation requires a plural: as,

Vīta§ illustrium (*Nepos*), *the lives of illustrious men.*

* See also § 152.
† Editions commonly have erroneously and contrary to the Mss. the singular. See Steinmetz.
‡ *Cervic-* probably meant a single vertebra.
§ See Servius Aen. L. 372. See also Fischer's Pseudo-Nepos, Preface, near the end.

1030 The singular is preferred with animals and vegetables where there is an allusion to the table, because they are considered in the mass, not counted: as,

> Villa ăbundat porco, haedo, agnō, gallīnā (*Cic.* de Sen. 16. 56), *the farm-house abounds with pork and kid and lamb* and fowl.*
>
> Lĕpŏrem et gallīnam et ansĕrum gustārĕ fas non pŭtant (*Caes. B. G.* v. 12), *hare and fowl and goose they think it an act of impiety to taste.*
>
> Pythăgŏricis interdictum ĕrat nē fābā uescĕrentŭr (*Cic.* de Div. I. 30. 62), *the Pythagoreans were forbidden to eat beans.*

1031 So also with other words where the mass does not admit of numeration: as,

> Puluinus rŏsā fartŭs (*Cic.* II. Verr. v. 11. 27), *a pillow stuffed with rose-leaves.*
>
> In uiŏlā aut in rŏsā (*Cic.* Tusc. v. 26. 73), *on violets or roses* (meaning the gathered flowers).

1032 In military language the singular is used at times for a plural†: as,

> Quoād insĕqui pĕdest pŏtuit (*Liv.* II. 25), *as far as the infantry could pursue.*
>
> Equĕs eōs ad castra ēgit (*Liv.* II. 25), *the cavalry drove them to their camp.*
>
> Hic miles māgis plăcuit (*Liv.* XXII. 57), *a soldiery of this kind was preferred.*
>
> Rōmānŭs irā ŏdiōquĕ pugnābat (*Liv.* III. 2), *the Romans fought under a feeling of indignation and hatred.*

DEFECTIVE SUBSTANTIVES.

1032.1 Undeclined substantives (§ 187) can only be used as nominatives or accusatives. But the names of the letters, and generally words spoken of as words, may be used as genitives, datives or ablatives, if an adjective or substantive in apposition fix the case.

---

* Observe that the omission of the indefinite article in English makes the distinction between the animal for table and the living animal.

† The singular however has its force, drawing attention to the individual. Thus, in the last phrase, 'each individual soldier has his own feelings of anger;' so again in the first sentence, 'a foot-soldier' would have been an equally good translation, signifying 'inasmuch as he was a foot-soldier.'

OMISSION OR ELLIPSIS OF SUBSTANTIVES.

1033. The masculine adjective is often used in speaking of men, the neuter in speaking of things; especially where the gender is distinguished in the termination. See § 1044.

1034. Some adjectives used as substantives may be seen in § 210; and to these may be added,

Stătīvā, hibernā, &c. (castrā *understood*).
Tertiāna-, quartāna-, &c. (fĕbrĭ- *understood*).
Circensēs, Saecŭlārēs, &c. (lūdī *understood*).
Trirēmi-, actuāria-, &c. (nāuĭ- *understood*).
Sŭburbāno-, Tuscŭlāno-, &c. (praedio- [n.] *understood*).
Rĕpĕtundārum (rērum *understood*).
Centensūmae, &c. (ūsūrae *understood*).
Agōnālĭă, Lĭbĕrālĭă, &c. (sācrā *understood*).
Prīmae, sĕcundae (partēs *understood*).
Tertia-, quarta-, &c. (parti- *understood*).
In postĕrum (diem *understood*).

1035. The genitive of a deity is often used with prepositions, the proper case of aedi- *a temple* being understood.

Hăbĭtābat rex ad Iŏuis* Stătōrĭs (aedem *understood*) (*Liv.* I. 41), *the king resided near the temple of Jupiter Stator.*

A Vestas (aedē *understood*) ductast (*Cic.* ad Fam. xiv. 2. 2), *she was taken away from the temple of Vesta.*

1036. But the Latin language does not copy the English in the use of the genitive of a person's name, meaning his house; but either inserts the word for house, or uses a preposition with the name of the person † as,

Vēnisti in dŏmum Laecae (*Cic.* in Cat. I. 4. 8), *you came to Laeca's.*

Dŏmī Caesăris dēprensust (*Cic.* ad Att. L 12. 3), *he was caught at Caesar's.*

1036.1 When a sentence contains two corresponding genitives governed

---

* This is like our own phrase, 'St. Paul's' for 'St. Paul's Church.'

† The use of the prepositions is as follows:—to Cicero's house, *ad Ciceronem* or *domum ad Ciceronem*; at Cicero's house, *apud Ciceronem*; from Cicero's house, *a Cicerone* or *a Cicerone domo*; and this even though Cicero be known to be absent. See these prepositions, §§ 1305. *o*; 1311. *c*; 1305. *h*.

by the same substantive, this substantive need for the most part only be expressed with the first genitive: as,

> Flēbat pāter dē fīlī mortĕ, dē pātris fīliŭs (*Cic.* II. Verr. I. 30. 76), *the father was weeping for the death of his son, the son for that of his father.*
>
> Quis est quī possit conferrĕ uītam Trĕbōnī cum Dŏlābellae ? (*Cic.* Phil. XI. 4. 9) *who is there who can compare the life of Trebonius with that of Dolabella ?*
>
> Meō iūdīciō stārĕ mālō quam omnium rĕlīquŏrum (*Cic.* ad Att. XII. 21. 5), *I choose to abide by my own judgment, rather than by that of all the rest.*

1036.2 As a wife, son, daughter or slave may be said to belong to a man, the genitive of the possessor is occasionally used without the substantives denoting those relations : as,

> Hasdrŭbal Gisgōnis (*Liv.* XXV. 37), *Hasdrubal, the son of Gisgo.*
> Vērāniă Pīsōnis (*Plin.* Ep. II. 20), *Verania, the wife of Piso*, more literally *Piso's Verania.*
> Flaccus Claudī (*Ter.* And. tit.), *Flaccus, Claudius's slave.*

Adjectives, &c.

1037 Adjectives and participles are attracted into the same case, gender and number as the substantive to which they refer.

Thus, from docto- or docta- *learned*, and hŏmŏn- *man* ; bŏno- or bŏna- *good*, mŭliĕr- *woman* ; grăui- *heavy*, ŏnĕs- *load*, we have :

Singular.

N. doctŭs hŏmo.	bŏnă mŭliĕr.	grăue ŏnŭs.
V. docte hŏmo.	bŏnă mŭliĕr.	grăue ŏnŭs.
Ac. doctum hŏmĭnem.	bŏnam mŭliĕrem.	grăue ŏnŭs.
G. doctī hŏmĭnis.	bŏnae mŭliĕris.	grăuĭs ŏnĕrĭs.
D. doctō hŏmĭnī.	bŏnae mŭliĕrī.	grăuī ŏnĕrī.
Ab. doctō hŏmĭnĕ.	bŏnā mŭliĕrĕ.	grăuī ŏnĕrĕ.

Plural.

N. doctī hŏmĭnēs.	bŏnae mŭliĕrēs.	grăuia ŏnĕră.
V. doctī hŏmĭnēs.	bŏnae mŭliĕrēs.	grăuia ŏnĕră.
Ac. doctōs hŏmĭnēs.	bŏnās mŭliĕrēs.	grăuia ŏnĕră.
G. doctōrum hŏmĭnum.	bŏnārum mŭliĕrum.	grăuium ŏnĕrum.
D.A. doctīs hŏmĭnĭbŭs.	bŏnīs mŭliĕrĭbŭs.	grăuĭbŭs ŏnĕrĭbŭs.

1038 Sometimes the gender and number of the adjective or participle are determined by the sense* rather than the form of the substantive : as,

Omnis aetas currĕre obuii (*Liv.* xxvii. 51), *all ages* i. e. *persons of every age kept running to meet him.*
Căpĭtă coniūrātiōnĭs uirgis caesi ac sĕcūrī percussī sunt (*Liv.* x. 1), *the heads of the conspiracy were flogged and beheaded.*
Concursus pŏpŭli mīrantium quid rei esset (*Liv.* i. 41), *a running together of the citizens, who wondered what was the matter.*
Eŏ nŭmĕrŏst qui semper sanctī sunt hăbĭtī (*Cic.* p. Arch. 12. 31), *he is one of a class who have ever been accounted sacred.*
Cētĕrā multĭtūdō dĕcĭmus quisque ad supplicium lectī (*Liv.* ii. 59), *of the great mass remaining, every tenth man was selected for punishment.*

1039 If a relative or other pronoun be the subject of a sentence which itself contains a predicative substantive, the gender and number of the pronoun are commonly determined by the latter: as,

Thēbae, quod Boeōtiae căpŭt est (*Liv.* xlii. 44), *Thebes, which is the capital of Boeotia.*
Iustă glōriă, qui est fructus uērae uirtūtis (*Cic.* in Pis. 24. 57), *the genuine glory, which is the fruit of true merit.*
Eă† quăternă mīlia ĕrant (*Liv.* xxi. 17), *these (legions) were each 4000 strong.*
Hōc ŏpŭs, hic lăbŏr est (*Virg.* A. vi. 129), *this is the task, this the labour.*

1040 If an adjective or participle refer to several nouns of different gender or number, the gender and number are commonly determined by one of the three rules following :

a. Most commonly the adjective agrees in number and gender with the noun to which it is nearest ;

b. Or, if the nouns be living beings, the masculine plural may be used ;

c. Or, if they be things without life, the neuter plural may be used : as,

---

* This is called the *constructio ad synesim.*

† Nay, we find in Livy, xxi. 55, *Duodeuiginti milia Romana erant,* ' the Romans amounted to 18,000 ;' for so all the best Mss.

a. Mens et animus et consilium et sententia civitatis positast in legibus (*Cic.* p. Clu. 53. 146), *the intellect, and soul, and forethought, and feelings of a state reside in the laws.*
Cingetorigi principatus atque imperium est traditum (*Caes. B. G.* VI. 8), *the chief post and the supreme command were handed over to Cingetorix.*
Numidae magis pedes quam arma tuta sunt (*Sal.* Jug. 74), *the Numidians owed their safety rather to their feet than their arms.*

b. Pater mi et mater mortui sunt (*Ter.* E. III. 3. 12), *my father and mother are dead.*

c. Labor uoluptasque, dissimillima natura, societate quadam inter se naturali sunt iuncti (*Liv.* V. 3), *toil and pleasure, utterly unlike as they are in nature, are still joined together in a sort of natural partnership.*

1041 As a plural adjective may be distributed between two substantives, so may a plural substantive between two adjectives. Thus,
Quarta et Martia legiones (*Cic.* ad Fam. XI. 19), *the fourth and the Martian legions.**

1042 Many words which were originally adjectives or participles are at times used as substantives, and as such may have adjectives or genitives attached to them: as,
Natalis meus (*Cic.* ad Att. VII. 5. 3), *my birthday.*
Vetus uicinus (*Cic.* p. Mur. 27. 56), *an old neighbour.*
Iniquissimi mei (*Cic.* II. Verr. V. 69. 177), *my greatest enemies.*
Paternus inimicus (*Cic.* p. Scauro, 2. 45. b.), *an hereditary enemy.*
Publicum malum (*Sal.* Cat. 57), *public misfortune.*
Praeclarum responsum (*Cic.* de Sen. 5. 13), *a glorious answer.*
Summa pectoris (*Cic.* ad Fam. I. 9. 15), *the highest parts of the breast.*
Occulta templi (*Caes.* B. G. III. 105), *the hidden recesses of the temple.*
Summum montis (*Sal.* Jug. 93), *the summit of the mountain.*
Medium diei (*Liv.* XXVI. 45), *the middle of the day.*

1043 The neuter adjective often found in the predicate of a sentence,

---

* Not unlike this is the use of two praenomina with the gens in the plural: as, *C. et L. Caepasii*, i.e. *Caius et Lucius Caepasii* (*Cic.* Brut. 69. 242), 'the two Caepasii, Caius and Lucius.'

when the subject is not of that gender, is to be considered as a substantive. Thus,

> Tristĕ lŭpus stăbŭlīs (*Virg.* Buc. III. 80), *a sad thing is the wolf unto the stall.*
>
> Vărium et mūtăbĭlĕ semper Fēmĭnă (*Virg.* A. IV. 569), *a thing of motley hue and ever changeable is woman.*

1. A neuter of an adjective is often used with prepositions, especially to form adverbial phrases: as,

> Stāre In occultō (*Cic.* p. Clu. 28. 78), *to stand in some dark corner.*
>
> In postĕrum prōuīdērunt (*Cic.* in Rull. II. 33. 91), *they provided for the future.*

So also de imprōuīsō *unexpectedly*, de intĕgrō *afresh*, sĭnĕ dŭbiō *without doubt.*

There is greater freedom in using as substantives those parts of an adjective which show their gender; as, for instance, the nominative and accusative of neuters. Thus the genitives of neuters of the third declension should be avoided in this construction, unless some other genitive less ambiguous accompany them. For example, we may say,

> Nīl hūmānī (*Ter.* Haut. I. 1. 25), *nothing like the conduct of a man*, where hūmānī is virtually a substantive; or,
>
> Nīl hūmānum, where hūmānum is an adjective.

But if the adjective be of the *i* declension, as cīuīli-, then we have no choice but nil cīuīlĕ, *nothing like the conduct of a citizen;* unless indeed two adjectives are united, as:

> Sī quidquam in uōbis, non dicō cīuīlis sēd hūmānī esset (*Liv.* V. 3), *if there had been aught in you of the feelings, I do not say of a citizen, but of a man.*
>
> Pŏtĭŏr ūtĭlis quam hŏnestī cūrā (*Liv.* XLII. 47), *it is better to concern oneself about the useful than the honourable.*

When the gender is not at once determined by the termination of the adjective, it is commonly better to use a substantive with the adjective: as,

Multīs hŏmĭnĭbŭs or multīs rēbŭs, rather than multīs alone.

The Roman gentile names, that is, the second names in *io*, are really adjectives, and hence are at times found with substantives of various genders attached to them: as,

Sulpicia horrea (*Hor. Od.* IV. 12. 18), *the Sulpician granaries.*
Octāuia porticūs (*Velle.* I. 11), *the Octavian portico.*
Iūlia lex (*Cic.* p. Balbo, 8. 21), *the Julian law.*
Cornēlia castra (*Caes.* B. C. II. 37), *the Cornelian camp.*

1047 The Romans use possessive adjectives formed from proper names instead of the genitive: as,

Extenditūr ūna
Horridā per lātōs āciēs Volcānia campos (*Virg. A.* X. 407),
Spreads unbroken
O'er the wide plain the bristling host of Vulcan.
Hērīlis filius (*Ter.* Ph. I. 1. 5), *master's son.*
Pompēiānūs exercitūs (*Caes.* B. C. III. 90), *Pompey's army.*

1048 Possessive adjectives include the notion of a genitive, and hence an adjective or participle, with or without a substantive, in the genitive case, is often attached to them; or it may be a relative sentence, referring to the noun implied in the adjective: as,

Quoi nōmen meum absentis hōnōrī fuissct, ei meas praesentis prēces non pūtas prōfuissē? (*Cic.* p. Planc. 10. 26) *do you think the prayers which I addressed in person were of no service to one to whom my mere name in my absence had been an honour?*

Vt meā dēfunctae mollītēr ossā cūbent (*Ov. Am.* I. 8. 108), *that my bones when I am dead may softly lie.*

Meam legem contemnīt, hōminis inimici (*Cic.* p. Sest. 64. 135), *he treats my law with contempt, but then I am his enemy.*

Vestrā consīlia accūsantur, qui mihi summum hōnōrem impōsuistis (*Sal.* Jug. 85), *it is your wisdom which is impeached, for it was you who imposed upon me the highest office.*

Vestrā, qui cum summa intēgrītātē uīxistis, hoc maxūme intērest (*Cic.* p. Sull. 28. 79), *you who have lived with the greatest integrity are most concerned in this.*

Vēiens* bellum ortumst, quibus Sābini armā coniunxērant (*Liv.* II. 53), *a war with Veii arose, with which city the Sabines had united their arms.*

1049 An adjective in agreement with the nominative often accompanies a verb where the English has commonly an adverb: as,

* 'Of or belonging to Veii.'

Et tibi Lŭbēns bĕnĕ făxim (*Ter.* Ad. v. 5.5), *and I would gladly serve you.*

In phy̆sĭcīs tōtust ălĭēnŭs (*Cic.* de Fin. I. 0. 17), *in natural philosophy he is altogether out of his element.*

Lŭpus grĕgĭbus nocturnŭs ŏbambŭlat (*Virg.* G. III. 538), *the wolf in presence of the flocks by night walks to and fro.*

Phĭlōtĭmus nullus uēnit (*Cic.* ad Att. XI. 24. 4), *Philotimus has not made his appearance at all.*

The adjectives prĭōr-, prīmo-, postrēmo-, prīncĭp-, sōlo- &c. are used in immediate connection with verbs in such a manner that the English translation often requires the insertion of the verb ĕs- *be* and the relative, or some other periphrasis: as,

Prīmă Sĭcĭlĭă prōuincĭast adpellātă (*Cic.* II. Verr. II. 1. 2), *Sicily was the first that was called a province.*

Hispănĭă postrēma omnium prōuĭnciārum perdŏmĭtast (*Liv.* XXVIII. 12), *Spain was the last of all the provinces to be thoroughly subdued.*

Stŏĭci sōli ex omnĭbŭs ēlŏquentiam uirtūtem essē dixērunt (*Cic.* de Or. III. 18. 65), *the Stoics are the only sect of the whole number who have declared eloquence to be a virtue.*

A neuter adjective is often used as an adverb. Thus,

Hŏdie aut summum crās (*Cic.* ad Att. XIII. 21. 2), *to-day or at farthest to-morrow.*

Dulcĕ* rīdentem (*Hor.* Od. I. 22. 23), *sweetly laughing.*

When substantives signifying agents have one form for the masculine, another for the feminine, they so far take the character of adjectives, that they must agree in number, gender and case with the word to which they refer: as,

Lēgis aeternae uis, quae quăsĭ dux uĭtae et măgistra offĭcĭōrum est (*Cic.* N. D. I. 15. 40), *the force of an eternal law, which is as it were the guide of life and the instructress in duty.*

Timor, non dĭŭturnus măgistĕr officĭ (*Cic.* Phil. II. 36. 90), *fear, no permanent instructor in duty.*

Other words commonly treated as substantives take a similar liberty between neuters and masculines: as,

---

* This is carried to a great extent by the poets, who use even the plural neuter in this way. The comparative neuter is the only form for a comparative adverb.

Măre Ocĕănum (*Caes.* B. G. III. 7), *the sea called Oceanus.*
Flūmen Rhēnum (*Hor.* ad Pis. 18), *the river Rhenus or Rhine.*
Erĭdănum ostium (*Plin.* III. 16), *the mouth of the Eridanus.*
Volturnŭs amnĭs (*Liv.* XXIII. 19), *the river Volturnus.*
Volturnum oppĭdum (*Plin.* H. N. III. 5.9), *the town Volturnum.*

1054 Although a substantive in Latin has commonly but one adjective attached to it, except where conjunctions are employed, this restriction does not apply, *a.* to pronominal adjectives, *b.* to numerals, *c.* to adjectives of quantity, *d.* to those which accompany verbs as part of the predicate, *e.* to the possessive adjectives, such as Plūtōnĭa (see § 1047), *f.* to three or more adjectives, with pauses to supply the place of conjunctions (see § 1435 *b.*): as,

    a. Eădem illa indiuīdua et sŏlĭdă corpŏră (*Cic.* de Fin. I. 6.18), *those same indivisible and solid bodies.*

    b. Duŏdĕcim mīlĭa Attĭcă tălenta dătō (*Liv.* XXXVIII. 38), *he shall pay 12,000 Attic talents.*

    c. Omnes rectae rēs atquĕ laudābĭlēs eō rĕfĕruntŭr (*Cic.* de Fin. I. 12.42), *all right and praiseworthy things are referred to this standard.*

    d. Princepsquĕ dĕcĭmă lĕgio ei grātiās ēgit (*Caes.* B. G. I. 41), *and the tenth legion was the first to thank him.*

    e. Et dŏmŭs exīlis Plūtōnĭă (*Hor.* Od. I. 4. 17), *and Pluto's shadowy house.*

    f. Eă uŏluptārĭă, dēlĭcātă, mollis hăbētur disciplīnă (*Cic.* de Fin. I. 11.37), *this is accounted a voluptuous, tender, effeminate school of philosophy.*

COMPARATIVES.

1055 The second of the objects compared is expressed by the ablative in short and simple phrases (§ 1015), but quam is employed for this purpose in longer or more complicated phrases, or when greater emphasis is desired. Thus,

    a. When the comparative adjective (or adverb) does not belong immediately to the two objects compared, quam is required : as,

    Fīlium frēquentiōrem cum illis quam sēcum cernēbat (*Liv.* XXXIX. 53), *he saw that his son was more frequently in their company than in his own.*

    b. But suppose that the adjective does belong to both, still if the first object be governed by a word which does not govern the second, the second should be in a distinct proposition of its own preceded by quam : as,

> Meliōrem quam egó sum suppōnō tibi (*Plaut.* Curc. II. 2. 6), *I give you as a substitute a better than myself.*
>
> Hŏmĭni non grātiōsiōrī quam Calidius est, Curidio argentum reddidisti (*Cic.* II. Verr. IV. 20. 44), *you paid the money to Curidius, a man not more influential than Calidius.*
>
> Pompēius dixit sē mūnītiōrem fŏrē quam Africānus fuisset (*Cic.* ad Q. Fr. II. 3. 3), *Pompey said that he should be better guarded than Africanus was.**

Obs. Yet even in this case, if the first object be an accusative, the second is often, though illogically, put in the accusative by attraction : as,

> Pătrem tam plăcĭdum reddo quam ŏuem† (*Ter.* Ad. IV. 1. 18), *I make your father as quiet as a lamb.*‡

c. But even when the two objects are under the same construction, quam should still be used with other cases than the nominative or accusative.

> *G.* Albānō non plūs ănĭmī ĕrat quam fĭdeī (*Liv.* I. 27), *the Alban had no more courage than honour.*
>
> *D.* His igitur quam phȳsĭcis pŏtius crēdendum exīstĭmās ? (*Cic.* de Div. II. 16. 37) *do you think then that we ought to trust these rather than the natural philosophers ?*
>
> *Abl.* Absoluērunt admīrātiōnē māgis uirtūtis quam iūrē causae (*Liv.* I. 26), *they acquitted (him) rather from admiration of his valour than for the goodness of his cause.*
>
> *d.* But *N.* Elĕphantō bēluārum nullā prūdentiŏr (*Cic.* N. D. I. 35. 97), *not one of all the great beasts has more intelligence than the elephant.*
>
> Ex ēius linguā mellē dulcior fluēbat ōrātiō (*Cic.* de Sen. 10. 31), *from his tongue flowed words sweeter than honey.*

* Here the difference of time, the one being future and the other past, made quam desirable.

† For *quam ouis est.*

‡ Examples of both these constructions occur in *Tibi, multo maiori quam Africanus fuit, me non multo minorem quam Laelium, et in republica et in amicitia adiunctorum esse pateris* (*Cic.* ad Fam. v. 7. 3), where *Laelium* stands for *quam Laelius fuit.*

Mĕliŏr est certă pax quam spērātă uictōriă (*Liv.* XXX. 30), *a certain peace is better than a hoped-for victory.*

Plūris est oculātus testis ūnus quam aurītī decem (*Plaut.* Truc. II. 6. 8), *one eye-witness is worth more than ten ear-witnesses.*

Acc. Săpiens hūmāna omnia īnfĕriōră uirtūtĕ dūcit (*Cic.* Tusc. IV. 26. 57), *a wise man looks upon all human things as inferior to virtue.*

Quō grăuiōrem inimīcum nōn hăbuī (*Q. Curt.* VI. 43), *a greater enemy than whom I never had.*

Ită sentio, Lătīnam linguam lŏcŭplētiōrem essĕ quam Graecam (*Cic.* de Fin. I. 3. 10), *my feeling is this, that the Latin language is richer than the Greek.*

1035. 1 The adjectives of dimension, such as māiŏr-, mĭnŏr-, longiŏr-, lătiŏr-, altiŏr-†, and the adverbs plūs, mĭnŭs, amplius, are often used without quam, yet so as not to affect the construction of the numerical phrase attached to them: as,

Plus septingentī captī (*Liv.* XLI. 12), *more than 700 were taken prisoners.*

Quinctius tēcum plūs annum uīxit (*Cic.* p. Quinct. 12. 41), *Quinctius lived with you more than a year.*

Constābat non minus dūcentos fuissĕ (*Liv.* XXIX. 34), *it was clear that there had been not less than 200.*

Nĕquĕ longius mīliă passuum octo ăbĕrant (*Caes.* B. G. V. 53), *nor were they more than eight miles off.*

Spătium nōn amplius pĕdum sescentōrum (*Caes.* B. G. I. 38), *an interval of not more than 600 feet.*

Obsīdes uigintī dăto, nē minōres octōnum dēnum neu maiōres quīnum quădrāgēnum (*Liv.* XXXVIII. 38), *hostages he shall give twenty in number, not younger than eighteen years of age, nor older than forty-five.*

Plus tertiā parte interfectā (*Caes.* B. G. III. 6), *more than a third part having been slain.*

A Caecīliō prŏpinquī minōrĕ centensūmis nummum mōuērĕ non possunt (*Cic.* ad Att. I. 12. 1), *from Caecilius his own immediate connections cannot get a sixpence at less than*

---

* With the relative the use of the ablative is alone admissible.
† *Altiŏr* (*Lucr.* IV. 415).

twelve per cent per annum (literally, one in a hundred per month).*

1055.2 A comparison of two qualities in the same object is expressed either by two comparatives, or by măgĭs and two positives: as,

Paullī contiō fuit uērior quam grātior pŏpŭlō (*Liv.* xxii. 38), *the harangue of Paullus was more true than agreeable to the citizens.*

Bellă fortius quam felicius gĕrĕrĕ (*Liv.* v. 43), *to conduct wars with more courage than good fortune.*

Artem iūris hăbēbĭtis măgis magnam quam difficilem (*Cic.* de Or. I. 42. 190), *you will then have a treatise on law rather bulky than difficult.*

1055.3 For the sake of brevity an ablative is sometimes used where the correct expression of the idea would require many words, especially with spē, ŏpīniŏnĕ, iustō, aequō.

Caesăr ŏpīniōnĕ cĕlĕrius uĕniet (*Cic.* ad Fam. xiv. 23), *Caesar will come more quickly than was expected.*

Amnis sŏlĭtō cĭtātiŏr (*Liv.* xxiii. 19), *the river running with greater rapidity than usual.*

1056 'Too great in proportion to something' is expressed by a comparative and quam prō ——: as,

Puluĕrem māiōrem quam prō nŭmĕrō excĭtābant (*Liv.* x. 41), *they raised a cloud of dust greater than might have been expected from their number.*

Proelium ătrōcius quam prō nŭmĕrō pugnantium (*Liv.* xxi. 29), *a battle more furious than was to have been expected from the number of combatants.*

1056.1 'Too great for something' is expressed by a comparative and quam qui —— or quam ŭt ——: as,

Maius gaudium ĕrat quam quŏd hŏmĭnes căpĕrent (*Liv.* xxxiii. 32), *the joy was too great for human beings to contain.*

Campānī māiōrĕ dēlīquĕrant quam quĭbŭs ignosci posset (*Liv.* xxvi. 12), *the people of Capua had been guilty of misconduct too grave to be pardoned.*

1056.2 'Too great' generally, without formal reference to a purpose

* Observe that all these constructions would remain correct in Latinity, even if the comparatives were struck out.

or standard, may be expressed by nimis and the positive, or by a comparative with the ablative aequō or iustō, or thirdly by a simple comparative: as,

> Vŏluptas quum māiŏr atquĕ longiŏr est, omne ănĭmi lūmĕn extinguit (*Cic.* de Sen. 12. 41), *when pleasure is too intense and continued too long, it puts out the whole light of the soul.*
> Libĕrius sī Dixĕrŏ quid (*Hor.* Sat. I. 4. 103), *too freely if I ought express.*

1056. 3 The simple comparative sometimes denotes only an excess beyond the average, and may then be translated by 'somewhat' or 'rather,' or by one of our diminutival adjectives in *ish*. In this sense the Latin comparative with a diminutival suffix in *culo* is also used, although it may also be used as a comparative.

> Sĕnectūs est nātūrā lŏquăciŏr (*Cic.* de Sen. 16. 55), *old age is naturally rather talkative.*
> Virgo grandiuscŭlă (*Ter.* And. iv. 5. 19), *a girl pretty well grown up; a biggish girl.*
> Thāis quam ĕgo sum māiusculast (*Ter.* E. iii. 3. 21), *Thais is a little older than I am.*

1056. 4 Atquĕ and ac in old writers and in poets are at times used in place of quam after comparatives: as,

> Nŏn Apollĭnis magis uerum atque hŏc responsumst (*Ter.* And. iv. 2. 14), *not Apollo gives a truer answer from his oracle than this.*
> Haud minŭs ac iussī făciunt (*Virg.* A. iii. 561), *not less than ordered do they.*

1056. 5 The degree of excess is expressed by the ablative of substantives (see § 1017), and by the ablatives eō or hōc and quō, tantō and quantō, multō and paulō, āliquantō and nihīlō; also by the numerical ablatives altĕrō-tantō or dŭplō, *as much again;* sesqui,[*] *half as much again,* &c. (see § 1018). But the accusative forms

---

[*] This word is probably an ablative, whose full form may have been *semi-siqui*, the latter part being the ablative of the obsolete positive *siqui-*, whence the comparative *siquior-* (but observe the different quantity), in the sense of 'following, second, inferior.' Thus *semis-esquis* contracted into *sesquis* would be like the German *anderthalb* or 1½, just as *semis-tertius* contracted into *sestertius* is equal to the German *dritthalb* or 2½. See § 272. It may be added that the assumed meaning of *sequi-* would account both for its being superseded by the comparative and also for its having no superlative.

in -um are not uncommon: as, multum improbior (*Plaut. Most.* III. 2. 139), aliquantum amplior (*Liv.* I. 7), quantum magis (*Liv.* III. 15).

SUPERLATIVES.

1057. The use of the superlative is chiefly in such constructions as the following:

a. Consilia sua optimo quoique probant* (*Cic.* p. Sest. 45. 96), *they satisfy all the best men of the excellence of their measures.*

Renuntiarunt ludos Ioui primo quoque die faciundos (*Liv.* XLII. 20), *they reported that games should be celebrated in honour of Jupiter on the earliest possible day.*

Multi mortales couuenere, maxime proximi quique‡, Caeninenses, Crustumini, Antemnates (*Liv.* I. 9), *a large number of people came to the meeting, chiefly the inhabitants of the several nearest states, Caenina and Crustumerium and Antemna.*

b. Optimus quisque maxime posteritati seruit (*Cic.* Tusc. I. 15. 35), *the best men always do the most to serve posterity.*

c. Vt quisque optime dicit, ita maxime dicendi difficultatem pertimescit (*Cic.* de Or. 1. 26. 120), *the nearer a man approaches perfection in speaking, the more is he alarmed at the difficulty of speaking.*

Ita, quam quisque pessime facit, tam maxime tutust (*Sal.* Jug. 31), *thus, the worse a man acts, the safer is he.*

d. Tam sum mitis quam qui lenissumus (*Cic.* p. Sul. 31. 87), *I am as mild as the gentlest man on earth.*

Tam sum amicus reipublicae quam qui maxime (*Cic.* ad Fam. v. 2. 6), *I am as attached to the country as any one living.*

Huic commendationi tantum tribuere quantum quoi tribuisti plurimum (*Cic.* ad Fam. XIII. 22), *to attach as much weight to this recommendation as you ever did to any one.*

---

* Literally 'make them to appear good.'

† This phrase should be contrasted with *altero quoque die, tertio quoque die*, &c. which imply the passing over one, two, &c. days every time. *Primo quoque die* therefore signifies 'the first day of all;' if that be impossible, then the next, and so on, allowing not a day to pass without an attempt.

‡ Plural, because each single state furnished a number.

Tē sīc tuēbōr ut quem dīligentissimē (*Cic.* ad Fam. XIII. 62), *I shall watch your interests with as much care as I ever did those of any friend.*

Dŏmus cŏlĕbrātūr ita ut cum maxŭmē (*Cic.* ad Q. F. II. 6.6), *my house is thronged as much as ever it was.*

Māter nunc cum* maxŭmē fīlium interfectum cūpit (*Cic.* p. Clu. 5.12), *she desires the death of her son now as much as ever.*

e. Quam pŏtuī maxŭmīs ĭtĭnĕrĭbŭs ăd Amānum exercĭtum duxī (*Cic.* ad Fam. XV. 4.7), *I led the army to the Amanus by the greatest possible marches.*

Stătue ălĭquem confectum tantis dŏlōrĭbus quantī in hŏmĭnum maxŭmī cădĕrĕ possunt (*Cic.* de Fin. I. 12.41), *picture to yourself any one exhausted by the greatest sufferings man's nature is capable of.*

Quantam maximam pŏtest uastĭtātem consŭlī ostendĭt (*Liv.* XXIII. 3), *he exhibits before the consul's eyes the greatest possible devastation.*

Ut pŏtuī accūrātĭssŭmē tŭ tūtātus sum (*Cic.* ad Fam. V. 17.2), *I have protected your interests with the greatest care in my power.*

f. Quam maxŭmas, quam prīmum, quam saepissŭmē grātiās ăget (*Cic.* ad Fam. XIII b. 6), *he will express his gratitude in the strongest possible terms, at the first possible opportunity, as often as possible.*

g. Quem ūnum nostrae cīuĭtātis praestantissĭmum audeō dīcĕrĕ (*Cic.* de Am. 1.1), *whom I venture to pronounce of all men in our country the most excellent.*

h. Ex Britannīs omnĭbus longē sunt hūmānissĭmī (*Caes.* B. G. V. 14), *of all the Britons they are by far the most civilised.*

Multō maxŭmă pars (*Cic.* p. leg. Man. 18.54), *by far the greatest part.*

In fidĭbŭs aures uel minŭmă sentiunt (*Cic.* de Off. I. 41. 146), *in the strings of musical instruments the ear perceives the very slightest differences of note.*

i. The superlatives which denote place or time, together with mĕdio-, which in power is a superlative, are used in agreement

---

* One might have expected *esse ut cum maxume.*

with a substantive to specify the *part* of it to which the superlative applies: as,

> Summus mons (*Caes.* B. G. I. 22), *the top of the mountain.*
> In extrēmō librō tertiō (*Cic.* de Off. III. 2. 9), *at the end of the third book.*
> Primā lūce (*Caes.* B. G. I. 22), *at daybreak.*

k. A superlative which in English would stand in the antecedent clause, in Latin is attached to the relative clause : as,

> P. Scīpiōnī ex multīs diēbus quōs in uītā laetissimōs uīdit, illō diēs clarissimus fuit (*Cic.* de Am. 3.12), *of the many joyous days which Publius Scipio saw in the course of his life, that day was the brightest.*

APPOSITION AND ATTRACTION.

1058 When one substantive is attached by way of explanation to another, it must agree with it always in case, and generally in number, and when practicable in gender: as,

> P. Vărius, uir fortissimus atque optimus ciuis (*Cic.* p. Mil. 27. 74), *Publius Varius, a most gallant gentleman and excellent citizen.*
> Duae urbes pŏtentissimae, Karthāgō atquĕ Nŭmantiă (*Cic.* p. leg. Man. 20. 60), *two most powerful cities, Carthage and Numantia.*
> Dēlĭciae meae Dīcaearchŭs (*Cic.* Tusc. I. 31. 77), *my darling Dicaearchus.*
> Pŏpŭlus Rōmānus uictor dŏmĭnusque omnium gentium (*Cic.* Phil. VI. 5. 12), *the Roman people, the conqueror and lord of all nations.*
> Omitto illās omnium doctrīnārum inuentricis Athēnās (*Cic.* de Or. I. 4. 13), *I omit that great inventress of every science, Athens.*
> Antĕ mē consŭlem (*Cic.* Brut. 15. 60), *before I was consul.*

1059 When the logical connection is lost sight of, and the construction is affected by the proximity of some connected word or idea, it is called attraction.*

---

* Observe that the German is logically correct in giving no termination to the adjective in the predicate. Still more logical would it have been to have given the adjective one fixed form under all circumstances. Cases and number and gender strictly belong to the substantive alone.

1060 It is thus that the adjective or substantive in the predicate is made to agree with the substantive in the subject: as,

N. Vŏlo ŏt esse ŏt hăbĕrī grātūs (*Cic.* de Fin. II. 22. 72), *I wish both to be and to be thought grateful.*

Acc. Crēdĭtur Pythăgŏrae audītōrem fuissē Nūmam (*Liv.* XL. 29), *it is believed that Numa was a pupil of Pythagoras.*

G. Captīuōrum nŭmĕrus fuit septem mīlium ac dŭcentōrum (*Liv.* X. 36), *the number of prisoners was 7200.*

Messī clārum gĕnūs Oscī* (*Hor.* Sat. I. 5. 54), *Messio's glorious race was Oscan.*

D. Vōbīs nŏcessest fortĭbus uĭrīs esse (*Liv.* XXI. 44), *you have no choice but to be brave.*

Fons ăquae dulcis quoi nōmĕn Arĕthūsa'st† (*Cic.* II. Verr. IV. 53. 118), *a spring of fresh water the name of which is Arethusa.*

Uti mīlĭtĭbūs exaequātus cum impĕrātōrē lăbos uŏlentĭbūs esset (*Sal.* Jug. c. 4), *in order that the general's taking an equal share in the labour might be gratifying to the soldiers.*‡

Abl. Fīliō suō măgistro ĕquītum creātō (*Liv.* IV. 46), *his son having been appointed master of the horse.*

Consŭlĭbus certiŏrĭbus factīs (*Liv.* IV. 46), *the consuls having been apprised.*

V. Rūfē mihi frustrā crēdĭte amīcō (*Catul.* 77. 1), *Rufus in vain believed to be my friend.*

1061 An attraction of case and gender is seen at times with the relative: as,

Raptim quĭbus quisquō pŏtĕrat ēlātīs, agmĕn implēuĕrat uiās (*Liv.* I. 29), *hastily carrying off what each could, a line of people in motion had filled the roads.*

Anĭmăl hoc quam uŏcāmŭs hŏmĭnem (*Cic.* de Leg. I. 7. 22), *this animal which we call man.*

But the different examples of attraction are also given in their several places.

* Some editors would make *Osci* here a nom. pl.
† For so we should read, and not *Arethusa est.*
‡ So again c. 84, *Neque plebi militia uolenti putabatur*; Tac. Agr. 18, *Ui quibus bellum uolentibus erat*; Macr. Sat. I. 7, *Si uobis uolentibus erit.* The idiom is possibly borrowed from the Greek: as, τῷ πλήθει οὐ βουλομένῳ ἦν τῶν Ἀθηναίων ἀφίστασθαι, Thuc. II. 3. This from Cortius.

NUMERALS.*

1002 Vno- *one* is used in the plural when a plural substantive constitutes a new unit.†

> Vni ex transrhēnānis lēgātos mīsērant (*Caes.* B. G. IV. 10), *they were the only people of those beyond the Rhine who had sent ambassadors.*
>
> Ex ūnis geminas mihi conficies nūptias (*Ter.* And. IV. 1. 50), *out of one marriage you will make me a brace of marriages.*
>
> Vnae atque altěrae scālas comminūtas (*Sal.* Jug. 60), *first one and then another ladder was broken to pieces.*

1003 Sescento- *six hundred* is often used vaguely for a very large number.

> In quō multā mōlestā, discessus noster, belli pěricūlum, militum imprōbitas, sescentā praetěreā (*Cic.* ad Att. VI. 4. 1), *in which there are many vexatious matters, our leaving the country, the danger of war, the violence of the soldiery, and a thousand things besides.*

1004 Mīli- *a thousand* in the singular is commonly an adjective; in the plural perhaps always a substantive.

> Mille ěquītes Gallia eōdem uersa in Pūnicum bellum hăbuit (*Liv.* XXI. 17), *Gallia lying in the same direction had a thousand horse as a protection against an attack from the Carthaginians.*
>
> Quo in fundō făcīlē mille hŏminum uersābātūr.(*Cic.* p. Mil. 20. 53), *on which land full a thousand men were engaged.*
>
> Děcem mīliă tălentum Găbīniō sunt prōmissă (*Cic.* p. Rab. Post. 8. 21), *ten thousand talents were promised to Gabinius.*

1005 If a smaller numeral be added to the thousands, then the construction of an adjective is preferred: as,

> Philippei nummi duŏdĕcim mīliă quădringenti uīgintī duŏ. (*Liv.* XXXIX. 5), 12422 *golden Philips.*

---

* Some remarks upon the construction of numerals have been made in the first part (§§ 253-272).

† Thus, many human beings make up one people; many letters of the alphabet go to a single letter or epistle. Sometimes the singular of a word happens not to be in use, and it may then be difficult to decide what was its meaning. Thus it is a question what was that meaning of *castro-* in the singular which caused its plural to signify 'a camp.'

But the genitive is still found at times: as,

> Philippeōrum nummōrum sēdĕcim milĭă trŏcentī uīgintī (*Liv.* XXXIX. 7), *of golden Philips 16320.*

1065. 1 An ordinal number is sometimes used elliptically, so as to imply an addition to the cardinal number immediately preceding: as,

   a. Where a nominative of an ordinal forms part of a predicate: as,

> Tū quŏtŭs ĕssē uĕlīs rescrībĕ (*Hor.* Ep. I. 5. 30), *be it yours to say how many you wish to be.*
>
> Dic quŏtŭs et quantī cūpĭās cēnārē (*Mart.* XIV. 217), *say what you wish to be the number to dine together, what the charge per head.**

   b. Where the ordinal is attached to one of the fractional divisions of the as (§§ 270, 272): as, sēmis tertĭŭs, contracted to sestertĭŭs, *half of the third unit†*, meaning altogether 2½. Thus,

> Trientem tertium pondō cŏrōnam auream dĕdit Iŏuī dōnum (*T. Quintius* ap. Fest. v. trientem), *he gave as a gift to Jupiter a gold crown weighing 2⅓ lbs.*
>
> Lignum bēs altĕrum (*Fest.* ibid.), *a log 20‡ inches in diameter*, or more idiomatically, *a 20-inch log.*
>
> Quartus quădrans (*Fest.* ibid.), 3¼.

   c. With tantum *as much*, expressed, or more commonly understood: as,

> Immo etiamsī altĕrum Tantŭm§ perdundumst, pérdam potius quám sinam (*Plaut.* Ep. III. 4. 81), *nay though I must lose as much again, lose it I will rather than permit this.*
>
> Ex eōdem sēmĭno ălĭūbi cum dĕcĭmō‖ rĕdit, ălĭūbi cum quintōdĕcĭmo ŭt ĭn Ĕtrūrĭā. In Sybărītāno dicuut ĕtiam cum centēnsĭmō rĕdīrē sŏlĭtum (*Varr.* R. R. I. 14. 1), *from the*

---

* Compare the corresponding Greek phrase: στρατηγὸς ἦν Ἡρακλείδης πέμπτος αὐτός, *Thuc.* I. 46; οἱ ἡρέθη πρεσβευτὴς δέκατος αὐτός, *Xen.* Hist. Gr. II. 2. 17.

† See note to § 1056.

‡ More literally '1⅔ feet broad.' The fuller phrase would be *bessem altĕrum latum*, or *bess' altĕrum l.*

§ Literally 'a second as much.'

‖ For *cum decimo tanto*, i. e. literally 'with a tenth as much.' The use of *tantum* 'as much' in the measure of crops is seen in *Plaut.* Trin. II. 4. 129, *Tribus tantis illi minus redit quam obseruerit.*

same seed there is in some lands a tenfold return, in others
fiftenfold, as in Hetruria. In the district of Sybaris they
say that the usual return is even a hundred for one.

Ager (Leontīnūs) ecficit cum octāuō, bĕnō ūt ĭgātur, uĕrum ūt
omnes di adiūuent, cum dĕcūmō (Cic. II. Verr. III. 47. 112),
*a return of eightfold from the land of Lentini is satisfactory;
but it needs the united blessing of all the gods to bring about a
return of ten for one.*

Frūmentā māiōrē quĭdem parti Ităliae quando cum quartō
respondĕrint uix mĕmĭnissē possŭmŭs (Col. III. 3. 4), *we
can scarcely remember a time when corn, so far at least as the
greater part of Italy is concerned, gave a return of four for
one.*

1066 The distributive numerals are often used in pairs: as,

Singŭlos singŭli pŏpŭli lictōres dĕdĕrunt (Liv. I. 8), *each of the
(twelve) states provided one lictor.*

Quīnā dēnā iūgĕra ăgri dăta in singŭlos pĕdĭtes sunt (Liv.
XXXV. 40), *fifteen jugers of land were given to every foot-
soldier.*

1067 The particular distributive bīno-, like gĕmĭno-*, is often used
of but two things when they match one another: as,

Bīnōs hăbēbat scўphōs (Cic. II. Verr. IV. 14. 32), *he had a pair
of cups.*

1068 The distributives bīno-, trīno-† &c. are used, like the plural
of ūno-, with plural substantives that have a singular sense: as,

Quīnis castrīs oppĭdum circumdĕdit (Caes. B. C. III. 9), *he surrounded the town with five camps.*

Littĕras reddĭdit trīnās (Cic. ad Att. XI. 17. 1), *she delivered
three letters.*

Trīnis cătēnis uinctus trahēbātūr (Caes. B. G. I. 53), *he was
being dragged along bound with three sets of chains.‡*

---

* *Duplĭci-* in its original sense is used where the two things lie flat
against each other, as *duplices palmae*, the joined hands in the act of
prayer, and *duplices tabellae* 'folded tablets.'

† Not *terno-* not *singulo-*.

‡ Even in speaking of one person the phrases are *inicere catenas
alicui, conicere in catenas, esse cum catenis*, as indeed the English phrase
is also plural. Hence in *Hor. Od.* III. 4. 80 we should probably read
Trecenas Pirithoum cohibent catenae.

1069   The poets occasionally use a distributive in place of the simple
number, and that both in the plural and singular: as,

   Dispar septēnis fistūlīs cannis (*Ov.* Met. II. 682), *an unequal
   pipe of seven reeds.*
   Gurgitĕ septēnō răpĭdus mărĕ submŏvĕt amnis (*Lucan,* VIII.
   445), *with sevenfold flood the rapid river bids the sea withdraw.*

1070   The word sestertio-, which is strictly only a numeral, 2½, is
commonly used in reference to money, and in that sense signified
originally 2½ asses or lbs. of bronze; but as the weight of Roman
money decreased to a great extent, and silver coin came into use,
sestertio- (or scstertio- nummo-, or nummo- alone) was eventually*
the name of a small silver coin worth about 2¼*d.*† of our money,
and was the ordinary unit of money. It is also used as an insig-
nificant sum of money.

   Prĕtĭum constĭtūtumst in mōdĭos sĭngŭlōs HS: III (*Cic.* II.
   Verr. III. 70, 163), *the price fixed was three sesterces the bushel.*
   Sestertium sescentā quādrāgintā mīliā dēferri ad sē dŏmum
   iussit (*Cic.* p. Clu. 25. 69), *he ordered* 640,000 *sesterces to be
   carried down to his house.*
   Ecquis est qui bŏnā Postumi nummō sestertiō sibi addīci velit ?
   (*Cic.* p. Rab. Post. 17. 45) *is there any one who would be
   willing to have the whole property of Postumus knocked down
   to him for a single groat ?*

1071   A million sesterces fall short of 10,000*l*. Hence the numbers
required, when the sesterce is the unit, soon became inconveniently
large, and the only mode the Romans had of expressing numbers
above 100,000 was by means of the numeral adverbs: thus,

   Accēpi uīciens dūcentā trīgintā quinquĕ mīlia, quādringentos
   septendĕcim nummōs (*Cic.* II. Verr. I. 14. 30), *I received*
   2,235,417 *sesterces.*
   Sestertium dēciens centēnā mīliā (*Cic.* II. Verr. I. 10. 28), *one
   million sesterces.*

   ⁎ Towards the close of the republic.
   † This would make the denarius about 9*d.*, which is slightly above
the usual estimate. But our antiquarians commit the strange error of
taking the *average* of existing denarii instead of the very largest for the
standard, as though coins could have *gained* weight by time.
   ‡ To be read perhaps *sestertii terni*; but the Mss. have nearly all
the mere symbols. See § 272.

1072 By way of brevity centēnă milĭă was dropped with the adverbs, causing no ambiguity, because the adverbs could only be used with sestertium in this sense: thus,

> Sestertium quădringentiens abstŭlit (*Cic.* II. Verr. I. 10. 27), *he carried off forty million sesterces.*
>
> Et eum tu accusăs ăvărĭtiae, quem dicis sestertium ŭlciens uŏluissĕ perdĕrĕ ? (*Cic.* p. Flac. 33. 63) *and do you accuse of avarice one who you say wished to throw away two million sesterces ?*

1073 Although sestertium as used with milĭă was in fact a genitive, it was found convenient to treat it as a neuter-substantive; so that sestertiă* was used as a nom. or acc. pl., and signified so many thousand sesterces.

> Căpĭt ille ex suis praediis sescēnă sestertia, ĕgo centēna ex meis (*Cic.* Parad. VI. 3. 49), *yonder man draws, let us suppose, 600,000 sesterces per annum from his estates, I 100,000 from mine.*

1074 Similarly with the adverbs it was found convenient to give to sestertium a genitive and ablative singular.

> Dĕcem pondo auri et argenti ad summam sestertii dĕciens in aerārium rettŭlit (*Liv.* XLV. 4), *he paid into the treasury ten pound weight of gold, and of silver to the amount of a million sesterces.*
>
> Nĕque in sestertiō ŭlciens pārum sē splendĭdē gessit, nĕque in sestertiō centiens affluentius uixit quam instĭtuĕrăt (*Nepos* in Attico 14), *as his establishment was sufficiently handsome when his income was two million sesterces, so he lived with no greater luxury than at first when his income was ten millions.*

1075. The construction of pondō† *by weight* or *pound,* and libra-m *pound,* in denoting weight, is very anomalous, the first having

---

* The word *sestertium* (nom.) is sometimes said to have been a coin. There in fact was no such coin and no such word. There is perhaps something parallel to the anomaly mentioned in the text in the practice of declining the genitive *cuius* of the relative as though it had been an adjective.

† *Pondo* would appear to have been originally an ablative 'by weight;' *libram, libras,* seem inexplicable. But in *Liv.* IV. 20 all the best Mss. have *libra,* which would admit a simple explanation 'by the scales,' and so, like *pondo,* come in a secondary sense to signify 'a lb.'

always the same form, the second being always an acc. singular or plural.

> Paterae aureae fuērunt dūcentae septuāgintā sex libras ferme omnes pondo, argenti decem et octō milia et trecentīs pondō (*Liv.* XXVI. 47), *there were 276 golden bowls all about a pound in weight, and of silver bullion 18,300 lbs.*

PERSONAL PRONOUNS.

1076 The nominatives of the personal pronouns are not commonly used, because the terminations of the verb already express the notion; but if there be any emphasis, then they are required.

> Quis tu hŏmo es? (*Ter.* And. IV. 1.11) *who are you?*
>
> Ego istum iŭvĕnem dŏmī tĕnendum censeō (*Liv.* XXI. 3), *I for my part think that this stripling of yours should be kept at home.*
>
> Natūrā tu illī pătĕr es, consĭliīs ĕgo (*Ter.* Ad. I. 2. 40), *by nature you are his father, as guardian I.*

1077 Similarly *he, she, it, they,* if emphatic, must be expressed by the proper pronoun, i-, ho-, isto-, or illo- (see below).

1078 These nominatives appear however at times to be required when there does not seem to be any emphasis upon them. Thus, in repeating a person's words in surprise, it is usual to insert the omitted nominative:

> M. Quid fēcit? D. Quid ille fēcĕrit? (*Ter.* Ad. I. 2.4) M. *What has he done?* D. *What has he done, ask you?*

Where the words *what* and *done* seem to require the special emphasis.

1079 So in confirming an assertion or answering a question, the nominative of the pronoun is required.

> Ego uēro ūtar prōrŏgātiōnē diēī (*Cic.* ad Att. XIII. 43), *yes, my friend, you are right, I shall avail myself of the postponement.*

Where the word *shall* is emphatic, not the pronoun.

1080 So again where quidem *it is true* introduces a word preparatory to a sed *but*: as,

> Deindē tuī mūnĭcĭpes, sunt illī quidem splendĭdissŭmī hŏmĭnes, set tămen pauci (*Cic.* p. Planc. 8. 21), *then as to your fellow-townsmen, they are, I grant, men of the highest station, but still only few in number.*

Orātōriās exercitātiōnes, non tū quidem rēliquistī, sed philōsŏ-
phiam illīs antepŏsuistī (*Cic.* de Fato, 2. 3), *your exercises
in oratory you have not abandoned, it is true, but you have
given philosophy the preference over them.*

Nos scītō dē uětěre illā nostrā sententiā prŏpě iam essĕ dēpulsos,
non nos quidem ut nostrae dignitātis sīmūs oblītī, sēd ūt
hăbeāmus rătiōnem ăliquando ětiam sălūtis (*Cic.* ad Fam.
I. 7. 7), *we, you must understand, have been almost weaned at
last from those old opinions of ours, not indeed so far as to
forget our dignity, but so as sometimes to take account of our
safety also.*

The singular tū and plural uōs* being commonly translated by
the same word *you*, it is often useful to insert some plural vocative
or other phrase with the latter, so as to prevent ambiguity.

Sī quid est quod mea ŏpera ŏpus sit uōbīs, ut tū plus uīdes,
Mănēbo (*Ter.* And. IV. 3. 23), *if there be any thing in which
you (and your young master) have occasion for my assistance,
as you (Davus) understand matters better than I do, I will
stay.*

The use of a first person plural for the singular—nōs for ĕgo,
nostĕr for mĕŭs—is occasionally met with in Latin, but more from
a feeling of modesty than pride. See dīcīmūs (*Cic.* p. leg. Man.
10. 47), and cohortātī 'sūmūs—pŏtuīmūs—arbĭtrārēmūr—ostendī-
mūs (*Cic.* de Div. II. 1. 1).

Sē, suo-, &c.

The reflective pronouns of the third person, both substantive
and adjective, are variously translated according to the word they
refer to. This word is commonly the nominative of the sentence:
as,

Eă praedia ăliīs cŏluit, non sĭbi (*Cic.* p. Rosc. Am. 17. 40),
these farms he cultivated for others, not for himself.

Tum illă rōiēcit se in eum (*Ter.* And. I. 1. 108), *then the other
threw herself back into his arms.*

Iustĭtĭă propter se est cŏlendā (*Cic.* de Off. II. 12. 42), *justice is
to be cultivated for itself.*

Non suī conseruandī causā prŏfūgērunt (*Cic.* in Cat. I. 2. 7),
it was not to save themselves that they ran off.

* The same ambiguity exists between the possessive adjectives *tuo-*
and *uestero-*, and may be removed in the same way.

Suā quae narrat flăcinora? (*Ter.* Haut. II. 1. 8) *what doings of his own does he recount?*

Vīne haec ignorārēt suōm patrem? (*Ter.* Ph. v. 6. 34) *the idea of this woman not knowing her own father?*

Aliēnā mēlius diiūdĭcant, quam suā (*Ter.* Haut. III. 1. 95), *they judge better of other people's affairs than their own.*

1084. Sē &c. and suo-, in a secondary sentence, may of course refer to the nominative or subject of that secondary sentence. They sometimes however refer to the agent of the main sentence, particularly if the secondary sentence express something in the mind of that agent : as,

Vir bŏnus nihil quoiquam quŏd in sē transfĕrat dētrahet (*Cic. de Off.* III. 19. 75), *a good man will not force any thing from any one to transfer it to himself.*

Sentit ănimus sē ui suā, nōn aliēnā mŏuērī (*Cic. Tusc.* I. 21. 55), *the mind feels that it is acted upon by a force of its own, not one from without.**

1085. Sē &c. and suo- sometimes refer to a noun not in the nominative, if that noun be substantially the subject : as,

A Caesăre inuītor†, sĭbi ut sim lēgātūs (*Cic. ad Att.* II. 18. 3), *I am invited by Caesar to be legate to him.*

Faustŭlō spes fuĕrat‡, rēgiam stirpem ăpud sē ēdŭcārī (*Liv.* I. 5), *Faustulus had entertained the hope that the children at nurse in his cottage were of royal stock.*

1086. Sē &c. and suo- sometimes refer to nouns not in the nominative, if placed near them : as,

Furnium per sē uīdi lŭbentissĭmē (*Cic. ad Fam.* x. 3. 1), *Furnius, so far as he himself is concerned, I saw with the greatest pleasure.*

Ratĭō ĕt ōrātĭō conciliat inter sē hŏmĭnēs (*Cic. de Off.* I. 16. 50), *reason and speech unite men to one another.*

---

* In *Caes.* B. G. I. 36, ad haec Ariouistus respondit &c., which chapter is all one sentence, there is much freedom in the use of these pronouns. Thus, in the last clause, *quod sibi Caesar denuntiaret se Aeduorum iniurias non neglecturum, neminem secum sine sua pernicie contendisse,—sibi* and *secum* refer to Ariouistus, *se* to Caesar, *sua* to neminem.

† Equivalent to *Caesar me inuitat.*

‡ Equivalent to *Faustulus spem habuerat.*

PERSONAL PRONOUNS.

Suas res Syrācūsānis restituit (*Liv.* XXIX. 1), *he restored to the Syracusans what belonged to them.*

Plăcet Stoĭcis suō quamquē rem nōmĭne adpellārĕ (*Cic.* ad Fam. IX. 22. 1), *it is a law with the Stoics to call every thing by its own name.*

Magōnem cum classĕ sua in Hispāniam mittunt (*Liv.* XXIII. 32), *they send Mago with his fleet to Spain.*

Rĕdĭmendĭ sē captīuis cōpiam făcĕrĕ (*Liv.* XXII. 58), *to give the prisoners an opportunity of ransoming themselves.*

Intĕr sē is used with active verbs for so intĕr sē : as,

Inter se adspĭclēbant (*Cic.* in Cat. III. 5. 13), *they kept looking at one another.*

The possessive pronouns often denote what is favourable to the party, especially in connexion with nouns signifying time or place : as,

Rŏgo ut nĕque occāsiōnī tuae dēsis, nĕquĕ suam occāsiōnem hostī dēs (*Liv.* XXII. 39), *I ask you neither to be wanting to an opportunity favourable to yourself, nor to give to the enemy one favourable to him.*

The possessive pronouns are often omitted in Latin where they are expressed in English : as,

Non dūbiumst quin uxōrem nolit fīlius (*Ter.* And. I. 2. 1), *there is no doubt that my son is unwilling to marry.*

Et eri semper lēnĭtas, uerēbar quorsum euāderet (*Ter.* And. I. 2. 4), *and my master's*[*] *constant gentleness, I was afraid what it would end in.*

Ipso-.

Ipso- is used with the personal pronouns and other nouns to denote emphasis :

Calpurnius custōdiā mīlĭtārī cinctŭs extinguĭtur ; Priscus se ipset interfēcit (*Tac.* Hist. IV. 11), *Calpurnius is surrounded by a guard of soldiers and put to death ; Priscus slew himself.*

Frātrem suum, dein se ipsumt interfēcit (*Tac.* Hist. III. 51), *he killed his brother, and then himself.*

---

[*] So in English we say 'master, father,' &c. for 'my master, my father.'

[†] Observe the difference between these two phrases.

Triennio ipsō minor quam Antōniūs (*Cic.* Brut. 43. 161), *exactly three years younger than Antonius.*

Ipsae diffluēbant cŏrōnae (*Cic.* Tusc. v. 21. 62), *the wreaths kept slipping down of themselves.*

Is, ŏt ipse Alpinūs amnis, difficillĭmus transĭtu est (*Liv.* xxi. 31), *this, itself too an Alpine river, is most difficult to cross.**

DEMONSTRATIVE PRONOUNS.

1091   Ho-, isto-, illo-, are called demonstratives, because the speaker in using them points to the things he speaks of.

Ho- is the demonstrative of the first person, and points to what is *near me*.

Isto- is the demonstrative of the second person, and points to what is *near you*.

Illo- is the demonstrative of the third person, and points to what is *distant* from both of us.

1092   Ho- *this* has the following uses: First, it points to something near the speaker: as,

Set quid hoc? Puĕr hercle'st. Mŭlier, tu spŏsuisti hunc? (*Ter.* And. iv. 4. 2) *but what is this (at my feet)? Faith, it's a baby. Woman, was it you put this baby down here?*

Hic uersus Plauti nōn est, hic est (*Serv.* ap. Cic. ad Fam. ix. 16. 4), *this verse is not Plautus's, this is.*

1093   Hence hic hŏmo may mean ĕgo, the speaker: as,

Vah, sŏlus hic homost, qui sciat diuinĭtus (*Plaut.* Curc. ii. 1. 33), *bah, your humble servant has not his match as a prophet.*

1094   Secondly, ho- refers to present time: as,

Ab illis hŏmĭnĭbūs ad hanc hŏmĭnum lĭbīdinem ac lĭcentiam me abdūcis? (*Cic.* ii. Verr. iii. 90. 210) *do you propose to draw me away from the men of those days to the self-indulgence and intemperance of the present race?*

Quid hoc pŏpŭlo obtĭnēri pŏtest? (*Cic.* de Leg. iii. 16. 37), *what measure can be carried with such citizens as we have now-a-days?*

---

* Whenever ipse- is used, the student should ask himself to what it is opposed.

1095 Ho- may also be used logically: First, at the beginning of a sentence referring to something immediately preceding: as,

Est genus hominum, qui esse primos se ómnium rerúm uolunt, Néc sunt—Hos conséctor (*Ter.* E. II. 2.17), *there is, you must know, a class of people who will have it that they are first in every thing, but are not so—These are the game I hunt down.*

1096 Secondly, as a so-called antecedent to a relative, when placed after that relative: thus,

Quam quisque norit ártem, in hac se exérceat (ap. *Cic.* Tusc. I. 18.41), *whatever art each knows, in that let him exercise himself.*

1097 Thirdly, when referring to what is coming: as,

Quórum ŏpĕrum haec ĕrat rătio (*Caes.* B. C. I. 25), *of these works the following was the plan.*

Hŏc ănimō scito omnis sánōs ut mortem seruitūti antĕpōnant (*Cic.* ad Fam. x. 27), *you must know that all men in their senses have determined upon this, to prefer death to slavery.*

1098 Isto- *that* (connected with *you*) has the following uses: First, it points to something near the person spoken to: as,

Istam quam hăbēs undo hăbes uestem ? (*Ter.* E. IV. 4.28), *that dress which you have got on, where did you get it from ?*

Tū tĭbī istas posthac comprimĭtō mănūs (*Ter.* Haut. III. 3.29), *you, sir, must keep those hands for the future to yourself.*

1099 Secondly, isto- refers to the second person, though there is no pointing: as,

S. Hōcĭne ăgĭs annōn ? D. Ego uēro istuc (*Ter.* And. I. 2.15), *S. Do you attend to what I am saying or not ? D. Yes, sir, I do attend to what you say.*

1100 Isto- signifies in itself neither praise nor blame, neither love nor hatred. The context may imply one or the other:

Bŏno ănimō fac sis Sostrătă; ĕt istam quod pŏtes fac consōlērĕ (*Ter.* Ad. III. 5.1), *keep up your spirits, Sostrata; and do your best to comfort your poor daughter there.*

Istuc est săpĕrĕ (*Ter.* Ad. III. 3.32), *there you show true wisdom, sir.*

Video de istis qui se pŏpŭlāris hăbēri uŏlunt, ăbessĕ non nēmĭnem (*Cic.* in Cat. IV. 5.10), *I perceive that of your would-be-thought friends of the people, a certain gentleman is absent.*

1101 Illo- *yonder, distant, former, other*, points to something comparatively distant : as,

> Tolle hanc pātīnam. Aufĕr illam offam porcīnam (*Plaut.* Mil. Gl. III. 1. 164), *take away this dish. Remove yonder rissole de porc.*
>
> Set quis illic est procŭl quem uideo? (*Ter.* Ad. III. 3. 84) *but who is yonder man there, whom I see in the distance?*

1102 Referring to something distant, though not visible : as,

> Ille suam semper ēgit uitam in ōtio, in conuīuiīs (*Ter.* Ad. v. 4. 9), *my brother there has always passed his time in idleness, in society.*

1103 Illo-, like ho-, may be used logically; that is, refer to the *words* of a sentence. When they are used together, ho- refers to the nearer word, illo- to the farther: as,

> Mēlius dē quibusdam ăcerbi inīmīci mĕrentur quam hī ămīci qui dulces uĭdentŭr. Illī uērum, saepĕ dīcunt; hī, nunquam (*Cic.* de Am. 24. 90), *bitter enemies deserve better of some persons than those friends who seem to be all sweetness. The former often speak the truth, the latter never.*

1104 Sometimes not the nearer *word* but the nearer* *thing* is marked by ho-, the more distant *thing* by illo- : as,

> Mĕliŏr est certā pax quam spērātā uictōrĭā. Haec in tuā, illa in Deōrum mānu est (*Liv.* XXX. 30), *certain peace is better than hoped-for victory. The one (peace) is in your own hands, the other (victory) in those of the gods.*

1105 A change of person is often marked by illo-, in which case the word *other* is often the best translation : as,

> Vercingetŏrix obuiam Caesări prŏfīciscĭtŭr. Ille oppĭdum Nŏuiŏdūnum obpugnāre instĭtuĕrat (*Caes.* B. G. VII. 12), *Vercingetorix sets out to meet Caesar. The other (viz. Caesar) had begun to besiege Noviodunum.*
>
> Aeŏlus luctantīs uentōs impĕrĭō prĕmĭt. Illī circum claustră frĕmunt (*Virg.* A. 1. 56), *Aeolus the struggling winds with sovereign sway restrains. They thus restrained around the barriers roar.*

* In this way are to be explained all those passages where *illo*- is said to be referred to the nearer word, and *ho*- to the farther word : as, for example, in *Liv.* XXV. 29, where *ille* and *illius* refer to Hiero as long dead, *hic* and *huius* to Hieronymus as only recently dead.

1106   Illo- also introduces something about to be mentioned, in opposition to what has been just mentioned: as,

Hōrum ĕgŏ sermōnē non mŏuēbăr. Illud, uērŏ dīcam, mē mŏuet, ăbessĕ tris cohortīs (*Cic.* ad Fam. III. 6. 5), *by what these men said to one another I was not annoyed. One thing however (I will be candid with you) does annoy me, and that is, that three battalions are absent.*

Illud tĭbi prōmittō, quicquid ĕrit ă tē factum, id sĕnātum com-prŏbātūrum (*Cic.* ad Fam. x. 16. 2), *one thing I promise you, whatever you do, that the senate will fully approve.*

1107   Illo- expresses distance in time, past or future: first past time: as,

Quid ille, ŭbi est Mĭlēsius? (*Ter.* Ad. iv. 5. 68) *well, and that gentleman from Miletus you were speaking of, where is he?*

Hei mĭhī quālis ĕrat! quantum mūtātūs ăb illo Hectŏrĕ qui rĕdīt exŭuiās indūtūs Achilli (*Virg.* A. II. 274), *alas, what was he like! How changed from that Hector of other days returning clad in Achilles' spoils!*

Ille ĕgŏ lībĕr, ille fĕrox, tăcui (*Ov.* Met. I. 757), *I once so free, so proud, was silent.*

1108   Hence illo- is applied to well-known personages of past times: as,

C. Sĕquăr, ŭt instĭtuī, dīuīnum illum uĭrum.
A. Plătōnem uidēlicet dīcis.   C. Istum ipsum, Attĭcĕ (*Cic.* de Leg. III. 1. 1),
C. *I will follow, as I have begun, that heaven-inspired man.*
A. *You mean Plato, no doubt.*   C. *The very same, Atticus.*

1109   Also to proverbs: as,
Vērum illud uerbumst, uŏlgo quod dīci sŏlet,
Omnis sĭbi 'sse mēlius malle quam altĕri (*Ter.* And. II. 5. 15),
*Too true 's the old saying in every body's mouth,
All men wish better to themselves than to their neighbour.*

1110   Ho- and illo- are used together to mark the connection of something present with something past: as,

Atăt hoc illud est;
Hinc illae lacrumae, haec illast misericŏrdia (*Ter.* And. I. 1. 98),
*Ah, ah! then, this explains that matter;
Hence all that weeping, hence that sympathy.*

1111   Illo- is also applied to future time: as,

Hic domus Aeneae cunctis dominabitur oris,
Et nati natorum, et qui nascentur ab illis (*Virg.* A. III. 97),
Here shall Æneas' house o'er every border rule,
His children's children and their children too.

1112   LOGICAL PRONOUNS.

                              a. *i-, eo-,* &c.

I-, eo-, &c., *this, that, the, he, she, it, a, one, such,* is never a demonstrative, and consequently it never takes the enclitic *ce;** it always refers to some word or words in the context.

1113   Commonly i- refers to a word preceding: as,

Eunti mihi Antium, uenit obuiam tuos puer. Is mihi litteras abs te reddidit (*Cic.* ad Att. II. 1. 1), *as I was going to Antium, there came across me your servant. This servant (or he) gave me a letter from you.*

Vnam rem explicabo eamque maxumam (*Cic.* de Fin. I. 8. 28), *one thing I will explain, and that the most important.*

1114   I- also refers to what follows: as,

Id tibi affirmo te In istis molestiis non diutius futurum (*Cic.* ad Fam. IV. 13. 4), *this I assure you of, that you will not be long in your present painful situation there.*

1115   I- is often used as an antecedent to a relative, and then may often be translated by the words *a, one, a man,* &c., especially if a reason be implied:

Si In eos quos speramus nobis profuturos, non dubitamus conferre officia, quales In eos esse debemus qui iam profuerunt ? (*Cic.* de Off. I. 15. 48) *if we do not hesitate to bestow our good offices on those by whom we hope to be benefitted, how ought we to behave towards those by whom we have already been benefitted ?*

Hostis apud maiores nostros is dicebatur quem nunc *peregrinum* dicimus (*Cic.* de Off. I. 12. 37), *he whom we now call* peregrinus *(foreigner) was called among our ancestors* hostis.

---

* The passage in Plautus (Merc. Prol. 91) is corrupt. See Bothe's edition.

Mĭnŭmē conuĕnit ex eo ăgrō qui Caesăris iussū diuĭdātŭr, cum mŏneri qui Caesăris bĕnĭfĭcĭō sĕnātor sit (*Cic.* ad Fam. XIII. 5. 2), *it is altogether inconsistent that a man who is a senator by Caesar's favour should be ejected from land which is in course of distribution under Caesar's order.*

Nam quō rĕdibo ore ăd eam quam contémpserim ? (*Ter.* Ph. v. 7. 24) *for with what face shall I go back to a woman whom I have thoroughly insulted ?*

1117 The relative clause often precedes, in which case this second pronoun is emphatic :

Hoc qui admīrātŭr, is se quid sit uir bŏnus nescīrē fătĕātŭr (*Cic.* de Off. III. 19. 75), *if any one wonder at this, let that man confess that he knows not what a good man is.*

Nōn est consentāneum, qui mĕtū non frangātŭr, eum frangī cŭpĭdĭtātē (*Cic.* de Off. I. 20. 68), *it is an inconsistency for a man to be proof against fear, and then not to be proof against temptation.*

1118 I- is used before a relative in such a manner as to denote the belonging to a class, and is to be translated by *such, the sort of person, one of those, the man to —, so — as to :* thus,

Nĕquĕ tu ĭs es qui quid sis nescĭās (*Cic.* ad Fam. V. 12. 6), *nor are you the person not to know what you are.*

1119 In this sense i- is often followed by ŭt : thus,

In eum res rēdiit iam lŏcum, ut sit nĕcessum (*Ter.* Haut. II. 3. 118), *matters are at last come to such a state that it is necessary.*

b. qui-, quo-, &c.

1120 The relative quo- or qua- and qui- agrees like other adjectives with its noun if expressed : as,

Intellexit diem instārē quō dĭē frūmentum mētīrī ŏportēret (*Caes.* B. G. 1. 16), *he saw that the day was close at hand, on which day it was required that he should measure out the corn.*

Causam dicit eā lēgē quā lēgē sĕnātōrēs sōlī tĕnentŭr (*Cic.* p. Clu. 57. 155), *he is making his defence under a law by which law senators alone are bound.*

1121   In the sentences just given the noun is expressed twice over.
This repetition is unnecessary; and commonly the noun which
should accompany the relative is omitted, so that the relative
agrees with the antecedent noun in number and gender, but has
its case determined by its own clause: as,

> Ab rēlĭquīs princĭpĭbus quī hanc temptandam fortūnam non
> exīstĭmābant (*Caes.* B. G. VII. 4), *by the other chiefs who
> thought that this risk ought not to be run.*
>
> Intrōmīssīs ĕquĭtĭbus, quōs arcessendōs cūrāuĕrat (*Caes.* B. G.
> V. 58), *horsemen having been let into the place, whom he had
> sent for.*
>
> Adeunt pĕr Aeduōs quōrum antīquĭtŭs ĕrat in iīs cīuĭtās
> (*Caes.* B. G. VI. 4), *they make their approach by means of
> the Aedui under whose protection the state had been from of
> old.*
>
> Quid uōs hanc mĭsĕram sectāmĭnī praedam, quĭbus licet iam
> esse fortūnātissimis? (*Caes.* B. G. VI. 35) *why do you pursue
> this wretched booty, you who have it in your power now to be
> the most fortunate of men?*
>
> Aduersāriōs suōs ā quĭbus paulo ante ĕrat ēiectus (*Caes.* B. G.
> VII. 4), *his opponents by whom he had been a little before
> expelled.*

1122   The relative may have a different noun from the sentence to
which it is attached: as,

> Erat lūnā plēnā, quī dies mărĭtĭmōs aestūs maxĭmōs efficĕrĕ
> consuēuit (*Caes.* B. G. IV. 29), *it was full moon, which day
> usually makes the sea-tides the greatest.*
>
> Cūmae, quam Graecī tum urbem tĕnēbant (*Liv.* IV. 44), *Cumae,
> which city Greeks then occupied.*

1123   A very common construction consists of the relative and its
so-called antecedent divided by the other words of the relative
clause: as,

> Habētis quam pĕtīstis făcultātem* (*Caes.* B. G. VI. 8), *you have
> now the opportunity you sought.*

---

* In sentences such as these it is a common habit in modern printing
to place the relative clause between commas, whereas the connection is as
close as between an ordinary adjective and its noun. Indeed it is useful
to translate such sentences in the exact order of the words: thus, ' In
the-which-followed winter;' ' The-which-you-sought opportunity.'

Ea quae secūta est hiēmē (*Caes.* B. G. iv. 1), *in the winter which followed.*

Ad eas quas diximus mūnītiōnēs (*Caes.* B. G. iii. 26), *to the fortifications which we have mentioned.*

1124. In the first and last of the phrases just quoted the noun belongs equally to both clauses. In the following it belongs to the relative clause:

Quōs in praesentiā tribūnos militum circum sē hăbēbat, sē sēquī iūbet (*Caes.* B. G. v. 37), *such tribunes of the soldiers as he had about him at the moment, he orders to follow him.*

1125. Thus, sometimes the noun of the main clause, more commonly that of the relative clause, is omitted. But if the noun be separated from the main verb by the relative clause, it sometimes takes its case from the relative clause, to which it is nearer: as,

Pōpulō ut placerent quās fēcisset fābulas (*Ter.* And. prol. 3), *that the plays he might write should please the people.*

Vrbem quam stătuō uestrast (*Virg.* A. i. 577), *the city which I am setting up is yours.*

1126. An antecedent is not always necessary: as,

Nēc ērat quod scriberem (*Cic.* ad Att. xii. 9), *nor was there any thing to write.*

Assēquēre quod uīs (*Cic.* ad Att. xi. 7. 3), *you will obtain what you wish.*

Hăbēbis quoi dēs littĕrās (*Cic.* ad Att. xi. 13. 5), *you will have some one to send a letter by.*

Interuēnit ēnim quoi mētuistī crēdō nē saluō cāpitē nēgāre non possēs (*Cic.* Phil. ii. 38. 99), *for there suddenly stepped forward one to whom you were afraid, I suppose, you could not say no without getting your head broken.*

Partō* quŏd ēusbās (*Hor.* Sat. i. 1. 94), *having acquired what you longed for.*

Bēne est oui Deūs obtŭlit parcā quod sătis est mănū (*Hor.* Od. iii. 16. 43), *'tis well with him to whom the Deity has offered with frugal hand what is enough.*

Diēs deindē praestĭtūtā căpĭtālisquē poenā qui non rēmigrasset Rōmam singŭlōs mētū suō quemque ŏbēdientiā fēcit (*Liv.*

---

* Here *quod eusbas* may be considered as a noun in the ablative.

vi. 4), *a day was then named, and capital punishment held out to any one who should not by that day have returned to Rome there to live, and this decisive measure made them all obedient, each individual being influenced by fear for himself.*

Praemia atque hŏnōres qui mīlĭtārĕ sēcum uŏluissent prŏpŏsuit (*Liv.* XXIII. 15), *he held out rewards and honours to such as should be willing to serve under him.**

1127   Such omissions fall for the most part under the four following heads: *a.* where the antecedent, if expressed, would be in the same case as the relative; *b.* where the verb immediately precedes or follows, and thus shows the connection; *c.* short relative phrases, where the antecedent would be a nominative or accusative; *d.* an antecedent dative before qui.†

1128   The relative in short phrases sometimes adapts its case to the main sentence: as,

Quem uīdēbĭtur praefĭcĭās (*Cic.* ad Att. VI. 3, 2), *you will place at the head of the business whom you think proper.*

Quō consuērat interuallo hostīs sĕquĭtŭr (*Caes.* B. G. 1. 22), *he follows the enemy at the interval he was accustomed to.* ‡

Raptim quĭbus quisquĕ pŏtĕrat ēlātīs (*Liv.* I. 29), *each hastily carrying out what he could.*

1129   When a relative referring to the preceding sentence is separated from its verb (or other governing word) by a conjunction or relative, it is convenient in the translation to substitute for the relative some proper form of the pronoun 'he' or 'this,' with an English conjunction if need be: as,

Quod postquam barbări fĭĕri ănĭmaduertĕrant (*Caes.* B. G. III. 18), *but when the barbarians saw that this was being done.*

Quŏd ūbi audītum est (*Caes.* B. G. III. 18), *and when this was heard.*

1130   When a relative is connected in meaning with two clauses, it generally adapts its case to the secondary clause, if that precedes the main clause: as,

---

* See also examples under § 1226, and *Liv.* III. 19. 6.

† This was probably at first owing to the similarity in sound between *qui* and *cui* or *quoi*, so that the case *d* would be virtually included in *a*; and then extended to the plural.

‡ The English often omit the relative, which however must always be supplied in translating into Latin.

Is ĕnim fuĕram, quoi* cum licēret magnōs ex ŏtiō fructus cā-
pĕrĕ, non dūbĭtāuĕrim mē grāuissŭmis tempestātĭbŭs ob-
uium ferrĕ (*Cic.* R. P. I. 4. 7), *for I had been one, who having
it in my power to derive great advantages from repose, still
did not hesitate to face the most fearful storms.*

Nam quid dē mē dīcam, quoi ūt omnĭā contingant quae uŏlo,
lĕvārī nōn possum? (*Cic.* ad Att. XII. 23. 4) *for what should
I say of myself, when, though every thing should befall me that
I wish, still I could not be relieved?*

Is quit albūs āternē fuŏrit ignōrās (*Cic.* Phil. II. 10. 41), *one of
whom you cannot say whether he was white or black.*

Quem nĭsi Sāguntīnum scĕlūs ăgĭtāret, respĭcĕrot profectō &c.
(*Liv.* XXI. 41), *and if Heaven's curse for his crimes at Saguntum had not been pursuing him, assuredly he would have looked
back at &c.*

1130. 1 When two relative clauses are combined (as by ĕt, quē, &c.),
and the cases of the two relatives should strictly speaking be different, the second may sometimes be omitted, when it would be a
nominative or accusative: as,

Bocchus cum pĕdĭtĭbŭs quos Vŏlux adduxĕrat, nĕque in priōrĕ
pugna affuĕrant, postrēmam Rōmănōrum ăciem inuādunt
(*Sal.* Jug. 101), *Bocchus, with the infantry which Volux had
brought up, and who had not been present in the preceding
battle, attack the rear of the Roman army.*‡

1130. 2 The adjectives tāli-, tanto-, and tŏt, as also the adverbs tam
and tum, are used as antecedents to the respective relatives quāli-,
quanto-, quŏt, quam and quum.

1131 The relative§ is often used in parentheses with the sense of
the logical pronoun i- or eo- : as,

---

* Rather than *qui cum mihi liceret*, &c. Hence probably we should read in Phil. II. 7. 17, *hac uero ne P. quidem Clodius dixit unquam*, quoi *quia iure fui inimicus, dolero a te omnibus uitiis tam cito superatum.*

† Had the *ignoras* preceded *albus*, the phrase would have been *quem ignoras*, &c.

‡ Sometimes the proper case of i- is supplied in the second clause, as *eos* in *Cic.* de Clar. Or. 74. 258.

§ So also the relative adverb *ut* is used for *sic* or *ita* in Ter. Ph. v. 2. 9. *Nouvi ego herele (ut homost) ne mutet sententiam*, 'I am only too much afraid faith (knowing the fellow's character) he may change his mind.' Compare Hec. III. 5. 10, *Sic sum*, 'it is my way.'

Quod sī mihi permīsissēs, qui meūs amŏr in tē est, confēcissem (*Cic.* ad Fam. VII. 2. 1), *whereas if you had left this matter altogether to me, such is my affection for you, I should have settled it.*

Quod sī facit, quā impūdentiast (*Cic.* p. Rosc. Com. 15. 45), *if he does this (and he has impudence enough to do it), &c.*

1131. 1 Logical pronouns,—and we here include, besides i- or eo-, all the pronouns so used, as ho- (§ 1095), illo- (§ 1103), and quo- (§ 1131),—are at times used in immediate agreement with a substantive, where a genitive of the pronoun with reī might have been expected: as,

Hōc mĕtū lātius ūăgări prohibēbat (*Caes.* B. G. V. 19), *by the alarm which thence arose he prevented (the troops from) wandering about to any great distance.*

Haec quidem est perfăcilis dēfensiō (*Cic.* de Fin. III. 11. 36), *the defence of this at any rate is a very easy matter.*

1132   I-dem.

I-dem *same* is employed in many constructions, the chief of which are the following:

Impĕrī nostrī terrārumque illārum idem est extrēmum (*Cic.* de Prov. Con. 13. 33), *our empire and that country have now the same boundary.*

Quaerĭtŭr idemnē sit pertināacia et persĕuĕrantiă (*Cic.* Top. 23. 87), *the question is, whether obstinacy and perseverance be the same thing.*

Acădēmīcŭs ĕt idem rhētŏr (*Cic.* N. D. II. 1. 1), *an academician and at the same time a professed speaker.*

Animus tē ergā est idem ac fuit (*Ter.* Haut. II. 3. 24), *my feeling towards you is the same as it was.*

Idem ăbeunt qui uĕnĕrant (*Cic.* de Fin. IV. 3. 7), *they go away the same that they came.**

Eōdem lŏcō rēs est quăsi eă pĕcūniă lēgātă nōn esset (*Cic.* de Leg. II. 21. 53), *the matter stands in the same position as if the said money had never been left.*

Idem nĕgas quidquam certī possē rĕpĕriri, idem tē compĕriassĕ dixisti (*Cic.* Acad. Pr. II. 10. 63), *on the one hand you say*

* With their opinions unaltered.

that nothing certain can be found by man, and yet on the other hand you also said that you had discovered so and so.

Nĕque ego ălĭtĕr accēpi ; intellexi tămĕn idem (Cic. ad Fam. ɪx. 15. 3), *nor did I take it otherwise ; I saw however at the same time &c.*

The construction with a dative or with cum belongs to the poets and the later writers : as,

Eōdem mēcum pătrĕ gĕnĭtŭs (Tac. Ann. ɪv. 2), *sprung from the same father as myself.*

Inultum qui sĕrult, ĭdém făcĭt occidenti (Hor. ad Pis. 467), *who saves a man against his will does the same as one who kills him.*

INTERROGATIVE PRONOUNS.

The use of the interrogative pronouns qui-, ŭtĕro- &c. falls under the two heads of direct* and indirect questions ; the former having commonly the indicative,† the latter nearly always the subjunctive : as,

Direct questions :

Quis tu es ? (Ter. And. ɪv. 1. 11) *who are you ?*

Quid ĭgĭtur sĭbi uolt pătĕr ? (Ter. And. ɪɪ. 3. 1) *what does my father mean then ?*

Indirect questions :

Quid rĕtĭneat per tē mĕmĭnit, non quid ămĭsĕrit (Cic. p. Deiot. 13. 38), *he remembers what he retains through you, not what he has lost.*

Quālis sit ănĭmŭs, ipse ănĭmus nescit (Cic. Tusc. ɪ. 22. 53), *what sort of thing the soul is, the soul itself knows not.*

---

* In the direct question the English language puts the nominative after the verb or its auxiliary, except indeed when the question is about the nominative itself and begins with ' who,' ' which,' or ' what.' Secondly, an interrogative pronoun or particle commences the sentence, unless indeed the question be about the act itself, in which case the verb or its auxiliary comes first. Thirdly, the mark of interrogation (?) is placed at the end of the sentence. On the other hand, the indirect interrogative is always attached to some word or phrase, generally to a verb. Secondly, the nominative, as in ordinary sentences, always precedes its verb. Thirdly, it is not entitled to the mark of interrogation.

† See below.

Both:

Quid factūrī fuistis ? Quamquam quid factūrī fuěritis dūbitem, cum uideam quid fēcěritis ? (*Cic.* p. Lig. 8. 24) *what would you have done ? And yet am I to doubt what you would have done, when I see what you actually have done ?*

Both:

Quid nunc fiet ? Quid fiat rŏgas ? (*Ter.* Ad. III. 1. 1) *what will become of us now ? What will become of us, ask you ?*

1135 A question is sometimes asked with a participle dependent upon the main verb, in which case it is commonly necessary for the English translator to substitute a verb for that participle, and at the same time to insert a relative before the original verb : as,

Vndĕ pĕtītum hōc in mē iăcĭs ? (*Hor.* Sat. I. 4. 70) *whence didst thou get this stone (which) thou throwest at me ?*

Quĭbus mōs undě dēductūs Amāzŏniā sěcūrī dextrās ŏbarmet, quaerěrě distŭlī (*Hor.* Od. IV. 4. 18), *but whence derived the custom which with Amazonian axe equips their arm, I ask not now.*

Cōgĭtātō quantīs lăbōrĭbus fundātum impěrium, quantā uirtūtě stăbĭlītam lībertātem ūnā nox paeně dēlěrit (*Cic.* in Cat. IV. 0. 19), *consider what labour was employed to found that empire, what valour to establish that liberty which a single night has almost annihilated.*

1136 Occasionally two questions are included in one sentence, and require to be separated in the translation : as,

Nihil iam ălĭud quaerěrě dēbětis, nĭsi ŭtěr ŭtri insĭdias fēcěrit (*Cic.* p. Mil. 9. 23), *you have now nothing else to inquire into but this, which of the two plotted against the other's life, which had his life so endangered.*

Cētěrōrum mīsěrābĭlĭŏr ōrātĭō fuit commĕmŏrantium ex quantīs ŏpĭbus quō rěcĕdĭssent Karthāgīnīensium rēs (*Liv.* xxx. 42), *the language of the rest was still more affecting, as they dwelt upon the powerful station from which, and the low depth to which the state of Carthage was fallen.*

1137 It may be observed, that the Latin language employs the indirect interrogation much more frequently than the English, which often prefers a mere relative with an antecedent substantive, or a substantive alone : as,

Nunc quid ăgendum sit consīdĕrātō (*Cic.* p. leg. Man. 2. 6), *consider now the business which you have to transact.*

Non sum praedīcātūrus quantās illē res dŏmī mīlītiaequŏ gessĕrīt (*Cic.* p. leg. Man. 10. 48), *I am not going to proclaim the greatness of his achievements at home and abroad.*

INDEFINITE PRONOUNS, &c.

1138 The simple qui- any is an enclitic,* and cannot occupy the first place in a sentence.

Omnĭā semper quae māgistrātūs illō dīcet, sĕcundīs auribus, quae ab nostrūm quō dicentŭr aduersīs accipiĕtīs ? (*Liv.* VI. 40) *will you always receive with a favourable ear what those magistrates say, and with an unfavourable ear what is said by any of us ?*

1139 The use of this word is frequent in sentences beginning with the relative or relative adverbs, and after si, nisi, ne, num : as,

Iam illis prōmissīs standum nōn est, quae coāctūs quis mĕtū prōmīsīt (*Cic.* de Off. 1. 10. 32), *lastly, there is another class of promises which are not binding, viz. those which one makes under the compulsion of fear.*

Quō quis uersūtior est, hōc inuīsior (*Cic.* de Off. II. 9. 34), *the more crafty a man is, the more is he disliked.*

Vbi sĕmĕl quis peiĕrāuĕrīt, eī credī posteā nōn ŏportet (*Cic.* p. Rab. Post. 13. 30), *when a man has once foresworn himself, he should not afterwards be believed.*

Num quŏd ĕlŏquentiae uestīgium appāret ? (*Cic.* de Or. I. 9. 37) *is there any trace of eloquence to be seen ?*

Hăbent lēgĭbus sanctum, sī quis quid dē rē publicā fāmā accēpĕrīt, ūtī ad māgistrātum dēfĕrat, nēuō cum quo ălio commūnicet (*Caes.* B. G. VI. 19), *they have it provided for by law, that if any one hear any thing by report on matters of state, he shall lay it before the authorities, and not communicate it to any other person.*

Sī quī grăuiŏrĕ uolnĕre accepto ĕquō dēcĭdĕrat, circumsīstēbant (*Caes.* B. G. I. 48), *whenever any one at all severely wounded fell from his horse, they formed around him.*

---

* This of course does not prevent the compounds *siqui-*, *nequi-*, &c. from being emphatic.

1140 In the phrases with sī-quī-, the main sentence has no connecting pronoun, the sī-quī- clause itself performing the office of a noun: as,

Sī quid est pābūlī* obruunt niuēs (*Liv.* XXI. 37), *what fodder there is, is buried under the snow.*

1141 Alīquī- *some, any*, is always emphatic, and is opposed to such words as *all, much, none*: as,

Vnum ālīquem nōmīnātō (*Cic.* p. Clu. 66. 185), *name some one or other.*

Sī nōs ād ālīquam ālīcūius commōdī ālīquandō rēcūpērandī spem fortūnā rēseruāuit, minus est errātum ā nōbīs (*Cic.* ad Fam. XIV. 4. 1), *if fortune has reserved us for any chance (however small) of recovering at any time (however distant) any thing desirable (in the slightest degree), then our error has been less.*

Est istuc quidem ālīquid, sed nēquāquam in istō sunt omnīā (*Cic.* de Sen. 3. 8), *what you say is, I grant, something, but it by no means includes the whole.*

Sī uīs esse ālīquid† (*Juv.* 1. 74), *if thou wishest to be somebody in the world.*

1142 The substantive‡ quī-quam and adjective ullō- signify *any* (if only one, and no matter what that one may be), and are used in negative, interrogative, conditional and comparative sentences: as,

Sine sōciīs nēmō quidquam tālē cōnātur (*Cic.* de Am. 12. 42), *without companions no one attempts any such thing.*

Idcircō cāpite et supercīliīs est rāsīs, ne ullum pīlum uīrī bonī bibere dicātur (*Cic.* p. Rosc. Com. 7. 20), *he goes with his head and his eyebrows shaved, that he may not be said to have a single hair of respectability about him.*

Et quisquam Iūnōnis nūmēn ādōret Praetereā? (*Virg.* A. 1. 52) *and is any one after this to worship the divinity of Juno?*

---

* Thus, *si quid est pabuli* may be considered to be the accusative case after the verb *obruunt.*

† So Juvenal, if we may trust the best and the majority of the Mss. (Madvig.)—Cicero uses both *sum aliquis* and *sum aliquid.*

‡ Quī-quam however is at times an adjective, and ullo- at times a substantive, in speaking of persons: as, *qui-quam*, Ter. Haut. 1. 1 29, Plaut. Ps. III. 2. 62; *ullo-*, Caes. B. G. L. 8. 3, Liv. v. 40, Cic. ad Fam. XIII. 26. 1.

Num censēs ullum ănĭmal, quod sanguĭnem hăbeat, sĭnē corde essē posse ? (*Cic.* de Div. I. 52. 119) *now do you think that any animal that has blood can exist without a heart ?*

Si ullă mea ăpŭd tē commendātĭō ŭlluit, haec ut ulleat rŏgō (*Cic.* ad Fam. XIII. 40), *if any recommendation of mine ever had weight with you, I beg that this may.*

Quamdiū quisquam ĕrit, qui tē dēfendĕre audeat, uīuēs (*Cic.* in Cat. I: 2. 6), *as long as there is a single living being who dares to defend you, you shall live.*

Cuiuis potest accidere, quod cuiquam potest (*Syr.* ap. Sen. de Tranq. An. 11), *that may happen to every one, which may happen to any one.*

Nihil est exitiōsius ciuitātĭbus quam quidquam ăgi per uim (*Cic.* de Leg. III. 18. 42), *nothing is more pernicious to a state than that violence should be resorted to in any thing.*

1143   Qui-piam is used like ălĭqui- :*

Quaeret quispiam (*Cic.* in Rull. II. 8. 20), *some one will ask.*

Forsităn ălĭquis ălĭquando eiusmŏdi quidpiam fĕcĕrĭt (*Cic.* II. Verr. II. 32. 78), *perhaps some one will some time or other have done something of this kind.*

Pĕcūniam si quoipiam fortūna ădēmit, aut si ălĭcūius ēripuit iniūrĭā, tămen consōlātŭr hŏnestās ĕgestātem (*Cic.* p. Quinct. 15. 49), *if money be taken from any one by misfortune, or wrested from him by the violence of some one, still integrity is a consolation to poverty.*

1144   Qui-uis and qui-lŭbet *any you please* are universal affirmatives, and may often be translated by *every one :* as,

Abs quīuīs hŏmĭnē bĕnĭfĭcium accĭpĕrĕ gaudeās (*Ter.* Ad. II. 3. 1), *one would be glad to receive a favour from any one.*

Mihi quiduis săt est (*Plaut.* Mil. Gl. III. 1. 155), *for me any thing is enough.*

Non cuiuis hŏmĭni contingĭt ădīrē Cŏrinthum (*Hor.* Ep. I. 17. 36), *it is not every man's lot to visit Corinth.*

---

* Except that it has never the meaning of 'something important,' which *ălĭqui-* often has.

† A superlative may often be substituted for them; as for example in the following sentences : 'the greatest stranger,' 'the least quantity,' 'only the most fortunate.'

234   SYNTAX.

Quem sĕquar ? Quemlĭbet, mŏdo ălĭquem (*Cic.* Acad. Pr. II. 43. 132), *whom am I to take for my guide ? Any body you please, provided it be somebody.*

1144.1   Qui-quŏ (N. quisquĕ) *every, all taken each by itself*, is opposed to ūnĭverso- *all united as a whole.* See examples under § 1037, *a, b, c.**

1145   Qui-dam *some* is used both generally, and in reference to particular objects which we either cannot or do not choose accurately to define. Hence it is often employed to soften some strong metaphor or epithet :

Sed sunt quidam† ĭtā uōce absŏni ŭt ĭn ōrātōrum nŭmĕrum uĕnīrĕ non possint (*Cic.* de Or. I. 25. 115), *but there are in fact some of so unmusical a voice that they can never be admitted into the number of orators.*

Accurrĭt quidam, nōtŭs mĭhī nōmĭnĕ tantum (*Hor.* Sat. I. 9. 3), *there runs up a certain person known to me by name alone.*

Nĕquĕ pugnas narrat, quod quidam‡ făcĭt (*Ter.* E. III. 2. 29), *nor does he talk of his battles, as a certain person does.*

Hăbet ĕnim quendam ăcŭleum contŭmĕlĭă quem păti ulrī bŏnī difficillŭmē possunt (*Cic.* II. Verr. III. 41. 95), *for insult has in fact a sort of sting in it, which a gentleman can with the greatest difficulty endure.*

Fuit ĕnim mirĭfĭcus quidam in Crassŏ pŭdōr (*Cic.* de Or. I. 26. 122), *for there was in fact in Crassus a bashfulness I had almost called astounding.*

1146   Qui-cunquĕ is commonly an adjective, and is used in three ways (of which however the first is by far the most common) : *a.* as *every one who*, in the same way as the ordinary relative is used ; *b.* without any antecedent, but so as to admit the insertion of such words as *no matter* before the *who* ; *c.* in the sense of *some one or other, the best I can.*

a. Quŏd ĕrit cumquĕ uĭsum, ăgēs (*Cic.* de Fin. IV 25. 69), *whatever you think proper, you will do.*

b. Quōcunque in lŏcŏ quĭs est, idem est ei sensŭs (*Cic.* ad Fam. VI. 1. 1), *wherever a person is, his feelings are the same.*

* See also § 349.
† Here Cicero has no particular persons in view.
‡ Here there is a particular person in view, viz. the braggart Thraso.

c. Quae sānāri pŏtĕrunt, quācunquĕ* rătiōnĕ sānābō (*Cic.* in Cat. II. 5. 11), *what parts admit of being healed, I will heal in the best way I can.*

1147 Qui-qui-† is commonly a substantive, and is used chiefly in the sense of *no matter who*, &c.; but at times as a relative in grammatical connection with the main clause:

Ago grātiās, quōquo ănĭmō făcĭs (*Cic.* Phil. II. 13. 33), *I thank you, no matter with what feeling you do it.*

Quicquid auctōrĭtātĕ possum, Id omnĕ tĭbi pollĭcĕŏr (*Cic.* p. leg. Man. 24. 69), *whatever power I possess in my name, I promise you the whole of it.*

1148 The chief constructions of ălĭŏ-‡ *one, some, other,* are the following:

Ălĭŭd est mălĕdĭcĕre, ălĭŭd accussārĕ (*Cic.* p. Cael. 3. 6), *it is one thing to abuse, one to accuse.*

Quae mĭnus tūta ĕrant, ălĭă fossis, ălĭă uallis, ălĭă turribus mūnĭēbat (*Liv.* XXXII. 5), *the parts which were less protected, he was fortifying, some with ditches, some with palisades, some with towers.*

Ipsi inter se ălĭīs ălĭī prōsunt (*Cic.* de Off. I. 7. 22), *they themselves mutually assist one another.*

Mē quŏtĭdie ălĭŭd ex ălĭo impĕdit (*Cic.* ad Fam. IX. 10), *for myself, one thing after another hinders me every day.*

Equĭtēs ălĭi ălĭā dīlapsi sunt (*Liv.* XLIV. 43), *the cavalry slipped off, some by one route, some by another.*

Iussit ălĭōs ălĭbi fŏdĕrĕ (*Liv.* XLIV. 33), *he ordered them to dig, some in one place, some in another.*

Quŏtannis ălĭum atque ălĭum dŏmĭnum sortĭuntŭr (*Liv.* XXXI. 29), *they take the chance of the lot every year, first for one master, then for another.*

Tĭmeō ne ălĭud crēdam atque ălĭud§ nuntĭēs (*Ter.* Hec. V. 4. 4),

---

* *Potero* might have been inserted.

† The use of *qui-qui-* in the sense of *qui-que-* is very rare, at any rate in the best writers.

‡ That *alio-* did not originally mean difference is shown by the fact that *aliqui-* is connected with it, and that its other derivative *altero-* in itself never signifies difference.

§ This shows the way in which *atque* alone came to be used after *alio-*.

I am afraid that I am giving credit to one thing, and you asserting another.

Longe ălĭă nōbīs ac tū scrīpsērās nuntiantŭr (*Cic.* ad Att. xi. 10. 2), *the accounts brought to us differ widely from what you write.*

Nōn ălĭŭs essem ătquĕ nunc sum (*Cic.* ad Fam. 1. 9. 21), *I should not have been a different person from what I now am.*

Lux longe ălĭast, sōlĭs et* lychnōrum (*Cic.* p. Cael. 28. 67), *there is a wide difference in the light of the sun and of a lamp.*

Lŭtātĭō quae ălĭă res quam cēlĕrĭtās uictōriam dĕdĭt? (*Liv.* xxii. 14) *what else but rapidity gave Lutatius the victory?*

Quĭd ĕnim ălĭud quam admŏnendī essētĭs ut mōrem trădĭtum ā pătrĭbus seruārētĭs? (*Liv.* xxii. 60) *for what else would there have been to do but to remind you of the duty of maintaining a custom handed down by your fathers?*

Quĭd est dīcĕre ălĭud, Quia indignos uestrā uŏluntātĕ creātūrī nōn estis, nĕcessĭtātem uōbīs creandī quos nōn uoltīs impōnam? (*Liv.* vi. 40) *what is this but to say: Since you will not willingly elect unworthy persons, I will impose on you the necessity of electing those whom you do not like?*

Rŏgāuit, numquĭd ălĭud ferret praetĕr arcam (*Cic.* de Or. ii. 69. 279), *he asked whether he was carrying any thing else besides a chest.*

1149   Altĕro- is used in the following constructions, being always limited to *one of two*, or *the second of many:*

Quōrum altĕr exercĭtum perdĭdit, altĕr uendĭdit (*Cic.* p. Planc. 35. 86), *of whom one has lost, the other has sold an army.*

Altĕrī dimicant; altĕrī uictōrem tĭment (*Cic.* ad Fam. vi. 3. 4), *the one party stake all upon war, the other look with terror to the conqueror.*

Miluo est quoddam bellum quăsi nătūrālĕ cum coruo; ergo altĕr altĕrĭŭs ōuă frangit (*Cic.* N. D. ii. 49. 125), *between the kite and the crow there is, as it were, a sort of natural war; consequently each breaks the other's eggs.*

Altĕrī altĕrōs ălĭquantum attrĭuĕrant (*Sal.* Jug. 79), *each nation had considerably reduced the power of the other.*

---

* When *et* or *que* are used in these phrases, the things compared are brought together. A pause too should precede. *Atque* is not so limited.

† See the note to § 324.

Vterquĕ nŭmĕrus plēnŭs, altĕr altĕrī dē causā hăbētŭr (*Cic.* Somn. Sc. 2), *both numbers are accounted full, the one for one reason, the other for another.*
Omnes quōrum in altĕrīus mānū uītă pŏsĭtast (*Cic.* p. Quinct. 2. 6), *all those whose lives are in the hands of another.*
Tū nunc ĕris altĕr ăb illo (*Virg.* Buc. v. 49), *thou shalt now be next after him.*
Ad Brūtum nostrum hos lĭbrōs altĕros quīnquĕ mittēmŭs (*Cic.* Tusc. v. 41, 121), *we shall send to our friend Brutus this second set of five books.*
Altĕrum tantum ĕquĭtĭbus dīuīsit (*Liv.* x. 46), *he gave to each horse-soldier as much again.*

1149.1 Nēmŏn- *no man, no one,* though properly a substantive, is found with appellations of persons, as nēmo cīuīs *no citizen,* nēmo Rōmānŭs *no Roman,* nēmo quisquam *no one whatever,* where however cīuīs, Rōmānŭs, quisquam, may be regarded themselves as adjectives. In place of the genitive and dative nullīŭs and nullī are preferred.

PRONOMINAL ADVERBS.

1150 The pronominal adverbs,* especially by the old writers, were often used as adjectives in connection with nouns: as,

Tēque ĭbĭdem peruoluam in lŭtō (*Ter.* And. iv. 4. 38), *and I will give you a good rolling in the same mud.*
Quid ĕgŏ nunc ăgam nĭsi in angŭlum ălĭquo ăbeam? (*Ter.* Ad. v. 2. 9) *what am I to do now, but take myself off into some quiet corner?*
Venit mĕdĭtātus ălĭcunde ex sōlō loco (*Ter.* And. II. 4. 3), *he is just come, after conning his lesson, from some solitary place.*
Modo quándam uidi uirginem hīc uīcīnĭae† (*Ter.* Ph. I. 2. 45), *I just now saw a maiden in this neighbourhood.*
Quō tendĭtĭs inquit; Quī gĕnŭs; undĕ dōmō? (*Virg.* A. vIII. 113) *whither haste ye, says he; who by race; from what home?*
Indĭdem ex Achaia ŏriundi (*Liv.* xxv. 15), *sprung from the same Achaia.*
Indĭdemne ex Amerĭā? (*Cic.* p. Rosc. Am. 27. 74) *what from the same Ameria?*

* Those forms of course being selected which accord with the relation of place expressed in the accompanying phrase.
† Hīc uīcīnĭae, both datives. See § 952. Nay in *Plaut.* Mil. II. 3. 2, hīc proxumae uīcīnĭae, for so the Palimpsest and Mss. C. D.

1151 The relative adverbs, like the relative itself, are often used without an expressed antecedent: as,

>Pergam quō coepi hoc iter (*Ter.* Hec. I. 2. 119), *I will continue this journey of mine to the place I started for.*

>Si rem servassem, fuit ubi negotiosus essem (*Plaut.* Truc. I. 2. 38), *if I had saved my money, I should have had something to employ myself upon.*

>Est, dis gratia, unde haec fiant (*Ter.* Ad. I. 2. 41), *there is, thanks to the gods, the wherewithal to do this.*

>Vāgārī quā uēlit (*Cic.* de Or. 1. 16. 70), *to wander along whatever road he pleases.*

1151.1 The adverbs of all pronouns used logically, especially those connected with the relative, may refer to antecedents of any gender or number, so that undĕ, for example, stands for ăb or ex quō, quā or quibus, quō for in or ad quem &c., ŭbi for in quō &c.: as,

>Omnĭbŭs undĕ pĕtītŭr, hoc consĭlī dĕdĕrim (*Cic.* ad Fam. VII. 11. 1), *to all defendants in a suit I would give this advice.*

>Pŏtest fĭĕri, ŭt is undĕ te audisse dicis, irātus dixĕrit (*Cic.* de Or. II. 70. 285), *it may be that the person from whom you say you heard it said so in anger.*

>Nĕquĕ praeter tō quisquam fuit, ŭbi nostrum ius contra illōs obtĭnērēmŭs (*Cic.* p. Quinct. 9. 34), *nor was there besides you any one before whom we could maintain our right against them.*

>Hŏmo ăpŭd eos quō sē contŭlit grātĭōsŭs (*Cic.* II. Verr. IV. 18. 38), *a man of influence among those to whom he betook himself.*

>Omnia quā uīsŭs ĕrat constrāta armīs (*Sal.* Jug. 101), *all the ground along which the eye could see was bestrewn with arms.*

VERB.

PERSONS, NUMBER, &c.

1152 The verb agrees in number and person with the agent (or nominative), and where it contains a participle, in gender also.

1152.1 Where there are two nominatives to a verb, the verb either, *a.* adapts itself to both, taking the plural form; or, *b.* to the nearer nominative.

a. Haec nĕque ĕgo nĕquĕ tū fēcimŭs* (*Ter.* Ad. i. 2. 23), *true, neither I nor you ever acted thus.*
Castŏr et Pollux ex ĕquis pugnārĕ uīsī sunt (*Cic.* N. D. ii. 2. 6), *Castor and Pollux appeared fighting on horseback.*
b. Et tu ĕt omnĕs hŏmĭnes sciunt (*Cic.* ad Fam. xiii. 8. 1), *you and all men know.*
Sĕnātus pŏpŭlusquĕ Rōmānŭs intellĕgĭt (*Cic.* ad Fam. v. 8. 2), *the senate and people of Rome perceive.*
Emissae eō cohortes quattuŏr et C. Annius praefectŭs (*Sal.* Jug. 77), *there were sent out to that place four battalions and C. Annius as governor.*

1152. 2 But of course when the compound sentence does not admit of being broken up into separate parts, a plural verb is required : as,
Iūs ĕt iniūriă nātūrā diiūdĭcantŭr (*Cic.* de Leg. i. 16. 44), *right and wrong are naturally distinguished from each other.*

1152. 3 The second person, as in English, is often used indefinitely, where we might also say 'a man.' (See § 1224.)

1152. 4 The third person plural, as in English, is often used indefinitely, especially with the adverb uolgō *promiscuously:* as, aiunt *they say,* fĕrunt *they carry the news about, they report.*

1152. 5 The compound tenses formed with fu- are rarely used. When found beside those with ĕs- they denote more forcibly precedence in point of time : as,
Lēges, quam quae lātae sunt, tum uĕrō quae prōmulgātae fuĕrunt (*Cic.* p. Sest. 25. 55), *both those laws which were passed, and above all those which (though never passed) were duly advertised.*
Armă quae fixa in păriĕtĭbus fuĕrant, ea hŭmī sunt inuentă (*Cic.* de Div. i. 34. 74), *arms, which had previously been fixed up on the walls, were found on the ground.*
Nĕque ăliter Carnūtēs interfĭciendī Tasgetiī consĭlium fuissĕ captūros, nĕque Eburōnēs ad castră uentūrōs esse (*Caes.* D. G. v. 29), *but for this (he said) neither would the Carnutes have conspired (as they had done) to put Tasgetius to death,*

---

* It need scarcely be noticed that 'we' has a twofold meaning, including with the first person sometimes the second person—*ego et tu, ego et uos*; sometimes the third, *ego et hic.* So also 'you' may include several persons addressed together, *tu et tu*; or may denote 'you' and 'he,' 'you' and 'they,' &c.

nor would the Eburones have been marching (as they then were) to the camp.

1152. 6 Fŏrem &c. is used in compound tenses by many writers* precisely as essem is.

1152. 7 The compound tenses made up of fu- with the participles in túro and endo are used only in hypothetical phrases: see §§ 709 to 721, and 1214.

Indicative Mood.

1152. 8 The indicative is employed in affirming, denying, and asking questions. The chief uses of this mood and its several tenses have been already stated.† Moreover, it is evidently sufficient to point out the cases where the other moods are required. Hence all further remark upon the indicative is nearly superfluous. However, it may still be useful to draw special attention to those cases where error is not uncommon.

1153 Conditional sentences may be divided into two general heads: 1. those which put an imaginary case, the non-existence of which is implied in the very terms, and which are here called hypothetical, such as, 'If he were here, he would tell us,' or 'If I had been ill, I should have consulted the physician;' in which cases it is clearly implied that 'the person spoken of is *not* present,' that 'I was *not* ill.' 2. Those suppositions which may be the fact or not, so far as the speaker professes to know, as, 'If I receive the letter, I will forward it.' This distinction being understood, it may be stated that conditional sentences of this second class have nearly always the indicative‡ in Latin in both clauses, although the English language may have the subjunctive: thus,

> Erras si id credis (*Ter.* Haut. 1. 1. 53), *you are mistaken if you believe that.*
>
> Perficiētur bellum, si urgēmŭs obsessōs (*Liv.* v. 4), *the war will be finished, if we at once press the besieged.*
>
> Si quŏd ĕrat grandĕ uas, laeti adfĕrēbant; si minŭs siusmŏdi quippiam uēnāri pŏtuĕrant, illă quidem certe pro lĕpuscŭlis căpiebantur, patellae pătĕrae tŭrĭbŭlă (*Cic.* II. Verr. IV.

---

* As Sallust, Livy, and the poets, but not Cicero.
† See §§ 431–478 and 575–591.
‡ But see below.

21. 47), *if any great vessel fall in their way, they brought it to him with joy; but if they were unable to run down any thing of that sort, then at any rate they would catch him as a sort of leveret, a plate, a chalice, a censer.*

Apud mē sīquid ērit ēiusmŏdī, mē imprūdente ērit (*Cic.* ad Att. I. 19. 10), *in my writings, if any thing of the kind exist, it will exist without my knowledge.*

Sī quī aut priuātīs aut pōpŭlīs eōrum dēcrētō non stētĭt, sǎ-crĭfĭcīis interdīcunt (*Caes.* B. G. VI. 13), *if any party, whether an individual or a state, abide not by their decision, they forbid them the sacrifices.*

Sēt sī tu negāris ducere, ǐbi culpam in tē trānsferet (*Ter.* And. II. 3. 5), *but if you refuse to marry, then he'll throw the blame on you.*

Grātissūmum mihi fēcĕris, sī ĭd eum ultrō uĕnĕris (*Cic.* ad Fam. VII. 21), *you will greatly oblige me if you will make the first move and call upon him.**

1154 Often the Indicative mood is in the clause of condition, followed by an imperative, or a subjunctive used as an imperative: as,

Sī mē dīlĭgis, postrīdiē kălendārum coena ăpŭd mē (*Cic.* ad Att. IV. 12), *as you love me, dine with me on the second.*

Sī quicquam inuenies mē mentītum, occīdito (*Ter.* And. V. 2. 22), *if you find that I have told any falsehood, kill me.*

Sī itĕst, factūrus ŭt sit officiŭm suum, Făciat; sīn aliter de hāc re est eius sentĕntia, Respŏndeāt mī (*Ter.* Ad. III. 5. 4), *if the fact be that he will do his duty, why let him do it; but if his purpose in this matter be otherwise, then let him give me an answer.*

1155 The indicative mood may be used without sī as a condition or supposition: thus,

Nĕgat quis,† nĕgo; aīt, aio (*Ter.* E. II. 2. 21), *a man says no, I say no; he says yes, I say yes.*

---

* It will be here seen that the conjunction may be used with every tense of the indicative; yet it is a common assertion in Latin grammars that the subjunctive denotes doubt or contingency, and that *si* takes the subjunctive.

† A mark of interrogation is often inserted, but is unnecessary.

1156 So also an indicative mood at the beginning of a sentence often expresses a concession, as introductory to something opposed : as,

Triumphāuit Sulla dē Mithridātē, sēd Itā triumphāuit, ūt ille pulsus regnāret (*Cic.* p. leg. Man. 3. 8), *true, Sulla did triumph over Mithridates, but his triumph was of such a nature, that the other, though defeated, still held royal power.*‡

1157 So also the double sīuē sīuē has the indicative mood : as,

Hōmǐnēs nōbǐlēs, sīuē rectē seu perpěram fǎcěrē coepěrunt, In ūtrōque excellunt (*Cic.* p. Quinct. 8. 31), *men of family, whether they commence a course of good or bad conduct, in either career become distinguished.*

1158 The doubled forms of the relative,* and those which have cumquě attached to them, take the indicative : as,

Quidquid ěrit, scrībēs (*Cic.* ad Att. xiv. 1), *whatever it be, you will write.*

Tu quántus-quantu's†, níl nísi sapiéntia's (*Ter.* Ad. iii. 3. 40), *you, every inch of you, are nothing but philosophy.*

Quamquámst scelestus, nón committet hódie unquam iterum ut uápulet (*Ter.* Ad. ii. 1. 5), *be he ever so great a scoundrel, he will not run the risk of a second thrashing today.*

Vtut erat, mansúm tamen opórtuit (*Ter.* Haut. l. 2. 26), *no matter how it was, he ought still to have staid.*

Hoc quōque ībō mēcum ěrit (*Plaut.* Aul. iii. 3. 1), *I will have this with me wherever I go.*

Quīcunque is est, eī mē prōfǐteǒr inīmīcum (*Cic.* ad Fam. i. 31. 3), *whoever that man may be, I declare myself his enemy.*

Dēiǒtǎrī cōpiās, quantaecunquē sunt, nostrās esse dūcō (*Cic.* ad Fam. xv. 1. 6), *the forces of Deiotarus, in their full extent, I look upon as ours.*

Quī ūbīcunquē terrārum sunt, Ibi est omnē reīpublǐcae praesǐdium (*Cic.* Phil. ii. 44. 113), *and wherever in the world they are, there is every thing that is to guard the country.*

1158.1 In relative propositions which limit something which is stated in general terms, the old writers, and even Cicero at times, used the indicative.

---

* See § 353–358.   ‡ See *Addenda*.

† Printed in the editions so that the verb wholly disappears; a common error in the text of Terence.

Cătōnem uěrō quis nostrōrum ōrātōrum, qui quidem nunc sunt, lěgit? (*Cic.* Brut. 17. 65), *but Cato—who of our orators, at least those now living, ever reads?*

Ex ōrātōribus Atticis antiquissimi sunt, quōrum quidem scriptā constant*, Pěriclēs ět Alcibiădēs (*Cic.* de Or. II. 22. 93), *of Athenian orators the oldest, at least among those whose writings are authenticated, are Pericles and Alcibiades.*

Quae tibi mandāui, uělim cūres, quod¹ eius tuā mŏlestiā făcěrě pŏtěris (*Cic.* ad Att. I. 5. 6), *these commissions I would thank you to attend to, as far as you shall be able without inconvenience to yourself.*

Tū tămen uělim ne intermittas, quŏd¹ aius făcěrě pŏtěris, scrībere ad me (*Cic.* ad Att. XI. 12. 4), *you however will I beg of you not cease, so far as you have it in your power, to write to me.*

Erus, quantum audio, uxōre excĭdit (*Ter.* And. II. 5. 12), *master, from what I hear, has lost the chance of a wife.*

Nīl locist socordiae, Quantum intellexi modo senis sententiam (*Ter.* And. I. 3. 1), *there is no room for stupidity, to judge from what I saw just now of the old man's feelings.†*

1159 Sentences which express repeated action have the indicative in the secondary clause in the best authors: as,

Quum uēr essě coepěrat, dābat sě lābōri (*Cic.* II. Verr. v. 10. 27), *at the beginning of every spring he gave himself up to business.*

Hostēs ŭbi ăliquos singŭlāris ex nāui ēgrědientis conspexěrant, impědītōs ădōriēbantŭr (*Caes.* B. G. IV. 26), *the enemy, whenever they saw any coming out of a ship by themselves, fell upon them before they could get clear.*

Si ā persěquendo hostis deterrēre nēquiuěrant, disiectōs ā tergō circumuěniēbant (*Sal.* Jug. 50), *if they could not deter the enemy from pursuit, as soon as they were scattered, they kept enclosing them on the rear.*

---

* So the Mss., not *constat.*   ‡ See § 922, last example.

† In such phrases as: *nam ego te, quod sciam, unquam ante hunc diem uidi* (*Plaut.* Men. III. 2. 35), *sciam* is probably an old indicative corresponding to *tuguam*; as it must be in *haud sciam an me opus sit quidem* (*Cic.* de Am. 14. 51), and in *haud sciam an iustiorumo triumpho* (*Liv.* IX. 15). It seems not unlikely that an erroneous interpretation of this *sciam* led to the use of the subjunctive in the parenthetic phrases, *quod meminerim*, &c. (See § 1195.)

Ut cūiusquĕ sors excĭdĕrat, ălăcĕr armă căpiēbat (*Liv.** xxi. 42), *every time the lot of any one fell out of the urn, delighted he took his arms.*

Epistolary Tenses.

1160 The use of the tenses in epistolary writing is occasionally very peculiar. The letters in ancient Italy being sent nearly always by private hand, and the roads with the facilities for travelling being very defective, a long time often elapsed between the writing and the receiving a letter. Hence it was not uncommon for the writer to make allowance for this interval, and to use those tenses which were suited to the time when the letter should be read: as,

Etsi nil sāne hăbēbam† nŏui, quod post accĭdisset quam dĕdissem ad tē Phĭlŏgĕni littĕras, tămen quum Phĭlōtĭmum Rōmam rĕmittĕrem, scribendum ăliquid ad tē fuit, &c. (*Cic.* ad Att. vi. 3. 1), *although I have indeed nothing new that has occurred, at least since I put my last in the hands of Philogenes for you, yet as I am sending Philotimus back to Rome, I am bound to write something to you.*

Hăbēbam acta urbāna usque ad Nōnas Martiās, e quĭbūs intellĭgēbam omniă pŏtiūs actum iri quam dē prōuinciīs (*Cic.* ad Att. vi. 2. 6), *I have the proceedings in the city down to the 7th of March, from which I am disposed to infer that the question of the provinces will be postponed sine die.*

Littĕrārum exemplum quās ad Pompēium scripsi, misi tĭbi (*Cic.* ad Att. iii. 8.4), *I enclose you a copy of a letter I have just written to Pompey.*

1161 Such terms as 'yesterday,' 'today,' 'tomorrow,' 'here,' are avoided for the same reason. Besides, it was far from the ordinary practice to affix a date of time and place, so that the words might have been unintelligible.

Pŭteŏlis magnūs est‡ rūmor Ptŏlĕmaeum esse in regnō. . . .

---

* Livy is not consistent in this construction. Examples of a subjunctive in him are: *ubi dīxisset* (i. 32), *quum uīdissent* (ii. 27), *quaecumque prehendisset* (iii. 11), *sicubi conseruā manūs esset* (xxi. 50), *ubi semel procubuissent* (xxii. 2), *ubi conuenissent* (xxii. 38).

† Otherwise the tenses should have been, *habeo, accīderit, dederim, remittam, est.*

‡ The epistolary tense would have been *erat.*

Pompēiīs in Cūmānum Pāternīs uēnit. Mīsit ad mē stā-
tim quī salūtum nuntiāret. Ad eum postrīdiē mānē uādē-
bam quum haec scripsī (*Cic.* ad Att. iv. 10), *we have a strong
report down here that Ptolemy has been restored to his throne.
.... Pompey arrived at his villa yesterday. He forthwith
sent one of his people with his compliments to me. I am going
to pay him a visit this morning.*
   Puteolī, April* 22.
Trīgintā diēs ērant ipsī, quum hās dābam littĕras, per quos nul-
lās ā uōbīs accēpĕram (*Cic.* ad Att. III. 21), *it is now exactly
thirty days since I heard from you.*

1162   Such change of tenses occurs chiefly at the beginning and end
of letters, where the writer has it more forcibly impressed upon
him that he is not in conversation. It is also confined for the
most part to those matters which are likely to be affected by the
interval of time that must elapse before the letter is read.

IMPERATIVE.

1163   The chief distinction between the two tenses is seen in §§ 592,
593. The future is chiefly used in laws.
   Dīuīs omnibus pontifices, singulīs flāmines suntō (apud Cic.
   de Leg. II. 8. 20), *for the gods in general there shall be a college of pontifices, each separate god shall have his flamen.*

1164   It is also used in the language of wills : as,
   Titius filius meus mihi hērēs estō (*Gaius*, II. 179), *my son
   Titius shall be my heir.*

1165   It is also used generally in reference to future time, more par-
ticularly if that time be fixed by any condition or otherwise : as,
   Vbi nōs lauĕrimus, sī uolēs lauātō (*Ter.* E. III. 5. 48), *when we
   have bathed, bathe if you will.*
   Quoquo hic spectabit, eō tu spectātō semul ;
   Si quo hic gradiētur, pariter tu progrĕdiminō† (*Pl.* Ps. III. 2. 69),

---

* The Festival of Pales was on the 21st.

† So the Mss., not *progredimĭnor* ; and indeed the passage requires
the singular. Moreover Madvig has proved, what Kvarup already maintained, that the form in *minor* does not exist. That in *mino* does exist,
and belongs to the singular. See Madvig, Opusc. II. 239.

Where'er he looks, thither must you look with him;
Where'er he marches, march you too forward by his side.
Cum ualetudini tuae consulueris, tum consulito navigationi (*Cic.* ad Fam. XVI. 4. 3), *when you have taken measures for your health, then and not till then take measures for your voyage.*

1166 The present is used in a less authoritative manner, and is applied both to the immediate occasion and to general directions.

Iuno Lucina fer opem (*Ter.* And. III. 1. 15), *Juno Lucina, aid me, I implore thee.*
Mihi crede (*Cic.* ad Fam. IX. 16. 8), *take my word for it.*
Iustitiam cole et pietatem (*Cic.* Somn. Sc. 3), *cultivate justice and affection.*
Vide quam rem agas (*Ter.* Ad. III. 2. 45), *have a care what you are after.*
Cave sis (*Ter.* E. IV. 7. 29), *be on your guard, if you please.*

1167 The present of the subjunctive mood is often used as an immediate imperative: as,

Efferant* quae secum huc attulerunt (*Ter.* Haut. IV. 4. 23), *let them bring out what they brought here with them.*
Quod boni datur, fruare† dum licet (*Ter.* Haut. II. 3. 102), *all the good that offers, enjoy while you may.*

1168 The presents cura and fac and the subjunctive velim are often prefixed to a subjunctive of a verb, with or without ut, and so express more forcibly what might have been expressed by a simple imperative of the latter verb: as,

Quare si quod constitutum cum podagra habes, fac ut in alium diem differas (*Cic.* ad Fam. VII. 4), *if then you have any engagement with the gout, mind you put it off to another day.*
Fac sciput te ut sies (*Ter.* And. II. 4), *mind you have your wits about you.*

---

* This subjunctive is due to an ellipsis of a verb which is occasionally supplied: as, *Treviros ulter censeo* (*Cic.* ad Fam. VII. 13. 2), 'I recommend you to fight shy of the Treviri.'

† Madvig would limit this use of the second person to the cases of a general nature, where 'you' means 'any one.' But he admits that there are some examples where 'you' is used in its definite sense, and himself quotes from Terence, *Si certum est facere, facias; verum ne post culpam conferas in me,* 'If you are resolved to do it, why do it; but do not afterwards throw the blame on me.'

Cūra ut quam primum uěniās (*Cic.* ad Fam. IV. 10), *take care and come as soon as you can.*

Tū ušlim ănimō săpientī fortīquĕ sīs (*Cic.* ad Fam. IX. 12), *do you meanwhile, I beg you, act with philosophy and firmness.*

1169 An affirmative in the future often expresses a direction with a confidence that it will be followed: as,

Tu intěrěā non cessābis ět eă quae hăbēs institūtă perpŏliēs (*Cic.* ad Fam. V. 12. 10), *you meanwhile will lose no time in giving the last polish to what you have in hand.*

Sīquid accidĕrit nŏuī, făciēs ut sciam (*Cic.* ad Fam. XIV. 8), *if any thing new occurs, you will let me know.*

1170 The present imperative is used at times to express a condition: as,

Tolle hanc ŏpīniōnem, luctum sustŭlĕrīs (*Cic.* Tusc. I. 13. 30), *once put an end to this opinion, and you will have put an end to all mourning for the dead.*

1171 A question may be so asked as to amount to an order: as,

Etiam tăcēs?* Egŏ căuēbo (*Ter.* Ad. IV. 2. 11), *hold your tongue; Syrus will be on his guard.*

Quin conscendīmŭs† Equōs? (*Liv.* I. 57) *come, come, let us mount our horses.*

Abin‡ hinc in malăm rem cum suspīciōne istāc, scelus? (*Ter.* And. II. 1. 17) *go and be hanged with your suspicions, you rascal.*

Non tu hinc ăbis? (*Ter.* E. IV. 7. 29) *be off, sir.*

1172 Hence in some phrases, such as those just quoted, the present imperative takes the place of the indicative: as,

Etiam§ tu hoc respondē, quid istic tibī negotist? Mihin? Ita. (*Ter.* And. V. 2. 8), *answer me this at once, what business have you in that cottage (which you have just left)? What business have I? Yes, you.*

---

* Literally 'Are you yet silent?' with a hint that he will soon be made so.

† Literally 'Why do we not mount our horses?'

‡ Literally 'Are you going? &c.; if not, I'll help you.' Pronounce *ăbĭn, sĭs*.

§ Pronounce *ĕtyam, qu'istic, ti* and *min*.

Quin* dīc, quid est (*Ter.* And. II. 6. 18), *come, come, sir, tell me what it is.*

Quin tu hoc audī (*Ter.* And. II. 2. 9), *come, come, listen to this.*

1173 Sentences of forbidding, &c. are variously formed. Nē with the future imperative is used in laws, and occasionally elsewhere : as,

Nocturnā mŭliĕrum sacrificiă nē suntō, praetĕr ollă quae prō pŏpŭlō ritē fīent ; nēue Initiantō, nisi ŭt assŏlet, Cĕrĕrī, Graecō sacrō (apud Cic. de Leg. II. 9. 21), *sacrifices by women at night there shall be none, save those which are duly made for the state ; nor shall they celebrate mysteries, except as is wont, to Ceres, according to the Greek rite.*

Bŏreā flantĕ, ne ărătō, sēmen nē iăcĭtō (apud Plin. XVIII. 77), *when the north wind blows, plough not, sow not.*

1174 Nē with the present imperative is found for the most part only in the old writers and the poets : as,

Ah nē meuī tantŏpĕrĕ (*Ter.* And. v. 2. 27), *oh, be not in such a passion.*

Quaeso ănĭmum nē despondē (*Plaut.* Merc. III. 4. 29), *I prithee despond not.*

Nimium nē crēdĕ cŏlōrī (*Virg.* Buc. II. 17), *trust not too much to the outside.*

1175 The subjunctive mood is used in forbidding, &c., but generally in the perfect tense. The use of the second person of the present subjunctive is rare, except when that person is used indefinitely.†

Nihil ignōuĕris, nihil grātiae causā fēcĕris, mĭsĕrĭcordiā commōtus nē sīs (*Cic.* p. Mur. 31. 65), *forgive nothing (they say), do nothing to oblige a friend, be proof against pity.*

Nē transiĕris Ibĕrum, nē quid reī tĭbi sit cum Săguntīnīs (*Liv.* XXI. 44), *cross not the Ebro (he says), have nought to do with the people of Saguntum.*

Ne me istoc posthac nōmine appellāssis (*Ter.* Ph. v. 1. 15), *do not call me by that name for the future.*

* In this way these two particles, *etiam* and *quin*, practically acquire a new meaning, just as *quidni*, ' why not,' comes to signify ' of course.' Compare too the secondary meaning of *numer* arising from its use in questions.

† These qualifications are from Madvig.

Nē quaesīs (*Ter.* Haut. IV. 4. 23), *ask no questions.*

Istō bōnō ūtāre dum adsit, quum absit nē rēquīrās (*Cic.* de Sen. 10. 33), *enjoy that blessing while you have it; when gone, grieve not for it.*

1176 The verbs cāuē, nōlī, nōlim, are frequently used in negative requests: as,

Cauneīs, i. e. cāuē ne eās (ap. *Cic.* de Div. II. 40. 84), *do not go.*

Cāuē tē essē tristem sentiat (*Ter.* And. II. 3. 29), *take care he does not perceive you are out of spirits.*

Cāuē dixĕrīs (*Ter.* Ad. III. 4. 12), *say it not.*

Nōlīte id uellē quod fiĕrī non pŏtest (*Cic.* Phil. VII. 8. 25), *do not wish for what is impossible.*

Hoc nōlim mē iŏcārī pŭtēs (*Cic.* ad Fam. IX. 15. 4), *do not, I pray you, suppose that I am joking in this.*

1177 The poets have many other imperatives used in negative requests, as fugĕ, mittĕ, parcĕ, &c.

Quid sit fūtūrum cras, fūgĕ quaerĕrĕ (*Hor.* Od. I. 9. 13), *what shall be tomorrow, shun to ask.*

Mittĕ sectārī (*Hor.* Od. I. 38. 3), *cease to search.*

Subjunctive.*

1178 A secondary clause or subordinate proposition is attached to the main clause or proposition in four ways: *a.* by a relative, *b.* by an interrogative, *c.* by an accessary conjunction, or *d.* by the construction called accusative and infinitive.

1178.1 With this subordinate relation must not be confounded the relation between two coördinate clauses, united by such words as ŭt or quĕ *and*, or else placed beside each other without any conjunction. Coördinate propositions are either both main propositions, or both subordinate clauses attached to the same main proposition.

1178.2 When a secondary clause beginning with a conjunction precedes the main clause, the secondary clause is called the *prŏtăsĭs* (putting forward), and the following main clause the *ăpŏdŏsĭs* (payment of a debt).

* The chief uses of the subjunctive have already been briefly pointed out in §§ 487-505 and 594-624.

1178. 3 The subjunctive is used where a proposition is put forward, not as a fact, but as a conception to be spoken of. Hence it is used in secondary clauses attached to the main clause of a sentence by a conjunction, or relative, or interrogative: 1st, where an object is expressed; 2d, where the assertions or thoughts of another than the speaker are stated; 3d, where that which does not exist is imagined, &c. But it will be practically more useful to deal with the separate cases.

1179 The *object*[a] or purpose of an action may be expressed by an imperfect of the subjunctive and the conjunctions ŭt, quō, quī, and the relative; or if the object be prevention, by ut nē, nē, quōmĭnŭs, and quīn: as,

Aliis nŏcent, ŭt in ălios lĭbĕrālēs sint (*Cic. de Off.* L. 14. 42), *they injure some, that they may be generous to others.*

Māgis mihi ŭt incommŏdet quam ŭt obsĕquātur gnātō (*Ter. And.* L. 1. 135), *more to annoy me than to oblige my son.*

Sĭbi quisquĕ tendēbat ut pĕrīcŭlō prīmŭst[†] suādēret (*Liv.* xxi. 33), *every one for himself was striving to be the first to get out of the danger.*

Obdūcuntur corticĕs truncī quō sint ā frīgŏrĭbus tūtiōrēs (*Cic. N. D.* ii. 47. 120), *the trunk of a tree is sheathed with bark, that it may be safer from the cold.*

Verbă rĕpertă sunt quae indĭcārent uŏluntātem (*Cic. p. Caec.* 18. 53), *words were invented to indicate the will.*

Gallīnae pullos pennis fŏuent nē frīgŏrē laedantūr (*Cic. N. D.* ii. 52. 129), *hens warm their chickens with their wings, that they may not be hurt by the cold.*

Vix mē contĭneo quīn inuŏlem in Căpillum (*Ter.* E. v. 2. 20), *I with difficulty restrain myself from flying at his hair.*

Ĕlĕfantōs in prīmam ăciem indūci iussit, sī quam iniĕcēro eă res tŭmultum possēt (*Liv.* xxvii. 14), *he ordered the elephants to be led into the first line, in hopes that this manœuvre might cause some confusion.*

1180 Hence also verbs of commanding, advising, begging, wishing, compelling, preventing, permitting, are followed by an imperfect of the subjunctive, and ŭt, or the negatives, ut nē, nē, quōmĭnŭs, quīn:

[a] See §§ 599, 607.

† *Prius* in the Mss., altered by some to *prior.*

Allŏbrŏgĭbŭs impĕrāuit ŭt his frūmentī cōpiam făcĕrunt (*Caes.
B. G.* 1. 28), *he commanded the Allobroges to supply them
with corn.*

Mŏnet ŭt in rĕlĭcuum tempŭs omnĭs suspĭcĭōnĕs uītet (*Caes.
B. G.* 1. 20), *he advises him for the future to avoid all suspicion.*

Per te ĕgo deōs ōro ut me adiŭuĕs (*Ter.* And. III. 3. 6), *by the
gods I beg you to assist me.*

Sĭnĭte ōrātōr ut sim* (*Ter.* Heo. prol. ll. 2), *allow me to be an
intercessor.*

1181   Not unfrequently the ŭt is omitted before the subjunctive in
short phrases: as,

Sĭnĕ me expurgem (*Ter.* And. v. 3. 29), *allow me to clear myself.*

Quō diē Rōmā te exĭtūrum pŭtes uĕlim ad mē scrībās (*Cic.* ad
Att. II. 5. 3), *I would wish you to write me word what day
you think you shall leave Rome.*

1181.1   But verbs of wishing, and also prŏhĭbē-, impĕra-, sĭn-, iŭbē-,
păti- (r.), and uĕta-, are also found with the accusative and infinitive, especially the passive infinitive; and indeed the last three of
these six verbs are but rarely found with ŭt.

1182   The *result* is expressed by the subjunctive. This construction
is common after verbs, &c. of accomplishing and happening: as,

Tempĕrantia effĭcĭt ŭt appĕtītiōnes rectae rătiōnī pāreant (*Cic.*
Tusc. IV. 9. 22), *self-restraint effects this, that the passions
wait upon right reason.*

Accĭdit ut prīmus nuntiāret (*Cic.* p. Rosc. Am. 34. 96), *it happened that he was the first to bring word.*

Nunquam accēdo quīn abs te ăbeam doctior (*Ter.* E. IV. 7. 21),
I never go near you without leaving you the wiser.

Non possunt multī rem āmittĕre ut non‡ plūres sēcum in eandem călămĭtătem trăhant (*Cic.* p. leg. Man. 7. 19), *it is
impossible for many persons to lose their property without
dragging a still larger number into the same calamity.*

---

* This has been altered to *exorator sim* by those who did not know
that the last syllable of *orator* might be long in Terence.

† The form *faxo* is used only parenthetically, and does not affect the
mood of the verb which accompanies it, which is always the future of the
indicative. *Faxo scies,* 'you shall know, trust me for that.' This has
been shown by Madvig in the second volume of his Opuscula.

‡ *Non* is required where the *result* is expressed; *ne* would be wrong.

Illud tibi affirmō, si rem istam ex sententiā gessĕris, fōre ūt absens ā multis, cum rēdiĕris ab omnĭbus collaudĕrē (*Cic.* ad Fam. I. 7. 5), *of one thing I assure you, and that is this, that if you carry the matter out satisfactorily, the consequence will be that even in your absence you will be praised by many, and when you return you will be lauded to the skies by all.*

Tantum ōpes crēuĕrant, ut mŏuĕre armā nec Mezentius, nĕque ulli ălii accŏlae ausi sint (*Liv.* I. 3), *so greatly had their power increased, that neither Mezentius nor any other of their neighbours dared to draw the sword.*

1183 With phrases which denote hindrance, opposition, avoiding, omission, doubt, the subjunctive is preceded by nē, quōmĭnŭs or quīn, but by the last, only in case there be with the main verb a negative to express the non-existence of the hindrance: as,

Impĕdior dŏlōre ănĭmi nē plūrā dicam (*Cic.* p. Sulla, 33. 92), *I am prevented by indignation from saying more.*

Per mē stetit* quo minus hae fierent nūptiae (*Ter.* And. IV. 2. 10), *it was my fault that this marriage did not take place.*

Nĕque ăbest suspĭciō quin ipsĕ sĭbi mortem conscĭuĕrit (*Caes.* B. G. I. 4), *nor is there wanting a suspicion that he was the author of his own death.*

Prorsus nihĭl ăbest quin sim miserrŭmŭs (*Cic.* ad Att. XI. 15. 3), *absolutely nothing is now wanting to complete my misery.*

Numquid† uis quin ăbeam? (*Ter.* Ad. II. 2. 39) *is there anything else I can do for you before I go?*

Făcĕrē non possum quin ad tē mittam (*Cic.* ad Att. XII. 27. 3), *I cannot but send to you.*

Non dŭbĭto quin mirēre (*Cic.* ad Att. XVI. 21), *I do not doubt that you are surprised.*

Quid est caussae quin cŏlōniam in Iānĭcŭlum possint dēdūcĕre? (*Cic.* in Rull. II. 27. 74) *what reason is there to prevent them from founding a colony on the Janiculum itself?*

1184 Impersonal phrases that signify an addition, &c. are generally followed by ut and the subjunctive: as,

---

* Forcellini is inaccurate in making *per me stat* equivalent to *rem in excusso*. The phrase can only be used of hindrances.

† A question is often equivalent to a negative. This, or a shorter form, *numquid uis?* was a civil mode of saying 'Good bye' (*Plaut.* Cap. I. 2. 88).

Rěliquumst ut dē fēlīcītātē paucī dicāmūs (*Cic.* p. leg. Man. 16. 47), *it remains for us to say a few words on good fortune.*

Accessit* eo ut mīlītēs ēius conclāmārint pācem sē uellē (*Cic.* ad Fam. x. 21.4), *there was added to all this that his soldiery cried out they wished for peace.*

1185 In the same way ūt and the subjunctive often follow the verb est with or without a substantive or neuter adjective: as,

Sěd est mōs hōmīnum ut nōlint eundem plūribus rēbūs excellěrē (*Cic.* Brut. 21.84), *but it is in fact a habit with the world not to allow that the same person excels in several things.*

Vērisimilě nōn est ut mōnūmentīs māiōrum pěcūniam antěpōněret (*Cic.* II. Verr. IV. 6. 11), *it is not likely that he valued money above the monuments of his ancestors.*

Atque ei ne intěgrum† quidem ěrat ut ciuibus iūrǎ redděret (*Cic.* Tusc. v. 21. 62), *but he had it not even in his power then to restore to his countrymen their rights.*‡

1186 Verbs &c. of *fearing* have the subjunctive, with ne if the object be not desired, with ūt if it be desired:§ as,

Věreor ne hoc serpat longius (*Cic.* ad Att. I. 13. 3), *I fear that this will creep further.*

Ornamenta mětuo ut possim rěcipere (*Plaut.* Curc. IV. 1. 3), *the ornaments I am afraid I shall not be able to recover.*

Haud‖ sānē pěrīcŭlumst nē non mortem aut optandam aut certē non timendam pŭtet (*Cic.* Tusc. v. 40. 118), *there is assuredly no risk of his escaping from the belief that death is an object to be desired, or at least not to be feared.*

---

* *Accedit* is often followed by *quod* and the indicative, particularly where the past or present is spoken of. So also *adde quod*.

† *Mihi non est integrum*, 'the thing is no longer entire; I have taken a step in it by which I am committed to a continuance in the same direction.'

‡ In such phrases as the preceding a notion of futurity is commonly implied, and hence it will generally, perhaps in good writers always, be found that an imperfect of the subjunctive is alone admissible. Even in the second sentence the idea is, 'It is not likely we shall find that &c.' It should be observed too, that the subjunctive phrase always follows.

§ Observe that the Latin inserts a negative where the English has none, and *vice versa*.

‖ This is an example of a practice common in Cicero, the crowding negatives in a sentence.

1187 The quality or quantity is often expressed by the subjunctive with **ut**, or the relative, preceded by some word signifying *so* or *such*.

>Non tam imperītus rērum ut non sciret (*Caes.* B. G. I. 44), *he is not so inexperienced in the world as not to know.*
>
>Rēs ēiusmŏdī cūius exĭtus prōuĭdērī possit (*Cic.* ad Fam. VI. 4), *a matter of such a kind that the issue of it can be foreseen.*
>
>Nĕque ĕnim tu is es qui quid sis nesciās (*Cic.* ad Fam. v. 12. 6), *nor indeed are you the sort of person not to know what is due to you.*
>
>Tantă pŭtābātur ūtĭlĭtas percĭpi ex bōbŭs, ut eōrum uiscĕrĭbus uoscī scĕlŭs hăbērētur (*Cic.* N. D. II. 64. 160), *so highly valued were the advantages derived from the ox, that to eat his flesh was deemed an impiety.*

1188 Sometimes the pronominal noun or adverb is omitted in the Latin, but the subjunctive still retained: as,

>Pĭnārĭus ĕrat uir ācĕr et qui nihĭl in fĭdē Sĭcŭlōrum rĕpōnĕret (*Liv.* xxiv. 37), *Pinarius was a man of energy, and not one to rely at all on the honour of the Sicilians.*

1189 In *indefinite* expressions the relative preceded by a verb signifying existence is followed by a subjunctive*: as,

>Sunt qui censeant (*Cic.* Tusc. I. 9. 18), *there are persons who think.*
>
>Inuenti autem multi sunt qui ĕtiam uĭtam prŏfundĕrĕ prō pătrĭā părātī essent (*Cic.* de Off. I. 24. 84), *and there have been found many who were ready to pour out their very lifeblood for their fatherland.*
>
>Quis est quin cernat? (*Cic.* Acad. Pr. II. 7. 20) *who is there who does not see?*
>
>Fuit antea tempus quum Germānos Gallī uirtūtĕ sŭpĕrārent (*Caes.* B. G. VI. 24), *there was formerly a time when the Germans were surpassed in valour by the Galli.*
>
>Est quātěnŭs ămīcĭtiae dărī uĕnĭă possit (*Cic.* de Am. 17. 61), *there is a line up to which friendship may be indulged.*
>
>Est ŭbi id ualeat (*Cic.* Tusc. v. 8. 23), *there are cases where this principle avails.*

---

* In these sentences the English language can always employ the word 'there.'

Nullă dŏmŭs in Sicilĭā lōcŭples fuit, ŭbi istĕ non textrīnum instĭtuĕrit (*Cic.* II. Verr. IV. 26. 58), *there was not a wealthy house in Sicily, but what that man set up in it a cloth manufactory.*

Inuentŭs est scrībă quidam qui cornicum ōcŭlos confīxĕrit (*Cic.* p. Mur. 11. 25), *there turned up a certain clerk, who caught the weasels napping.**

1190   There are many phrases apparently similar to these where the indicative is found, but in most of these it will be seen that the relative clause is the subject, and what precedes it the predicate: as,

Quis illic est qui cóntra me astat? (*Plaut.* Pers. I. 1. 13) *who is the man yonder who stands facing me?*

Here the person alluded to is altogether definite.

Sunt autem multī qui ērĭpiant ăllis quŏd ăllis largiantŭr (*Cic.* de Off. I. 14. 43), *and indeed those who rob one set of men to lavish what they thus rob on another set, are a numerous class.*

1191   Sometimes est-qui, sunt-qui† are to be looked upon as nouns, equivalent to nonnēmo, nonnulli, and are then followed by the Indicative: as,

Set ĕst-quod suscensĕt tibi (*Ter.* And. II. 6. 17), *but he is annoyed with you about a certain matter.*

Sunt-quos curricŭlō pulvĕrem Olympĭco
Collēgissĕ iŭvat (*Hor.* Od. I. 1. 3),

To some on Olympic course to have swept up dust is maddening joy.

Sunt-qui ĭtă dicunt impĕrĭă Pīsŏnis sŭperbă barbăros nĕquīuissĕ pătī (*Sal.* Cat. 10), *some do say that the barbarians could not bear the tyrannical commands of Piso.*

Est-ŭbī peccat (*Hor.* Ep. II. 1. 63), *sometimes (the world) goes wrong.*

1192   After digno-, idōneo-, apto-, ūno-, sōlo-, primo-, &c., what is necessary to complete the predicate is expressed by the *relative* or ŭt with the subjunctive:‡ as,

---

* Literally 'pierced the eyes of the crows.'

† Nay Propertius (III. 7. 17) has *est-quibus* for a dative. Compare too the Greek ἔστιν οἱ.

‡ But an infinitive also in later writers, as *legi dignus* (Quint. X. 1. 96). See also § 1255.

Liuiānae făbŭlae non sătis dignae sunt quae ĭtĕrum lĕgantŭr (*Cic.* Brut. 18.71), *the plays of Livius do not deserve a second reading.*

Idōneus nōn est qui impĕtret (*Cic.* p. leg. Man. 19.57), *he is not a fit person to obtain his request.*

Sōlŭs es, Caesar, cūiŭs in uictōriā cĕcĭdĕrit nēmō nĭsi armātŭs (*Cic.* p. Deiot. 12.34), *you are the only conqueror, Caesar, in whose victory no one fell unless armed.*

1193 After comparatives, quam qui- or quam ŭt is followed by the subjunctive: as,

Māiōrēs arbōrēs caedēbant quam quas ferrē cum armis miles posset (*Liv.* XXXIII. 5), *they were cutting down trees too heavy for a soldier to carry in addition to his arms.*

Fĕrōciŏr ōrātiō uīsa est quam quae hăbenda ăpud rēgem esset (*Liv.* XXXI. 18), *the speech was looked upon as in too high a tone to be addressed to a king.*

Nĭmis laetă rēs est uīsa, māiorquē quam ŭt eam stătim căpĕre ănĭmō possent (*Liv.* XXII. 51), *the suggestion seemed too delightful and too grand for him to grasp immediately.*

Sĕnior iam ĕt infirmior quam ut contentiōnem dicendī sustĭnēret, obmūtuit et concĭdit (*Liv.* XXXIII. 2), *being now advanced in years and too weak to support any violent effort in speaking, he suddenly lost his voice and fell to the ground.*

1194 A predicate is limited and explained by qui- and the subjunctive:* as,

Peccassĕ mihi uīdeor qui ā tē discessĕrim (*Cic.* ad Fam. XVI. 1.1), *I did wrong, I think, in leaving you.*

Satin sānu's, mē qui id rŏgĭtes ? (*Ter.* And. IV. 4.10) *are you quite in your senses to ask me that ?*

1195 So also a relative clause with a subjunctive (but not to the exclusion of the indicative)† is used at times parenthetically: as,

---

* Quippe qui-, utpote qui-, ut qui-, are also used in this way, but with greater emphasis. The indicative is found in some writers in these phrases.

† See § 1158.1. Many passages are unduly put forward as examples under this head by both Madvig (§ 364, Anm. 2) and Zumpt (§ 559): as, *quod sine molestia tua fiat* (*Cic.* ad Fam. XIII. 23), *qui modo tolerabili condicione sit* (*Cic.* in Cat. IV. 8.16), *quod rerum dici uellet* (*Cic.* II. Verr. IV. 16.36).

Refertae sunt ōrātiōnes centum quinquāginta, quās quidem
adhūc inuēnērim et lēgerim, et uerbis et rēbus illustribus
(*Cic. Brut.* 17. 65), *the hundred and fifty orations are replete,
at least such of them as I have hitherto come across and read,
with brilliant language and brilliant matter.*

Něque ěrat in exercitū, qui quidem pědestria stīpendia fěcisset,
uir factis nōbilior (*Liv.* vii. 13), *nor was there a soldier in
the army, at least of those who had served on foot, more distinguished for his deeds.*

1106. In *indirect questions*, i. e. where an interrogative pronoun or
conjunction and verb are attached to some verb or phrase, the
verb following the interrogative* is in the subjunctive: as,

Nātūrā dēclārat quid uēlit (*Cic. de Am.* 24. 88), *Nature pro-
claims what she wishes.*

Těneo quid erret, et quid ăgam hăbeo (*Ter. And.* iii. 2. 18), *I
twig what his mistake is, and know what to do.*

Ex captiuis cognōuit quo in lŏco hostium cōpiae cōnsēdissent
(*Caes. B. G.* v. 9), *he learnt from the prisoners where the
enemy's forces were posted.*

Ignōrābat rex ūter cōrum esset Orestēs (*Cic. de Am.* 7. 24), *the
king knew not which of the two was Orestes.*

Ex hoc quantum bŏni sit in ămicitia, iūdicari pŏtest (*Cic. de
Am.* 7. 23), *from this a judgment may be formed, how much
happiness there is in friendship.*

Existit quaestiō num quando ămici nŏui uětěribus sint antě-
pōnendi (*Cic. de Am.* 19. 67), *there rises the question, whether
at any time new friends are to be preferred to old friends.*

Cum incertus essem, ŭbi essēs (*Cic. ad Att.* i. 9), *being uncer-
tain where you were.*

Discent quemadmŏdum haec fiant (*Cic. de Am.* 12. 41), *they
will learn how these things are done.*

Dŭbito an Vĕnŭsiam tendam (*Cic. ad Att.* xvi. 5. 3), *I am at a
loss whether to make for Venusia.*

Cōpiās suās, iūdiciōně non conduxěrit, ăn ĕquitum aduentū
prohibitus, dŭbium est (*Caes. B. G.* vi. 31), *whether it was*

---

* Care must be taken not to confound the relative and interrogative.
Scio quid quaeres meum, 'I know the question you wish to put;' but
scio quod quaeris, 'I know the answer to it.' Compare *Ter. And.* iii. 3. 4,
ti quid te ego uelim, ti quod tu quaeris scies.

from design that he omitted to collect his forces, or because he was prevented by the arrival of our cavalry, is doubtful.

Dŏleam necne dŏleam nihil intĕrest (*Cic.* Tusc. II. 12. 29), *whether I am hurt or not hurt, makes no difference.*

Id uīsŏ, tūn ăn illī insăniant (*Ter.* And. III. 3. 3), *the object of my visit is to see whether it be you or they that are mad.*

Dē puĕrīs quid ăgam, nōn hăbeō (*Cic.* ad Att. VII. 19), *what to do with the boys, I know not.*

Hanc (palūdem) sī nostrī transīrent, hostēs expectābant (*Caes.* B. G. II. 9), *this (morass) the enemy were waiting to see whether our men would cross.**

1197   In the older writers, and occasionally in Horace and Virgil, an indicative is found in indirect questions: as,

Sī nunc mĕmŏrārĕ uĕlim, quam fĭdēli ănĭmo in illam fuī, uēre possum (*Ter.* Hec. III. 5. 21), *if at this very moment I wished to mention how faithful I have been towards her, I could do so with truth.*

Vĭdĕ ut discĭdit lăbrum (*Ter.* Ad. IV. 2. 20), *see how he has cut my lip open.*

Adspĭce ŭt antrum
Siluestris rāris sparsit labruscā răcēmis (*Virg.* Buc. V. 6),
See how the wild labruscat†
Has sprinkled the cave with scattered grapes.

1198   An interrogative clause sometimes accompanies the phrase quid ais, or the imperatives dīc, cĕdŏ, or the indicative quaesŏ, but without being dependent on them: as,

Quid ais‡, ubi intellēxeras I'd consilium căpere, cur non dixti extemplo Pămphilō? (*Ter.* And. III. 2. 37) *just tell me this: When you saw that they were going to play that game, why did you not immediately tell Pamphilus?*

Dīc§ mĭhi, plăcetnē tĭbi ēdēre iniussū meō? (*Cic.* ad Att. XIII.

---

* It has been already noticed (§ 495) that in these indirect questions there is often an ambiguity whether the existing time or future time be meant. Compare §§ 594 and 600.

† 'A wild vine.'

‡ The phrase *quid ais* is also used in expressing surprise at something heard: as, 'What do you say? surely I misunderstand you,' or 'You don't say so.'

§ This *dic mihi*, like the conjunction *rho*, is merely a mode of inviting a person's special attention to some coming question. The French in the same way use *dis-moi.*

21. 4) *be so good as to answer me this: Do you approve of your publishing the book without my authority?*

Cĕdŏ, quid iurgābit tēcum? (*Ter.* And. II. 3. 13) *pray, what quarrel will he have with you?*

Quaesō, quŏtiens dīcendumst tĭbi? (*Plaut.* Most. IV. 2. 32) *how often must I tell you, prithee?*

1199 The phrase nescĭŏ-qui- is to be looked upon as a trisyllabic word partaking of the nature of an adjective. Hence there is no irregularity in the construction with an indicative : as,

Aliī nescĭŏ-quō pacto obdūruērunt (*Cic.* ad Fam. v. 15. 2), *others somehow or other have become hardened.*

1200 A similar union accounts for the indicative in such phrases as,

Sālēs in dīcendō nīmium-quantum* uālent (*Cic.* Or. 26. 87), *jokes tell immensely in oratory.*

Id mīrum-quantum* prōfuit ad concordiam cīuĭtātis (*Liv.* II. 1), *this conduced wonderfully to harmony among the citizens.*

Immānō-quantum ănĭmī exarsēre (*Sal.* ap. Non.), *the men fired up beyond all measure.*

Reported Speech or Thoughts (OBLIQUA ORATIO).

1201 When the words or thoughts of another are reported and not in the first person, it is called the *obliqua oratio*, and all secondary clauses, that is, clauses dependent upon the relative or upon conjunctions, are in the subjunctive mood. Compare the following passages :

Sēnātū reique publĭcae *ĕgŏ* non *dēro*, si audacter sentenliās dīcĕrĕ *uultis*; sin Caesărem *respĭcĭtis* atque ēius grātiam *sĕquīmĭni*, ut sŭpĕrĭōrĭbus *fēcistis* tempŏrĭbus, *ĕgŏ* mihi consĭlium *cāpiam*, nēquĕ sĕnātūs auctōrĭtātī *oltempĕrābō†*, *I will not be wanting to the senate and the country, if you are willing to express your opinions boldly ; but if you look to Caesar, and make his favour your object, as you have done on recent occasions, then I will take my measures for myself, and will not be guided by the authority of the senate.*

---

* Still the original phrase must have been, *nimium est quantum ualeant, mirum est quantum profuerit*, &c. Compare the Greek phrase θαυμαστον ὁσον.

† See Caesar, B. C. L 1.

Sĕnātū reique publicae sē non dēfŭtūrum pollĭcētur, si audacter sententiam dīcĕrĕ vĕlint ; sin Caesărem respĭciant atque ēius grătiam sēquantŭr, ut sŭpĕrĭōrĭbus făctūrīnt tempŏrĭbus, sē sĭbi cousilium captūrum nĕquĕ sĕnātūs auctōrĭtāti obtempĕrātūrum, *he promises that he will not be wanting &c.*

1202 Or the tenses might be thrown into past time (which is more commonly used) by writing pollicēbatūr or pollĭcĭtūs est, uellent, respĭcĕrent, sēquĕrentŭr, făcissent.

1202.1 In the *obliqua oratio*, as compared with the *directa oratio*, the changes are as follows :

The main tenses, which are indicatives in the original speech, are changed to the accusative and infinitive.

Imperatives are changed to imperfects of the subjunctive.

Subjunctives remain subjunctives.

Direct interrogatives in the indicative are changed to the accusative and infinitive, provided the person was either the first or third ; but if it was the second person, then the subjunctive is required.*

With regard to the tenses, imperfects remain imperfects, and perfects remain perfects ; but which of the imperfects or perfects is to be preferred, depends upon the tense of the indicative verb to which the whole is subjoined.

The pronouns ho- (in its original sense) and isto- have no place in the *obliqua oratio*, any more than ĕgŏ, tū, nōs, uōs, &c. Illo- commonly supplies the place of the second person. See *Sal.* Jug. ca. 61, 62, 64, 65, 77.

All this however does not prevent the use of the indicative mood in the midst of the *obliqua oratio*, where the writer chooses to say something of his own.

1203 Sometimes the *obliqua oratio* is introduced by a verb of recommending &c. with the subjunctive mood, and this is followed by an infinitive ; before which in the English some word signifying *to say* must be inserted : as,

Cēnsēbant ut noctu iter făcĕrent, possĕ prĭūs ĭd angustias uĕnīri quam sentīrentŭr (*Caes.* B. C. 1. 67), *they recommended that they should march by night, observing that they might make their way to the pass before they were perceived.*

* See Madvig's Opuscula, vol. ii. p. 208.

1204 At other times the *obliqua oratio* is introduced by a verb of saying, &c. with the Infinitive mood, and this is followed by a subjunctive; before which in the English some word signifying *to recommend* &c. must be inserted: as,

> Dŏcent suī iūdĭcī rem nōn essĕ; proinde hăbeat rătiōnem postĕrĭtātĭs (*Caes.* B. C. I. 13), *they point out that it is not a matter for them to decide upon, and they recommend him therefore at once to consider the consequences.*

1205 Without a formal use of the *obliqua oratio*, a verb in a dependent clause may be in the subjunctive mood, when it expresses the thoughts or words or alleged reasons of another.

> Aristīdes, nonne ŏb eam caussam expulsust pătriā, quod praeter mŏdum iustūs esset ?ª (*Cic.* Tusc. v. 36. 105) *Aristides again, was he not driven from his country on the very ground that he was just beyond measure?*
>
> Făbiō dictă diēs est, quod lēgātŭs in Gallos pugnasset (*Liv.* vi. 1), *notice of trial was given to Fabius, for having fought against the Galli when ambassador.*
>
> Aedem deō Iŏuī uŏuit, si eō dĭē hostes fūdisset (*Liv.* xxxI. 21), *he vowed a temple to the god Jupiter, if he routed the enemy that day.*

1206 In these cases the power of the subjunctive may be expressed by inserting such words as *they said* or *they thought:* for example, in the last sentence but one the English might have been, 'because he was just *they said* beyond measure.'

1207 Sometimes the verb *to say* or *think* is expressed in these phrases, and unnecessarily put into the subjunctive mood: as,

> Illĕ pĕtĕrĕ contendit ut rĕlinquĕrētur, partim quod mărĕ tĭmēret, partim quod rĕligiōnĭbŭs impĕdīrī sēsē dīcĕret (*Caes.* B. G. v. 6), *the other zealously entreated to be left behind, partly because he was afraid of the sea, partly because he was prevented, he said, by religious scruples.*

ª The subjunctive mood may be thus used, when the writer speaks of a feeling which moved himself at a *former* time: as, *Mihi Academiae consuetudo non ob eam caussam solum placuit, quod . . . , sed etiam quod esset ea maxuma dicendi exercitatio* (*Cic.* Tusc. ii. 3. 9), 'For myself the practice of the Academy pleased me, not merely because . . ., but also because it afforded the best exercise in speaking.' (Madvig).—*Occurrebant (mihi) colles campique et Tiberis et hoc caelum, sub quo natus educatusque essem* (*Liv.* v. 54).

Here *impediretur* would have expressed the same, though less forcibly; on the other hand, *timeret* might have been translated, 'he was afraid, he said.'

> Cum Hannĭbălis permissu exisset dē castris, rĕdĭit paulō post, quod se oblītum nesciō-quid dĭcĕret (*Cic.* de Off. I. 13. 40), *after leaving the camp with Hannibal's permission, he returned shortly after, because he had forgotten something or other, he said.*

> Lēgātos suos multi dē prōuinciā dēcēdĕrē iussērunt, quŏd illōrum culpā sē minus commŏdē audīre arbitrārentŭr (*Cic.* II. Verr. III. 59. 134), *many (governors) have directed their lieutenants to leave a province, because through the misconduct of these lieutenants they themselves, they thought, had got a bad name.*

> Quem qui rĕprendit, in eō rĕprendit, quod grātum praeter mŏdum dicat esse (*Cic.* p. Planc. 33. 82), *and he who censures him, censures him for being, he says, grateful beyond measure.*

1208 It has been said above that the subjunctive is used in speaking of that which does not exist. Thus, what is denied is in the subjunctive after a conjunction: as,

> Istos tantum ăbest ŭt ornem*, ŭt efficī non possit quin eōs ōdĕrim (*Cic.* Phil. XI. 14. 36), *so far from complimenting those persons you speak of, I cannot be prevented from hating them.*

> Tantum ăbŭrat ut binos scribĕrent, uix singŭlos confēcērunt (*Cic.* ad Att. XIII. 21. 5), *so far from copying two sets (of the work), they with difficulty completed one.*

> Pŭgīlēs in iactandis caestĭbŭs ingĕmiscunt, non quod dōleant, sed quiā prōfundendā uōce omnĕ corpŭs intendĭtŭr (*Cic.* Tusc. II. 23. 56), *the boxer in throwing out the caestus utters a groan, not because he is in pain, but because by sending out the voice every muscle in the body is strained.*

> Nōn eō dicō quō mihi uĕniat in dŭbium tuā fĭdēs (*Cic.* p. Quinct. 2. 5), *I do not say this because your word is doubted by me.*

> Maiōrēs nostri in dŏmĭnum dē seruō quaeri nōluĕrunt, non

---

* The rule applies of course to *ornem*, not to the other subjunctives in this sentence.

quis non posset uērum inuĕnīrī, sed quia uidēbātūr indignum essĕ (Cic. p. Mil. 22. 59), *our ancestors were unwilling that evidence should be drawn by torture from a slave against his master, not because the truth could not be got at, but because (in this case) there seemed to be something degrading.*

Non quin confīdĕrem diligentiae tuae (Cic. ad Fam. XVI. 24. 1), *not that I in any way distrusted your carefulness.*

Another example of the subjunctive employed in speaking of what does not exist, is seen in *hypothetical** sentences, both in the clause of condition and the clause of consequence. These sentences are conveniently divided into present and past.

   a. Hoc nec sciō, nec si sciam, dicĕre ausim (Liv. praef.), *this in the first place I do not know, and secondly, if I did know, I should not venture to say.*

   Tū si hic sis, aliter sentias (Ter. And. II. 1. 10), *you yourself, if you were in my situation, would feel differently.*

   b. Quid făciam, si furtum fĕcĕrit ? (Hor. Sat. I. 3. 94) *what should I do, were he to commit a theft ?*

   c. Nonně săpiens, si fāme ipsē conficiātūr, abstŭlĕrit cĭbum altĕri ? Minūmē uērō (Cic. de Off. III. 6. 29), *would not a wise man, if he were himself on the point of being starved, rob some other of food ? Assuredly not.*

   d. Id si accĭdĕrit, simŭs armāti (Cic. Tusc. 1. 32. 78), *if that were to happen, we should be ready armed.*

   e. Si frātĕr esset, qui măgis mōrem gĕrĕret ? (Ter. Ad. IV. 5. 74) *if he had been a brother, how could he have been more obliging ?*

   f. Si quis hoc gnatō tuo Tuŏs sĕruŏs faxeit†, quālem habērea

* See above, § 1153 and §§ 496, 497, 498.

† That *faxit* is inadmissible here, even Madvig would allow, although he denies the existence of the word *faxem*. Moreover the explanation of the form *faxo* given in § 566 is confirmed by a line in the same scene, *Pol si istuc faxis, haŭ sine poena fěceris*; for the law of the Latin language requires that the two verbs should here be in the same tense (see Madvig's own Gr. § 340, obs. 2), and the difference of form is agreeable to a peculiarity of the iambic senarius, which, while it admits contracted forms in the middle, prefers the uncontracted at the close of the line, as *periclum* and *periculo*, Plaut. Cap. III. 5. 82; *norit* and *nouerit*, Ter. And. Prol. 10; *sit* and *siet* or *siet*, And. II. 5. 13, Haut. III. l. 47; *fac* generally, but *face* at the end, And. IV. 1. 56, v. 1. 2; besides a large number of words which are commonly monosyllabic in pronunciation except in the last place, as *mihi*, Aud. IV. 4. 4, Haut. III. 1. 101. Madvig's

grātiam? (*Plaut.* Cap. III. 5. 54) *if any slave of yours had done the same for your son, what would your gratitude have been like?*

Si hās inimīcitiās cāuērĕ pŏtuisset, uīuĕret (*Cic.* p. Rosc. Am. 0. 17), *if he had been able to guard against the enmity of this party, he would have been now alive.*

g. Absque eō esset, recte ēgo mihi uīdīssem (*Ter.* Ph. I. 4. 11), *if it had not been for him, I should have taken good care of myself.*

Rēgnumne hic tu pŏssidēs? Si pŏssiderem, ornātus esses ex tuis uirtūtibus (*Ter.* Ad. II. 1. 21), *are you lord paramount here? If I had been, you should have had a dressing such as your special merits deserve.**

h. Nĕcassem tē uerbĕrĭbus, nĭsĭ—īrātūs essem (*Cic.* R. P. I. 38. 59), *I should have flogged you to death, if I had not—put myself in a passion.*

Dēlētūs exercitus fŏret, nĭ fūgientis siluae texissent (*Liv.* I. II. 22), *the army would have been annihilated, had not the woods covered them in their flight.*

1210   It will be seen that in hypothetical sentences with the *present* tenses (whether imperfect or perfect), the condition, though not fulfilled at the present moment, is not an impossibility, for it may yet perhaps be fulfilled.

1211   The *past* tenses in hypothetical sentences (both imperfect and perfect) allude to past time, or at any rate to an obstacle in past time affecting the present state of things. In either case it is now too late to alter matters; and therefore these tenses often imply not only the non-existence of a state of things, but also impossibility.

1212   The tenses in hypothetical sentences are determined in the usual way. If the imperfect be used in the conditional clause, the notion of the verb is not completed before that in the clause

view is, that *faxo* and such forms are the equivalents of the Greek τυψω, ψησω, and consequently simple, not perfect futures. See his Opuscula, vol. ii. p. 60, &c. This is clearly wrong.

* It should be remembered that in the *obliqua oratio* the subjunctive will be found after *si*, even when the construction is not that which we have called hypothetical, but the ordinary sentence of condition, which in the *directa oratio* would be in the indicative.

of the consequence. On the other hand, a perfect tense in the conditional clause generally* denotes an action completed before what is expressed in the clause of the consequence. As regards the past tenses of hypothetical sentences, in the clause of the consequence the past-imperfect is used to denote a continued state of things, or something not yet completed, whereas a single occurrence is expressed by the past-perfect.

1213 Thus the general construction of sentences containing the word *if*, is, that the hypothetical, *i.e.* those which put a case, the non-existence of which is implied, have the subjunctive in both clauses, while in other cases the indicative is required in both clauses.

1214 The apparent exceptions to this rule are for the most part to be explained by the sentences being elliptical. Thus in hypothetical sentences the participles in *turo* and *endo* are often found in the clause of consequence; and, if so, always attended by an indicative: as,

Sī mē triumphārē prohibērent, testīs cītātūrus† fuī rērum ā mē gestārum (*Liv.* xxxvIII. 47), *if they had attempted to prevent my triumphing, I should have called up witnesses of my achievements.*

Illī ipsī quī rēmansērant rēlictūrī āgrōs ērant, nīsī littēras mīsīsset (*Cic.* II. *Verr.* III. 52. 121), *even those who had remained behind would have abandoned the lands, if he had not sent the letter.*‡

Quid quod sī Andrānōdōrō consīliā prōcessīssent, Hēraclēne cum cēterīs fuit seruiendum†, *nay, if the plans of Andranodorus had succeeded, Heraclea must have become a slave with the rest of the people.*

Sī priuātūs esset, tāmēn ad tantum bellum is ērat dēligendus

---

* This word is inserted with a view to such a sentence as, *Id si fecisses, per mihi gratum fecisses*, where however the real consequence is expressed in *pergratum*, 'I should have been greatly your debtor.'

† Literally 'I intended to call them,' for which our translation substitutes, by no very violent inference, 'I should have done so.' The latter literally translated would have been *citauissem*.

‡ That is, 'They were preparing to leave, and' (though the author omits expressly to say so) 'no doubt would have done so.'

§ This passage occurs in *Liv.* xxiv. 26, with the alterations required by the *obliqua oratio*, viz. *sibi* and *fuerit* in place of *Heracleae* and *fuit*. Compare a similar change in the same chapter of the phrase, *Si effugium patuisset in publicum, impleturas urbem tumultu fuerunt*.

(*Cic.* p. leg. Man. 17. 50), *if he had been in a private station, still for so serious a war he was the man who ought to have been selected.*

1215. A similar explanation accounts for the following phrases:—

Nĭ mĕtuam pătrem, hăbeo quod mŏneam prŏbē (*Ter.* And. v. 4. 15), *if I were not afraid of my father, I could give him an excellent* hint.*

Id ĕgŏ, sī tū nŏgēs, certŏ sciot (*Ter.* Haut. iv. 1. 10), *even if you were to deny this, I know it for certain (and consequently your denial of it would be fruitless).*

Admŏnēbăt mē rēs ŭt intermissiōnem ēlŏquentiae dēplōrārem, nī uĕrērer nē dē me ipsŏ uĭdōrer quĕrī (*Cic.* de Off. ii. 19. 67), *I was reminded by the matter before us that I ought to lament the disappearance of eloquence from among us; and should have yielded to the suggestion, had I not feared that I might be thought to be urging a merely personal complaint.*

Sī per Mŏtellum lĭcĭtum esset, mātrēs illōrum, uxōrēs, sŏrōres uĕniĕbant (*Cic.* ii. Verr. v. 49. 129), *their mothers, wives, sisters were coming (and would actually have come), if Metellus had permitted.*

Multă mē dehortantŭr ă uōbis, nī stŭdium reīpublĭcae sŭpĕret (*Sal.* Jug. 31), *many considerations dissuade me from troubling you (and they would probably prevail), if my love for my country did not outweigh them.*

Pons ĭter paene hostĭbus dĕdit, nĭ ūnus uir fuisset (*Liv.* ii. 10), *the bridge all but offered a passage to the enemy, (and would have done so completely,) had it not been for one brave man.*

Quod nī prŏpĕrē pernōtuisset, haud multum ăb exĭtĭō lēgātī ăbĕrant (*Tac.*‡ Ann. i. 23), *and if this had not speedily become generally known, (they would have put an end to the lieutenant-general, for even as it was), they were not far from so doing.*

---

* Literally 'I have an excellent hint to give, and but for the reason assigned I would give it.'

† Of course 'my knowledge' is in no way conditional upon 'your speaking the truth or not.'

‡ Tacitus abounds in this construction: see in the very same chapter, *ferrum parabant, ni . . . . interiessent.*

1216   Such sentences as the following are mere instances of ordinary exaggeration forthwith corrected*:—

Mē truncūs īllapsus cĕrĕbrō Sustŭlĕrat, nīsī Faunūs Ictum Dextrā lĕuasset (*Hor.* Od. II. 17. 27), *Horace a trunk down gliding on his skull had carried off, (or at least would have done so), had not Faunus with his hand lightened the blow.*

1217   The verbs of duty and power, already expressing in themselves what is less forcibly implied in the subjunctive mood, generally retain the terminations of the indicative in hypothetical sentences: as,

Hunc pātris lŏcō, sī ullo in tē pīctās esset, cōlĕrĕ dĕbŭbās (*Cic.* Phil. II. 38. 99), *this man you ought to have respected as a father, if you had had any affection in you.*

Consŭl essē qui pŏtui, nīsi hunc uitae cursum tŏnuissem ā puĕritiā ‡ (*Cic.* R. P. I. 6. 10) *how could I have been consul, if I had not kept strictly to this course of life from my boyhood?*

1218   In the same way the verb 'to be' in the indicative is accompanied by adjectives†, and occasionally substantives, when the hypothetical form of the sentence might have suggested the subjunctive: as,

Longumst sī tībi narrem quamŏbrem id făciam (*Ter.* Haut. II. 3. 94), *it would be tedious if I were to tell you why I do so.*

Aequiūs ĕrat id uŏluntātē ßĕrī (*Cic.* de Off. I. 9. 28), *it would have been better if it had been done willingly.*

Nonnē fuit sătius tristīs Amăryllīdīs Iras Atque sŭperbā pātī fastidiā ‡ (*Virg.* Buc. II. 14) *had it not better been Amaryllis' bitter wrath and haughty whims to brook?*

Quantō mēlius fuĕrat‡ in hōc prōmissum pătris nōn essē scrutātum‡ (*Cic.* de Off. III. 25. 94) *how much better would it have been, if in his case his father's promise had not been kept?*

1219   The conjunction in hypothetical sentences is sometimes omitted, as in English; but in this case the verb is commonly placed first: as,

---

* It should be observed, that in sentences of this character the *nisi* or *si* commonly follows.

† Particularly adjectives of propriety.

‡ The past-perfect tense in place of a simple perfect is common in such phrases, and also with the verbs of duty and power.

Rōges mē, nihil fortassē respondeam (*Cic.* N. D. I. 21.57), *were you to ask me, I should perhaps make no answer.*

Darēs hanc uim Crasso, in forō saltāret (*Cic.* de Off. III. 19.75), *had you offered this power to Crassus, he would have danced in the forum.*

1220 Very frequently the conditional clause is omitted: as,

Stāre putēs, ādeō prōcēdunt tempōrā tardē (*Ov.* Trist. v. 10.5), *you would think (if you were here) that time was standing still, so slowly does it advance.*

Reos dicērēs (*Liv.* II. 35), *you would have said they were on their trial (had you been there).*

Hoc confirmāuĕrim, ēlŏquentiam rem ūnam esse omnium difficillimam (*Cic.* Brut. 6.25), *this I would maintain (if there were occasion), that eloquence is the one thing of all most difficult to attain.*

1221 Thus, mālim *I should prefer,* nōlim *I should be unwilling,* uelim *I should wish,* are modest expressions, not partaking of the rudeness of mālo *I prefer,* nōlo *I won't,* uŏlo *I insist;* while mallem, nollem, uellem, signify *I should have preferred &c.,* and refer either to past time, or to what is now impossible. Hence,

Nollem* factum (*Ter.* Ad. II. 1.11), *I wish it had never been done,* i. e. *I beg your pardon.*

1222 The consequence also is at times omitted: as,

O si sub rastrō crĕpet argentī mihī sēriă (*Pers.* II. 10), *oh, if neath the harrow a jar of silver were to crack for me.*

1223 The consequence† again is generally omitted in sentences containing quăsi *as if,* or equivalent words: as,

Quăsi uĕrō consilii sit rēs (*Caes.* B. G. VII. 38), *as if forsooth it were matter for deliberation.*

Mē iŭuat, uĕlut si ipse in partē lăbōris fuĕrim, ad fīnem belli peruēnissē (*Liv.* XXXI. 1), *I am delighted, as though I had myself shared the toil, to have arrived at the close of the war.*

---

* Literally 'I should have wished it not done.' The suppressed condition may have been, *Si optando poterirem quae facta sunt infecta reddere.* *Nolim factum* would signify, 'I should be sorry to have it done.'

† Thus in the second sentence the fuller form would have been, 'I am as much delighted as I should have been if &c.'

Eius crūdēlitātem, uĕlut sī cōram ădesset, horrēbant (*Caes. B. G.* I. 32), *they kept shuddering at this man's bloodthirstiness, as though he had been present.*

Sic quaestŏr est factus, quam si esset summō lŏcō nātŭs (*Cic. p. Planc.* 25. 60), *he was made quaestor with the same facility, as if he had been born in the highest station.* *

1224   When the second person is used to denote generally *one, a man*, the subjunctive commonly enters into secondary clauses, whether preceded by a relative or conjunction : as,

In excĭtandō plūrŭmum uălet, sī laudēs eum quem cohortēri (*Cic.* ad *Fam.* xv. 21. 5), *in rousing to action, the greatest effect is produced, if one praises the person whom one is encouraging.*

Bŏnus segnior fit, ŭbi neglēgās (*Sal.* Jug. 31), *the good man becomes less active, when you neglect him.*

Tantum rĕmănet, quod rectē factis consĕcūtus sis (*Cic.* de Sen. 19. 69), *that only is left behind, which a man has obtained by good deeds.*

1225   Secondary clauses which are attached to clauses in the subjunctive or infinitive mood and form an essential part of the idea therein expressed, are themselves in the subjunctive mood : as,

Si lūcē quŏquŏ cănes lātrent, quom Deos sălūtātum ăliqui uĕnĕrint, his crūră suffringantur, quŏd ācres sint quom suspiciō nullă sit (*Cic. p. Rosc. Am.* 20. 56), *if even in the light dogs were to bark, when any persons come to a temple to offer their prayers, they would have their legs broken for being so watchful when there is no ground for suspicion.*

1226   Hence verbs of *promising* and threatening, inasmuch as they express in one word 'the saying that something will be done', take a subjunctive of the condition : as,

Praemium prŏpŏsuit qui‡ inuēnisset nŏuam uŏluptātem (*Cic.*

---

* See § 499. In the four examples here given the tenses in the indicative mood with a negative would have been respectively, *consili res non est, in parte laboris non fui, non aderat, non erat summo loco natus*. Thus it is only the mood that is here altered by the hypothetical form of the sentence.

† This remark is from Madvig.

‡ For the omission of the antecedent *si* see § 1126.

U

Tusc. v. 7. 20), *he promised a reward to the man, who should find a new pleasure.**

1227 By the omission of the governing verb the subjunctive appears to carry with it a meaning which really belongs to that verb.

a. Possibility, pŏtest esse ŭt understood. This construction however is very rare unless some such word as forsĭtăn, forsăn,† accompany the subjunctive: as,

Vĕlim dēs ŏpĕram, quod commŏdō tuō fiat (*Cic.* ad Fam. xiii. 27.3), *I would beg you to give your assistance, so far as may be done without inconvenience to you.*

Me miseram, forsan hĭc mihl paruam habĕtt fĭdem (*Ter.* E. i. 2.117), *alas, maybe my friend here may have little faith in me.*

Nĭmium forsĭtăn haec illī mīrentūr (*Cic.* ii. Verr. iv. 56.124), *those people may perhaps admire these things overmuch.*

Năque id făcio, ut forsĭtan quĭbusdam uĭdear, sĭmŭlătiōnē (*Cic.* ad Fam. 1. 8. 2), *nor do I do this, as some perhaps may think, by way of make-believe.*

b. Permission and concession, such a verb as sĭn- *permit,* or cēd- *grant,* being understood: as,

Fruātur‡ sāne hoc sōlăciō (*Cic.* de Prov. Con. 7.16), *let him enjoy forsooth this consolation.*

Vt§ dēsint uīres, tămĕn est laudandă uŏluntas (*Ov.* Pont. iii. 4.70), *though strength be wanting, praiseworthy still the will.*

Fuĕrit cŭpĭdus, fuĕrit īrātus, fuĕrit pertĭnax, scĕlĕris ŭĕrō crīmĭnĕ lĭceat mortuō cărēre (*Cic.* p. Lig. 6.18), *he may have been ambitious, he may have been revengeful, he may have been obstinate; but the charge of impiety at any rate allows him, now that he is dead, to be clear of.*

Vt ĕnim cĕtĕrĭ părīā Tubĕrōnī cum Vărō fuissent, hoc certē

---

* See § 303.

† The *an* at the close of these words is no doubt identical with the Greek *ἄν*; but as this takes the form *κεν* in Homer, we probably have in it only a variety of our verb *can.* Compare our *may-be* and the French *peut-être.* Moreover the root *can* was not a stranger to the Latin language, for it virtually occurs in the old form *as-quin-unt* for *nequeunt.*

‡ Observe that the concessive tenses nearly always commence a clause, unless *modo* or *dum* accompany them.

§ 'Even granting that.'

praecĭpuom Tŭbĕrōnis fuit (Cic. p. Lig. 9. 27), *for even allowing that every thing else had been shared by Tubero with Varus, this at least was the peculiar qualification of Tubero.*

Sit clarus Scipio, ornētur eximiă laude Africānūs, hăbeātur uir ēgrĕgius Paullus, sit aeternā glōriā Mărĭūs, antĕpōnātūr omnĭbus Pompeiūs, ĕrit prŏfecto intĕr hōrum laudēs ălĭquid lŏci nostrae glōriae (Cic. in Cat. iv. 10. 21), *let Scipio be renowned, let Africanus be covered with especial glory, let Paullus be accounted a great man, let Marius enjoy eternal fame, let Pompey take precedence of all, still there will assuredly be amid the glories of these men some room for our fame also.*

Nĕ sit summum mălum dŏlor, mălum certo est (Cic. Tusc. ii 5. 14), *granting that pain is not the greatest evil, an evil is certainly is.*

Mănent ingĕnĭă sĕnĭbus, mŏdŏ permăneat stŭdium (Cic. de Sen. 7. 22), *the intellect remains with the aged, provided only there still remain energy.*

Seruōs est nemō, quī mŏdŏ tŏlĕrābĭli condĭcĭōnē sit seruĭtūtis, quī nōn audāciam ciuium pĕrhorrescat (Cic. in Cat. iv. 8. 16), *there is not a single slave even, if his position as a slave be but tolerable, that does not shudder at the audacity of men who call themselves citizens.*

Id quoque possum fĕrre, mŏdo si reddat (Ter. Ad. ii. 1. 51), *that also I can put up with, provided only he pay.*

Tŭ fors quid me fiat parui pendis, dum illi consulas (Ter. Haut. iv. 3. 37), *you perhaps care little what becomes of me, provided only you secure your master there.*

Hŏmĭnes, quamuis* in turbĭdis rēbus sint, tămĕn interdum ănĭmis rĕlaxantūr (Cic. Phil. ii. 16. 39), *men, allowing that they are in circumstances as troubled as you please, still at times unbend.*

c. Indirect interrogative, rŏgās understood: as,

A. Quid fēcit? B. Quid illĕ fĕcĕrit? (Ter. Ad. i. 2. 4) A. *What has he done?* B. *What has he done, ask you?*

d. Wishing, uis, prĕcŏr, &c. understood: as,

---

* The poets, together with Livy and later writers, use *quamuis* with an indicative, and vice versa *quanquam* with a subjunctive: as, *quamuis est rusticus* (Virg. Buc. iii. 84), *quanquam moueretur* (Liv. xxxvi. 34).

Quid fāciam? (*Ter.* E I. 1.1) *what would you have me do?*
Quid fācĕrem? (*Ter.* E. v. 1.15) *what ought I to have done?*
Valeant quī intĕr nos discidiúm nolunt (*Ter.* And. iv. 2.13), *farewell to those who insist upon tearing us asunder.*
Nē uiuam si id tibi concēdō (*Cic.* ad Fam. vii. 23. 4), *may I die if I grant you that.*
Dispĕream nī Submossēs omnīs (*Hor.* Sat. i. 9. 47), *may I be utterly destroyed, if thou wouldst not have made the whole of them move off.*
Atque ita me di ament ūt ego nunc non tām meapte cuūsa Laetōr quam illius (*Ter.* Haut. iv. 3. 8), *and so may heaven love me, as I am delighted now not so much on my own account as on his.*

e. Demanding, postūlant? &c. understood : as,

Tu ūt unquam tē corrigās! (*Cic.* in Cat. i. 9. 22), *you ever correct yourself!*
Hīcine ut tibi respóndeat! (*Ter.* Ph. v. 8.3), *this man answer you!*

f. Duty, ŏportet &c. understood : as,

Vīlicūs iniussū dōminī crēdat nēminī (*Cato.* R. R. 5. 3), *a bailiff should lend to no one without his master's authority.*
Pŏtius dicĕret nōn esse aecum (*Cic.* de Off. iii. 22. 88), *he should rather have said, it was not fair.*
Sūmeret Alicūnde (*Ter.* Ph. ii. 1. 69), *he should have borrowed it from some one.*
Frūmentum ne ēmissēs (*Cic.* ii. Verr. iii. 84. 195), *you should not have bought the corn.*

g. The object is often expressed elliptically, more particularly in a parenthesis, which ought always to be brief : as,

Vēre ut dicam† (*Cic.* ii. Verr. v. 09. 177), *to speak candidly.*
Sēnectūs est nātūrā lōquācior‡, ne ăb omnibūs eam uĭtiis uidear uindĭcārē (*Cic.* de Sen. 16. 55), *old age is naturally somewhat talkative, so you will not charge me with defending it from every fault.*

* See § 1247 and note.
† Perhaps in this example 'permission' is the notion understood, dabis ueniam.
‡ Hoc dīco understood, 'I say this that I may not appear &c.'

Vix incēdo inānis, ne ire pŏsse cum onĕre existŭmes (*Plaut. Am.* I. 1. 174), *I can scarcely walk with nothing about me, so do not suppose that I can get on with a load.*

1228 For the sake of brevity, such a verb as existŭmes or dicam is often omitted in sentences like that just given. Thus Plautus might have said in the last example, Vix incēdo Iuānis, ne Irē possim cum ŏnĕrē: as,

Nōuam cam pŏtestātem ūripuĕrē pătribus nostris, nē nunc dulcēdinē sēmel captī fĕrant dēsīdĕrium (*Liv.* III. 52), *this power, when yet unknown to them, they wrested from our fathers; much less now, having once tasted the sweets of it, will they tolerate the loss.*

Mortālĭā factă pĕribunt, Nĕdum sermōnum stĕt hŏnōs (*Hor. Ep.* II. 3. 68), *deeds will perish, much less will the glory of words survive.*

Vix in ipsis tectis frīgus uītātur, nĕdum in mărī sit făcĭle ăbesse ăb Iniūriā tempŏris (*Cic. ad Fam.* XVI. 8), *even in a roofed building it is difficult to avoid the cold, much less is it easy at sea to escape being hurt by the weather.*

Erat ĕnim multō dŏmicĭlium hūiŭs urbĭs aptiŭs hūmānĭtātĭ tuae quam tōtă Pĕlŏponnēsus, nĕdum Pătrae (*Cic. ad Fam.* VII. 28. 1), *for in those days this city was better suited as a residence to one of your refined habits, than any part of the Peloponnesus, let alone Patrae.*

1229 Quum or cum in clauses signifying a *reason* for or against any thing is followed by a subjunctive: as,

Quum uītă sĭne ămīcis mĕtūs plĕnā sit, rătio ipsă mŏnet ămīcītiās compărārĕ (*Cic. de Fin.* I. 20. 66), *seeing that life without friends is full of danger, reason itself warns us to form friendships.*

Quae quum omnĭă factă sint, tămĕn ūnă sōla ĕrat ciuĭtas Māmertīnă, quae lēgātos qui istum laudārent mīsĕrint (*Cic.* II. *Verr.* II. 5. 13), *in spite of all these doings, Messana was the one sole city that sent an embassy to speak in favour of the accused.*

Sĕd eă quum contemplărī cŭpĕrem, uix adspĭciendī pŏtestas fuit (*Cic. de Or.* I. 36. 101), *but although I was eager to have a good stare at these things, I could scarcely get a look at them.*

Quae quum ita sint (*Cic.* In Cat. I. 5. 10), *this being the case.*

1230 Quum as an adverb of time in the past tenses has the subjunctive mood, being translated with the imperfect by *while* or *as*, with the past-perfect by *after:* as,

Quum ācerrimē pugnārētur, sŭbĭtō sunt Aedui uisi ab lătĕrĕ nostris ăpertō (*Caes.* B. G. VII. 50), *as the battle was proceeding with the greatest spirit, there suddenly appeared a body of Aedui on the exposed* flank of our men.*

Quum dies complūres transissent, sŭbĭtō pĕr explōrātōres certior factūs est (*Caes.* B. G. III. 2), *after many days had already passed by, he was suddenly informed by his scouts.*

1231 Quum followed by tum, in the sense of *not only, but also*, has generally the indicative, occasionally the subjunctive: as,

Quum multae rēs in phĭlŏsŏphiā nēquāquam sătis explĭcātae sint†, tum perdifficĭlis quaestio est dē nātūrā deōrum (*Cic.* N. D. I. 1. 1), *while there are many things in philosophy which have been by no means fully explained, one of the most difficult is the inquiry about the nature of the gods.*

1231.1 After antĕ-quam and prius-quam, *a.* a subjunctive is used, where the speaker would imply the non-occurrence of the act; & an indicative, where he would imply the occurrence of the act, and therefore particularly where a negative precedes, and above all in past sentences. In other cases there seems to be some indifference as to the mood.

a. Subj. Nŭmĭdae, priusquam ex castris subueniretur, in proxĭmos collis discēdunt (*Sal.* Jug. 54), *the Numidians went off to the nearest hills, before assistance came from the camp.*

Antĕquam hŏmĭnes nĕfāriī dē meo aduentu audīrē pŏtuissent, in Măcĕdŏniam perrexi (*Cic.* p. Planc. 41. 98), *before the villains could hear of my approach, I went straight on into Macedonia.*

Antĕ lĕuēs pascentŭr in aethĕrĕ cerui, Quam nostro illius labātur‡ pectŏrĕ uoltus (*Virg.* Buc. I. 60), *sooner aloft in air*

---

* *i. e.* the right, which had no shields to protect them.

† The examples of this construction are not numerous, and what there are seem open to doubt. In some perhaps, instead of *tum* we should read *tamen*, and translate the *quum* by 'although.'

‡ Yet in a similar passage (A. IV. 27) Virgil has *uiolo* and *resoluo*.

shall graze the hart, than from this breast his features pass away.

b. *Ind.* Nĕquĕ prius fŭgĕrĕ destĭtērunt, quam ad flūmen peruēnērunt (*Caes.* B. G. I. 53), *nor did they stop flying, before they reached the river.*

Nĕque antĕ dīmīsĭt eum, quam fĭdem dĕdĭt (*Liv.* XXXII. 10), *nor did he let him go, till he gave his word.*

Non dēfătĭgābŏr, antĕquam illōrum uĭas percĕpĕrō (*Cic.* de Or. III. 36. 145), *I will not give in, before I fully understand their ways.*

Ante ălĭquantō quam tū nātŭs ĕs (*Cic.* ad Fam. x. 3. 2), *a considerable time before you were born.*

INFINITIVE.

1232 The infinitive* is an undeclined neuter substantive, which denotes in the most general way the action or state expressed by the verb. The use of it, as of other undeclined substantives (§ 149), is in strictness limited to the nominative and accusative, indeed almost exclusively to the latter. (Yet see § 1255.)

a. It seems to occupy the place of a nominative in such sentences as,

Docto hŏmĭnĭ uĭuĕre est cōgĭtārĕ (*Cic.* Tusc. v. 38. 111), *with the educated man to live is to think.*

Non cădĭt autem inuĭdēre in săpĭentem (*Cic.* Tusc. III. 10. 21), *but envy is incompatible with the character of the wise man,* or *the wise man is not susceptible of envy.*

b. It occupies the place of an accusative in such sentences as,

Stŏĭcĭ īrascī nescĭunt (*Cic.* de Or. III. 18. 65), *the Stoic knows not anger.*

Emŏrī cŭpĭo (*Ter.* Haut. v. 2. 18), *I long for death (that I may get out of my misery).*

1233 Hence the infinitive is occasionally, though very rarely, found after prepositions which govern the accusative: as,

Intĕr optŭmē uălēre et grăuissŭme aegrōtārĕ nihil dīcēbant intĕressĕ (*Cic.* de Fin. II. 13. 43), *between the best health and the severest sickness there is no difference they said.*

---

* In the Greek language this is so completely the fact, that the article may be prefixed to it in all its cases. The English also treat their infinitive as a substantive, when they place before it the preposition 'to.'

Quod crimen dicis praeter āmāssē meum ? (*Ov.* Her. VII. 164)
what charge dost allege against me, except the having loved ?

1234 Hence also a neuter adjective occasionally accompanies the infinitive : as,

Viuĕre ipsum turpe est nōbīs (*Cic.* ad Att. XIII. 28), *life itself is disgraceful to us.*

Tōtum hoc displīcet phīlŏsŏphārī (*Cic.* de Fin. I. 1. 1), *all this acting the philosopher offends me.*

1235 The most common use of the infinitive is as the object of active verbs, particularly those which signify *wish, power, duty, habit, knowledge, intention, commencement, continuance, cessation :* as,

Artēriae mīcāre non dēsinunt (*Cic.* N. D. II. 9. 24), *the arteries never leave off throbbing.*

Intuēri sōlem aduorsum nēquīts (*Cic.* Somn. Sc. 5), *you cannot gaze directly upon the sun.*

Et nesció-quid tibi sum oblitus hódie, ut uolui, dicere (*Ter.* And. v. 1. 22), *and somehow or other I forgot to tell you to-day, as I intended.*

Vincĕre scis, uictōria ūtī nescis (*Liv.* XXII. 51), *you know how to gain a victory, you know not how to use a victory.*

1236 Some verbs besides an accusative of the person* take a second accusative of the *thing* expressed by an infinitive : as, dŏce-† *teach,* iūbe- *bid,* uĕta- *forbid,* sīn- *permit,* cōg- *compel,* mŏne- *warn,* horta- (r.) *encourage,* impĕdī- *hinder,* prohĭbe- *prevent,* &c. Thus,

Dŏcēbo eum posthac tăcēre (*Cic.* in Rull. III. 2. 4), *I will teach him to be silent for the future.*

Hĕrus mē iussit Pamphĭlum obseruārĕ (*Ter.* And. II. 5. 1), *master has ordered me to keep an eye upon Pamphilus.*

Ab ŏpĕre lēgātōs discēdĕrĕ uĕtuĕrat (*Caes.* B. G. II. 20), *he had forbidden the lieutenants to leave the work.*

Me enim impĕdit pŭdŏr ăb hŏmĭnē grăuissĭmo haec exquīrĕrĕ (*Cic.* de Or. I. 35. 163), *for I cannot for shame urge this request on one of his dignity.*

1237 After the passive too of many of the verbs given in the preced-

---

* See Madvig, Gr. 390.

† All these verbs, except the first two or three, are also found with a subjunctive following. See §§ 1180, 1181.

ing section the infinitive is used, the accusative of the preceding construction, which expressed the person, becoming now the nominative: as,

> An sum ětiamnunc Graecē lŏquī dŏcendūs? (*Cic.* de Fin. II. 5. 15) *or am I at this time of life to be taught to speak Greek?*
> Consŭles iūbentur scrībĕre exercĭtum (*Liv.* III. 30), *the consuls are directed to enrol an army.*
> Mūrōs ădīrē uĕtĭtī sunt (*Liv.* XXIII. 10), *they were forbidden to approach the walls.*
> Prohĭbĭtī estĭs in prōuinciā pĕdem pōnĕrĕ (*Cic.* p. Lig. 8. 24), *you were prevented setting foot in the province.*

1238 Verbs of *saying*[*], *hearing*, *feeling*, *thinking*, *knowing*, are followed by an accusative and infinitive[†] : as,

> Thălēs ăquam dixit esse ĭnĭtium rērum (*Cic.* N. D. I. 10. 25), *Thales said that water was the beginning of things.*
> Perlŭbentĕr audīuī tē essē Caesărī fămĭlĭārem (*Cic.* ad Fam. VII. 14. 2), *I heard with very great pleasure that you were on intimate terms with Caesar.*
> Tē multum prōfēcissē sentiō (*Cic.* ad Fam. V. 13. 2), *I feel that you have advanced matters greatly.*
> Spēro nostram ămīcĭtiam nōn ĕgērĕ testĭbŭs (*Cic.* ad Fam. II. 2), *I hope that our friendship needs not witnesses.*
> Tibi eos scio obtempĕrātūros măgis (*Ter.* Ad. IV. 5. 70), *I know that they will more readily comply with your wishes.*

1239 An abstract substantive or a neuter pronoun which conveys the same meaning as the verbs of the last section, may be followed by the construction of the accusative and infinitive: as,

> Illa ŏpīniō tollētur, Crassum non doctissĭmum fuisse (*Cic.* de Or. II. 2. 7), *that opinion shall be put an end to, that Crassus was not a most learned man.*
> Dē hōc ipsō, nihil esse bŏnum nisi quod hŏnestum esset, dispŭtāuit (*Cic.* Tusc. II. 25. 61), *he held an argument on this very point, that there is nothing good except what is right.*

1240 An impersonal passive of saying, thinking, &c. is sometimes

---

* See §§ 911, 912. 1, also § 1202 with note, and § 1203.
† The same applies to phrases such as *fama est*, *auctor sum*, *certiorem te facio*, &c.

used with an accusative and infinitive, particularly with the perfect tense or the participle in *endo*: as,

> Nuntiatum est īdem Scīpiōnem cum legiōne (*Caes.* B. C. III. 36), *word was brought that Scipio was close at hand with a legion.*
>
> Ibi dīcendumst nullam esse rempublicam (*Cic.* R. P. III. 3 L. 43), *there we cannot but acknowledge there is no constitution.*

1241 Sometimes the same idea is expressed by the personal passive together with the nominative and infinitive: as,

> Caesar ā Gergouiā discessisse audiēbātūr (*Caes.* B. G. VII. 59), *reports reached them from time to time that Caesar had left Gergovia.*
>
> Voluntāriā morte interiisse crēditus est (*Tac.* Hist. IV. 67), *he was believed to have perished by his own hand.*
>
> Gladiōrum multitūdo dēprehendi posse indicābātur (*Cic.* p. Mil. 24. 64), *secret information was given by more than one person, that a large number of swords might be seized.*
>
> Perspectust ā mē dē tē cōgitāre (*Cic.* ad Fam. I. 7. 3), *I saw clearly that he was thinking of you.*

1242 Verbs of *wishing, permitting, bidding, hindering,* &c. are followed by the accusative and infinitive†: as,

> Corpora iuuenum firmāri labōre uoluerunt (*Cic.* Tusc. II. 15. 36), *they wished the muscles of young men to be strengthened by labour.*
>
> Dēlectum habēri prohibēbō (*Liv.* IV. 2), *I will prevent the levy of troops from being held.*
>
> Rem ad arma dēdūci studēbat (*Caes.* B. C. I. 4), *he was eager that matters should be brought to a contest of arms.*

1243 The verbs, iūbe- *bid*, uĕta- *forbid*, prohibē- *prevent*, impera- *command*, may be used passively with a passive infinitive‡: as,

---

* See § 911 and note.

† The construction with the subjunctive with many of these verbs is more common. See § 1160.

‡ This construction is widely different from that noticed in § 1237. The *tu* which is the nominative to *iussu's* would be the accusative after *renuntiare* in the active construction; whereas in *consules iubentur scribere exercitum*, the word *consules* would be the accusative after *iubent* itself.

Iussū's rēnuntiārī cōnsŭl (*Cic.* Phil. II. 32. 79), *directions were given that you should be returned as consul.*

In lautūmiās dēdūcī impĕrantŭr (*Cic.* II. Verr. v. 27. 68), *an order is given that they should be conducted down into the stone-quarries.*

The perfect passives, coeptŭs est, dēsĭtŭs est*, are preferable to the active when a passive infinitive is used: as,

Mătĕriă coepta ĕrat comportārī (*Caes.* B. G. IV. 18), *they had begun carrying timber.*

Pāpīsĭŭs est uŏcārī dēsĭtŭs (*Cic.* ad Fam. IX. 21. 2), *he ceased to be called Papirius.*

The verbs which express the *emotions* of the mind† are followed by an accusative and infinitive to express the cause of the emotion‡: as,

Haec perfecta esse gaudeo (*Cic.* p. Rosc. Am. 47. 136), *I am delighted that these matters are settled.*

Tantum sē sŭŭs ŏpīniōnis dēperdĭdĭsse dŏlēbant (*Caes.* B. G. v. 54), *they were hurt that they had lost so much of their reputation in this respect.*

A predicate consisting of a neuter adjective, or a substantive, or an impersonal verb, is accompanied by the accusative and infinitive to express the subject: as,

Nōn est rectum mĭnōrī pārērĕ māiōrem (*Cic.* Univ. 6), *it is not fitting that the superior should obey the inferior.*

Făcĭnŭs est uincīrī cīuem Rōmānum (*Cic.* II. Verr. v. 66. 170), *it is a serious matter for a Roman citizen to be bound.*

Omnĭbus bŏnīs expĕdit saluam esse rempublĭcam (*Cic.* Phil. XIII. 8. 16), *it is for the interest of all good men that the country should be free from danger.*

---

* So in the old writers there occur such phrases as *nequitur comprimi* (*Plaut.* Rud. IV. 4. 20), *retrahi nequitur* (*Plaut.* ap. Fest.), *id forum nequitum exaugurari* (*Cato* ap. Fest.), *suppleri queatur* (*Lucr.* I. 1045), and perhaps *ulcisci nequitur* (*Sal.* Jug. 31).

† This construction is similar to *horret tenebras, id gaudeo*, &c. See §§ 401, 893, 909.

‡ The construction with *quod* is more common, and in some cases that with *cum* is admissible. See § 1455 I.

Hos trūcīdāri ŏportēbat* (*Cic. in Cat.* 1. 4. 9), *these men ought to have been butchered.*

Corpus mortāle ăliquō tempŏre intĕrīrĕ nĕcessest* (*Cic. de Inv.* II. 57.170), *mortal flesh must some time or other perish.*

1247 Broken sentences consisting of an accusative and infinitive are often used interrogatively to express any strong feeling, as indignation about the present or past, rarely about the future: as,

Ex illā fămīliā tam inlībĕrālĕ făcĭnŭs esse ortum?† (*Ter. Ad.* III. 4. 2) *to think that so ungentlemanly a proceeding should have originated with that family!*

Tē istā uirtūte in tantās aerumnās incĭdisse? (*Cic. ad Fam.* XIV. 1. 1) *that you with your merit should have fallen into such troubles!*

Mēne incoptō dēsistĕrĕ uictam? (*Virg. A.* I. 41) *Juno indeed desist from what she has begun, defeated!*

1248 The accusative that precedes the infinitive performs the same office as the nominative in the other moods, and it is for this reason often called the *subject-accusative.* There is this difference however between the infinitive and the other moods, that the latter have suffixes to denote the different persons, so that the nominative need not be expressed by a separate pronoun. With the infinitive the subject-accusative pronoun is nearly always expressed: as,

Scrībĭs, *you write;* but, dīco tē scrībĕrĕ, *I say that you write.*

1249 But even with the infinitive the subject-accusative pronoun is occasionally omitted if both the infinitive and the main verb have the same subject‡: as,

Confĭtēre hūc eā spē uēnisse (*Cic. p. Rosc. Am.* 22. 61), *confess that you came here with this hope.*

Id nescīrĕ Māgō dixit (*Liv.* XXIII. 13), *Mago said that he did not know this.*

---

* *Oportet* and *necesse est* are also at times used with the subjunctive, but rarely with *ut.* *Necesse est* prefers a dative to an accusative if it be a person, as, *homini necesse est mori* (*Cic. de Fat.* 9. 17).

† The construction of *ut* with the subjunctive refers to the future. See § 1227 *c.*

‡ This infinitive is dependent upon some such phrase as *credendum est.*

§ See also § 879.

Rēfractūros carcĕrem mĭnăbantŭr (*Liv.* vi. 17), *they kept threatening that they would break open the prison.*

1250 On the other hand, the reflective pronouns are sometimes used unnecessarily with verbs of wishing : as,

Grātum sē uĭdēri stŭdet (*Cic.* de Off. ii. 20. 70), *he is anxious to be thought grateful.*

Attĭcum sē dīci ōrātōrem uŏlēbat (*Cic.* Brut. 82. 284), *he insisted on being called an Attic orator.*

1251 When to the construction of the accusative and infinitive a short clause is attached by means of a relative or the conjunction quam, the same construction, by a species of attraction, is at times introduced into this clause also : as,

Affirmāuī, quiduīs mē pŏtius perpessūrum, quam ex Itălia exĭtūrum* (*Cic.* ad Fam. ii. 16. 3), *I solemnly declared that I would suffer any thing rather than leave Italy.*

Antōniŭs aiēbat sē tantīdem frūmentum aestūmassĕ, quantī Săcerdōtem† (*Cic.* II. Verr. iii. 92. 215), *Antony kept declaring that he had valued the corn at the same price as Sacerdos.*

Suspĭcor tē hisdem rēbus quĭbus me ipsum‡ commŏuĕrī (*Cic.* de Sen. 1. 1), *I suspect that you are moved by the same circumstances as myself.*

1252 There are constructions where the infinitive seems to supply the place of a genitive : as,

Nĭsī quem fortĕ lŭbīdo tĕnet pŏtentiae paucōrum lībertătem suam grātĭfĭcārī§ (*Sal.* Jug. 31), *unless perchance a fancy possesses any one for sacrificing his liberty to gratify the power of a few.*

Tempŭs est hinc ăbīrĕ mē (*Cic.* Tusc. i. 41. 99), *it is time for me to go away.*

Summa ēludendī occăsĭost mi nūnc senes, Et Phaedriae curam ădĭmerĕ§ argentāriam (*Ter.* Ph. v. 6. 2), *I have a glorious opportunity now of dodging the old people, and relieving Phædria of his anxiety about money.*

---

* For *quam ex Italia exirem.*   † For *quanti Sacerdos aestumasset.*
‡ For *quibus ipse commouear.*   § For *adimendi.*

1253 In narrative the infinitive is at times used as the main verb* with the power of the past-imperfect of the indicative; and when so used, is called the *historic infinitive:* as,

> Consŭlem anceps cūra ăgĭtāre ; nollĕ dĕsĕrĕrĕ sŏcios, nollĕ mĭnŭĕre exercĭtum (*Liv.* xxxiv. 12), *a twofold anxiety troubled the consul; he was unwilling to desert the allies, he was unwilling to diminish the army.*
>
> Ego instāre ut mihi respondēret, quis esset (*Cic.* II. Verr. II. 77. 168), *I meanwhile kept pressing him to tell me who he was.*
>
> Iste ūnumquodquŏ ŭăs in mănŭs sūmĕrĕ, laudāre, mĭrāri† (*Cic.* II. Verr. IV. 27. 63), *your worthy praetor kept taking into his hands and praising and admiring every separate vase.*

1254 After the words părāto- *ready, prepared,* and insuēto- *unaccustomed,* an infinitive is at times used by good writers,‡ and in the poets and later writers after contento- *contented,* suēto- and assuēto- *accustomed:* as,

> Omnĭă perpĕti părāti, maxime ā rē frūmentāriā lăbōrābant (*Caes.* B. C. III. 9), *prepared to endure the worst, they suffered most in the article of grain.*
>
> Id quod părāti sunt făcĕre (*Cic.* p. Quinct. 2. 8), *the which they are prepared to do.*
>
> Insuētus vēra audīre (*Liv.* xxxi. 18), *unaccustomed to hear the truth.*

1255 Some writers, especially the poets, use the infinitive in many constructions where good prose writers employ a different form of words: as,

> Frūges consūmĕre nāti§ (*Hor.* Ep. I. 2. 27), *born to consume grain.*

---

* In such a phrase as *iamque dies consumptus erat, quum tamen barbari nihil remittere,* &c. (*Sal.* Jug. 98), the verb *remittere* is still the main verb.

† For a copious use of the historic infinitive see *Caes.* B. G. III. 4, where there occur in succession, *decurrere, conicere, repugnare, mittere, excurrere, ferre, superari.*

‡ Cicero more commonly however uses *ad* with the gerund.

§ In this and the following sentences more legitimate phrases would have been: *ad fruges consumendas, ad pellendos inimicos, committendae pugnae, exeundi, qui cantaretur, ut adsset,* the supine *visum, habenda* or *quae habeat, ad sequendum, persequendi.* The use of the adjective with an infinitive is very common in the lyric poetry of Horace.

Non mihi sunt uīrēs inimīcos pellĕrĕ (*Ov.* Her. I. 109), *I have not strength to drive away my foes.*

Auidus committĕrĕ pugnam (*Ov.* Met. v. 75), *eager to join battle.*

Nulla hinc exīrĕ pŏtestas (*Virg.* A. ix. 739), *no power of going out from hence.*

Puĕr ipsĕ fuit cantārī dignŭs (*Virg.* Buc. v. 54), *the boy himself was worthy to be sung of.*

Virum tŏt ădīrĕ lăbōrēs impŭlit (*Virg.* A. I. 14), *she urged the hero to encounter so many toils.*

Pĕcūs ĕgit altōs Vīsĕrĕ montīs (*Hor.* Od. I. 2. 7), *he drove his cattle to visit the lofty mountains.*

Illŏ suō mŏriens dat hăbērĕ nĕpōti (*Virg.* A. ix. 362), *he again dying gives them to his grandchild to keep.*

Cĕlĕrem sĕquī Aiăcem (*Hor.* Od. I. 15. 18), *Ajax swift to follow.*

Nĕcessĭtūdo persĕquī (*Sal.* Jug. 82), *the necessity for pursuing.*

1256 The Latin language often admits the perfect infinitive where the English language uses the simple infinitive; but it will be seen in such cases that the completion or consequences of the action are regarded more than the action itself. This distinction applies especially to phrases of regret or satisfaction in the future tenses, also to phrases of wishing and prohibition, &c.: as,

Contentī sīmŭs id ūnum dixissĕ (*Vell.* II. 103), *let us be satisfied with this one observation.*

Quiessĕ ĕrit mĕlĭūs (*Liv.* III. 48), *you had better be quiet.*

Bacchās nē quis ădīssĕ uĕlit (*Inscr.* S. C. de Bacc.), *let no one wish to approach the priestesses of Bacchus.*

Magnŭm sī pectŏrĕ possit Excussissĕ deum (*Virg.* A. vi. 78), *in hopes she may have power to shake from her breast the mighty god.*

Sŏciīs maxŭmē lex consultum essĕ uolt (*Cic.* in Caecil. 6. 21), *the law wishes to provide for the interests of the allies above all.*

1257 On the other hand, while the English express past time by the perfect infinitive after the auxiliary verbs *could*, *might*, *ought*, the Latin writers generally consider it sufficient to express the past time in the main verb, and to use with it the simple infinitive: as,

Licuit in Hispăniam īrĕ (*Liv.* xxi. 41), *I might have gone to Spain.*

Hoc ĕgŏ cūrārĕ non dēbuī (*Cic.* ad Fam. v. 2. 9), *this I ought not to have cared for.*

1258 Still not unfrequently both the main verb of duty and the infinitive are in the perfect tense; as,

Tunc dĕcuit flēssĕ (*Liv.* xxx. 44), *then was the time for weeping.*
Quod iampridem factum esse ōportuit (*Cic.* in Cat. 1. 2. 5), *what ought to have been done long ago.*
Adulescenti morem gestum opŏrtuit (*Ter.* Ad. II. 2. 6), *you ought to have humoured the younger.*

1259 In the compound tenses of the infinitive, both active and passive, the verb esse is often omitted: as,

Dēnēgārat sē commissūrum mihi gnātam suam uxōrem (*Ter.* And. 1. 5. 6), *he had declared that he would not trust his daughter in marriage to me.*
Omnīs uōs ōrātōs uōlo (*Ter.* Haut. prol. 26), *I must entreat you all.*
Nēque tu hoc dīces, tibi non praedictūm. Caue (*Ter.* And. 1. 2. 34), *nor shall you say that no previous notice was given you. So be on your guard.*

1260 The future infinitive, both active and passive, is often expressed by the circumlocution of fŏrĕ with ut and an imperfect subjunctive* (called the *periphrastic future*): as,

Spēro fŏre ut contingat id nōbis (*Cic.* Tusc. 1. 34. 82), *I trust that we are destined to have this happiness.*
Pompēius dixĕrat fŏre uti exercitus Caesăris pellĕrĕtŭr (*Caes.* B. C. III. 80), *Pompey had foretold that Caesar's army would be routed.*

1261 The participle in *turo* with fuisse is exclusively used as a hypothetical tense: as,

An Pompēium censes tribus suis consŭlātibus laetātūrum fuissĕ, si sciret se in sōlitūdine Aegyptiōrum trŭcidātum iri ? (*Cic.* de Div. II. 9. 22) *or do you think that Pompey would have gloried in his three consulships, if he had known that he was to be butchered in a desert of Egypt?*

---

* This construction is the only one where the verb has no participle in *turo*. Observe however that the periphrastic future differs from the simple future by being unlimited in point of time.

Nisi nuntii dē victōriā pĕr ĕquitēs essent allāti existimābant, fŭtūrum fuisse ūti oppĭdum āmittĕrētŭr (*Caes.* B. C. III. 101), *they were of opinion that if the news of the victory had not been brought by men on horseback, the town would have been lost.*

A future passive may be expressed by the impersonal passive infinitive of i- *go* and the accusative supine: as,

Arbitrantur sē bĕnifīcos ultum īri (*Cic.* de Off. I. 14. 43), *they think they shall be considered kind.**

A future-perfect passive is at times expressed by the infinitive fŏrĕ and the perfect passive participle: as,

Dēbellātum mox fŏrĕ rēbantŭr (*Liv.* XXIII. 13), *they thought that the war would be shortly brought to a close.*†

PARTICIPLES AND VERBAL SUBSTANTIVES.

Participles are partly like adjectives, partly like verbs. Like adjectives they agree with some noun in case, gender and number. On the other hand they are derived from verbs, denote an act, and govern the same case as the verb from which they are derived. The tense or time of a participle depends upon the verb which it accompanies.

The participle in *enti* is an imperfect, and corresponds to the English participle in *ing*: as,

Gŭbernātor clāuom tĕnens sĕdet in puppi (*Cic.* de Sen. 6. 17), *the pilot holding the tiller sits on the stern;*—i. e. the pilot holds the tiller and sits at the stern. Here tĕnens refers to present time, because sĕdet is present.

Arantī Cincinnātō nuntiātumst eum dictătōrem essĕ factum (*Cic.* de Sen. 16.56), *word was brought to Cincinnatus ploughing, that he had been made dictator;*—i. e. as Cincinnatus was ploughing, word was brought to him that he had been made dictator. Here ărantī refers to past time, because nuntiātumst is past.

---

* More literally, 'that people are going to look upon them as kind.' The beginner should take care not to confound this supine with the perfect passive participle.

† For the significations of the tenses see also §§ 509, 511, 512, 513.

Croesus Halyn pĕnĕtrans magnām peruortĕt ŏpŭm uim (quoted by Cic. de Div. II. 56. 115), *Croesus penetrating to the Halys will overturn a mighty power;*—i. e. when Croesus shall penetrate to the Halys, he will overturn a mighty power. Here pĕnĕtrans refers to future time, because peruortet is future.

The participle in *enti* is often best translated by the conjunctions *as*, *while*, &c., with the proper tense of the indicative mood.

1266 The participle in *enti* is sometimes used where the act is completed, but only just completed: as,

Rōmam uĕniens cōmĭtĭa ĕdixit (*Liv.* XXIV. 7), *immediately upon his arrival at Rome he proclaimed the day for the election.*

1267 Similarly the participle in *enti* is sometimes used when the act has not yet begun, but will commence forthwith: as,

Discēdens in Ităliam lēgātis impĕrat ūti nāuis rĕfĭciendas cūrārent (*Caes. B. G.* v. 1), *immediately before setting out for Italy he gives orders to the lieutenants to have the ships repaired.*

1268 The participle in *tūro** is used by the best writers rarely except in connection with the verbs *es- be* and *fu- be*; with the former to denote *intention* or *destiny*, with the latter to denote *what would have happened under a certain hypothesis.*

1269 In Livy and the later writers it is often used at the end of the main clause of a sentence with the same significations: as,

Dīlābuntŭr in oppĭdā, moenĭbus sē dēfensūri (*Liv.* VIII. 29), *they slip away into different towns, intending to defend themselves by means of fortifications.*

Dĕdit mihi quantum pŏtuit, dătūrŭs amplius si pŏtuisset (*Plin. Ep.* III. 21), *he gave me as much as he was able; and would have given me more, if he had been able.*

1270 The perfect participle in *to* had probably at first only an active signification. It still retains this power in those verbs which are called reflectives or deponents, and traces of it also appear in the poetical construction: Membrā sŭb arbŭto Strātŭs (§ 892).

1271 Still in the ordinary language the participle in *to* is nearly al-

---

* See §§ 517 and 702-711.

PARTICIPLES AND VERBAL SUBSTANTIVES.   307

ways used as a passive, unless the verb whence it is formed be employed exclusively as a reflective or a deponent.* Thus, with scrīb-ĕrĕ *to write*, we have scripto- *written, being written, having been written;* but with sĕqu-ī *to follow*, sĕcūto- *having followed.*

1272   At the same time there are not a few perfect participles from reflective or deponent verbs which are at times used passively : as,

Sĕnectūtem ŭt ădĭpiscantŭr omnēs optant, eandem accusant ădeptam (*Cic.* de Sen. 2. 4), *old age all pray that they may attain to, yet abuse when it is attained.*

Virtūs experta atquĕ perspectă (*Cic.* p. Corn. 6. 16), *merit that has been tried and proved.*

Partitot exercĭtū (*Caes.* B. G. VI. 33), *having divided his army.*

Euersio exsĕcrātae cŏlumnae (*Cic.* Phil. I. 2. 5), *the overthrow of the accursed pillar.*‡

1272.1 Although, when the simple verb is not transitive, the passive is commonly used only as an impersonal, still the poets take liberties in this respect, especially in the perfect participle : as,

Triumphātaeŝ gentĕs (*Virg.* G. III. 33), *nations that have been triumphed over.*

1273   A few participles in *to* from deponents appear at times to be used as imperfects : as, ŏpĕrāto-, fărĭāto-, ūso-, sĕcūto-, ueoto-, sŏlĭto-, &c. Thus,

Vidit se ŏpĕrātum (*Tac.* Ann. 11. 14), *he saw himself sacrificing (in a dream).*

Conclāmant sŏcii laetum paeānă sĕcūti (*Virg.* A. x. 738), *his comrades following pour forth the happy paean.*

1274   The participle in *to* is at times used with the verb hăbe- *have*, by which circumlocution a sort of perfect indicative of the active voice is produced : as,

Hăbes iam stătūtum quid ŭbi ăgendum pŭtĕs (*Cic.* ad Fam. IV.

---

* Still there are exceptions. *Cenato-* is equivalent to *quum cenavisset*, and has nothing of the passive signification. Other exceptions are *pranso-, poto-, nupta-, exosa-, iurato-, coniurato-, adulto-,* &c. See also §§ 392, 393.

† Literally 'his army having been divided.'

‡ Others are *consulato-, confesso-, emenso-, emerito-, pacto-, perfuncto-, populato-,* &c.

§ But for the simple verb, *triumphare de gentibus.*

2. 4), *you have at last determined what course you deem it right to pursue.*

Rōmānī in Asiā pecūniās magnās collŏcātās hăbent (*Cic.* p. leg. Man. 7. 18), *Romans have invested large sums of money in Asia.**

1275 The participle in *to* is used with the futures of the verbs *dăgĭve* and *redd- give back*, so as to form a future perfect; but the phrase further denotes that the act is done for another person: as,

Sic strātās lĕgiōnes Lătīnōrum dăbō, quemadmŏdum lĕgātum iăcentem uīdētis (*Liv.* VIII. 6), *I will lay the legions of the Latins low for you, just as you see their ambassador lying on the ground.*

Hoc ĕgo tĭbi ecfectum reddam (*Ter.* And. IV. 2. 20), *this I will effect for you.*

1276 The participle in *to* in agreement with a substantive is largely used, where the English language commonly prefers an abstract noun. Thus,

Barbărŭs eum ŏb īram interfecīt dŏmĭnī obtruncāuit (*Liv.* XXI. 2), *a barbarian cut him down out of revenge for the murder of his master.*

Māiŏr ex cīuĭbūs āmissīs dŏlor quam laetĭtĭā fūsīs hostĭbus fuit (*Liv.* IV. 17), *there was more sorrow for the loss of their fellow-countrymen than delight at the rout of the enemy.*

Ab condĭta urbe ad lībĕrātam (*Liv.* I. 60), *from the foundation of the city to its liberation.*

Post nātōs hŏmĭnēs (*Cic.* Brut. 62. 224), *since the creation of man.*

1277 The neuter nominative of the participle in *to* is occasionally used (by Livy for example) as the subject of a verb. Thus,

Audītum omnem exercĭtum prŏfīcīscī laetĭtĭam ingentem fēcit (*Liv.* XXVIII. 26), *the hearing that the whole army was setting out caused unbounded joy.*

Dēgĕnĕrātum in ăliīs artĭbŭs huic quŏque dĕcŏri offecit (*Liv.* I. 53), *his degeneracy in other qualities stood in the way of his credit in this respect also.*

---

* More literally 'they have large sums invested.' From this construction arose the formation of the perfect in the languages derived from the Latin.

PARTICIPLES AND VERBAL SUBSTANTIVES.   309

Diū non perlītātum tēnuĕrat dictātōrem ne antĕ mĕrīdiem signum dărĕ posset (*Liv.* VII. 8), *a long delay in obtaining a successful issue to the sacrifices had prevented the dictator from giving the signal before noon.*

1278 The ablative of the participle in *to* is used at times as an ablative absolute with a whole sentence for its substantive: as,

Expŏsĭtō quid inīquĭtas lŏci posset (*Caes.* B. G. VII. 52), *having explained to them what consequences unfavourable ground could produce.*

Edicto ut quicunque ad uallum tendĕret pro hoste hăbērētŭr (*Liv.* X. 36), *having proclaimed that whoever made for the entrenchment would be dealt with as an enemy.*

Permisso seu dīcĕrĕ prius seu audīrĕ mallet, ītā coepit (*Liv.* XXXIV. 31), *permission having been given him to speak first or to listen, as he preferred, he began thus.*

Audīto Marcium in Ciliciam tendĕrĕ (*Sal.* Fragm. V.), *having heard that Marcius was hastening into Cilicia.*

1279 The ablative of the participle in *to** is occasionally used absolutely even without a noun: as,

Nōn est peccātō mi ignosci aecum (*Ter.* Hea. V. 1. 10), *I am not entitled to be forgiven if I offend* (more literally, *an offence having been committed*).

1280 An ablative of the participle in *to*, with or without a noun in agreement, is used with ŏpŭs est†: as,

Nihil ĕrat cur prŏpĕrāto ŏpŭs esset (*Cic.* p. Mil. 19. 49), *there was no reason why they need make haste.*

Prius quam incīpias, consulto; et ŭbi consŭluĕris, mātūrē facto ŏpŭs est (*Sal.* Cat. 1), *before you commence, you must deliberate; and when you have deliberated, you must act with due haste.*

1281 As the Latin language is for the most part without a participle for the perfect active, the following circumlocutions are in use.

 a. The ablative absolute: as,

---

* Some ablatives of this kind have virtually become adverbs: as, auspicato, litato, &c.

† *Vsus est* is found with the ablative of the participle in *to* in the older writers. The construction is consistent with the use of the same phrase in connection with other ablatives. See § 999.

Hac parte copiārum aucta Itĕrum cum Săbĭnis confligĭtŭr (*Liv.* I. 37), *having increased this part of his forces, he engages again with the Sabines.*

b. Quum with the past-perfect subjunctive, or ŭbi with the simple perfect indicative: as,

Quum ab sĕdē suā prōsĭluisset āmōvērique āb altārĭbus iŭvĕnem jussisset (*Liv.* II. 12), *having leapt down from his seat and ordered the young man to be moved away from the altars.*

Vbi eō uĕnit, prŏpĕ trĭbūnal constĭtit (*Liv.* II. 12), *having arrived there, he at once posted himself near the tribunal.*

c. An accusative of the perfect passive participle dependent upon the main verb: as,

Gallum caesum* torquē spŏliāuit (*Liv.* VI. 42), *having slain the Gaul, he stripped him of his collar.*

1282 The participle in *to* is a perfect, and its tense or time depends upon the verb which it accompanies. Thus,

a. Omnĭă quae dīco dē Planciō, dīco expertūs in nōbīs (*Cic.* p. Planc. 9. 22), *all that I say about Plancius, I say having made trial of him in my own person.* Here expertūs is a present-perfect, because dīco is a present—I have had experience of his great worth, and therefore speak with certainty.

b. Consĕcūtŭs id quŏd ănĭmō prŏpŏsuĕrat, rĕceptui cănī iussit (*Caes.* B. G. VII. 47), *having obtained what he had proposed to himself, he ordered the signal for retreat to be sounded.* Here consĕcūtŭs is a past-perfect, because iussit is a past —He had obtained what he wished, and so he sounded a retreat.

c. Nōn admissi, Karthāgĭnem prōtĭnūs ībunt (*Liv.* XXI. 9), *if not admitted, they will proceed straightway to Carthage.* Here admissi is a future-perfect, because ībunt is a future; and indeed if the conjunction si be used, the phrase will at once become: si admissi nōn ěrunt. Thus the perfect participle which accompanies a future tense is far from expressing a fact.

1283 The gerund is a neuter substantive in *endo* which denotes the

---

* Often a better translation is effected by two verbs: as, 'he slew him and stripped him &c.'

action or state expressed by the verb. It differs from the infinitive, in that it is declinable, and that through all the cases (including, what is commonly omitted, the nominative). Also like an ordinary substantive it may be governed by some few prepositions (in, ab, de, ex, rarely pro, with the ablative; and with the accusative by ad, ob, inter, rarely in, circā, antē).

Nom. Iŭvĕnī pārandum, sĕnī ūtendumst (*Sen.* Ep. 36), *earning belongs to the young, using to the old man.*

Acc. Hŏmo ăd intellĕgendum nătust (*Cic.* de Fin. II. 13. 40), *man is born to understand.*

Gen. Dīcendī difficultātem pertīmescīt (*Cic.* de Or. I. 26. 120), *he dreads the difficulty of speaking.*

Deus bŏuem ărandī causā fēcit (*Cic.* N. D. II. 14. 37), *God made the ox for the purpose of ploughing.*

Dat. Tēlum fŏdiendo ăcūmĭnātum (*Plin.* XI. 2), *a weapon pointed for digging.*

Abl. Virtūtēs cernuntŭr in ăgendō (*Cic.* Part. Or. 23. 78), *the manly virtues are seen in action.*

The simple ablative of the gerund is used at times in such a manner that the nominative of the ordinary imperfect participle might be substituted for it; as,

Miscendo* consilium prĕcesquĕ, nunc ōrābant nē se exūlārĕ pătĕrētur, nunc mŏnēbant nē mōrem pellendī rēgēs inultum sĭnĕret (*Liv.* II. 9), *mixing advice and entreaties together, they one moment begged him not to suffer them to remain in exile, another warned him not to leave the practice of expelling kings unpunished.*

The gerund is followed by the same case as the verb to which it belongs: as,

Viam quam nōbīs quŏque ingrĕdiundumst (*Cic.* de Sen. 2. 6), *the road which we also have to travel.*

Suŏ quoiquĕ iūdĭcioest ūtendum (*Cic.* N. D. III. 1. 1), *each must use his own judgment.*

Diălectīcast ars uēra ac falsă diiūdĭcandī (*Cic.* de Or. II. 38. 157), *logic is the art of judging between truth and falsehood.*

---

* Equivalent to *miscente*. It is probably to this use of the gerund that the Italian and Spanish languages are indebted for their imperfect participle in *ado*. So also *reportando* (*Liv.* XXV. 8. 10), *omnia temptando* (*Sal.* Jug. 76).

312   SYNTAX.

    Tribuendō suom quoiquĕ (*Cic.* de Off. 1. 5. 14), *by allotting to every man what belongs to him.*
    Mōri māluit falsum fatendō (*Cic.* Part. Or. 14. 50), *he preferred to die through confessing a falsehood.*

1286 The gerund being a substantive may also have a genitive after it (but this usage seems limited to the genitive of the gerund): as,
    Rēiciundī trium iūdĭcum lēgēs Cornēliae făciunt pŏtestātem (*Cic.* II. Verr. II. 31. 77), *the Cornelian laws give the power of challenging* three jurymen.*
    Ego ēius uĭdendī cŭpĭdūs (*Ter.* Hec. 3. 3. 12), *I desirous of seeing* her.*
    Suī purgandī† causā (*Caes.* B. G. IV. 13), *for the sake of clearing* themselves.*

1287 *Gerundive.*—When a noun in the accusative‡ would accompany the gerund, the construction is commonly altered so that this noun takes the case of the gerund, and the gerund, now called a gerundive, takes the number and gender of the noun: as,
    Dīligentia cōlendast§ nōbīs (*Cic.* Or. II. 35. 148), *we must cultivate a habit of precision.*
    Coniungo mē cum hŏmĭnĕ măgĭs ad uastandam§ Ĭtăliam quam ad uincendum părātō (*Cic.* ad Att. VIII. 15), *I am uniting myself with a man who is better prepared for devastating Italy than for concluding the war victoriously.*
    Nĕquĕ rēs ullā quae ad plācandos§ deos pertĭnēret praetermissast (*Cic.* in Cat. III. 8. 20), *nor was any thing omitted which was thought likely to appease the gods.*

* The insertion of the preposition 'of' after these participles would make the phrases vulgar; but a vulgar phrase is generally an old one. In fact the formation of the Latin participle in *endo* from an abstract substantive called the gerund is exactly parallel to the origin of our own participle in *ing* from a substantive in *ing*. With us the substantive was the older form; and the use of the participle originated in such a phrase as, 'the house was a-building' (i. e. 'in building'), 'I was a-hunting of a hare.'

† The pronominal genitives in *i*, even when they refer to a plural noun, require that the gerund should be a genitive singular.

‡ The same construction is also admissible with the four reflective verbs, *ut-* 'use,' *fru-* 'enjoy,' *fung-* 'discharge,' and *pot-* 'make oneself master.'

§ All the best Mss. have *uastandam* and *placendos*, as Madvig has pointed out; not, as our editions, *uastandum*, *placendum*.

Initā sunt consilia urbis dēlendae, ciuium trūcīdandōrum, nōminis Rōmāni extinguendī (*Cic.* p. Mur. 37. 80), *plans were formed for destroying the city, butchering the citizens, extinguishing the Roman nation.*

The two constructions of the neuter gerund with a noun dependant upon it, and the gerundive in agreement with the noun, are not to be used indifferently. The construction with the gerund was the earlier one, and so belonged to the older writers*, but still maintained its ground in certain phrases†. In those which are commonly considered the best writers, the construction with the gerundive was for the most part preferred‡. Indeed, when the phrase is attached to a preposition governing the accusative, the gerundive construction is adopted almost without exception.

The use of the gerundive with the accusative is very common after the verbs lŏca-, condūc-, cūra-, rĕdim-, da-, suscip-, &c.: as,

Mŏnŭmentum ei marmŏreum făciundum lŏcārunt (*Cic.* ad Fam. iv. 12. 3), *they placed the making a marble monument in his hands,* i. e. *they contracted with him that he should build the monument.*

Cŏlumnam conduxĕrat făciundam (*Cic.* de Div. ii. 21. 47), *he had undertaken the erection of a pillar,* or *he had contracted to erect.*

Pontem in Ărări făciendum cūrat (*Caes.* B. G. i. 13), *he has a bridge built over the Arar.*

The gerundive is often omitted in these phrases for the sake of brevity: as,

Si Rhŏdiis turpĕ nōn est portōrium lŏcārĕ§, ne Hermacreonti quidem turpest condūcĕrĕ (*i. e.* exigendum understood) (*Cic.* de Inv. i. 30. 47), *if it is not disgraceful in the Rho-*

---

* *Mihi hae noctu agitandumst uigilias* (*Plaut.* Trin. iv. 2. 27), 'I have to keep watch to-night;' *aeternas poenas in morte timendumst* (*Lucr.* i. 112), 'they have to dread eternal punishment when dead.'

† See §§ 1285, 1286.

‡ Madvig has carefully examined this question in his *Opuscula*, i. 380, &c. He there points out that in the phrase *ad occupandum Vesontionem* (*Caes.* B. G. i. 38) there is no violation of the rule, *Vesontionem* being masculine, like *Narbo Martius* in the same country.

§ Hence the connection between the two significations of *lauare*, to place' and 'to let,' the latter alone surviving in the French *louer*.

dians to let the port dues, neither is it disgraceful in Hermocreon to farm them.

Anserĭbus cibarĭă lŏcantŭr (i. e. praebendă understood) (Cic. p. Rosc. Am. 20. 56), *the providing food for the (sacred) geese is farmed out.*

1291 This construction is used with impĕra- impose*, the gerundive being always omitted: as,

Equĭtes impĕrat ciuĭtātĭbŭs (i. e. cōgendōs understood) (Caes. B. G. VI. 4), *he imposes upon the states the providing horse-soldiers,* or *he commands them to provide him with cavalry.*

1292 The genitive of the gerundive is used† to denote a tendency, fitness or purpose, more particularly in connection with the verb ĕs- be: as,

Quae diūtīnae obsĭdĭōnis tŏlĕrandae sunt (*Liv.* XXX. 9), *whatever is of use for supporting a long blockade.*

Quae ĭcmĕre ăgĭtăuĕrant, eă prōdendi impĕri Rōmāni, trādendae Hannĭbāli uictōriae ĕrant (*Liv.* XXVII. 9), *the hasty measures they had taken, tended to sacrifice the Roman empire, to betray the victory into the hands of Hannibal.*

Cētĕra in duŏdĕcim tăbŭlis mĭnuendi sunt sumptūs (*Cic.* de Leg. II. 23. 59), *the other regulations in the twelve tables have for their object a diminution of expense.*

Armă cēpit, non prō suā iniūriă, sed lēgum ac lĭbertātis subuertendae‡ (*Sal.* Fragm. Or. Philippi c. Lep.), *he has taken up arms, not to avenge any wrong done to himself, but to upset our laws and our liberties.*

1293 The dative§ also of the gerundive is used to denote fitness or purpose: as,

Quăsĭ firmandae uălĕtūdĭnĭ in Campāniam concessit (*Tac.* Ann. III. 31), *he retired into Campania as if to improve his health.*

---

* That this is the literal translation of impera- is consistent with the translation of separa-, dispara-, compara-, appara-, 'put apart, in different places, together, before a person.'

† Particularly by Livy.

‡ This construction is commonly explained, but whether rightly is doubtful, by an ellipsis of causa. It often occurs in Tacitus.

§ Tacitus has even the ablative in this sense: *explenda simulatione*, Ann. XIV. 4.

PARTICIPLES AND VERBAL SUBSTANTIVES. 315

> Qui ŏnĕrī fĕrendō ĕrant (*Liv.* II. 9), *such as were capable of bearing the burden.*
>
> Nec soluendo aeri aliēnō respublica ĕrat (*Liv.* XXXI. 13), *nor was the state in a condition to pay its debts.*
>
> Dĕcemuirōs ăgrō Samnītī mētiendō diuidendōquĕ creat (*Liv.* XXXI. 4), *he appoints ten commissioners for the purpose of measuring and dividing the Samnite territory.**

1295 The construction of the gerundive with the verb ĕs- *be*, in the sense of duty, is only a particular case of what has been already noticed in § 966, and the dative of the person in fact belongs to the verb ĕs rather than to the gerundive.† Thus,

> Vt ŭbi ambŭlandum, ungendum, sic mihi dormiendum (est‡) (*Cic.* ad Att. IX. 7. 7), *as you must walk, must anoint yourself, so I must sleep;*—which would be more literally translated, *as walking, as anointing belongs to you, so does sleeping to me.*

1296 The frequent use of the gerund and gerundive with ĕs- *be*, in the sense of *duty* or *fitness*,§ led the mind at last to attach the notion of duty to the gerundive itself, so that the latter is at times used as an equivalent of an adjective in *bĭlĭ*. Thus,

> Nec tē, iŭuĕnis mĕmŏrandĕ, silēbo (*Virg.* A. X. 793), *nor thee, ever-memorable youth, will I pass by in silence.*

---

* The last three phrases are common. See § 984.

† So in such a phrase as *legionem in Morinos ducendam Fabio dedit* (*Caes.* B. G. V. 24), the dative *Fabio* is dependent not upon *ducendam*, but upon *dedit*; and again, the accusative after *dedit* is not *legionem*, but *legionem ducendam*, 'the duty of conducting the legion.' But although the dative case commonly accompanies the gerund and gerundive, yet there are occasional examples even in Cicero where ab and the ablative occur, especially when the verb takes a dative of its own, and a second dative in the sense of the agent would cause ambiguity. Thus, *quibus est a nobis consulendum* (*Cic.* p. leg. Man. 2. 6), 'whose interests you must consult.'

‡ *Est mihi* admits the translation, 'I have;' and precisely in the same way, *est mihi ambulandum* may be well translated by 'I have to walk.' Thus the origin of the dative in this phrase is without difficulty.

§ The notion of *possibility* is sometimes expressed by the participle in *endo*, but it occurs in the best writers only with a negative or *uix*: as, *malum uix ferendum* (*Cic.* de Fin. IV. 19. 53), 'an evil scarcely to be endured.' For the use of this participle with *fu-* 'be' in *hypothetical sentences*, see §§ 715-721.

1297 The phrases denoting duty at the same time refer commonly to the future time for the performance of the act; and indeed generally, as the gerund or gerundive is strictly an imperfect, the completion of the act must belong to future time. Hence the idea of futurity gradually attached itself to this form, and grammarians have given it, though inaccurately, the name of a future participle. That it is truly an imperfect* is well seen in such phrases as :

Inter ăgendum (*Virg.* Buc. ix. 24), *while driving.*
In pātriā dōlendā occūpāti et sunt et fuērunt (*Cic.* de Off. i. 17. 57), *they both are and have been for some time occupied in blotting out their fatherland from the face of the world.*

1298 The so-called verbal adjective in *bundo* is really a participle, and so sometimes found with an accusative: as,

Vītābundus castra hostium (*Liv.* xxv. 13), *carefully avoiding the enemy's camp.*

1299 The verbal substantive in *tu* is used in the accusative† after verbs of motion to denote the object : as,

Ad Caesărem grătūlātum conuēnērunt (*Caes.* B. G. i. 30), *they came from different quarters to Caesar to congratulate him.*
Quinquĕ cohortīs frūmentātum mīsit (*Caes.* B. G. vi. 36), *he sent five cohorts to get corn.*
Id rescītum īrī crēdit (*Ter.* Ad. i. 1. 45), *he believes that people are going to find it out,* or *he believes that it will be found out.*

1300 It governs the same case as the verb from which it is derived : as,

Pācem pĕtītum ōrātōres mittunt (*Liv.* i. 15), *they send ambassadors to seek peace.*
Lēgātos mittunt rŏgātum auxīlium (*Caes.* B. G. i. 11), *they send ambassadors to ask aid.*

1301 The verbal substantive in *tu* is used in the ablative with certain adjectives: as,

---

* Something like an imperfect participle is seen in the so-called adjective *secundo-* (i. e. *sequundo-*) 'following, second.'

† This accusative of the verbal in *tu* is often called the supine active, and the ablative of the same the supine passive; but there is nothing passive in the latter, and therefore the distinction is inappropriate. A similar error exists in our own language in the foolish practice now beginning to prevail of saying, 'a house to be let,' instead of 'a house to let.'

Diffĭcĭlĕ dictu est (*Cic.* de Off. II. 14. 48), *it is difficult to say* (literally, *in the saying*).

Optŭmum factu est (*Cic.* ad Fam. VII. 3. 1), *it is the best thing to do*.

The verbal in *tion* sometimes governs the same case as the verb from which it is derived ; as,

Iustĭtĭa est obtempĕrātĭō scriptis lēgĭbŭs (*Cic.* de Leg. I. 15. 42), *justice is obedience to written laws*.

Dŏmum rĕdĭtĭōnis spē sublātā (*Caes.* B. G. I. 5), *the hope of returning home having been taken away*.

PREPOSITIONS.

Ab (or ā before some consonants) seems to have signified originally *proximity*; and hence it was well suited to denote the quarter from which an action commenced, and therefore the source and origin of things. Thus it signifies:

a. The *quarter at or near which*, expressed by *at*, *in*, *on*, &c.: as,

Ā fronte ĕt ab sĭnistrā partē nūdātis castrīs (*Caes.* B. G. II. 23), *the camp being laid bare in front and on the left*.

Gallia ab Sēquănis et Heluĕtĭīs adtingit Rhēnum (*Caes.* B. G. I. 1), *Gallia reaches to the Rhine at the parts occupied by the Sequani and Helvetii*.

Isthmus duŏ măria ăb occāsu ĕt ortū sōlis fīnĭtĭmă dĭrĭmĭt (*Liv.* XLV. 28), *the isthmus divides two adjoining seas on the west and the east*.

Ā mātrĕ Pompēium arctissĭmō contingēbat grădū (*Suet.* Aug. 4), *he was very nearly related to Pompey on the mother's side*.

Apud sŏcrum tuam prŏpe ā meis aedĭbus sĕdēbās (*Cic.* in Pis. 11. 26), *you were sitting at your mother-in-law's near my house*.

b. With the verb sta- *stand*, &c., *by*, *on the side of*, *in favour of*: as,

Nēmo ā sĕnātu et bŏnōrum causā stētit constantiŭs (*Cic.* Brut. 79. 273), *no one stood more firmly by the senate and the cause of good men*.

Hōc nihĭlō măgis ăb aduorsāriis quam ā nōbis făcit (*Cic.* de Inv. I. 48. 90), *this tells no more for our opponents than for us*.

Vĭdē ne hoc tōtum sit ā mē (*Cic.* de Or. I. 13. 55), *have a care lest the whole of this argument be in my favour.*

c. *In, in respect of, in point of, as regards :* as,

Sŭmŭs ēnim impărātī, cum ā mīlĭtĭbus tum ā pĕcūnĭā (*Cic.* ad Att. VII. 15. 3), *for we are indeed unprepared, not merely in point of troops, but even of money.*

Antōnĭŭs ăb ĕquĭtātū firmŭs essĕ dīcēbātŭr (*Cic.* ad Fam. X. 15. 2), *Antony was said to be strong in cavalry.*

d. The department *in which* the services of an officer or servant are called for, and thus arises a name for the *office* : as,

Hŏmĭnēs hăbet quōs ăb ĕpistŏlīs et lĭbellīs et rătĭŏnĭbŭs appellat (*Tac.* Ann. XV. 35), *he has persons whom he calls secretaries, registrars, accountants.*

Phĭlēmŏnem, ā mănū seruum, simplĭcī mortĕ pūnĭit (*Suet.* Jul. 74), *his amanuensis Philemon he punished by simply putting to death.*

Antĭŏchus Tĭ. Claudī Caesărĭs ā bĭblĭŏthēcā (*Inscr.* ap. Grut. 584. 6), *Antiochus, librarian to Tiberius Claudius Caesar.*

e. *At*, in reference to time ; as,

Summissŭs ā prīmō, post exsultāuit audācĭŭs (*Cic.* Or. 8. 26), *subdued at first, he afterwards burst out in a bolder style.*

f. *From*, the point of departure : as,

Mātūrat ăb urbĕ prŏfĭciscī (*Caes.* B. G. I. 7), *he hastens to set out from the city.*

Ab Rōmā lēgātī uēnērunt (*Liv.* XXI. 9), *ambassadors came from Rome.*

g. *With*, after verbs signifying *commencement* : as,

Caedīs ĭnĭtĭum fēcisset ā mē (*Cic.* Phil. V. 7. 20), *he would have made a beginning of the massacre with me.*

Ab hīs sermo ŏrītur, respondet Laelĭŭs (*Cic.* de Am. I. 5), *with these the conversation commences, Laelius replies.*

h. *From*, the commencement of time : as,

Ab hōrā septĭmā ad uespĕram pugnātum est (*Caes.* B. G. I. 26), *the battle continued from one o'clock until evening.*

Tuās ĕpistŏlās ā prīmō lēgo (*Cic.* ad Att. IX. 6. 5), *I am reading your letters from the beginning.*

Quibūs ā puĕris dēditī fuimūs (*Cic.* de Or. I. 1. 2), *to which we have been devoted from our boyhood.* *

i. From, the commencement of a series : as,

Carneădēs est quartūs ăb Arcĕsĭlā (*Cic.* Acad. II. 6. 16), *Carneades is fourth in the line from Arcesilas.*

j. Immediate succession of time, translated by *with, after :* as,

Ab his praeceptis contiōnem dīmīsit (*Liv.* XLIV. 34), *with these injunctions he dismissed the assembly.*

Ab hoc sermōnē prōfectūs est (*Liv.* XXII. 40), *immediately after this conversation he set out.*

k. With verbs signifying *to pay,* the source whence the money proceeds : as,

Tĭbi quod dēbet, ăb Egnătiō soluet (*Cic.* ad Att. VII. 18. 4), *what he owes you, he will pay by a draft on Egnatius.*

Rĕlĭquam pēcūniam ă Făbĕriō rĕpraesentābĭmūs (*Cic.* ad Att. XII. 25), *the rest of the money we will pay at once by drawing on Faberius.*

l. With personal pronouns and the names of persons, *from their house :* as,

A. Unde est ? B. A nōbīs (*Ter.* And. IV. 4. 15), A. *Where did it come from ?* B. *From our house.*

Ab Andriast ancilla haec (*Ter.* And. III. 1. 3), *this maid-servant is from the Andrian woman's house.*

Haec cistella, numnam hinc ab nobis domast ? (*Plaut.* Cist. IV. 1. 0) *this casket, pray did it come from our house here ?*

m. A motive, *from, out of, in consequence of :* as,

Tanto ardōrē mīlĭtum est ūsūs ăb ira inter condĭciōnes pācis interfectae stătiōnis (*Liv.* XXIV. 30), *he was so warmly supported by his soldiers, from their anger at the troops on guard having been killed during a negociation.*

Nōn ā cŭpĭdĭtātē sōlum ulciscendi ăgrum nostrum inuādent (*Liv.* V. 5), *not merely from the desire of revenge will they invade our territory.*

n. The *agent* with passive verbs, expressed by the preposition *by :* as,

* Literally 'from boys,' an idiom which agrees with our own.

Ab sŏciis ūnĭcē dīlĭgēbātŭr (*Cic.* p. Planc. 9. 24), *he was most highly esteemed by his colleagues.*

Ā mē tŭ cōactŭs es cōnfĭtērī (*Cic.* II. Verr. v. 30. 76), *you were compelled by me to confess.*

o. What is considered as an agent, with intransitive verbs : as,

Māre ā sōlē collūcet (*Cic.* Acad. Pr. II. 33. 105), *the sea is made a mass of light by the sun.*

Nihil est ūălentĭŭs, ā quo intĕrĕat (*Cic.* Acad. Post. I. 7. 29), *there is nothing stronger (than itself) by which it may be destroyed.*

p. Removal, separation, distance, expressed commonly by *from*: as,

Ab dēlectātiōne omni nĕgŏtiis impĕdīmŭr (*Cic.* p. Mur. 19. 39), *we are prevented from taking any amusement by business.*

Proxĭmīs ā tectis ignis dēfendĭtŭr aegre (*Ov.* Rem. Am. 625), *an adjoining fire is warded off from buildings with difficulty.*

Ab inimīcōrum audāciā tēlisquē uĭtam dēfendĕrē (*Cic.* p. Mil. 2. 6), *to defend our lives against the audacity and weapons of our enemies.*

Ipse ab hōrum turpĭtūdĭne abhorrēbat (*Cic.* p. Sest. 52. 112), *he himself turned away in horror from the baseness of these men.*

Mīlĭā passuum tria ab eōrum castrīs castrā pōnĭt (*Caes.* B. G. I. 22), *he pitches his camp three miles from their camp.*

Obs. In many of these constructions a mere ablative is sufficient (see § 1023), but before persons the preposition ab is required.

q. Ab is sometimes placed before the measure of the distance, instead of the place measured from : as,

Ab mīlĭbus passuum octō uentō tĕnēbantŭr (*Caes.* B. G. IV. 22), *they were detained by the wind eight miles off.*

Pŏsĭtīs castrīs ā mīlĭbus passuum quīndĕcim auxĭlia expectārē cōnstĭtuunt (*Caes.* B. G. VI. 7), *having encamped at a distance of fifteen miles, they resolve to wait for the allied troops.**

1304. In composition with verbs ab denotes, *a. removal, absence*: as, aufĕr- *carry away*, ăbĕs- *be absent*; hence ăbūt- (r.) *use up. b. down*:

---

* See Maltbine's Greek Grammar, Transl. II. 876, ἀπὸ σταδίων τεσσαράκοντα τῆς θαλάττης.

ra, ăbĭo- or ăbĭcĭ- (abĭĭci-) *throw down*, absorbe- *suck down*, abstrūd-* *thrust down*, afflīg-* *dash down*, appŏs- or ăpŏs-* *set down*.†

In composition with adjectives ăb denotes *absence, difference*: as, āmenti- or ămens- *without mind, mad*, absōno- *out of tune or time*.

    Ad signifies—*a. Motion to* (i. e. *up to*, not *into*) : as,

Exercĭtum ad Căsĭlīnum dūcĭt (*Liv.* XXIII. 17), *he leads his army to* (*the walls of*) *Casilinum*.

Mūnītiōnem ad flūmen perdūxĕrat (*Caes.* B. C. III. 66), *he had carried the fortification to the* (*bank of the*) *river*.

    b. To what time : as,

Ad id dūbiae seruārant ănīmōs (*Liv.* XXI. 52), *up to that time they had kept their minds in a state of doubt.*

    c. To what extent : as,

Omnēs ad ūnum idem sentiunt (*Cic.* de Am. 23. 86), *they have all to a man the same feeling.*

Seruī ad quattuor mīlĭa hŏmĭnum Căpĭtōlĭum occŭpāuĕrĕ (*Liv.* III. 15), *the slaves to the number of 4000 men seized the Capitol.*

Incautōs ad sătiĕtătem trŭcīdābītĭs (*Liv.* XXIV. 38), *unprepared as they will be, you will butcher them till you are tired.*

Ad‡ uīgintī mātrōnis per uiātōrem accītīs (*Liv.* VIII. 18), *as many as twenty ladies having been summoned by the messenger.*

    d. Direction, to, towards : as,

Via ad Casĭlīnum obsessa (*Liv.* XXII. 15), *the road to Casilinum being occupied by the enemy.*

Vergit ad septemtriōnēs (*Caes.* B. G. I. 1), *it inclines to the north.*

    e. Purpose, for : as,

Multa sunt ănĭmaduorsa herbārum gĕnĕra ad morsūs bestiārum (*Cic.* de Div. L 7. 13), *many kinds of herbs have been discovered for the bites of beasts.*

---

* See § 451. 1.

† Compare the German *ab-gehen* 'go down,' and Sansk. *ava* 'down.'

‡ In this usage the numeral alone depends upon the preposition, the substantive adapting its case to the rest of the sentence. See § 1055. 1.

Ad lūdos pĕcūniae dēcernuntŭr (*Cic.* ad Q. F. I. 1. 9. 26), *money is voted for the games.*
Ad ăgrum instruendum utres nōn ĕrant (*Liv.* vi. 5), *they were too weak (in purse) to stock a farm.*
Pĭlus Rōmānŏs ăd insĕquendum tardābat (*Caes.* B. G. vii. 26), *the marsh made the Romans slow to pursue.*

f. To, in reply : as,

Ad illă quae mē măgis mōuērunt respondēbō (*Cic.* p. Cael. 11. 27), *I will reply to those other points which moved me more.*

g. In respect of, looking to : as,

Vĭr ăd ūsum pĕrītŭs, ad fortūnam fēlix (*Cic.* p. Font. 15. 43), *a man of experience as regards the world, and favoured in respect to fortune.*

h. In addition to : as,

Sī ad cētĕrā uolnĕra hanc quŏquĕ plāgam inflīxissēs (*Cic.* in Vat. 8. 20), *if in addition to the other wounds you had inflicted this blow also.*
Ad hoc prōmissă barba et căpĭllī effĕrāuĕrant spĕciem ōris (*Liv.* II. 23), *in addition to this a long beard and long hair had given a savage character to his face.*

i. By, of future time : as,

Nōs hīc te ăd mensem Iānuārium expectāmŭs (*Cic.* ad Att. I. 3. 2), *we expect to see you here by the month of January.*
Nescio quid intersit ūtrum nunc uĕniam, ăn ad dĕcem annōs (*Cic.* ad Att. xii. 46), *I know not what it matters, whether I come now or ten years hence.*

j. Near, before, off, to, over (all in the sense of nearness) : as,

Ad Geronium constĭtĕrat bellum (*Liv.* xxii. 32), *before Geronium the war had come to a standstill.*
Classis quae ăd Sĭcĭliam ĕrat (*Liv.* xxvii. 22), *the fleet which was lying off Sicily.*
Cănunt ad tībiam clārōrum uĭrōrum laudēs (*Cic.* Tusc. iv. 2. 3), *they sing the praises of great men to the flute.*
Nonnunquam ăd uīnum dĭsertī sunt (*Cic.* p. Cael. 28. 67), *they are sometimes eloquent over their wine.*

k. In comparison to, by the side of : as,

Nihil ad nostram hanc (*Ter.* E. II. 3. 69), *nothing to this one of ours.*

Terra ad ūnīuersī caelī complexum quāsī punctī instār obtinet (*Cic.* Tusc. I. 17. 40), *the earth, compared to what the whole heavens embrace, is as it were but a point.*

l. In accordance with, after : as,

Catō uītam ad certam ratiōnis normam dirigit (*Cic.* p. Mur. 2. 3), *Cato shapes his life by the strict square of reason.*

Vīxit ad aliōrum arbitrium, nōn ad suum (*Cic.* p. Mur. 9. 19), *he has lived according to the pleasure of others, not his own.*

m. Among, before (in the same sense as apūd) : as,

Minus clādis, cēterum non plūs animōrum ad hostīs erat (*Liv.* X. 35), *there was less loss, but not more confidence among the enemy.*

Senātōrum superbiam ad plēbem crīminantur (*Liv.* III. 9), *they attack the tyranny of the senators before the commonalty.*

n. Immediately upon, in consequence of, at : as,

Ad fāmam obsidiōnis dēlectūs habērī coeptūs est (*Liv.* IX. 7), *at the report of a siege, a levy of troops was commenced.*

Nēc ad ducis cāsum perculsa magis quam irrītāta est multitūdō (*Liv.* IX. 22), *and the great mass of the men were not so much panic-struck as roused to fury at the accident to their chief.*

o. Before a word denoting a person, *to the house of* that person: as,

Magnī dōmum concursūs ad Afrānium* fīebant (*Caes.* B. C. I. 53), *great crowds kept flocking to the house of Afranius.*

Nēque dōmum unquam ad mē littěras mittam quīn adjungam eas quās tibī reddī uēlim (*Cic.* ad Fam. III. 8. 10), *nor shall I ever send letters to my own house, without adding to the packet a letter for you.*

Deuertit Clōdius ad sē (*Cic.* p. Mil. 19. 51), *Clodius turned out of the road to his own house.*

p. With a noun denoting the *department* in which a servant's offices are looked for, whence arises a name for the *office* (see āb, § 1303 *d.*) : as,

---

* And this phrase is used although Afranius himself was in Spain at the time. See § 1303 *l.*

Licinum seruom sibi habuit ad manum (*Cic.* de Or. III. 60. 225), *he had a slave Licinus for his amanuensis.*

Puer quis ex aula capillis Ad cyathum statuetur unctis? (*Hor.* Od. I. 29. 7) *shall some page from the palace with perfumed locks be stationed beside the wine-ladle?*[a]

1306   Ad in composition with verbs denotes—*a. motion to:* as, ád-i-go to, *approach*, acced- *step up to.* *b. addition:* as, acced- *be added*, ascrib-[†] *enroll with.* *c. nearness:* as, aside- *sit near*, adiace- *lie near*, assurg- (alicui) *rise to (a person).* *d. assent, favour:* as, annu-nod assent, arride- *smile on,* acclama- *express assent by acclamation, cheer.* But see § 1308. 1, &c.

1307   Aduersūs or -um (old form aduorsūs or -um) is literally translated by our *to-wards.* It denotes:

a. Motion towards: as,

Quis haec est, quae me aduórsum incedit? (*Plaut.* Per. II. 2. 18) *who is this woman, that is coming towards me?*

Impětum aduersus montem in cohortīs faciunt (*Caes.* B. C. I. 46), *they make a charge up*[‡] *the mountain upon the cohorts.*

b. Opposite, facing, before (without motion): as,

Lero et Lerina aduersūs Antipŏlim (*Plin.* III. 11), *Lero and Lerina opposite Antipolis.*

Egóne ut te aduórsum méntiar, matér mea! (*Plaut.* Aul. IV. 7. 9), *I tell a falsehood before you, mother!*

c. Conduct towards (good or bad, friendly or unfriendly): as,

Quónammódo mē géram aduorsus Caesārem? (*Cic.* ad Fam. XI. 27. 5) *how in the world am I to bear myself towards Caesar?*

Id grátum fuisse aduórsum te, habeo grátiam (*Ter.* And. I. 1. 15), *that this was pleasing to you, I feel grateful.*

d. To counteract, against: as,

Sunt tămen quaedam rĕmědiă propria aduersus quaedam us-

---

[a] In very late writers, as Vegetius, *ad* was used to denote the means: as, *ad spongiam detergere* (III. 4. 2), *ad coriam cannam exuoare* (III. 3. 12), *ad siphonem paulatim infundes* (I. 10. 2), *ad acum pars auriculae signatur* (III. 2. 27), *perforare ad acum* (Ibid. 28).

[†] See § 451. 1.

[‡] He who goes up a mountain goes *facing* it. Compare the use of the ablative absolute, *aduerso monte ire*, and § 1320 *b.*

nĕnā (*Cels.* v. 27. 12), *there are however certain specific remedies against certain poisons.*

e. At variance with, in opposition to : as,

Pĕcūniae concĭliātae aduorsum lēgēs, aduorsum rempublĭcam (*Cic.* II. Verr. III. 84. 194), *money quietly obtained in opposition to the law, in opposition to the interests of the country.*

f. Aduorsum is used adverbially with i- *go* &c. and a dative of the person : as,

Cesso hĕrŏ meo īre aduorsum ! (*Plaut.* Cas. III. 6. 6) *why do I not at once go to meet my master !*

1308 Am, rarely if ever used except in composition, when it signifies, *a.* with verbs, *round :* as, anquīr- *look round for*, amplect- (r.) *embrace*, ăm-ĭo- or ăm-ĭcĭ- *throw round*. *b.* in adjectives, *on both sides :* as, ancīp- or ancīpĭt- *two-headed*.

1308. 1 Ana (= ανα), used in its full form only as an adverb, and only in medical* prescriptions, signifies *distribution* or *each :* as,

Sacchări, erui pollĭnĭs, ăna unciam ūnam (*Veg.* Art. Vet. III. 65. 6), *sugar, and the flour of black vetches, one ounce of each.* Fŏlĭi cappărĭs, fŏlĭi mirti siluestris, fŏlĭi cūpressi ăna uncias tres dilĭgentissĭmē dētĕrĕs (*ibid.* III. 2. 6), *take of caper-leaves, wild-myrtle-leaves, cypress-leaves, three ounces each, and pound them as fine as possible.*

1308. 2 An† *up* (= ανα) is found only in composition. The form in which it appears greatly varies. *a.* In ăn-hēla- it retains its correct form. *b.* Frequently it has the consonant assimilated to that which follows, as in accŭmŭla-, addormīsc-, allĕua-, ammŏue-, apprehend-, acquīesc-, arrĭg-, assĭccā-, attĕr-. *c.* Sometimes the consonant is altogether lost, as in a-gnōsc-, a-scend-. *d.* More commonly it is attracted into the form of the familiar preposition ăd, thus changing the dental liquid for a dental mute, as in ădāresc-, ădĕd-, ădĭm-, ădōlesc-, ădūr-. *e.* Not less frequently it is attracted into the form of the familiar preposition in, by an easy change of the vowel‡, as in incĭp- or incĭpi-, ĭnhorre-, ĭntŭmesc-, ĭmbu-, ignōsc-.§

---

* As the medical art at Rome was in the hands of Greeks, Greek words obtained admission into this part of the language.

† See § 834 *b.* and note.

‡ So in, the negative prefix, corresponds to the privative αν.

§ Even ām-ĭt- (ămitt-) represents the c.r. of αν-ιημι.

1308. 3 An *up*, like its equivalent *ana*, has the following meanings: *a. up*, as anhēla- *send up (a blast of air), make a violent expiration;* ascend- *climb up,* accŭmŭla- *heap up,* adiūva- *lift up and so aid,* allēva- *raise up,* apprehend- *take up,* arrĭg- *erect,* adaequa- *raise to a level with,* inhorre- *bristle up,* intŭmesc- *swell up,* instĭtu- *set up.* *b. back,* as inhĭbe- *hold up or back,* inclīna- *bend back,* inflect- *bend back,* infrĭng- *refract.* *c. again,* as agnosc- *recognise,* ammŏne- or admŏne- *remind,* adsurg-* *rise up again,* instaura- (=restaura-) *celebrate anew,* ingĕmĭna- *redouble.* *d. reversal of a preceding act,* as ignosc- *forget,* acquiesc- *repose after labour.* *e. loosening, opening,* as adăpĕri- *open up,* ĭnăra- *plough up,* infind- *cleave open, plough up.* *f. commencement,* as ădāma- *fall in love,* addormisc- *fall asleep,* aduespēram- *begin to be dusk,* ambūr- *begin to burn, singe,* imbu- *wet for the first time,* informa- *give a first shape to,* immĭnu- *impair (what was entire),* incĭp- *or* incĭpi- *take up, begin.* *g. separation, removal, disappearance,* as ădĭm-† *take up and so take away,* ampūta- *cut off,* assicca- *dry up,* ădāresc- *dry up (intr.),* infrĭng- *break off,* incīd- *cut off,* intăbesc- *melt away.* *h. through,* as ădĭg- *drive through, transfix,* admisce- *mix up or thoroughly.* *i. intensity,* as accīd- *cut deep into,* ĕdĕd- *eat deep into,* attonde- *cut (the hair) close,* ădūr- *burn a deep hole in,* attĕr- *rub a deep hole in,* afflīg- or afflīci- *produce a deep impression on, seriously affect.*

1308. 4 An signifies *up* in the adjective acclīui- *uphill.*

1309   Antĕ. *a. Before* in place: as,

Immŏlābat antĕ praetōrium (*Cic.* de Div. I. 33. 72), *he was sacrificing before his tent.*

Antĕ trĭbūnal tuum M. Fanni, antĕ pĕdes uostros iūdĭcem, caedēs ērunt (*Cic.* p. Rosc. Am. 5. 12), *before your tribunal, Marcus Fannius, before your feet, gentlemen of the jury, will murders be committed.*

b. The same without a case: as,

Flŭuĭus ab tergo, antĕ circăquĕ uĕlut rīpā praecepa, ōram tŭmŭli omnem cingēbat (*Liv.* XXVII. 18), *a river in the rear, in front and on the sides something like a precipitous bank shut in the whole circuit of the eminence.*

* See *Liv.* XXI. 36. 7, XXII. 2. 6, and *ad-insurg-* XXII. 4. 2.
† Compare *as-ups-*.

c. *Before* a person (rare): as,

Dīcĕrĕ causam antĕ iūdicem (*Cic.* I. Verr. 3. 9), *to make a defence before a judge.*

d. Motion *forward* (without a noun): as,

Vt si aut mănĭbūs ingrĕdiātŭr quis, aut nōn antĕ sed rētrō (*Cic.* de Fin. v. 12. 35), *as if a person were to walk upon his hands, or to walk, not forwards, but backwards.*

e. *Before* in order: as,

Quem antĕ mē dīlĭgo (*Balb.* ap. Cic. ad Att. VIII. 15 A.), *whom I esteem above myself.*

f. *Before* in time (which is the ordinary meaning of the word): as,

Multo antĕ noctem cōpiās rēduxit (*Liv.* XXVII. 42), *long before night he led the forces back.*

g. *Before* in time without a noun: as,

Et fēci ante et făcio nunc (*Cic.* ad Fam. XV. 14. 3), *I have done so before, and I do so now.*

Paucis antĕ diēbūs oppĭdum obpugnārant (*Liv.* XLI. 11), *a few days before (this) they had assaulted the town.*

Anno antĕ quam mortuŏst (*Cic.* de Am. 3. 11), *the year before he died.*

h. This preposition, as well as *post*, often causes this ablative to be changed for an accusative by attraction, as if it depended upon the preposition. Thus,

Chalcīdem diēs antĕ paucos prōdĭdĕrat (*Liv.* XXXI. 24), *he had betrayed Chalcis a few days before.*

Sulci ante annum fiunt quam vīneăĕ consĕruntŭr (*Col.* V. 5), *the furrows are made a year before the vineyards are planted.*

Lătīnae fēriae fuēre antĕ diem tertium nōnas Maiās (*Liv.* XLI. 10), *the Latin festival was two days before the nones of May,* i. e. *the 5th of May.*

i. Hence another preposition may be placed before antĕ: as,

Caedem contŭlisti in antĕ diem quintum kălendas Nŏvembris (*Cic.* in Cat. I. 3. 7), *the massacre you fixed for the fourth day before the kalends of November,* i. e. *October the 28th.*

Supplĭcătĭo indicta est ex antĕ diem quintum īdūs Octōbris cum eō die in quinquē diēs (*Liv.* XLV. 2), *a thanksgiving* was proclaimed to continue from the fourth day before the ides of October inclusive for five days, i. e. from the 11th to the 15th of October.

1310 Antĕ in composition with verbs signifies *before in place, time and excellence*: as, ante-i- *walk before, live before, surpass*; antĕ-cēd-.* *precede in place, in time, in quality.*

1311 Apŭd (ăpŭt) is for the most part limited to persons. It denotes:

a. Near, with places (rarely): as,

Apŭd oppĭdum Cybistrā castrā fēcī (*Cic.* ad Fam. xv. 4. 4), *I encamped near the town Cybistra.*

Apud forum modo e Dāuo audīuī (*Ter.* And. π. 1. 2), *I heard it just now from Davus near the forum.*

Cīuīcam cŏrōnam ăpud Brĭtannĭam mĕrītŭs ĕrat (*Tac.*† Ann. xvi. 15), *he had earned a civic crown among the Britons.*

b. Near, with persons: as,

In lectō Crassŭs ĕrat, ĕt ăpŭd eum Sulpĭcius sĕdēbat (*Cic.* de Or. π. 3. 12), *Crassus was on the couch, and near him Sulpicius was sitting.*

Apŭd exercĭtum est (*Cic.* π. Verr. iv. 22. 49), *he is with the army.*

Auet ănĭmŭs ăpŭd illud consĭlium dīcĕrĕ (*Cic.* Phil. v. 5. 13), *my soul longs to speak before that bench of judges.*

c. At the house of a person‡, even though he be away: as,

Brūtum ăpŭd mē fuissĕ gaudeo (*Cic.* ad Att. xv. 3. 2), *I rejoice (to hear) that Brutus has been at my house.*

Dŏmī easē ăpud essē archĭpīrātas dixit duōs (*Cic.* π. Verr. v. 29. 73), *there were at his house, he said, two of the chief pirates.*

d. Metaphorically *in one's senses*: as,

Non sum apŭt me (*Ter.* Haut. v. 1. 48), *I am all abroad, am lost, am out of my senses.*

Proin tu fāc apud tē ut sies (*Ter.* And. π. 4. 5), *do you then at once take care you have all your wits about you.*

---

* See § 451. 1.

† This use of *apud* with the names of countries is almost peculiar to Tacitus.

‡ See §§ 1303 *b*, 1305 *a*.

e. In the time of: as,

Apud pătres nostrōs (*Cic.* p. Mur. 36. 75), *among our fathers*, i. e. *in the times of our fathers.*

Apud saeclum prius (*Ter.* E. II. 2. 15), *in the preceding generation.*

f. In the mind: as,

Praemia ăpŭd me minŭmum uălent (*Cic.* ad Fam. I. 9. 11), *rewards with me have very little weight.*

Apud uĭros bŏnos grătiam consĕcūtī sŭmŭs (*Cic.* ad Att. IV. 1. 3), *we have obtained influence with good men.*

g. In authors: as,

Vt ille ăpud Tĕrentium (*Cic.* de Fin. v. 10. 28), *like that old man in Terence.*

De sĕpulcris nihil est ăpud Sŏlōnem amplius quam . . . . (*Cic.* de Leg. II. 26. 64), *on the subject of sepulchres there is nothing in the laws of Solon more than . . . .*

1312   Ar (of the same meaning as ăd), rarely if ever used except in composition*, and then it signifies—*a. to:* as, arcesse- *and* arcicall to (you), send for ; aruŏca- *call to* (you), aruŏla- *fly to,* aruĕna- *one lately arrived, a stranger. b. presence:* as, arbĭtero- *a person present, a witness, umpire, judge;* arfu- *be present* (whence arfuit).

1313   Circā.   *a. About, round,* in reference to place : as,

Custōdes circa omnis portas missi ne quis urbe ēgrĕdĕrētŭr (*Liv.* XXVIII. 26), *guards were sent round to all the gates to prevent any one from leaving the city.*

Cānes circā se hăbēbat (*Cic.* II. Verr. I. 48. 126), *he had dogs about him.*

b. The same without a noun : as,

Lŭpă sitiens ex montibus qui circā sunt ad puĕrīlem uāgītum cursum flexit (*Liv.* I. 4), *a thirsty wolf out of the mountains which lie around, upon hearing the crying of a child turned its course thither.*

c. About, as to time : as,

Postĕro diē circā eandem hōram cōpiās admŏuit (*Liv.* XLII. 57), *the next day about the same hour he moved up his troops.*

* But see *Plaut.* Truc. II. 2. 17.

d. *About*, as to number: as,

Deindĕ pĕr īnsĕquentīs diēs circā singŭlās hēmīnās ēmittendum (*Cels.* VII. 15), *then during the following days about an hemina is to be drawn off each day.*

e. *About, upon, concerning, in reference to* (chiefly in the later writers): as,

Hi circā consilium ēligendī successōris in duas factiōnes scindĕbantŭr (*Tac. Hist.* I. 13), *these were dividing themselves into two parties upon the question of electing a successor.*

1314 Circĭtĕr. a. *About*, as regards place (rare): as,

Vt ŏpīnor, lŏca haec circĭtĕr excĭdit mihi (*Plaut.* Cist. IV. 2. 7), *I fancy it was hereabouts I dropt it.*

b. *About*, as to time: as,

Circĭtĕr idūs Sextīlīs pŭto me ād Icōnium fŏrē (*Cic.* ad Fam. III. 5. 4), *about the ides of Sextilis, i.e. August 13th, I calculate I shall be in the neighbourhood of Iconium.*

c. *About*, as to number (the chief use of the word): as,

Diēs circĭter quindĕcim īter fēcērunt (*Caes.* B. G. I. 15), *they marched for about fifteen days.*

1315 Circum, *round*, whether in rest, or circular or other similar motion: as,

Terrā circum axem sē conuortĭt (*Cic.* Acad. Pr. II. 39. 123), *the earth turns round its axis.*

Ex eā turrī quae circum essent ŏpĕrā tuērī sē possĕ confīsī sunt (*Caes.* B. C. II. 10), *from this tower they felt confident that they should be able to defend the works which lay around.*

Puĕros circum āmīcos dīmittĭt (*Cic.* p. Quinct. 6. 25), *he sends the servants round to his friends.*

Paucae, quae circum illam essent, mănent (*Ter.* E. III. 5. 33), *a few women remain to wait upon that lady.*

1316 Cĭs. a. *On this side of, within*, as regards place: as,

Saepe ăb his cĭs Pădum ultrāque lēgiōnes fūsae ĕrant (*Liv.* V. 35), *the legions had been often routed by them on this side of the Padus and beyond it.*

b. *Within*, in regard to time (only in Plautus): as,

Nūlla, ĭnxim, cĭs diēs paucōs sĭet (*Plaut.* Truc. II. 3. 27), *I would make it wholly disappear within a few days.*

1317 Cis in the composition of adjectives signifies *on this side of*: as, cīsalpīno-, cisrhēnāno-, cispādāno-, *on this side the Alps, the Rhine, the Po*.

1318 Cĭtrā. *a. On this side of, within,* as regards place: as,

Erat ēnim cum suis nāuĭbus cĭtrā Vēliam mīliā passuum triā (*Cic.* ad Att. xvi. 7. 5), *for he was in fact with his fleet three miles on this side Velia.*

b. The same without a noun: as,

Tēla hostium cĭtrā cădēbant (*Tac.* Hist. iii. 23), *the missiles of the enemy kept falling short.*

c. Within, as to time : as,

Lōcĭs ūlĭgĭnōsĭs cĭtrā kălendās Octōbrĭs sēmĭnārē conuĕnĭt (*Col.* ii. 8), *on wet lands it is right to sow before the 1st of October.*

d. Short of, in degree : as,

Peccāuī cĭtrā scĕlŭs (*Ov.* Tr. v. 8. 23), *my guilt is short of impiety.*

1319 Clam and the diminutive clanculum are used only before persons, in the sense of *without their knowledge* :

a. As prepositions : as,

Sibi nunc uterque cóntra legiónés parat
Patérque filiúsque clam alter álterum (*Plaut.* Cas. pr. 50),
*Against each other now are they preparing armies,
Both sire and son, each unknown to each.*

Emptast clam úxōrem et clam fīlium* (*Plaut.* Merc. iii. 2. 2), *she has been purchased unknown to my wife and unknown to my son.*

Aliī clanculum pătrēs quae făciunt (*Ter.* Ad. i. 1. 27), *what others do without their fathers' knowledge.*

b. They are often used adverbially without a substantive.

1320 Cŏntrā. *a. Overagainst, facing :* as,

Quinctius trans Tiberim contra eum lōcum ūbī nunc nāuālĭă sunt, quattuor iūgĕrum cōlĕbat ăgrum (*Liv.* iii. 26), *Quinctius was cultivating a farm of but four jugers on the other side of the Tiber, opposite where the dockyard now is.*

---

* So Ritschl from the palimpsest ; but otherwise the best Mss. have uxore and filio.

Aspicĕ-dum contrā mē (*Plaut.* Most. v. 1. 56), *just look me in the face.*

b. *Up*[*] : as,

Dūcēnāriā duō contrā scālās fěrēbat (*Plin.* v. 20), *he would carry two two-hundred weights up stairs.*

c. Metaphorically, *opposition, against :* as,

Res Rōmānā contrā spem uōtāque ēius rēsurgēbat (*Liv.* xxiv. 45), *the power of Rome was rising again contrary to his hope and his prayers.*

d. *Towards,* of the feelings or behaviour : as,

Elĕphantī tantā narrātur clēmentiā contrā mĭnus uălĭdōs ŭt &c. (*Plin.* VIII. 7), *the kindness of the elephant towards the weak is said to be so great that &c.*

e. *The reverse* (with or without a case) : as,

In stultĭtiā contrast (*Cic.* p. Clu. 31. 84), *in folly it is just the reverse.*

Quod contrā fit ā plērisquĕ (*Cic.* de Off. 1. 15. 49), *whereas the contrary of this is done by most people.*

f. *Weighed against* (and with a dative case apparently) : as,

Non cārust auro cŏntrā (*Plaut.* Ep. III. 3. 30), *he is not dear at his weight in gold.*

Cōram. a. *In the presence of,* only before persons ; as,

Mĭhī ĭpsī, cōram gĕnĕrō meō, quae dīcĕre ausu's ? (*Cic.* in Pis. 6. 12) *even to me, in the presence of my son-in-law, what language did you dare to use ?*

Prĕcēs ad uos conuerto, disque et pătriă cōram obtestŏr (*Tac.* Ann. iv. 8), *I turn my prayers to you, and before the gods and my country implore you.*

b. Frequently without a substantive : as,

Quăsĭ tēcum cōram lŏquĕrer (*Cic.* ad Fam. II. 9. 2), *as if I had been talking with you face to face.*

Cum. a. *With,* chiefly in the case of persons ; as,

Văgāmŭr ēgentes cum coniŭgĭbŭs et lĭbĕrīs (*Cic.* ad Att. VIII. 2. 3), *we wander about in poverty with our wives and children.*

---

[*] Because he who moves facing the stairs ascends them. See *aduersum,* § 1307 a.

Tēcum essē uehēmenter uellim (*Cic.* ad Fam. v. 21. 1), *I should be infinitely delighted to be with you.*

b. A relation between two parties is expressed by the dative of the chief party, and cum with the other: as,

Tēcum mihi rēs est (*Cic.* p. Rosc. Am. 30. 84), *my dealings are with you.*

Intercēdunt mihi inimīcītiae cum istīus mūliĕris uirō (*Cic.* p. Cael. 13. 32), *there is a disagreement existing between me and the husband of that woman.*

c. *With* or *in*, in the sense of *wearing*: as,

Nolo me in uia Cum hac ueste uideat (*Ter.* E. v. 2. 67), *I must not have him see me in the street in this dress.*

Cēnāuit cum tŏgā pullā (*Cic.* in Vat. 13. 31), *he dined in a black toga.*

Ipse esse cum tēlō (*Sal.* Cat. 27), *he himself went about armed.*

d. Two nouns are at times united by cum, so as to have a common predicate or adjective or genitive attached to them: as,

Ipse dux cum aliquot principibus capiuntur (*Liv.* XXI. 60), *the general himself with a considerable number of the leading men are taken.*

A'bin hinc in malam rem cum suspicione istāc scelus! (*Ter.* And. II. 1. 17) *go and be hanged, you and your suspicions, you scoundrel.*

Pĕdem cum uōce rĕpressit (*Virg.* A. II. 378), *he checked his foot, and checked his voice.*

Induit albos cum uittā crīnīs (*Virg.* A. VII. 417), *she puts on locks and fillet white alike.*

Cimini cum monte lăcum (*Virg.* A. VII. 697), *the lake and mountain of Ciminus.*

e. *With*, denoting coincidence of time: as,

Summi puĕrōrum ămōres saepe ūnā cum praetextā pōnuntūr (*Cic.* de Am. 10. 33), *the strongest attachments of boys are often laid aside together with (at the same time as) the prætexta.*

Păriter cum ortū sōlis castrā mētābātūr (*Sal.* Jug. 106), *precisely as the sun was rising he was measuring out a camp.*

f. *With*, *in*, &c., to express accompanying feelings, circumstances: as,

Athēniēnsēs cum silentio audītī sunt (*Liv.* XXXVIII. 10), *the Athenians were heard in silence.*

Flāminī corpus magnā cum cūrā inquīsītum nōn inuēnit (*Liv.* XXII. 7), *the body of Flaminius he made search after with the greatest care, but did not find it.*

g. The immediate consequences, expressed by *to*: as,

Vēnit Lampsācum cum magnā călămitāte et prŏpe pernicīe ciuitātis (*Cic.* II. *Verr.* I. 24. 63), *he came to Lampsacum* to the great damage and all but utter ruin of the citizens.*

h. *With*, in comparisons: as,

Conferte hanc pācem cum illō bellō (*Cic.* II. *Verr.* IV. 52. 115), *compare this peace with that war.*

Cum meum factum cum tuō compăro (*Cic. ad Fam.* III. 6. 1), *when I compare my conduct with yours.*

i. *With*, in the sense of *against*, with verbs denoting contest: as,

Cum omnibus sălūtis meae dēfēnsōrĭbus bellă gĕrunt (*Cic. p. Sest.* 2. 4), *they wage war with all who defend my life and fortunes.*

Hannibal dē imperiō cum pŏpŭlō Rōmānō certāuit (*Cic. de Or.* II. 18. 76), *Hannibal contended for empire with the Roman people.*

j. Cum eō, followed by ŭt and a subjunctive, is employed to express an addition or qualification: as,

Lānŭuinis sacrā suā redditā, cum eo ŭt aedes Iūnōnis commūnis Lānŭuinis cum pŏpŭlō Rōmānō esset (*Liv.* VIII. 14), *to the people of Lanuvium their sacred property was restored, on the condition that the temple of Juno should be in common between the burgesses of Lanuvium and the people of Rome.*

Vnum gaudium affulsĕrat, cum eo ŭt appārēret haud prŏcŭl exĭtiō fuissĕ classem (*Liv.* XXX. 10), *one joy had shone upon them, together with the certainty that the fleet had been at one time on the verge of destruction.*†

1323 Cum or cŏn in composition with verbs signifies—a. *union*: as, conclūr-‡ *run together*, co-i- *meet*, consŭl- [*sit together*], *deliberate.*

* *Lampsacum*, not *Lampsacus*, is the nominative in Cicero. See II. *Verr.* I. 24. 63.

† See also § 1065. 1, examples 2, 3, 4.

‡ See § 431. 1.

b. completeness (in the way of destruction): as, comĕd- *eat up*, com-būr-* *burn up*, contŭd-* *hammer to pieces*, confīc- or conficī- *dispatch*, concīd- *cut to pieces*. *c. completeness* (in the way of success): as, confīc- or confīcī- *make up*, consĕqu- (r.) *overtake, obtain*, consecta- (r.) *hunt down*. *d. with a great effort:* as, cōnĭc- or cōnĭcĭ- *hurl*, conclāma- *cry out loudly*, collŏca- *place with care, place for a permanence*, concŭt- or concŭtĭ- *shake violently*, comprehend- *seize firmly*. *e. in harmony:* as, concĭn- *and* consŏna- *accord, harmonise*, consenti- *agree (in feeling)*. *f.* the same as *be* in English, at once changing the construction of the verb and adding *completeness:* as, constēr-* *bestrew* or *pave*, collīn- *besmear*. (See § 905.)

1324 Cum or cŏn in adjectives denotes *union:* as, conscio- *sharing knowledge*, commūni- *shared in common*, commŏdo- *having the same measure, fitting*, coniŭg- *yoked together, yokemate*.

1325 Cum or cŏn with substantives denotes *fellow:* as, conseruo- *fellow-slave*, commilĭtōn- *fellow-soldier*, consŏcĕro- *one of two fathers-in-law*.

1326 Dē. *a. Down, down from:* as,

Ruunt dē montĭbŭs amnēs (*Virg. A.* IV. 164), *adown the mountains rush the rivers*.

Clĭpĕā dē cŏlumnis dempsit (*Liv.* XL. 51), *he took the shields down from the pillars*.

Atque haec ăgĕbantŭr in conuentū pălam dē sellā† (*Cic.* II. Verr. IV. 40. 85), *and what is more, these remarks were made in court openly from the chair.*

b. The *source from* which: as,

Hoc audiuī dē pătrĕ meŏ (*Cic. de Or.* III. 33. 133), *this I heard from my father.*

Millĕ iūgĕrum dē Pilio ēmit (*Cic. ad Att.* XIII. 31. 4), *he bought a thousand jugers (of land) of Pilius.*

Pĕcūniam nŭmĕrāuit dē suō (*Cic. ad Att.* XVI. 16 A. 3), *he paid the money down out of his own pocket.*

Virtūs, quam tū nē dē făcĭē quĭdem nostī (*Cic. in Pis.* 32. 81), *Virtue, whom you know not even by sight.*

c. Part of, one or more of: as,

* See § 451. 1.
† Which was on elevated ground.

Dē tuīs innŭmĕrābĭlĭbŭs in me offĭcĭis, ĕrĭt hoc grātissŭmum (*Cic.* ad Fam. XVI. 1. 2), *of your innumerable kindnesses to me, this will indeed be the most welcome.*

Hăbĕātur sānē ōrātor sed dē mĭnōrĭbŭs (*Cic.* Opt. gen. Or. 4. 9), *let him be accounted indeed an orator, but one of an inferior class.*

d. The *material* of which any thing is made : as,

Prīmum sĭbi fēcĭt pōcŭlă dē lŭtō (*Tibul.* I. 1. 31), *he first made him cups of dirt.*

Dē frātrĕ quid fīet* ? (*Ter.* Ad. v. 9. 39) *what will become of my brother?*

e. Motives, causes, suggestions, variously translated, as by *under, for, on,* &c. : as,

Iustīs dē caussīs rătĭōnes dēferrī prŏpĕrāuī (*Cic.* ad Fam. v. 20. 2), *for good reasons I made haste to give in my accounts.*

Quōrum dē sententĭā tōtă res gesta est (*Cic.* p. Sull. 19. 55), *under whose advice the whole matter was conducted.*

f. Down *upon, on* : as,

Dē grădū cōnārī (*Liv.* XXXIV. 39), *to fight their best on foot.*

Etiamsī cĕcĭdĕrit, dē gĕnū pugnat (*Sen.* de Prov. 2), *even if he fall, he fights on his knee.*

Non possum, inquit, tĭbi dīcĕrĕ, nescio ĕnim quid dē grădū făciat—tanquam de essĕdārio interrŏgārētŭr (*Sen.* Ep. 29), *I cannot tell you, says he, for I know not what he could do fighting on foot—as though the question had been about a chariot-soldier.*

g. On (a topic), *over, about, of, concerning* : as,

Nĭhil dīco dē meo ingĕnĭō (*Cic.* in Caecil. 11. 30), *I say nothing of my own abilities.*

Rēgŭlus dē captīuīs commūtandis Rōmam missŭs est (*Cic.* de Off. I. 13. 39), *Regulus was sent to Rome about an exchange of prisoners.*

Dē me autem suscĭpĕ paulisper meas partīs (*Cic.* ad Fam. III. 12. 2), *on the other hand, as regards myself, put yourself in my position for a moment.*

Africānus dē Nŭmantinīs trĭumphāuĕrat (*Cic.* Phil. XI. 8. 18), *Africanus had triumphed over the people of Numantia.*

* Literally 'will be made.' See § 1003.

h. With words of time the meaning is somewhat doubtful. It would seem however that here also the notion of a part (see subdivision e.) prevails, and that the determination as to what part is only to be inferred from the context. Thus the best translation perhaps is our preposition *by* or *in the course of*: as,

>Vt iŭgŭlent hŏmĭnem, surgunt dē noctē lătrōnes (*Hor.* Ep. I. 2. 32), *to murder man, rises by night the robber.*

>Coepērunt ĕpŭlārī dē diē (*Liv.* xxiii. 8), *they began banqueting by daylight.*

>Dē tertiā uĭgĭliā exercĭtum rēdūcit (*Caes.* B. C. II. 35), *in the course of the third watch he leads back the army.*

i. At times dē is used with a noun to denote immediate succession of time, *directly after*: as,

>Non bŏnus sompnŭs est dē prandiō (*Plaut.* Most. III. 2. 8), *sleep directly after breakfast is not good.*

>Iamque ădĕrit multō Priămi dē sanguĭnē Pyrrhus (*Virg.* A. II. 662), *and soon will Pyrrhus be here, fresh from the streaming blood of Priam.*

1327 Dē in composition with verbs denotes—*a. down*: as, dēm- (for de-im-) *take down*, dēmĭt-* *let down*. *b. removal*: as, dētondē- *shear*, dēcortĭcā- *strip off the bark*. *c. absence*: as, dēes- or rather dēe- *be wanting*, dēbe- (for dehibe-) *owe*, dēfĭc- or dēfĭci- *fail*. *d. prevention*: as, dehorta- (r.) *dissuade*, dēprĕca- (r.) *pray a thing may not be*. *e. unfriendly feeling*: as, dēspĭc- or dēspĭci- *despise*, dērĭde- *laugh at*. *f. partially*: as, dēperd- *lose in part*, dēpĕri- *perish in part*, dērŏga- *take part away (by a rogation)*. *g. intensity* (?): as, dēpŏpŭla- (r.) *lay thoroughly waste*, dēāma- *love to distraction†*.

1328 Dē with adjectives denotes—*a. down*: as, dēclīuĭ- *sloping downwards*. *b. absence*: as, dēmenti- or dēment- *without mind, idiotic*.

1329 Dĭ or dĭs (dĭr) is used only in composition. With verbs it denotes—*a. division*: as, dĭuĭd- *divide*, dĭd- *distribute*, dīscrīb-* *distribute by writing*, dīlāb-* *slip away in different directions*. *b. difference*: as, dīscrĕpa- *sound a different note*, dissenti- *feel differently*. *c. the reverse of the simple notion*: as, dīsplĭce- *displease*, dīffĭd-*

---

* See § 431. 1.

† In this last sense the prefix was perhaps originally the preposition *dī* or *dīs*. See § 1329 d.

distrăt, *discing- ungird*. *d. intensity*: as, *dilauda- bepraise*, *discŭp-* or *discŭpĭ- desire to distraction*.

1330. *Dis* in the composition of adjectives denotes—*a. difference*: as, *discŏlōr- of different colour* or *colours*, *discordi-* or *discord-* (from *corda- a musical string*) *sounding a different note*. *b. negation*: as, *dissĭmĭli- unlike*, *dispări-* or *dispăr- unequal*.

1331. [Ec], ē, *ex* may be looked upon as the opposite to *In*, just as *Ēb* in its ordinary senses is to *Ăd*; and an attention to this distinction is often a useful guide in the translation of the English preposition *from*. It denotes—*a. out of* (with motion): as,

Tēlum ē corpŏre extraxit (*Cic.* p. Rosc. Am. 7. 19), *he drew the weapon out of the flesh*.

Eum éxturbasti ex aedibus (*Plaut.* Trin. I. 2. 100), *this man you bundled out of the house*.

b. Off, i. e. *from on* (and it may be observed that *In* signified *on* as well as *in*): as,

Ex ĕquis dēsĭliunt et pēdĭbus proeliantŭr (*Caes.* B. G. I. 2), *they leap off their horses and fight on foot*.

Nĭsi ō campo in căuam hanc uiam dēmittĭmŭs ĕquŏs (*Liv.* XXIII. 47), *unless we ride down from the plain into this hollow road*.

c. On, from, when a person is *in* or *on* a place and directs his efforts thence: as,

Castŏr et Pollux ex ĕquis pugnārē uisī sunt (*Cic.* N. D. II. 2. 6), *Castor and Pollux were seen fighting on horseback*.

Contiōnārī ex turri altā sŏlēbat (*Cic.* Tusc. v. 20. 59), *he was wont to harangue the people from a high tower*.

d. The material of which any thing is made, *of*: as,

Expōnit multum argentum, non paucă pōcŭla ex aurō (*Cic.* II. Verr. IV. 27. 62), *he displays much silver, and not a few cups of gold*.

Stătua ex aerĕ factast (*Cic.* II. Verr. II. 21. 50), *a statue was made of bronze*.

Qui ĕrat tōtŭs ex fraude et mendăciŏ factŭs (*Cic.* p. Clu. 26. 72), *who was made up entirely of roguery and lying*.

e. A change from one character to another, *from*: as,

Quaero ex tē sisne ex pauperrŭmō dīues factŭs (*Cic.* in Vat.

12. 29), *I ask you whether or no from being very poor you have become rich.*

Sic hŏmĭnes saepe ex fūcōsis firmī suffrāgātōrēs suādunt (*Q. Cic. de Pet.* 27), *in this way men often turn out firm from having been deceitful supporters.*

f. The preceding construction is also used to denote an intermediate condition : as,

Pallĭdum ē uĭrĭdī et mollē fŏlium hăbet (*Plin.* XXI. 90), *it has a palish green and soft leaf.*

g. Of, signifying part of, preceding the whole : as,

Nēmō ē dĕcem sānā mente est (*Cic. de Leg.* III. 10. 24), *not a man of the ten is of sound mind.*

Fūfĭus, ūnŏs ex meis intĭmīs (*Cic. ad Fam.* XIII. 3), *Fufius, one of my most intimate friends.*

h. The commencing point of time *whence* measurement proceeds, expressed by *from :* as,

Ex kălendis Iānuārīis ād hanc hōram inuĭgĭlāuī reipublicae (*Cic. Phil.* XIV. 7. 19), *from the first of January to the present hour I have kept a close watch upon the interests of the country.*

Ex eā diē septentriōnes uentī fuārē (*Cic. ad Att.* IX. 6. 3), *from that day the wind continued in the north.*

i. Immediate succession of time, *after :* as,

Ex consŭlātu est prŏfectŭs in Galliam (*Cic. Brut.* 92. 318), *immediately after his consulship he set out for Gallia.*

Oppĭdum ex ĭtĭnĕre expugnārē (*Caes. B. G.* II. 12), *to storm the town immediately on his arrival.*

Diem ex die expectābam (*Cic. ad Att.* VII. 26. 3), *I was waiting day after day.*

j. Source of information with verbs of asking, hearing, &c. : as,

Sēd ălĭquĭd ex Pompēiō sciam (*Cic. ad Att.* V. 2. 3), *but I shall learn something from Pompey.*

Hoc te ex ălĭīs audīrē mālo (*Cic. ad Att.* V. 17. 2), *this I prefer your hearing from others.*

Quaesŭī ex Phania, quam in partem prōuinciae pŭtāret tē uelle ut uĕnīrem (*Cic. ad Fam.* III. 6. 1), *I asked Phania into what part of the province he supposed you to wish me to come.*

k. Cause: as,

Grâuiter claudicâbat ex uolnĕre ob rempublicam acceptŏ (*Cic. de Or.* II. 61. 249), *he was very lame from a wound received in his country's service.*

Arctiūs ex lassĭtūdĭnĕ dormīsbant (*Cic. de Iuv.* II. 4. 14), *they were sleeping somewhat soundly from fatigue.*

l. That on which any thing depends physically or morally: as,

Vĭdētis pendēre ăliōs ex* arbŏrĕ, pulsārī autem ăliōs et uerbĕrārī (*Cic.* II. Verr. III. 26. 66), *you see some hanging from a tree, others again beaten and flogged.*

Ex quō uerbō tōta illă causă pendēbat (*Cic. de Or.* II. 25. 107), *on which word the whole of that cause depended.*

m. The authority upon which a person acts: as,

Ex sĕnātus consultō Manlius uincŭlis lĭbĕrātŭr (*Liv.* VI. 17), *under a decree of the senate Manlius is released from prison.*

Rēs ex fuedĕrĕ rĕpĕtunt (*Liv.* XXI. 10), *they demand redress under the treaty.*

n. The standard *by* which any thing is measured: as,

Nōn est ex fortūnā fĭdes pondĕrandă (*Cic.* Part. Or. 34. 117), *it is not by success that fidelity is to be measured.*†

Ex ēuentu hŏmĭnes de tuō consĭlio exīstĭmābunt (*Cic. ad Fam.* I. 7. 5), *the world will judge of your prudence by the result.*

o. As suggested by, *in accordance with*: as,

Stătuēs ūt ex fĭdē fāmā rĕque meā uĭdēbĭtŭr (*Cic. ad Att.* V. 8. 3), *you will decide as shall appear to be in accordance with my honour, character and interest.*

Te ex sententiā nāuĭgassē gaudeō (*Cic. ad Att.* V. 21. 1), *I am delighted that your voyage has been satisfactory.*‡

Piscis ex sententiā Nactŭs sum (*Ter. Ad.* III. 3. 66), *I have fallen in with a dish of fish to my heart's content.*§

---

* Very frequently *ab* is used with this verb.

† Literally 'weighed.'

‡ Literally 'that you have sailed according to your wishes or feeling.'

§ The phrase *ex mei animi sententia* is ambiguous, meaning either 'to my heart's content,' or 'on my word of honour' (literally 'according to the feeling of my heart'). Hence the pun in Cicero (*de Or.* II. 64. 260). *Nasica censori, quum ille—Ex tui animi sententia tu uxorem habes? —Non hercule, inquit, ex mei animi sententia.*

p. In proportion : as,

Făcĭt haerēdem ex deunciā Caecīnam (*Cic.* p. Caec. 6. 17), *he makes Caecina heir to eleven-twelfths of his property.*

Ex partē magnā tĭbi assentĭŏr (*Cic.* ad Att. vii. 3. 3), *I agree with you in a great measure.*

q. The quarter *on* or *at* which : as,

Vna ex partē Rhēnō contĭnentūr (*Caes.* B. G. i. 2), *on one side they are shut in by the Rhine.*

r. The liquid in which any thing more solid is dissolved, is preceded by ex : as,

Resinam ex melle Aegĭptiam* uorāto, saluom fēceris (*Plaut.* Merc. i. 2. 28), *take a bolus of Egyptian gum mixed in honey, and you will make it right.*

Cŭcŭmĕris silvestris pars intĕrĭŏr ex lactē . . diluitūr (*Cels.* v. 21. 1), *the inner part of a wild cucumber is dissolved in milk.*

[Ec], 6, ex in composition with verbs denotes—*a. out :* as, exĭmĕ- *take out*, exī- *go out*, ēgrĕdĭ- or ēgrĕdī- (r.) *march out*, ecfĕr- or effĕr- *carry out*, expōn-† *set forth*. *b.* removal by the act expressed in the simple verb : as, excanta- *remove by charms*, ēdormī- *sleep off*, ex- terrē- *frighten away*. *c. escaping* by means of the act expressed in the simple verb : as, ēsulta- *escape by moving on one side*, ēlucta- (r.) *get away by wrestling*, ecfŭg- or ecfŭgi- *escape by flight*. *d. obtaining an end* by the act of the simple verb : as, extŭd-† *hammer out*, ēuestīga- *trace out*, ēlăbōra- *work out*, exsēqu- *follow out, attain*. *e. publicity :* as, ēdīc-† *proclaim*, ēnuntia- *divulge*. *f. ascent :* as, ēmerg- *emerge*, ēueh- *carry up* or *raise*, exsist- *stand up*. *g. completeness :* as, ēdisc- *learn by heart*, exŭr- *burn up*, ēmērē- (r.) *complete one's service*. *h. change of character* with verbs formed from adjectives and substantives : as, expia- *make clean, atone for*, ec- fĕra- *make savage*, ecfēmina- *convert into a woman*. *i.* removal of what is expressed by the noun whence the verb is formed : as, exossa- *I bone* (as a fish), ēnōda- *I make smooth by removal of knots*. *j. the reverse :* as, explīca- *unfold*, exaugŭra- *deprive of a religious character*, exauctōra- *discharge* (i. e. relieve a soldier of the obliga-

---

* So Ms. B, not *Aegyptiam*.

† See § 431. 1.

‡ Perhaps immediately from the adjectives exossi- 'boneless,' enodi- 'without knots.'

tion expressed by the Latin auctōrāmento-). *k. distance*: as, exaudi- *hear in the distance* or *on the outside*.

1333 In adjectives formed from substantives this preposition denotes *absence*: as, ēnerui- *without muscle*, exsompnī- *sleepless*, extorri- (*for* exterri-) *banished*.

1334 Ergā with an accusative. *a. Facing* (very rare): as,

Tonstrīcem Suram Nouisti nostram, quae hās nunc ergā aedīs habet* (*Plaut.* Truc. II. 4. 51), *you know our coiffeuse Sura, who lives now facing this house.*

b. Towards (of friendly feeling): as,

Eōdem mōdo ergā amīcōs affectī sūmus quo ergā nosmēt ipsōs (*Cic.* de Am. 16. 56), *we are disposed in the same way towards friends as towards ourselves.*

c. Against (of unfriendly feeling, rare): as,

Quasi quid fīlius Meus dēliquisset mē ergā (*Plaut.* Ep. III. 3. 8), *as if my son had committed any offence against me.*

1335 Extrā.† *a. Without* (no motion): as,

Hī sunt extrā prōuinciam trans Rhŏdănum prīmī (*Caes.* B. G. I. 10), *these are the first people without the province on the other side of the Rhone.*

b. The same without a noun: as,

Extrā ēt intūs hostem habēbant (*Caes.* B. C. III. 69), *they had an enemy without and within.*

c. Metaphorically: as,

Extrā causam id est (*Cic.* p. Caec. 32. 94), *that is foreign to the question before us.*

Dīco omnia extrā culpam fuissĕ (*Cic.* II. Verr. v. 51. 134), *I affirm that all were blameless.*

Sed mehercŭlēs extrā iŏcum hŏmo bellūs est (*Cic.* ad Fam. VII. 16. 2), *but really without joking he is a pleasant fellow.*

d. Except: as,

Extrā dūcem paucosquē praetĕreā, rēlīquī in bellō rāpācēs, in ōrātiōnē crūdēlēs (*Cic.* ad Fam. VII. 3. 2), *except the chief*

---

* This reading is partly conjectural.
† For the preposition *ex, e,* see § 1331.

and a few besides, the rest were rapacious in the field, bloodthirsty in language.

Nēuē nāuigātō citrā Calicadnum extrā quam sī quī nāuis lēgātōs portābit (*Liv.* XXXVIII. 38), *neither shall he navigate the sea on this side of Calicadnus, always excepting the case of a ship carrying ambassadors.*

1336 In is used with the ablative and accusative; with the former when there is no motion,* with the accusative when there is motion.

In with the ablative denotes—*a. In*, in reference to place: as,

In eō conclāuī eī cūbandum fuit (*Cic.* de Div. II. 8. 20), *in that chamber he would have had to sleep.*

Attulit in cāueā pullōs (*Cic.* de Div. II. 34. 72), *he brought the chickens in a cage.*

In hortīs cum uīcīnō suō ambulābat (*Cic.* Acad. Pr. II. 16. 51), *he was walking in the park with his neighbour.*

b. On or over: as,

Nēmō eum unquam in equō sēdentem uīdit (*Cic.* II. Verr. v. 10. 27), *no one ever saw him on horseback.*

Equitāre in arundine longā (*Hor.* Sat. II. 3. 248), *to ride on a long reed.*

Pōns in Ibērō prope effectus erat (*Caes.* B. C. I. 62), *the bridge over the Ebro was nearly finished.*

c. Among: as,

Caesaris in barbarīs erat nōmen obscūrius (*Caes.* B. C. I. 61), *Cæsar's name was not well known among the barbarians.*

Exercitum in Aulercīs collocāuit (*Caes.* B. G. III. 29), *he quartered the army in the country of the Aulerci.*

d. Included in, part of: as,

Nihil praeter uirtūtem in bonīs dūcere (*Cic.* de Fin. III. 3. 10), *to look upon nothing but manliness as entitled to a place among blessings.*

Capitō in decem lēgātīs erat (*Cic.* p. Rosc. Am. 9. 26), *Capito was one of the ten deputies.*

e. In, in the sense of *within the range of*, but only in certain phrases: as,

* That is, no motion in relation to the noun; or rather, no motion from the *exterior* of it to its *interior*.

Cum in sōle ambŭlo, cŏlōrŏr (*Cic.* de Or. II. 14. 60), *when I walk in the sun, I get browned.*

Istă mŏdĕrătio ănĭmi in ŏcŭlis clărissĭmae prōuinciae atque in auribŭs omnium gentium est pŏsĭtă (*Cic.* ad Q. F. 1. 1. 2. 9), *that power of self-control you possess lies under the eyes of a most distinguished province, and within the hearing of all nations.*

f. In, denoting the position *in which* a person is, as regards the feelings of others: as,

Difficĭle est dictū, quanto in ŏdiō sīmŭs ăpŭd extĕrās nătiōnēs (*Cic.* p. Leg. Man. 22. 65), *it is difficult to say in what detestation we are held among foreign nations.*

Eă cīuĭtas tĭbi ūna in ămōrĕ fuit (*Cic.* II. Verr. IV. 1. 3), *that state was the special object of your affection.*

Ăpŭd eum sunt in hŏnōre ĕt in prĕtiō (*Cic.* p. Rosc. Am. 28. 77), *they are respected and valued by him.*

g. In, before persons, signifying *in the case of, in what concerns them:* as,

Respondit se id quŏd in Neruiis fēcĭssĕt factūrum (*Caes.* B. G. II. 32), *he replied that he would do the same as he had done in the case of the Nervii.*

Idem in bŏnō seruō dici sŏlet (*Cic.* de Or. II. 61. 248), *the same is commonly said of a good slave.*

h. Dressed in, wearing, armed with: as,

Pătĭbŭlo adfixŭs, in isdem ănŭlis quos gestābat (*Tac.* Hist. IV. 3), *fixed to the gallows with the same rings on, which he wore (when alive).*

Trĭfĭdă Neptūnŭs in hastā (*Val. Fl.* I. 641), *Neptune armed with a three-fanged spear.*

i. In respect of, in reference to: as,

Vexātŭr ăb omnĭbŭs in eō lĭbrō quem scripsit dē uĭtā beātā (*Cic.* Tusc. V. 9. 24), *he is attacked by all in reference to the book which he wrote on a happy life.*

j. A period of time *in the course of* which a thing happens is often preceded by In: as,

Vix tĕr in anno audīrĕ nuntium possunt (*Cic.* p. Rosc. Am. 46. 132), *they can receive news scarcely three times in the year.*

Hae res contrā nos făciunt in hōc tempŏrĕ (*Cic.* p. Quinct. I. 1), *these things make against us under present circumstances.*

Fere in diebus paúcis quibus haec ácta sunt Chrysis uicina haec mŏritur (*Ter.* And. I. 1. 77), *within a few days or so after this occurred, my neighbour here Chrysis dies.*

 k. The simple verbs of placing, such as pōs- *put,* lŏca- *place,* stătu- *set up* (even though motion be implied in them), take *in* with an ablative in the best writers, and that whether used in their simple sense or metaphorically : as,

  Tăbūlae testămenti Rōmam ĕrant adlātae, ŭt in aerărĭō pōnĕrentŭr (*Caes.* B. C. III. 108), *his will had been carried to Rome, that it might be deposited in the treasury.*

  Omnem cūram in sīdĕrum cognĭtiōnĕ pŏsuērunt (*Cic.* de Div. I. 42. 93), *they employed all their thoughts in the study of the stars.*

  Apud Pătrōnem te in maxŭmā grătiā pōsui (*Cic.* ad Att. v. 11. 6), *I have caused you to be in very high favour with Patro.*

1337 In with an accusative denotes—*a. Into :* as,

  Glădium hosti in pectŭs infixit (*Cic.* Tusc. IV. 22. 50), *he drove the sword into the enemy's breast.*

  Paene in fŏueam dēcĭdi (*Plaut.* Per. IV. 4. 46), *I all but fell into a ditch.*

  Inde ĕrat brĕuissĭmŭs in Britanniam trāiectŭs (*Caes.* B. G. IV. 21); *from thence was the shortest passage to Britain.*

 b. On to : as,

  Filium in hŭmĕros suŏs extŭlit (*Cic.* de Or. I. 53. 228), *he lifted his son on to his shoulders.*

  Dēiŏtărum in ĕcum sustŭlĕrunt (*Cic.* p. Deiot. 10. 28), *they lifted (the aged) Deiotarus on to his horse.*

 c. Among (with motion) : as,

  Cohortīs quinque in Ebŭrōnes misit (*Caes.* B. C. V. 24), *he sent five cohorts into the country of the Eburones.*

 d. The new form or character into which any thing is changed has *in* before it : as,

  Ex hŏmĭnĕ sē conuortit in bēluam (*Cic.* de Off. III. 20. 82), *he changes himself from a man into a beast.*

  Aquă mărina in dimidiam partem dēcŏquenda est (*Col.* XII. 24), *the sea-water must be boiled down to one-half.*

e. The object *on* which any thing is spent or employed : as,

Nullus těruncius insūmĭtūr* in quemquam (*Cic.* ad Att. v. 17. 2), *not a farthing is spent on any one.*

Māiōrem sumptum in prandium fēcērunt (*Cic.* II. Verr. iv. 10. 22), *they spent a larger sum on a breakfast.*

f. Direction of sight or thoughts *on* or *to* an object : as,

In quōios fortūnas nōn ŏcŭlos dēfīgit? (*Cic.* Phil. xI. 5. 10) *on whose property does he not fix his eye?*

In te ūnum sē tōtă convortet cīvĭtās (*Cic.* Somn. Sc. 2), *the whole body of citizens will turn their thoughts to you alone.*

g. Direction of power *towards* or *over* an object : as,

Vĭri in uxōres uĭtae nĕcisque hăbent pŏtestātem (*Caes.* B. G. vI. 19), *the husband has power of life and death over the wife.*

Nĕ tamdiū quidem dŏmĭnūs ĕrit in suŏs? (*Cic.* p. Rosc. Am. 28. 78) *shall he not even for this little time be master over his own people?*

h. Feeling *towards*, whether friendly or hostile (though more frequently the latter) : as,

Ad impiĕtātem in deōs, In hŏmĭnēs adiunxit iniūriam (*Cic.* N. D. III. 34. 84), *to impiety towards the gods he added outrage to man.*

Si fĕrae partūs suos dīligunt, quā nōs in lībĕros nostrōs indulgentia esse dēbēmūs? (*Cic.* de Or. II. 40. 168) *if wild beasts love their offspring, what ought to be our kindness towards our children?*

i. Purpose† (even though not attained), *for, to*: as,

Nullă pĕcūniă nĭsi in rem mīlĭtārem est dătă (*Cic.* p. Rab. Post. 12. 34), *no money was given except for military purposes.*

In hanc rem testem Sicīliam cĭtābo (*Cic.* II. Verr. II. 59. 146), *I will call Sicily itself as a witness to prove this fact.*

j. Tendency, sense of words, &c., *for, to, as* : as,

---

* Yet with *par-* and *consĭmĭ-* the best writers prefer *in* with the ablative.

† This usage was carried to a great extent by the later writers, but is more limited in Cicero, who instead of such a phrase as *in honorem alĭcuius*, would have said *honoris alĭcuius causa*. (See Madvig, Opusc. I. p. 167.)

Ego quaé in rem tuam sint, eâ uelim faciās (*Ter.* Ph. II. 4. 9), *as for me, whatever course may be for your interest, that I should wish you to adopt.*

In eam sententiam multā dixit (*Cic.* ad Att. II. 22. 2), *he said much to this effect.*

Haec in suam contūmēliam uertit (*Caes.* B. C. I. 8), *all this he interpreted as an insult to himself.*

k. Resemblance (resulting from an act), manner, form, *after*: as,

Pēditum agmēn in mōdum fūgientium ăgēbātūr (*Liv.* XXI. 41), *the infantry was hurrying along so as to look like a body of runaways.*

l. In distributions the unit is expressed by **in** and an accusative plural with or without the adjective **singulo**-, while the English is expressed by *every, each, the,* &c.: as,

Iam ad dēnārios quinquāginta in singulos mŏdiōs annōnā peruēnĕrat (*Caes.* B. C. 1. 52), *the price of corn had now reached to fifty denaries the bushel.*

Quingēnos dēnārios prētium in căpită stătuĕrant (*Liv.* XXXIV. 50), *they had fixed 500 denaries as the price per head.*

Tempŏra in hōras commūtāri uidēs (*Cic.* ad Att. XIV. 20. 4), *the state of things changes you see every hour.*

Vĭtium in dies crescit (*Cic.* Top. 16. 62), *vice increases every day.*

m. The future in phrases of time expressed by *for, until,* &c.: as,

Ad cēnam hŏminem inuĭtāuit in postĕrum diem (*Cic.* de Off. III. 14. 58), *he asked the man to dinner for the next day.*

Sermōnem in multam noctem prōduximus (*Cic.* Somn. Sc. 1), *we kept up the conversation until late at night.*

n. In some phrases denoting the position of a party, the verb *es- be* is used with **in** and an accusative, although no motion or change is expressed*: as,

Pulcerrŭmum dūcēbant ăb extĕris nātiōnĭbus quae in ămīcĭtiam pŏpŭlī Rōmānī dĭciōnemque essent, iniūrias prōpulsāre (*Cic.* in Caecil. 20. 66), *they deemed it a most glorious*

---

* This originated, says Madvig (Lat. Gr. § 230, obs. 2, note), in an inaccuracy of the pronunciation, where the distinction between the accusative and ablative rested on the single letter *m.*

duty to ward off outrage from foreign nations who stood in the relation of friends and vassals to the Roman people.

Quum uostros portūs in praedōnum fuissē pŏtestātem sciātis (*Cic.* p. leg. Man. 12. 33), *when your own harbours have been, you are aware, in the possession of pirates.*

1338 In when compounded with verbs* denotes—*a. into:* as, Inienter, Indūc-† *lead in. b. upon:* as, iniūg-† *place (as a yoke) upon*, indu- *put on*, indūc-† *draw on*, impĕra- *impose. c. against:* as, Infĕr- *carry against*, Illid- *dash against*, inuide- *look with envy at. d. at, over:* as, ingĕm- *groan at*, illăcrŭma- *weep over. e. privacy:* as, Inaudi- or Indaudi- *hear as a secret.* But see §§ 1308. 2, 1308. 3.

1339 Infrā denotes *below. a.* In regard to place, with or without a noun; as,

Argentum ad māre infra oppĭdum exspectābat (*Cic.* II. Verr. IV. 23. 51), *he was waiting for the silver by the sea-side below the town.*

Infrā nihil est nĭsi mortālĕ; sŭprā lūnam sunt aeterna omniă (*Cic.* Somn. Sc. 4), *below there is nothing but what is mortal; above the moon every thing is eternal.*

b. Of time: as,

Hŏmērus nōn infrā sŭpĕriōrem Lўcurgum fuit (*Cic.* Brut. 10. 40), *Homer was not of a later date than the elder Lycurgus.*

c. Of number: as,

Hiĕmĕ pauciōra oŭă sūbicĭtō, non tămĕn infrā nŏuēnă (*Plin.* XVIII. 26), *in winter you must place fewer eggs under them, not a smaller number however than nine at a time.*

d. Of magnitude: as,

Vrī sunt magnĭtūdĭnē paulo infrā ēlĕfantōs (*Caes.* B. G. VI. 28), *the urus in size is a little below the elephant.*

e. Of worth: as,

---

* *In* in the composition of adjectives signifies *not*, but has no connection with the preposition. On the other hand, verbs are never compounded with the negative *in*. *Ignora-* 'be ignorant' seems to be an exception, but only seems, for it is formed from the adjective *ignaro-*, which as an adjective was entitled to the negative prefix before the simple adjective *gnaro-*. Substantives compounded with *in* 'not' are at times found, but only in the ablative, as *iniussu* 'without permission.'

† See § 451. 1.

Infrā se omnia hūmāna dūcet (*Cic.* de Fin. III. 8. 29), *he will deem every thing human below him, i. e. unworthy his attention.*

1340 Intĕr denotes *between* or *among.* *a.* Of place : as,

Mons Iura est inter Sēquănōs ĕt Heluētiōs (*Caes.* B. G. 1. 2), *Mount Jura lies between the Sequani and the Helvetii.*

Inter sōbrios bacchāri uĭdētŭr (*Cic.* Or. 28. 99), *he seems to be acting Bacchus among sober people.*

b. Of time, *between, during* : as,

Dies quādrāgintā quinque inter bīnos lūdos tollentŭr (*Cic.* II. Verr. II. 52. 130), *forty-five days between the two festivals shall be struck out.*

Hoc inter cōnam dictāuī (*Cic.* ad Q. F. III. 1. 6. 19), *I have dictated this during dinner.*

c. Mutuality : as,

Inter se aspĭciēbant (*Cic.* in Cat. III. 5. 13), *they kept looking at one another.*

Cicĕrōnes puĕri āmant inter sē (*Cic.* ad Att. VI. 1. 12), *the young Ciceros are great friends.*

1341 Intĕr in composition with verbs denotes *between* : as, interpōs- *place between.* But see § 1342. 1.

1342 Intĕr is compounded with nouns forming both substantives and adjectives—*a.* with the sense *between* : as, interuallo- (n.) *the space between two stakes in a palisade, an interval,* intertignio- (n.) *the space between two beams,* internuntio- *a messenger who goes backwards and forwards between two people.* *b. within* : as, inter-cŭti- or -cŭt- *within the skin.* *c. between,* as regards time ; as, interlūnio- *the interval when no moon is visible.*

1342. 1 Inter—from in or ān *up* = *ana* (see § 834, and compare § 308. 1) —denotes *a. up* : as, intellĕg- *pick* or *gather up* (information), *perceive,* interturba- *stir up,* intermisce- *mix up.* *b. again* : as, interpŏla- *full* (cloth) *again, vamp up anew.* *c. reversal* of a preceding act : as, interīlĭg- *unyoke,* interquiesc- *repose after labour.* *d. separation, removal, disappearance* : as, interrūp- *break off,* intermīttlaue- *off* or *let out* (the fire), interclūd- *shut off,* intercīd- *fall away, escape,* interfrīg- *break off,* interārresc- *dry up,* interbĭb- *drink up,* interdīc- *forbid,* intermina- (r.) *warn off with threats.* *e.* especially of disappearance by death, as inter-fĭc- or -fĭci- *make away with, kill*, intĕrĭm- *take off, kill*, intĕri- *pass away, die*, inter-mŏr- or -mŏri- *die off*, internĕca- *kill off*, interfrīgesc- *die of cold* (hence *be neglected and so become obsolete*). *f. through*: as, inter-fŏd- or -fŏdi- *dig through*, interspīra- *breathe through*, inter-fŭg- or -fŭgi- *fly through*, interlūce- *and* interfulge- *shine through*.*

1343   Intrā denotes *within*. *a.* Of place without motion : as,

     Intrā părĭĕtes meos dē meā pernĭcĭē consĭlĭa ĭncuntŭr (*Cic.* ad Att. III. 10. 2), *plans are entered into within the walls of my house for my own destruction.*

     Antiŏchum intrā montem Taurum regnārē iussērunt (*Cic.* p. Sest. 27. 58), *they decreed that Antiochus should rule within Mount Taurus.*

   b. Of place with motion : as,

     Intrā portas compelluntŭr (*Liv.* VII. 11), *they are driven within the gates.*

   c. Metaphorically : as,

     Epŭlāmŭr ūnā non mŏdō non contrā lēgem sĕd ĕtiam intrā lēgem (*Cic.* ad Fam. IX. 26. 4), *we feast together not only not against the law, but even within it.*

     Quīdam phrĕnĕtĭci intrā uerbă dēsĭpiunt (*Cels.* III. 18), *some lunatics show the disease only in words.*

   d. Of number (particularly in regard to time), *within, during*: as,

     Intrā annos quattuordĕcim tectum non sŭbiĕrant (*Caes.* B. G. I. 34), *for fourteen years they had not passed under a roof.*

     Intrā paucos diēs oppĭdum căpĭtŭr (*Liv.* II. 25), *within a few days the town is taken.*

1344   Intrō *in* is used in composition with verbs of motion or direction : as, introi- *enter*, intrōdūc- *lead in*, intro-spic- or -spĭci- *look in*.

1345   Iuxtā† (root iŭg- *yoke, join*) denotes—*a.* Proximity of place, *close by*: as,

---

* This *inter* became soon in a great measure obsolete, so that many of the words belong exclusively to the older writers, Cato, Plautus, Lucretius. It may be useful to compare the meanings of this *inter* with those of *an* and its representatives, § 1308. 2.

† This word is scarcely to be met with in Cicero. In Tacitus it is very common.

Iuxtā mūrum castrā pōsuit (*Caes.* B. C. I. 16), *he pitched his camp near a wall.*

b. The same with motion, *nearly to :* as,

Iuxtā sēdītiōnem uentum (*Tac.* Ann. vi. 13), *matters came nearly to a sedition.*

c. Proximity of time, *immediately after :* as,

Nēque ēnim conuēnit iuxta inēdiam prōtīnus sătiētātem essē (*Cels.* II. 16), *nor indeed is it reasonable that immediately after fasting there should be a full meal.*

d. Nearness in quality, *akin to :* as,

Vēlōcĭtas iuxtā formīdinem est (*Tac.* Ger. 30), *speed is akin to fear.*

Eōrum ēgō ullam mortemquē iuxta aestŭmo (*Sal.* CaL 2), *the life and death of such men I look upon as much the same.*

e. Equality without a noun, *equally :* as,

Sōlō caelōquē iuxtā* griui (*Tac.* Hist. v. 7), *the soil and atmosphere being equally unhealthy.*

1346 Ob denotes—a. *Towards,* with motion (but only in very old writers) : as,

Ob Rōmam noctū lēgiōnes dūcĕrĕ coepit (*Enn.* ap. Fest.), *he began to lead the legions by night towards Rome.*

b. *Against, before,* with or without motion : as,

Follem sĭbi obstringĭt ob gŭlam (*Plaut.* Aul. II. 4. 23), *he binds a bladder before his mouth.*

Lānam ob oculum habēbat (*Plaut.* Mil. Gl. v. 1. 37), *he had a piece of wool over his eye.*

Mors et ŏb ŏcŭlos saepĕ uersātast (*Cic.* p. Rab. Post. 14. 30), *death often passed to and fro before his eyes.*

c. *Against, for,* in accounts, where money is set against the thing purchased, pledged, &c., or the thing purchased, &c. against the money : as,

A'ger obposĭtust pĭgneri Ob dĕcem mnas (*Ter.* Ph. iv. 3. 56), *my land has been put as a pledge against ten minæ,* i. e. *has been mortgaged for that sum.*

---

* In this sense a dative is found: as, *res parva se iuxta magnis difficilis* (*Liv.* xxiv. 19), 'a little matter, but equally difficult with great matters.'

Quin ărrăbōnem ā me ăccēpisti ob mŭlĭĕrem (*Plaut.* Rud. III. 6. 23), *nay you received from me earnest-money for the woman.*

Āĭt se ob ăsĭnos fērre argentum (*Plaut.* As. II. 2. 80), *he says that he has brought the money to pay for the asses.*

Est flăgĭtĭōsum ob rem iūdĭcandam pĕcūnĭam accĭpĕrĕ (*Cic.* II. Verr. II. 32. 78), *it is indeed a scandalous thing to take money for giving a verdict.*

d. A purpose or reason, *for*, *on account of*: as,

Haec ĕgo ad te ŏb eam caussam scrībo ut iam dē tuā quŏquĕ rătĭōnĕ mĕdĭtērĕ (*Cic.* ad Fam. 1. 8. 3), *all this I write to you with this object, that you may consider the course of proceeding you also should now adopt.*

Vērum id frustra ăn ob rem făcĭam, in uestrā mānū sĭtum (*Sal.* Jug. 31), *but whether I am doing this in vain or to some purpose, is in your hands, my friends.*

1347. Ob in composition with verbs signifies—*a. to, towards*: as, ŏbigo *to*, ostend- *hold out to*, occŭr-* *run to meet*. *b. before*: as, obambŭla- *walk before*, obuŏlīta- *keep flying before*, obuersa- (r.) *pass to and fro before*, obīĭne- *hold in the presence of* (an enemy). *c. shutting, obstructing*: as, obd- *put to*, obstru- *build up*, obsīde- *blockade.* *d. against* (physically): as, oblucta- (r.) *struggle against*, offend- *strike against.* *e. against* (morally): as, obnuntĭa- *bring an unfavourable report*, obtrecta- *depreciate*, ōbēs- *be injurious.* *f. upon*: as, occulca- *tread upon*, opprĭm- *crush*, obtĕr- *trample upon.* *g. covering, affecting the surface*: as, obdūc-* *draw over*, offŭd-* *pour over*, occalle- *grow hard on the surface.*

1348. Pălam *openly*, *publicly*, *in the presence of many*. *a.* With an ablative (or perhaps dative): as,

Indĕ rem crĕdītŏrī pălam pŏpŭlō soluit (*Liv.* VI. 14), *upon this he paid the money to the creditor in the presence of the people.*

b. The same without a case; as,

Arma in templum† lūce et pălam comportābantŭr (*Cic.* in Pis. 10. 23), *people were carrying arms into the temple in daylight and openly.*

1349. Pĕnĕs denotes—*a. In the hands of, in the possession of*: as,

---

* See § 451. 1.   † Al. *templo.*

Pĕnĕs eum est pŏtestās (*Cic.* ad Fam. IV. 7. 3), *the power is in his hands.*

Istaec pĕnes uos psaltriast ? (*Ter.* Ad. III. 3. 34) *is that singing-girl at your master's house?*

Serui centum dies pĕnĕs accusātōrem fuērĕ (*Cic.* p. Mil. 22. 60), *the slaves for a hundred days were in the custody of the accuser.*

Culpa tē'st penes (*Ter.* Hec. IV. 1. 20), *the fault lies with you.*

Pĕnes te ĕs ?* (*Hor.* Sat. 2. 3. 273) *are you in your senses?*

Pĕr denotes—*a. Through*, with motion : as,

It hastā Tāgō per tempŭs ŭtrumque (*Virg.* A. IX. 418), *passes the spear through Tago's either temple.*

Heluĕtii pĕr angustias suas cōpias transduxĕrant (*Caes.* B. G. I. 11), *the Helvetii had led their forces through the defile.*

b. Through, as seen through : thus,

Nātūrā membrānās ŏcŭlōrum perlūcidas fēcit ut pĕr eas cernī posset (*Cic.* N. D. II. 57. 142), *nature made the membranes of the eye transparent, that they might be seen through.*

Quod uidēbam equidem, sed quāsī per cālīgĭnem (*Cic.* Phil. XII. 2. 3), *which I saw all the time it is true, but only through a cloud as it were.*

c. When a similar thing occurs at consecutive points of a line : as,

Inuitati libĕrālĭter per dŏmōs (*Liv.* I. 9), *generously invited to all the houses*, i.e. *some to one, some to another.*

Quid hoc negotist quod omnes homines fābulantur pĕr uias ? (*Plaut.* Cist. v. 1. 1) *what is this business which all the world is talking about in every street of the town?*

d. Of time, *during, through, for* : as,

Tĕnuistī prōuinciam per dĕcem annōs (*Cic.* ad Att. VII. 9. 4), *you have clung to the province during ten years.*

Rŏgō tĕ nē tē uias pĕr hiĕmem committās (*Cic.* ad Fam. XVI. 8), *I beg you not to expose yourself to the danger of travelling during the winter.*

e. The means by which a thing is done, *through, by, by means of* : as,

* Compare this with a similar use of *apud* above.

Quŏd ădĕptŭs est per scĕlŭs, id per luxŭriam ĕcfundĭt (*Cic.* p. Rosc. Am. 2. 6), *what he has obtained through impiety, he is squandering in luxury.*

Quŏmĭnus discessĭō fĭĕrĕt pĕr aduorsărios tuŏs est factum (*Cic.* ad Fam. I. 4. 2), *it was owing to your opponents that a division did not take place.*

f. When the means employed are deceitful, *per* may be translated by *under.* In this case the nouns employed are such as spĕcie- *appearance*, nōmĕn- *name*, causa- *cause*, &c.: thus,

Per spĕciem ăliĕnae fungendae uĭcis suăs ŏpes firmăuit (*Liv.* I. 41), *under pretence of acting for another, he strengthened his own power.*

Aemŭlătiōnis suspectos per nōmĕn obsĭdum ămŏuĕbat (*Tac.* Ann. XIII. 9), *those suspected of rivalry he was endeavouring to get rid of under the name of hostages.*

g. When the agent does not act through any intermediate means, he is said (though incorrectly) to act through himself: as,

Quoscunquĕ nŏuis rĕbŭs ĭdōneos crēdĕbat, aut per se aut pĕr ălios sollĭcĭtăbat (*Sal.* Cat. 39. 0), *all those whom he thought well fitted for taking part in a revolution, he was working upon, either himself or by means of others.*

Nihĭl audactŭr ipsĭ per sĕsē sinē P. Sullā făcĕrĕ pŏtŭĕrunt (*Cic.* p. Sul. 24. 67), *they could do nothing daring of themselves without the aid forsooth of Publius Sulla.*

h. With phrases denoting *hindrance, &c.,* the point where the hindrance exists is expressed by *pĕr through*: as,

Vtrisque adpăruit nihil pĕr altĕros stărē quō mĭnŭs inceptă persĕquĕrentŭr (*Liv.* VI. 33), *to each nation it was evident that there was no obstacle on the part of the other to prevent them from carrying out their intentions.*

Per dūces, non per mīlĭtes stĕtĕrat, nē uincĕrent (*Liv.* III. 61), *it had been the fault of the generals, not the soldiers, that they had not conquered.*

i. With verbs denoting *permission* or *power*, the person who might have stood in the way is expressed by *pĕr*: as,

Dīglădientŭr illi per mē lĭcet (*Cic.* Tusc. IV. 21. 47), *they may fight it out for me,* i. e. *as far as I am concerned.*

Quam et per uălĕtŭdĭnem et pĕr anni tempus nāuĭgărĕ pŏtĕrĭs, ad nos uēnī (*Cic.* ad Fam. xvi. 7), *when both your health and the season of the year permit your sailing, come to us.*

j. By, in entreaties, to express the person or object in consideration of which the favour is asked*: as,

Pĕr ĕgŏ tē deōs ōro (*Ter.* And. v. 1. 15), *I entreat you by the gods.*

Pĕr ĕgŏ tē fīlī quaecunquĕ iūrĕ līberos iungunt pārentĭbus prōcor quaesōquĕ (*Liv.* xxiii. 9), *by all the ties, my son, which bind a child to a parent, I pray and entreat thee.*

k. Hence in oaths, *by:* as,

Iūrārem per Iŏuem Deosquĕ Pēnātis me eă sentīrĕ quae dīcĕrem (*Cic.* Acad. Pr. ii. 20. 65), *I would have sworn by Jupiter and the Household Gods that I really felt what I said.*

1351. Pĕr‡ in composition with verbs denotes—*a. through:* as, perdūc-† *lead through,* perflu- *flow through.* *b. completion:* as, perficor -fĭcĭ- *complete,* permīt-† *let go altogether, abandon* (to others), perōrā- *conclude a speech.* *c. destruction:* as, pĕri- *perish,* perd- [fordo], *destroy,* pĕrim- *kill*‖.

1352. Pĕr in composition with adjectives denotes—*a. through:* as, pernoct- *lasting all night,* peruigil- *awake all night,* pĕrenni- *lasting through endless years.* *b. very*¶: as, perlūcī- *very light,* permagno- *very great.* *c. destruction:* as, periūro- *violating an oath,* perfĭdo- *breaking faith.*

---

* This in fact is only another example of the *meaus* noticed in § *e.* A weak party approaches an offended superior through some third party; as for instance in Caesar, B. G. vi. 4, the Senones, in applying for his mercy, *adeunt per Aeduos.*

† Observe how the preposition is separated from its noun in these examples.

‡ In *expergisc-* (v.) 'wake up,' the preposition is *por,* the old form being *exporgisc-* i. e. *exporrigisc-.* Again in *porhibe-* the old form was probably *porhibe-.* Compare *perinde,* a corruption of *proinde* or rather *porinde.*

§ See § 451. 1.

‖ The *per* signifying *destruction* is perhaps of a different origin. At any rate it is the same as the German prefix *ver,* seen in *verthun* 'destroy;' and as our English *for,* seen in the obsolete *fordo* i. e. 'destroy,' *forswear, forget,* &c.

¶ The prefix *per* 'very' is often separated from the simple adjective: as, *per mihi mirum uisumst* (*Cic.* de Or. i. 49. 214), 'it seemed very wonderful to me.'

1353 Pōnĕ (closely connected with post) signifies *behind*. *a.* With a noun : as,

Pōne nos recēde (*Plaut.* Poen. III. 2. 34), *step back behind us.*

Vinctae pōnĕ tergum mănūs (*Tac.* Hist. III. 85), *his hands were bound behind his back.*

b. Without a noun : as,

Et ante et pōne, ĕt ad laevam ĕt ad dextram, et sursum et deorsum [mŏuēbātŭr] (*Cic.* de Un. 13 ad fin.), [*it moved*] *forward and backward, to the left and to the right, upward and downward.*

Pōnĕ sĕquens (*Virg.* A. x. 226), *following behind.*

1354 Post denotes *behind, after. a.* Of place : as,

Flūmĕn ĕrat post castrā (*Caes.* B. G. II. 9), *there was a river in the rear of the camp.*

Sĕd magnum mĕtuens sĕ post crātērā tĕgēbat (*Virg.* A. IX. 346), *but behind a vast bowl in his fear he hid him.*

b. The same without a noun : as,

Caedĕre incĭpiunt seruos qui post ĕrant (*Cic.* p. Mil. 10. 29), *they begin to cut down the slaves who were in the rear.*

c. Of time, *after, since :* as,

Post tuum discessum bīnās ā Balbō ; nihil nŏuī (*Cic.* ad Att. xv. 8), *since your departure two* (*letters*) *from Balbus ; no news.*

Hoc sexenniō post Vēios captos factumest (*Cic.* de Div. I. 44. 100), *this occurred six years after the capture of Veii.*

Post diem quintum quam barbări ĭtĕrum mălē pugnāuĕrant, lēgātī ā Bocchō uĕniunt (*Sal.* Jug. 102), *on the fifth day after the second defeat of the barbarians, an embassy from Bocchus arrives.*

d. The same without a noun : as,

Initiō meā sponte eum, post inuītātū tuō mittendum duxi (*Cic.* ad Fam. VII. 5. 2), *at first of my own motion, afterwards at your invitation, I thought it right to send him.*

Post paucīs diēbūs* ălios dĕcem lēgātōs addūxērunt (*Liv.* xL. 47), *a few days after they brought other ten ambassadors.*

Sĕnātus post paulō* de hīs rēbūs hăbĭtūs est (*Liv.* v. 85), *a senate was held soon after on this subject.*

* Or these may possibly be datives dependent upon post, as in *postibi*. Compare §§ 957, 958, and the use of *contra* with *eum*.

e. Metaphorically : as,

Vbi pĕrĭcŭlum aduĕnit, inuĭdia et sŭperbiă post fuĕrĕ (*Sal.* Cat. 23), *when danger approached, envy and pride fell into the rear.*

1355 Post in composition with verbs signifies—*a. after*, of place : as, postscrīb-* (*Tac.*), *write after. b. after*, of time : as, postfacto- *done afterwards,* postgĕnĭto- *born afterwards. c. after*, in importance : as, postpōn-* and posthăbe- *deem of secondary importance.*

1356 Prae denotes *before. a.* Of place : as,

Tĭbĕrim, prae se armentum ăgens, nandō trāiĕcit (*Liv.* 1. 7), *he swam across the Tiber, driving the herd before him.*

Stillantem prae sē pŭgiōnem tŭlit (*Cic.* Phil. 11. 12. 30), *he carried the dripping dagger before him.*

Also as an adverb : thus,

I prae (*Ter.* And. 1. 1. 144), *go first.*

b. The same metaphorically : as,

Cētĕrī tectiōrēs ; ĕgō semper me dīdicissē prae mē tŭlī (*Cic.* Or. 42. 146), *the others are more reserved; I ever avowed the fact that I once studied the subject.*

c. The cause (but chiefly in negative sentences), *for*: as,

Sōlem prae iăcŭlōrum multĭtŭdĭne non uĭdēbĭtĭs (*Cic.* Tusc. 1. 42. 101), *you will not see the sun for the number of darts.*

Nec lŏquī prae maerōrĕ pŏtuit (*Cic.* p. Planc. 41. 99), *and he could not speak for grief.*

Prae lassĭtūdĭne opus est ut lauem (*Plaut.* Truc. 11. 3. 7), *I am so fatigued I must take a bath.*

Crēdo prae ămōre exclusti hunc fŏrās (*Ter.* E. 1. 2. 18), *I suppose it was for love you shut him out.*

d. *In comparison with, by the side of*: as,

Rōmam prae suā Căpuā inrīdēbant (*Cic.* in Rull. 11. 35. 06), *they will laugh at Rome compared with their own Capua.*

1357 Prae in composition with verbs denotes—*a. before*: as, praemĭt-* *send in advance*, praebe- (*i. e.* praehĭbe-) *hold before*, *present*, praesta- *place* or *stand before. b. before*, in the sense of *passing by* : as, praeflu- *flow by*, praenāuĭga- *sail by. c. at the head of*, in com-

* See § 451. 1.

mand: as, prae&-*be in command,* prae-fic- *or* -fici- *place in command.* d. *at the extremity:* as, praerōd-* *gnaw at the end,* praeclūd-* *close at the end.* e. *superiority:* as, praesta- *and* praecell-* *surpass.* f. *before,* in time: as, praecerp- *gather too soon,* praedic-* *say beforehand,* praesāgi- *feel beforehand.* g. *the doing a thing first for others to do after:* as, prael-rē uerbā *to tell a person what he is to say,* prae-cīp- *or* -cipi- *teach,* praescrīb-* *enjoin by writing.*

1358 Prae in the composition of adjectives denotes—*a. before,* of place: as, praecīp- *or* praecīpit- *head-first.* b. *before,* of time: as, praescio- *knowing beforehand.* c. *at the extremity:* as, praeusto- *burnt at the end,* praeācūto- *sharp at the end.* d. *very:* as, prae-alto- *very deep,* praeclāro- *most glorious†.*

1359 Praetĕr denotes—*a. Passing by:* as,

Praeter castrā Caesăris suas cōpiās transduxit (*Caes.* B. G. 1. 48), *he led his own troops past Caesar's camp.*

Serui praetĕr ŏcŭlos Lolli haec omnia fĕrēbant (*Cic.* II. Verr. III. 25. 62), *the slaves kept carrying all these things along before the eyes of Lollius.*

b. *Beyond,* in amount or degree: as,

Lăcus praeter mŏdum crēuērat (*Cic.* de Div. I. 44. 100), *the lake had risen above its usual level.*

Hoc mihi praecīpuum fuit praetĕr illōs (*Cic.* p. Sul. 3. 9), *this belonged especially to me above others.*

c. *Besides,* I. e. *in addition to:* as,

Praeter sē dēnōs ad conlŏquium addūcunt (*Caes.* B. G. 1. 43), *they bring to the conference ten men each besides themselves.*

Praetĕr auctōritātem, uīrēs quŏque ad coercendum hăbēbat (*Caes.* B. C. III. 57), *besides the authority of a name, he had the physical means also for compulsion.*

d. *Except,* excluding: as,

---

* See § 451. 1.

† This formation is scarcely if at all found in Cicero; for *praeearius-* (II. Verr. IV. 48. 107) has been altered into *perearius-* by Zumpt on the authority of Mss.

‡ This signification and the last are not so opposite as may at first seem. Thus in *neque uestitus praeter pellis habent quicquam* (*Caes.* B. G. IV. 1), either translation is admissible without any difference of meaning. See also § 1233. 1.

Omnibus sententiis praetēr ūnam condempnātust (*Cic.* p. Clu. 20. 55), *he was found guilty by all the votes save one.*

Frūmentum omnĕ praeter quod sēcum portātūri ērant combūrunt (*Caes.* B. G. I. 5), *they burn up all the grain except what they purposed to carry with them.*

Prīmō clāmōre oppĭdum praetŏr arcem captum est (*Liv.* VI. 33), *at the first shout all the town but the citadel was taken.*

In the sense *except* praetĕr may be used like a conjunction, so as to be followed by a noun in the same case as some preceding noun:

Cētĕrae multĭtūdĭnī diem stătuit praeter rērum căpĭtālium dampnātis (*Sal.* Cat. 36), *he fixes a day for the rest of the multitude, except those convicted of capital offences.*

c. Contrary to: as,

Nihīl eī praetĕr ipsĭus uŏluntātem accĭdit (*Cic.* in Cat. II. 7. 16), *nothing happened to him contrary to his own wish.*

Multa impendērĕ uĭdentur praeter nātūram (*Cic.* Phil. I. 4. 10), *many things seem likely to happen out of the usual course of nature.*

1360 Praetĕr in composition with verbs signifies *passing by:* as, praetĕri- *go by,* praetermīt- *let go by.*

1361 Prō denotes—*a. Before,* of place: as,

Praesidĭā prō templīs omnĭbus cernĭtĭs (*Cic.* p. Mil. 1. 2), *you see troops before all the temples.*

Laudātī prō contiōne omnes sunt (*Liv.* XXXVIII. 23), *they were all commended in front of the assembled army.*

b. Before, with the notion of defending, *in defence of:* as,

Prō nūdātā moenĭbus pătriā corpŏra oppōnunt (*Liv.* XXI. 8), *in defence of their native city, now stripped of its walls, they present their bodies to the enemy.*

Egŏ prō sŏdāli et prō meā omnī fāmā dēcernō (*Cic.* de Or. II. 49. 200), *I am fighting the last battle for my friend and for my own character altogether.*

Haec contrā lēgem prōque lēgĕ dictā sunt (*Liv.* XXXIV. 8), *such were the arguments urged against and in favour of the law.*

c. In place of: as,

Lūbenter uerba iungēbant, ut sodes* prō sī audēs, sis prō sī uīs (*Cic.* Or. 45. 154), *they were fond of joining words, as* sodes *for* si audes, sis *for* si uis.

Quoi lēgātūs et prō quaestōrē fuerat (*Cic.* I. Verr. 4. 11), *under whom he had been lieutenant and proquaestor*, i. e. *deputy-quaestor*.

d. *Equivalent to, as good as, as, for :* as,

Prō occīsō rĕlictust (*Cic.* p. Sest. 38. 81), *he was left for dead.*

Cōnfessiōnem cēdentis hostis prō uictōriā hăbeō (*Liv.* XXI. 40), *the confession of a retreating enemy I look upon as a victory.*

Id sūmunt prō certō (*Cic.* de Div. II. 50. 104), *this they assume as certain.*

e. *In payment for, in return for, for :* as,

Mīsimus qui prō uectūrā soluěret (*Cic.* ad Att. I. 3), *we have sent a person to pay for the freight.*

f. *In consideration of, for :* as,

Hunc ămāre pro eius suāuitātē dēbēmūs (*Cic.* de Or. 1. 55. 234), *this man we ought to love for his own sweetness of character.*

Tē prō istīs factīs ulcīscăr (*Ter.* E. v. 4. 19), *I'll punish you for those doings.*

g. *In proportion to, considering, in accordance with :* as,

Proelium ătrōcius quam prō nŭmĕrō pugnantium ēditŭr (*Liv.* XXI. 29), *a fiercer battle is fought than could have been expected from the number of the combatants.*

Prō multĭtūdine hŏminum et prō glōriā belli angustōs hăbent finīs (*Caes.* B. G. I. 2), *considering the number of inhabitants and their military reputation, their territories are confined.*

Dĕcet, quidquid ăgās, ăgĕrĕ prō uīribŭs (*Cic.* de Sen. 9. 27), *it is right that whatever you do, you should do to the best of your power.*

Hīs raptim prō tempŏre īnstrūctīs (*Liv.* XXX. 10), *these men being hastily drawn up as well as the circumstances admitted.*

h. *For, in favour of :* as,

Hoc non mŏdō non prō mē, sed contrā me est pŏtius (*Cic.* de

---

* An error no doubt of Cicero's. Sodes must be for si uelis, l and d being interchanged, as in so many words; odor and olor, lacruma and dacruma, Vlixes and Olysses.

Or. 111. 20. 75), *this, so far from being for me, is rather against me.*

1362 Pŏr and prō in composition with verbs signify—*a. forward*: as, prōgrĕd- *or* prōgrĕdi- (r.) *advance*, porrĭg- *stretch out*, prōcŭr-* *run forward*. *b. out*: as, prōdi- *come forth*, prōsĭli- *leap out*. *c. to a distance*: as, prōfŭg- *or* prōfŭgi- *fly to a distance*, prōterre- *frighten off*, prōsĕqu- (r.) *follow for some distance*, prohĭbe- *keep off*. *d. downwards*: as, prōflīga- *knock down*, prōtĕr- *trample down*. *e. extension*: as, prōmīt-* *allow to grow long*. *f. publicity*: as, prōfĭte- (r.) *declare publicly*, prōmulga- *advertise (a law)*, proscrīb-* *offer a reward for the life of*, prōnuntia- *announce publicly*. *g. progress, profit*: as, prōfĭc- *or* prōfĭci- *make progress, advance*, prōdēs- *be of service*. *h. in place of*: as, prōcūra- *take care of in place of another*. *i. before*, in time: as, prōlud- *rehearse beforehand*. *j. postponement or continuation*: as, prōdīc-* *name a future day*, prōfĕr- *postpone*, prōrōga- *continue for a longer period (by enactment)*.

1363 Prō in the composition of adjectives denotes—*a. downward*: as, prōclīui- *downhill*. *b. negation*: as, prōfundo- *bottomless*, prōfāno- *not sacred, profane*.

1364 Prō in composition with nouns of relationship denotes greater distance, expressed in English by *great*: as, prōnĕpōt- *great-grandson*, prōāuo- *great-grandfather*, prōsŏcĕro- *wife's grandfather*.

1365 Prŏpĕt denotes *near*. *a.* Of place: as,

Ipsīus cōpiae prŏpe hostium castrā uīsae sunt (*Caes*. B. G. I. 22), *his own forces were seen near the enemies' camp*.

b. The same without a case, or with ăb and a noun : as,

Quis hic lŏquitur prŏpĕ ? (*Plaut*. Rud. I. 4. 11) *who is talking close by here?*

Bellum tam prŏpe ă Sĭcĭliā, tămĕn in Sĭcĭliā non fuit (*Cic*. II. Verr. v. 2. 6), *the war though so near Sicily, yet was not in Sicily*.

c. The same metaphorically : as,

Prŏpĕ sēcessĭōnem plēbis res uēnit (*Liv*. VI. 42), *matters came almost to a secession of the commonalty*.

---

* See § 451. 1.   † See also § 908.

d. *Near*, of time : as,

Prope adest quum alieno more uiuendumst mihi (*Ter.* And. I. 1.125), *the time is at hand when I shall have to live in accordance with another's ideas.*

1366 Propter (from prope) denotes—*a. Near*, with or without a case : as,

Propter Platonis statuam consedimus (*Cic.* Brut. 6. 24), *we took our seats near a statue of Plato.*

Duo filii propter cubantes ne senserunt quidem (*Cic.* p. Rosc. Am. 23. 64), *his two sons sleeping close by were not even aware of it.*

b. On account of, for, through : as,

Tironem propter humanitatem et modestiam malo saluom, quam propter usum meum (*Cic.* ad Att. VII. 5. 2), *I wish Tiro to recover more out of regard to the delicacy and modesty of his character than for any benefit to myself.*

Nam non est aecum me propter uos decipi (*Ter.* Ph. v. 7. 34), *for it is not reasonable that I should be a loser through you.*

1367 Re (or red) in composition with verbs signifies—*a. backward :* as, retrah- *drag back*, renuntia- *carry word back*, repet- *go back*, reformida- *draw back in fear. b.* hence *reflection* of light or sound : as, resona- *re-echo*, refulge- *shine brilliantly. c. in return :* as, rependo- *repay*, referi- *strike in return*, red-d- *repay. d. opposing an effort in the other direction :* as, retine- *hold back*, reuinci- *bind back*, retice- *keep back* (a secret). *e. refusal :* as, renu- *refuse by a shake of the head*, recusa- *make some excuse and so decline. f. reversing some former act :* as, rescid-* *cut down again* (that which has been erected), remit-* *let go again* (that which has been stretched), requiesco- *repose* (after labour), rescisc- *discover* (that which it has been attempted to conceal), recalesce- *grow warm again. g. reversing the act expressed in the simple verb†:* as, refig-* *unfix*, resigna- *unseal*, reclud- *open*, retog- *uncover*, resera- *unbolt. h. putting away from sight, concealing, sheltering :* as, relega- (*leave behind*), *banish far away*, recond- *put away into some secret place*,

---

* See § 451. 1.

† Hence the adjective recidiuo- 'rising again' shows that reuid- once signified 'rising again after falling or being felled,' as the new shoots from the stump of a chestnut- or oak-tree.

rĕ-cĭp- or -cĭpi- *receive and shelter. i. remaining behind* when the greater part is gone: as, rĕmănē- *remain behind*, rĕsĭdē- *remain still at the bottom. j. change of state:* as, red-d- *render, make,* rĕdĭg- *reduce to some state.* k. repetition:* as, rĕflōrēsc- *blossom a second time.*

Rĕtrō by the later writers is compounded with verbs of motion, and signifies *backwards:* as, rĕtrōgrădi- (r.) *march backwards* (*Plin.*).

Sē in the old writers is used as a preposition with the ablative, and signifies *separation or without:* as,

Si plus minus sēcuērunt, sē fraude estō (*XII. Tables*, ap. Gell. XX. 1), *if they cut more or less, it shall be without detriment (to them).*

Sē (or sĕd) in composition signifies—*a.* with verbs, *separation:* as, sēced- *withdraw*, sēpōn-† *put aside. b.* in adjectives, *absence:* as, sēcūro- *free from care,* sēcord- or sŏcord- *senseless, spiritless.*

Sĕcundum (*i.e.* sĕquendum, from sĕqu- (r.) *follow*) denotes—
a. Following: as,

I tū sĕcundum (*Plaut.* Am. II. 1. 1), *do you come after me.*

b. Along: as,

Lĕgiōnēs iter sĕcundum măre sŭpĕrum făciunt (*Cic.* ad Att. XVI. 8. 2), *the legions are marching along the upper sea.*

c. Behind, without motion: as,

Volnŭs accēpit in căpĭtĕ sĕcundum aurem (*Sulpic.* ad Cic. Fam. IV. 12. 2), *he received a wound in the head behind the ear.*

d. After, of time: as,

Spem ostendis sĕcundum cŏmĭtĭă (*Cic.* ad Att. III. 12. 1), *you hold out a hope of improvement after the elections.*

Sĕcundum uindēmiam (*Cato*, R. R. 114), *after the vintage.*

e. Second in order, next to: as,

Sĕcundum tē nihil est mihi ămīcius sōlĭtūdĭnē (*Cic.* ad Att. XII. 15), *next to you I have no better friend than solitude.*

---

* To this head belongs the use of *redi-* In such phrases as, *Iam res in eum rediit locum* (*Ter.* Haut. II. 3. 118), 'matters are at last come to this state;' *ad eum summa imperi redibit* (*Caes.* B. C. I. 4), 'the chief command will devolve on him.'

† See § 451. 1.

f. In accordance with: as,

Omnia quae secundum naturam fiunt sunt habenda in bonis (*Cic. de Sen. 19.71*), *every thing that happens in accordance with nature is to be reckoned among blessings.*

g. In favour of: as,

Pontifices secundum eum decreuerunt (*Cic. ad Att. iv. 2.3*), *the pontifical college decreed in his favour.*

1372 Sine denotes *without:* as,

Homo sine re, sine fide, sine spe (*Cic. p. Cael. 32.78*), *a man without money, without credit, without hope.*

Infero mari nobis nauigandumst, Ego iam cum fratre an sine? (*Cic. ad Att. viii. 3.5*) *we must sail along the lower sea. True; but just tell me, with my brother or without him?*

1373 Sub has for its original meaning *up,* as is seen in its derivatives the adjectives supero- *above,* summo- *highest,* the prepositions super *upon,* supra *above;* and above all in the use of sub itself in the composition of verbs*. It is found with both accusative and ablative.

1374 Sub with the accusative denotes—*a. Up to:* as,

Sub primam nostram aciem successerunt (*Caes. B. G. i. 24*), *they came up to our first line.*

b. Under, with motion: as,

Exercitus sub iugum missus est (*Caes. B. G. i. 7*), *the army was sent under the yoke.*

Totamque sub arma coactam Hesperiam (*Virg. A. vii. 43*), *and all Hesperia to arms compelled‡.*

c. Within reach of things from above (with motion): as,

Vt sub ictum uenerunt, talorum uis ingens effusa est In eos (*Liv. xxvii. 18*), *the moment they came within throw, an enormous quantity of missiles was showered upon them.*

Quod sub oculos uenit (*Sen. de Ben. i. 5*), *what comes within the range of the eye.*

* See § 1376. Indeed our own word *up* is the very same word as *sub;* and the Greek *hupa-* 'highest,' the title usually given to the Roman consul, is a superlative from the same root.

† The sense of *to* belongs to the accusative termination, and not to the preposition.

‡ Compare the common phrase without motion, *sub armis sum.*

Ea quae sub sensus subiecta sunt (*Cic.* Acad. Pr. II. 23. 74), *those things which are brought within reach of the senses.*

d. Subjection to dominion, *under* (with action) : as,

Sub pŏpŭli Rōmāni impĕrium cĕcĭdĕrunt (*Cic.* p. Font. 1, 12), *they fell under the dominion of the Roman people.*

e. In phrases of time, *immediately after;* and sometimes, though rarely, *just before:*

Sub eas littĕras stătim rĕcĭtātae sunt tuae (*Cic.* ad Fam. x. 16. 1), *immediately after these dispatches, yours were read out.*

Afrīcum bellum sub rĕcentem Rōmānam pācem fuit (*Liv.* XXI. 2), *the war with the Afri followed close upon the peace with Rome.*

Sŭb haec dicta omnes mănūs ad consŭles tendentes prōcŭbŭērunt (*Liv.* VII. 31), *immediately after these words they all prostrated themselves, stretching out their hands to the consuls.*

Quid lătĕt ut mărīnae Fīlium dīcunt Thētĭdis sub lăcrĭmōsā Trōiae Fūnĕră ? (*Hor.* Od. I. 8. 13) *why skulks he, as did sea-born Thetis' son they say on the eve of Troy's mournful carnage ?*

Sŭb with the ablative signifies—a. *Under* (without motion)* : as,

Sub terrā sempĕr hăbĭtāuĕrant (*Cic.* N. D. II. 37. 95), *they had always lived underground.*

Hostes sub monte consēdĕrant (*Caes.* B. G. I. 21), *the enemy were encamped under a mountain.*

b. *Within reach of things above* (without motion) : as,

Adprŏpinquāre nōn ausae nāues, nē sŭb ictū sŭperstantium in rūpĭbus pīrātārum essent (*Liv.* XXXVII. 27), *the ships did not dare to approach, lest they should be within shot of the pirates stationed above on the cliffs.*

Iam lūcescēbat, omniăquĕ sŭb ŏcŭlis ĕrant (*Liv.* IV. 28), *it was now getting light, and all that was passing below was visible.*

c. Inferiority, subjection (without action), *under:* as,

---

* *Under* with motion is at times expressed by the ablative; for instance, when the mind dwells upon the state that follows rather than the act, or when other prepositions are added to signify the precise motion. Thus, *sub terra uiui demissi sunt in locum saxo conseptum* (*Liv.* XXII. 57), 'they were let down alive into a stone chamber underground.'

Mātris sŭb impĕriost (*Ter.* Haut. II. 3. 4), *she is under her mother's rule.*

Vir impĭgĕr et sŭb Hannĭbălē măgistro omnis belli artis ēdoctūs (*Liv.* XXV. 40), *a man of energy, and who had been thoroughly instructed in the art of war under Hannibal.*

d. In conditions, *under:* as,

Iussit ei praemium tribui sŭb eā condĭcĭōnē nē quid posteā scrībĕret (*Cic.* p. Arch. 10. 25), *he ordered a reward to be given him, under the condition that he should never write again.*

e. In phrases of time—*during, in, just at:* as,

Nē sŭb ipsā prŏfectĭōnē mīlĭtēs oppĭdum ĭrrumpĕrent, portās obstruit (*Caes.* B. C. I. 27), *that the soldiers might not burst into the town during the very embarkation, he builds up the gates*.

1376 Sŭb in composition with verbs denotes—*a. up:* as, subaeh-*carry up* (as a river), sŭm- (*i. e.* sŭblm-) *take up*, surg- (*i. e.* surrig-) *rise*, subdūc-† *draw up*, sustine- *hold up*. *b. under:* as, sŭbes- *be under*, subiāce- *lie under*, submerg- *sink*. *c. assistance:* as, subuĕni- *come to assist*, succŭr-† *run to assist*. *d. succession:* as, succin- *sing after*, succlāma- *cry out after*. *e. in place of:* as, sufflo- or suffĭci- *appoint in place of*, suppō-† *put in place of*, substĭtu- *set up in place of*. *f. near:* as, sŭbes- *be at hand*, subsĕqu- *follow close after*. *g. underhand, secretly:* as, surrip- or surrĭpi-*snatch away secretly*, sŭborna- *equip secretly*, subdūc-† *withdraw quietly*. *h. in a slight degree:* as, subride- *smile*, sŭbaccusa- *accuse in a manner*. *i. abundance‡:* as, sufflo- or suffĭci- and suppĕt- *be abundant.*

1377 Sŭb in the composition of adjectives denotes—*in a slight degree:* as, sŭbobscūro- *rather dark*, subfusco- *dusky.*

1378 Subtĕr is used generally with an accusative, rarely with an ablative, often without a noun. It signifies—*a. Under:* as,

Iram in pectŏrĕ, cŭpĭdĭtātem subter praecordiă lŏcăuit (*Cic.*

---

* Compare the use of *sub* with an accusative in phrases of time.
† See § 451. 1.
‡ This sense is connected with that of *sub* 'up.' Compare the opposite, defic- or defĭci- 'be low, wanting.'

Tusc. I. 10. 20), *anger he placed in the breast, desire under the midriff.*

Ferre iuuat subter densa testudine casus (*Virg. A. IX. 514*), *they glory beneath the close array of shields to bear each chance.*

Omnia haec, quae supra et subter, unum esse dixerunt (*Cic. de Or. III. 5. 20*), *all these bodies, which are above and below, form one whole they said.*

b. Metaphorically, *in subjection, under:* as,

Virtus omnia subter se habet (*Cic. Tusc. V. 1. 4*), *virtue holds every thing in subjection to her.*

1379 Subter in composition with verbs signifies—*a. under:* as, subterlab-* *glide underneath.* *b. secretly:* as, subterduc-* *withdraw secretly.*

1380 Super is followed both by an ablative and an accusative. With an ablative it signifies—*a. Over* (without motion): as,

Destrictus ensis cui super impia Ceruice pendet (*Hor. Od. III. 1. 17*), *o'er whose unholy neck a drawn sword hangs.*

b. *Upon* (without motion): as,

Poteras requiescere mecum Fronde super uiridi (*Virg. Buc. I. 80*), *thou mightest have reposed with me upon green leaves.*

c. *Concerning:* as,

Quid nuncias Super anu ? (*Plaut. Cist. IV. 1. 7*) *what news do you bring about the old woman ?*

Vellem cogites quid agendum nobis sit super legatione (*Cic. ad Att. XIV. 22. 2*), *I wish you would consider what we must do concerning the embassy.*

1381 Super with an accusative denotes—*a. Upon* (with motion): as,

Imprudens super aspidem assidit (*Cic. de Fin. II. 18. 59*), *unwittingly he sits down upon an asp.*

Alii super uallum praecipitantur (*Sal. Jug. 58*), *others are thrown headforemost upon the stakes.*

b. *Above* in order (as at table): thus,

Nomentanus erat super ipsum (*Hor. Sat. II. 8. 23*), *Nomentanus lay above him.*

* See § 451. 1.

c. *Beyond* (but with a notion of greater height*): as,

Proxĭmē Hispānĭam Maurī sunt, sŭper Nŭmĭdĭam Gaetŭlī (*Sal.* Jug. 10), *next to Spain are the Moors, beyond Numidia the Gætuli.*

d. *More*, in amount: as,

Sătis sŭperquā dictumst (*Cic.* N. D. II. 1. 2), *enough and more than enough has been said.*

e. *Besides:* as,

Pūnĭcum exercĭtum sŭper morbum ĕtĭam fămēs affēcit (*Liv.* XXVII. 46), *the Punic army, besides sickness, suffered severely also from famine.*

1382. Sŭpĕr in composition with verbs signifies—*a. over:* as, sŭperuěnĭ- *pass over*, sŭpĕrēmĭne- *project above*, sŭperfŭd-† *pour over*. *b. abundance:* as, sŭpĕrā- *abound*. *c. remaining over, survival:* as, sŭpĕrĕs- *remain over, survive*. *d. in addition:* as, sŭpĕraddŭo-† *bring in addition*.

1383. Sŭprā denotes—*a. Upon*, with motion: as,

Sub terrā hăbĭtābant nĕque exĭĕrant unquam sŭprā terram (*Cic.* N. D. II. 37. 95), *they lived underground, and had never come out above the ground.*

Et saltū suprā venābŭlā fertur (*Virg.* A. IX. 553), *and with a bound he flies upon the spears.*

b. *Upon*, in contact with: as,

Nēreĭdes sŭprā delphīnos sĕdentēs (*Plin.* H. N. XXXVI. 5. med.), *Nereids seated upon dolphins.*

c. *Over*, at some distance above: as,

Ecce sŭprā cǎpŭt‡ hŏmo lĕvis ac sordĭdus, sed tămĕn ĕquestri censū, Cătĭēnŭs; ĕtĭam is lenĭētŭr (*Cic.* ad Q. F. I. 2. 2. 6), *see, there is ready to pounce down upon my head a fellow devoid of principle and honour, but yet of equestrian station, I mean Catienus. Even he shall be appeased.*

---

* For example, in the instance quoted Sallust used the word because they were farther from the sea, and therefore probably higher.

† See § 451. 1.

‡ Dr. Butler (Latin Prepositions, p. 121) has given this passage to prove that *supra caput* means 'exceedingly.' He connects it with *levis*, though the words are separated by *homo*.

d. *Above*, in order (as at table) : thus,

Accŭbuĕram ăpŭd eum et quidem sŭprā me Attĭcŭs, infrā
Verrĭŭs (*Cic.* ad Fam. IX. 20. 1), *I had just sat down to dinner at his house, and by the way Atticus sat next above me, Verrius below.*

e. *Above*, in amount: as,

Caesa eō diē sŭprā milĭă uīgintī (*Liv.* XXX. 35), *there were slain on that day above twenty thousand.*

Etsī haec commĕmŏrātĭō uĕreor nē sŭprā hŏmĭnĭs fortūnam
essĕ uīdeātŭr (*Cic.* de Leg. II. 16. 41), *and yet what I am going to mention will be thought, I fear, to exceed the lot of man.*

f. *In addition to, over and above, besides:* as,

Sŭprā bellī Săbīnī mĕtum id quŏque accessĕrat (*Liv.* II. 18), *besides the fear of a Sabine war, there was this further trouble.*

g. In reference to former times, *before:* as,

Paulō sŭprā hanc mĕmŏrĭam seruī ūnā crĕmābantŭr (*Caes.* B. G. VI. 19), *a little before the times which those now living can recollect, the slaves (of the deceased) used to be burnt with him.*

h. In referring to a preceding part of a book or letter, *above:* as,

Vt sŭprā dēmonstrāuĭmŭs (*Caes.* B. G. VI. 34), *as we have shown above.*

Tĕnŭs (from tĕn- or tend- *stretch*), which always follows its noun, signifies *reaching to*, and is used—*a*. With an accusative (very rarely) : as,

Rēgĭō quae uirgĭnĭs aequŏr ăd Helles
Et Tănaïn tĕnŭs immensō descendit ăb Eurō (*Val. Fl.* 1. 537),
*The region which to the maiden Helle's sea
And far as the Don from the vast East descends.*

b. With an ablative of the singular, particularly with words in *a* or *o**: as,

Antĭŏchus Taurō tĕnŭs regnārĕ iussust (*Cic.* p. Deiot. 13. 30), *it was ordained that Antiochus should rule only as far as the Taurus.*

c. With an ablative of the plural (very rarely) : as,

---

* This form was probably at first an accusative, *Taurom*.

Pectŏrĭbusquĕ tĕnus mollĕs ērectōs in auras
Nārĭbūs et pătŭlō partém mărīs suŏmĭt ōre (*Ov. Met.* xv. 512),
*Chest-high upraised into the moving air
From wide-spread mouth and nostrils vomits out
One half the sea.*

d. With a genitive of the plural, particularly in the consonant declension ; as,

Et crŭrum tēnŭs ā mentō pălĕārĭā pendent (*Virg. G.* iii. 53),
And leg-deep from the chin the dewlap hangs.

1385   Trans signifies—*a. On the other side of*: as,

Cōgĭto interdum trans Tĭbĕrim hortōs ălĭquos părărĕ (*Cic.* ad Att. xii. 19. 1), *I think at times of purchasing some park on the other side of the Tiber.*

b. To the other side of: as,

Trans Alpīs transfertŭr (*Cic.* p. Quinct. 3. 12), *he is carried to the other side of the Alps.*

1386   Trans in composition signifies *across*: as, transmĭt-† *or* trāmĭt-*send across*, transi- *go across*.

1387   Vorsŭs (uorsum, uersūs, uersum) signifies *direction*: as,

Brundŭsĭum uorsŭs ĭbās (*Cic.* ad Fam. xi. 27. 3), *you were going in the direction of (or towards) Brundusium*‡.

1388   Vorsŭs is also used in conjunction with the prepositions Ad and In : as,

Ad ōcĕănum uersus prōfĭcisci iŭbet (*Caes.* B. G. vi. 33), *he orders him to set out in the direction of the ocean.*

In Ĭtălĭam uorsus nāuĭgātūrūs ĕrat (*Sulpic.* ad Cic. ad Fam. iv. 12. 1), *he was about to sail towards Italy.*

1389   Vls *on the other side of*, with an accusative (but rarely used) : as,

Sācra ūt uls et cis Tĭbĕrim fiunt (*Varr.* L. L. iv. 15), *sacrifices are offered both on yonder and on this side of the Tiber.*

1390   Vltrā denotes—*a. On the other side of, beyond* : as,

Vltrā Sĭlĭānam uillam est uillŭlă sordĭda et ualdē pŭsillă (*Cic.* ad Att. xii. 27. 1), *on the other side of Silius' country-house is a cottage of mean appearance and very small.*

---

* See also § 803. † See § 451. 1.
‡ See also § 798.

b. *To the other side of, beyond:* as,

Paulo ultrā eum lŏcum castrā transtŭlit (*Caes.* B. C. III. 66), *he moved the camp to a spot a little beyond that place.*

c. Metaphorically : as,

Sunt certi dēnĭquĕ fīnes
Quōs ultrā citrāquĕ nĕquit consistĕrĕ rectum (*Hor.* Sat. I. 1.106),
*There are in fine fixed limits
Beyond and short of which truth cannot halt.*

Nōn ultrā hēmīnam āquae assūmit (*Cels.* IV. 2. 4), *he takes not more than a pint-and-a-half of water.*

d. The same without a noun : as,

Estne ăliquid ultra, quŏ prōgrĕdi crūdēlĭtas possit ? (*Cic.* II. Verr. v. 45. 119) *is there any thing beyond this to which bloodthirstiness can go ?*

In the examples already given, it has been seen that prepositions are at times placed after their nouns, although their name implies the contrary*. In the old language this appears to have been the case with perhaps every preposition, and the practice prevailed to the last in some legal phrases. It may further be observed that—*a.* The preposition cum is always placed after the ablatives of the personal pronouns: as, mēcum, tēcum, sēcum, nōbiscum, uōbiscum, and for the most part after the ablatives of the simple relative : as, quōcum, quācum, quicum, quĭbuscum. *b.* The prepositions tĕnŭs and uorsŭs always follow their case. *c.* The disyllabic prepositions generally are more apt to occupy the second place than those which are monosyllabic. *d.* The relative†, and the pronoun ho- *this*, when it occurs at the beginning of a sentence, have a tendency to throw the preposition behind them.

---

* It may be useful to compare the meaning of the term *case* with that of the term *preposition.* They both denote primarily the relations of place. They are both so intimately connected with the noun as to be pronounced with it, and even written with it, although printers have as regards prepositions abandoned the authority of the best inscriptions and manuscripts. Thirdly, as the case-ending is always added as a suffix, so also in the old language was the preposition. Hence there is no original distinction, either in essence or form, between a case-ending and a preposition. These considerations may perhaps tend to create in the mind a clearer notion of what a case is.

† This explains the form *quaed,* as compared with *ades,* and also *quamobrem, quemadmodum, quocirca.*

e. When an emphatic adjective or genitive accompanies a noun, this emphatic word commonly comes first, and is immediately followed by the preposition, which must then be considered as an enclitic attached to it, and should be pronounced accordingly.

1392. The preposition is occasionally separated from its noun. The words which may come between are included for the most part under the following heads : *a.* an adjective belonging to the noun ; *b.* a genitive belonging to it; *c.* an adverb or case attached to that noun when it is a gerund or participle ; *d.* the enclitics nē, quē, uē, although in the case of the monosyllabic pronouns the noun as well as the preposition commonly precede these enclitics*; *e.* the conjunctions which commonly occupy the second place in a sentence, as autem, ĕnim, quĭdem, tămĕn, uĕrō.

1393. The preposition may attach itself to the adjective in place of the substantive, or even to a genitive which depends upon the substantive, and the substantive itself be removed to a distance ; or, lastly, the preposition occasionally is found before the verb†.

1394. Whether a preposition is to be repeated or not before each of two nouns, is to be decided by the intimacy of the connection between them. When that intimacy is close, the nouns may be considered as one, and a single preposition will be sufficient. Thus, the Aulerci and Lexovii being close neighbours in the map of Gallia, one preposition is enough in—

> Exercĭtum ĭn Aulercis Lexŏuiisquĕ conlŏcāuit (*Caes.* B. G. III. 20), *he posted the army in the country of the Aulerci and Lexovii.*

1395. On the other hand, if the nouns be looked upon as very distinct, two prepositions are requisite : as,

> Sătis ĕt ad laudem ĕt ăd ūtĭlĭtātem prŏfectum arbĭtrātŭr (*Caes.* B. G. IV. 19), *he thinks that sufficient progress has been made both for glory and for utility*‡.

---

* See §§ 836, 837.

† As, *dum longus inter saeuiat Ilion Romanosque pontus* (*Hor.* Od. III. 3. 37).

‡ Hence the preposition *inter* is often repeated: as, *interest inter animum fortuito entegressas et inter omnes naturalis* (*Cic.* de Fat. 9. 19). So also *Cic.* de Fin. 1. 9. 30, Parad. 1. 3. 14.

1396 When the antecedent and relative are dependent upon the same preposition, the preposition may for brevity's sake be omitted in the relative clause, if the verb be not expressed: as,

> Mē tuae littĕrae nunquam in tantam spem adduxērunt, quantam illōrum (*Cic.* ad Att. III. 19. 2), *as for myself, your letters have never led me to entertain so strong a hope as those of other friends.*

1397 If two prepositions have a common noun, that noun must be repeated in Latin (except in the case of those disyllabic prepositions which are used adverbially): as,

> Hoc non mŏdŏ non prō mē, sed contrā me est pŏtiūs (*Cic.* de Or. III. 20. 75), *this, so far from being for, is rather against me.*

ADVERBS.

1398 An adverb, as its name implies, is commonly attached to a verb, and usually precedes it; but if the adverb is emphatic, it may commence or end the whole sentence; or if unemphatic, it may occupy the non-emphatic, that is, the second place* in a clause.

1399 An adverb may of course be used with participles, and this usage is sometimes retained by them even when they have become virtually substantives: as, facto- (n.), dicto- (n.), responso- (n.), &c. Thus,

> In ŏdium addūcentŭr aduorsăriī, sī quŏd ēorum sŭperbē, crūdēlĭter, mălĭtĭōsē factum prŏfŏrētŭr† (*Cic.* de Inv. I. 10. 22), *the opposite parties will be brought into discredit, if any tyrannical, cruel, or spiteful act of theirs be brought forward.*
> Suī nēgōtī bĕnē gĕrens (*Cic.* p. Quinct. 19. 62), *a good manager of his own affairs.*
> Pol mĕī patris bĕne părta indīlĭgentĕr Tŭtātur (*Ter.* Ph. v. 3. 5), *faith he takes poor care of what my father earned so creditably.*

1400 An adverb often accompanies adjectives and adverbs, but is rarely found with substantives, and perhaps only under one of the

---

* See § 1473.

† Observe that if *factum* had not been a substantive, the pronoun must have been *quid*, not *quod*. See § 306.

two conditions: a. that the substantive shall be in apposition; b. that it shall be interposed between a substantive and its adjective or dependent genitive: as,

    a. Mārius septǐmum consul dŏmī suae est mortuŭs (*Cic.* N. D. III. 32. 81), *Marius in his seventh consulate died at his own house.*

    Pŏpŭlus, lātē rex (*Virg.* A. I. 21), *a city that ruleth far and wide.*

    b. E't heri semper lēnitas uerēbar quorsum euāderet (*Ter.* And. I. 2. 4), *and master's constant gentleness, I was afraid what it would end in*.*

    Omnes circā pŏpŭlī (*Liv.* XXIV. 3), *all the states around.*

1401   Adverbs are used in some phrases with the verb es- *be*, when an adjective or participle might have been expected: as,

    Vtī nēquē uos cāpiāmīnī ēt illī frustrā sint (*Sal.* Jug. 85), *that you may not be deceived, and that the other party may be disappointed.*

    Aput ustōrēs dicta impūne ērant (*Tac.* Ann. I. 72), *among our ancestors mere words were unpunished.*

    Vēliae fuī sānē lŭbentēr ăpud Talnam nostrum (*Cic.* ad Att. XVI. 6. 1), *at Velia I was indeed most comfortable at our friend Talna's.*

NEGATIVE PARTICLES.

1402   The simplest form of the Latin negative is ne†. On the other hand, nōn has some other element added to the simple negative, and is therefore more emphatic. Hence nōnī is used with the

---

* Even here it is far from certain that *semper* does not belong to *uerebar*.

† The same is the form of the English negative as it appears in our old writers. It also enters into the formation of *never* from *ever*. The particle enters into the formation of many Latin words: as, nĕquí- 'be unable,' nĕfas, nĕfaste-, nĕfario-, nĕfando-, nĕuis 'thou wilt not,' in which it is short; and the following with a long ē, nēue, nēdum, nēmon- nĭquam, nĕquitiĕ-, nēquaquam, nēquiquam. Other words into which *ne* enters are nunquam, nāliquam, neuter (old form ne-cuter), as also the phrase ne minus. See also § 761.

‡ Non may possibly be formed from ne and unum, just as our English *no* is a corruption of *none*, i. e. *ne one*. Compare the German *nein* from *ne ein*. Indeed the old Latin writers use the form *nenu*, which seems more clearly to be a contraction of *ne unum*.

indicative, and with the subjunctive when a result is expressed, in which case the subjunctive evidently assumes the meaning of the indicative*.

1403 When nōn affects a single word in a sentence, it precedes it; when it affects a whole sentence, it commonly precedes the verb. Occasionally, in order that it may have great emphasis, nōn is placed at the beginning of a sentence, or at the beginning of the predicative part of a sentence, and in these cases it often becomes difficult to give a translation which shall not greatly alter the order of words† : as,

Nōn hos pălus, non silvas mŏrantŭr (*Caes.* B. G. vi. 35), *no marsh, no woods restrain them.*

1404 In sentences containing a main verb of thinking or saying, the negative, which really belongs to the infinitive mood, is at times for emphasis placed before these main verbs : as,

Nōn existŭmāuit suis similibus prŏbāri possē se esse hostem pătriae, nĭsī mihi esset inĭmīcŭs (*Cic.* Phil. II. 1. 2), *he thought that the men of his own stamp could never be satisfied he was a public enemy to his country, unless he was a private enemy of mine*‡.

1404.1 Nĕ, haud (hau), nōn, are all proclitics§. Hence the form of the verbs nesci-, hausci- (so in Ritschl's Plautus); and hence such an order of words as :

Vt iam liceat ūnā conprehensiōne omniă complecti, non-dūbĭtantemquĕ dicĕre, omnem nātūram essĕ scrutātricem sui (*Cic.* de Fin. v. 9. 26, ed. Madvig), *so that we may now in-*

---

* In the same way the French use the strengthened negatives, *ne..pas, ne..point, ne..rien*, in such phrases as *je n'irai pas, je n'irai point, je ne vois rien*, &c., where the particles *pas, point, rien*, severally represent the Latin nouns *passum, punctum, rem*. On the other hand their subjunctive mood commonly takes a simple *ne*.

† In the commencement of Horace's Satire (I. 6), *Non quis Maecenas &c. naso suspendis adunco Ignotos*, the negative is separated from the verb to which it belongs by nearly five lines.

‡ In the same way the Greeks use the order οὐκ ἔφη, although the negative belongs to the following infinitive. In Latin also *nega-* probably owes its formation to the same principle, the negative in this word too belonging always to the accompanying infinitive.

§ So also οὐκ (οὐ) is commonly a proclitic; and similarly our *not* (cánnot, knów-not) is an enclitic.

clude all in one general assertion, and without hesitation say
that nature is always self-preserving.

1405 Between nĕ* and quidem the word (or words, if intimately
connected) on which the emphasis lies is always interposed: as,

Egō ne ūtīlem quidem arbĭtrŏr essĕ nōbis fŭtūrārum rērum
scientiam (*Cic.* de Div. II. 9. 22), *for my part I do not think
it even expedient for us to know the future.*

Nē sī cŭpiam quidem (*Cic.* in Pis. 28. 68), *not even if I desired it.*

1405. 1 Besides *not*—*even*, the ordinary meaning of nĕ—quidem, it is
sometimes to be translated *neither*†: as,

Nē Vărius quidem dŭbĭtat cōpiās prōdūcĕrĕ (*Caes.* B. C. II. 33),
neither does Varius hesitate to lead out his forces.

Huic ut scĕlus, sic nē rătĭō quidem dēfuit (*Cic.* N. D. III. 28. 68),
*as this woman (Medea) was not deficient in villany, so neither
was she in wit.*

Si illud, hoc; nōn autem hoc; Igĭtur ne illud quidem (*Cic.* de
Fin. IV. 19. 55), *if that be true, then this must be so; but this
is not true; consequently neither‡ is that.*

1406 Where in English the conjunction *and* is followed by a negative pronoun or adverb, the Latin language commonly prefers nĕquĕ accompanied by an affirmative pronoun or adverb: as,

Nĕque ex castris quisquam discessĕrat (*Sal.* Cat. 30), *and not a
man had left the camp.*

Nĕque ullam sŏciĕtātem confirmāri posse crēdidi (*Cic.* Phil. II.
35. 89), *and I thought that no alliance could be ratified.*

Nĕque est usquam consĭliō lŏcŭs (*Cic.* de Off. II. 1. 2), *and there
is nowhere room for deliberation.*

1406. 1 In writers after the Augustan period nĕc often has the power
of *not even*: as,

Pătris iussā nec pŏtuissĕ fīlium dētrectārĕ (*Tac.* Ann. III. 17),
*the orders of a father it was not even in the power of a son to
decline (let alone the will).*

---

* As *quidem* is itself a word of strong affirmation, it was enough to use
the simple negative *ne*.

† In German *auch nicht*. See Madvig ad Cic. de Fin. p. 816.

‡ This distinction has been thoroughly established by Madvig (ibid.),
who has dealt with all the apparent exceptions in Cicero, Sallust, &c.

.... Nec puĕri crēdunt, nĭsī qui nondum aerĕ lăvantur (*Juv.* II. 152), (*all this*) *not e'en our bairns believe, save those, Who for the penny-bath are yet too young.*

Sed nec Tĭbĕrĭō parcit (*Suet.* Oct. 86), *but not even Tiberius does he spare.*

1407 Similarly an intention to prevent any thing is expressed in Latin by nē and an affirmative pronoun or adverb, although the English often uses the conjunction *that*, followed by a negative pronoun or adverb: as,

Ut dăret ŏpĕram nē quŏd his collŏquium inter se esset (*Liv.* XXIII. 34), *that he should take care that they should have no conference with each other.*

Dispŏsĭtīs explōrātōrĭbus nēcūbi Rōmāni cōpias transdūcĕrent (*Caes.* B. G. VII. 35), *scouts being placed at different points, that the Romans might not lead their forces over at any point.*

Tū tămĕn eās ĕpistŏlas concerpĭtō nēquandō quid ēmānet (*Cic.* ad Att. x. 12. 3), *you however will tear up those letters, that nothing may ever ooze out.*

1408 On the other hand, where a result is denoted, the conjunction ūt is employed with the negative pronouns, &c.: as,

Tantīs impĕdĭōr occūpātĭōnĭbŭs ut scrībendī făcultās nullă dĕtŭr (*Cic.* ad Fam. XII. 30. 1), *I am hindered by so many engagements, that I have no opportunity of writing.*

Obuiam mihi sic est prōdĭtum, ut nihil posset fĭĕrī ornātĭūs (*Cic.* ad Fam. XVI. 11. 2), *they came out to meet me in such a manner, that nothing could be more complimentary*.

1409 But when the negative affects a single word, *and not* is expressed by et nōn: as,

Vĕtŭs et nōn ignōbĭlis dīcendī măgistĕr (*Cic.* Brut. 91. 315), *an old and not unknown professor of oratory.*

* Thus in the following tables the words in the first column belong to clauses of purpose, those in the second to clauses of result:

ne . . . . ut non.	ne quando .	ut nunquam.
ne quis . } ut nemo.	ne unquam	
ne quisquam	ne-cubi . .	ut nusquam.
ne quid } ut nihil.	ne ullus .	ut nullus.
ne quidquam		

Incrēdībĭlĭs ănĭmŭs et nōn ūnĭus uĭrī uīrēs (*Cic.* p. Mil. 25. 67), *a spirit past belief, and a power of work such as no single man ever had.*

1409. ¶ Again, when *and not* introduces an idea directly opposed to what precedes, *et nōn* or *ac nōn* are required: as,

Illī iŭdĭces, sī iŭdĭcēs, et non parrĭcīdae pătriae nōmĭnandī sunt (*Cic.* p. Planc. 29. 70); *those jurymen, if indeed they are to be called jurymen, and not rather parricides of their fatherland.*

Quăsī uĕrō mē tuo arbĭtrātu, et non meō grātum esse ŏportĕat (*Cic.* p. Planc. 29. 71), *as if forsooth your opinion and not my own ought to decide the measure of my gratitude.*

Quid tū fēcisses, sī tē Tărentum et non Sămărŏbrĭuam mīsissem ? (*Cic.* ad Fam. VII. 12) *what would you have done, if I had sent you to Tarentum, instead of Samarobriva ?*

Nullă res rectē pŏtest admĭnistrārī, sī ūnusquisquē uĕlit uerbă spectāre, et nōn ad uŏluntātem ēius qui eă uerba hăbuĕrit accēdĕrē (*Cic.* de Inv. II. 47. 140), *nothing can be executed properly, if every separate person is to look to the words only, instead of complying with the intention of him who used those words.*

Non dīcĕrem, sī puĕrī esse illam culpam, ac non pătris exĭstĭmārem (*Cic.* II. Verr. III. 68. 159), *I should not have said so, if I had thought that was the boy's and not the father's fault.*

Plūrĭbus uerbis ad tē scrībĕrem, sī res uerbă dēsīdĕrāret, ac non prō se ipsā lŏquĕrētŭr (*Cic.* ad Fam. III. 2. 2), *I should have written to you at greater length, if the subject had needed words, and not itself spoken in its own behalf.*

Quī pŏtes rĕpĕrīre ex eō gĕnĕre hŏmĭnum qui te ăment ex ănĭmo ac non sui commŏdī causā sĭmŭlent ? (*Cic.* ad Q. F. I. 1. 5. 15) *how are you to find men of that class who love you sincerely, instead of pretending to do so for their own advantage ?*

1410   The adjective *nullo-* and the indeclinable noun *nihil* are occasionally used emphatically for *nōn* and *nē* : as,

Nihil nĕcessest (*Cic.* ad Att. VII. 9. 6), *there is no necessity.*
Sextŭs ăb armis nullus discēdit (*Cic.* ad Att. XV. 22), *Sextus has not a thought of laying down the sword.*

1411   An accumulation of negatives is common in Latin, so as to produce a strong emphasis (but attention must be paid to the position of *non* in such phrases*): as,

   a. Non nihil ūt in tantīs mălīs est prŏfectum (*Cic.* ad Fam. XII. 2. 2), *some progress has been made, considering the very unhappy position we are in.*

   Pŏpŭlus sŏlet non nunquam dignos praetĕrīrĕ (*Cic.* p. Planc. 3. 8), *the citizens are wont at times to pass by the worthy.*

   Sē non nollē dixit (*Cic.* de Or. II. 18. 75), *he said he was no way unwilling.*

   b. Tuum consĭlium nēmō pŏtest non laudārĕ (*Cic.* ad Fam. IV. 7. 2), *the course you are pursuing no one can avoid praising.*

   Aperte ădūlantem nēmō non uĭdet (*Cic.* de Am. 26. 99), *a man who openly flatters, every one sees through.*

   Nihil nōn aggrĕdientŭr hŏmĭnēs (*Liv.* IV. 35), *men will attack any thing.*

1412   After a general negative, a second negative may be introduced under either of the following circumstances — *a.* when some word or phrase is made emphatic by being placed between *nē* and *quidem*; and *b.* when the main clause is divided into two or more, of which each has its own negative† : as,

   a. Aduentus noster nēmĭnī nē mĭnūmō quĭdem fuit sumptui (*Cic.* ad Att. V. 14. 2), *our arrival was not even the least expense to any one.*

   Nōn ēnim praetĕreundumst ne id quĭdem (*Cic.* II. Verr. 1. 60. 155), *for we must not pass over even this.*

   b. Sic hăbeas nihil tē mihi nec cārĭŭs essĕ nec suāuĭŭs (*Cic.* ad Att. V. 1. 5), *be assured that there is nothing either dearer or sweeter to me than yourself.*

---

* Thus,

non nihil = aliquid.	nihil non = omnia.
non nemo } = aliquis.	nemo non = omnes.
non nullus }	nullus non = omnis.
non nunquam = aliquando.	nunquam non = semper.
non nusquam = alicubi.	nusquam non = ubique.

Similarly *non modo —, non tantum —*, mean ' so much and more besides ;' whereas *modo non —, tantum non —*, mean ' something just short of —.'

† Occasionally a double negative with the power of a single negative occurs through carelessness: as, *quos non miseret neminis*, ' who don't pity no one.' (*Cato* ap. Fest. v. *nemini*.)

1413   After clauses containing words compounded with nĕ, a second
clause is sometimes introduced which requires that the affirmative
notion*, instead of the negative, should be supplied : as,

Nĕgant Caesărem in condĭcĭŏnĕ mansūrum, postŭlātăque haec
ăb eo interpŏsĭta essĕ, quŏmĭnŭs ā nōbis părārētŭr (*Cic.* ad
Att. vii. 15. 3), *they say that Caesar will not abide by the
terms, and that these demands have been put forward by him
to prevent our making preparations.*

Nēmo extŭlit eum uerbis qui ĭtă dixisset ut qui ădessent in-
tellĕgĕrent quid dicĕret, sed contempsit eum qui mĭnŭs id
făcĕrĕ pŏtuisset (*Cic.* de Or. iii. 14. 52), *no one ever extolled
a man for speaking so as to make himself intelligible to those
present, but all despise one who is unable to do so*†.

1414   A negative will often extend its influence over a second clause
attached to the first by aut or uĕ : as,

Nĕquĕ consistendi aut ex essĕdis dēsĭliendī făcultātem dĕdĕrunt (*Caes.* B. G. v. 17), *nor did they give (them) an opportunity of halting or leaping down from their war-chariots.*

Nōn ŭbĭuis cōrămuŏ quĭbuslĭbĕt (*Hor.* Sat. i. 4. 74), *not any
where or before any people.*

1414.1   A negative prefixed to two clauses may be used to deny not
each separate clause, but the combination. Thus in the following
example each of the three negatives affects what has been included
for the nonce in brackets.

Nōn ĕnim (dixi quĭdem sed non scripsi), nec (scripsi quidem sed
nōn ŏbii lēgătiōnem), nĕc (ŏbii quidem sed non persuāsi Thē-
bānis) (*Quint.*‡ ix. 38. 55), *for you must not suppose that I
spoke, and then abstained from writing; or that I wrote indeed,
but took no part in the embassy; or that I did take part in the
embassy, yet failed to persuade the Thebans.*

* *i. e.* for *nega-* 'deny,' *dic-* 'say ;' for *nol-* 'be unwilling,' *uol-* 'wish ;'
for *nemo* 'no one,' *omnes* 'all.' As regards *neque-* see § 1404. Compare
too *Hor.* Sat. i. 1-5, *nemo ... uiuat, laudet* (i. e. *omnes laudent*); Liv.
xxvi. 2, *nemo memor esset, praesidio mollis essent*; Plaut. Trin. iii. 2. 62,
nolo ... , sei ...

† Observe that *nemo extulit* has caused *contempsit* to be an aorist as
well as a singular, though a plural present is required by the sense.

‡ Translating Demosthenes p. Cor. c. 55.

1415 The negative in nē — quidem, when followed by a common predicate, often extends its influence over a preceding clause beginning with non mŏdŏ or non sŏlum : as,

> Amentātiō non mŏdŏ ămīcō sed nē līběrō quidem dignast (*Cic. de Am.* 24. 80), *flattery is unworthy not merely of a friend, but even of a freeman.*
> Sĕnātuī non sŏlum iŭuāre rempublĭcam, sed nē lūgēre quidem licuit (*Cic. in Pis.* 10. 23), *the senate were forbidden not merely to assist, but even to mourn over their country*".

1416 In imperative sentences, and in subjunctive clauses dependent upon ŭt or nē, nēuĕ is used rather than nĕquĕ or et nē : as,

> Suis praedixĕrat ut Caesăris impĕtum excipĕrent nēuĕ sē lŏcō mŏuērent (*Caes. B. C.* III. 92), *he had told his men beforehand to wait for Caesar's attack, and not move from their ground.*
> Hŏmĭnem mortuom in urbĕ nēuĕ sĕpĕlītō nēue ŭrĭtō (apud *Cic. de Leg.* II. 23. 58), *neither bury nor burn a corpse in the city.*

1416.1 Haud *not* (in old writers often hau) is used chiefly before adjectives and adverbs, but also in the phrase haud scio or hau scio *I know not.*

INTERROGATIVE PARTICLES.

1417 The simplest interrogative particle is the enclitic nĕ, which is affixed to that particular word on which the question turns, whether verb, substantive, adjective or particle : as,

> Pŏtestnĕ uirtus, Crassĕ, seruirĕ ? (*Cic. de Or.* I. 52. 226) *is it possible, or is it not possible, Crassus, that virtue should be a slave?*
> Apollinemnĕ tū Dēlium spŏliāre ausŭs ĕs ? Illĭnĕ tū templō tam sanctō mănūs impiās afferre cōnātŭs ĕs ? (*Cic.* II. *Verr.* I. 18. 47) *was Apollo of Delos the god whom you dared to despoil? Was that the temple with all its sanctity on which you attempted to lay your unholy hand?*

" It is in such passages as these that non modo is said to be used for non modo non. The distinction is well seen in *Cic. p. leg. Man.* 13, 39 : Quoius legiones sic in Asiam peruenerunt, ut non modo manus tanti exercitus, sed ne uestigium quidem quoiquam pacato nocuisse dicatur. ... Non modo ut sumptum faciat in militem nemini uis adfertur, sed ne cupienti quidem quoiquam permittitur.

Núllon egó Chrométis pacto adfínitatem effúgere potero ? (*Ter. And.* I. 5. 12) *is there no way in which I shall be able to escape a marriage into Chremes' family ?*

A. Quid coeptás Thraso ? *B.* Egóne ? (*Ter.* E. v. 7. 1) *A. What are you after, Thraso ? B. What am I after ?*

Sicine ágis ? (*Ter.* Ad. I. 2. 48) *is this the way you act ?*

Ilicone crédere ea quae dixi oportuit te ? (*Ter.* E. v. 6. 11) *if you must needs believe what I said, ought you to have done so at once ?*

1418   A question is often asked without any interrogative particle : as,

Rógitas ? Nón uides ? (*Ter.* E. iv. 4. 8) *do you ask ? Don't you see ?*

Néquoo te exoráre ut maneas tríduom hoc ? (*Ter.* Ph. III. 2. 4) *can I not prevail upon you to wait the next three days ?*

Clódius insídias fécit Milóni ? (*Cic.* p. Mil. 22. 60) *did Clodius waylay Milo ?**

1419   In direct† questions the particle num commonly implies the expectation of an answer in the negative, and nonnĕ one in the affirmative : as,

Num facti piget ? Num eiús color pudóris signum usquam indicat ? (*Ter.* And. v. 3. 6) *is he sorry for his conduct ? No. Does his cheek show any sign of shame ? No.*

Quid cănis, nonnĕ simĭlis lŭpō ? (*Cic.* N. D. I. 35. 97) *well and the dog, is he not like the wolf ? Of course he is.*

1420   In simple indirect questions (not commencing with an interrogative pronoun‡) nŭ is commonly employed, sometimes num : as,

Videamus primum, deōrumnĕ prōuidentiā mundus rĕgātur ; deindĕ, consūlantnĕ rebūs hūmānis (*Cic.* N. D. III. 25. 65), *let us consider first whether the universe is governed by the foresight of the gods ; secondly, whether they provide for the welfare of man.*

Spŏcŭlāri iussi sunt, num sollicitāti ănimi sŏciōrum a rēge

---

* In many of these cases it would be perhaps better to consider the words as an assertion either put ironically or in the name of the other party. Thus, 'Clodius waylaid Milo, you say.'

† See § 1134 and note.

‡ Such as qui-s, ubi, unde, quo, quando, &c.

ēssent (*Liv.* XLII. 19), *they were directed to be on the look-out to find whether the king had been tampering with the allies.*

1421 The particle ăn is not used in the simple direct question; and in the simple indirect the best writers seldom use it except in the phrases nescio ăn, haud scio ăn, dŭbĭto ăn, incertum ăn : as,

> Est id quidem magnum atque haud scio an maxĭmum, sed tĭbi commūnĕ cum multis (*Cic.* ad Fam. IX. 15. 1), *true, that is an important matter, and I would almost venture to say the most important of all, but still it is common to you with many.*
>
> Hoc dĭiūdĭcārī nescio an numquam*, sĕd hoc sermōnĕ certĕ non pŏtest (*Cic.* de Leg. I. 21. 50), *the decision of this point I am strongly inclined to think can never take place, but certainly not through the present conversation.*
>
> Mŏriendum certe est, ĕt id incertum ăn hōc ipsō diē (*Cic.* de Sen. 20. 74), *die we must, some time or other, and possibly this very day.*

1422 The use of sī (and sī fortĕ) in indirect questions is very rare, except in phrases where *hope* or *expectation* is expressed or implied (*if perchance*) : as,

> Expectābam sī quid de eō consĭlĭō ad mē scrībĕrēs (*Cic.* ad Att. XVI. 2. 4), *I was waiting to see whether you would write any thing to me about this plan.*
>
> Circumfunduntūr ex rēlĭquis partĭbus, sī quem ădĭtum rĕpĕrīrĕ possint (*Caes.* B. G. VI. 37), *they pour round on the other sides, in hopes they may find some place to enter at.*

1423 The term *disjunctive question* is used to denote those cases where one or more alternatives are added (which in English are preceded by the word *or*). The forms used, alike for direct and indirect questions, are the four which follow : *a.* ŭtrumt ———,

---

* In many of the ordinary editions the negative in these phrases has been deprived of its first letter. Thus Ramshorn, p. 710, quotes *nescio an ulli* from *Cic.* ad Fam. IX. 9. 2, though the best Mss. have *nulli*. See Orelli's edition. So also *Cic.* ad Att. IV. 3. 2.

† *Num* is limited in its use to the simple question. Yet at times it appears to be used in disjunctive questions, because at the close of that simple question which alone was intended at starting, it suddenly occurs to the writer (see § 1426) to draw attention to the absurdity of some alternative, which he attaches as usual by the particle *an*. See Madvig's Opusc. II. 230.

ăn* ——; b. —— nĕ, ăn ——; c. ——, ăn ——; d. ——, —— nĕ: as,

a. Utrum nescis quam altē ascendĕris, an prō nihilo id pŭtas? (Cic. ad Fam. x. 26. 3) *which is the right explanation of your conduct; that you do not know to what a high station you have risen, or that you set no value upon it?*

Id ĭgĭtŭr, ŭtrum hāc pĕtītiōne an proxŭmā praetor fīās (Cic. ad Fam. x. 26. 2), *the question is this, whether you are to be praetor this election or next.*

b. Eā ferarumne ăn hōmĭnum causā gignĕrē uidētŭr? (Cic. N. D. II. 62. 156) *is it for the wild-beasts think you or for man that it (the earth) produces these things?*

Quaero eum, Brūtūnĕ sĭmĭlem mālīs, ăn Antōnī (Cic. Phil. x. 2. 5), *I ask whether you would wish him to be like Brutus or Antony.*

c. Sortiētŭr, an nōn? (Cic. Prov. Cons. 15. 37) *shall he cast lots or not?*

Postrēmō, fŭgĕre an mănēre tūtius fŏret, ĭn incerto ĕrat (Sal. Jug. 38), *lastly, whether to fly or stay were the safer, was a matter of doubt.*

d. Sunt haec tuā uerbă, necnĕ †† (Cic. Tusc. III. 18. 41) *are these your words or are they not?*

Nihĭl intĕressĕ nostrā pŭtāmus, ualeāmŭs aegrīnĕ sīmŭs (Cic. de Fin. IV. 25. 69), *it makes no difference to us we think, whether we are well or ill.*

1424 The forms, —— nĕ, —— nĕ; ăn ——, ăn ——, are found in the poets (and but rarely elsewhere): as,

Qui tĕneant orās, hŏmĭnēsnĕ fĕraene,
Quaerĕrŏ constĭtuit (Virg. A. I. 312),
*Who occupy the borders, men or beasts,
He resolves to ask.*

---

* Care must be taken not to confound with disjunctive questions those in which, although the English language uses the same particle, there is really no opposition between the parts, but all may be equally denied or affirmed, so that *aut* and not *an* must be interposed: as, *quid ergo, solem dicam aut lunam aut caelum deum?* (Cic. N. D. I. 30, 84) 'what then, shall I apply the name of god to the sun, or to the moon, or to the sky?'

† *Ne* in the second part of a direct question is rare, and perhaps limited in the best writers to the form *necne*. So *utrum* ——, *necne* occurs in an indirect question. The Pseudo-Nepos has *utrum* ——, *natresne*, &c.

Saepĕ mănūs ŏpĕri tentantēs admŏuĕt, an sit Corpŭs ăn illŭd ĕbur (Ov. Met. 10. 254), *oft his hands he moveth to the work, trying whether that before him be flesh or ivory.*

1425 The old construction with ŭtrum has after it —— nĕ, ăn —— : as,

Vtrúm, studĭone id sibi habet an laudi putat Fore, si perdiderit gnătum? (Ter. Ad. III. 3. 28) *does he look upon this as an amusement, or does he think it will be a credit to him, if he ruin his son?*

Vtrum ĕrat ūtĭlius, suismĕ seruire an pŏpŭlō Rōmāno obtempĕrărĕ? (Cic. II. Verr. IV. 33. 73) *which was the more expedient course, to be slaves to countrymen of their own, or to meet the wishes of the Roman people?**

1426 It has been seen that ăn is the particle ordinarily used before the second part of a question. Hence ăn (or an uĕrō) is well adapted for those cases where a statement is immediately followed by the alternative put in the form of a question: as,

Nĕcessest quicquid prōnunties, id aut esse aut nōn esse. An tū diălecticis nē imbūtus quidem ĕs? (Cic. Tusc. I. 7. 14) *what you put forward must needs either be or not be. Or are you not acquainted with even the A B C of logic?†*

Ad mortem tē Cătĭlīnă dūci iampridem ŏportēbat—an uĕrō Scipiō Graccum priuātūs interfĕcit, Cătilinam nos consŭles perfĕrēmŭs? (Cic. in Cat. I. 1. 3) *death, Catiline, ought long ago to have been your fate—or does any one really pretend, that when Scipio, though a private man, slew Gracchus, the consuls of Rome are to tolerate Catiline?*

Nōs hic te exspectāmŭs ex quōdam rūmōre, ăn ex littĕris tuis ăd ălios missis (Cic. ad Att. I. 3. 2), *we meanwhile are ex-*

---

* The particle *ne* is at times added to the interrogative pronouns and also to the particles *num* and *an*: as, *quine*, *quone*, *quantusne*, *ubine*, *utrumne*, *numne*, *anne*. But care must be taken to distinguish those elliptical phrases where the relative and not the interrogative pronoun precedes *ne*. Thus, *Ter.* Ph. v. 7. 29: De. *Argĕntum iube reserībi*. Ph. *Quodne egŏ discripsi porro illis quibus debui?* De. '*Order the money to be repaid.* Ph. What, the money which I paid away forthwith to those creditors I spoke of?' And again, *Ter.* And. IV. 4. 29: *Quemne egŏ heri uidi ad uŏs adferri uĕsperi?* 'What, the child which I myself saw being carried to your house yesterday evening?'

† Which must be the case if you deny my proposition.

pecting you here on the authority of some rumour, or (am I right?) letters of yours to some other people.*

1427   An answer in the affirmative may be expressed by ĕtiam, Ită or Ita est, sic or sic est, uĕrum, uĕrŏ, factum, sānĕ, maxŭmē, quidnī ?, admŏdum, oppĭdŏ, plānē, &c., by a personal pronoun with uĕrō, or lastly by the verb of the preceding sentence repeated :† as,

Hăccin tua domūst? Ita (*Plaut*. Am. 1. 1. 206), *is this your house? Yes.*

Nŏuī ūbi quidnam scrībam ?—quid ?—ĕtiam (*Cic.* ad Att. 1. 13. 5), *have I any news to write to you?—any news?—yes.*

P. Itáne patris his conspectum uéritum hinc abiisse ? G. Admŏdum. P. Phánium rclíctam solam ? G. Sic ?. P. Et irátúm senem ? G. Oppido (*Ter.* Ph. 2. 2. 1), P. *Do you really mean that, afraid to face his father, he is gone off ?* G. *Precisely.* P. *That Phanium has been left by herself ?* G. *Just so.* P. *And that the old man is in a passion ?* G. *Exactly.*

A. Daane hoc ? B. Dŏ sānĕ (*Cic.* de Leg. 1. 7. 21), A. *Do you admit this ?* B. *Yes, I do admit it.*

1428   An answer in the negative may be expressed by nōn, mĭnŭmē, nihil mĭnŭs, &c. : as,

Cognitōrem adscrībit Sthĕnĭō. Quem ? Cognātum ălĭquem ? Nōn. Thermĭtānum ălĭquem ? Ne id quidem. At Sĭcŭlum ? Mĭnŭmē (*Cic.* II. Verr. II. 43. 106), *he appoints a person to act as attorney for Sthenius. Whom, think you? Some relative? No. Some inhabitant of Thermæ? Not even that. Still a Sicilian of course? By no means.*

1429   Imŏ seems to have signified properly an assent with an important qualification (but from carelessness it is used at times where the correction amounts to a total denial) : as,

Vīuīt ? Imo ĕtiam in sĕnātum uĕnīt (*Cic.* in Cat. 1. 1. 2), *is*

---

* Hence in Tac. an is used almost with the sense of an? : as, Ann. II. 42, *finem vitae sponte an fato impleuit*, 'he ended his life by an act of his own, or was it by a natural though sudden death.'

† At times the affirmation is understood without a formal expression ; as when a reply begins with *at* 'true but,' *at enim* 'true but beyond a doubt,' *et quidem* 'true and no less truly.'

‡ Just as *si* 'so,' 'yes,' is used in French &c.

he alive? Yes indeed he is, and more than that, comes into the senate.

Caussa ĭgĭtur non bŏna est? Imo optŭmă, sĕd ăgētur foedĭ-sūmē (*Cic.* ad Att. ix. 7. 4), *the cause then is not a good one? Nay, the best of causes, but it will be supported most disgracefully.*

A. Sīc hunc dēcĭpis? D. Imo ĕnimuero A'ntĭpho, hĭc me dēcĭpit (*Ter.* Ph. 3. 2. 43), A. *Is this the way you cheat this poor fellow?* D. *Not exactly so; it is this poor fellow, Antipho, who is cheating me**.

COPULATIVE CONJUNCTIONS.

1430   Of the three copulative conjunctions, ĕt, quĕ, atquĕ (ăc), the enclitic quĕ is more particularly employed to attach something subordinate to what precedes and unites two things more closely together into one; as,

Sōlis et lūnae rĕlĭquōrumquĕ sīdōrum ortūs (*Cic.* de Div. 1. 56. 128), *the rising of the sun and moon and the other stars.*

Sĕnātus pŏpŭlusquĕ Rōmānŭs (*Cic.* Phil. iii. 15. 38), *the senate and people of Rome.*

1431   Long phrases are connected commonly by ĕt, sometimes by quĕ, rarely by atquĕ; whereas all three are employed to connect words or short phrases, except that quĕ is never attached to those demonstrative pronouns or adverbs which end in *c.*

1432   When two words or phrases are to be united, a still stronger union is effected by employing a pair of conjunctions. Thus, *a.* ĕt —— ĕt —— is employed either with single words or long phrases. *b.* —— quĕ, —— quĕ is used in the connection of relative clauses, and sometimes with a pair of words the first of which is a pronoun; and also generally in the poets. *c.* —— quĕ, ĕt ——† is limited to single words, of which again the first is often a pronoun. *d.* even ĕt ——, —— quĕ occurs, but again rarely except with single words: as,

---

* A friend and former colleague suggested that *imo* is merely a contraction of *in modo* 'in a manner,' and referred to the arguments I had put forward elsewhere ('Alphabet,' p. 141), to show that *modo* when used as an adverb had a monosyllabic pronunciation.

† This form occurs in Sallust, not in Cicero.

a. Nihil est ĕnim simŭl ĕt inuentum et perfectum (*Cic.* Brut. 18. 70), *for nothing was ever both invented and perfected at once.*

b. Quīquō Rōmae, quīque in exercĭtu ĕrant (*Liv.* XXII. 26), *both those at Rome and those in the army.*

Mēquē regnumquē meum (*Sal.* Jug. 10), *both myself and my sceptre.*

Alit fontemque ignemquē fĕrēbant (*Virg.* A. XII. 119), *others the limpid stream and fire were bearing.*

c. Sēque et cohortem (*Liv.* XXV. 14), *both himself and the cohort.*

d. Id et singŭlīs ūnĭuersīsquē semper hŏnōrī fuit (*Liv.* IV. 2), *this was ever an honour alike to individual leaders and to the whole mass of those who followed.*

1433 When more than two things are to be united, of which no one is to be more closely united to one than to another, the following forms are admissible:

 a. ĕt ——, ĕt ——, ĕt ——.
 b. ——, ĕt ——, ĕt ——.
 c. ——, ——, —— quĕ.
 d. ——, —— quĕ, —— quĕ*: as,

a. Is, ĕt in custŏdiam cīuis dĕdit, et supplicātiōnem mihi dēcrēuit, ĕt indĭces praemiīs affēcit (*Cic.* in Cat. IV. 5. 10), *this person has ordered citizens into custody, has voted a public thanksgiving in my name, has rewarded the informers.*

b. Admīrārī sŏleō grāuĭtātem et iustĭtiam et săpientiam Caesăris (*Cic.* ad Fam. VI. 6. 10), *I always admire the high principle, and justice and wisdom of Caesar.*

c. Vrbem pulcerrŭmam flōrentissŭmam pŏtentissŭmamque esse uŏluērunt (*Cic.* in Cat. II. 13. 29), *they wished Rome to stand foremost in splendour, prosperity, and power.*

d. A cultū prōuinciae longissime absunt, minĭmēque ĭd eos mercātōres saepē commeant, proxĭmīquē sunt Germānīs (*Caes.* B. G. I. 1), *they are farthest from the civilisation of the province, are visited very rarely by merchants, and lie nearest to Germany†.*

* Very rarely ——, atque (ac) ——, atque (ac) ——.

† The poets often attach a *que* to the first, as well as all the following members of a series: as, *oblītus rēgisque ducumque meīque* (*Ov.* Met. XIII. 276), 'forgetful of prince, of chiefs, of me.'

1434. When of the words or phrases to be united, the union is to be closer between some than others, more than one of the conjunctions ĕt, quĕ, atquĕ must be used; and thus the Latin language has great power in grouping together the different parts of a sentence according to their importance*: as,

> Caedēs atque incendia, et lēgum intĕrĭtum, et bellum cīvīle ac dōmestĭcum, et tōtīus urbĭs atque impĕri occāsum apprŏpinquārĕ dixērunt (*Cic.* in Cat. III. 8. 19), *massacres and conflagrations, the annihilation of law, civil and domestic war, the downfall of the city and the empire, all these were approaching they said.*
>
> Illud signum sōlĭs ortum, et fŏrum cūriamquĕ conspĭcĭt (*Cic.* in Cat. III. 8. 20), *yonder statue looks upon the rising sun, and the forum and senate-house†.*
>
> Nāuĭgantēs indĕ pugnātum ad Lilўbaeum fāmaque etĭ captās hostium nāuĭs accēpērĕ (*Liv.* XXL. 50), *as they were sailing thence they received the news that a battle had been fought off Lilybaeum, and that the enemies' ships had been all put to flight or‡ taken.*
>
> Ităquĕ prōductĭs cōpĭĭs ante oppĭdum consīdunt; et proxīmam fossam crātĭbŭs intĕgunt atqueĭ aggĕre explent, sēque ăd ēruptĭōnem atque omnĭs cāsus compărant (*Caes.* B. G. VII. 79), *accordingly having led out their forces they take a position before the town; and the first ditch which presented itself they bridge over with hurdles, orĭ fill up with earth, at the same time that they prepare against a sally and every other mischance§.*

1435. There are three modes by which an enumeration is made so as

---

* Cicero at times in his orations purposely uses *et* alone throughout a long period to connect all the single words and phrases and clauses, whether long or short; his object being rather to deluge his hearer's mind with a torrent of ideas, than to place them in due subordination before him.

† The omission of the word *the* before *senate-house* has the same effect of bringing the latter pair of nouns nearer together, as the change of conjunction has in Latin.

‡ This disjunctive use of *et* and *atque* is not uncommon.

§ If every one of the three conjunctions be translated by *and*, the repetition at once offends the ear and confuses the mind. The variety of stops in our modern printing enables us to make that distinction visible to the eye, which the Romans made sensible to the ear also by a variety of conjunctions. See 'Journal of Education,' IV. 135.

to be highly impressive:—*a.* that already mentioned (in § 1433) with the prefixed and repeated *ĕt* (called *Polysyndeton*); *b.* a simple enumeration without conjunctions (called *Asyndeton*); *c.* a repetition of some word at the beginning of each clause (called *Anaphora*): thus,

- *b.* Sempĕr audax, pĕtŭlans, lŭbīdĭnōsūs (*Cic.* p. Sull. 25. 71), *always daring, mischievous, sensual.*
- Quid uŏlŭĕrit, cōgĭtārit, admīsĕrit, nōn ex crīmĭne est pondĕrandum (*Cic.* p. Sull. 25. 69), *his criminal wishes, intentions, actions, are not to be measured by the charges of his accuser.*
- *c.* Erepti estis sĭnĕ caedē, sĭnĕ sanguĭnĕ, sĭne exercĭtū, sĭnĕ dīmĭcātiōnĕ (*Cic.* in Cat. III. 10. 23), *you have been rescued without a massacre, without bloodshed, without an army, without a struggle.*

1436   An omission of a conjunction is—*a.* common in the old language and public formulae between two words; *b.* the regular construction with words or phrases opposed to one another; and *c.* occasionally used in a light and lively style for the sake of brevity: as,

- *a.* Rŏgātĭōnem prōmulgāuit, uellent iūbērentnĕ* Phĭlippō rēgī bellum indīci (*Liv.* XXXI. 6), *he put up a public notice of his intention to take the pleasure and order of the people for declaring war against king Philip.*
- Lex Aeliă Sentĭă (*Gaius*, I. 6. 18), *the law passed by Ælius and Sentius.*
- Vsus fructūst est iūs aliēnīs rēbūs ūtendi fruendi saluā rārum substantĭā (*Paul.* in Dig. VII. 1. 1), *the usufruct is the right to the use and produce of property belonging to others, without detriment to the property itself.*
- *b.* Nō cursem hūc illuc uiā dēterrŭmā (*Cic.* ad Att. IX. 9. 2), *that I may not keep running first to this place and then to that along the worst possible road.*
- Omniă, mĭnŭmă maxŭma, ad Caesărem mitti sŏlēbam (*Cic.* ad Q. F. III. 1. 3. 10), *all the news, from the most unimportant to the most important, I knew was regularly sent to Cæsar.*

* More literally 'he advertised a bill asking whether they wished and ordered that war should be declared against king Philip.'

† Thus what was originally two independent words became almost one; still the accusative is *usum fructum*.

Quum diu anceps fuisset certāmĕn, et Săguntīnīs* quiă praetĕr spem rĕsistĕrent crēuissent ănīmī, Poenus quiă non uīcisset prō uicto esset, clāmōrem rĕpente oppīdānī tollunt (*Liv.* XXI. 9), *when the contest had been for a long time doubtful, and the spirit of the Saguntines was increased because they had up to this time made a resistance beyond their hopes, whilst the Carthaginian was as good as defeated because he was not already victorious, the townspeople suddenly set up a shout*‡.

Sullă pŏtuit, ĕgo non pŏtĕro † (*Pomp.* ap. Cic. ad Att. IX. 10. 2), *was Sulla able, and shall not I be able ?*

c. Adĕrant prŏpinqui, ămīcī (*Cic.* II. Verr. I. 48. 125), *his connexions, friends were present.*

In fĕrīs Ĭnessĕ fortĭtūdĭnem saepĕ dīcĭmŭs, ŭt ĭn ĕquīs, in leōnĭbŭs (*Cic.* de Off. I. 16. 50), *we often attribute courage to a beast, as the horse, the lion.*

1437 When clauses follow one another without any conjunctions to connect them, the same order is commonly used in each (except that an inversion is admissible in the last clause): as,

Ad hoc praeusti artus, nīuĕ rĭgentes nerui, quassātă fructĭque armă, claudi ac dēbĭlēs ĕquī§ (*Liv.* XXI. 40), *in addition to this their limbs frostbitten, their muscles stiffened by the snow, their arms shattered and broken, their horses lame and exhausted.*

Is mōtus terrae multārum urbium magnas partīs prostrăuit, mărĕ flūmĭnĭbŭs ĭnuexit, montīs lapsu ingentī prŏruit (*Liv.* XXII. 5), *this earthquake threw down a great portion of many cities, carried the sea up rivers, caused fearful avalanches*‖.

---

* In the passages where long clauses are opposed, the writer takes care to place opposed words at the beginning of each clause, as here: *Saguntinis..., Poenus...* Where the phrase is a short one, this is not necessary, as in *Cic.* in Cat. II. 11. 25, *quibus nos suppeditamus, eget ille.* 'of which we have abundance, while he has none.'

† This conjunction is almost necessary in the English translation when two opposed clauses are attached by a conjunction to another sentence.

‡ Compare also the use of such opposed clauses after *an* in § 1426; and see 'Journal of Education,' IV. p. 140, &c.

§ After *nervi* the editions have *membra torrida gelu*; which, to say nothing of the substantive preceding the epithet, is evidently a mere marginal interpretation of *praeusti artus*.

‖ Here again our editions insert after *prostrauit, auertitque curos rapidas amnes*, which is evidently an interpolation.

1438. With adjectives and adverbs of comparison*, the conjunctions ĕt and quŏ are used in such a manner that the two things compared are brought together and under a common construction, while the adjective or adverb of comparison either precedes or follows the things compared; or is interposed after the first of the things compared, as a sort of enclitic. Thus, if we include the double and single use of each conjunction, there are six varieties:

a. Strēnuī mīlītīs et bŏnī impĕrātōrīs officiă, sĭmŭl exsĕquēbātŭr (*Sal.* Cat. 60), *he was performing the parts at once of a zealous soldier and a good general.*

b. Quoī-sĭmŭl et Volcatiō pĕcūniă nŭmĕrātast (*Cic.* II. Verr. III. 76. 176), *the money having been paid to him and Volcatius at the same time.*

c. Nihīl est ēnim sĭmŭl ĕt inuentum et perfectum (*Cic.* Brut. 18. 70), *for nothing was ever invented and brought to perfection both at the same time.*

d. Aliēnātā mentē sĭmŭl luctū mĕtūquē (*Liv.* XXIV. 26), *their minds distracted by the double feeling, of sorrow (for their mother's death) and fear (for themselves).*

e. Hoc, principiúm-sĭmŭl ōmenquē bellī (*Liv.* XXI. 29), *this, at once a commencement and an omen of the war.*

f. Părĭter, cōmĭtīque ŏnĕrīquē tĭmentem (*Virg.* A. II. 729), *fearful alike for his companion and for the load he bore.*

1439. The use of atquē with adjectives and adverbs of comparison is much more free, as neither an identity of construction nor the close union of the things compared is essential. Thus,

Mē cŏlīt ĕt obseruat aeque atque illum (*Cic.* ad Fam. XIII. 69. 1), *he pays as much respect and attention to me as to him.*

Sī quī dīcātŭr īllum occīdīsse ac nōluĕrīt (*Cic.* de Inv. II. 7. 23), *if a person were charged with having killed a different person from what he had intended.*

Pār dēsīdĕrium suī rēlīquīt ac Ti. Graechus rēlīquērat (*Cic.* p. Rab. 5. 14), *he died as much regretted as Tiberius Gracchus had done.*

1440. Et is occasionally used in the sense of 'also,' 'too,' even in

---

* This word is here used in a wide sense, so as to include such adjectives as aeque-, par- or pari-, simil-, dissimili-, idem, uno-, duo-, duplici-, and the adverbs aeque, pariter, simul, una, &c.

the best writers*, but for the most part only in certain combinations: as, sĕd ĕt, sĭmŭl ĕt, sīc ĕt, ĕt ipsī.

1441 Quĕ and ŭē in the poets are sometimes placed, not after the second of the two words compared, but after a word which is the common predicate of both clauses : as,

Insānum te omnes puĕrī clāmentquĕ† puellae (*Hor*. Sat. II. 3. 130), *the madman ! all would exclaim, both boys and girls*‡.

1442 The poets take the liberty of placing quĕ behind a later word than the first of its clause, particularly in a pentameter line : as,

Quum maestūs ăb alto
Iliŏn, ardentes respĭcĕretquĕ deos (*Tibul*. II. 5. 21),
*As in sadness from the deep
On Ilion and the burning gods he was looking back.*

1443 The construction nĕquĕ —— ĕt ——, and also that of ĕt —— nĕquĕ —— deserve attention, because they differ from the English idiom. Thus,

Pătēbat uia, et certă nec longă (*Cic*. Phil. XI. 2. 4), *a road lay open to them which had the double advantage of being certain and not long.*

Vŏluptātēs ăgrĭcŏlārum, nĕc ulla impĕdiuntur sĕnectūte, et mihi ad săpientis uītam proxŭmē uīdentūr accĕdĕrĕ (*Cic*. de Sen. 15. 51), *the pleasures of the farmer (have a twofold recommendation : they)‡ are never obstructed by old age, however advanced, and they seem to me to approach most nearly to the life a wise man would lead.*

DISJUNCTIVE CONJUNCTIONS.

1444 The difference between autĭ and uĕl, though commonly trans-

---

* See Allen's 'Doctrina Copularum,' p. 52.

† A construction that probably began with a repetition of the predicate: *puerī clāmant clāmentque puellas*. Other instances are to be found in Horace; as, *mutatosque*, Od. I. 5. 5; *horribilique*, II. 19. 24; *medius que*, II. 19. 28; *laetique*, II. 19. 32: and in Tibullus; as, *peruigilque*, I. 1. 51; *aequiterque*, I. 3. 56. See Orelli ad *Hor*. Od. II. 19. 28.

‡ See Allen's 'Doctrina Copularum,' p. 120.

§ Or the words within brackets might have been omitted, and the word 'and' exchanged for 'at the same time that.'

‖ See § 840, notes † and ‡.

lated by the same word in English, is marked. Aut divides two
notions essentially different, while uel marks a distinction either
not essential in itself or unimportant in the mind of the speaker,
so that it is often used to correct a mere expression. When they
are repeated, the distinction becomes still more marked. In the
construction aut —— aut ——, the denial of one clause is an affirmation of the other. Whereas in the construction uel —— uel
—— all the clauses may coexist or not, the speaker merely expressing his indifference as to a choice between them. Lastly, uel
is used with superlatives and in other phrases with the sense of
even, or perhaps more precisely *if you like**.

 a. Audendum est áliquid úniuersis, aut omnia singulis pāti-
endā (*Liv.* vi. 18), *we must make a bold effort in a body, or
else every individual must suffer the worst.*

 Aut occubuissem hŏneste, aut uictōres hŏdie uiuĕrēmūs (*Cic.
ad Att.* iii. 15. 4), *either I should have fallen honourably, or
else we should have been now living as conquerors.*

 b. Magnūs hŏmo, uel pŏtius summūs (*Cic.* Brut. 85. 293), *a
great man, or rather the greatest of men.*

 Vna atque altĕra aestas uel mētū uel spē uel poepā uel prae-
miis uel armis uel lēgibus pŏtest tōtam Galliam sempiternis
uinculis adstringĕrĕ (*Cic.* Prov. Cons. 14. 34), *one or two
summers, by the influence of fear or hope or punishment or
rewards or arms or laws (I care not which), may bind all
Gallia in eternal chains.*

 c. Vidētur uel mŏri sătius fuisse quam esse cum his (*Cic. ad
Att.* ix. 6. 7), *it seems to me that even death would have been
better than to live in the company of these people.*

 Vestrā causā me lŏqui quae lŏquor, uel ea fidēs sit (*Liv.* xxi.
13), *that it is for your sake that I say what I do say, let even
this be a security to you.*

 Cūiūs eō tempŏre uel maxŭma ăpud rēgem auctōrĭtās ērat (*Liv.*
xxxvi. 41), *whose influence with the king at this time was the
very greatest*†.

---

 * It will be seen that all the meanings here given to *uel* are consistent
with its being in origin an imperative of *uol-* 'wish,' in the sense of ' make
your own choice.' See § 840, note †.

 † The use of *ue* agrees nearly with that of *uel*, from which it is probably formed; but it is always an enclitic, and occurs more frequently in
poetry than in prose.

VARIOUS CONJUNCTIONS AND ADVERBS.

The conjunction **at** denotes rather addition than opposition. It is commonly employed after a concession, especially—

a. After **si**, in the sense of *yet, still*: as,

Si minus supplicio affici, at custōdiri ŏportēbat (*Cic.* II. Verr. v. 27. 69), *if it was not right they should be severely punished, still they ought to have been guarded.*

Si non bŏnam, at ălĭquam rătĭōnem afferrĕ sŏlent (*Cic.* II. Verr. III. 83. 195), *they usually bring forward, if not a good reason, yet some reason.*

b. In a reply, when a proposition of the other party is assented to, but at the same time rendered useless for his purpose by some addition: as,

Nunquam nĭsi hŏnōrĭfīcentissĭmē Pompēium appellat.—At in ēius persōnā multă fēcit aspĕrĭūs (*Cic.* ad Fam. VI. 6. 10), *he never speaks of Pompey except in the most complimentary terms.—Precisely so, but in dealing with him he acted on many occasions somewhat roughly.*

c. Hence it is employed to anticipate an opponent's objection, in which case the verb inquies or dīcēs is commonly omitted, and not unfrequently the particle ĕnim or uĕrō added: as,

At sunt mōrōsi et diffīcĭles sĕnĕs (*Cic.* de Sen. 18. 65), *but you will tell me, old men are cross and difficult to please.*

At ēnim Q. Cătŭlŭs ăb hac rătĭōnĕ dissentit (*Cic.* p. leg. Man. 17. 51), *true, I shall be told, but Quintus Catulus dissents from this view.*

d. It denotes a sudden emotion of the mind, and is employed in sudden transitions in a speech: as,

Exi foras scelĕste. At etiam rēstĭtas? (*Ter.* E. IV. 4. 1) *get out of the house, you scoundrel. What! do you still resist?*

Narrābat se hunc neclĕgĕre cognatūm suom. At quem uirum? (*Ter.* Ph. II. 3. 19) *he often told me that this kinsman took no notice of him. And yet what a noble creature he was!*

e. Hence the repeated form attăt, i. e. atattăt*, is used to mark a sudden discovery: as,

* See § 24.

Attāt hoc illūd est (*Ter.* And. L 1. 98), *ah, ah, I see it then, this explains that business.*

1446. Autem strictly denotes *again*, and is never used in the sense of opposition, but real addition. It never occupies the first place in a clause. Its significations are—

a. *Again:* as,

Tum autem hoc timet (*Ter.* And. L 5. 34), *then again she is afraid of this.*

Sed quid ego haec autem nēquīquam ingrātā rēvolvo ? (*Virg.* A. π. 101) *but why do I again in vain turn o'er these unwelcome thoughts ?*

Porro autem ālio (*Ter.* Ph. L 1. 14), *and ere long with another again.*

b. *On the other hand:* as,

Nēque ēnim tu is es qui quid sis nesciās ; nēque autem ēgo sum ītā dēmens ūt &c. (*Cic.* ad Fam. v. 12. 6), *nor indeed are you the person not to know what is due to you, nor on the other hand am I so mad as &c.*

c. *And* or *now* (especially in a parenthesis) : as,

Diŏgěnem ădŭlescens, post autem Pānaetium audiěrat (*Cic.* de Fin. π. 8. 24), *he had attended the lectures of Diogenes when a young man, and afterwards those of Panætius.*

Nēminem conuēni (conuēnio autem quŏtīdiē plūrīmos) quīn omnēs mihi grātiās ăgant (*Cic.* ad Fam. IX. 14. 1), *I have met no one (and I daily meet very many), but they all thank me.*

d. *But* or *now*, especially in adding the new propositions of a syllogism : as,

Si ămitti ulla beāta pŏtest, beāta esse non pŏtest. Quis ēnim confidit sibi semper id stăbile permansūrum quod frăgile sit ? Qui autem diffīdat perpĕtuïtāti bŏnōrum suōrum, tīmeat nĕcessest, ne ăliquando āmissis illis sit miser. Bĕătūs autem esse in maxĭmārum rērum tīmōrē nēmō pŏtest. Nēmō igĭtūr esse beātus pŏtest (*Cic.* de Fin. π. 27. 86), *if happiness can be lost, it cannot be happiness. For who feels sure that that will always remain stable to him which is in itself frail ? But if a man feels no security in the continuance of his blessings, he must needs be afraid of some time or* other losing them, and so becoming miserable. But no one can be happy when in fear about matters of the greatest importance. Consequently no one can be happy.

c. Autem is also used in catching up some objectionable word or phrase, where we insert some such expression as *did I say?*

Numquis testis postūmum* appellāuit? testis autem, num accusātōr? (*Cic.* p. Rab. P. 5. 10) *now did any witness mention the name of Postumus? Witness did I say, did the accuser?*

Intellĭgis quam meum sit scīrĕ quid in rē publicā fīat; fīat autem, immō uĕro ĕtiam quid fŭtūrum sit (*Cic.* ad Att. v. 13. 3), *you understand how much it concerns me to know what is doing in the public world; doing did I say, nay even what will be done.*

In Āfricam* transcendes; transcendĕs autem dicō? hōc ipso annō duos consŭles, ūnum in hispāniam*, altĕrum in Āfricam* misērunt (*Liv.* xxi. 44), *you will cross over into Africa. Will did I say, this very year they have sent their two consuls, one into Spain, the other into Africa.*

1447 Dēmum is strictly an adverb of time, and signifies—*a. At last,* a very long time having preceded: as,

Ego nōnce maritus ănno demum quinto et sexagēnsumo Fiam! (*Ter.* Ad. v. 8. 15), *I become a bridegroom now for the first time in my sixty-fifth year!*

Nunc dēmum uĕnis? Cur passu's? (*Ter.* Ad. ii. 2. 25) *are you come now for the first time? Why did you put up with it so long?*

Quartā nix dēmum expōnimŭr hōrā (*Hor.* Sat. I. 5. 23), *at last at ten o'clock (and then with difficulty) we land.*

b. Nothing short of, especially with the pronoun i- or eo-: as,

Sic ĕnim sentio, id dēmum esse misĕrum quod turpĕ sit (*Cic.* ad Att. viii. 8), *for I feel that that, and that alone, is wretched which is base.*

Idem uelle ĕt ĭdem nolle, eă dēmum firma ămĭcĭtia est (*Sal.* Cat. 20), *an identity of desires and dislikes, that and nothing short of that constitutes lasting friendship.*

1448 Dum is strictly an adverb of time, and signifies—*a. While, as long as* (nearly always with the indicative):

* To copy the Mss. where proper names have no capitals.

Dum haec dīcit, abiit hōra (*Ter.* E. II. 3. 49), *while he was saying this, an hour passed away.*

Dum haec in uěnětīs* gěrunturt, titurius in fīnīs unellōrum* peruěnit (*Caes.* B. G. III. 17), *while these things were going on among the Veneti, Titurius arrives in the territories of the Unelli.*

Dum lătīnē* lŏquentur littěrae, quercŭs huic lŏcō non děrit (*Cic.* de Leg. I. 1. 1), *so long as literature shall talk Latin, this spot will not be without its oak.*

Diem insěquentem quiěuěrě mīlĭtes, dum praefectŭs urbis uīrēs inspĭcěret‡ (*Liv.* XXIV. 40), *the next day the soldiers rested, that the general might in the interval examine the strength of the city.*

b. *Until* (nearly always with the indicative mood, unless a purpose be intended): as,

Expectābo dŭm uěnit (*Ter.* E. I. 2. 126), *I shall wait until he comes.*

Expecta ămăbō tē, dum attĭcum* conuěniam‡ (*Cic.* ad Att. VII. L 4), *wait, I pray you, until I can see Atticus.*

c. *Provided that* (always with the subjunctive): as,

Oděrint, dum mětuant (ap. *Cic.* Phil. I. 14. 34), *let them hate, provided they fear.*

Omnia hŏnestă neclěgunt, dum mŏdō pŏtentiam consěquantŭr (*Cic.* de Off. III. 21. 82), *they neglect all that is honourable, if they can but attain political power.*

d. *Yet, a while,* as an enclitic after negatives (including uix) or a present of the imperative: as,

Vixdum ěpistŏlam tuam lěgěram cum curtius* uěnit (*Cic.* ad Att. IX. 2 A. 3), *I had scarcely yet read your letter, when Curtius called.*

Lěgātiōně děcrětā necdum missā (*Liv.* XXI. 6), *when the embassy had been decreed, but not yet sent.*

Adesdum, paucis tě uŏlo (*Ter.* And. I. 1. 2), *here a moment, I want a few words with you.*

1449 Enim must commonly be translated by the English conjunction *for*, but at times retains what was probably its earlier signification

---

* See p. 397, note.   † See § 458.
‡ The subjunctive, to denote a purpose.

indeed, as in ēnimuērō indeed, indeed, nēque ēnim nor indeed, ĕtĕnim and indeed, Ĕtĕnim* true you will say, but in fact, sĕd ĕnim but indeed, &c.: as,

    Enimuēro dauet, nil locist sēgnitiae nec socŏrdiae (Ter. And. I. 3. 1), indeed, indeed, Davus, there is no room for sloth or stupidity.

    Quid tūtē tecum? Nihil enim (Plaut. Most. III. 1. 24), what are you saying to yourself? Nothing, I assure you.

1450. Iam is an adverb of time, and often differs from nunc just as eō tempŏrĕ differs from hoc tempŏrĕ. It commonly denotes something extreme in point of time: as,

    a. *Already* (sooner than might have been expected): as,

    Hermae tui pentĕlĭcī iam nunc mē dēlectant (Cic. ad Att. I. 8. 2), your Mercuries of Pentelic marble already now charm me (before I have seen them).

    Haec iam tum cum ādĕrās offendēre eiūs ănimum intellĕgēbam (Cic. ad Att. I. 11. 1), this, already when you were with us, I perceived annoyed him.

    b. *At last* (later than might have been expected): as,

    Postŭlo ut rĕdeat iam in uiam (Ter. And. I. 2. 19), I expect him to return at last into the right path. (He has gone astray long enough.)

    c. *Presently*: as,

    Dē quibus iam dicendi lŏcŭs ĕrit (Cic. Brut. 25. 96), of which I shall presently have an opportunity of speaking.

    d. *Then again, lastly* (to denote a transition from one subject to another): as,

    Iam quantum dicendi grăuĭtātē uălĕat, uos saepĕ cognostis (Cic. p. leg. Man. 14. 42), then again how impressive he is as a speaker, you yourselves have often witnessed.

    e. Iam iamquĕ, of what is expected *every moment*: as,

    Quanquam ipsĕ iam iamque ădĕro (Cic. ad Att. XIV. 22. 1), and yet I myself shall be with you forthwith.

1451. Ită; so differs from sīc so as the logical i- or eo- *this* from the demonstrative ho- *this*.

---

* See § 1445 c.   † See p. 397, note.

‡ The oldest form of the neuter pronoun *id*. Compare the Gothic neuter *thata*, whence our *that*.

a. *So* (*so exceedingly*), pointing to a coming *ut that*: as,

Inclūsum in cūriā sēnātum hăbuĕrunt Ită multos diēs ŭt intĕriĕrint nonnullī fămē (*Cic.* ad Att. VI. 2. 8), *they kept the senate shut up in their house so many days that some died of hunger.*

b. *So* (*so little*, or with a restrictive sense), with the same construction: as,

Itā triumphārunt, ŭt illĕ pulsus sŭpĕrātusquĕ regnāret (*Cic.* p. leg. Man. 3. 8), *they triumphed, it is true, yet so that the other, routed and overpowered though he was, was still a sovereign.*

c. *So*, referring to the preceding sentence: as,

Itā sunt omniă dēbĭlĭtātă (*Cic.* ad Fam. II. 5), *to such an extent is every thing exhausted.*

Ita est (*Ter.* E. I. 2. 44), *yes, it is so.*

d. *So*, corresponding to a preceding or following *as* (ŭt &c.): as,

Vt quisque optĭmē graecē scit, Ita est nēquissŭmŭs (*Cic.* de Or. II. 66. 265), *as each man is better acquainted with Greek, so is he a greater rogue.*

e. *So**, in expressing a prayer: as,

Itā mē Di ăment, nonnihil tĭmeo (*Ter.* E. IV. 1. 1), *so may the gods love me, I am somewhat frightened.*

f. Ut ... Itā *although* ... *yet*: as,

Vt a procliis quiētem hăbuĕrant, Itā non noctē, non die unquam cessāuĕrant ăb ŏpĕrē (*Liv.* XXI. 11), *although they had had rest from fighting, yet they had never ceased either by day or by night from working.*

g. Itā† ... sī *on the one condition ... that*: as,

Pācis Ita ălĭquă spēs est, sī uōs ut uicti audiātis (*Liv.* XXI. 13), *of peace there is not the slightest hope, except on the condition that you listen to the terms offered as men who are conquered.*

---

* Sic is used in the same way: *sic te diua potens cypri ... regat*, *Hor.* Od. I. 3. 1.

† So also *sic* is used in Horace (Ep. I. 7. 69): *sic ignouisse putato Me tibi, si cœnas mecum.* Indeed *sic* is only *si* with the demonstrative suffix added. Compare the use of *so* in English for *if*: 'So you dine with me, I'll forgive you.'

ITA. NAM. QVIDEM.

A. This, referring to an accusative and infinitive following* : as,
Ită constĭtŭī, fortĭtĕr esse ăgendum (*Cic.* p. Clu. 19. 51), *this I resolved upon, that I must act with firmness.*

i. So (so very), with the words by which the degree is to be measured, not expressed (especially after negatives) : as,
Sīmŭlācră praeclără, sed nōn īta antīquă (*Cic.* ii. Verr. iv. 49. 109), *figures of great repute, but not so very old.*

1452 Nam, while it commonly signifies *for*, has two other meanings which deserve attention :

a. Thus, for example (introducing a particular instance after a general proposition)†. *b.* It often assigns a reason why a particular name or fact which might have been expected is not included in a series or argument just preceding. Thus,

b. Nam quod nēgas tē dŭbĭtārĕ quin magna in offensā sim ăpud pompēium hoc tempŏrĕ, non uĭdĕō causam cūr ĭtă sit (*Cic.* ad Att. ix. 2. 2), *I purposely pass over your statement that you have no doubt of my having given great offence to Pompey, for this simple reason, that I do not see any reason why it should be so.*

Nam maeciam, non quae iūdĭcārĕt, set quae reĭcĕrētŭr essĕ uŏluisti (*Cic.* p. Planc. 16. 38), *I omit the Maecian tribe, for in presenting that tribe you intended it to be, not one of those to furnish a jury, but the one to be challenged by your opponents.*

1453 Quidem‡ gives emphasis to the word or words before it, and its meanings deserve great attention. They are—

a. At least : as,

Ut mihi quidem uĭdētŭr (*Cic.* de Fin. i. 7. 23), *so it seems to me at least.*

Meā quidem sententĭā pācī sempĕr est consŭlendum (*Cic.* de Off. i. 11. 35), *in my opinion at least (whatever others may think) peace ought ever to be the object of our counsels.*

b. Nē ... quidem§ *not even :* as,

---

* Sic is used in the same way.

† See Caes. B. G. iii. 28 ; Pl. Trin. L 2. 46, Men. i. 1. 20, Pers. iv. 2. 2.

‡ The same in meaning and perhaps in form as the Greek γε. See 'Alphabet,' p. 141.

§ See §§ 1405, 1412, 1413.

Id nē fērae quidem făciunt (Cic. de Fin. i. 10. 34), *this even the wild-beast does not do.*

Nē id quidem est explōrātum (Cic. ad Att. x. 8), *even that is not certain.*

c. Et quidem *and indeed, nay:* as,

Mē cum Gabīniō sententiam dīcĕre, et quidem illum rŏgāri priŭs (Cic. ad Att. x. 8), *that I should give my opinion in the same room with Gabinius, and indeed he be asked his first!*

d. Et quidem, and qui-quidem (in replies), assenting to what is said, and at the same time ironically adding what renders the assent useless: as,

Torquem dētraxit hosti.—Et quidem sē texit nē intĕrīret.—At magnum pĕrīcŭlum ădiit.—In ŏcŭlis quidem exercĭtūs (Cic. de Fin. i. 10. 35), *he tore the collar from his enemy's neck.—Yes, and (excuse my adding) covered himself with his shield, that he might not be killed.—But still he incurred great danger. —Certainly, in the eyes of the army.*

At ĕrat mēcum sĕnātŭs—et quidem ueste mūtātā. At tōta Ītălĭă conuēnĕrat—quoi quidem uastĭtātis mĕtŭs infĕrēbātŭr (Cic. p. Planc. 35. 87), *but the senate, you say, were with me. They were, and (you have forgotten to add) dressed in mourning. But all the inhabitants of Italy had assembled to support me. They had, and (by way of encouragement I suppose) were daily threatened with the devastation of their property.*

e. Qui-quidem *which by the way:* as,

Quō quidem in bellō uirtūs ēnĭtuit ēgrĕgĭă · m · Cătōnis proăuī tuī (Cic. pro Mur. 14. 32), *in which war by the way, the valour and abilities of your great-grandfather M. Cato shone conspicuous.*

Dē triumphō tĭbi assentior, quem quidem tōtum făcĭle abiēcĕrō (Cic. ad Att. ix. 7. 5), *about the triumph I agree with you, and by the way I shall readily at once abandon all idea of it.*

f. *It is true, certainly* (a concession commonly followed by sēd): as,

Făcis ămīcē tū* quidem, sed mihi uĭdēris ălĭud tu hŏnestum

* See § 1080.

iūdicāre atque ĕgo existŭmem (*Cic.* ad Att. VIII. 2. 2), *you act like a friend I grant, but still you seem to me to hold a different opinion of what is right and proper from that which I entertain.*

Ignosco ĕquidem* tibi, sed tū quŏquĕ mihī uĕlim ignoscās (*Cic.* ad Q. F. III. 1. 3. 7), *I forgive you certainly, but I must beg you too to forgive me.*

g. Similarly in a transition from one subject to another, the last clause of the preceding matter has a quidem, while the new matter is introduced with an autem. Thus,

Ac dē prīmō quidem officī fontē dixīmus. Dē trĭbūs autem rĕlĭquīs lātissĭmē pătet ĕă rătiō quā sŏcĭĕtās hŏmĭnum contĭnētŭr (*Cic.* de Off. I. 6. 19 et seq.), *and we have now said enough of the first source of duty. Of the three which remain, the most extensive in its operations† is the principle by which society is held together.*

Quŏd (in origin only the neuter of the relative, signifying *this* or *that*) is translated by the words *that, because,* &c. In the older constructions it is generally preceded by some part of a logical pronoun. The difference in use between quŏd and ŭt in the sense of *that,* lies chiefly in this, that quŏd commonly precedes a statement of facts past or present in the indicative, ŭt commonly introduces purposes or results expressed in the subjunctive. The uses of quŏd belong for the most part to the following heads:

a. That, the fact that, after a logical pronoun (see §§ 301 &c., 1112 &c.): as,

Eo ipsō quod nĕcesse ĕrat solui, făcultas soluendi impĕdiēbātŭr (*Liv.* VI. 34), *by the very fact that it was necessary payment should be made, the means of making that payment were obstructed.*

Hōrum fortissimi sunt belgae, proptĕrĕā quŏd ā cultū prōuinciae longissĭmē absunt (*Caes.* B. G. I. 1), *of these the bravest are the Belgæ, for the reason that they are furthest removed from the civilisation of the province.*

Praeterquam quŏd admissi audītīquĕ sunt, eā quŏquĕ nānā

---

* I. e. *ego quidem,* and perhaps pronounced *ikem* or *ike.*
† Literally 'extends most widely.'

lēgātio fuit (*Liv.* xxi. 10), *beyond the fact that they were admitted and heard, this embassy also was without effect.*

b. As quid why is used for propter quid, so quŏd is commonly used for propter quŏd, that is *because.* Thus,

Grātiās ăgĭmus dŭcĭbus uestrīs, quŏd ŏcŭlīs măgīs quam auribus crēdĭdērunt (*Liv.* vi. 26), *we thank your generals for that they gave credit to their eyes rather than to their ears.*

In uiam quod tē dās* hoc tempŏrĕ, nihīl est (*Cic.* ad Fam. xiv. 12), *there is no reason why you should expose yourself to travelling at this season.*

Laudat āfricānum quod fŭĕrit† abstĭnens (*Cic.* de Off. ii. 22. 76), *he praises Africanus for having been temperate.*

c. *In that,* where quum or the relative itself might have been used (see § 1455 h.): as,

Bĕnĕ făcĭtis quŏd ăbōmĭnāmĭnī (*Liv.* vi. 18), *you do well in rejecting it as something impious.*

Fēcistī mihi pergrātum quod sērāpiōnis librum ad mē mīsisti (*Cic.* ad Att. ii. 4. 1), *you have done what is most agreeable to me, in sending me Serapion's book.*

d. Quŏd often introduces a clause which serves as the nominative or accusative to the main verb, or stands in apposition to a noun. Thus,

Accēdit quod mīrīficē ingĕnīis excellentĭbus dēlectātūr (*Cic.* ad Fam. vi. 6. 6), *there is added the fact, that he is wonderfully charmed with men of extraordinary genius.*

Mitto quŏd omnis meas tempestātes sŭbiĕris (*Cic.* ad Fam. xv. 4. 12), *I pass over your having encountered, as you say, all the storms to which I have been exposed.*

Me ūnā consōlātiō sustentat, quod tĭbi nullum ă mē piĕtātis officium dēfuit (*Cic.* p. Mil. 36. 100), *for myself but one consolation supports me, I mean the fact, that no duty demanded of me by affection has been wanting to you.*

e. Quŏd often introduces a sentence, which is to be the subject of remark, when the English may be expressed by *with regard to the fact that,* or more simply. Observe too that *a.* if the sentence so introduced be a present or past fact, the indicative is required; *b.* if it be a future possibility, the subjunctive: as,

* See § 1189.   † See § 1203.

a. Quod scrībis tē sī uellim ad mē uentūram, ĕgŏ uĕrŏ tē istīc essĕ uŏlo (*Cic.* ad Fam. xiv. 3. 5), *as to your offer to come to me if I wish it, I do not wish it (my dear Terentia); on the contrary, I wish you to remain where you are.*

Quod mē uŏtas quidquam suspĭcārī..., gĕram tĭbi mōrem (*Cic.* ad Att. iii. 20. 3), *you forbid me to harbour any suspicion—I will oblige you.*

Quŏd ad crīmĭna attĭnet, quĭbus mōtī bellum indīxistis, uel ītāri eā tūtum censēmŭs (*Liv.* vi. 26), *as regards the charges which induced you to declare war, we think it safe for us even to confess them.*

b. Tum quod tē postĕrius purgēs, hūius non fēciam (*Ter.* Ad. ii. 1. 8), *then as to your trying afterwards to clear yourself, as you perhaps will, I shall not value it at this.*

Nam quŏd dē argento spērem, aut posse postulem mē fallere, Nĭhil est (*Ter.* Haut. iv. 2. 4), *for as to my entertaining any hope about the money, or expecting to be able to take them in, that's at an end.*

f. Non quŏd *not because, not that* (or more commonly non quō*), with a subjunctive, is used to deny a reason, or to guard against an inference (see § 1208): as,

Nullō mŏdŏ prorsūs assentior, non quod diffĭcĭlĕ sit mentem ăb ŏcŭlis sēuŏcārĕ; sed quō māgĭs sēuŏco, eō mĭnŭs id quod tū uis possum mentē comprehendĕrō (*Cic.* N. D. iii. 8. 21), *I by no means give an unqualified assent, not that I find it difficult to abstract my thoughts from what I see with my eyes, but because the more I do this, the less able am I to grasp with my mind the idea you wish me to grasp.*

g. Quŏd, like quum (see § 1455 g), is used to denote duration of time: as,

Iăm diu est quod uĕntri uictum nŏn datis (*Plaut.* Am. i. 1. 146), *it is now a long time since you gave my belly any food.*

h. Quid quŏd often introduces a new and striking fact when the literal translation would perhaps be: *what would you say to the fact that ——?* but the idea may often be more simply expressed by *nay*. Thus,

---

* Not only is non quo more common, but the examples with non quod seem apt to have a following d, as *difficile* here, and *doleam* § 1208, ex. 3; and so are open to suspicion.

Quid quod sēnātūs eos nōluit praeessē prōuinciīs, qui non praefuissent ? (*Cic.* ad Att. VI. 6. 3) *nay the senate decreed that those should preside over the provinces, who had not already done so.*

i. Quŏd followed by a conjunction, as sī, nisī, ŭtĭnam, ŭbi, &c. is often used to connect a new sentence with what precedes; in which case it often admits such a translation as *but, whereas, and.* Thus,

Quod sī tū uălērēs, iam mihi quaedam explōrāta essent (*Cic.* ad Att. VII. 2. 6), *whereas if you had been in health, some points would have been cleared up for me before this.*

Of quom, quum, or cum*, the chief uses are as follow :—

a. To denote time, with the past-imperfect subjunctive, *while,* i. e. at some point of time in a long period. Thus,

Ad hannĭbălem, quum ad lăcum ăuerni esset, quinquĕ nōbĭlēs iŭuĕnēs ab tărentō uēnērunt (*Liv.* XXIV. 13), *there came to Hannibal, while he was near the lake of Avernus, five young men of high family from Tarentum.*

b. Time with the past-perfect subjunctive, *after*, *when :* as,

Cum hostīs fūdisset, moenia ipsa oppugnāre est adgressūs (*Liv.* VIII. 16), *after routing the enemy, he advanced to storm the fortifications themselves.*

c. In indefinite expressions†, quum, when preceded by a verb signifying existence, is followed by a subjunctive : as,

Erit illud prŏfectō tempus quum grăuissŭmi hŏmĭnis fĭdem dēsīdĕrēs (*Cic.* p. Mil. 26. 69), *there assuredly will come the time when you will feel the loss of so high-principled a man.*

d. When a time is precisely defined, as for instance by the two particles tum quum, the indicative is used even with the past tenses, both perfect and imperfect : as,

Tum quum in āsĭā res magnās permulti āmīsērant, scīmus rōmae fīdem concĭdisse (*Cic.* p. leg. Man. 7. 19), *at the time*

---

* In form an old accusative of the relative. Compare the English *when*, the old accusative of *who*, as *then* is of *the*.

† Yet after postquam, ubi, and ut, in a sense nearly the same, the indicative aorist is used.

‡ See § 1189.

when very many lost vast properties in Asia, we know that at Rome credit was knocked down.

Quid quum dăbās his lĭtērās, nōn eōs ad mē uentūrōs arbĭtrābārē? (*Cic.* ad Fam. III. 7. 3) *well, and when you were handing the letter to them, did you think that they would not come to me?*

e. When, used with the perfect and the other tenses in a manner not included under the heads *a*, *b*, *c*, and requiring commonly the indicative: as,

Quum se intĕr ĕquĭtum turmās insinuāuĕrunt*, ex essēdis dĕsĭliunt (*Caes.* B. G. IV. 33), *their habit is, when they have worked their way among the squadrons of cavalry, to leap down from their chariots.*

Quum caesăr in galliam uĕnit, altĕrius factiōnis princĭpēs ĕrant aedui, altĕrius sēquănī (*Caes.* B. G. VI. 12), *when Caesar first came into Gallia, the Ædui were at the head of one party, the Sequani of the other.*

Longum illud tempus, quum nōn ĕro, măgis mē mŏuet quam hoc exĭguom (*Cic.* ad Att. XII. 18. 1), *that long period, when I shall no more exist, has more influence with me than the present short span.*

Cum inde ăbeot, iam tum incēperat Turba intĕr eos (*Ter.* E. IV. 4. 58), *when I came away, there had already commenced a row between them.*

Iam addicta atque abdūcta erat, quom ad portum uenio (*Plaut.* Merc. III. 4. 31), *she had already been knocked down (by the auctioneer) and carried off, when I got to the harbour.*

f. When, where the time or circumstances are first defined, and then follows quum with an indicative verb, which is in substance the main verb of the sentence: as,

Lĕgēbam tuas lĭttĕras, quum mihi ĕpistŏla affertŭr ă leptā, circumuallātum essē pompēium (*Cic.* ad Att. IX. 12. 1), *I was in the act of reading your letter, when behold despatches*

---

* This reading, not insinuauerint, is justified by the Mss. and required by the idiom of the language. It is one of many such passages corrupted by editors. See Madvig ad Cic. de Fin. v. 15; and above § 1159.

† A present with the power of an aorist seems to have been the idiom of the language in phrases of this kind. Compare in this same play respicio (II. 3. 50), aduenio (II. 3. 53), perit (III. 3. 16). See also § 458.

are brought me from Lepta, stating that Pompey was completely blockaded.

Commŏdum ad tē dĕdĕram littĕras, cum ad mē diŏnўsius fuit (*Cic.* ad Att. x. 16. 1), *I had only that moment sent off a letter to you, when Dionysius made his appearance here*[*].

g. It is used to express a long period down to the present inclusive: as,

Hánc domum Iam múltos annos ĕst quom possideo ĕt colo (*Plaut.* Aul. prol. 3), *this house I have occupied and taken care of these many years.*

Multi anni sunt cum ille in aerĕ meo est (*Cic.* ad Fam. xv. 14. 1), *it is now many years that that man has been in my debt.*

Quia séptem menses súnt, quom in hasce aedis pedem Nemo intro tetulit (*Plaut.* Most. ii. 2. 39), *because for the last seven months not a soul has set foot in this house.*

h. With two indicative verbs in the same tense, it expresses identity of action as well as identity of time (when the best translation is by the preposition *in*): as,

Quae quum tăces, nulla essĕ concēdis (*Cic.* p. Rosc. Am. 19. 54), *in the very fact that you say nothing about these matters, you acknowledge that they amount to nothing.*

Praeclārē făcis quum puĕrum dĭlĭgĭs (*Cic.* de Fin. iii. 2. 9), *you act a most noble part in thus loving the child.*

Lŏco illē mōtŭs est cum est ex urbĕ dēpulsŭs (*Cic.* in Cat. ii. 1. 1), *in driving him out of Rome, we dislodged him from his (military) position.*

i. When used as an equivalent for quŏd, it has an indicative: as,

Grātŭlor tĭbi quum tantum vălēs ăpŭd eum (*Cic.* ad Fam. ix. 14. 3), *I congratulate you on your having such influence with him.*

j. Quum, *since*, *as*, *although*, used to denote a reason† *for* or *against*, requires the subjunctive. Thus,

---

* Literally 'at my house.' See § 1161.

† The text of Cicero, particularly in the sixth and following books of the miscellaneous letters, has often quum or quando where the best Mss. have the more correct reading quoniam, viz. where a reason is given and an indicative mood follows. See Wunder's V. L. ex codice Erfurtensi, praef. p. 97 &c. See also § 1229.

Qui cum ūnā domō iam capī nōn possint, in aliās domōs exeunt (*Cic.* de Off. 1. 17. 54), *and as at last they cannot all be contained in one house, they move off into other houses.*

Druentia quum aquas uim uehat ingentem, nōn tamen nāuium patiens est (*Liv.* xxi. 31), *the Durance, although it carries with it a tremendous volume of water, still is not able to float ships.*

k. Quum followed by tum* unites two clauses, the first of which deals with what is general, or common, or old, while the latter opposes to it that which is special, or strange, or new. Hence the tum is often accompanied by emphatic adverbs, such as maxumē, imprimis, uērō, &c. In this construction sometimes the subjunctive mood, more commonly the indicative, follows quum. Not unfrequently the quum is used without any verb of its own. Thus,

Quum plūrumas commoditātēs amīcitiā contineat, tum illa praestat omnibus (*Cic.* de Am. 7. 23), *among the very many advantages which friendship possesses, the most important of all is this.*

Quum ipsam cognitiōnem iūris auguriī consequī cupiō, tum mercūle tuis studiīs ergā mē delector (*Cic.* ad Fam. iii. 9. 3), *at the same time that I am eager to acquire a knowledge of the augural law for its own sake, I am upon my word charmed with your zeal in my favour.*

Quōs ego senātōres uīdī, qui acerrumē cum cōlōrā, tum hoc iter pompēī uituperārent (*Cic.* ad Att. vii. 5. 4), *what senators have I seen most fiercely attacking every thing that had been done, but above all this march of Pompey's!*

Vērō always gives great emphasis to the word before it. Its chief uses are as follows:—

a. Added to ēnim *indeed,* giving it greater power: as,

Enimuērō daue nīl locist segnitiae nec socordiae (*Ter.* And. 1. 3. 1), *indeed, indeed, friend Davus, there is no room now for sloth or stupidity.*

b. In answering questions† emphatically, in which case it commonly follows either the verb or a personal pronoun which stands first in a sentence. Thus,

---

* See § 1231. † See §§ 378, 586, 1079, 1427.

Egŏ uĕrō Apūliam prŏbō (*Cic.* ad Att. x. 7.1), *yes, my friend, you are right; I do approve of Apulia (as the place for you to go to).*

c. It is particularly used after the pronoun i- or eo-, as also after the particles of time, tum, ŭbi, ŭt, to introduce the end of a climax, *then beyond all mistake, then with a vengeance:* as,

Hoc sĕnātuī cūram iniēcit nē tum uĕrō sustĭnēri sēdĭtiō non possĕt (*Liv.* v. 7), *this filled the senate with alarm lest their last hope should now be destroyed, and the sedition should be indeed past resistance.*

Vt uĕrō* nŭmĭdās insēquentĕs ăquam ingressī sunt, tum rĭgēre omnĭbus corpŏrĭ (*Liv.* xxi. 54), *but the moment that, in pursuit of the Numidians, they entered the water, then beyond all mistake the bodies of all the men became numbed with cold.*

Id uĕrō ĭta accendit ănĭmōs ut pĕr omnē fās atquĕ nĕfās sĕcūtūrī uĭndĭcem lībertātis uĭdērentŭr (*Liv.* vi. 14), *this indeed completed their indignation, enraging them to such a degree that they seemed ready to follow the assertor of their liberties even to the violation of every divine and human law.*

d. As a connecting particle it may be translated by *but;* yet some words should always be inserted to express the importance of the matter added: as,

Certior factŭs est trīs iam cōpiārum partīs heluētios transdūxissĕ, quartam uĕrō partem citrā flūmen rĕlĭquam essĕ (*Caes.* B. G. I. 12), *he received information that the Helvetii had conveyed over three parts of their forces, but that the fourth part fortunately was still on his side of the river.*

1457 Vt is translated by *that* or *to, as, how, when,* &c. Its constructions are as follows:

a. *That, to,* to express an object (always with an imperfect subjunctive)‡: as,

---

* Observe that the full translation of *uero* after *ut* or *ubi* is not given until the apodosis as it is called of the sentence. To understand the force of *uero* in this passage, it should be known that the Roman troops had come out of their camp without sufficient clothing, without breakfast, in a winter-day amid snow and wind.

† *Vt* is in origin only another form of *quod.* The difference in form is explained by the several changes which have occurred in *illud* and *illui,* in *quoius* and *cuius,* in *cuei* and *ubi.*

‡ See § 1179.

Ab ărătro abduxĕrunt cincinnātum, ut dictātŏr esset (*Cic.* de Fin. II. 4. 12), *they took Cincinnatus from the plough, that he might be dictator.*

Sĕd (ūt ĭd eā quae coniunctiōrā rēbus tuis sunt renortăr) (*Cic.* ad Fam. I. 8. 5), *but (to return to what is more closely connected with your affairs*).

Vt te omnes di deaeque pérduint (*Ter.* Haut. IV. 6. 6), *oh that all the gods and goddesses would destroy thee!*

Hos lăbōres timeo ut sustineās (*Cic.* ad Fam. XIV. 2. 3), *these labours I am afraid you will not support.*

b. That, so that, to, so as to, to express a result (always with a subjunctive)† : as,

Sōl efficit ūt omniă flōreant (*Cic.* N. D. II. 15. 41), *the sun causes every thing to blossom.*

Siciliam Itā uexāuit ūt eā restĭtuī in antīcum stătum nullō mŏdŏ possit (*Cic.* I. Verr. 4. 12), *he has harassed Sicily to such a degree that it cannot by any means be restored to its former condition.*

c. That, in the sense of *granting that, even allowing that, although*‡, in which case it commonly begins the sentence (still with a subjunctive) : as,

Sĕd ūt fuĕrīs dignior, non compĕtītŏr in culpast (*Cic.* p. Planc. 4. 10), *but even allowing you were the more worthy of the two, it is not your competitor who is in fault.*

Vērum ūt hoc non sit, praeclărum spectăcŭlum mihi prŏpōnŏ (*Cic.* ad Att. II. 15. 2), *but even supposing this is not so, I promise myself a glorious sight.*

d. That, to think that, the idea of ——! in elliptical phrases of indignation or ridicule§ : as,

Pătŏr ūt ōbesse filiō dēbeat ! (*Cic.* p. Planc. 13. 31), *the idea of a father being bound to damage his son !*

e. In explanation of some preceding word, *namely* (still with a subjunctive) : as,

Quŏd ipsi diēbus uigintī aegerrĭmē confēcērunt, ut flūmen transīrent, ille ūnō diē fēcĕrat (*Caes.* D. G. I. 13), *what they themselves had completed with the greatest difficulty in twenty*

---

* See § 1227 g.   † See §§ 1182, 1187.
‡ See § 1227 b.   § See § 1227 e.

days, namely the passage of the river, the other had done in a single day.

f. How (with an indicative in direct, a subjunctive commonly in indirect sentences): as,

Vt ŭălĕs ? (*Plaut.* Most. III. 2. 29) *how do you do ?*

Audīstī ut mē circumstĕtĕrint (*Cic.* ad Att. I. 16. 4), *you heard how they planted themselves round me.*

g. As, to express similarity, often with *sic* or *Ita so* to correspond with it. An indicative is required in this and all the following constructions. Thus,

Ită est, ut scrībis* (*Cic.* ad Att. VII. 8. 1), *it is as you say.*

Ipsĕ rex, sic ut sompno excĭtŭs ĕrat, sēmĭnūdus fūgit (*Liv.* XXIV. 40), *the king himself, just as he was when roused from sleep, with but half his clothes on, runs off.*

Hŏmo ŭt ĕrat fŭrĭōsus respondit (*Cic.* p. Rosc. Am. 12.33), *the fellow with his usual madness replied.*

Illi, ŭt est hŏmĭnum gĕnus suspīciōsum, hoc arbĭtrantŭr (*Cic.* in Caecil. 9. 28), *those* (*Sicilians*), *with that readiness to suspect which characterises their nation, hold this opinion.*

h. As, to judge from what ———. Thus,

Vt stăm rem uideo, stĭust obsaturābere (*Ter.* Haut. IV. 8. 29), *to judge from what I see of that business of yours, you will have your fill of it.*

i. As was to be expected ———. Thus,

Vt ăb īrātŏ uictŏrĕ (*Liv.* XXI. 12), *as might be expected from an angry conqueror.*

j. As, so far as is possible, making allowance for ——— (in elliptical phrases, no verb following the conjunction‡). Thus,

Multum ut tempŏrĭbŭs illis uăluit dīcendō (*Cic.* Brut. 7. 27), *he had great power in oratory, making allowance for those times.*

Non nihil ŭt in tantis malis est prōfectum (*Cic.* ad Fam. XII.

---

* Literally 'write,' the extract being from a letter in answer to one from Atticus.

† See § 238, note.

‡ Some such phrase as *fieri potest* understood. This construction must be carefully distinguished from another elliptical use of *ut* with *fieri solet* understood, 'as naturally happens.' See Heindorf ad Hor. Sat. I. 6. 30.

2. 2), *some progress has been made, considering the very bad state of affairs.*

k. To express contrast, rather than similarity, when the ūt and ītă may be translated by *though, yet.* Thus,

Vt lŏcus prŏcul mūrō sătīs aecūs ăgendīs uīneīs fuit, ītă haudquāquam prospĕrē, postquam ĭd ēffectum ŏpĕris uentumst, coeptīs succēdēbat (*Liv.* xxi. 7), *although the ground at a distance from the wall was sufficiently level for bringing up the vineæ, yet when they came to the actual employment of them, no success whatever attended their efforts.*

l. As applied to time, ūt commonly signifies immediate succession, *the instant that,* and is most frequently followed by the aorist of the indicative: as,

Fūgă sătellĭtum, ut iăcentem uīdĕrĕ rēgem, factast (*Liv.* xxiv. 7), *a flight among the guards took place the moment they saw the king lying on the ground.*

m. It is also used to denote the point from which a period of time commences, but with the same notion of *immediate* succession, *from the very moment that:* as,

Vt Cătĭlīna ērūpīt ex urbĕ, semper uīgĭlāuī (*Cic.* in Cat. iii. 1. 3), *from the very moment that Catiline sallied from Rome, I have ever been on the watch.*

Vt ăb urbĕ discessī, nullum ădhūc intermīsī diem, quin ălĭquid ad tĕ littĕrārum dărem (*Cic.* ad Att. vii. 15), *from the time of my leaving the city, I have never yet allowed a single day to pass, without sending you something in the way of a letter.*

Vt primum fŏrum attĭgī, spectāuī semper ut tĭbi possem quam maxĭme essĕ coniunctūs (*Cic.* ad Fam. v. 8. 3), *from my first setting foot in the forum to the present hour I have ever made it an object to be as closely as possible united with you.*

ORDER OF WORDS.

In the simplest form of sentence, viz. one which denotes an action, the common order is the nominative, the accusative, the

---

* Other examples are: *ut semel emigrauimus* (*Plaut.* Most. ii. 2. 39), *uxorem ut duxit* (*Ter.* Hec. v. 1. 25), *ut uenit* (*Hor.* Sat. ii. 2. 128), *ut tetigi* (*Ov.* Trist. iii. 8. 27), *ut fluxit* (*Hor.* Epod. 7. 19), *ut equitauit* (*Hor.* Od. iv. 4. 42).

verb; *i. e.* first the quarter whence the action proceeds, then the direction of that action, lastly the action itself. Any words belonging to the nominative and accusative commonly follow them, while those belonging to the verb commonly precede it. The latter consist of adverbs or adverbial phrases which express the time, manner, means, and generally the attending circumstances.

1459 But as the grammatical connection between Latin words is expressed in the terminations of those words, a greater freedom of position is admissible than would be practicable without ambiguity in English. Hence the words of a Latin sentence are commonly placed with a view to marking their relative importance and emphasis,* and on this principle must the arrangement of the Latin sentence be studied.

1460 The most conspicuous place in a sentence or clause of a sentence is the first. Hence this place is allotted to an emphatic word. Thus, Cæsar's Gallic war properly begins with the word *Gallia*. Again, in the seventh chapter there occurs a sentence beginning with *Cæsar*,† because the preceding paragraph spoke only of what the other party, the Helvetii, were doing. Hence a sentence thus beginning with the nominative of a proper name should have some such words as *on the other hand, meanwhile*, &c. inserted after the nominative, to give it a sufficient prominence in English.

1461 A still greater emphasis is given to *other* words‡ when placed at the commencement of a sentence, because the very inversion of the ordinary order draws the greater attention to them: as,

Susceptum§ cum săguntīnis bellum, hăbendum cum rōmānis est (*Liv.* xxi. 10), *we began the war with Saguntum, we must conduct it against Rome.*

---

* Emphasis always implies an opposition to some other word expressed or understood; and the student would do well in each case to ask himself what the opposed word or notion is.

† See also the sentences beginning with *Dumnorix*, c. 9; *Helvetii*, c. 11; *Cæsar*, c. 18; or *Liv.* xxi. c. 3, *Hanno*; c. 5, *Hannibal*; c. 7, *Hannibal*; c. 11, *Saguntini.*

‡ See the examples in interrogative sentences, § 1417. See also the position of the verb in cases of concession, §§ 1156, 1227 *b*, and in hypothetical conditions, § 1219; also § 1436 *b*, third example.

§ Still *susceptum* in the Latin is only a participle; but the English translation would lose its force if the sentence began with 'the war.'

The word *est**, commonly the most unimportant word in a sentence, acquires a strong accent when placed first in a sentence or clause (see § 1080, 1st example; § 997, 3d example); but *est* and *ĕrat* are also found in the first place when a formal narrative or description commences† : as,

Erant in eā lēgiōnĕ fortissimi uiri centūriōnes qui &c. (*Caes. B. G.* v. 44), *now there happened to be in that legion two very brave officers, with the rank of centurions, who &c.*‡

Est in sēcessū longō lŏcŭs &c. (*Virg. A.* i. 159), *there is in a deep recess a place &c.*

Relatives, interrogatives, and conjunctions naturally occupy the first place in their several clauses. If they give up this place to another word, the strangeness§ of the transposition gives unusual emphasis to the word thus occupying the first place : as,

Nos túa progénies, caeli quibus ádnuis árcem (*Virg. A.* i. 254¶), *we, thine own progeny, to whom thou promisest the height of heaven.*

Adeon rem rĕdisse, pătrem ŭt extimescam (*Ter. Ph.* 1. 3. 1), *to think that matters should be come to this, that a father should be the object of my dread !*

Posthác si quidquam, nil precor (*Ter. Ph.* 1. 2. 92), *if aught occur hereafter, I offer no prayer (for him).*

Ego illius ferrĕ possum magnificā uerba, Verbā dum sunt (*Ter. E.* iv. 6. 3), *I can bear that fellow's grand words, so long as they are mere words.*

---

* Thus in Greek, ἐστί, generally an enclitic, has an accent when it commences a sentence.

† The monosyllabic verbs *dat, fit, it*, seem at times to occupy the first place when not emphatic. Possibly their very brevity is a reason for giving them this advantage, lest they be wholly overlooked. See a parallel case in § 1489, note §.

‡ See also I. 6, *Frant*; III. 12, *Erant* &c.; v. 6, *Erat*; v. 23, *Erat* &c.; vi. 38, *Erat.* See also *Virg. A.* ii. 21.

§ This doctrine of emphasis growing out of a strange position is well exemplified in the heroic verse. The most natural place for a sentence to begin is at the beginning of a verse. But there occur passages where a sentence begins in the sixth foot; and in such cases the isolated word is always specially emphatic in good writers. See Bentley ad *Lucan.* I. 231, and *Journal of Education,* iv. 356. Perhaps too, when a sentence terminates with a word in the first foot of a line, that equally isolated word should be one of importance.

¶ Compare also v. 1, *Troiae qui* &c.; 392, *Tyrios qui* &c.; and III. 656, *ingens cui* &c.

1464. It should be recollected that there are many actual pauses in a sentence where the printer inserts not even a comma. The word which follows such a pause must, for the purposes of emphasis, be considered a commencing word*.

1465. It must be recollected too that many little words, as ŭt, sī, ĕt, nĕo, sĕd, ns, nŏnt, ĭn, quamt, and the prepositions, are at times proclitics‡, that is, pronounced with the word which follows them, so that they must not be deemed to be first words to the exclusion of the following word. See Addenda.

1466. The last place in a sentence is often an emphatic one: as,

Qui hŏnos post conditam hanc urbem hăbĭtust tŏgāto antĕ mĕ nēmĭnī (*Cic.* Phil. II. 6. 13), *an honour which since the foundation of this city was never paid to any one wearing a toga before me.*

Aliŭd ĭtĕr hăbĕbant nullum (*Caes.* B. G. I. 7), *other road they had none.*

Apŭd helvētios longē ditissimus fuit orgĕtŏrix (*Caes.* B. G. I. 2), *among the Helvetii by far the richest man was Orgetorix.*

Nam ex his praĕdiis talĕnta argenti bina capiēbat statim (*Ter.* Ph. v. 3. 6), *for from these farms he received two talents of silver every year invariably.*

Animos nestros temptābunt semper, ulres nōn expĕrientŭr (*Liv.* IV. 5), *your courage and your feelings they will attempt to master, aye without intermission; of your actual strength they will make no trial.*

1467. It has been stated that the ordinary place of a verb is at the end, and that it is emphatic at the beginning of a sentence. When placed elsewhere it has the power of making the preceding word or words emphatic|| : as,

---

* Thus in the ordinary hexameter there is frequently a pause after the first two feet and a half, which is followed by an emphatic word: as in *Virg.* Buc. x. 75,—

Gálla, cúius amor } tantúm mihi créscit in hóras,
Quántum uére nouo } ulridis se súbicit álnus;—

where *uiridis* means 'with the sap flowing freely,' not 'green.'

† See § 1404. 1.

‡ In the Mss. these little words are very often, if not generally, written in immediate connection with the following word.

§ See § 28.

|| The reason of this appears to be, that the predicate of a sentence is

Săguntum uestri circumsĭdent exercĭtŭs : mox karthāgĭnem circumsĭdēbunt rōmānae lĕgĭōnēs (*Liv.* xxi. 10), *Saguntum is besieged by your armies : ere long Carthage will be besieged by the legions of Rome.*

Vtĭnam prō dĕcŏrĕ tantum et non prō sălūte esset certāmĕn (*Liv.* xxi. 41), *oh that the struggle had been one for glory only and not for existence.*

Vt seruēmĭnī dest* uōbīs ănĭmus ? Quid, sī mŏriendum prō pătria esset, făcĕrētĭs ? (*Liv.* xxiii. 60) *when the object is to save yourselves, does your courage run low ? What then would you have done, if you had had to die for your country ?*

Prius semprōniō per cĭuium agmen quam pĕr hostiúm† fuit ērumpendum (*Liv.* xxii. 60), *Sempronius had to force a passage through the ranks of his own countrymen before he forced one through those of the enemy.*

1468   Sometimes the word thus placed before the verb is not itself so emphatic as the word with which it is intimately connected, and which then stands at the end of the sentence : as,

O Geta, Prouinciam cepisti duram (*Ter. Ph.* i. 2.22), *oh Geta, the duty you undertook was a hard one.*

Maecēnās ătăuīs ĕdĭtĕ rēgĭbus (*Hor. Od.* i. 1.1), *Maecenas sprung of royal line.*

1469   An adjective‡ or dependent genitive, if emphatic, commonly precedes its substantive; whereas when not emphatic, it commonly follows§. Thus,

Saepe et contemptūs hostis cruentum certāmĕn ēdĭdit, ĕt inclĭtī pŏpŭlī rēgesquĕ perlĕuī mōmentō uictⁱ sunt (*Liv.* xxi.

commonly the more emphatic part, and that the verb is commonly the chief part of the predicate. Observe too that a participle in its own clause has the same influence.

* So generally in Mss., not *deest*.

† The comma usually inserted after *hostium* is inadmissible, as the *fuit* should be pronounced almost as though it were attached to it like an enclitic.

‡ In the phrase *tuom officium facere* 'to do your duty,' it would at first seem that *tuom* has no title to the emphatic position which it commonly, though not always occupies in this phrase; but the answer is, that *officium* (= *opificium*) originally meant not 'duty,' but 'work,' so that the phrase literally translated is, 'to do your own work, not another person's.'

§ When a substantive is very short compared to its adjective, the former commonly precedes, as *aes alienum, res familiaris*.

43), *if a despised foe has often maintained* a bloody *contest, not less often have* renowned *states and monarchs been conquered by the* slightest *blow.*

Pulchrum erit campāni, rōmānum impĕrium uestrā fĭdē, uestris uĭrĭbus rĕtentum esse (*Liv.* XXIII. 5), *it will be a proud reflection, men of Capua, that the empire of* Rome *herself was saved from falling by your fidelity, by your power.*

1470   A still stronger emphasis belongs to the adjective or dependent genitive when it throws* as it were its substantive to the end of the sentence† : as,

Dē quō quum dispŭtārem, *tuam* mihi dări uellem cotta ēlŏquentiam (*Cic.* N. D. II. 59. 147), *in discussing which I should have wished your eloquence, Cotta, to have been given to me.*

Hoc ŭbi iŭuentus rōmāna indĭcĭmus bellum (*Liv.* II. 12), *such the war which we, the youth of Rome, declare against you.*

Bonds me absente hic cŏnfecistis nŭptias (*Ter.* Ph. II. 1. 28), *a pretty marriage you have knocked up here in my absence.*

E quĭbūs ūnŭs ĕuel quĭdŭĭs aspergĕrē cunctos, Praetĕr eum qui praebĕt, ăquā (*Hor.* Sat. I. 4. 87), *one of whom delights to sprinkle with any (the dirtiest) water all save him who acts purveyor.*

Nĕc cum *huiusmodi* ūsus uenit ŭt conflictarēs malo (*Ter.* Ph. III. 3. 21), *and have never been called upon to struggle with a misery of this kind.*

Nam per *hius unam*, ut audio, aut uiuam aŭt moriar sentĕntiam (*Ter.* Ph. III. 1. 19), *for on his one vote it depends, I hear, whether I am to live or die.*

1470.1   And generally any qualifying word may in this way be separated from the word qualified : as,

Itā patrem adolescĕntis facta haec tŏlerare audiō uiolenter (*Ter.* Ph. v. 1. 4), *so very furiously is the young man's father offended I hear with these proceedings.*

---

* This wide separation of the adjective and substantive would cause confusion, but that the great emphasis of the adjective causes it still to be ringing in the ear when we come to the substantive.

† Compare in the first book of the Aeneid, v. 647, *patrius amor, rapidum Achaten*; v. 661, *noua consilia*; v. 673, *nostro dolore*; v. 675, *Iunonia hospitia*; v. 679, *magno amore*; v. 680, *nostram mentem*; v. 688, *notas uoltus.*

1471 The demonstrative pronouns, and the logical pronoun i- or eo-, commonly occupying the place before the substantive, appear to acquire a special emphasis when placed after it: as,

Te appī tuumquĕ cǎput sanguine hōc consĕcrō (*Liv.* III. 48), *thee Appius, and thy head with this blood I devote.*

1471.1 Numerals are often placed at the end of a sentence or clause.*

Gallia est omnis diuīsa in partīs trīs (*Caes.* B. G. I. 1), *Gallia as a whole is divided into three parts.*

1472 Nouns in apposition and the genitive commonly follow the substantive to which they belong, and therefore have an emphasis when prefixed to the substantive: as,

Vnī consŭlī scrutīniō ius fuit dīcendī dictātōris (*Liv.* XXII. 31), *to Servilius alone, as consul, belonged the power to name a dictator.*

Sēd ĭtā forsĭtan dĕcuit cum foedĕrum ruptōrĕ dūcē ac pŏpŭlō deōs ipsōs commĭttĕre ac prōflīgārĕ bellum, nos qui sĕcundum deos uiŏlātī sūmus, commissum ac prōflīgātum confĭcĕrĕ (*Liv.* XXI. 40), *but perhaps it was fitting that, with a general and a people who habitually violate treaties, the gods themselves should commence the war and break the neck of it†, and that we who next to the gods have been injured should then come in and finish it.*

Fābius pŏtens uir, quum inter sui corpŏris hŏmines, tum ĕtiam ad plēbem (*Liv.* VI. 34), *Fabius, a man of influence not merely among the men of his own body‡, but also with the commonalty.*

1473 As an emphatic word demands a large share of the attention, it tends to prevent the mind from dwelling on the word or words which follow. Hence as the first place in a sentence or clause is allotted to emphatic words, so the second place is adapted to unimportant words§, which are inserted here although unconnected with the adjoining words: as,

---

* A habit borrowed probably from the form of accounts, where the numbers are placed at the end of the lines in a vertical column for the convenience of addition.

† Literally 'to give the knock-down blow which all-but finishes.'

‡ i.e. class or order.

§ Such words should be read most faintly, so as not to attract attention.

Iānuā sē ac pariētibus texit (*Cic.* p. *Mil.* 7. 18), *he protected himself behind the gate and the walls of his house.*

An hūiūs illī lēgis mentiōnem făcĕre ausūs esset? (*Cic.* p. *Mil.* 12. 33) *or would he have dared to make mention of this law?*

Hunc illī ē nāuī ēgressum comprehendērant atque in uincŭlīs conīēcĕrant (*Caes.* B. G. IV. 27), *this man had no sooner disembarked than they had seized him and thrown him into prison.*

Magnus ibi numĕrus pĕcŏris repertŭs est (*Caes.* B. G. V. 21), *a great number of sheep was found there.*

Magnam haec rēs caesărī difficultātem adfĕrēbat (*Caes.* B. G. VII. 10), *no little difficulty did this occasion to Caesar.*

Rĕsistēs autem sī sătis firmus stĕtĕris, sī te nĕque collēgae uānā glōriā nĕque tuā falsa infāmiā mōuĕrit (*Liv.* XXII. 39), *and resist him you will, if you stand firm enough, if — nor your colleague's empty glory, nor your own ill-founded disgrace affect you.*

Vnō diē intermissō gallī, atque hoc spătiō magnō crātium numĕrō effectō, mĕdiā nocte ad mūnītiōnēs accēdunt (*Caes.* B. G. VII. 81), *having allowed one day to pass (without any attack), and having in this interval made up a great quantity of hurdles, at midnight the Gauls quietly advance to the lines.**

Quōs sibi caesărī oblātōs gāuīsus rĕtĭnērī iussit (*Caes.* B. G. IV. 13), *delighted that these men should be thrown in his way, Caesar ordered them to be detained*‡.

1474   It is because of their enclitic character§ that autem, quidem, quŏque, &c. never occupy the first place in a clause or sentence. Igitŭr, ĕnim, uĕrō, are occasionally found at the beginning, and

---

* Many editors would place a comma before *Galli*, thus giving it an importance it does not deserve. It is in fact a sort of enclitic, and should appear in the English translation in the least prominent place. Similarly a comma should follow, not precede the word *Caesar* or *Galba* in the first line of the following chapters,—B. G. II. 2, II. 7; III. 5, III. 28; IV. 6, IV. 15, IV. 20; V. 7, V. 11.

† Here both *sibi* and *Caesar* have the nature of enclitics.

‡ For the enclitical position of a word which refers equally to two words or to two clauses, see § 1438 b and s.

§ The vocative when in the first place is of course emphatic. Otherwise it is commonly an enclitic, and should be thrown in after an emphatic word.

ORDER OF WORDS. 421

then have more importance than when they occupy their more ordinary place after the first word.

1475 In short* sentences, words which are opposed to one another are either brought close together, or placed as far apart as possible, in the latter case occupying the two emphatic positions of first and last.

> Hostis hostem occīdĕrĕ uŏlui (*Liv.* II. 12), *I wished to slay the enemy of my country.*
> Hospĕs necauit hŏspitem (*Plaut. Most.* II. 2. 48), *he strangled one who was his own guest.*
> Cum hānc sibi uidebit praesens praesentem ēripi (*Ter. Ad.* IV. 5. 34), *when he shall see her torn from him before his very face.*
> Rătiō nostrā consentit, pugnat ōrătiō (*Cic. de Fin.* III. 3. 10), *our principles agree, our language is at variance.*
> Něc ad mortem minūs ănimi est, quam fuit ad caedem (*Liv.* II. 12), *nor have I less courage to die myself, than I had but now to slay another.*
> Mihi măgis littĕrae suut exspectandae ā tē, quam ā mē tĭbi (*Cic.* ad Fam. IX. 10), *I have a better right to expect a letter from you, than you from me.*

1476 When two clauses opposed to one another contain the same word in different cases or tenses, that common word usually precedes the words opposed.

> Si cīuis uester, sīcŭt *ad pācem pĕtendam* uēnit, ĭtă *pācis condĭciōnes* rettŭlisset, sŭperuăcāneum hoc mihi fuisset ĭtĕr (*Liv.* XXI. 13), *if your countryman, who came to ask for peace, had in the same patriotic spirit reported the terms of that peace, this visit would have been superfluous for me.*
> Vincĕrĕ scis, uictōria ūti nescis (*Liv.* XXII. 51), *how to gain a victory, you know; how to use a victory, you do not know.*
> Non sōlum călămĭtātĕ, sĕd ĕtiam călămĭtātis formīdĭnĕ lībĕrātōs (*Cic.* p. L Man. 6. 16), *relieved not merely from ruin, but also from the fear of ruin.*
> Et făcĕ prō thălămi fax mihi mortis ădest (*Ov. Her.* 21. 172), *and in lieu of the marriage-torch the torch of death awaits me.*

* See § 1435 *b* note, and § 1437.

APPENDIX I.

ON THE CRUDE-FORM VIEW OF LANGUAGE, ITS TRUTH AND ITS PRACTICAL ADVANTAGES.[*]

As the very phrase 'crude form' is yet strange to the ears of most scholars, it may be useful to explain what is meant by it; to establish the truth of the new system; and to show the practical advantages which it offers even for elementary instruction.

In the first place, it may be noted, if only to conciliate the attention of readers, that upon the system of crude forms every Sanskrit grammar is constructed.

"Inflection", says Professor Wilson (§ 48 of his Grammar, 2d ed.), "whether of declension or conjugation, is contrived by the Sanskrit grammarians on the same principle. It consists of two parts: 1, the *anga*, 'body,' or inflective base, that is the word itself; and 2, of certain particles, which, being attached to the base, complete the inflected word". He goes on to say, at the latter part of § 51, "there is but one general declension in Sanskrit grammar"; and though it is convenient to divide nouns into classes, yet even then, he adds, "no arrangement admits of more ready reference than that which classes them according to their final letters."

Again, in § 167, he founds the system of conjugation on the *dhâtu*, or 'crude verb;' observing also, in § 171, that "the verb in its inflected form is composed of two elements: 1, the *anga*, or 'base,' the modified verb to which the inflections are subjoined; and 2, certain letters or syllables which constitute the inflectional terminations, and are subjoined to the base."

The exhibition of the Greek[†] and Latin languages upon the

---

[*] Chiefly reprinted from the *English Journal of Education* (Bell), New Series, Nos. 48 and 50 (Dec. 1850 and Feb. 1851).

[†] See the *Elements of Greek Grammar* by Joseph G. Greenwood, Esq., now Principal of Owen's College, Manchester.

crude-form system is in perfect accordance with the passages we here quote from Professor Wilson's Grammar, and with the remarks of Bopp in his *Vergleichende Grammatik*, § 112, &c.

The first proposal in print to apply the principle to the analysis of the classical languages was made by the present writer in a review of Zumpt's Latin Grammar in the first Number of the *Journal of Education*, published by the Society for the Diffusion of Useful Knowledge in 1830 (pp. 98–100 and 105). The system had been previously expounded in the classical lecture-rooms of the University of London (now University College).*

In endeavouring to give a more distinct exposition of the system of crude forms, we shall, for the sake of brevity, for the most part limit our observations to the Latin language.

In the ordinary grammars it is the practice to start from the nominative of a noun, and from the infinitive or first person of the present indicative of a verb. Now the nominative of a noun is something more than the naked word, as it also expresses a certain relation to the sentence. So again, the first person of a verb includes in its termination a representative of the pronoun 'I'. The infinitive mood in like manner presents to us a suffix, by means of which the notion of the verb is expressed in the form of an abstract substantive. Thus, in every one of these three cases we have some foreign matter, so to say, added to the pure metal.

Now the principle of the crude-form system is to get rid of this foreign matter, and thus to exhibit the simplest form of a word, or, as Bopp expresses it, *die Grundform, die nackte Wortgestalt*. But it would be thought a false step to introduce that which, though in a certain sense more true and more philosophical, would involve a complicated process of analysis. To such an objection the supporters of the crude-form system answer, that their principles are not only true, but at the same time are recommended by extreme simplicity. Thus they affirm, with Professor Wilson, that on the crude-form system there is at bottom but one declension and but one conjugation; and if for some purposes it is still

---

* In the year 1836 was published the *Bromsgrove Latin Grammar* by the Rev. G. A. Jacob, M.A. (late Scholar and Tutor of Worcester College, Oxford); which is drawn-up in a great measure, but far from uniformly, upon the crude-form system. Mr. Jacob subsequently published a Greek Grammar upon the same plan.

convenient to divide nouns and verbs into classes, these classes depend upon one simple and unvarying rule, viz. the characteristic or last letter.

But examples will best explain what is meant. In the fourth declension, that of *gradus* for example, the same letters down to the vowel *u* inclusive, appear in every case both of the singular and plural, except in the dative and ablative of the latter, and the doubt which this one exception might suggest is removed by the occurrence of such forms as *verubus*, *acubus*. From the fact of the five letters *gradu* being thus common to all the inflected forms, it becomes to some extent probable that the several ideas of number and case are distinguished by the letters which follow *gradu*. Similarly in the fifth declension, *dies* for example, the three letters *die*, being constant, tend to a similar conclusion. In the third declension, nouns such as *turris*, *avis*, differ much in several of the case-endings from *rex*, *homo*, *aetas*. The former exhibit an *i* in nearly every case; for we have *turrim* in the acc. singular, and *turris*, *avis*, as well as *turres*, *aves* in the acc. plural; *turri*, *avi*, as well as *turre*, *ave* in the abl. sing. Nay, even a plural nom. such as *turris* is well established as an archaic variety. Thus an *i* presents itself in every case of both numbers. On the other hand, we never meet with an acc. *regim*, nor with such plural cases as *regis* or *regium*. Under these circumstances there are strong reasons for separating the consideration of such words as *rex* from those nouns which have a nominative in *is*. Looking then, in the first instance, to *turris* as an example of a class, we find *turri* in every case. To proceed: in the nouns of the first declension, as *musa*, an *a* is traceable through every case of both numbers, if we include in our view such datives as *equabus*, *duabus*, *ambabus*, and the Greek forms μούσαις, &c.

In the nouns so far discussed, the parts common to every case are *gradu*, *die*, *turri*, *musa*; and so we have come across classes which end in four out of the five Latin vowels. There remains one declension, the second, and one vowel, viz. *o*. Now the nouns of this declension exhibit the vowel in question in the dat. and abl. of the singular, in the gen. and acc. of the plural, as *domino*, *dominorum*, *dominos*. The corresponding Greek declension helps us out in many of the other cases, as δοῦλος, δούλοιο or δούλου, δοῦλον, δοῦλοι, δούλοις. But we need not depend on the Greek alone. Cicero also wrote *servos*, *servom*, rather than *servus*, *ser-*

uum; and so in all words where the ordinary ending of these cases would give us the combination -*uus,* -*uum*. Again, Cicero's genitive of *qui* was *quo-ius,* not *cuius*. So also we may fairly assume that *nullíus* with its long *i* is a contraction of *nullo-ius,* a genitive which bears a marked affinity in its termination to the Homeric genitive λογοιο. We may the more safely assume that *nullíus* is only a reduced form of *nulloíus,* because a long *i* in Latin often corresponds to the diphthong οι of the Greek, as in *dominí* (nom. pl.), *dominís,* compared in respect of ending to δουλοι, δουλοις. In the nom. pl. Terence wrote *Adelphoe;* and *oloe* is said to have been used as an archaic form for the nom. *illi*. At any rate, as regards the abl. pl. Festus says: *'aboloes* dicebant pro *ab illis.'* Thus the sing. vocative alone in this declension presents any difficulty. But the change to a short *e* is seen even in the nom., as in *ille, iste, ipse;* and that the last of these grew out of an old *ipsos* is pretty well established by the fact that the old writers give us a nom. *ipsus*. In truth, it is nearly a law of the Latin and other languages, that any short final vowel is soon reduced to a short *e*. Thus *magis, scriberis, aetatis*, scripserunt,* when deprived of the final consonants, become at once *mage, scribere, aetate, scripsere*. Add to this, that a vowel *o* is wholly unknown to the terminations of the other declensions. From all these facts it is inferred that in the second declension the part essential to the noun, as opposed to case-endings, terminates in the vowel *o*.

But we have passed over that portion of the third declension which differs in the mode of forming the cases from *turris*. Examples of such nouns are, if we define them by their nominatives, *rex, nux, lapis, paries, uirtus, aetas, pater, consul, hiemps, ratio, homo, puluis,* &c. Upon any grammatical system such words present anomalies in the nominative case. In the other, or so-called oblique cases, the difficulties are few; and it will be found that the essential part of these words ends in a consonant, viz. *rêg-, nûc-, lapid-, pariĕt-, uirtût-, aetât-, hiĕm-;* and again, *patĕr-, consŭl-, ratiôn-, homôn-, puluis-*. The modification or loss of the final consonant which ensues in the first seven of these nouns on the addition of an *s* to form the nominative, is nearly parallel to what happens in the formation of the perfect tenses, *rexi, duxi, diuisi, misi, rumpsi;* and this was to be expected, as the same consonants

* See Grammar, § 909 note.

are brought into juxtaposition. As regards *pulvis, cucumis* and *cinis*, the final *s* of the nominatives in reality performs a double office. In other words, *pulvius* would have been theoretically a more correct form; and hence it is that the last syllable of this nominative is at times found long, as in Virg. Aen. x. 478, *et uersa pulvis inscribitur hasta*. That the base of *pulvis* must put in a claim to an *s*, is proved by the diminutive *pulvisculus* as compared with *navicula, canicula, fraterculus*. The oblique cases *pulverem, pulveris*, &c. confirm this, for the syllable *er* in these words represents the *is* of the base, just as *er* in *scripserunt* corresponds to the middle syllable *is* of *scripsistis*, and the *er* of the reflective or passive *scribir-is* to the *is* of the simple verb *scribis*. The change of *s* between vowels into *r* is familiar to every Latin scholar. It must also be admitted, on consideration, that while *i* is the vowel which the idiom of the language prefers before *s*, a short *e* is all but required before *r*.

The absolute disappearance of the final *s* in the nominatives *pater, consul, ratio, homo*, and the loss in addition of a liquid from the end of the last pair of words, will need a fuller discussion, and shall be considered presently.

Thus far we have dealt only with the declension of nouns. As regards the verbs, the question is exceedingly simple. No one will have any difficulty in assigning *ama, mone, reg*, and *audi*, as the essential elements in the conjugation of the verbs *ama-re, mone-re, reg-ere*, and *audi-re*. The only parts of the verb *amare* which fail to exhibit an *a* after the *m* are the first person *amo* of the indicative present, and the whole of the present subjunctive, *amem*, &c. But a contraction of *ama-o* into *amo* would be perfectly parallel to what is seen in the Greek grammar in τιμῶ, τιμᾷς; and the compression of *ama-am, ama-as, ama-at*, &c. (which the analogy of *scrib-am, scrib-as, scrib-at*, &c. would have led us to expect) into *amem, ames, amet*, &c. is a matter of no extraordinary character, considering the intimate connection between a long vowel *e* and the simple *a*. A Greek scholar is of course familiar with this fact; and in the Latin perfect *eg-i* (as compared to the present *ag-o*) we seem to have a word which has been contracted from a perfect of reduplication *a-ag-i*. In the second conjugation we should have been able to trace the vowel *e* throughout all the deduced forms, if we had taken for our example any of the verbs *fle-re, ne-re, de-le-re*, or *ex-ple-re*, for in these the perfect and so-called supines still exhibit an *e* in the base of the word. And even among those verbs which commonly form the perfect in -*ui*, as *moneo*, *habeo*, &c., the archaic forms, such as *habeuit*, seem to imply an old perfect *habeui*; for *habuit* must have been a contraction of *habeuerit*, just as *amasso* and *amassim* are admitted to be contractions from old forms *amaueso* and *amauesim*, which preceded *amauero* and *amauerim*. Lastly, the conjugation of *audi-re* in no single instance fails to retain the *i*.

Thus we reduce the four conjugations to the four heads, of verbs in *a*, in *e*, in consonants, and in *i*. The question here suggests itself, how is it that there are not six conjugations to correspond to the six declensions? in other words, what has become of the conjugations in *o* and in *u*? To speak first of the verbs in *u*: the class exists, and as examples of it may be taken the verbs *nu-ere*, *plu-ere*, *acu-ere*, *metu-ere*; but the vowel *u* is rarely subject to contraction with a following vowel, so that it was found unnecessary to separate verbs of this class from those which ended in a consonant. On the whole however it is perhaps desirable, for simplicity's sake, to make a *u* conjugation; and in fact in the third person of the plural of the present indicative these verbs have a peculiarity which distinguishes them from such verbs as *reg-ere*, *scrib-ere*; we mean that *metuunt* and *acquuntur*, though supported by the authority of our grammars and ordinary editions, are not so legitimate, if manuscripts are to be trusted, as *metuont* and *sequntur*. Secondly, an advantage is gained by the separation of verbs in *u* from verbs in a consonant, in the complete analogy of the perfects *col-ui*, *audi-ui*, *ne-ui*, *ama-ui*, *gno-ui*, *plu-ui*, where we have the same suffix added without distinction to a verb ending in a consonant, and to verbs in all the five vowels, *i*, *e*, *a*, *o*, *u*. *Pluuit* was the only perfect known to Livy; and the older writers generally adopted either the form *annuuit*, or at least *annuit* with a long *u*, thus distinguishing the perfect from the present. But there still remains a vacancy caused by the non-appearance of a class of verbs in *o*. Such vacancy can only be filled by a wretched remnant of a conjugation. The forms *gno-ui*, *gno-tum* (*noui*, *notum*), the participles *potus* and *aegrotus*, all point to bases in *o*, viz. *gno-*, *po-*, *aegro-*. The present of the first exhibits a somewhat fuller form in the so-called inceptive *gnosc-o*. That there was once a verb *po-* 'drink,' is proved by the substantives *po-tion-*, *po-culo-* (nom. *potio*, *poculum*), by the frequentative *po-ta-re*, and by the Greek τσ-σω, στσω-σω. Again, a verb *aegro-o* from the adjective *aegero* (nom. *aeger, aegra*, &c.) would be in perfect keeping with the Greek verb δουλο-ω from the noun δουλο- (nom. δουλος). Unfortunately there was a tendency in the Latin language to force all those verbs which are formed from substantives or adjectives of the second declension into the first conjugation. Thus from the substantives *dono-, domino-* (nom. *donum, dominus*), and from the adjectives *misero-, denso-* (nom. *miser, densus*), were deduced the verbs *dona-re, domina-ri, misera-ri, densa-re*. The readiness which exists in the Latin language to interchange the vowels *a* and *o* is well seen in *ignora-re*, from an adjective *ignaro-* (nom. *ignarus*), while the simple adjective *gnaro-* (nom. *gnarus*) is deduced from the verb *gno-* (*gnosco* or *nosco*).

The application of the crude-form system to verbs was virtually adopted in the Latin grammar which was used in the Charter-House during the headship of the Rev. Dr. Russell, as the three conjugations of *amare, monere* and *audire* were treated as contract verbs, *amao amo, amais amas, amait amat*, &c. It has at times been objected to this view, that a contraction of *amait* to *amat* ought to have led to a long vowel in the last syllable of *amat*. The argument is valid, but yet no way damages the theory, for the syllable was originally long, as indeed is seen in the passive *amātur, monētur, audītur*, whereas from *regit* comes *regĭtur*. It is thus that the old writers, as Plautus, Terence, &c. never hesitate to treat the third person of a tense as having a final long syllable, whenever the corresponding vowel is long in the first and second persons of the plural. Examples may be seen in the "Prolegomena" to Ritschl's Plautus, p. 182, &c., such as *velĭt, audĭīt, fūīt, solēt, attinēt, habēt, sīt, dāt, fuēt, mavulīt, afflictāt, egēt, desiderēt, ĭt, lubēt*, though followed in every example he quotes by a word with an initial vowel. There are not wanting similar examples in Virgil and Horace; but editors and teachers complacently get over the difficulty by attributing the unusual length to the so-called principle of cæsura, or to poetical license. What therefore at first view appeared as a defect in the theory of crude forms, only tends to prove the validity of the system.

In the irregular verbs the system of crude forms has its usual superiority. The conjugation for example of the so-called substantive verb, in both Greek and Latin, becomes more intelligible, and therefore more easy to remember, when attention is paid to the form of the base. *Sum* and εἰμί, when examined by themselves, appear utterly unconnected; but a light is thrown even upon these, and still more decidedly on many other parts of the conjugation, when *is* is regarded as the point of departure. Varro, for example, tells us that *esum*, *esumus*, *esunt* were the old forms, which, losing their initial vowel, became severally *sum*, *sumus*, *sunt*. That ἐσ-μι* in Greek should be changed to εἰμί was to be expected from the habitual tendency of that language to suppress the sibilant. Further, an attention to the crude form *is* at once explains the so-called adjectives, but really participles, *absens*, *praesens*, which are but reduced forms of *ab-es-ens*, *prae-es-ens*. Again, the beginner in Greek is somewhat confused at times by the similarity in many parts of the verbs εἰμί ' I am' and εἶμι ' I go'. He will have most of his doubts at once solved by the knowledge that the former has ἐσ, the latter ἰ, for its base.

We next proceed to examine the proposition that all the Latin declensions in reality belong to one type. In the process of word-building the chief difficulty arises from the fact, that if vowels are brought together, contraction commonly results; while if consonants are placed in juxtaposition, the one or the other is frequently modified, so as to harmonise with the other. Hence it follows that where the choice presents itself, we should select for our first consideration those forms, where, of two syllables brought into contact, either the first ends in a consonant and the second begins with a vowel, or *vice versa*, where a vowel at the end of the first is followed by a consonant at the beginning of the second. Now it so happens that among the suffixes which have the office of denoting cases, the majority commence with a vowel. Hence the consonant declension for the most part exhibits the cases in a fuller and less modified form. Thus to take the accusative, *reg-em* assigns a whole syllable to the case-ending, whereas in *turri-m*, *die-m*, *musa-m*, *seruo-m* (or *seruu-m*), *gradu-m*, a vowel has been lost. The same applies to the plural accusatives *reg-es*, *turri-s* (*turres*), *die-s*, *musa-s*, *seruo-s*, *gradu-s*. Similarly in the ablatives of the singular, *reg-d*, *turri* (*turrí*), *diē*, *musā*, *seruō*, *gradū*, the first gives us a letter *d* as the representative of the case, whereas contraction absorbs this vowel in all the vowel declensions, yet at the same time leaves a trace of the same termi-

* The modern Lithuanian, or the language now spoken around Memel and Riga, conjugates its substantive verb, *esmi*, *esi*, *esti*, &c.

nation in the length of the final vowel, as arising from contraction.

The genitival *is* of *reg-is* would lead us to expect from analogy *turri-is*, *die-is*, *musa-is*, *seruo-is*, *gradu-is*, not one of which occurs. This fact at first sight appears somewhat fatal to the theory; but a closer inspection will remove much of the difficulty, and the satisfactory removal of a difficulty ought to be held a strong confirmation of a theory. Now the forms *gru-is*, *su-is*, *anu-is* (the last in Terence) really exhibit what is demanded; and the long *u* in *gradus* gen. has always been held to be the result of contraction from *graduis*. Secondly, in the first and fifth declensions the older language has at least two forms, *musai* and *musas* (as in *pater-familias*, to say nothing of the Greek gen. σοφίας), *diei*, *dies* and *die*. Now it is evident that all these varieties would grow out of *musa-is* and *die-is*. By the loss of the *s* we obtain *musai* and *diei*, and then by an ordinary contraction *musae* and *die*; while the absorption of the *i* in *musais* and *dieis* gives us *musas* and *dies*. In the second declension, although *seruo-is* is unknown, yet in *nullius*, or rather *nullo-ius*, we get even more than the suffix wished for; and a termination *us* harmonises better with the Greek genitival suffix *os* than the ordinary Latin suffix *is*. Thus in the celebrated Bacchanalian inscription we find *senatu-os* for the genitive of *senatu-*.

But there still remain the genitives *auis*, *turris*, which refuse even in their quantity to justify the theory of a previously existing *aui-is* or *turri-is*. The explanation probably is this: the Latin language had some twenty verbs which blended together the third and fourth conjugations, as *facio*, *iacio*, *orior*, *gradior*, which in the first person singular and third plural follow the analogy of the fourth, but in the other persons that of the third conjugation. Nay, as we look further and further back into the language, we find such forms as *parire* for *parere*, *morimur* for *morimur*, *euenat* for *eueniat*, &c. Similarly in the declensions they seem at times to have had double forms, one ending in a consonant, one in the vowel *i*. Thus by the side of *naui-* 'a ship' we may assume a shorter form *nau-*: compare the Greek ναυ-ς. Thus *nau-is* would be a legitimate genitive, and *nau-fragus*, *nauta* need not be deemed contractions from *naui-fragus*, *naui-ta*. So *au* in *auceps*, *auspex*, may have been an original *haso*, signifying 'bird,' from which the gen. *au-is* with a short *i* is regularly formed. In fact, we have probably in this tendency to double forms the explanation of the confusion by which the Romans themselves were led to force the nouns ending in a consonant and those ending in a vowel *i* into a common declension.*

In the genitives plural *die-rum*, *musa-rum*, *servo-rum* we have a common suffix; while in *reg-um*, *sui-um*, *gradu-um* we only miss the *r*, the addition of which would bring them into perfect agreement with the preceding trio. Now this *r* really represents the *s* which formed the essential part of the genitival suffix in the singular, it being a law of the Latin language to change an *s* into *r* whenever it is thrown between vowels, as in such neuters as *opus*, *operis*, in the verb *ese*, *eram*, *ero*, &c. But this *s* of the genitive is itself lost in *musai*, *musae*, in *servi*, in *Vlixi*, *Achilli*, *Cleomeni* (for *Vlixis*, *Achillis*, *Cleomenis*), and in *diei*. Hence there is nothing very surprising in the disappearance of its representative *r* in the plural. Besides, *caelicolum*, *amphorum*, *nummum*, *duum*, and even *dierum*, *specierum*, are more or less familiar contractions for *caelicolarum*, *amphorarum*, *nummorum*, *duorum*, *dierum*, *specierum*. Lastly, it is a well-known fact that *nucerum*, *bouerum* were the old forms of *nucum*, *boum*. And these two words by the way justify the theory at which we have hinted already, that the plural cases are in reality formed from the singular genitive by the addition of a suffix for plurality. Thus *nucer* and *bouer*, of the two archaic forms *nucerum*, *bouerum*, represent the singular genitives *nucis*, *bouis*, precisely as from the base *cinis* or *puluis* we have a genitive *ciner-is*, *puluer-is*. Thus *musarum* is for *musas-um*, of which *musas* is an old genitive singular. In the Greek language this *s* falling between vowels is of course lost as usual, and we have μουσων instead of μουσασ-ων. Similarly theory would give us for the noun γενεσ- (nom. γενος) a singular genitive γενεσ-ος, but in place of this the Greek ear preferred γενε-ος; while the Latin has *gener-is*.

What we have said of the plural genitive being formed directly from the singular genitive has its parallel in the accusative. Thus *musam*, *servom* should be considered as the Latin mode of writing what would have appeared in Greek as *musm* and *servon*. The

* Indeed there is strong reason for believing that the final *i* is in origin a diminutival suffix, the special power of which was soon lost. In other words the two forms *nou-* and *noui-* stood to each other in the same relation as our *lad* and *laddie*.

addition of an *s* as the symbol of plurality would have given us *musans*, *seruons*; but as *n* was never pronounced in Latin, any more than in Greek, before the consonant *s*, it was at last omitted in writing, and so there arose *musas*, *serus*, but of course with a long vowel. In the Cretan dialect of the Greek language such a form as δουλονς for the accusative plural was in ordinary use; but the Attic dialect substituted δουλους, precisely as the nominative of οδοντς became not οδοντς but οδους.

The Latin dative *reg-i* would suggest other datives, *auii*, *dici*, *musai*, *serusi*, *gradui*. Of these *dici* and *gradui* occur in the ordinary language; *musai* is an archaic variety of *musae*; and even in the second declension *quoi*, as we have already observed, exhibits the desired form. But *gradui* and *dici* are often contracted into the disyllables *gradu* and *dic*. Moreover the Greek grammar habitually so far suppresses the final *i* as to make it subscript, which seems very like retaining it as an etymological symbol, while in pronunciation it was altogether destroyed. Hence *servō* agrees substantially with δουλῳ. Besides, the Latin datives *nulli*, *utri*, &c. are evidently representatives of *nulloi*, *utroi*, as *nullius*, *nulli* nom. pl., *nullis*, stand for *nulloius*, *nulloi*, *nullois*.

We have said that *i* is the ordinary suffix of a singular dative. An older form must have been *bi*. Such is seen in the so-called adverbs, but originally datives, *i-bi* (nom. *i-s*), *u-bi* (or *cubi*, as seen in *si-cubi*, *num-cubi*, *ne-cubi*, from the relative), *ali-bi* (archaic nom. *ali-s*), *utro-bi* (nom. *uter*), *ubi-que* (nom. *quisque*), *no-bi-s*,[*] *uo-bi-s*; secondly, in the plural datives *reg-i-bus*, *avi-bus*, *die-bus*, *equa-bus*, *duo-bus*, *acu-bus*; thirdly, in the Homeric datives ι-φι, βιη-φι, ουρανο-φι, στηθεσ-φι; fourthly, in the Sanskrit datives of the dual and plural *nau-bhy-am* and *nau-bhy-as* from *nau-* 'a ship,' as well as the plural instrumental case *nau-bhi-s*. But if it be admitted that a *b* once belonged to the dative suffix, it remains to be explained how it came to disappear, as in *musis* and *servis*. This objection will be answered if it be shown that those very forms which long retained a *b* have since lost it. Now the four little words, *tibi*, *sibi*, *ubi*, *ibi* have all lost the labial in the French derivatives *toi*, *soi*, *ou*, *y*. Again, the three prepositions *ab*, *sub*, *ob* are subjected to the same curtailment, in *a*, in *asporto* (for *absporto*), in *suspendo*, *suscito*, *sustollo* (for *subs-*), and in *ostendo* (for

---

[*] *Sibi*, *tibi* are omitted in this enumeration, because there is reason to believe that the bases of these words have a claim to the *b*.

obs-tendo). The two verbs *iubeo* and *habeo* also lose their *b* at times, the first in *jussi, jussum*, the second in the derived substantive *a-mentum* for *habi-mentum* 'something to hold by,' and also in the French present *j'ai, tu as, il a, ils ont*. The persons *avons, avez* do indeed retain the *b* virtually in the form of a *v*; but when the French add this present tense to the infinitive in order to make a future, 'I have to ——,' the syllable *av* falls off from both *av-ons* and *av-ez*, as seen in *finir-ai, finir-as, finir-a, finir-ons, finir-ez, finir-ont*. Similarly the conditional of the French verb is always made up by attaching the past tense *avais*, &c. to the infinitive, but in this process the syllable *av* again disappears, and we have *finir-ais*, &c. The German verb *hab-en* and our own *have* suffer in the same way. Thus the German *haben* in the present exhibits *hat* not *habt*, and in the past tense *hatte* not *hab-te*; while we say *has, had*, rather than *haves, haved*.

Hence with a knowledge that the *b* in Latin words had no safe footing, we may boldly infer that from an old dative *musa-bi* were formed first *musai* and ultimately *musae*; and from a plural *musa-bi-s*, on the one hand *musa-bus*, on the other, with the loss of the *b, musais, musis*. For the vowel-changes compare the three words *quairo* (the old form), *quaero, in-quiro*.

The nominative has been reserved to the last, because it contains what has been deemed by some a grave difficulty. Although *s* is visibly the suffix of the nominatives *reg-s* (*rex*), *sui-s, die-s, Aenea-s, seruo-s* (*seruus*), *gradu-s*, yet it has been objected that neuters, with few exceptions, are without the final sibilant, that the same is true of nearly every nominative of the first declension, of such words as *puer* in the second, and of *pater, consul, ordo, ratio* in the third declension.

With regard to neuters, the identity of the nominative and accusative in every instance is a difficulty which must attach to every grammatical system, as much as to that founded upon crude forms. Perhaps the cause may lie in this, that in the simplest form of sentence, viz. one consisting of a nominative, a verb, and an accusative, as *dominus seruum caedit*, the action expressed in the verb proceeds from the nominative to the accusative, from the master to the slave; and so the idea of the nominative in origin was identical with that of an agent. But an agent having life must of necessity be either masculine or feminine. Thus a neuter noun would have no claim to serve as a nominative, and

F F

consequently could not in strictness be entitled to the nominatival suffix s. Again, if neuters had at first no nominative, there was little use in a distinctive mark for an accusative, these two cases being under ordinary circumstances specially opposed to each other. But in the second declension a special difficulty presents itself. In other neuter nouns the nominative, vocative and accusative obtain their identity by the omission of all case-endings, and at times by sacrificing a portion even of the crude form, whereas with nouns in *o* an *m* seems to be attached, in violation of the general rule as regards the accusative, and with still less justification in the nominative. This difficulty is one which will be considered in the next appendix (§ xxii.), and we hope solved. It is mixed up with a somewhat recondite question.

The *s** in the first declension, it must be admitted, is only found in masculine nouns, and even they are of foreign origin, as the word above quoted, *Aeneas*. Still there is so close a connection between the first declension of the Latin and the first declension of the Greek language, that any thing proved for the one has a bearing upon the other. Thus the ς of ταμίας and πολίτης leads to rather a strong belief that the Latin also must once have possessed such a letter, although no longer found in what is left of the language. But it has been said that the office of this ς in the Greek words is not that of denoting a nominative, but to mark a gender. The assertion is founded solely on the accident that the masculine nouns take an ς in the nominative, which the feminine nouns have discarded. But even the masculine nouns appear without this letter in many phrases of Homer, as νεφεληγερέτα Ζεύς, μητίετα Ζεύς, ἱππότα Νέστωρ, &c.; and Cicero too preferred the forms without a sibilant in the Greek words *Archyta*, *Aristagora*, as well as in the names of his countrymen *Sulla* and *Cinna*. Moreover, an argument such as that of the Greek grammarians might just as well be used in proof that *s* in Latin is a mark of the feminine gender, seeing that of *acer*, *acris*, *acre*, the middle form *acris* is generally feminine. We have a parallel error in the Icelandic grammarians. This language, it is well known, has a general tendency to employ the letter *r* where the classical and other kindred languages have an *s*. Accordingly an *r* is found as an ending of many nominatives; but it happens to be limited for the most

---

* The greater part of this argument was first printed in an article in the *Classical Museum*, No. xix. p. 59.

part to those of a masculine gender. Hence, in § 141 of his Grammar, Rask calls it the sign of the masculine. Unfortunately for his doctrine, *ku-* 'a cow', *su-* 'a sow', also take an *r* to form the nominatives *kyr*, *syr* (§ 170); and in § 159 he has the candour to say, "In the oldest times there were also many feminines in *r*, e.g. *adr* 'a vein', afterwards *ad*, *áfr* 'river', afterwards *á*," &c. But a comparison of the Greek and Latin grammars will present us with evidence to prove that even feminine nouns of the *a* declension were not averse to the nominatival *s*. In the Greek language it is the ordinary doctrine that σοφια and σοφιη are but dialectic varieties of the same word. If we may extend the same doctrine to the Latin language, we are entitled to say that there is no substantial distinction between *luxuria* and *luxuries*, *tristitia* and *tristities*, *materia* and *materies*, words which (as Madvig observes) rarely form their genitives, datives and ablatives after the model of the fifth declension.

We next consider those nouns whose crude form ends in a liquid, as *patĕr-*, *consŭl-*, *ratiōn-* or *ordŏn-*. Our theory as regards these words is, that the *s*, originally added, was first assimilated to the preceding liquid; that by a second change one of these two liquids was dropped, but so dropped that the preceding vowel by its increased length was made to compensate for the loss; and thirdly, that this long syllable was finally deprived of its length. A triple assumption such as this, of course requires strong proof in the way of analogy; and it is believed that the nine arguments which are presented in the following paragraphs will be thought to contain such proof.

1. The four Greek verbs σπειρω, στελλω, φαινω, and νεμω, to take these as examples of classes, have for their respective bases the syllables σπερ, στελ, φαν, and νεμ. From these, if the regular formation had been followed, we ought to have had, as first aorists, εσπερσα, εστελσα, εφανσα,* ενεμσα. Assimilation would have changed them to εσπερρα, εστελλα, εφαννα, and ενεμμα; and again, the suppression of one of the liquids, together with the fitting compensation by increase in the length of the vowel, would give us, what is actually found, εσπειρα, εστειλα, εφηνα, ενειμα.

2. As the feminine of adjectives ending in a consonant was often formed by the addition of the syllable σα, e.g. τυπτον-σα,

---

* Aorists εκερσα, κελσα, εκερσα occur in Homer. See Addenda.

χαρισ-σα, Φοινισ-σα, for ruττοντ-σα, χαριεντ-σα, Φοινικ-σα, so from the crude forms μακαρ-, ταλαν-, τερεν- should have been formed μακαρ-σα, ταλαν-σα, τερεν-σα, which, if our view be correct, passed through an intermediate μακαρ-ρα, ταλαν-ρα, τερεν-ρα, to μακαιρα, ταλαινα τερεινα.

3. The Latin superlative ended commonly in *sumo-* or *rimo-*; but in *acer-rimo-*, *deter-rimo-*, *simil-limo-*, the *s* has assimilated itself to the preceding liquid, *r* or *l*.

4. The Latin infinitival suffix *ère* appears to have grown out of an older form *èse*, as seen in *es-se* 'to be' (for *ès-èse*). This view is confirmed both by the universal habit of the old language to present an *s* between vowels where the later language preferred *r*, as in *Fusius*, *asa*, afterwards *Furius*, *ara*; and by the occurrence of a passive infinitive *dasi* (see Forcellini), which of course implies an active infinitive *dase* for *dare*. Hence *vel-le*, *nol-le*, *mal-le* have in *le* a substitute for an older *re*, as that was a substitute for *se*.

5. In the Icelandic tongue, as we have already said, an *r* instead of an *s* is the ordinary nominatival suffix of masculine nouns. But when such a noun ends in *n* or *l*, the *r* is at times assimilated, so that from a base *ketil-* 'kettle', *graen-* 'green', *span-* 'spoon', we have the nominatives *ketill*, *graenn*, *spann*. Again, some words whose base has a final *r*, as *dör-* 'spear', are not afraid to take a second *r* in the nom., as *dörr*. And if the base ended in *s*, the old language at times even added a second *s* for the nominative. Thus from *is-* 'ice', *laus-* 'loose', were formed old nominatives *iss*, *lauss*. We have here, by the way, a case precisely parallel to the theoretic nominative *pulviss* mentioned above. But in the later Icelandic language there was a tendency, as was to be expected, to discard one of two similar consonants at the end of a nominative; and thus what was a virtual symbol of the nominative wholly disappeared. In § 139 of Rask's Grammar it will be seen that the nouns which were thus truncated had a base ending in the letters *r*, *l*, *n* and *s*, i.e. the very endings which are subject to the same mutilation in Latin. We have here then a simile which really runs on all fours, and which alone ought to settle the problem. But to proceed.

6. The Icelandic verb in the third person regularly takes an *r* corresponding to the *s* of English, as from the base *tel-* 'tell', *hann telr* 'he tells'; yet from *skin-* 'shine', the old writers preferred *skinn* for *skinr* 'shines', and this *skinn* afterwards became *skin* (§ 93).

7. The genitive plural in Icelandic has regularly a suffix *ra* (corresponding to the Latin *rum*, and so a corruption of *rum*), yet from *hin-* 'the', and *gamal-* 'old', the gen. pl. is *hin-na, gamal-la* (§ 93).

8. The ordinary termination of the neuter comparative in Icelandic is *ara* or *ra*,* as *kaldara* 'the colder'; but from *vaen-* 'fair', *sael-* 'happy,' are formed the comparatives *vaen-na, sael-la* (§ 199).

9. The Latin language is specially apt to discard any final *e* which follows an *r*. Thus for *videbaris, videreris*, we find in preference *videbare, viderere*. Again, although the analogy of the Greek δις, τρις, the Latin *bis* (*duis*), and our own *twice, thrice*, would have led us to expect *tris* and *quatris* in Latin, yet we find nothing but *ter* and *quater*. It is therefore no matter for surprise, if instead of *puerus, paters, lintris*, which strict theory demands, we find *puer, pater, linter*. But the Greek nominatives πατηρ, χειρ, τερην, from the several crude forms πατερ-, χερ-, τερεν-, exhibit the long vowel of compensation; and so also does the Latin more frequently than is commonly believed, as *patēr* in Virgil:

> Ostentans artemque pater arcumque sonantem. Aen. v. 521.
> Concilium ipse pater et magna incepta Latinus, &c. xi. 469.
> Congredior. Per sacra pater et concipe foedus. xii. 13.

What we have said would account for such nominatives as *ration, homon*; but even these are not found. The difficulty is however cleared up when we call to mind that while the Greeks wrote Στραβων, the Romans preferred *Strabo*. Nay the Greeks themselves changed ρηων to ρης. See Addenda.

So much for the singular. In the plural nominative a comparison of *reg-es* with the forms exhibited in the other declensions leads us to the conclusion that *avis* (archaic), *gradūs*, and *dies* have all by contraction lost an *e* before the final *s*, whereas *musae*, standing for *musa-es*, has lost the sibilant itself. Lastly, *serui* (βουλοι) must be considered as contracted from *serues*, and this reduced from an obsolete *seruo-es*.

Thus all the Latin declensions appear to have been moulded upon one common type.

We will close these remarks with a word or two of comment on an objection, to which reference has already been made. Even if

* This suffix in the Mœso-Gothic has a sibilant in lieu of the liquid *r*.

we admit your system to be founded on the firmest basis of philological truth, it requires much complicated argument to prove its truth, and for that reason would be found utterly impracticable in the instruction of the young. The answer is simple. The proofs are for the learned alone. The business of the pupil is to learn the contrary process, by which from the bare word or crude form the so-called cases are formed by the addition of syllables or letters. This process is far easier than that put forward in the old grammars. Thus the Latin words for 'king', 'bird', 'thing', 'wing', 'slave', 'step', are presented for the first time to the beginner in the forms *reg-*, *aui-*, *re-*, *ala-*, *seruo-*, *gradu-*. From these he is taught to build up the different cases. In this process he has at once an advantage over those who follow the old course. He can never be at a loss for the declension, as the last letter is an invariable guide. Nay, he may throw aside all consideration of the order in which the declensions follow, as the terms 'consonant declension', '*i* declension', &c. are at once simple and sufficient. Thus he is saved from many traps which are set for one who uses the Eton Grammar. For example, the words *puer*, *linter*, *pater* are only deceitful guides to the declension until we know some other case or cases; whereas the crude forms *puero-*, *lintĕri-*, *patĕr-* at once give a direction which cannot be mistaken. A treacherous similarity exists between *equus*, *uirtus* and *senatus*, between *seruos* and *arbos*, between *dies* and *paries*; but there is no chance of the pupil referring to the same declensions *equo-*, *uirtūt-* and *senatu-*, or *seruo-* and *arbŏs-*, or *diŏ-* and *pariĕt-*.

We now pass from the familiar matters of declension and conjugation to a part of grammar usually much neglected—the general doctrine of derivation; and we shall still find that the crude forms of nouns and verbs give us a safer foundation on which to build. Thus from the substantives *ciui-*, *fide-*, *uita-*, *tribu-*, we more readily proceed to the adjectives *ciui-li-*, *fide-li-*, *uita-li-*, *tribu-li-*, than we can from the nominatives *ciuis*, *fides*, *uita*, *tribus*. Still more decided is the advantage in deducing directly from the crude forms *mari-*, *Roma-*, *bello-*, *tribu-*, rather than from the nominatives *mare*, *Roma*, *bellum*, *tribus*, the derivatives *marino-*, *Romano-*, *Bellona-*, *tribuno-*. Again, the diminutives *nauicula*, *uirguncula*,[*] *diecula*, *sucula*, *ratiuncula*, are with little

[*] Zumpt, through looking to the nominatives, speaks of *uirguncula* as formed by the addition of a suffix *uncula*.

difficulty referred to the crude forms *naui-*, *uirgŏn-*, *did-*, *su-*, *ratiōn-*.

The light which the study of Latin throws upon the etymology of our own tongue is a secondary but still an important consideration. Here again the crude forms have a marked advantage over the nominatives. Thus our English adjectives *re-al*, *reg-al*, *gradu-al*, *manu-al*, *vertic-al*, *nation-al*, are less easily referred to the nominatives *res*, *rex*, *gradus*, *manus*, *uertex*, *natio*, than to the crude forms, which present themselves at once to the eye. The same, or nearly the same, is true of the words *lapid-ary*, *avi-ary*, *sanguin-ary*, *salut-ary*, *station-ary*.

In what has been hitherto said, the chief stress has been laid upon the forms of words. But there is another consideration of even greater moment for the student. To give the name of nominative to what is really something more than the mere expression of a name has naturally led to the utter neglect of that something more; and the logical view of language has only confirmed the error. On the other hand, when we know that the nominative is really a case, in other words that it expresses a relation between the word and the other members of a sentence, we have much light thrown on the nature of the Latin language. We then see that the special office of the nominative is to define the source of the action implied in the verb. Nor let it be objected that such a view is traversed by the employment of nominatives with a passive verb, for the passive is at bottom a reflective verb.* Nay the construction of a passive sentence only confirms what we have said; for the moment the true agent is formally expressed in a passive, the preposition *ab* is called in aid; so that in the two sentences *dominus seruum caedit* and *seruus caeditur a domino*, *dominus* and *a domino* are equivalent phrases.

APPENDIX II.

ON TRACES OF AN OLD *diminutival* SUFFIX, MORE OR LESS LIKE THE KELTIC *agh*, IN THE LATIN VOCABULARY.

A DISCUSSION, ill-fitted for admission into the body of a school-grammar, may yet deserve a place here; and I am desirous that my more precise views should be accessible to the reader of these

* See Grammar, §§ 375-379, and the two notes * pp. 59 and 60.

pages. Still, for details, that is for the full arguments, which alone can carry conviction, I must refer to the paper, as printed in the *Transactions of the Philological Society of London* for 1856. Here I can give only an abstract.

I. *Introduction.*—The Gaelic suffix *ach* or *ag* 'little' has its representative in the final syllables of the various Scotch diminutives, lass-*ock* and lass-*ow*, lass-*ick* and lass-*ie*, 'a little lass.' But the Latin and Greek also have intimate relations with the Keltic. Again, as our own tongue throws off final gutturals in *way*, *day*, *honey*, *Norway*, &c. (German *weg*, *tag*, *honig*, *Norweg*, &c.), so the Latin also loves to drop a *g*, as in *maior* (=*mayor*), *nuvolo*, *milo*. Yet as with us derivatives sometimes restore the *g*, for example in *Norweg-ian*, so is it in Latin. Another mode of avoiding a guttural with us is to substitute a labial sound for it, as in *laugh*, *rough*. This habit also prevails in Latin. Lastly, diminutives in form often discard their diminutival power, as French *sol-eil*, Italian *fratello*, *sorella*; and these are apt to stand alone in a language, without any primitive to contrast with them.

II. *Agh*, as seen in substantives: *lim-ac-* 'slug.' In Greek occur some 60 examples, as ῥοδ-ακ- 'dwarf-rose,' ϝαλλ-ακ- 'youth,' μειρ-ακ- 'young person.' The Latin substantives of the first declension have lost a final guttural, as shown by the derived adjectives *rosac-eo-*, *ferulac-eo-*, *membranac-eo-* (24 of them), and *vernac-ulo-*. To the double-diminutives, Gaelic *cur-ach-an* 'a coracle,' Scotch *lass-ick-in*, German *veil-(i)ch-en* 'a little violet,' correspond Latin *ferul-ag-on-*, &c. (about 20); and hence it is inferred that *ferul-ac-* or *ferul-ag-* were older forms of *ferul-a-*. Plants in the form *ferul-ag-*, *lapp-ag-*, would correspond to our *charl-ock*, *shamr-ock*, *sour-ock* (sorrel).

III. *Agh* in verbs. A diminutival suffix added to verbs generally denotes a succession of petty acts, as *twinkle*, *sprinkle*, *hobble*. So with Latin verbs which take the suffix *agh*. The guttural still traceable in a few of these verbs, which therefore adhere to the third conjugation, as *plang-*, *frang-*, *trah-*, *stra(g)-* whence *stravi*, sb. *strage-*, adj. *stragulo-*. In the great majority the loss of it has transferred the verbs to the first conjugation, in which however it is seen that the final *a* is something foreign to the root, as *cub-a-re*, *lav-a-re*, beside *cumb-ere*, *lav-ere*. The guttural again traceable in derivatives, as *or-ac-ulo-*, *lav-ac-ro-*.

IV. *Agh* in verbs supplanted by *ab* (for *abh*). Latin generally has *b* at the end of syllables where Greek has φ. Hence a final *b* is seen attaching itself to verbs of the *a* conjugation in the derived adjectives *medicab-ili-*, *laudab-ili-* (over 400), compared with *ut-ili-*; in the sbs. *vocab-ulo-*, *venab-ulo-*, compared with *jac-ulo-*; in *dolab-ra-*; and in the frequentatives (note this idea) *plorab-undo-*, *contionab-undo-* (over 60). But if *ab* be thus adapted to denote continuity of time, it may well be the element seen in *am-ab-am*, and even in *am-ab-o*, so that *am-ab-o* will strictly be an imperfect present. Similarly *ero*, ἔσομαι, εἰμί, are in form presents, in power futures.

V. *Ab* for *ag* in substantives after a guttural, as *cann-ab-i-* 'hemp,' and otherwise, as, *tr-ab-* (=*dor-ab-*?) 'tree.'

VI. As *agh* denotes what is habitual in all Manx verbs and many Manx adjectives, so it enters into such Greek words as κολ-αξ- 'flatterer,' φεν-αξ- 'cheat,' λαλ-αγ- 'prattler' (above 20), and into the Latin *bib-ac-*, *ed-ac-*, *loqu-ac-* (about 50).

VII. Ax, so common in Greek sbs., gives place to *ec* or *ic* in Latin. Thus to πάλλαξ-, ὕραξ-, συνδαξ- correspond *pellec-*, *sorec-*, *podec-*. The lists of words in *ex* and *ic* (together over 60) very generally exhibit the idea of smallness, as *culec-* 'gnat,' *pulec-* 'flea,' *cimec-* 'bug.' So too, as plants and small birds with us often and in our diminutival suffixes *ock* and *ow*, the Latin also has for plants *ulec-*, *rumec-*, *carec-*, *vitec-*, *frutic-*, *scandic-*, *salic-*, *filic-*, *tamaric-*; and for birds *perdic-*, *fulic-*, *cornic-*, *coturnic-*, *soric-*.

VIII. *Agh* in sbs. becomes *ug* or *uc*, so as to lie nearer our own *ock*. Latin examples *cruc-*, *frug-es*. The word *crux* (=σκόλοψ) examined.

IX. *Agh* reduced to a mere guttural, as in our own *park* for *parr-ock*. *Arc-*, *calc-*, *falc-*, *lanc-*, *merc-*, analysed.

X. Our *ec* often, yet not always, reduced to *ĕ* in the body of such words as *ros-ĕ-tum* for *ros-ec-tum*, i. e. *ros-agh-tum* (see *rosac-eo-* in § 1). Sometimes the two forms, as *virectum* and *virētum*, *dumectum* and *dumētum*, exist beside each other.

XI. As the Scotch reduce *lassock* to *lassow*, so the second Latin declension owes its existence chiefly to a similar loss; but the adj. *aprug-no-* still bears traces of an older *aprogh-* 'a wild boar;' and similar evidence is found in *hordeac-eo-*, *sebac-eo-*, *foliac-eo-*, *bulbac-eo-* (19 such), as well as in *rapic-io-*, *tribunic-io-*, &c.

XII. As the Scotch reduce *lassick* to *lassie*, so *ensic-ulus*, *canic-ula*, *retic-ulum* tell us that *ensi-*, *cani-*, *reti-* had once a final guttural. Again in the fifth declension *plebec-ula*, *diec-ula* bear witness that *plebe-*, *die-* had once a final *c*; which is confirmed as to the latter by a comparison of our *day* and the German *tag*. In the fourth declension the argument would have been smoother, if we had found *onuc-ula* and *genuc-ulum*, rather than *anic-ula* and *genic-ulum*. But we know historically that *genibus* grew out of *genubus*. Moreover as γονυ (*genu*) : *knee* : : δορυ : *tree* : : *genuc-ulum* : *knuck-le*. This seems to establish the legitimacy of *genuc-ulum*. Plautus too by his twice-employed adjective *meticulosus*, implies a sb. *metic-ulus*. Observe too that as *lassis* : *lass*, so *cani-* : *can-*; and a a.v. *can-* 'dog' is consistent with *can-um* gen. pl., and with κυν-ος, &c. So with *op-um*, *juven-um*.

XIII. *Agh* in sbs. sometimes doubly represented, as in *verben-ac-a-*, *form-ic-a-*, *xumb-uc-o-*, *fur-c-a-*. So *occlulo-* has the like suffix d thrice over.

XIV. The softened *ow*, for *ock*, seen in English adjectives, as *shall-ow*, *yell-ow*, virtually occurs in the Greek βραχ-υ-, γλυκ-υ-, ελαχ-υ-, &c., and so is represented in the Latin equivalents *brev-i-*, *dulc-i-*, *lev-i-*,—an argument confirmed by the derivatives *brevic-ulo-*, *dulcic-ulo-*, *levic-ulo-*. *Truc-*, i.e. *tor-uc-*, retains the suffix in greater purity.

XV. *Agh* in adjectives also sometimes doubly represented, as in *fl-acc-o-* (=μαλ-ακ-ο-), *plan-c-o-*, *gil-b-o-*, *fl-av-o-*, *gil-v-o-*, *cur-v-o-*, *tor-v-o-* (comp. *tr-uc-*), *ard-u-o-*, &c.

XVI. Some adjectives in *o* are deduced from genitival forms, as *patrius*, *igneus*; and so no way connected with our suffix.

XVII. *Agh* in verbs reduced first to *ug* or *uc*, and then to *u*, as in *flu-*, *fru-* (r.), *stru-*, *viv-*, *volv-*, *solv-* (with *lu-*), *ferv-*, *loqu-*, *nu-*, *ru-*, *spu-*, *scru-* (*scru-ta-ri*, σκαλ-ευ-ευ), &c.

XVIII. *Agh* in verbs reduced to *ec* or *ic*, as *spec-*, *plec-* of *plect-*, *nec-* of *nect-*, *flec-* of *flect-*, and (*g*)*nic-* of (*g*)*nisi*, (*g*)*nixus*.

XIX. *Agh* in verbs reduced to a simple guttural, as *mer-g-*, *spar-g-*, *ter-g-*, *verg-* 'incline,' *ver-g-* 'pour,' *ful-g-*, *par-c-*, *pos-c-*, *ves-c-* (r.), *ul-c-* (*ulciscì*), *torqu-e-*.

XX. *Agh* in verbs supplanted by a labial, first by *p*. Examples such as *carp-*, *rup-*, *scalp-*, *serp-*, *trep-*, are examined.

XXI. Secondly by *b*, as *scrib-* (=γραφ-), *f*(*e*)*rib-* (τρυβ-) implied in *trivi*, *tribulum*; *o*(*e*)*r-ib-* implied in *cr-ib-ro-* n., *glub-*. An extinct *b* claimed for some other secondary verbs on the evidence of derivatives, as *vol-ub-*, *sol-ub-*, *fl-eb-*, *ten-eb-*, *lug-ub-*, *illic-ib-*, *sal-ib-*, in place of *volv-*, *solv-*, *fle-*, *tene-*, *luge-*, *illici-*, *sali-*.

XXII. Thirdly by *m*. The direct interchange of χ and μ appealed to in support of this doctrine. Examples of such verbs in *m* considered, as *frem-*, *prem-*, *trem-*, *crem-a-re*, and a vb. *crem-* implied in the sb. *crem-or*. The *m* which appears in the alleged suffixes *men* (μεν) and *mentum* claimed for the preceding verb, so that we should rather divide the several elements, as in *orn-am-entum*, *mon-um-entum*, *teg-um-en*, ον-ομ-εν- or ον-υμ-εν-, &c. The same argument applied to the infinitive τυπτ-εμ-εν, &c. The paper then reverts to substantives; and after noticing the fact that the suffix *om* of *bottom*, *fathom*, is represented in the oldest German by *am* and *um*, as *pod-um* or *pot-am* and *vad-um*, treats this suffix as a labialised *agh*. Thus the old German *var-am* corresponds to our *brake* (=*bar-agh*) 'fern;' and *potam* not only to the Latin *fundo-*, but also to its equivalents πυθ-αρ- and *pod-es-*. Hence *om* (*um*), the strange ending of the nominatives and accusatives of Latin neuters, *ervom*, *bellum*, is justified as representing *ervogh*, *bellogh*, older forms, it is thought, than *ervo-*, *bello-*. Hence too αριμον-, Ἴλιυμ- (Ἴλιον-), form adjectives αριαο-ο-, Ἰλιαο-ο-.

XXIII. *Agh* in verbs passes through *ea* or *eh* to *e*, as *ver-e-* (r.) beside *verec-undo-*. The cases of *suade-*, *dense-*, *rube-*, *tene-*, *late-*, *sate-*, *luge-*, *exple-*, *spre-vi*, *cre-vi* considered.

XXIV. *Agh* in verbs passes through *ic* &c. to *i*. If the adj. *leni-* stand for *lenigh*, so also must the verb *leni-*; and similarly with like cases. Derivatives too, as *orig-on-*, claim a guttural in behalf of *ori-* (r.), &c.

XXV. *Agh* in verbs exchanges its guttural for a sibilant, as ταρασσ- (beside ταραχ-η); so in Latin *incipis-*, *potes-*. The French forms *finissant* &c., and our own *finish*, show that the Latin sb. and vb. *fini-* stood in place of *fin-igh*. So also the Italian *finisco* brings in with its own claim one for all *inceptive*, or, as Homer treats them, *iterative* verbs; and these two meanings alike accord with the power assigned to our suffix in § III.

XXVI. *Eo* or *ic* &c. exchange the guttural for a *t*, chiefly after a preceding guttural, like our own *gobb-et* for *gabb-ock*, *giml-et* for *giml-ick*, *spig-ot* for *spig-ock*. But the license is often carried beyond the excuse, as in *emm-et* for *emm-ock*. Thus *abiet-* stands for *abiec-*, witness the adj. *abieg-no-*. *Vell-ic-a-re*, *fod-ic-a-re*, *more-ic-a-re* have our suffix in the legitimate form, *ic*; but frequentative verbs generally have changed *ic* for *it*, as *ag-it-a-re*, which with no less than 300 similarly constituted verbs, may plead in excuse a preceding guttural; but not so *enitare*, *saltare*, *pultare*. *Aedilit-io-* &c. we know stands for *aedilic-io-*, and perhaps *brevit-er* for *brevic-er* &c.

XXVII. Our *ic* reduced to *it* in other forms. Such comparatives as *trist-ic-ior*, *laet-ic-ior* (afterwards *tristit-ior*, *laetit-ior*), established on good ms. authority; and hence *tristit-ia-*, *laetit-ia-*, explained as similar to *grat-ia-*. The same explanation proposed, more or less doubtingly, for words of the form *nav-it-a-*, *serv-it-io-* n., *mon-it-ion-*, *serv-it-ut-*, *fund-it-or-*, *mult-it-udon-*, *nov-ic-io-* and *nov-it-io-*, *subdit-ic-io-* and *subdit-it-io-*.

XXVIII. *Agh* &c. change the guttural for a *d*, as in *ϝα-ιδ-* beside *ϝϝαιϝα*, *ϝαϝ-ϝιον*. Hence *rubedon-*, *albedon-*, in place of the classical *robigon-*, *albugon-*, &c. *Mult-ic-ud-on-* (if the older form) would have a valid excuse for *d* in place of *g*.

XXIX. The many changes of vowel, which have been here assigned to our suffix, justified by the law which assimilates vowels in adjoining syllables. Thus a Greek writes μαλασσ-, ερισσ-, μελισσ-, ορυσσ- (ο being habitually followed by υ rather than by another ο). So a Roman preferred: 1. *ar-a-*, *ar-at-ro-* n., *ar-ab-am*, *ar-ab-ili-*, *al-ao-er* (al- 'raise'); 2. *gem-eb-undo-*, *frem-eb-undo-*, *trem-eb-undo-*, *ver-e-* (r.), *ver-eo-undo-*, *ten-e-*, *ten-eb-am*, *ten-eb-ra-*, *ten-eb-ra-*, *cel-eb-eri-*, *fer-et-ro-* n., *ver-et-ro-* n., *pet-ess-*, *nec-esse*, *c(e)r-e-vi*, *sp(e)r-e-vi*, *f(e)r-e-to-*; 3. *nit-ib-undo-*, *rid-ib-undo-*, *rid-ic-ulo-*, *in-cip-iss-*, *vic-issim*; 4. *lug-ub-ri-*, *luc-ub-ra-re*; or with not identical, yet kindred vowels, as 5. *lat-e-*, *lat-eb-ra-*, *scat-eb-ra-*, *sal-eb-ra-*, *lac-ess-*, *fac-ess-*, *cap-ess-*, *par-e-*, *man-e-*, *alg-e-*, *ard-e-*; or 6. *quer-ib-undo-*, *c(e)r-ib-ro-* n., *t(e)r-i-vi*, *t(e)r-i-to-*, *t(e)r-ib-ulo-* n., *vert-ig-on-*; or again, 7. *vol-uo-ri-*, *vol-up-i-*, *vol-ub-ili-*, *vol-um-en-*, *in-vol-uc-ro-* n., *sol-u-to-*, *sol-ub-ili-*, *tol-u-tim*, *doc-uu-* *ento-*, *mon-um-ento-*, *in-col-um-i-*. Some exceptions from this law considered. A convincing example of vowel-assimilation is seen in the series of words: *a*, παλλαξ m. 'a youth;' *e*, Lat. *pellex* f. 'a concubine;' *i*, *fillie* 'a young mare;' *o*, Scotch *pollock* 'a young fish,' πωλος 'a foal;' *u*, Lat. *pullus*, either a colt or chicken, —where the words are at bottom identical, and in themselves denote merely 'a little young one.'

XXX. The many changes of consonant which have been assigned to our suffix explained, partly from the desire to avoid gutturals, especially repeated gutturals, partly on the principle that aspirates readily interchange. By way of example, the irregularities of the verb φερ- (Sanskrit *bhri* or *dhri*) considered in Greek, Latin and English.

INDEX.

The numerals refer to the sections, not to the pages, except where the letter p. is prefixed. The letter n. means note. Latin words and parts of Latin words are in italics.

a conjugation, 519, 522, 523.
a declension, 89-99, p. 424.
ab, 810, 816, 1303, 1304.
abd-, 542.
abdica-, 1028.
abest ut, 1208.
ablo-, 1304.
abin, 1171.
ablative, 50, 51, 989, p. 429, *i*; absolute, 1013; 'by' or 'with,' 1000; for dat. 1019; 'from,' 1021; in *d*, 50, 1021; 'in point of,' 997; of circumstances, 1009; of degree, 1017; of gerund, 1294; of means, 1000; of penalty, 1005.1; of measure, 1014; of price, 1005; of quality, 1010; of road, 1008; of time, 992; of 'where,' 991; with comparative, 1015, 1055, 1055 *d*; with *fac-fi-*, 1003; with prep., 1025; with verbs of buying, 1005; of removal, 1023; of sacrificing, 1006.
abs, 810 n.
absunti-, 725.
abstine-, 940.
abstract nouns, 907.
ac, 1480 &c.
ac non, 1409. 1.
accent, 22-28.
accessary conjunctions, 846.
accliui-, 1308. 4.
accusative, 45, 46, 369, 884; singular, p. 429; plural, p. 429, p. 431; after active verb, 888; after adj. in *bundo*, 1298; after deponents, 891; after intransitives, 893; after participles in *to*, 892; after

quo, 918; after substantives, 907; cognate, 894; and Inf. 911, 1248; factitive, 896; for nom. 912; of time, &c. 913; two together, 896-902; with verbs of calling, 827; of feeling, 889.
accusing, adj. of, 933; verbs of, 944.
active verb, 367; conjugated, 575.
acu-, 297. L.
ad, 1305, 1306.
adeuna-, 1308. 3.
adaequa-, 1308. 3.
adeo, 799.
adim-, 1308. 3.
adig-, 900.
adipes, 1026.
adjectives, 211-239; concord of, 1037; as sub., 936, 1034, 1042; for adv., 1049, 1051; gender of, 1040; place of, 1468; possessive, 1047, 1084 *s*; in predicate, 1000; suffixes of, 225-234; in *a, o, i*, have lost a guttural, p. 442, xiv. xv., p. 444, xxvii.; in *ab-ili*, p. 441, iv.; in *ae*, p. 441, vi.; in *ae-co*, p. 440, ii., p. 441, xi.; in *ae-o*, p. 443, xxii.; in *bundo*, 1298; in *ic-io*, p. 441, xi; in *ti-io*, p. 443, xxvi.; of comparison, 1438; of fitness, &c., 936.
admodum, 797.
admone-, 1308. 8.
adsurp-, 1308. 3.
adula-, 979.
aduersus, 1307.
aemula-, 979.
aetate gen., 909 n.
afflig-, 1304.

agnosc-, 1308. 3.
ai-, 739.
adverbs, 767, 1398; in *a*, 366, 793; in *am*, 782, 791; in *bi*, 366, 765; in *ē*, 768; in *im*, 790; in *dē*, 366, 700, 800; in * īs*, 783; in *iter*, 773, p. 443, xxvi.; in *bis*, 777; in *o*, 366, 771, 789, 1056; in *per*, 778; in *sccus*, 801; in *tenus*, 803; in *tim*, 779, 780; in *tro*. 788; in *um*, 792; in *us*, 781 &c.; in *vorsum*, 798; in predicate, 1401; of comparison, 1438, 1439; place of, 1398; pronominal, 366, 1150; with partic., 1399; with sub., 1400.
ai- vb, 739.
ali-, 320, 327.
alio-, 110, 111, 327, 1148.
aliqui-, 1141.
alphabet, 2.
alter differs from *alteri*, 324.
altero-, 110, 111, 330, 1148.
alterius, 111, 380.
am, 834 a, 1308.
ambur-, 1308. 3.
amplius, 1055. 1.
an, 1421 &c.; use of, 1426; a proclitic, 1465; repeated, 1424.
an 'up,' 834 b, 1308. 2.
ana, 1308. 1.
anaphora, 1435.
Anglo-Saxon superl., 836 a.
animi, 935 n.
annona-, 210.
annuit, p. 427.
ante, 1309.
antid, 802.
antecedent omitted, 1126, 1151.
antequam, 1231. 1.
anu-, 142, 207, 1.
aorist, 445, 446, 585, 586, 614.
appos-, 1304.
apposition, 1052, 1058, 1472.
apud, 815 n., 1311.
apprehend-, 1308. 3.
ar, 1312.
araxa, 567.
arassere, 568.
arduo-, 355. 1. n.
as, divisions of the, 270.
asking, vbs. of, 902.
asyndeton, 1435.
at, 1443.

atque (*ac*), 1430, 1438; for *quam*, 853; with comp., 1056. 4.
attraction, 1039, 1055 & obs., 1059, 1125, 1251.
au, 882 n.
auersa-, 904.
axis gen., why short, p. 430.
aut, 840; differs from *uel*, 1444.
autem, 1446; place of, 1474.

benigno-, 238.
blandi-, 971.
bookkeeping, phrases of, 982.
bou-, 157.
buying, vbs. of, 846, 1005.

c, 11.
cani-, 190.
can-um gen. pl. explained, p. 441.
capess-, 754.
cardinal numbers, 247, 252, 253.
care-, 1023.
case, 42, 1391 n.
cassum, 540.
ce suffix, 289, 293, 319, 792, 1112 n.
cēdo, 731, 1198.
cela-, 898.
centena milia, 1072.
certa-, 956.
ceruices, 1026.
cetera, 918.
cimex-, 207, 1.
circa, 1313.
circiter, 1314.
circum, 1315.
circumda-, 906.
cis, 1316.
cito, 772.
citra, 1318.
clam, 782, 1319.
claud-, 760 n.
coeptus est, 1244.
cognate acc., 402, 894.
collectives, 195. 1.
comparative, 240-246, 838, 1015, 1055, 1193.
comparison, adj. and adv. of, where placed, 1438.
composition, 35; of verbs, 758.
condona-, 975.
conditional sentences, 1153.
conduc-, 1289.
cēnsui-, 819 n.
conjugation, 518; a, 519, 522, 523;

INDEX. 447

c, 386, 819, 524, 525; *i*, 519, 528, 529; *o*, 519, 520; *u*, 519, 525, 527; consonant, 518, 521; of verb active, 876 &c.; deponent, 685; impersonal, 699; part. in *turo* with *ex-* and *su-*, 702 &c.; passive, 685; pass. impers. 701; reflective, 570, 636 &c.
conjunctions, 839; omitted, 1436; postponed, 1463.
consocio-, 957.
consonant conjugation, 518, 521.
consonant declension, 55, 87.
conspergo-, 905.
consul/- vb., 555. 2.
as urul for *consuls*, p. 135.
contra, 1320.
contract verbs in Latin, p. 126.
contracted perfect, 563-7.
copula, 874.
copulative conjunctions, 840, 1430 &c.
coram, 1321.
corona-, 210.
cred-, 981 a.
crude form, 41, p. 422; in Sanscrit grammar, p. 422; simplicity of, p. 138.
cui bono? 983 a.
cuiusmodi, 311.
cum prep., 820, 1322, 1323, 1391.
cum conj., 1453.
cum maxume, 1057 d, p. 226.
cura-, 1168, 1289.
custom, vbs. of, 1007.

da-, 549, 732, 975, 1275, 1289.
dative, 49, 110 n., 850; doubled, 982; dat. ethic, 978; in poets, 986, 988; of attraction, 985; of fitness, 1293; of motion to, 987; of name, 985; of part. in *rudo*, 1293; of person concerned, 877; of person whose body is concerned, 972; of purpose, 984; of serving as, 983; plur., p. 433; sing., p. 432; with adj., 961; with adv., 962; with gerundive, 967; with perfect particip., 967; with static vbs., 963; with sbs., 969; with vbs. of giving, 973; with vbs. of taking away, 973.
dê, 1325-8.
dd as a suffix, 366, 800.

debui, 1257.
decuri, 964.
deciens, 1071.
declension, 54; first or *a*, 89-99; second or *o*, 100-24; third or *i*, 125-39; third or consonant, 55-87; fourth or *u*, 140-44; fifth or *e*, 145-8; vowel, 98; irregular, 157; mixed, 148-1; reduced to one, p. 423, 429.
defective nouns, 149, 1032.
defung-, 1023.
demonstratives, 286, 1091.
denum, 1447.
denario-, 1070.
deo-, 158.
deponent verbs, 399, 400; conjugated, 685.
derivation, 34; of verbs, 740 &c.; from prep., 832.
desiderative verbs, 755.
desin-, 940.
desitus est, 1244.
deterior-, 812, 814, 824.
di, 1329, 1330.
dio-, 534.
dicam omitted, 1228.
digno-, 1016, 1192.
diminutives, 188 &c. and Appendix II.
diminutive verbs, 750.
direct interrogative, 302.
dirim-, 812.
discrib-, 1329.
disjunctive conjunctions, 1444; question, 1423.
distributive numbers, 249, 252, 252, 1066.
diti-, 221.
doce-, 553, 556, 898, 1236.
domi, 114, 952, 1036.
domo-, 152.
domum, 836, 1036.
duo-, 534.
dum, 1448.
duo-, 117, 118, 130.
duplici-, 1067 a.

e, 1331.
e declension, p. 424.
ed, 304, 366.
eo, 611, 813, 817, 1331.
ecasior, 891.
ess, 862.

ecfer-, 811.
edepol, 861.
ego, crude form of, 271 a.
eho, 862 a.
elision, 29.
ellipsis of sb., 1033; of main verb, 1227; of verb of requesting, 1204; of verb of saying, 1203.
em-, 1005 n.
emolumento-, 330 a.
emphasis decides order of words, 1459.
emphatic adjective precedes, 1468; emphatic genitive precedes, 1468, 1472.
enclitics, 27, 1473.
enim, 1449; place of, 1474.
eo, adv., 304, 366, 789.
epicoene, 190.
epistolary tenses, 1160.
epol, 861.
equidem, 336, 1453 f. n.
equo-, 121. 1.
erat first, 1462.
erga, 1334.
es-, 'eat,' 722; 'be,' 723.
esse omitted, 1259.
est first, 1462.
et, 1430 &c.; 'also,' 'too,' 1440; a proclitic, 1465.
et mos, 1409.
et—neque, 1443.
et, que, and *atque* opposed, 1434.
ethic dat., 978.
etiam, 1171.
etiam nun, 806.
ex, 1331.
excess, degree of, 1056.6.
exerce-, 555.2.
existumes, 1228.
extent of place, &c., 913.
expergisc-, 555. 8.
extra, 1335.

fac, 1168.
facititive acc., 896.
fastidi-, 939.
farem, 566, 1209 a. f.
faro, 566, 1209 n.t.
fearing, verbs of, 1186.
feeling, verbs of, 393, 872, 889, 939, 939, 1245.
feminine suffixes, 191.
fer-, 729.

fi-, 736, 1003.
ferri, 736 n.
fig-, 535.
first word emphatic, 1460, 1461.
foras, 886.
forbidding, sentences of, 1173-7.
fore, 725.
forem, 725.
fore ut, 1260.
foris, 952.
forgiving, verbs of, 973.
fractions, 268-272.
frag-, 535.
frequentative verbs, 745.
frio-, 1002.
fru-, 1001, 1287 n.
fu-, 723, 723.1, 1152.5.
fugi-, 558.
fullness, adj. of, 931; verbs of, 941.
fung-, 1287 n.
future, 439, 441, 447, 448, 466-469; f. perfect, 476; f. perf. subj., 803, 805, 1226; f. perf. pass., 1263; f. periphrastic, 1260; f. for imperative, 1170.

genders, 39, 183 &c., 1040.
genitive, 47, 48, 919; sing., p. 430; plur., p. 431; emphatic, 1391 e, 1469, 1470; after gerund, 1286; after neut. pron., 932; in *ius*, 110 n.; in point of, 935; objective, 927; of cause, 929; of connection, 926; of definition, 926.1; of quality, 927; of removal, 930, 940; of tendency, 1292; partitive, 922; place of, 1468, 1472; possessive, 924; subjective, 921; with adj., 929; with adv., 923; with gerund, 1286; with possessive, 1048; with subs., 920; with verbs, 938.
gentile name, 1046.
genu-, p. 442, xii.
genus, 917.
gerund, 435, 634, 1284-6, 1294, 1295.
gerundive, 1287 &c.
giving, verbs of, 973.
Glycerio-, 208.
gratifico-, 971.
Greek acc., 916; nouns, 106 &c.
gus-? 748.

habe-, 386.
habessit, origin of form, p. 127.

INDEX

hara, 1404. 1.
haud, 1416. 1.
historic present, 449 a., 455; hist. infin., 1253.
he-, 295-300, 1092 &c.
hoc adv. 300.
hactine, 293.
hodie, 804.
hordeo-, 207. 2.
horsum, 366 n.
hora, 1035, 1303 L, 1305 a., 1311 a.
hujus, 847.
hujus, 114, 982.
hypothetical sentences, 496-9, 705, 1153, 1209, 1223.

i consonant, 9.
i conjugation, 519, 528, 529.
i declension, 125-39, p. 424.
i- or *eo-*, 302, 1113 &c.
i-y, 25.
i- verb, 737.
iace-, 386.
iam, 1450.
ibi, 304, 366.
i-dem, 342. 1, 1132.
igitur, place of, 1474.
ignaro-, 1338 a.
ignosce-, 762 n., 979, 980, 1308. 3.
ilico, 797.
illi, *illim*, adv., 298, 366.
illo-, 287 &c., 1101 &c.
illo adv., 298, 366.
*ima-? 748.
imbu-, 1308. 3.
immine-, 1308. 3.
imo-, 823, 1429.
impera-, 1281.
imperative, 421, 422, 424, 479, 593, 1153, 1173.
imperfect, 439 &c.; conjugated, 556; in fin. 506-13; past, 459-63.
impersonal verb, 371, 393, 699-701, 872; conjugated, 699, 700; passive, 383, 701.
in, 913, 1336.
incip-, 1308. 3.
inde, 304, 365.
indefinite pronouns, 1138 &c.
indicative, 1152. 8; for subj. 1215; of concession, 1156; of supposition, 1155.
indirect interrogative, 318, 494, 495, 1196, 1197.

indirect oration, 492, 1291.
indirect question, 1196.
infero-, 822.
infinitive, 430-2, 506-13, 1232 &c.; after adj. 1254; after relative or conjunction, 1251; and acc. 1238-1240; as a gen., 1252; historic, 1253; imperfect, 509, 512, 513, 625; in poets, 1255; of hypothesis, 1261; of indignation, 1247; passive, 1244; perfect, 510, 511, 628; with prep., 1233.
infitias, 886.
informo-, 1308. 3.
infra, 1339.
inhibe-, 1308. 3.
inquam, 102.
inser-, 906.
insiar, 833. 1.
instructo-, 1254.
intelleg-, 818.
inter, 1340, 1341, 1393 a., 1395 a.
inter, 'up,' 818, 834 d., 1342. 1.
inter se, 1087.
interclud-, 1342. 1.
interdic-, 1023, 1342. 1.
interest, 910, 948.
interfic-, 1342. 1.
interi-, 1342. 1.
interim, 797.
interimo-, 1342. 1.
interjections, 660.
interlunio-, 210. 1.
intermit-, 1342. 1.
interpola-, 1342. 1.
interrogative, direct, 308, 1184, 1417-1419, 1423, 1425, 1426; double, 1136; indirect, 318, 494, 495, 1196, 1197, 1420-1424; particles, 1417; pronouns, 1134 &c.
intra, 1343.
intransitive verb, 373, 378, 394; used transitively, 401-403.
intro, 1344.
intumesc-, 1308. 3.
inurid-, 979, 1023, 980.
invicto-, 765.
ipso-, 326, 1090.
iri, 1262.
irregular nouns, 149 &c.
irregular verbs, 592 &c.
is eu id, 302.
isti adv., 299.
istim adv., 299.

isto adv., 299.
isto-, 286, 288, 1098.
ita, 1431.
iterum, 822.
iug-, 535.
Iuppiter, 160.
ius-iurando-, 161.
iuxta, 1345.

k only before *a*, 6.
Karthagini, 931.
Keltic suffix *agh* in Latin, p. 439.

l or *ll*? 257
lab-, 533.
lapiderum, 376 n.
last word emphatic, 1468.
last word in an hexameter beginning a clause, 1463 n.
latum, 543.
leaves, 1031.
letters, number of, 2.
libera-, 940 n.
libram, 1075.
licet, 807 n.
licuit, 1257.
lintar, for *lintris*, p. 437.
liquids, order of, 2.
loca-, 1289.
logical pronoun, 301, 1112.
loqu-, 398.
lucta-, 956.

macte, 883.
Madvig referred to in notes, 725, 815, 951, 1141, 1163, 1165, 1175, 1182, 1193, 1202, 1205, 1209, 1224, 1236, 1287, 1288, 1337 f., 1337, 1404. 1, 1425, 1405. 1.
magis, 776. 1.
maior, 1055. 1.
malam rem, 886.
malim, 1221.
mallem, 1221.
malum, 863.
mandca-, 210.
manu-, 207. 1.
masculine suffixes, 191.
matrimo-, 1019.
meat, 1030.
medo-, 979, 980.
medica-, 979.
medius fidius, 861.
memini, 390, 943.

memory, verbs of, 943.
mercule, 861.
merg-, 535.
Mileti, 951 n.
mill-, 257, 1064.
minor-, 1055. 1.
minus, 776. 1, 1055. 1.
mira-, 939.
mirum—quantum, 1200.
misce-, 956.
mixed numbers, 1065. 1 &.
modera-, 979.
modo, 794.
moods, 423 &c.
mori- conjugated, 857.
musas for *musans*, p. 432.

nam, 1452.
nē, 1173, 1179, 1225, 1402; a proclitic, 1465; differs from *ut non*, 1408 n.; *ne—quidem*, 1405, 1453 &.
nē, ' verily,' 862.
nĕ, 1417, 1420; affixed to interrogatives, 1425 n.; repeated, 1424.
nearness, adj. of, 955.
nearness, verbs of, 956.
nec, 534.
nec a proclitic, 1465; 'not ven,' 1406. 1.
necesse est, 1246 n.
nedum, 1228.
nope-, 1404 n.
negatives accumulated, 1411.
negative particles, 1402.
negative repeated, 1412.
neg-leg-, 634 h., n.
nemon-, 1149. 1.
neque—et—, 1443.
neque quisquam, 1406.
nequitur, 1244 n.
nescio, 410 n.; *nescio an*, 1421.
nescio-qui-, 1199.
neue, 1416.
neuter nom. in *um*, p. 443, xxii.
neuter nom. rejects *s*, why? p. 41. 2.
neuter passives, 392.
neuter pronouns, 909.
neuter suffixes, 194.
nig- or *nic-*, 182.
nihil for *non*, 1410.
nimis, 776. 1.
nimium-quantum, 1200.
nisi-, 535. 3; 1001.

INDEX. 451

'no,' how expressed, 1428.
nolim, 1221.
nollem, 1221.
nominative, 44, 48, 368, 867; for voc., 880; form of, p. 425; plur., p. 437; power of, p. 433, 439; singular, p. 437 &c.
non, 1402; a proclitic, 1465; place of, 1403.
non modo for non modo non? 1415.
non nemo, 1411 a.
non quin, 1208.
non quo, 1208.
non quod, 1454 f.
non-emphatic words, where placed, 1467.
nôui, 389.
nos, 1082.
noun in apposition, where placed, 1472.
nonne, 1419.
nub-, 533, 977.
nuceram, 376 a.
nudiustertius, 805.
nullo- for non, 1410.
num, 1419, 1423 a.
number, 52; differs from English idiom, 1025; concord of, 1040.
numerals, 247 &c.; place of, 1471. L.
numquid uis, 1183 a. †.
nuncine, 792.
nuper, 778.

o conjugation, 519, 520.
o declension, p 424.
o final in verbs, 410.
ob prep., 1346; in comp., 1347; = cre, 830 a.
obiter, 797.
objective gen., 927.
obliuisc-, 943.
obliqua oratio, 492, 1201.
obsolete-, 885. L.
oculo-, 207. 3.
oi, 390.
officio-, 1469 a.
om-it-, 1308. 2.
opes-, 999.
opitula-, 742 1 a.
oportet, 1246 a.
opus est, 1280.
order of words, 1458.
ordinal numbers, 248, 252, 261, 1055. L.

ordo for ordinis, p. 435.
owner, 1036. 2.

paenitet, 689, 988.
pag-, 535.
palam, 782, 1348.
parato-, 1284.
parc-, 979, 980.
pare-, 956.
'part of,' 1057. i.
paril- verb, 398.
participle, 436, 514 &c., 1264; for abstract differs from adj., 934 a.; in endo, 1296; in endo with es-, 712; in endo with fu-, 715; in enti, 1285; in to, 1270; in turo, 1251, 1258; in turo with es-, 702; in turo with fu-, 705; perfect, 892; perfect, circumlocution for, 1281; question in, 1135.
particles, 764.
partitive gen., 922, 925.
pasc-, 1001.
passive, 379, 380, 570; conjugated, 655; impersonal, 701, 981; of saying and thinking, 1241.
past imperfect, 459-65, 580-2; past perfect, 473; ind. 588, 589; subj. 621-4.

pater for pateris, p. 435.
pater, p. 437.
pause in hexameter, 1464 a.
penalty, gen. of, 945.
praes, 1349.
praes, 947 a.
per, 1350; in comp., 1351; of destruction, 1351 a. f.
per me stat, 1163 a.
perd-, 1351.
perfect, 439 &c., 442, 443, 478, 833 &c.; form of, 471; conjugation of, 561; contracted, 563-7; present, 473; infin. 510, 511, 1255-1258; of intransitives, 477; third person of, 472 a.; use of, 478.
perinde, 800.
permission, subj. in, 489.
personal pronouns, 274, 1076.
personal suffixes, 405 &c.
personal verb, 370.
plag-, 535.
plural suffixes of nouns, 52; of verbs, 414 &c.
plural for sing., 1026.

plus, 243 n., 776. 1., 1065. 1.
porna-, 973 n.
polling-, 818.
polysyndeton, 1435.
pondo, 1075.
pone, 1353.
per, 818, 834 s, 1362.
porro, 788.
possessive adj., 1047; gen., 824-25.
pronouns, 359.
postid-, 386.
postrem, 728.
post, 1354; in comp., 1355.
postilla, 802.
postquam, 958 n.
postumo-, 823.
poti- verb, 942, 1287 n.
prae, 1356; in comp., 1357.
praedito-, 542 n.
praeter, 1359; in comp., 1360.
predicate, 874.
prepositions, 808, 830, 914 n., 1233, 1303, 1397; case after, 914 n.; change of form in, 809 &c.; Latin compared with Greek, 830 n., 834 n.; meaning of, 1391 n.; omitted, 1396; place of, 1391-3.
present tense, 449, 452-8; ind., 578-9; historic, 449 n., 455; perf., 472; subj., 594-602; perf. ind., 584, 587; perf. subj., 613-620.
price, 1005.
primo-, 823, 1050.
primor-, 838 n.
principal parts, 531 &c.
prior-, 823.
priusquam, 1231. 1.
pro, 1361; in comp., 1362-4.
proclitics, 28, 835, 1404. 1, 1465.
prodes-, 727.
prob, 862 n.
prohibe-, 1237.
proinde, 800.
pronominal adverbs, 366, 1150.
pronouns, 273 &c.; demonstrative, 286, 1091, 1471; gender of, 1039; indefinite, 1138 &c.; interrogative, 1134 &c.; logical, 301, 1112; personal, 274, 1076; possessive, 359, 1088; reflexive, 278-85, 1083-89.
prope, 1365.
propter-, 908.
propter, 1366.

pronum, 798.
Pseudo-Nepos, 851 n.†; 1423 n.
pudet, 938.
puer for *puerus*, p. 437.
pulvis, 9, p. 426.
punishment, verbs of, 975 n.
purpose, 490, 1407.

q, 6.
qui, 315, 316.
quam with comp., 1055; with sup., 1057 s.; a proclitic, 1465.
quamquam, 358, 791.
quamuis, 352, 791, 1287 b.
quando, 795, 1455 j.
quandoquidem, 857 n.
quanti, 946 n.
quasi, 499, 1223.
quauis, 366.
que, 840 n., 1430 &c.; displaced, 1441.
quer-, 555. 2.
qui- verb, 738.
qui- or *quo*-, 305, 1120-21; 'any,' 1138; -*d*-, 1131.
qui-cunque, 1146, 1158.
quid sis, 1198.
quidni? 1172 n.
quidquod, 1454 b.
qui-dam, 343, 1145.
quidem, 857 n., 1080, 1403, 1415, 1455; place of, 1474.
qui-lubet, 1144.
qui-nam, 346.
qui-piam, 345, 1143.
quippe qui with subj., 1194 n.
qui-quam, 344, 1142.
qui-que, 347-50, 922. 1.
qui-qui-, 1147, 1158.
qui-uis, 351, 1144.
quod, 1454; with *sius*, 922.
quondam, 792.
quoniam, 1455 j. n.
quoque, place of, 1474.
quoto-, 248, 1065. 1.
quum, 1229, 1281 b, 1455.

'rather,' 1056. 2.
ratio for *rationis*, p. 435.
re- sb., 910 n.
re, 'back,' 1367.
recidiuo-, 1367 n. †.
reciprocal verbs, 398.
redim-, 1289.

INDEX. 453

reduplication, 471.
radii, 472 n.
refert, 910, 948.
reflexive pronoun, 278-85, 1083-9;
omitted, 1249.
reflexive verb, 374 &c.; 398-400;
conjugated, 570, 636.
reperum, 876 n.
relative, 3.7, 1120-91; attraction
of, 1051; double form of, 353-8,
1158; postponed, 1463.
remit-, 975.
repeated action, 1159.
reported speech, 1201.
reppuli, 553. 2.
re-publica-, 163.
rescisc-, 1367.
result, subj. of, 491, 1406.
retine-, 1367.
retro, 1368.
rite, 770.
Ritschl, 1319 n., 1404. 1.
rise-, 391.
road by which, 1008.
roga-, 903.
roots, 30.
rossi-, 1031.
rx-, 396.
rup-, 533.
ruri, 952.
rus, 886.
rursus, 798.

s final lost in nom., p. 133.
sacrificing, vbs. of, 1005.
sanguis-, p. 9.
salis, 776. 1.
scilicet, 807.
scrib-, 533.
se, 1083, 1369; crude form of, 280.
second person, 1152. 3, 1175,
1224.
second word non-emphatic, 1473.
secondary clauses, 1225.
secundum, 1371.
secus, 917.
sed, 834, 1369; a proclitic, 1465.
seditios-, 815 n.
semel, 264 n.
semper, 776.
sen- or *sens*-, 164, 207, 1.
sense supersedes form, 1088.
ser-, 542 n.
serrocino-, 745 n.

serui-, 871.
sescenti-, 1063.
sestertio-, 272, 1070.
sestertium, 1075.
showing, vbs. of, 975.
si, 496-9, 1153, 1154, 1159, 1209;
omitted, 1219; as an interrogative, 1422; a proclitic, 1465.
sic, 300, 1451 g, n.
simple voice, 405.
simplici-, 264 n.
simul, 853, 854.
sin-, 1236.
sincero-, 264 n.
sine, 1372.
sing. for pl., 1032.
si-qui-, 1139, 1140.
sius, 1157.
smelling, vbs. of, 895.
sodes, 1361, o, n.
solo-, 110, 1050, 1192.
sordido-, 553. 1 n.
sorti- vb., 398.
sparg-, 533.
spondeo, 410 n.
static verb, 885, 391.
sto- pron., 288 n.
strengthened form of verb, 451. 1.
studo-, 939.
suade-, 979.
sub, 913, 1873-6.
sůbici-, 612 n.
subject, 874.
subject-accusative, 911, 1248-50.
subjective gen., 921.
subjunctive, 427-9, 481-505, 1178
&c.; as a future, 500-5, 1226;
for imperat. 1167; in commands,
486, 1180; in concessions, 1227
b; in elliptical sentences, 1227;
in hypothesis, 496-9, 1209 &c.;
in indirect questions, 494, 495,
1196; in obliqua oratio, 1201-6;
in parenthesis, 1195; in permission, 489, 1180; in purpose,
490, 1179; in results 491, 1192;
of duty, 1227 f; of indignation,
1227 e; of possibility, 1227 a;
of prayer, 1227 d; translated as
indic., 491, 493, 494; with *ut*
qui, 1194 n.
substantive, number of, 1026; in
predicate, 1060; in a, e, i, u, c,
have lost a guttural, p. 440, ll.

&c.; in *ab-ulo*, p. 441, iv.; in *ac-ulo*, p. 440, iii.; in *ac-ro*, p. 440, iii.; in *ag-on*, p. 440, iii.; in *an-ente* &c. p. 443, xxii.; in *c*, p. 441, ix.; in *io-ulo*, p. 441, xii.; in *ec* or *ie*, p. 441, vii.; in *ec-ula*, p. 441, xii.; in *ed-on*, p. 444, xxvii.; in *et*, p. 443, xxvi.; in *i-to*, p. 441, x.; in *io-ulo*, p. 441, xii.; in *il-ia*, p. 444, xxvii.; in *il-udon*, p. 444, xxvii.; in *il-ut*, p. 444, xxvii.
subter, 1378; in comp., 1379.
suffix, 32; of adj., 225-234; of masculine subs., 191, 192; of feminine, 193; of neuters, 194; personal, 406 &c.
sum, sunt, explained, p. 429.
summo-, 823.
suo-, 361, 1084.
suppedita-, 396.
supellex-, 818.
super, 1380; in comp., 1382.
superlative, 240-46, 1057; from prep., 838.
supine, 433, 434, 887, 998, 1299-1301.
supra, 1383.
susvip-, 1289.
susum, 798.
syllable long by nature, 14; long by position, 15; short, 13.
symbols, numerical, 251.
syntax, 866.

tag-, 535.
taking away, verbs of, 873.
tanquam, 1223.
tanti, 946 n.
tantum, 1068.1 a.
te as a dat., 977 n.
telling, verbs of, 875.
tempera-, 979.
'temple,' 1038.
tene-, 380.
tenus, 437 &c.
tenses of Latin verb, 451 &c.
tenus, 1384, 1391 b.
tepefac-, 758.
ter, 783, p. 437.
terp-, 534.
'that of,' 1036. L
third person, quantity of, 412.
tig-, 535.

time, difference of, 1017; how long, 915; within which, 993-5; when, 992.
'too,' 1036.
torque-, 553.
towns, 884, 951, 980, 1021.
traic-, 900.
trans, 1386.
transitive verb, 372; used reflectively, 391-7.
trusting, verbs of, 874, 1002.
tu, crude form of, 275.

v consonants = *w*, 10, 25.
v conjugation, 519, 526-7.
v declension, 140-4, p. 424.
ubi, 315, 386, 953-4.
ubique, 347, 366.
ue, 1444, n.; displaced, 1441.
vel, 840, 1057 k.
velle, how formed, p. 436.
vend-, 542.
venum, 866.
vere-, 939.
vero, 1458; place of, 1474.
veso-, 1001.
veto-, 1236, 1237, 1248.
vic-, 534.
vicem, 917.
vicinus, 1071.
vicinius, 1150.
ullo-, 834, 1142.
uls, 1389.
ultumo-, 823.
ultra, 1390.
ultro, 788.
ultumo-, 823.
unde, 305 n.; 915, 1150.
undeclined subs., 1032. L.
uno-, 1082.
vorsus, 1387, 1391 b.
ut, 316, 796, 1481; a proclitic, 1465.
uti-, 1001, 1287 a.
utinam, 796.
utique, 347, 796.
utut, 358, 796.
ut qui with subj., 1194 n.
utrum, construction of, 1428.

vegetables, 1030.
verb, 367 &c.; after emphatic word, 1467; derivation of, 740; diminutive, 750; frequentative, 748;

impersonal, 371; of saying, &c., 1238; of wishing, 1242; place of, 1458, 1461, 1467; in *a*, 522; in *ay*, p. 440, liii.; in *ayna*, 745 n.; in *e*, 386, 324; p. 443, xxiii.; in *eo* or *ic*, p. 442, xviii.; in *exo* or *iss*, p. 443, xxv.; in *ess* or *iss*, 754, p. 443, xxv.; in *g*, p. 442, xix.; in *i*, 528, p. 443, xxiv.; in *iía*, p. 443, xxvi.; in *m*, p. 442, xxii.; in *o*, 519, p. 427; in *p*, p. 442, xx.; in *t* final long, p. 428; in *turi*, 755; in *u*, 526, p. 427, p. 442, xvii.; in *ab*, *ob*, *ib*, *b*, p. 442, xxi.; inceptive, 752; intransitive, 373-8; irregular, 392; of accusing, 944; of buying, 846; of commanding, &c., 1180; of comparing, 956 n.; of duty, 1217; of fearing, 1186; of feeling, 393, 889, 938-9; of hindrance, 1138; of memory, 943; of requesting omitted, 1204; of saying omitted, 1205; of smelling, 895; of wishing, 1242; passive, 380 &c.; personal, 370; place of, 1437, 1467, 1468; plural suffixes of, 414 &c.; reciprocal, 398; reflective, 374 &c., 398-400; static, 385-91; transitive, 372.

verbal sb., 1264; in *tion*, 1309; in *tu*, 687, 1299. *

vi-, 165.

vita-, 1029.

vocative, 43 n., 682; for nom. 883; place of, 1474 a.

vocifera-, 742. 1 a.

val-, 733.

vowels, order of, 3; vowel silent, 24; vowel-assimilation, p. 444, lxix.

weather, 1027.

words opposed, place of, 1475.

worth, gen. of, 947

x, last letter, 2; = *ks*, 5; or rather xx, 813 n.

y not a Latin letter, 2.

'yes,' how expressed, 1427.

z not a Latin letter, 2.

ADDENDA ET CORRIGENDA.

§§ 44, 45, 50, for *beam* read *tree, beam.*

236, to [quadra] append as note: Brackets in the form [ ] denote obsolete or theoretic words.

885, add after *infitias* the words *exequias, suppetias.*

958, transfer first example to § 959.

1158, *add:* Other examples are seen in: *Laudabunt* alii ... — *tu nec tam* &c., *Hor.* Od. 1. 7. 1 ; *Est ut ulro uir* ... — *aequa lege Necessitas* &c., Od. III. 1. 9 ; *Optat* quietem ..., *Optat* Prometheus..., *Optat* supremo ... — *sed uctant leges Iouis*, Epod. 17. 65.

1228,	*line* 10	*for* Mortalia facta	*read* Facta
„	„ 19	„ better	„ much better
1295,	„ 1 and 4	„ gerundive	„ gerund or gerundive
1408,	„ 4	„ so many engagements	„ engagements so important.

1465, *add:* In collating a Ms. (Harl. 1. ?) of Liv. VI. 1–17, many years ago, at the British Museum, I found the above words written as proclitics, the number of times here stated: *ut* 19, *si* 8, *nisi* 1, *seu* 1, *et* 1, *nec* 7, *ne* 7, *non* 23, *aut* 1, *at* 1, *an* 2, *quam* 4. Also *qui* 2, *quae* 1, *qua* 1, *quo* 1, *quod* 4, *quum* 6, *quin* 2, *tum* 4, *tam* 1, *iam* 2, *sic* 2, *se* 9, *te* 1, *etiamsi* 1. Further, 251 monosyllabic prepositions against 48 not so written, and 10 disyllabic prepositions against, 7 not so written. The same collation exhibited written as enclitics: *sum* 1, *sunt* 1, *est* 3, *quae* 1, *sim* 2, *erat* 5, *erant* 1, *se* 7, *sui* 1 ; *quisque* 2, *tamen* 1, *enim* 1, and even *summsui* for *summo ui* (compare *summopere*).

Page 135, *l.* 32: attach to the word 'assimilation' the note : † So αρσην θαρσος τυρσος of Ionic and Old Attic became in later Attic αρρην θαρρος τορρος.

„   „ *l.* 35 : attach to the word 'compensation' the note : ‡ So κτεννω γεννατο (for εγενσατο ?) of the purer Aeolic became in Attic κτεινω εγεινατο, and εγερρω φθερρω became ηγειρω φθειρω. See Liddell and Scott under N and P, where however the change is reversed.

„   437, *l.* 15. To χειρ append the note : ¦ A nominative χερς appears in an epigram of Timocreon's, in Hephaestion περι μετρων 1 : ᾁ συμβουλευω χερς αυω, τους δε τυφα.

www.ingramcontent.com/pod-product-compliance
Lightning Source LLC
Chambersburg PA
CBHW031958300426
44117CB00008B/818